National Memories

National Memories

Constructing Identity in Populist Times

EDITED BY
HENRY L. ROEDIGER, III
AND JAMES V. WERTSCH

OXFORD
UNIVERSITY PRESS

Oxford University Press is a department of the University of Oxford. It furthers the University's objective of excellence in research, scholarship, and education by publishing worldwide. Oxford is a registered trade mark of Oxford University Press in the UK and certain other countries.

Published in the United States of America by Oxford University Press
198 Madison Avenue, New York, NY 10016, United States of America.

© Oxford University Press 2022

All rights reserved. No part of this publication may be reproduced, stored in a retrieval system, or transmitted, in any form or by any means, without the prior permission in writing of Oxford University Press, or as expressly permitted by law, by license, or under terms agreed with the appropriate reproduction rights organization. Inquiries concerning reproduction outside the scope of the above should be sent to the Rights Department, Oxford University Press, at the address above.

You must not circulate this work in any other form
and you must impose this same condition on any acquirer.

Names: Roediger, Henry L., III, editor. | Wertsch, James V., editor.
Title: National memories : constructing identity in populist times / Henry L. Roediger, III, James V. Wertsch.
Description: New York, NY : Oxford University Press, [2022] | Includes bibliographical references and index.
Identifiers: LCCN 2021052756 (print) | LCCN 2021052757 (ebook) | ISBN 9780197568675 (hardback) | ISBN 9780197568699 (epub) | ISBN 9780197568705 (digital-online)
Subjects: LCSH: Nationalism and collective memory—Case studies. | Populism—Case studies. | Political psychology—Case studies.
Classification: LCC JC311 .N29175 2022 (print) | LCC JC311 (ebook) | DDC 320.54—dc23/eng/20220206
LC record available at https://lccn.loc.gov/2021052756
LC ebook record available at https://lccn.loc.gov/2021052757

DOI: 10.1093/oso/9780197568675.001.0001

1 3 5 7 9 8 6 4 2

Printed by Integrated Books International, United States of America

Contents

Preface ix
Introduction xi
Contributors xv

SECTION I. HISTORICAL ORIGINS OF NATIONAL MEMORY AND POPULISM IN AMERICA

1. When We Forget   3
   Strobe Talbott

2. City on a Hill: Pilgrims, Puritans, and the Origin of America   20
   Abram Van Engen

3. Europe in 1989, America in 2020, and the Death of the Lost Cause   35
   David W. Blight

4. Charlottesville and the End of American Exceptionalism   41
   Jeffrey K. Olick

SECTION II. CASE STUDIES OF NATIONAL MEMORY AND POPULISM IN AMERICA

5. Finding a Way Forward: Memory and the Future in American National Narratives   65
   Christina Simko

6. The Weight of the Past: Ecological Perspectives on a Contested Confederate Monument   87
   David Cunningham

7. From Hero to Villain: Stability and Change in Popular Beliefs About Christopher Columbus   115
   Amy Corning and Howard Schuman

8. Psychological Aspects of National Memory: An American Case   146
   Jeremy K. Yamashiro

SECTION III. COMPARATIVE STUDIES OF NATIONAL MEMORY AND POPULISM FROM AROUND THE WORLD

9. Social Representations of History, Living Historical Memory, and Historical Charters: Refining Collective Memory Toward a Theory of Political Culture Change 169
James H. Liu, Sarah Y. Choi, Robert Jiqi Zhang, Roosevelt Vilar, and Moh. Abdul Hakim

10. Decades Later: What World War II Events Are Remembered as the Most Important Ones? Implications of Data Collected in 12 Countries 190
Magdalena Abel, Sharda Umanath, and Krystian Barzykowski

11. National and State Narcissism as Reflected in Overclaiming of Responsibility 209
Henry L. Roediger, III, Adam L. Putnam, and Jeremy K. Yamashiro

12. United States's and Germany's Collective Memories of Pride and Shame for American and German History 236
Sharda Umanath and Magdalena Abel

SECTION IV. CASE STUDIES OF NATIONAL MEMORY AND POPULISM FROM AROUND THE WORLD

13. Persistence of Collective Memory over 3,000 Years: The Case of Ancient Versus Modern Israel 259
Yadin Dudai

14. National Pasts as Political Presents: War Memory in East Asia 280
Carol Gluck

15. How China Remembers the Korean War and the Limit of Statist Nationalism 300
Zhao Ma

16. Using a Golden Age: National Memory of Georgia's Favorite King 324
Nutsa Batiashvili

17. Collective Memory and Mass Movements: When Mobilization
    Requires Neither Leadership nor Political Elites   343
    Rauf Garagozov

SECTION V. CONCEPTUAL FRAMEWORKS FOR THE STUDY OF NATIONAL MEMORY AND POPULISM

18. Mass Movements and Coalitional Psychology: Mobilization
    Requires Neither Tribalism nor Gullibility   369
    Pascal Boyer

19. Toward a Dynamical—in the Field—Approach to
    Collective Memory   389
    Alin Coman

20. How Collective Memories Emerge: A Cognitive
    Psychological Perspective   409
    Suparna Rajaram, Tori Peña, and Garrett D. Greeley

21. Populist Beliefs: Byproducts of an Adaptive System?   434
    Elizabeth J. Marsh, Matthew Stanley, and Morgan K. Taylor

22. The Narrative Tools of National Memory   454
    James V. Wertsch

Index   473

Preface

This volume grew out of a conference held at Washington University in St. Louis in May 2019. The conference brought together leadings scholars from various disciplines to discuss "National Memory in a Time of Populism." The perspectives and methods used to study the topic varied greatly across participants, by design. We hoped to encourage people to work outside their disciplinary boundaries and to be informed by researchers using different techniques and frameworks. The readers of this volume will have to decide about the success of our efforts, but the participants in the conference ended up being very enthusiastic about the product. Because they heard each other's presentations (and often read each other's chapters), their own chapters have been enriched and improved. All participants in the conference, save one, submitted chapters to the book.

Our conference and this book could not have occurred without support from many organizations and people. Financial support for the conference came from the American Academy of Arts and Sciences and from Washington University in St. Louis. We owe a debt of gratitude to both institutions for making our hopes for this conference come true. We especially thank Jonathan Fanton and David Oxtoby, past President and President of the American Academy of Arts and Sciences, respectively, for their support. We also thank Mark Wrighton, Chancellor Emeritus of Washington University, and Barbara Schaal, Dean Emerita of Arts and Sciences, for their generous contributions to our project. Andrew Martin, Chancellor of Washington University, was kind enough to make remarks at the conference banquet. In addition, we owe a huge debt of gratitude to Kristin Williams, Angie Rahaman, and Latonya Barnes, staff members of the McDonnell International Scholars Academy at Washington University, who helped organize the conference and who made it run smoothly. We thank Declan Saviano, an undergraduate student at Washington University, for his great efforts in helping us prepare the volume for publication.

At Oxford University Press, we thank Joan Bossert for believing in our project from the outset. When she retired, we were lucky to inherit the efforts of our new editor, Abby Gross. Abby has helped steer us through the publication process.

Producing a volume of this magnitude is a team effort, as our acknowledgments here attest. We appreciate the great assistance we have had in editing this volume.

Introduction

The "new nationalism" that has burst on the scene in recent years surprised just about everyone. What was thought to be an atavistic, spent force surfaced not only in regions where nationalism had a long history but also in places such as the United Kingdom and the United States. It is not entirely clear whether the forms that nationalism is taking today are all of a kind or whether they are similar to those of the past, but a thread that runs throughout the entire discussion is the importance of memory. At least since Ernst Renan gave memory a central role in defining a nation, it has been widely accepted that a usable past is crucial to answering his question, What is a nation?

With these issues in mind, we convened a group of distinguished scholars from throughout the world in 2019 to discuss "National Memory in a Time of Populism." Our meeting was sponsored by the American Academy of Arts and Sciences and Washington University in St. Louis, and it brought together colleagues from across the natural sciences, social sciences, and humanities. Many came with a background of research and writing on national memory, and others were applying their disciplinary expertise to the issue for the first time, but everyone brought something valuable to the discussion. This volume arose from our meeting, and its chapters were enriched by authors having heard each other's presentations.

We undertook this effort at a time when interest in memory studies was exploding in the humanities and social sciences. New publications, research networks, and professional organizations had sprung up everywhere, and our goal was to harness the energy that ensued. In addition to its focus on national communities, memory studies took a "transcultural turn" (Erll, 2021) around 2010 in an effort to address increasingly important projects that extend beyond the nation. This called into question the "methodological nationalism" that accepts the nation as the normal or default focus of scholarship.

It hardly needs saying that none of the contributors to this volume came to our discussion to celebrate nationalism. Indeed, they were likely to agree with Romila Thapar's comment that "history is to nationalism what the poppy is the opium addict."[1] But their goal remained one of understanding national memory in the hopes of addressing its powers and its dangers, thus leaving the task of integrating this effort with transcultural memory studies a project for the future.

The chapters of this volume employ a range of methods and concepts, making it somewhat artificial to arrange their content into neat categories. We have nonetheless grouped them into sections based on geographical region or disciplinary perspective. In addition, a couple of other themes run across these sections. The first is resistance to assumptions about the power of top-down state efforts to control national memory. These assumptions surface in routine comments about the power of modern states and the media to control information about the past. Such comments tend to be about others (seldom ourselves!) and are reflected in claims such as "Of course those people believe that, it's all they were taught in school!"

We do not deny that elites and state authorities often try—and to some degree succeed—in their top-down efforts to control national memory. But claims that leave it at that are too glib, if not fundamentally misguided. Instead of being a matter of state authorities creating images of the past at will, national memory turns out to reflect complex negotiations that also involve cultural, social, and mental forces coming from the community. The distinguished scholar of nations and nationalism Ernest Gellner is perhaps best known for his recognition of the role of the state, through formal education, to shape nationalism. But in formulating his claims, he also noted that the process is one that "*takes pre-existing cultures* and turns them into nations" (italics added), suggesting powerful bottom-up forces. Memories held by the populace determine whether people will either resist or be persuaded by top-down efforts.

In line with this interactive model, the state does not create national memory or identity out of nothing but, rather, engages with a particular set of cultural resources. These resources have been the object of inquiry for many of the contributors to this volume. In particular, several of them have spent years studying narratives that are what Alisdair MacIntyre called the "stock of stories" that guide a culture as it seeks to answer views of who we are and how we are to act. These provide semiotic resources and mental habits to be harnessed in more or less effective ways, and they sometimes even

---

[1] https://www.bing.com/videos/search?q=youtube+romila+thapar&view=detail&mid= E5AD1683CB9A5BBF3B16E5AD1683CB9A5BBF3B16&FORM=VIRE.

serve as a sort of "brake" on what top-down efforts can do. In this volume, authors examine such issues under the heading of collective narcissism, implicit attitudes, narrative templates, and so forth. The result is that top-down efforts are viewed as being shaped as much by bottom-up forces from a national community as vice versa.

A second general theme running through much of this volume concerns the dynamic and highly contested nature of national memory. This dynamism is so prevalent that it might be more appropriate to speak of national *remembering* rather than memory. Instead of being a fixed narrative or a body of information, such remembering is typically characterized by memory activists, competing narratives, generational change, and other forces. The term "remembering" occasionally surfaces in the following chapters, but its slightly cumbersome nature in English makes it difficult to use. The spirit of the term, however, can be seen throughout.

We have organized the 22 chapters of this volume into five general sections. The first two focus on American national memory and identity, including their history and current status. The third and fourth sections consider how national memory and identity play out in other places throughout the world, and the fifth section outlines general conceptual frameworks for studying national memory and identity. At every point along the way, the reader will find insights from a surprising array of sources in the humanities and social sciences.

As they made their contributions to this volume, the authors worked to connect with other perspectives. This involved reading others' chapters and incorporating ideas from them in building their argument. The product is an account of what leading experts the social sciences and humanities have to offer when trying to understand national memory. We hope readers find this product as exciting and insightful as we have.

Contributors

Moh. Abdul Hakim
Universitas Sebelas Maret
Surakarta, Indonesia

Magdalena Abel
Department of Experimental Psychology
University of Regensburg
Regensburg, Germany

Krystian Barzykowski
Institute of Psychology
Jagiellonian University
Krakow, Poland

Nutsa Batiashvili
Department of Anthropology
Free University of Tbilisi
Tbilisi, Georgia

David W. Blight
Department of History
Yale University
New Haven, CT, USA

Pascal Boyer
Departments of Anthropology and Psychology
Washington University in St. Louis
St. Louis, MO, USA

Sarah Y. Choi
School of Psychology
Massey University
Palmerston North, New Zealand

Alin Coman
Department of Psychology and Princeton School of Public and International Affairs
Princeton University
Princeton, NJ, USA

Amy Corning
Institute for Social Research
University of Michigan
Ann Arbor, MI, USA

David Cunningham
Department of Sociology
Washington University in St. Louis
St. Louis, MO, USA

Yadin Dudai
Department of Neurobiology
Weizmann Institute of Science and Global Professor
New York University
New York, NY, USA

Rauf Garagozov
Uppsala University
Uppsala, Sweden

Carol Gluck
Department of History
Columbia University
New York, NY, USA

Garrett D. Greeley
Department of Psychology
Stony Brook University
Stony Brook, NY, USA

James H. Liu
School of Psychology
Massey University
Palmerston North, New Zealand

Zhao Ma
Department of East Asian Languages and Cultures
Washington University in St. Louis
St. Louis, MO, USA

Elizabeth J. Marsh
Department of Psychology and Neuroscience
Duke University
Durham, NC, USA

Jeffrey K. Olick
Department of Sociology and History
University of Virginia
Charlottesville, VA, USA

Tori Peña
Department of Psychology
Stony Brook University
Stony Brook, NY, USA

Adam L. Putnam
Department of Psychology
Furman University
Greenville, SC, USA

Suparna Rajaram
Department of Psychology
Stony Brook University
Stony Brook, NY, USA

Henry L. Roediger, III
Department of Psychological and Brain Sciences
Washington University in St. Louis
St. Louis, MO, USA

Howard Schuman
Institute for Social Research
University of Michigan
Ann Arbor, MI, USA

Christina Simko
Department of Anthropology and Sociology
Williams College
Williamstown, MA, USA

Matthew Stanley
Department of Psychology and Neuroscience
Duke University
Durham, NC, USA

Strobe Talbott
Foreign Policy Program
Former President, Brookings Institution
Washington, DC, USA

Morgan K. Taylor
Department of Psychology and Neuroscience
Duke University
Durham, NC, USA

Sharda Umanath
Department of Psychological Science
Claremont McKenna College
Claremont, CA, USA

Abram Van Engen
Department of English
Washington University in St. Louis
St. Louis, MO, USA

Roosevelt Vilar
School of Psychology
Massey University
Palmerston North, New Zealand

James V. Wertsch
Department of Anthropology
Washington University in St. Louis
St. Louis, MO, USA

Jeremy K. Yamashiro
Department of Psychology
University of California, Santa Cruz
Santa Cruz, CA, USA

Robert Jiqi Zhang
School of Psychology
Massey University
Palmerston North, New Zealand

SECTION I

HISTORICAL ORIGINS OF NATIONAL MEMORY AND POPULISM IN AMERICA

For the past several decades, America has not been considered to be a particularly nationalistic country. Indeed, it prided itself as the leader of efforts to form global alliances, often using a somewhat self-congratulatory national narrative to back this up. To be sure, this narrative occasionally led to tragic ventures, such as the Vietnam War and the war in Iraq, but the story of America as a special nation striving to take leadership in global affairs on the basis of higher ethical values generally served to frame the national discourse.

As Strobe Talbott notes in Chapter 1, this status as an international leader may have come to an abrupt halt with the election of President Donald Trump. In an extraordinary break with tradition, Trump went out of his way to sully the moral framework grounded in Enlightenment ideas that guided America's founders. Talbott's account expands the usual notion of national memory by going beyond concrete events and actors and placing virtue and character at the center of the memory project. The importance of George Washington, for example, stems from the fact that he was an exemplar of the high character needed to create the republic he and his compatriots envisioned, making him an index of something larger and more abstract.

As Talbott notes, King George reacted to the news that Washington wanted to retire to his plantation rather than cling to power by exclaiming, "If he does that, he will be the greatest man in the world." Washington's role in the emerging national narrative was as someone who modeled civic responsibility and the peaceful transfer of power, and it was part of a story that underpinned the American project for centuries. And it is something that stood in stark contrast to Trump's dismissive views of civic virtue and his efforts to cling to power. Going forward, the issue will be whether the sort of national narrative Talbott envisions, one that grew out of the model provided by Washington and other early figures, is sufficiently strong and flexible to survive the attacks of populist demagogues.

The other chapters in this section show that the national narrative against which Trump's destructive efforts played out was hardly straightforward before he came along. In Chapter 2, Abram Van Engen notes, for example, that the frequently used story of a "city on a hill" emerged over history in ways that involve complexities that are seldom appreciated. Like any national narrative, the story of America is shaped by the beginning assigned to it, and in this case Van Engen shows how John Winthrop's 1630 sermon concerning a city on a hill had a complex narrative of its own. The city on a hill story has been dusted off and used since 1960 as if it were a clear narrative, but he outlines how fracture lines between New England and Virginia—North and South—were part of America's origin story from the outset.

In Chapter 3, David Blight elaborates on this struggle in American politics in the aftermath of the Civil War—a process that continues to the present day. Specifically, he argues that the Lost Cause tradition is "one of the most deeply ingrained mythologies in American history" and is at the root of some of today's most contentious debates, including those that provided fuel for Donald Trump's demagoguery. In Blight's view, this is part of an ongoing struggle between justice and reconciliation that may be gaining rather than losing steam today. Blight envisions the dynamics and contestation in this case in general terms, making it possible to see parallels with Europe after the fall the Soviet Union.

Jeffrey Olick pursues a related line of reasoning about the tensions of American national remembering in Chapter 4 on Charlottesville, Virginia, and the end of American exceptionalism. He contrasts America's celebration of its perceived exceptionalism with the rise of the politics of regret that surfaces in national remembering in Europe. Drawing on the sociology of culture, he outlines the fault lines that are reflected in America's inattention to past injustices, as well as some of the forces that may lead to change. Explicit or implied comparisons with how the politics of regret has played out in Europe provide a background against which Olick considers the powerful case study of deadly demonstrations that took place in 2017 in Charlottesville.

1
When We Forget

Strobe Talbott

> President Trump may not know a lot about the framers, but they certainly knew a lot about him.
> —Jamie Raskin, lead manager for the second Senate trial, February 9, 2021

All countries have sagas. The populace wants to know how their patch on the planet came to be the homeland of their ancestors. If they were ancient empires or remnants of ones, their histories were blurred by myth and memory mixed with dreams.

The American narrative is different. It's an open book. Scholars have mined virtually all the facts and details from the American Revolution. The protagonists chronicled what they were doing and why, and not just for their contemporaries but also for posterity, so that future generations would accept, understand, and embrace the fundamentals.

These practical visionaries could see beyond the age of the divine right of kings. In their modern republic, the citizenry would reign and the government would serve. They aspired to that ideal, but they were also realists. They knew their faults and those of their constituents. Therefore, they put safeguards in place to protect against human frailty. Inevitably, over two and half centuries, there have been instances of folly, tragedy, and corruption emanating from the top. But only one chief executive has tried, blatantly, to transmogrify the United States from a representative democracy into a personal dictatorship. Donald J. Trump came dangerously close to succeeding, and even though now out of office, he is determined to be a major and disruptive force in the political fray.

The 45th president has degraded America's canonical memory. He has scorned the Declaration of Independence and the Constitution because they are liberal at their core, whereas Trumpism is despotic at its core.

The first six presidents did their best to safeguard a set of noble principles and durable institutions for their successors to steward and advance. George Washington, John Adam, Thomas Jefferson, James Madison, James Monroe, and John Quincy Adams were particularly worried that their radical experiment in liberty might not survive. After all, in their time, tyranny was the global norm. Their letters and speeches were often flares shot over the horizon in the hope that posterity would heed their warnings of backsliding.

As they leaned into the future, they borrowed the wisdom of the past. The American republic had a rich backstory. The Founding Fathers of America were children of the European Enlightenment. In the 17th century, Britain was in the forefront of that movement. While explorers were sailing to far parts of the globe in search of trade or conquest, philosophers back home were turning inward. After probing the workings of their own minds, they postulated that all *Homo sapiens* who come squalling into the world have the same faculties, which would mean, ideally, that the entire human race should have equal status and equal rights.

Freethinkers on both sides of the English Channel exchanged their ideas with peers. Their dissemination of pamphlets and treatises were often referred to as the Republic of Letters. This unfettering of rigorous reason and bold imagination created a vast, kaleidoscopic configuration of science, literature, music, architecture, theater, and medicine.

The initial waves of British settlers crossing the Atlantic left the Enlightenment behind for almost 100 years. Their motherland was too far away, and they were too busy taming a wilderness.

That changed at the dawn of the 18th century. Literacy was rising in the colonies, and London publishers had a brisk business with the bookshops in American cities. When the leaders of the Revolutionary Generation came into their own, they were schooled in the syllabus of the Enlightenment. They were men of affairs: landed farmers, lawyers, publishers, educators, scientists, and physicians who began lighting lamps while knowing they were also playing with fire.

They were not determinists, expecting that the arc of history, by itself, would bend toward equality, justice, liberty, and peace. Realization of those ideals required constant, judicious, and ethical human agency. Progress was fragile, susceptible to human weakness or malevolent strength. They were cautious optimists, not utopians. They knew they were neither saints nor angels (most did not believe in either such beings).

In their youth, several of them who rose to the leadership of the Revolution had been profoundly attracted to the European savants. Benjamin Franklin was the iconic example. In his teens, he plunged into the English philosophers' dense tomes. Soon he was in London as an apprentice printer by day and a budding philosopher by night, using the press to publish his own treatise weighing in on the existence of God, a subject that he would steer away from for the rest of his life. In a letter to a friend many years later, Franklin said, "The great Uncertainty found in Metaphysical Reasons disgusts me, and I quitted that of Reading, for others more satisfactory."[1] Quite of few of his comrades agreed. Thomas Paine, the English-born political theorist and pamphleteer for the Revolution, put it succinctly: "My own mind is my own church."[2]

Franklin was also searching for ways to improve people's lives, whether with a better wood-burning stove, urinary catheter, faster route across the Atlantic, or inoculation for smallpox. In all his enthusiasms, whether vocational or recreational, he followed a three-step method: first, follow your curiosity; second, understand what makes a thing work; and third, apply your resourcefulness to invent something new or to make the old one work better.

America's man for all seasons spent much of his long life promoting the tenet that new ideas must be given a chance rather than be squelched by orthodoxy or, worse, repressed by an overbearing government. In his mid-20s, he wrote a full-throated defense of free speech and free press. He founded the first successful lending library in the English-speaking world. His achievement inspired other colonies to make it easier for their citizens to acquire knowledge and, therefore, to come to sound opinions.

He also conceived and initiated a college in Philadelphia that would educate students from the working class with those more privileged. The Academy and Charitable School was later named the University of Pennsylvania.[3]

In 1775, as Franklin neared his eighth decade, the Continental Congress appointed this inveterate correspondent to be the first postmaster of the

---

[1] From Benjamin Franklin to Benjamin Vaughan, 9 November 1779, Founders Online, National Archives, last modified June 13, 2018, http://founders.archives.gov/documents/Franklin/01-31-02-0035
[2] Thomas Paine, *Age of Reason: Being an Investigation of True and Fabulous Theology* (New York: 1975), p. 6.
[3] Franklin was the inaugural president for six years, then a trustee for the rest of his life.

United States. That made him the official in charge of America's own Republic of Letters, integrating all 13 states in the last months before the Declaration of Independence was signed. Before his service to the Revolution and what came after, he had already helped lay the foundation for a society ready for a new polity.

Although Benjamin Franklin was the arch druid of the Revolution, for most of his life he thought of himself as a loyal Englishman. That changed in January 1774 when he was in London working for a peaceful resolution after years of the colonists' escalating outrage against British taxation without representation. Ordered by parliamentarians to a chamber known as the Cockpit in Westminster, he stood stoically while the members shouted, hurled insults, and treated him like a villain who had committed a capital crime. When asked how the colonists would react if British soldiers were sent to enforce compliance, he responded, "They will not find a rebellion; they may indeed make one."

Angry and sorrowful, he left a country that he had loved and returned to a home he loved more.

The younger founders-to-be were more inclined to separate from the Crown. John Adams, at age 29 years, sensed the Tea Party was a turning point. He had been honing his intellect in his teens, probing the lessons of history, and envisioning America's destiny: "Let it be known that British liberties are not the grants of princes or parliaments, but original rights, conditions of original contracts, coequal with prerogative and coeval with government—That many of our rights are inherent and essential."[4]

He took a dim view of 17th-century Enlightenment philosophers' belief that rigorous logic could master almost all phenomena, including human behavior. "Reason holds the helm, but passions are the gales." He was a realist in an age of idealism. "Cold will still freeze, and fire will never cease to burn; disease and vice will continue to disorder, and death to terrify mankind." He added that "sobriety" was essential for the truly enlightened, lest pretty lights obscure the hard truths and reality.[5]

The young Thomas Jefferson, however, was intoxicated. At the age of 16 years, he had come under the thrall of William Small, a teacher at the

---

[4] David McCullough, *Adams*, op. cit., pp. 421–2, and Joseph Ellis, *Passionate Sage: The Character and Legacy of John Adams* (New York: Norton paperback, 1994), p. 92.
[5] Diary of John Adams, Massachusetts Historical Society, https://www.masshist.org/digitaladams/archive/doc?id=D11. McCullough uses this the entries in *Adams*, op. cit., p. 62.

College of William and Mary in Williamsburg, Virginia. Small, a Scott, was an adherent of a branch of the Enlightenment flourishing in his homeland. He introduced Jefferson to the writings of Francis Hutcheson, a professor at the University of Glasgow, who stressed that the state had no right to interfere or violate "moral sense" inherent in all humans at birth.

Jefferson credited Small, who "probably fixed the destinies of my life . . . a man profound in most of the useful branches of science, with a happy talent of communication, correct and gentlemanly manners, and an enlarged and liberal mind."[6]

Just out of college, Jefferson balanced a private law practice with an increasing affinity for statecraft. He could see that the Enlightenment had not only jumped the Atlantic but also was showing much more vitality than in the Old Country.

In 1766, he saddled his horse and left Virginia for the first time in order to be inoculated against smallpox in Philadelphia (largely due to Benjamin Franklin). He then proceeded to New York, where he watched soldiers from the local British garrison skirmish with crowds of locals and Sons of Liberty, a clandestine organization active throughout the colonies.

Upon returning home, he had a sense that he and the colonies were part of something vast and expanding, bound together by similar cultures and aspirations, dynamism in society, breakthroughs in science and medicine, and a shared cause.

Proud as he was of his own country, in his stately home overlooking Charlottesville, Virginia, he hung three portraits of Englishmen from the previous century. Among them was John Locke, with whose work Jefferson was most intimate. Locke laid out the basics for an enlightened nation and government: sovereignty of the individual, religious toleration (separation between church and state), separation of powers, with no one above the law. These essentials were incorporated into the Declaration of Independence and the Constitution.

The other two paintings were of Francis Bacon, the father of empiricism, and Isaac Newton, the father of modern science. Jefferson referred to them as "my trinity of the three greatest men the world had ever produced."[7]

---

[6] https://wwnorton.com/college/history/america-essential-learning/docs/TJefferson-Autobiography-1821.pdf
[7] https://www.monticello.org/site/research-and-collections/john-locke-painting

Jefferson was adamant that widespread education and a robust, responsible journalism were critical for a health body politic. Late in life, he wrote,

> If a nation expects to be ignorant & free, in a state of civilisation, it expects what never was & never will be. The functionaries of every government have propensities to command at will the liberty & property of their constituents. There is no safe deposit for these but with the people themselves; nor can they be safe with them without information. Where the press is free and every man able to read, all is safe.[8]

The man who would be eulogized as "first in war, first in peace, and first in the hearts of his countrymen" considered himself a proper Englishman until the age of 43 years. His metamorphosis began when Britain's barrage of revenue policies hit Virginia hard, infuriating planters, businessmen, and land speculators. But it was not until the winter of 1768–1769, when Parliament threatened to arrest the ringleaders of the growing resistance and bring them to England to be tried for treason, that George Washington countenanced active protest, although not revolution. He supported an embargo of British goods:

> At a time when our lordly Masters in Great Britain will be satisfied with nothing less than the deprivation of American freedom, it seems highly necessary that something shou'd be done to avert the stroke and maintain the liberty which we have derived from our Ancestors; but the manner of doing it to answer the purpose effectually is the point in question.
>
> That no man shou'd scruple, or hesitate a moment to use a[r]ms in defence of so valuable a blessing, on which all the good and evil of life depends; is clearly my opinion; Yet A[r]ms I wou'd beg leave to add, should be the last resource; the de[r]nier resort. Addresses to the Throne, and remonstrances to parliament, we have already, it is said, proved the inefficacy of; how far then their attention to our rights & privileges is to be awakened or alarmed by starving their Trade & manufactures, remains to be tryed.[9]

Here was a faithful Briton, well past the midpoint of his life—a professional soldier for whom war was not a glorious abstraction—invoking Enlightenment ideals of freedom and liberty, suggesting he was now being pulled in two directions.

---

[8] https://www.loc.gov/resource/mtj1.048_0731_0734/?sp=4&st=text
[9] Papers of Washington Colonial Series, letter to George Mason, April 5, 1769.

Five years later, when Britain blockaded Boston Harbor, Washington agreed to attend the First Continental Congress, hoping for an outcome that would be a compromise with the Crown. But by the following spring, Britain sent a contingent of soldiers to arrest the ringleaders of colonial militias. The British called them traitors; Americans called themselves patriots.

George Washington, who had shied away from philosophy, was an improbable hero of the Enlightenment. His dearest ambition—constantly thwarted—was a pastoral life. Yet, even though he would not be classed as an intellectual, he had qualities crucial to leadership of the American Revolution and the American Enlightenment.

Once in command of the Continental Army, he displayed sound instincts that were ideological as well as military. On his way from Philadelphia to Massachusetts to take up his duties in a region that was already at war, Washington gave a speech to the New York provincial Congress. "When we assume the soldier," he said, "we did not lay aside the citizen."[10]

Dispensing with the royal "we," he took up the republican one.

Eight years later when the war was won, when a formal peace with Britain was yet to be signed, he issued a circular letter to the states acknowledging the intellectual impetus of the American cause was provided by bold thinkers in Europe—including, by obvious implication, Great Britain:

> The foundation of our Empire was not laid in the gloomy Age of ignorance and superstition, but at an Epocha when the rights of Mankind were better understood and more clearly defined, than at any former period—The researches of the human Mind after social happiness have been carried to a great extent, the treasures of knowledge acquired by the labours of Philosophers, Sages and Legislators, through a long succession of years, are laid open for our use and their collected wisdom may be happily applied in the establishment of our forms of Government. The free cultivation of letters, the unbounded extension of Commerce, the progressive Refinement of manners, the growing liberality of sentiment, and, above all, the pure and benign light of Revelation, have had a meliorating influence on Mankind and encreased the blessings of Society.[11]

---

[10] Ron Chernow, *Washington*, p. 193: "[Washington] minted a beautiful phrase that must have resonated deeply among his listeners: 'When we assumed the soldier, we did not lay aside the citizen.' The citizen-soldier passed this first test of his political skills with flying colors. Given with perfect pitch, he new how to talk the language of peace even as he girded for war."

[11] https://press-pubs.uchicago.edu/founders/documents/v1ch7s5.html

When King George heard that Washington was retiring to his plantation, he was said to remark in astonishment, "If he does that, he will be the greatest man in the world."[12]

Washington would have been the most contented man in the world if only he could retire to Mount Vernon for the rest of his days. Instead, he was lured back to duty and leadership.

Heeding voices of the Enlightenment, he presided over the Constitutional Convention to make sure that the United States would be truly united within a federal system of government.

Once again out of obligation, he was elected to the highest office of the land. Many urged him to accept the title Your Majesty or His Highness, or both, and that he would serve a lifetime presidency. He refused.

In his first inaugural address, Washington laid out his guiding principles:

> I behold the surest pledges, that as on one side, no local prejudices, or attachments; no separate views, nor party animosities, will misdirect the comprehensive and equal eye which ought to watch over this great assemblage of communities and interests: so, on another, that the foundations of our National policy will be laid in the pure and immutable principles of private morality; and the pre-eminence of a free Government, be exemplified by all the attributes which can win the affections of its Citizens, and command the respect of the world.

He used his celebrity to make the American people believe that there was such a thing as an American nation, although the concept was, at best, a hope for the future. Given his success in galvanizing a Continental army out of militias from 13 colonies, banging on a beggar's bowl for the necessary funds, Washington already had a reputation for pulling together diverse entities, goals, and people who could imagine themselves part of one cause and one land. In his first year as president, he spent a month in New England, visiting 60 towns and hamlets. His constituents took pride in their president, and much of his charisma was his rectitude.

Aware of his deficiencies and appreciative of others' skills, Washington was uncomfortable being treated as a demigod. Because the Constitution was mute on the subject of a cabinet, he established one of his own consisting of five men recruited for their diverse opinions on what he called "interesting

---

[12] https://msa.maryland.gov/msa/mdstatehouse/html/gwresignation.html

questions of National importance." Rather than opening meetings with his own views, he listened to theirs before deciding on a course of action.

He was a virtuoso of silence. Often, he did not need to give an order. Instead, he let his subordinates deliberate among themselves, waiting for them to come up with a solution that he favored and then giving them the nod. He convened meetings to solicit opinions and insights of men from different regions. Once he had surveyed others' thinking, he had confidence in his own judgment.

Washington believed that wise and benevolent statecraft relied on statesmen virtuous in their personal ethics: perspicacity, charity, and, above all, honesty with themselves as well as others. He wanted—indeed, insisted—that his closest colleagues hold to the same standard. Soon after the inauguration, he wrote a note to James Madison: "As the first of everything, in our situation will serve to establish a Precedent, it is devoutly wished on my part, that these precedents may be fixed on true principles."[13]

A few days later, Washington sent another note to his vice president, John Adams: "The President in all matters of business & etiquette, can have no object but to demean himself in his public character, in such a manner as to maintain the dignity of Office," adding a particular trait that he frowned upon: superciliousness.[14]

Despite Washington's lack of formal schooling, he was determined learn the fields of statesmanship. He acquired a membership at the New York Society Library in his first year in office. The records show that he borrowed two hefty works in his first year: *The Law of Nations* by Emer de Vattel—a Swiss disciple of the 17th-century Dutch Enlightenment jurist Hugo Grotius—and a volume of recorded debates in the British House of Commons. His selection of these tomes suggests what was on his mind: He wanted to learn about international governance in the Old World and the workings of the mother of all parliaments.

A newly inaugurated leader of a newly constituted republic was reverting to a habit from his youth when his mother oversaw his lessons, much of them moral precepts: He was doing his homework.

Seven years later, in his farewell address, Washington reiterated what he believed was the first commandment of rational and honorable statecraft: "It is substantially true that virtue or morality is a necessary spring of popular

---

[13] https://clintonwhitehouse3.archives.gov/WH/glimpse/presidents/html/gw1.html
[14] https://founders.archives.gov/documents/Washington/05-02-02-0182

government." This ethos, he believed, would be paramount to those who came after him in the highest office in the land.

The Revolutionary Generation contributed six men to the presidency, spanning 40 years. They shared astonishing experiences, heroic achievements, and mortal dangers. During the band-of-brothers years, while the republic was fragile, they tried to paper over their philosophical, political, and personal differences. That was more difficult with the rise of political parties, which represented opposing ideologies; the cloak of comity began to wear thin.

Jefferson and Alexander Hamilton despised each other, and each wrote excoriating letters to Washington trying to get the other fired from the cabinet. Adams turned on Jefferson for supporting the French Revolution, with its bloody reign of terror. Jefferson, for his part, turned on Adams, beating him for a second term.

Adams snubbed Jefferson by slipping out of Washington in the early hours of his inauguration day, and there followed a sad silence of a dozen years between the two men. They had been partners during the writing of the Declaration of Independence and were close personal friends during the late 1780s, when Jefferson was minister to France and Adams was America's man in London.

The feud began to thaw on January 1, 1812, when Adams sent a cordial note to Jefferson at Monticello, beginning an exchange of 158 letters that lasted for 14 years. The scope of their correspondence seemed to probe almost every field of knowledge, much of it an extensive curriculum on the Enlightenment. On certain disputes of the past, they found common ground; on others, they agreed to disagree. Disagreement, they knew, was not just inevitable: It was, and remains, sacred ground for a democracy. A free people thrive on argument, as long as it is in the spirit of dialogue.

"I have thus stated my opinion on a point on which we differ," Jefferson wrote,

> not with a view to controversy, for we are both too old to change opinions which are the result of a long life of enquiry and reflection; but on the suggestion of a former letter of yours, that we ought not to die before we have explained ourselves to each other.[15]

---

[15] https://founders.archives.gov/documents/Jefferson/03-06-02-0446

A threatened friendship had been rescued. But Jefferson and Adams never saw each other again. They stayed close to their homes, Monticello, Virginia, and Quincy, Massachusetts, respectively. During the 14 years of correspondence, their minds met regularly in a highly personal version of the Republic of Letters; this ended shortly before their deaths, within 5 hours of each other, on July 4, 1826—the 50th anniversary of the Declaration of Independence.

Jefferson had directed that his gravestone note only his three proudest accomplishments: author of the Declaration of Independence, author of the Statute of Virginia for religious freedom, and father of the University of Virginia. Other contributions to his country and his world can be noted elsewhere.

As for Adams, he lived long enough to see his son John Quincy in the White House, but he was spared seeing him soundly beaten by Andrew Jackson. The Adams presidents were also the first and second to be voted out of office after one term.

With the passing of the Revolutionary Generation, America entered a series of new eras. A few presidents rose to greatness, whereas others tried their best but failed. Even those who brought disgrace to the office paid lip service to the norms and laws that they skirted or violated. Why? Because they wanted to keep their niches in the pantheon that the founders had built for their successors.

Not Donald Trump. He used his tenure to construct a temple to himself. Now we know what happens when a malignant narcissist accrues extreme political power: He aspired to an earthly, personalized form of the divine right of kings. Freethinkers of the 17th century challenged that inane hubris.

When Trump accepted the Republican Party's nomination in Cleveland, Ohio, in July 2016, his peroration brought down the house. It consisted of four words, starting with his favorite: "I am your voice!" The founders would have sensed the acrid odor of tyranny. In their republic, citizens must retain their own voices and exercise their right to think for themselves. That principle was at the core of the founders' philosophy. They also revered empiricism, the rigorous pursuit of reality and facts that underlines pragmatic governing.

Trump had been a master of chicanery and falsehood throughout his career, so it was not a surprise that his first sentence was also his first lie as president: "I do solemnly swear that I will faithfully execute the office of President of the United States, and will to the best of my ability, preserve, protect and defend the Constitution of the United States."

For the next 4 years, Trump constantly offended the oath and much of the Constitution, starting with the preamble with its inclusive pronoun:

> We the People of the United States, in Order to form a more perfect Union, establish Justice, insure domestic Tranquility, provide for the common defen[s]e, promote the general Welfare, and secure the Blessings of Liberty to ourselves and our Posterity, do ordain and establish this Constitution for the United States of America.

A new president's own plans and goals must conform with those of the framers, whose first and foremost aspiration was a cohesive nation. They knew that perfection was not in the reach of mortals, but they could try. Hence, "a more perfect union."

That phrase connoted ceaseless progress in constructing a government and nurturing a society based on the ideals of the Declaration of Independence: "We hold these truths to be self-evident, that all men are created equal, that they are endowed by their Creator with certain unalienable Rights, that among these are Life, Liberty and the pursuit of Happiness."

E pluribus unum was an early and durable motto. It has often carried a dual meaning: The American states are united in a single country, and all citizens have the same rights and responsibilities, regardless of ethnicity, gender, faith, and country of origin.

Trump rejected both definitions. As candidate, he ran on a brazen self-serving platform of division and conflict. The framers' "We the People" connotes the citizenry, whereas Trump's version was "*my* people"—those who let him be their voice and gave him their votes. All others were losers and scum.

As for justice, Trump dispensed rewards to those who pleased him and castigated those who did not.

And then there is another word—cherished by the framers: tranquility. It means civil peace. Trump thrived on making enemies of his fellow citizens. He defiled all of the arch principles and virtues undergirding the supreme law of the land. Trump not only tried to adulterate American democracy to his solipsism but also had considerable success. He cowed the Republican Party that had scorned him until its leaders surrendered.

He turned American foreign policy on its head, cozying up to authoritarian regimes while diluting ties with allies that had shared America's traditional democratic values dating back to the founders.

How mournful it is to read in the Declaration of Independence the determination to resist the "injuries and usurpations" of a tyrant and "[t]o prove this, let Facts be submitted to a candid world." For 4 years, a candid world had to resign itself to dealing with "alternative facts" delivered by a megalomaniac master of mendacity in the White House.

Not only was Trump the first modern president to scoff openly at the founders' ethics, ideology, and laws, but also he was the only one who has jettisoned rational policymaking. He felt that he could get away with that as long as the issues at hand were in the realm of politics, laws, institutions, and the perversions of human agency. That was largely why Trump had such a dismal record of useful and sensible statecraft. Most of his enterprises were shams, whether in foreign policy, legislation, education, and health.

Yet, at the close of 2019, his bizarre stratagems had achieved many of his desires. The stock market was on a roll, and Trump might have had a clear path to a second term.

Then, a novel virus caught the entire world off guard. Trump reacted as though he knew more than all the medical experts. He had a campaign to run and win, and nothing and no one was going to change that focus. The pandemic killed almost 400,000 Americans in 2020, a staggering toll that could have been mitigated if Trump had used his executive power and listened to medical scientists to combat the plague. Instead, he let it rage while assuring his devotees that the scare was a hoax.

Trump was used to staring down his fellow beings, flouting their laws, splintering their institutions, and scorning their governments—including his own. Mother Nature, however, was an exception. She wouldn't bend to bullying.

Trump's spell was weakened, but at a devastating price for his fellow citizens. If he had the sense to see a reality that required urgent and massive expertise, he would have blunted the carnage and probably captured his cherished second term.

There was another upheaval in 2020, but this one was a perennial upheaval of human passions. White supremacism had always been near the core of Trumpism, but it came boiling up to the surface of his strategy to ensure victory. In the spring, as protests spread against police brutality in inner cities nationwide, he used his baroque campaign rallies and social media to warn his followers that Black Americans were a threat to White suburbs. He ordered federal military forces to quell demonstrations with tear gas and encouraged armed fascists to menace Black marchers who were largely peaceful.

When election day came, opinion polls showed that more voters disapproved of Trump's handling of the protests than those who approved. The margin was close to the election result.[16]

Trump had long worried about Joseph Biden as his challenger for the 2020 campaign. He fabricated a conspiracy theory that Biden's son, Hunter, had conducted illegal business in Ukraine. Trump tried to bully the president of Ukraine, Volodymyr Zelensky, to go along with the scam. He was desperate for American military aid to combat Russia's 2014 occupation of Ukraine. In July 2019, Trump put the screws to Zelensky: The price of the American armaments was a Ukrainian public investigation into phantom scandal that might knock Biden out of the race for the White House.

American presidents have wide oversight of foreign relations, including conducting diplomacy with their counterparts abroad. However, the Ukraine caper was a bald-faced case of extortion, having nothing to do with American policy and everything to do with threatening Zelensky to stoke a lie that would smear Trump's rival in domestic politics. (Trump held up the security assistance for 55 days over the summer. Zelensky did not bend to his demands.)

As the real truth leaked out, so did the real scandal. In February 2020, the Democratic majority in the House of Representatives impeached Trump on the charge of abuse of power, only to fall short when the Republican majority in the Senate acquitted him.

There was the rub. Trump's base was a minority in the American electorate, but it was powerfully influential in the Republican party in the heartland. Motivated by fealty or fear, a formidable band of Republicans in Congress and state houses demonstrated a herd immunity against their scruples and their own oaths to the Constitution. Both worked to Trump's advantage.

Of all the founders, Hamilton was the most prescient. He warned that:

> a dangerous ambition more often lurks behind the specious mask of zeal for the rights of the people, than under the forbidding appearance of zeal for the firmness and efficiency of government. History will teach us, that the former has been found a much more certain road to the introduction of despotism, than the latter, and that of those men who have overturned the liberties of republics the greatest number have begun their career, by paying

---

[16] https://thehill.com/hilltv/what-americas-thinking/533251-poll-majority-disapprove-of-trumps-handling-of-capitol-riots

an obsequious court to the people, commencing Demagogues and ending Tyrants.[17]

He returned to that concern several years later:

> The truth unquestionably is, that the only path to a subversion of the republican system of the Country is, by flattering the prejudices of the people, and exciting their jealousies and apprehension, to throw affairs into confusion, and bring on the civil commotion. A man unprincipled in private life desperate in his fortune, bold in his temper, possessed of considerable talents, having the advantage of military habits—despotic in his ordinary demeanour—known to have scoffed in private at the principle of liberty.
>
> Those then, who resist a confirmation of public order, are the true Artificers of monarchy—not that this is the intention of the generality of them. Yet it would not be difficult to lay the finger upon some of their party who may justly be suspected . . . when such a man is seen to mount the hobby horse of popularity—to join in the cry of danger to liberty—to take every opportunity of embarrassing the General Government & bringing it under suspicion—to flatter and fall in with all the non sense of the zealots of the day—It may justly be suspected that his object is to throw things into confusion that he may "ride the storm and direct the whirlwind."[18]

The storm that Trump conjured up after the ballots were counted following the November 3, 2020, election had no precedent in American history. He used his favorite tools, bigotry and falsehood, although he used them more audaciously than ever before. He accused the Democrats of stealing the election by faking Biden ballots and demanded a recount that would nullify legitimate votes in Democratic strongholds. It was a naked attempt to disenfranchise Black, Brown, and immigrant voters. The thief played the victim.

In the weeks after Biden's victory, angry legions of Trump supporters swarmed into the streets throughout the country. Some staged riots and threatened violence. Meanwhile, a squad of Trump lawyers fanned out to the swing states that tipped to Biden with baseless claims of fraud that were quickly thrown out by judges around the states as well the Supreme Court.

---

[17] https://founders.archives.gov/documents/Hamilton/01-04-02-0152
[18] https://founders.archives.gov/documents/Hamilton/01-12-02-0184-0002

Trump was deeply involved, egging on his minions and threatening administrators from both parties who had overseen a remarkably efficient and nearly faultless national election.

But Trump would not give up. "Big protest in D.C. on January 6th," Mr. Trump tweeted on December 19, one of several of his tweets promoting the day. "Be there, will be wild!"

That was the day that the Congress would affirm Biden's victory, with Vice President Mike Pence overseeing the counting of the ballots in a pro forma ceremony. Nevertheless, Trump was hoping Pence would go off script and disqualify enough of Biden's winnings to cause a constitutional crisis. Pence did not have such power. As he wrote in a letter to Trump, "The presidency belongs to the American people, and to them alone."

Trump had yet another play, and this one was deadly. At noon, he went to the Ellipse near the White House where 2,000–2,500 excited marchers were waiting. "We will never give up," he said, "We will never concede. It will never happen. You don't concede when there's theft involved. Our country has had enough. We will not take it anymore." The pep talk ran over an hour. At the end, he urged everyone to walk down Pennsylvania Avenue to give Republicans "the kind of pride and boldness that they need to take back our country."

Then he returned to the White House, where he watched on television as all the world could see the U.S. Capitol vandalized, blood was shed, people died. According to his staff, the president was delighted by the insurrection that he had fomented.

The 45th president of the United States was the first to go to war against his own government. He lost, at least for the time being. He was impeached by the House of Representatives twice, but he also was acquitted twice by the Senate because a guilty charge requires a two-third votes.

A sizable majority of Americans had known that Trump had been lying about the election win. Many wanted dearly to have *their* country back after 4 dreadful years. Before they saw the reports from the national capital during that surreal afternoon, many believed that Trump's reign was finally and truly over. They thought they could breathe again. But now they had to brace themselves for new brazen crimes to keep him in power. That was plausible. Trump had his own millions who believed in him or were frightened of him. That is likely to be the case for some time.

But there have been competing voices.

At the end of Joe Biden's inauguration address, he said: "And so today, at this time and this place, let us start afresh. All of us. Let us listen to one another. Hear another. Show respect to one another." It was part of his pledge to be a president for all his fellow citizens. It was also redolent of Jefferson's appeal to Adams for good faith, especially in disputes: Americans, in all our multiplicity and passion, must try not to die before we have explained ourselves to one another.

Several weeks later, when Trump, a private citizen, was holed up in Florida, stewing new schemes to upend American democracy, Jamie Raskin, the lead of the Senate trial, brought into the proceedings:

> Ben Franklin, a great champion of the Enlightenment, an enemy of political fanaticism and cowardice, and of course another great Philadelphian, once wrote this: "I have observed that wrong is always growing more wrong until there is no bearing it anymore, and that right, however opposed, comes right at last." Comes right at last. Think about that. This is America, home of the brave, land of the free. The America of Ben Franklin, who said, "If you make yourself a sheep, the wolves will eat you." Don't make yourself a sheep. The wolves will eat you. The America of Thomas Jefferson, who said at another difficult moment, "A little patience and we shall see the reign of witches pass over, their spirits dissolve, and the people, recovering their true sight, restore their government to its true principles." The America of Tom Payne, who said, "The mind, once enlightened, cannot again become dark."

That's something to remember.

2

City on a Hill

Pilgrims, Puritans, and the Origin of America

Abram Van Engen

A national memory is a national story. Every story can be told any number of ways, but one factor remains necessary to each: a beginning. When does a nation begin?

How a nation settles on a starting point can reveal a good deal about the processes of national memory as they take shape. Are starting points obvious? Are they assigned by national leaders? Do they arise from public and cultural events? What potential beginnings are erased, forgotten, or ignored in order to celebrate another? And which actors are assigned the most prominent roles? In short, how a nation begins its story reveals a great deal about the formation and consequences of national memory.[1] Where, when, and with whom does a nation begin?

In some cases, it might seem like an easy question to answer. Take the case of the United States. The Declaration of Independence was published to the world on July 4, 1776. Early citizens celebrated the Fourth of July across every colony, and today, citizens all across the nation still mark the day with fireworks. What more is there to say?[2]

The problem is that any chosen beginning will find itself in the midst of history, and therefore its own beginnings will extend back before it. It is one thing to ask citizens when the United States of America begins. Answers will almost surely agree. It is another thing to ask them when "America" began and what that has to do with the nation that has "America" in its name. America is something other, larger, and older than the United States, and yet its longer, larger history often informs

---

[1] For more on this point, see especially Yamashiro et al. (2022), and see Chapter 5 in this volume.
[2] On the celebration of the Fourth of July as an early rite practiced in various and sometimes competing ways to create a national identity, see Waldstreicher (1997).

Abram Van Engen, *City on a Hill* In: *National Memories*. Edited by: Henry L. Roediger and James V. Wertsch, Oxford University Press. © Oxford University Press 2022. DOI: 10.1093/oso/9780197568675.003.0002

national memory, including how we understand the story and origins of the United States.

Early citizens of the recently independent United States recognized the problem themselves, and many began casting about for histories that would extend national memory into a pre-national time. What they hoped to shore up was a sense of identity that could bind citizens together. Virginians, for example, had long identified themselves as Virginians. Now, as citizens of the United States, they had to nurture a shared sense of identity with people from, for example, Massachusetts—a very different culture with its own history and memories. What could people from these two places share in common? As Joyce Appleby (2000) has aptly explained, "Because political union preceded the formation of a national identity, the first generation was forced to imagine the sentiments that might bind the nation together" (p. 240). A nation meant a national identity, but no national identity preceded the nation. One had to be invented and then ingrained. "The Revolution had offered patriots the rhetorical opportunity to treat America's social diversity as a summons to a new kind of nationhood," Appleby adds, "but a successful War for Independence did not supply the shared sentiments, symbols, and social explanations necessary for an integrative national identity" (p. 262).[3]

In the early years of the 1800s, increasingly more Americans called for a national identity based in memory—in a shared narrative of the past. The nation needed a national history in order to have a common story that could be felt, lived, embraced, and embodied by all—an account of how they had come together as a nation in order to tell them who they were. Scholars of nationalism often refer to this as "temporal depth," which basically means the culturally shared memories (whether imagined or actual) that bind individuals together as mutual citizens. A shared story of the country's past, it has been argued, is an essential feature of national identity.[4]

It was in this moment—in the early republic shortly after the War of 1812 when a "euphoria of nationalism" (Howe, 2007, p. 71) swept across the country—that an unlikely set of figures suddenly gained national prominence: the Pilgrims.

---

[3] For two essential starting points on the role of culture and imagination in the creation of nationalism, see Anderson (1991) and Hobsbawm and Ranger (1983).

[4] On the role of narratives in creating a nation, see Simon During (1990) and Chapter 22 in this volume. Thomas Allen (2008), in a review of debates about nationalism and its relation to representation, gives some credence to During's position, especially in this period, but also tempers it with the work of Anthony D. Smith.

The story of the *Mayflower* had long been known and variously celebrated in New England, especially in Massachusetts, but beyond its regional salience, the landing of the Pilgrims had little relevance for others. The general insignificance of the Pilgrims makes sense. After all, if one is looking for a starting point to American history, it might seem strange to begin with a people who were not the first to live here, nor the first Europeans to arrive, nor the first English settlers to call it home. In so many ways, the Pilgrims were late to the game. Beginning any story with them, especially a national story of the United States—whose first president hailed from Virginia—would seem odd. Yet increasingly, the Pilgrims became the origin story of the nation. How that happened can give us insights into the processes of national memory.

It began with a speech—but not just any speech and not just by any orator. Daniel Webster had already become one of the most well-known and influential Northerners in the nation. He had successfully argued crucial cases before the Supreme Court, and he would go on to become a powerful senator and eventually the Secretary of State. In 1820, he was asked to give an address in Plymouth to commemorate the bicentennial of Pilgrim Landing. And when he did so, in rapturous terms, he emphasized that the history "of our native land" (Webster, 1826, p. 2) began at Plymouth Rock. Which "native land" did he mean? Was Webster referring to New England (the usual reference until then in Pilgrim celebrations), or did he mean the relatively new United States? As Webster moved through the speech, it became clear that he had a much larger, national meaning in mind. Because the Revolution began in Massachusetts, Webster argued, a Massachusetts origin of the nation naturally made sense. In Webster's tale of the nation, Plymouth led to Lexington (with hardly a side glance at Virginia, and only to dismiss it). The beginning of the nation came not in 1776 but in 1620, when Pilgrims landed at Plymouth Rock.

From the moment Webster delivered this speech, the notion of Pilgrim origins began to spread. Webster's stature, in addition to his oratorical prowess, helped make the story stick. The address was printed and distributed widely. John Adams (as cited in Remini, 1997) soon proclaimed Webster "the most consummate orator of modern times" and announced that

> this Oration will be read five hundred years hence with as much rapture, as it was heard; it ought to be read at the end of every Century, and indeed at the end of every year, for ever and ever. (p. 186)[5]

---

[5] Henry Cabot Lodge (1887), in his own enthusiastic biography of Webster, claimed that the Plymouth oration "was received with a universal burst of applause. It had more literary success than

In this case, what we find is the particular influence of a powerful individual whose words were printed and broadly distributed. It is a top-down model for the creation of national memory.[6]

Or is it? Anthony D. Smith, one of the leading scholars of nationalism, has argued that narratives of the nation are never simply imposed on a people. They gain force only by expressing the desires of a people at a given time and place. Nations are "*felt* and *willed*" by citizens, not just invented or constructed by elites (Smith, 2000, p. 59). In the case of Webster, regional celebrations of Plymouth Rock had existed long before he made this speech. The people invited him there for a reason. There was already an opening for the memory of this beginning—a culturally celebrated commencement situated at Plymouth Rock—to become the beginning of a new national memory. In other words, there was an interplay between forces from the ground up and the power and forcefulness of Webster himself, top-down.

Other factors also contributed to the spread of this story. However prominent Webster might have been in the North, he was not loved in the South. And the South seemed to be where the true power of the nation lay. In 1820, at the time of Webster's address, James Madison was president of the United States. He was the fourth Virginian (out of the first five presidents) to hold the office. And what did Virginia care for Plymouth Rock?

To understand the spread of the Pilgrims as a new origin story of America, two elements become especially important: (a) the content of the story and (b) the method of its delivery. What Webster preached at Plymouth was a message many Anglo-Americans wanted to endorse. The Pilgrims, Webster said, came for liberty. They established freedom as the substance of American identity. And the creation of a new nation on July 4, 1776, simply extended that freedom more broadly. "At the moment of their landing," he declared, "they possessed institutions of government, and institutions of religion: and

---

anything which had at that time appeared, except from the pen of Washington Irving" (p. 123). More generally, Webster's speeches (including this one) "were attended by political luminaries, reprinted on three continents, and read in politically influential circles in Europe and Spanish America" (Gustafson, 2007, p. 121).

[6] Many scholars agree that Webster's speeches of the 1820s were integral to making Pilgrim Landing and Plymouth Rock into a national origin myth. Before then, Pilgrims hardly mattered, and certainly not beyond New England. As Conforti (2001) summarizes, "The founding of Plymouth itself remained an uncommemorated, even obscure, local event overshadowed for most of the colonial era by the 'Great,' expansive Puritan migration to New England" (p. 171). Bendroth (2015) adds, "For much of the early nineteenth century, Plymouth Rock was the pride of New England but not much anywhere else" (p. 27). Webster would change that. For a summary of Webster's influence, see Sheidley (1998, Chapter 5).

friends and families, and social and religious institutions, framed by consent, founded on choice and preference, how nearly do these fill up our whole idea of country!" (Webster, 1826, p. 25). The story of the Pilgrims as it came to be told gave Anglo-Americans a certain pride in their identity. They could claim that the United States, unlike other countries, represented a unique experiment in liberty. Fleeing persecution abroad, the Pilgrims established freedom here.

To rehearse such a story, a good deal would have to be ignored or erased. It should not surprise us that the fact of slavery in New England was quickly forgotten because the supposed establishment of freedom was precisely what enabled the Pilgrims to become an origin story more generally. The prior and ongoing presence of Native Americans was also pushed out of the tale. Rather than being a people with lands and governments and rights, they became a piece of the vacant wilderness on which a new story of freedom could unfold. In one of the most fundamental lectures on the topic of national history and memory, the French scholar Ernst Renan remarked already in 1882, "Forgetting, I would even go so far as to say historical error, is a crucial factor in the creation of a nation, which is why progress in historical studies often constitutes a danger for [the principle of] nationality" (Renan, 1990, p. 11). This process has been called "firsting" by the Native American scholar Jean O'Brien (2010), who chronicles the way local historians wrote Indians out of existence by identifying the "first" English settler in the town and celebrating the town's (English) origins. In many cases, including Plymouth, the English village that emerged was built on the very site that had once been a Native American village, the fields already cleared for planting and the land already prepared. But by calling English settlers the "first," the prior could be ignored. This was certainly the case with the Pilgrim myth at the moment of its creation. Not only were Native Americans erased but so too were other English colonists, and not just in Virginia but even in New England, where plenty of English boats had already come (and already spread the plague that enabled the Pilgrims to settle where they did). Erasure and forgetting are an essential feature of national memory. With the Pilgrims, all motives, actions, and peoples other than the Pilgrim pursuit of liberty were set aside.

The content of the tale, then, explains one reason why people began to pick up the story of the Pilgrims and make it their own. But the method of distribution remains equally important. How did people even hear about the Pilgrims? In what context was this tale encountered?

Here the crucial factor is the cultural power of textbooks. Beginning in 1820, the same year as Webster's speech, a national craving for history combined with new schooling requirements to create a booming market for schoolbooks. What had been only a sparse trickle of publications here and there between 1775 and 1820 soon became a flood. Literary journals soon devoted significant space specifically to reviewing all the new textbooks coming rapidly into print. In the decade of the 1820s, which saw multiple commemorations (200 years since Pilgrim Landing and 50 years since the start of the American Revolution), textbooks became bestsellers and continued rising in sales until they were "out-performing the nearest genre of book by over five to one" (Joyce, 2015, p. 43).[7]

These schoolbooks exercised an outsized influence on the creation and consolidation of national history. The stories they contained traveled beyond the confines of school because the books themselves were designed from the start to reach not just students but also families. They were the reference books of the new nation, set next to the family bible with perhaps a few other books in the home, and for many Americans, they constituted "very nearly the sole source of information on American history" (Van Tassel, 1960, p. 91). As a result, textbooks became the makers, keepers, and distributors of national memory.[8]

They did not all agree. Variations could be found from book to book, but because many of the textbook writers hailed from New England—including the most prominent and bestselling ones (Samuel Goodrich, Charles Goodrich, Salma Hale, and Emma Willard)—the Pilgrims held a unique space and function in these histories.[9] Perhaps the best way to

---

[7] For the numbers of editions per decade, see Callcott (1959, p. 473). Callcott claims that five editions appeared between 1775 and 1820. Nietz (1961) says that "only eight or nine American history textbooks were published in our country before 1820, and apparently none had a wide circulation" (p. 234). The journals devoting book reviews to textbooks were the *United States Literary Gazette* (established 1824) and the *American Journal of Education* (established 1826) (see Van Tessel, 1960, pp. 89–90). For more on the dramatic rise of historical interest in the 1820s and 1830s, especially in New England, see Harlow Sheidley (1998, Chapter 5). For the rise and role of schoolbooks more generally in the era, see Charles Monaghan and E. Jennifer Monaghan (2010). Monaghan and Monaghan, like others, identify 1820 as a turning point. As Calcott (1970) observes, "Never before or since has history occupied such a vital place in the thinking of the American people as during the first half of the nineteenth century" (p. 25).

[8] According to Adams (2008), history textbooks were "the most widely read books of any genre in the United States before the twentieth century" (p. 49). Joyce (2015) observes, "Textbook publishers targeted entire families as likely consumers of their product" (p. 56).

[9] For the top four textbook writers, see Alfred Goldberg (1941). Gretchen Adams (2008, p. 50) names the top six: these four plus Jesse Olney and Marcius Wilson. By 1860, New England comprised only 10% of the U.S. population, yet the region produced half of the nation's historians (see Callcott, 1970, p. 68). As the literary historian Joseph Conforti (2001) aptly summarizes, "New Englanders dominated American historical writing from the seventeenth well into the twentieth century" (p. 6).

understand how they served is to explore the table of contents in Emma Willard's *A History of the United States, or Republic of America*, first printed in 1828 and then reprinted 53 times over 45 years (her history textbooks sold more than 1 million copies).[10] Willard organized American history by a series of turning points that bracketed off distinct epochs. In doing so, she could follow chronology but still set apart the Pilgrims. That is, her histories begin with Columbus but then quickly mark the "first epoch" as comprised by "Portuguese, English, Spanish, and French Discoveries" in the years 1578–1619. By locating Jamestown, New Amsterdam, and other colonial settlements in the era of "discovery," Willard could effectively move them out of the era of true beginnings. The moment of true beginning comes instead in the "Second Epocha," starting with the "landing of Mr. Robinson's congregation at Plymouth" and covering the years 1620–1642 (Willard, 1828, pp. iii–v).

What set the Pilgrims apart, for Willard, was their cause. Where others came for gold, she claimed, the Pilgrims came for God. And while others stumbled to establish themselves in ways marked by misery and deceit, the pure-hearted Pilgrims established the cause of liberty as the enduring attribute of what it means to be American. This distinction of the Pilgrims from all the rest (pursuing God and freedom, not gold and gain) remained an enduring feature of the Plymouth myth. Portraying the Pilgrims' Mayflower Compact as the origin of the United States, Willard (1828) wrote, "In their character and in their institutions, we behold the germ of that love of liberty, and those correct views of the natural equality of man, which are now fully developed in the American constitution" (p. 46).[11] This was the myth, the national memory, printed and reprinted in countless textbooks distributed throughout the nation. Schoolbooks took Webster's speech and spread it to children and families in every state.

---

[10] For printing counts, see Baym (1991, pp. 4–5). Baym adds, "The intended audience for this text, then, was the entire literate population." For the estimate of more than 1 million books, see Barry Joyce (2015, p. 45).

[11] As John Seelye (1998) notes about the cultural use of a Pilgrim origin myth, "Certainly the Pilgrims stand out from all the other early settlers of the North American continent, whether the French of Canada, the Spanish of Florida and Mexico, or the English at Roanoke and Jamestown, as remarkable exemplars of 'pure' motives, distinct from the rest in having only a secondary interest in the commercial aspects of colonial enterprise" (p. 10). Seelye's is one of the best and most comprehensive sources tracking the American cultural and collective memory of Pilgrims and Puritans over time. For a good source concerned more broadly with the memory and making of "New England," see Conforti (2001).

By the time the French nobleman Alexis de Tocqueville arrived in the United States in 1831, the idea of Pilgrim origins had become so widespread that he adopted it into his massively influential tome *Democracy in America* (first published in English in 1838). In Chapter 2 of that widely celebrated work, Tocqueville identifies Puritan New England as "the germe of all that is to follow . . . and the key to almost the whole work"—the origin, in short, of the nation (Tocqueville, 2007, pp. 27–28). In Virginia, said Tocqueville, "No lofty conceptions, no intellectual system directed the foundation of these new settlements." It was left to New England to initiate America, for "the foundation of New England was a novel spectacle, and all the circumstances attending it were singular and original." The principles established by Pilgrims and Puritans, Tocqueville insisted, "spread at first to the neighbouring states; they then passed successively to the more distant ones; and at length they imbued the whole confederation" (p. 28). Those principles, he went on, now

> extend their influence beyond its limits over the whole American world. The civilization of New England has been like a beacon lit upon a hill, which, after it has diffused its warmth around, tinges the distant horizon with its glow. (pp. 30–31)

The idea of America as a "beacon lit upon a hill," a veiled citation of Matthew 5:14, opens one further complication to the making of national memory. For in the rise of Ronald Reagan, many years later, the United States repeatedly became identified as a "shining city on a hill"—a reference, Reagan said, to the sermon of John Winthrop, the first Puritan governor of Massachusetts Bay, which he delivered on the *Arbella* shortly before stepping ashore in 1630. In other words, Reagan turned to the Puritans, and to an origin story of their motives and consequences, in order to ingrain the memory of a beginning that would mark the continuing identity and purpose of America ever since. Established as a "city on a hill," Reagan said in the 1970s and 1980s, the United States needed to revive its place in the world in order to stay true to its founding vision.

We have seen how the myth of Pilgrim origins spread and what it erased as it took its place at the origin of a nation that would not emerge until many years later. The rise of the phrase "city on a hill" tells an equally curious and mysterious story of national memory. For when Winthrop delivered his sermon in 1630, it quickly fell on deaf ears. No one marked the day of his auspicious announcement, not even Winthrop himself. And the sermon, which he might or might not have delivered aboard the *Arbella*—which he might or might not have delivered *at all*, in fact—was never printed, barely distributed, and never remembered or remarked upon for a full 200 years after Winthrop's arrival. Tocqueville never cited the sermon because by the time his book appeared, no one yet had heard of it. The first anyone knew of Winthrop's supposed sermon was a few months after the publication of Tocqueville's book, when a manuscript of the sermon was found buried in the archives of the New-York Historical Society. If Winthrop's sermon declaring that "we shall be as a city upon a hill" is the foundation of the nation, it is a foundation invented after the fact.[12]

The moment Winthrop's sermon became famous, moreover, was not the moment it was found. Published in 1838, *A Model of Christian Charity* (Winthrop's "city on a hill" sermon) again passed quickly and quietly away, languishing in *The Collections of the Massachusetts Historical Society*. For another century, it was hardly a national text and certainly not a part of any national memory. Throughout the 19th century, the phrase "city on a hill" appeared here and there in relation to a few political entities (as Tocqueville's usage demonstrates), but by and large it was an expression attached almost exclusively to the church. Americans did not refer to the United States as a "city on a hill." They used that phrase instead to designate Christians, clergymen, apostles, missionaries, and emissaries of Christ.

What moved this phrase from an expression of the church to a slogan of the nation was, finally, the Cold War. In that context, scholars and politicians often worked together to shore up American traditions while setting apart the United States as a beacon of liberty, a counter to everything represented by the communist Soviet Union. One scholar in particular, an influential Harvard professor named Perry Miller, located in the Puritans the source of all things American. And it was he who began to emphasize, again and again, that Winthrop's 1630 "city on a hill" sermon had established the identity and purpose of the United States.

To make this claim, Miller had to do something that, in context, would seem rather drastic: He downplayed the Pilgrims. On the other hand, his story of America as a "city on a hill" actually depended on a different point of origin—the arrival of a large band of Puritans in 1630, a full 10 years

---

[12] For a history of this sermon and of American exceptionalism more broadly, see Van Engen (2020). See also Chapter 4 in this volume.

later, in a different colony under a different magistrate having a distinct relationship with England. As any historian of the era knew, the Pilgrims and Puritans were actually separate people living in side-by-side colonies with contrasting views and goals. The Pilgrims were *separatists*—that is, they officially separated from the Church of England. Because the monarch was the head of the Church of England, this act of separation was perceived as treasonous. The Pilgrims were harried out of England, first settling in the Netherlands before a small, poorly outfitted band of 102 Pilgrims made an attempt at starting over in America in 1620 aboard the *Mayflower*. They never had much money, and they never flourished. The Puritans were different. They sought the reform of the Church of England and never separated from it. When they came to New England, they had a charter from the King and quite a few resources. Moreover, they came in force—almost 1,000 in the great wave of 1630 that founded Boston. The Pilgrims eventually achieved a patent for Plymouth Colony, but through much of the 17th century, Pilgrims and Puritans lived in separate jurisdictions.

In highlighting the 1630 "city on a hill" sermon of the Puritan governor John Winthrop as the true origin of America, Miller had to disregard and set aside the already established myth of Plymouth Rock and the coming of the Pilgrims 10 years earlier. The Pilgrims, for Miller, represented nothing more than a washed-up group of refugees who came to shore with no clear ideas and no sense of purpose. They languished with little consequence in a minor colony that was eventually swallowed up by the main event: the creation and consolidation of Massachusetts Bay. It was the coming of Winthrop and the Puritans in 1630, Miller said, that really mattered. The *Mayflower* was a mistake when it happened (it was headed to Virginia), and it remained a mistake of national memory to celebrate it. No clear beginning could be identified in 1620. The nation that Miller wanted to sketch—its true founding, its "first" clear statement of principles and purpose—came in 1630 with Winthrop's declaration that "we shall be as a city upon a hill."

Miller's many publications and lectures helped reshape American historical narratives, but they operated primarily in academic spheres. Miller always wanted to be a public intellectual, but he never achieved broad influence. Instead, his ideas were taken up by textbooks and fellow scholars, who gradually turned to Winthrop's sermon after having largely ignored it for the past century. Where Emma Willard sang a paean of praise to the Pilgrims, for example, she hardly noted the arrival of Winthrop and certainly never cited his supposedly foundational speech. That remained the case in

American history textbooks up until the Cold War, when suddenly the arrival of Winthrop and his "city on a hill" declaration began to appear as a turning point in American history. Anthologies of American literature likewise ignored Winthrop's sermon until the Cold War, when rather suddenly they made it not just a canonical piece of the American literary tradition but even the founding and origin of American letters. In other words, beginning in the 1950s, scholars and schoolbooks began to situate Winthrop and his sermon in a prime position, an originating vision of the nation that was about to come.

It was in the wake of this work that John F. Kennedy, in 1961, became the first president to incorporate Winthrop's "city on a hill" sermon into American political rhetoric. As he prepared to leave his beloved Massachusetts for the White House, he spoke to the state's general court one last time, telling them that Winthrop had been his mentor all along. "I have been guided by the standard John Winthrop set before his shipmates on the flagship *Arbella* 331 years ago," Kennedy said,

> as they, too, faced the task of building a new government on a perilous frontier. "We must always consider," he said. "That we shall be as a city upon a hill—the eyes of all people are upon us." Today the eyes of all people are truly upon us.

For Kennedy, Winthrop's words rang with both hope and fear—a warning and a call to all Americans who dared to lead before a watching world.

In the decades after Kennedy, each president made some use of Winthrop's sermon, but no one popularized the "city on a hill" line or implanted it in American collective memory quite as forcefully as Ronald Reagan. Whereas in 1820, Daniel Webster had used a powerful speech to shape the making of American schoolbooks, in the 1970s the gradual reshaping of textbooks and anthologies preceded and became crystallized in the powerful speeches and rhetoric of one particular politician. The relationship was reversed, but the pieces remained in place: A re-schooling of the American public went hand-in-hand with the remaking of national memory by one influential individual. By the end of the 20th century, Reagan's rhetoric had so ingrained itself that almost no one—including almost no scholars of American history and literature—knew or remembered that Winthrop's "city on a hill" sermon had languished unpublished and unknown for more than 200 years.

Reagan achieved his purpose, moreover, by purposefully blending the two origin stories. Since 1820, Pilgrim Landing had gained a special place in commemorations of the nation. Since the 1950s, Winthrop's speech (delivered 10 years after Pilgrim Landing) had gained prominence. Reagan made them one. The Puritan Winthrop represented, for Reagan, "an early Pilgrim, an early freedom man" (Reagan, 1989). By deliberately and consistently calling Winthrop a "Pilgrim" through many years, Reagan was able to celebrate both Plymouth Rock and Winthrop's "city on a hill" sermon. Both were blended together as the founding moment of freedom, and together the Pilgrims of Winthrop's "city on a hill" called us to carry the torch of liberty forward from generation to generation.

For more than 20 years after Reagan's last usage of it in his 1989 Farewell Address, Winthrop's 1630 sermon became part of the common political lexicon both left and right. In attempting to defeat Reagan's successor, the Democrat's nominee, Michael Dukakis, turned to Winthrop's sermon as the founding moment of American history. But unlike Reagan or Bush, Dukakis (1988) tried to cite other lines in Winthrop's sermon as fundamental to the meaning of America:

> "We must," said Winthrop, "love one another with a pure heart fervently. We must delight in each other, make each other's conditions our own, rejoice together, mourn together, and suffer together. We must," he said, "be knit together as one."

For Dukakis, Winthrop's monumental founding sermon, *A Model of Christian Charity*, established America on the central principle of *community*. On the left, these lines from Winthrop's sermon—the lines about rejoicing, mourning, and suffering together leading to a common American community—became more important than the phrase "city on a hill." Bill Clinton, Barack Obama, Elizabeth Warren, and numerous other politicians on the left have all turned to Winthrop's sermon, and all of them have quoted the same lines as Dukakis. In other words, following Reagan, Winthrop's sermon—which initially had gone unknown—had become so famous that politicians both left and right viewed it as foundational. They fought about which lines mattered most because both sides accepted the invented tradition of its original historical significance.

That has changed only recently, and only through the rise of Donald Trump's "America First" rhetoric. In the 2016 election, Trump never turned to

Winthrop's sermon, never called America a "city on a hill," explicitly rejected American exceptionalism, and told virtually no history of America at all (apart from a vague gesture that America had once been great). It was the opposition to Trump—from both liberals and conservatives—who turned to the language of "city on a hill" (see Van Engen, 2018). And in the years since Donald Trump has taken power, Winthrop's sermon has seen some decline in collective recitation, even as the opponents of Trump still often turn to this sermon and try to keep up the fading image of a city on a hill.

Although the story of Winthrop's sermon may be in the process of a dramatic change right now, the constants in its history are nonetheless telling. Pilgrim and Puritan origin stories arose and spread through the combined efforts of schools and speeches—national lecterns and national textbooks. But the form and method of distribution do not explain everything. These origin stories took hold also because of what they allowed so many Americans to say and think about themselves. By sidelining Virginia, where slavery and its horrors could never be entirely ignored, Pilgrim origin stories enabled a national memory and a national story dedicated to the progress of liberty. The painful memories of New England—the stories of Native Americans cheated, murdered, and enslaved, the enslaved Africans in New England homes, the selling and separating of families by Pilgrims and Puritans, the investments in slave ships and the money made by New England merchants—these dismally unfree aspects of the Pilgrim and Puritan story were quietly muted for a national origin devoted to something purer, something nobler, something good.[13]

The work of national memory is seldom meant to give us an accurate picture of the past—though it is often presented as such. Instead, it exists to guide the present generation into the future. Origin stories, with all their inventions and erasures, have ever been made, marked, and remembered because they establish a national identity and give the nation a sense of purpose, wrongs to right and rights to defend or uphold. As much as historians attempt to set the record straight, origin stories will always have a powerful hold on the public. For national memories are, in the end, national stories. And every story—whatever else it has or does, whatever work it attempts to achieve, whatever it includes or erases—can only be a story if it starts.

---

[13] For more on this impulse in national collective memory, see Chapter 11 in this volume. And for more on the way national memory spreads, see Chapter 19 in this volume.

Where and when does the United States begin? In time immemorial? At the ice bridge of the Bering Strait? In 1492 when Columbus sailed the ocean blue? In 1607 at Jamestown? In 1619 with the arrival of the first enslaved Africans? In 1620 with the coming of the Pilgrims? In 1630 with an unmarked and unpublished sermon? In 1776 with a declaration? In 1783 with a treaty? In 1789 with a Constitution? The answers will always be contested, but they will always be forthcoming. For whatever other national memories come and go, the memory—the making, the *firsting*—of a beginning will always recur. And how the story starts, in all its many different guises, will be used again and again to tell us where we stand and who we are.

References

Adams, G. A. (2008). *The specter of Salem: Remembering the witch trials in nineteenth-century America*. University of Chicago Press.

Allen, T. (2008). *A republic in time: Temporality and social imagination in nineteenth-century America*. University of North Carolina Press.

Anderson, B. (1991). *Imagined communities: Reflections on the origin and spread of nationalism* (rev. ed.). Verso.

Appleby, J. (2000). *Inheriting the revolution: The first generation of Americans*. Harvard University Press.

Baym, N. (1991). Women and the Republic: Emma Willard's rhetoric of history. *American Quarterly*, *43*(1), 1–23.

Bendroth, M. (2015). *The last Puritans: Mainline Protestants and the power of the past*. University of North Carolina Press.

Callcott, G. H. (1959). History enters the schools. *American Quarterly*, *11*(4), 470–483.

Callcott, G. H. (1970). *History in the United States, 1800–1860: Its practice and purpose*. Johns Hopkins University Press.

Conforti, J. (2001). *Imagining New England: Explorations of regional identity from the Pilgrims to the twentieth century*. University of North Carolina Press.

Dukakis, M. (1988). *Address accepting the presidential nomination at the Democratic National Convention in Atlanta*. The American Presidency Project. Retrieved October 22, 2020, from https://www.presidency.ucsb.edu/documents/address-accepting-the-presidential-nomination-the-democratic-national-convention-atlanta

During, S. (1990). Literature—Nationalism's other? The case for revision. In H. K. Bhabha (Ed.), *Nation and narration* (pp. 139–153). Routledge.

Goldberg, A. (1941). School histories of the middle period. In E. Goldman (Ed.), *Historiography and urbanization: Essays in American history in honor of W. Stull Holt* (pp. 171–188). Johns Hopkins University Press.

Gustafson, S. M. (2007). Histories of democracy and empire. *American Quarterly*, *59*(1), 107–133.

Hobsbawm, E., & Ranger, T. (Eds.). (1983). *The invention of tradition*. Cambridge University Press.

Howe, D. W. (2007). *What hath God wrought: The transformation of America, 1815–1848*. Oxford University Press.

Joyce, B. (2015). *The first U.S. history textbooks: Constructing and disseminating the American tale in the nineteenth century*. Lexington Books.

Kennedy, J. F. (1961). *The city upon a hill speech*. John F. Kennedy Presidential Library and Museum. Retrieved October 22, 2020, from https://www.jfklibrary.org/learn/about-jfk/historic-speeches/the-city-upon-a-hill-speech

Lodge, H. C. (1887). *Daniel Webster*. Houghton, Mifflin.

Monaghan, C., & Monaghan, E. J. (2010). Schoolbooks. In R. Gross & M. Kelly (Eds.), *A history of the book in America: Vol. 2. An extensive republic: Print, culture, and society in the new nation, 1790–1840* (pp. 304–318). University of North Carolina Press.

Nietz, J. (1961). *Old textbooks*. University of Pittsburgh Press.

O'Brien, J. (2010). *Firsting and lasting: Writing Indians out of existence in New England*. University of Minnesota Press.

Reagan, R. (1989). *Farewell address to the nation*. The American Presidency Project. https://www.youtube.com/watch?v=FjECSv8KFN4

Remini, R. V. (1997). *Daniel Webster: The man and his time*. Norton.

Renan, E. (1990). What is a nation? (M. Thom, Trans.). In H. K. Bhabha (Ed.), *Nation and narration* (pp. 8–22). Routledge.

Seelye, J. D. (1998). *Memory's nation: The place of Plymouth Rock*. University of North Carolina Press.

Sheidley, H. (1998). *Sectional nationalism: Massachusetts conservative leaders and the transformation of America, 1815–1836*. Northeastern University Press.

Smith, A. D. (2000). *The nation in history: Historiographical debates about ethnicity and nationalism*. University Press of New England.

Tocqueville, A. d. (2007). *Democracy in America* (I. Kramnick, Ed.; H. Reeves, Trans.). Norton.

Van Engen, A. (2018, January 9). American exceptionalism and America first. *Religion and Politics*. Retrieved October 22, 2020, from https://religionandpolitics.org/2018/01/09/american-exceptionalism-and-america-first

Van Engen, A. (2020). *City on a hill: A history of American exceptionalism*. Yale University Press.

Van Tassel, D. (1960). *Recording America's past: An interpretation of the development of historical studies in America, 1607–1884*. University of Chicago Press.

Waldstreicher, D. (1997). *In the midst of perpetual fetes: The making of American nationalism, 1776–1820*. University of North Carolina Press.

Webster, D. (1826). *A discourse, delivered at Plymouth, December 22, 1820: In commemoration of the first settlement of New-England* (4th ed.). Wells & Lilly.

Willard, E. (1828). *History of the United States, or Republic of America*. Barnes.

Yamashiro, J. K., Van Engen, A., & Roediger, H. L., III. (2022). American origins: Political and religious divides in US collective memory. *Memory Studies*, 15(1), 1–18. doi:10.1177/1750698019856065

3
Europe in 1989, America in 2020, and the Death of the Lost Cause

David W. Blight

Figure 3.1 Protesters call for the removal of a Robert E. Lee statue in Richmond, Virginia, in June, 2020
Photo courtesy of Alex Broening.

In November, 1989, when the Berlin Wall suddenly began to crumble and then fall, much of the world watched in awe.[1] Could it be true that Communism was about to collapse? For seventy years, it had been a system, an ideology, that ordered large swaths of the globe. Now a whole vision of history—a vision meant to maximize freedom, but which had turned, over time, into tyranny—seemed to be leaving the stage.

Many people still possess, as I do, little pieces of concrete from the Berlin Wall. And many of us feel some awe in seeing, during these past few weeks, Confederate monuments in America likewise reduced to pieces, relics of the collapse, after a hundred and fifty-five years, of the public vestiges of the Lost Cause tradition. The summer of 2020, like the autumn of 1989, could mark the death of a specific vision of history. If so, it has taken a long, long night—to borrow from Robbie Robertson and the Band—to drive old Dixie down.

We should not celebrate too much as monuments topple and old slave-auction blocks are removed. History did not end when the Soviet Union dissolved, and it will not end now, even if a vibrant movement sweeps a new age of civil rights into America. Most of all, we must remember what the Lost Cause is and was before we try to call it past. As so many now understand—whether they have read William Faulkner or Toni Morrison or the thousands of scholars who have reshaped American history in the past three generations—slavery, the Civil War, Reconstruction, and segregation are never purely historical. They still haunt the air we breathe, or cannot breathe. They are what W. E. B. Du Bois once called, in 1901, our "present-past." They are a history never to be erased, even if and when the bronze Jefferson Davis and Robert E. Lee can be carried out of the U.S. Capitol and left at the Smithsonian Castle, for a decision on their final resting place.

The Lost Cause is one of the most deeply ingrained mythologies in American history. Loss on an epic scale is often the source of great literature, stories that take us to the dark hearts of the human condition. But when loss breeds twisted versions of history to salve its pain, when it encourages the revitalization of vast systems of oppression, and when loss is allowed to freely commemorate itself in stone and in sentimentalism across the cultural landscape, it can poison a civil society and transform itself into a ruling regime.

---

[1] This chapter is reprinted by permission of *The New Yorker*, in which it originally appeared as https://www.newyorker.com/culture/cultural-comment/europe-in-1989-america-in-2020-and-the-death-of-the-lost-cause.

Some myths are benign as cultural markers. Others are rooted in lies so beguiling, so powerful as engines of resentment and political mobilization, that they can fill parade grounds in Nuremberg, or streets in Charlottesville, or rallies across the country.

The Lost Cause ideology emerged first as a mood of traumatized defeat, but grew into an array of arguments, organizations, and rituals in search of a story that could regain power. After the Civil War, from the late eighteen-sixties to the late eighteen-eighties, diehards, especially though not exclusively in Virginia, and led by former high-ranking Confederate officers, shaped the memory of the war through regular publications and memoirs. They turned Robert E. Lee into a godlike Christian leader and a genius tactician, one who could be defeated only by overwhelming odds. Their revolution, as the story went, was a noble one crushed by industrial might, but emboldened, in the eighteen-seventies, by righteous resistance to radical Reconstruction, to black suffrage, and to the three Constitutional amendments that transformed America.

The Lost Cause argued that the Confederacy never fought to preserve slavery, and that it was never truly defeated on the battlefields of glory. Lost Cause spokesmen saw the Confederacy as the real legacy of the American Revolution—a nation that resisted imperial and centralized power, and which could still triumph over rapid urbanization, immigration, and strife between labor and capital. Above all, the Lost Cause seductively reminded white Americans that the Confederacy had stood for a civilization in which both races thrived in their best, "natural" capacities. The slaughter of the Civil War had destroyed that order, but it could be remade, and the whole nation, defined as white Anglo-Saxon, could yet be revived.

By the eighteen-nineties, the Lost Cause had transformed into a widespread popular movement, led especially by Southern white women in the United Daughters of the Confederacy (U.D.C.), and by an increasingly active United Confederate Veterans association (U.C.V.) and its widely popular magazine, *The Confederate Veteran*. The first commander-in-chief of the U.C.V. was General John B. Gordon, a leader of the Ku Klux Klan in Georgia and a former governor and senator for that state. Gordon became famous for his particular brand of reconciliation, which involved popular lectures that humanized soldiers on both sides of the war, and for his tales of the "kindliest relations" between masters and slaves in antebellum times. He is one of the ten former Confederates for whom United States military forts are named across the South.

From the eighteen-nineties through the First World War, as Jim Crow laws and practices spread across Southern states, and as lynching became a ritual of terror and control, it was organizations like the U.D.C. and U.C.V. that placed hundreds of monuments, large and small, all over city squares and town centers. By 1920, virtually no one in the South, black or white, could miss seeing a veterans' parade, or a statue of a Confederate soldier leaning on his musket with sweet innocence and regional pride. Schools, streets, and parks were named for Confederates. And, at one dedication after another, the message sent to black Southerners was that the Lost Cause was no longer lost. It had, instead, become a victory narrative about the overturning of Reconstruction and the reëstablishment of white supremacy. The myth had become the ruling regime, which governed by law and by violence, and because it controlled the story. What's more, the nation largely acquiesced to, and even applauded, this dogged Southern revival.

The language of the Lost Cause, as well as its monumental presence, is now what many of us desire to banish. But as we do so it is useful to hear its chords, since they still echo today in precincts of the American right. In 1868, Edward A. Pollard, the former editor of a Richmond newspaper, in his book "The Lost Cause Regained," urged "reconciliation" with conservative Northerners, as long as it was on Southern terms. "To the extent of securing the supremacy of the white man," he wrote, "and the traditional liberties of the country . . . she [the South] really triumphs in the true cause of the war." Such an achievement would take years, but it did come. When a former Confederate officer, John T. Morgan, addressed a meeting of the Southern Historical Society, in 1877, he framed the preceding nine years as the "war of Reconstruction." The South, he maintained, had just won this "second war," and therefore no one "need inquire who was right or who was wrong" in the first war. This was never easy for Union veterans to swallow, but it was how white supremacy became an integral part of the process of national reconciliation.

The ultimate sick soul who had to be healed was Jefferson Davis, the former President of the Confederacy, whose large memorial has now been toppled in Richmond. After he was released from prison, in 1867, without ever having been tried for treason, Davis gave a heartbeat to the Lost Cause story. His two-volume, 1,279-page memoir, "The Rise and Fall of the Confederate Government" (1881), is the longest and most self-righteous legal brief on behalf of a failed political movement ever produced by an American. Davis laid all responsibility for secession and the war on the "unlimited, despotic power" of the North. To Davis, slavery was in no way the cause of the conflict, and yet, like almost all Lost Causers, he went on at great length to defend the enslavement of blacks. Black people had already been enslaved in Africa, Davis argued. In America, they had been "trained in the gentle arts of peace and order," and advanced from "unprofitable savages to millions of efficient Christian laborers." The "magic word of 'freedom' " had ruined this peaceful world like the "tempter . . . the Serpent in Eden."

Confounding as these arguments may seem to most twenty-first-century minds, Lost Cause spokesmen were deadly serious, and their ideas propped up a story that many Americans still accept. Around Memorial Day in Richmond, 1890, when the spectacular Robert E. Lee equestrian statue was unveiled before a crowd of up to a hundred and fifty thousand people, a Lee cult seemed in total triumph. Confederate flags waved everywhere. A women's memorial association had managed to wrangle many factions into agreement on a design and artist for the statue, and on elaborate ceremonies to anoint it. Twenty-five years after Appomattox, the general who had led the crusade to divide and destroy American democracy stood high astride his monument, the first in a series of statues that became Monument Avenue. Much of the Northern press called the statue evidence that Lee had become, as the New York *Times* put it, a "national possession."

Not everyone was celebrating, of course. Many black men, needing jobs, had worked on the crews that pulled and set the giant granite structure into place. The three black men on the Richmond City Council had voted against an appropriation for the Lee monument. And John Mitchell, the editor of the Richmond *Planet*, the city's black newspaper, wrote that those who wore the "clinking chains of slavery" had a perfect right to denounce the spectacle of the unveiling and all that lay behind it. Black men, Mitchell said, helped "put up the Lee Monument, and should the time come will be there to take it down." The state of Virginia apparently wishes to do just that, in an act that many of us who have studied these matters thought would never occur. When it does, one can hope that a line of black citizens might be given pride of place in holding the ropes.

What comes after this change in commemoration will determine whether we are truly witnessing the death of the Lost Cause. Structural racism remains present in nearly every corner of the United States—in the material worlds of health care, economic inequality, and policing, and in our politics, which are split between a white-people's party and a party trying in fits and strides to be a voice of pluralism. When the Berlin Wall opened and then fell, and as Eastern European countries began to move from Communism to democracy, we learned that their path was not easy. Some, like Hungary, have collapsed into authoritarianism. Russia itself, now run by a dictator, is a mockery of democracy that tries its best to poison our own.

The term used for the great changes spurred, in 1989, by the reunification of Germany was *die Wende*, which can be translated as the *turning*, or the *change*. When the Cold War came to an end, societies and minds seemed to be opening, and democracy seemed to have new traction. Around that time, in the early nineties, I was a visiting Fulbright professor in Germany. I travelled all over the country and, at one particular stop, in a small provincial town near Dresden, I lectured to a room full of East German high-school teachers, who were just beginning to develop curricula that might include U.S. history. My host was a local school principal named Matthias, who had been born near the end of the Second World War, in Dresden. His family had escaped the city in 1944, just before its near-total destruction. He grew up amid the rubble, and he had spent his entire life under the East German Communist regime and its controls on thought and behavior.

Die Wende was challenging and overwhelming for Matthias. Once, over dinner, he told me that he did not think he and his generation could adapt to what capitalism and democracy would bring. He was more hopeful for his son's generation: He thought it had a chance to secure not just a future but a new history, a story true to reality. Then he uttered something that I will never forget. He said, "I know your country. I have been to your country with my fingers on a map." He spoke at length of how he had memorized American states and their capitals. He had never been to the country, but, for him, America was an idea to wrestle with, its political creeds an obsession.

The statues are being toppled, but the story that built them remains. If Matthias could visit America, one hopes that he would see a country trying to transcend that story—trying, like his son, to capture not just a brighter future but a truer sense of the past. If he were here, I would tell him of a history full of suffering, hypocrisy, and tragedy, along with sublime creativity and advancement. I would tell him how Americans have been rewriting this history for a long time, and we could talk to each other about the link between public memory and the grind of progress. It would be the beginning, I think, of a long conversation. But if this is to be our 1989, we must make the most of it. The whole world may be watching.

4
Charlottesville and the End of American Exceptionalism

Jeffrey K. Olick

It is always difficult, even risky, to try to explain, let alone recognize, a significant transformation while in the midst of it. Yet, the editors and contributors to this volume face an urgent challenge to apply the knowledge we have gained from our work on social and political memory in diverse times and contexts to the dizzying crisis in which we presently find ourselves, much as this present is always a moving target. Like collective memory itself, *scholarship* on collective memory processes can provide orientation within the flux of time, since it begins from the recognition that, as unique—and uniquely challenging—as our moment may seem, we have seen similar things, or at least similar processes, before and elsewhere. Like collective memory itself does, analytically placing our own moment against such backgrounds is part of the process of understanding where we are and why we are there.

What, then, does the accumulated body of research and theory in what has come to be known as "memory studies" tell us about our present moment, and about the changing circumstances of national memory that in many ways define it? At the broadest level, the place to start is to recognize that, like everything else, memory has a history: Both memory's forms and salience change over time. In some epochs, for instance, collective memory comes to us through oral epic, in others through "scientific" historiography. Sometimes memory is transmitted within families, and sometimes across mass media; sometimes these mass media are centralized and uniting, other times multiple and dividing; and these patterns change over time. Something similar can be said about nations and of the role of memory in them. As Ernest Renan wrote in 1882, "A heroic past with great men and glory . . . is the social capital upon which the national idea rests" (Renan, 1990, p. 19). Similarly, "forgetting . . . is an essential factor in the creation of nations" as

Jeffrey K. Olick, *Charlottesville and the End of American Exceptionalism* In: *National Memories*. Edited by: Henry L. Roediger and James V. Wertsch, Oxford University Press. © Oxford University Press 2022. DOI: 10.1093/oso/9780197568675.003.0004

well, and "unity is always brutally established" (p. 11). But Renan also recognized that "nations are not eternal. They have a beginning and they will have an end" (p. 20). These are some of the reasons why, according to Renan, "the progress of historical studies often poses a threat to nationality" (p. 11). Something similar might be said about memory studies as well because memory studies takes the apparent malleability and transformation of the past as its first axiom.

Within the 20th century more narrowly, and more directly to the point at hand, we have seen a widespread transformation in the landscapes of national memory from heroic monuments built at the beginning of the last century to celebrate glories, through memorials of sacrifice after World War I intended to stoke resentment, to lamentations of grief and despair after World War II meant to warn us not to forget what our inhumanity has wrought (Mosse, 1991; Winter, 1995). But while few today would think of representing the past by sculpting, for example, a military leader on a rearing stead, iconoclasm—the destruction of monuments—faces strong taboos, and new forms and attitudes must contend with the durability of the old ones. There is no rule, after all, that for every new monument, an old one must be taken down; indeed, there is quite a bit of antipathy toward doing so. Newer approaches are thus often layered on top of, or next to, the old ones: Ours is a mnemonic landscape of complex histories and competing temporalities in which it is difficult to find the very unity asserted by claims to national identity. Yet we do seem to be moving between different overall regimes—from the heroic to the tragic, from the monumental to the memorial, from the proud to the critical. This is, in my view, quite a good thing.

In doing so, however, we have faced strong forces of reaction and resistance: Over large parts of the world since approximately the turn of the 21st century, despite having faced the legacies of our inhumanity (or sometimes because of how uncomfortable it has been to do so), we have seen the rise of populist movements formed at least in part in reaction to the sensibilities that have led us to re-examine our difficult pasts in these ways. A hallmark of many of these movements has been that their adherents are often angry about the trajectory of memory politics in particular, with its diminution of heroes, its challenges to national mythologies, and its insistence on regret. For populists, the trajectory toward regret in our memory politics has been the project of corrupt elites who have foisted their apologetic weakness on a population whose complicity, if that is even the right word, is only that they allowed themselves to be misled. As such, populism often seems to entail a commitment to never saying you are sorry; the people have nothing to be sorry about, quite in contrast to the elites.

American Exceptionalism

In the United States, this populism bears strong similarities—even draws on tropes of—both older and contemporaneous populisms elsewhere. In another respect, however, there has once again often seemed to be an American exception, as has been claimed in so many other regards (Müller, 2016). For decades, that is, other societies have been examining the legacies of their pasts in vigorous and consequential public debates. From the late 1960s, though with particular visibility in the 1980s, for instance, West Germany experienced paroxysmal public controversies over the legacies of the Holocaust for its politics, and the centrality of its memory to German political culture; since the so-called Stockholm Declaration of 2000,[1] recognition of the importance of the Holocaust in European collective memory—even in societies that bear very little or no responsibility for it— has been ensconced internationally as a basic commitment of European nation-states. In a different context, Japan has been forced to acknowledge its history of colonial brutality as well as its atrocities against both China and Korea. Canada, Australia, and New Zealand, among others, in turn, have begun working through the legacies of their settler colonialism. And truth and reconciliation commissions have become a routine part of so-called transitional justice. Where once we celebrated the triumphs of the past, now we mourn its losses and atone for our errors. And debates over whether, and how, to do so have often been national news throughout the world, or at least in many places other than the United States, which has in many respects been late to the game.

To be sure, during the past few decades, the United States has not been entirely free of significant public debates about the past: Epochal trends have a force of their own. Indeed, what I (Olick, 2007) have elsewhere termed the "politics of regret" has been part of the American discourse as well. For instance, the Vietnam Veterans Memorial is one of the best-known examples

---

[1] On January 27–29, 2000, in the context of increasing right wing violence in Europe, representatives of 45 governments convened at the Stockholm International Forum on the Holocaust, marking the 55th anniversary of the liberation of Auschwitz. The declaration signed at the meeting recognized the "unprecedented" nature of the Holocaust and the special responsibilities this demanded, and it committed its signatories to active programs of Holocaust education and remembrance.

of what James Young (2002) called a "counter monument," marking what was widely viewed as a loss or shame for the United States; the memorial is a wound in the ground, a jagged scar through the landscape, stimulating humility and self-examination. In the early 1990s, to take another example, plans were made for an exhibit at the Smithsonian Institution presenting the history of, and critical reflection on, the United States's use of an atomic bomb on Hiroshima in World War II. In both cases, however, reaction modified the critical impulse: A more "traditional" addendum was made to the Vietnam memorial in the form of "realist" statues of soldiers; at the Smithsonian, veterans' and other groups prevented the inclusion of critical information in the exhibit, which was reduced to a contextless presentation of the airplane—the Enola Gay— that had delivered the bomb. More recently, a project led by *The New York Times* to center the history of slavery in U.S. political culture—the so-called 1619 Project named to mark the arrival of the first African slaves— has been widely vilified and has been answered with a 1776 Project—the date of the U.S. Declaration of Independence— intended to "uphold our country's authentic founding virtues and values and challenge those who assert America is forever defined by its past failures, such as slavery."[2]

The most significant "exception" in U.S. memory politics, however, has undoubtedly been the extent to which the defeated Southern insurrection of the 1860s has been positively, even heroically, commemorated in the United States, and especially the extent to which such commemoration has gone unchallenged. According to data gathered by the Southern Poverty Law Center (2019), for instance, as of 2016 there were more than 1,700 state-sponsored symbols honoring Confederate soldiers, leaders, and institutions in the United States. Although the overwhelming majority were in the former Confederate states, they were not limited to these states. There is a widespread cliché, containing significant truth when it comes to memory, that the North won the war but the South won the peace (Savage, 1996). Myths of an honorable "lost cause" have been allowed to flourish unchallenged, just as Confederate flags and the unofficial Confederate anthem *Dixie* have been staples of American popular culture.

Emblems of discredited pasts have certainly persisted elsewhere in the world, but it is difficult to think of a more vivid example than the iconography of the "lost cause" and the celebration of its "heroes," many of them depicted on the aforementioned steads. Much the same is true of the memory of the

---

[2] Full statement is available at https://1776unites.com.

Indigenous peoples whose "pacification" is somehow part of the nation's heroic self-narrative. The persistent iconography of the "American Indian," whether it is used in mascots for professional and collegiate sports teams, names of roadways, coinage, branding or other commercial uses, is truly astounding. Populism elsewhere in the world has in many respects been a reaction to examination of the most potent challenges to national pride in the historical record; American populism has come about without quite the same penetration of regret to the general population, to say nothing of official policy, that has often taken place elsewhere. Whereas in Germany every school child learns of the atrocities of the Holocaust (or at least has since the late 1960s), slavery and even the real lessons of the Civil War remain obscured in American political discourse, which has not seemed to have had the same "coming to terms" with the past, rather than organized forgetting of it, that has taken place elsewhere. This gives American populism a somewhat different cast; the mighty here are less used to falling, and the threat of doing so is perhaps greater in a nation that views itself as a "city on a hill," an exception in nearly every regard.

Yet, even in this grim landscape, there are signs that the American discourse is changing, even quite dramatically. Is the American exception in collective memory coming to an end? If so, why now? (Ironically, of course, it is also true that changes in American memory politics are leading other nations to re-examine aspects of their problematic pasts as well—most prominently colonialism—in ways that had heretofore received less regretful attention than the more recent legacies of World War II.[3]) In the following sections, I examine, as a sociologist and drawing on sociological approaches, both the structures and contingencies in this unfolding mnemonic transformation with an eye toward explaining it. Yet, the conclusion has to be that the process of transformation, still underway as everything always is, is simultaneously over- and underdetermined. Examination of this complexity raises the further, and perhaps more basic, question of why the long status quo held at all. To be sure, the answer to this question has to do with interests, identities, and power, as is always the case. But it also has to do with the peculiar structures of inattention that have enabled and underwritten a peculiar kind of mnemonic ignorance (in the active sense of the word).

---

[3] Cross-cultural mnemonic influences and exchanges such as this are captured and extended by Michael Rothberg's (2009) work on what he terms "multidirectional memory." For her part, Astrid Erll (2011) refers to "travelling memory."

The Old Regime

In 2005, sociologists Howard Schuman, Barry Schwartz, and Hanna D'Arcy published an important paper in *Public Opinion Quarterly*, putatively following up on a long tradition of inquiry into the connections—and often disconnections—between "elite" and "popular" discourses. In particular, the authors were interested in whether elite critiques of historical figures—heroes—were being taken up in wider opinion; this interest stemmed in part from questions about whether public beliefs about the collective past match the images of the past presented in museums, textbooks, academic discourse, etc. Noting a rise in "minority rights" during the previous half-century, the authors began from the observation that this "revolution" had "spurred attempts to revise beliefs about important individuals and events from the past" (Schuman et al., 2005, p. 3) In other work from around the same time, Schwartz (2003, 2009) was documenting and analyzing the transformation in Abraham Lincoln's reputation from that of savior of the Union to emancipator of the slaves. Schwartz and colleagues (2005) sought to measure the effectiveness of what they termed "a far more radical attempt to change American collective memory" (p. 3), namely the putative effort by intellectual and political "elites" to transform Christopher Columbus's status as a hero who "discovered" America to a "villain" whose arrival heralded the destruction of the native Americans. Noting what they termed an "assault on the meaning of Columbus's landfall in 1492" on its 500th anniversary in 1992 (p. 3), they charted the spread of this "elite" discourse through reference works, children's and school books, and the mass media.

Yet despite the prevalence of the "assault" on Columbus's reputation, the opinion survey at the heart of Schwartz et al.'s (2005) study showed that this critical view had *not* in fact disseminated very widely.[4] With the exception of slightly higher inclinations among Native American and other minorities to adopt the critical view, "traditional" views of Columbus remained much more common. To be sure, Schuman et al.'s paper is substantially more nuanced than it is possible to summarize here: In particular, the paper found that although critical views did not penetrate, there was a modest retreat from the most strongly "heroic" versions, which the authors attribute, following Schwartz's extensive work on Lincoln, to a general decline in heroic

---

[4] Chapter 7 in this volume indicates somewhat more change more recently.

narratives in American society; and they date the beginnings of this decline, moreover, to the period *before* the civil rights movement—a period in which, that is, there was an intentional and significant effort to change American political culture and collective memory. Nevertheless, this paper showed clearly that despite the rise of a critical discourse in intellectual and other circles, institutions of American collective memory were proving quite recalcitrant to change, a circumstance that has only begun to change significantly after the 2019 events in Charlottesville, Virginia.

The same resistance is also clear to the naked eye. Consider, for instance, efforts to get Yale University to rename one of its residential colleges, named for U.S. Vice President John C. Calhoun, who was a vigorous defender of slavery. There had been calls for such a change since the 1960s (Caplan, 2015). Yet it was not until after a White supremacist's murderous attack on an African American church in South Carolina (in Calhoun's home state and located on Calhoun Street) in 2015, resulting in the South Carolina governor's decision to remove the Confederate flag from the state house (which incidentally had first been placed there only in 1962), that university leadership began to take such calls seriously. Even then, despite vigorous debates throughout 2016, the university decided not to change the name, citing alumni opinion, among other factors. University President Peter Salovey only changed this decision in 2017, following the murderous riot that took place in Charlottesville in August of that year; the college was finally renamed for Grace Hopper, a pioneering mathematician and computer scientist who had earned her PhD at Yale, but not before decades of refusal to consider doing so, and not before a deliberate process after the South Carolina massacre, but before the Charlottesville riot, had reaffirmed the decision not to make the change.

Consider as well discussions about reparations for slavery in the United States. Every year since 1989, congressman John Conyers, Jr. proposed that Congress convene a commission to study the issue, but to no avail. In 2014, the writer Ta-Nehisi Coates published a much-discussed article in *The Atlantic* making "The Case for Reparations," yet like Conyers's proposal or the decades-long calls to Yale (and other institutions) to remove symbols honoring the United States's racist leaders, the discussion remained at the edges of popular consciousness, the kind of (attempted but failed) radical intervention foisted on the masses by disconnected elites. Only since Charlottesville has there been more serious further discussion about varieties of reparations, including for the notorious Tulsa Massacre of 1921.

The same is true of debates over whether to remove statues of Confederate "heroes" in Charlottesville and elsewhere. Although frustration with the markers of the Confederacy around Charlottesville was long-standing for some, a new trajectory began at least as early as 2012. In February of that year, a 17-year old African American named Trayvon Martin was shot to death by a leader of the "neighborhood watch" in a gated community in Sanford, Florida, leading to vigorous protests; the shooter, George Zimmerman, was later acquitted of murder charges, and subsequent demonstrations in the wake of the acquittal saw the birth of the "Black Lives Matter" hashtag. About a month after the shooting, during a panel discussion in Charlottesville with well-known University of Virginia historian Edward Ayers at the annual Virginia Festival of the Book, Charlottesville City Council member Kristin Szakos asked whether the city should consider removing its prominent Confederate monuments. According to news reports, the question elicited a shocked gasp from those present, and Ms. Szakos subsequently received threats. The Black Lives Matter (BLM) movement, in turn, grew significantly in 2014 following the police killings of Michael Brown in Ferguson, Missouri, and Eric Garner in New York City. Yet negative public opinion about the BLM movement remained dominant until the May 2020 murder in Minneapolis of George Floyd, which galvanized public attention and radically changed levels of support for the movement.

For more than 10 years since Schuman et al.'s (2005) paper documented the failure of elite efforts to transform public historical consciousness, the regime that had been in place since the end of "Reconstruction" and the institution of "Jim Crow" in the U.S. South thus held firm. Popular discourse in the United States ignored, vilified, romanticized, or exploited memory of the Indigenous peoples of North America, often turning "Indians," along with their partners the "cowboys," into kitsch. Few Americans spent any time contemplating the often intentional extermination of these people(s) or thinking about what happened to them as extermination. Slavery, of course, is widely referred to (although not accepted by all) as America's "original sin," yet the atonement for that sin, supposedly complicated by the fact that so many Americans do not trace their own roots to before the Civil War, has never fully taken place. In (some) contrast to the Holocaust in Germany, slavery in the United States is considered rather ancient history. The "progress" of civil rights, moreover, is often taken as proof that the problem has been rectified.

Breaking the Dam

So, what—if anything—has changed, and why? Throughout 2015, especially following the South Carolina attack, numerous Southern cities debated whether they needed to make changes to their commemorative landscapes. Indeed, New Orleans Mayor Mitch Landrieu had already begun the effort in 2015 but finally executed the removal of New Orleans's Robert E. Lee statue only in May 2017, and this had to be done under the cover of darkness. In Charlottesville, a combination of players, including City Council member Wes Bellamy as well as a high school student, Zyahna Bryant, who started a petition to encourage the city to remove its Confederate monuments from their prominent places in the downtown area, led to the appointment of a Blue Ribbon Commission on Race, Memorials and Public Spaces, which recommended in February 2016 that the city transform the monument by adding context (see the previous discussion of the layering of new on old commemorative forms). In the same month, however, the City Council voted instead to move the statue from its central position and rename the park from Jackson Park to Justice Park. This vote immediately faced legal and other challenges.

In turn, the Charlottesville debate became a focal point for so-called Alt-Right groups for a number of reasons. First, Charlottesville was the birthplace of three early U.S. presidents (Thomas Jefferson, James Madison, and James Monroe); in addition, the explorers Meriwether Lewis and Richard Clark, whose expedition to the West expanded the reach of the United States even farther following the Louisiana Purchase in 1803 had, were from the area and were associated with and commemorated in the city. Second, Jefferson's Charlottesville estate, Monticello, was the embodiment of both the Enlightenment spirit that animated the American Revolution—and the author of the Declaration of Independence—and a prime example of human exploitation: Like many other early leaders of the American republic, Jefferson was a slave holder (owning more than 600), and his use of enslaved people on his technologically innovative plantation made even starker the contradiction within the great humanist's, and by extension the nation's, worldview. Beyond this, Jefferson had fathered as many as six children with the enslaved half-sister of his legal wife, Martha, Sally Hemings. For decades, historians, various commemorative foundations, and "legitimate" family members denied and disputed that there had been a sexual relationship between Jefferson and Hemings (who likely would have been 14 years old when it began). This debate was particularly vigorous following the publication of an exhaustive study by historian Annette Gordon-Reed in 1997. It was only in 2000 that the Thomas Jefferson Foundation accepted that DNA analysis indicated Jefferson's paternity of at least some of Hemings's children. Finally, the University of Virginia, built in Charlottesville by Jefferson, was the alma mater of two neo-Nazi leaders, Richard Spencer and Jason Kessler, who led the Unite the Right rally in Charlottesville on August 11 and 12, 2017, aimed in part as a reaction to the city's efforts to move the Robert E. Lee statue.

Although, as of this writing, the Lee statue, as well as another of Thomas "Stonewall" Jackson, remain in place in Charlottesville (ironically, since the debate over the Charlottesville monuments is what started the removal process elsewhere), the Unite the Right rally—and in particular U.S. President Donald Trump's reaction to it, in which he seemed to equate the neo-Nazis with left-wing counterprotesters—led to further pressure to remove Confederate statuary. One of the most visible such efforts was the removal of a Lee–Jackson monument in Baltimore on August 16, 2017—immediately after the Charlottesville riot. In the years since, there has in fact been a widespread movement to reconsider the presence not only of the Confederate past but also other markers of discreditable figures, or figures whose discreditable pasts had been suppressed in collective memory or not considered important enough—or possibly even intertwined with—their supposedly commemorable legacies. Perhaps most prominent was the June 2020 decision—1 month after the police murder of George Floyd in Minneapolis—after many years of ineffective calls, of Princeton University to rename the Wilson School of International and Public Affairs, in recognition of U.S. President Woodrow Wilson's overt racism and implementation of White supremacist policies.

Indeed, the May 2020 murder of George Floyd unleashed a veritable floodgate of commemorative reconsideration, resulting in the removal of monuments along Monument Avenue in Richmond, Virginia, the former capitol of the Confederacy, as well as Confederate and other markers throughout the U.S. South, including a particularly divisive one at Mississippi State University, where resistance was long and heavy to any reconsideration of Confederate symbols and legacies (a move led in part by players on the university's football team) (see Chapter 6, this volume). The iconoclastic moment, however, spread quickly beyond markers of the Confederacy to include a wide variety of historical figures, not only around the United States but also in other countries, including European figures who had been involved in the slave trade or who stood for colonial exploitation.[5] In the United Kingdom, debate extended even to wartime Prime Minister Winston Churchill. And in the United States, reconsideration of Christopher Columbus was no longer a matter for the intellectual fringes, as the 2005 paper by Schuman et al. found (see Chapter 7, this volume).

Sociological Perspectives

How, then, can a sociological approach help us understand these transformations? First, it is important to note that the use in the previous discussion of the term "collective memory" is not merely metaphorical, a catch-all for both individual opinions about and public representations of the national past. Rather, the term collective memory is meant to link the varieties of different ways we represent the past—both our own and that of our groups—to ourselves and to each other. In this view, and by extension, national memory is not reducible to what individuals remember, especially because most people do not have personal experience of the events that constitute the national past; the ways in which individuals think about both their own and their shared group pasts are shaped by frames that operate at levels and in media beyond individual neurological and cognitive processes. By the same token, personal experience of public representations of the past is a crucial part of the politics of public memory because shared memory is only genuinely collective if it is cognitively and emotionally resonant with the people it addresses. An implication of this, of course, is that public memory addresses different people in different ways. This is why it is not surprising, for instance, that Schuman et al. (2005) found a greater penetration of critical frames of Columbus in Native American and African American attitudes. Public representations of the national past, oppositional efforts to build, change, or maintain them, and individual experiences together constitute the domain of collective memory, in which what individuals remember and official representations constitute each other in both iterative and interactional manners.

A further axiom of sociological approaches to memory has often been that memory takes place in the present, not in the past. What happened does not change, but its relevance in the present does. Collective memory,

---

[5] See again Rothberg (2009) and Erll (2011) on multidirectional and traveling memory.

or collective remembering, is the process of making that relevance actual. In later work inspired by this "presentist" approach, first articulated by Maurice Halbwachs in the 1920s (Halbwachs, 1992), numerous scholars have thus emphasized the ways in which the past is made and remade in the present for present purposes. Such continuous transformations in national memory are readily apparent even in a landscape dotted with the remains of older memory. Indeed, as discussed later, we often simply walk by or build around the remnants of earlier memory, which are often inconvenient.

National memory, then, is subject to numerous vicissitudes of time. For instance, sometimes older representations remain simply because they are large and heavy, because they are habitual and traditional. These dynamics we might call "inertial," as I have elsewhere (Olick & Robbins, 1998). They may also either remain or change because of their "fit" or "resonance" with contemporary culture. If a particular image of the past—for instance, the American flag—continues to symbolize values for which people continue to stand, it will persist. If, however, an older symbol or image no longer jibes with contemporary values—for instance, the image of the Aunt Jemima brand of pancake syrup (Kern Foxworth, 1994), the name Sambo's for a restaurant, or the names Redskins or Indians for a sports team—it is ripe for change. Finally, a particularly powerful strand in the presentist sociology of memory emphasizes instrumentalism with and about the past: Actors with specific agendas work to make changes happen (or, conversely, to prevent them) (see Chapter 14, this volume); attachment to a particular view of the past, or to a particular set of historical symbols, can be both the object of interested action and a reason for it.

For many recent sociologists, however, such instrumentalism can sometimes be taken too far: "The past," they find, is not in fact infinitely malleable; efforts to make and remake images of the past in present contexts for present purposes often face significant constraints. And this has clearly been the case in the efforts to end American exceptionalism and embrace more critical views of the collective past. To be sure, the Confederate statues were built by particular people for particular reasons in particular times, namely by powerful groups to demonstrate and perpetuate not just White supremacy (a fact) but White supremacism (an ideology) in moments when it might have been challenged (e.g., the "progressive era" of the 1920s or during the civil rights movement of the 1960s). Similarly, those who worked to remove the statues faced both active pushback from groups that saw their identities and ideologies as at stake and indifference by many people who, for a variety of reasons and in a variety of ways, did not feel themselves invested in these representations and debates.

Within the more recent sociological literature, then, a number of theorists have proposed models that explain when and how much collective memory changes, rather than assuming it is always fictive and malleable. Michael Schudson (1989), for instance, has developed a tripartite model that views the malleability of the past as shaped by (1) "the structure of available pasts," (2) "the structure of individual choice," and (3) "conflicts about the past among a multitude of mutually aware individuals and groups" (p. 108).

It might be worth explaining briefly how Schudson's (1989) model applies in the present context. Regarding the first point, even defenders of the "lost cause" ideology cannot claim that the war was not terrible or that slavery was not an abomination. While for some time, Jefferson's defenders could deny claims about his paternity of the Hemings's children, DNA evidence is to some extent undeniable (although there were some efforts to attribute paternity to Jefferson's brother). Given this structure of available pasts, "conservative" and farther right players had available to them only other strategies, including minimalization, obfuscation, and relativization. For instance, some claimed that slavery was, for the most part, not terrible or was a necessary stage in some sort of economic development; they claimed that slaves were for the most part well cared for and happy; and they claimed that most Southerners were not slave holders and were not fighting to defend the institution but, rather, their homes, their land, and their "way of life," just like anyone would: Symbols of the Confederacy, in this view, are just ordinary emblems of proud identity.

In terms of individual choices, moreover, it is important to understand why defenders of the statues and the Confederacy in general chose to do so in light of all the vast changes that had occurred in American society, in the valence of racism, and the identity of the South (after all, a supposed "New South" had replaced the old). There are, of course, prominent examples of individuals who chose a different path—for instance, examining and repudiating their own families' legacies (although very rarely their financial consequences) (e.g. Ball, 1998). For those seeking to change the commemorative landscape, the task was often visceral and urgent: The fight against the legacies of the Confederacy was very much a contemporary fight for life and liberty. For many, the monuments stood not only for an execrable past but also for the continued presence of its murderous ideology.

Regarding the structure of conflict, it has been fascinating to watch the shifting constellations, including, ranging from right to left: alt-right radicals; more "mainstream" defenders of Southern pride and others who want to keep the monuments; Whites and others who initially did not support BLM or the removal of the monuments but who did so after George Floyd's murder, but some of whose support for BLM diminished after property damage and rioting during some protests; BLM organizers and supporters participating in nonviolent action; and more radical vandals and others who tired of "legal" mechanisms and took it on themselves to do what several years of political action had not been able to accomplish. Who is considered to be in the mainstream and who on the fringes, and what values they express, is also a shifting terrain, as we can see, for instance, in the quick retrenchment from BLM as the summer of 2020 unfolded. In this category, however, one cannot underestimate the impact of Donald Trump's presidency and the groups that view themselves empowered by it. When neo-Nazis came to Charlottesville, they did so with a sense of tacit support from a White supremacist leader.

Several other sociological models as well provide insights into the kind of factors that must be taken into account in any thorough examination of the causes of mnemonic change [the kind of change Schuman et al. (2005) showed had not yet occurred in the early 2000s]. In her analysis of commemorative politics in Israel, for instance, Vinitzky-Seroussi (2002) points out that fundamental differences in the political cultures of different societies must also be taken into account. Comparing the politics surrounding the Vietnam Veterans Memorial in the United States to those surrounding the commemoration of the assassination of Israeli Prime Minister Yitzhak Rabin, Vinitzky-Seroussi argues that sometimes it is the remembered event that is ambiguous and thus divisive, but sometimes it is the society that is profoundly fragmented, resulting in "fragmented commemoration" in which different parties commemorate the same history differently. Such a process is clearly at work in the United States, in which different identity groups project different meanings onto the symbols of the Confederacy, and there seems little shared between them. There are, in other words, some issues on which different conflict parties simply cannot even agree to disagree. For many on the left (and now center), the imagery of the Confederate flag or of what they view as traitorous leaders is too much to bear, which is why many do not find the addition of context to statues that are allowed to remain a sufficient solution.

Robin Wagner-Pacifici and Barry Schwartz (1991), Gary Alan Fine (2001), and Christina Simko (2012; see also Chapter 5, this volume), for their part, have all emphasized the role of so-called "agents of memory" or "mnemonic entrepreneurs" in bringing about mnemonic change (or in resisting it) (see also Vinitzky-Seroussi & Teeger, 2010), but always within complex contexts. Simko (2012), in particular, who refers to agents as "carrier groups," has emphasized the multidimensionality of contexts in which agency is but one factor, including the nature of the events (e.g., the Charlottesville riot or the murder of George Floyd), audiences, and the traditions and trajectories of discourses leading up to a particular moment (in this regard, it is important to note that traditions can work in different directions—for instance, in the argument that tearing down monuments amounts to changing or denying history or, contrarily, that demands for change have reached a tipping point). In my own work (Olick, 2007), I have also emphasized the role of media of memory, and in the present context there is no understating the role of ubiquitous cell phone cameras, which can be—though are not always—very effective at breaking through barriers to empathy and understanding.

The Social Production of Indifference

Collective memory is indeed a continual work in progress, a reaction to the changing needs of the present. Yet, as the previous narrative showed, the rate of change is not constant over time. Transformation in collective memory happens in fits and starts. In many contexts—especially the political context of public commemoration—it requires significant effort by well-placed actors. And even the most concerted efforts by the best-placed such actors often fail, or at least take a very long time, and face the extraordinary complexities of wide varieties of resistance. For instance, well-placed (and especially well-funded) factions can exert outsized power in the name of resistance. And institutional factors can prove to be powerful impediments to change, even when such change is desired. As a brief example, anti-removal advocates in Charlottesville were able to use the law, which includes a prohibition against removing war memorials, as a way to prevent removal of the Lee and Jackson statues in Charlottesville, while other statues elsewhere were successfully removed through legal and extra-legal means.

All of this analysis of when, where, why, and how national collective memory changes, however, leaves a perhaps more profound question unanswered: Namely how is it that people who view themselves as decent have been able to tolerate the persistence of monuments to unspeakable brutality, terrible crimes, and immeasurable suffering, some of it ongoing? The vivid images of a Minneapolis police officer kneeling on George Floyd's neck for 8 minutes and 46 seconds were shocking indeed. But were they really that new? What cognitive and moral structures have produced the kind of indifference—let us not even speak of support—for what intelligent people must know is an ongoing outrage?

To be sure, the psychoanalytic tradition has offered us a powerful vocabulary for understanding such attitudes (Cohen, 2001)—projection, denial, repression, avoidance, etc.—and I have reported on the applicability of such concepts in the German contexts in previous work (Olick & Perrin, 2010). In the present context, however, I have found the work of the "cognitive sociologist" Eviatar Zerubavel particularly insightful. First, few since Halbwachs have explained as clearly as Zerubavel the basic constituents of a sociological understanding of memory. "The work on memory typically generated by psychologists," Zerubavel (1996, pp. 284–285) argues, perhaps too polemically, "might lead one to believe that the act of remembering takes place in a social vacuum." To be sure, social psychology is a vibrant field, and cognitive psychology (including the excellent work of many contributors to this volume) has also sought, like Zerubavel, to avoid treating its subjects as what he calls "mnemonic Robinson Crusoes" (p. 285). For his part, however, Zerubavel begins by explaining that we often require verification of our memories by others, and even our most individual memories are often supported and corroborated by our intimates. Following Halbwachs very closely, he shows that "many of our earliest 'memories' are actually recollections of stories we heard from them about our childhood. In an odd way, they remember them for us!" (p. 285). Similarly, other people can also block our access to certain events even in our own lives—for instance, by denying that they ever happened (see Chapter 20, this volume). This is what many contemporary commentators have referred to as "gaslighting." And so Zerubavel lays a firmly sociological starting point for even the consideration of private memory.

With regard to group memberships, moreover, Zerubavel (1996) outlines how we go through a process of "mnemonic socialization" into "mnemonic traditions," which entail "rules of remembrance" (p. 283). For instance, we moderns are all required to remember birthdays and government identification numbers and certain rules of the game ("ignorance of the law is no defense"). Mnemonic traditions, moreover, also require us (and train us) to remember certain things about them: the names of our political leaders, the fact that a particular Monday is a holiday, the past (after all, whoever forgets it is condemned to repeat it, which is a pretty nasty threat). As a result of all of this, "The sociology of memory ... highlights the impersonal aspect of our recollections. ... Much of what we remember we did not experience personally. We do so as members of particular families, organizations, nations, and other *mnemonic communities*" (Zerubavel, 1996, p. 285).

In addition to providing a clear vocabulary for approaching memory sociologically, Zerubavel's later work also calls our attention to an important piece of the puzzle of atrocious memories: Namely he analyzes what are commonly called "conspiracies of silence" (Zerubavel, 2006). Yet the term conspiracy implies an intentionality that need not necessarily obtain. This is because denial and avoidance, like everything else, are socially organized (see Cohen 2001). We need, in other words, to learn to ignore the "elephant in the room." And often, this learning is so successful that we are not consciously aware that we are doing it. Indeed, the conspiracy of silence into which one enters becomes part of the mnemonic tradition and is passed on to future generations. It is nearly a cliché at this point, for instance, for self-critical Southern writers to begin by saying they had a sense, so deep that they could not even articulate it to themselves, that something was amiss in their family histories; topics were avoided and narratives contained strange silences.

Within this framework, it is clear that more work remains to be done to understand the ways in which our attention has been socially organized. How many of us, after all, can name even the most prominent historical markers in our daily ambit? The elephant is not just in the room but sometimes in the middle of the street! How, in other words, have we all learned our indifference? Many of us have had the luxury of ignoring statues and markers and honorifics commemorating histories that, if we examined them closely, we would find abhorrent. But we routinely walk by them without notice, without stopping to look or read, without doing what monuments and memorials (although the former perhaps less than the latter) ask us to do: stop and think about the past. Our children look to us, just like we looked to our parents when we were children, to see how upset they should be about all the terrible things in the world. Do we walk by the homeless person without looking?

More likely without seeing, because we learn not to, and then really do not. It is tempting to say we would not tolerate particularly obvious offenses—no Hitler Avenue or Manson Boulevard—but the evidence says otherwise. There is, as the title of yet another of Zerubavel's books states, a great deal *Hidden in Plain Sight* (Zerubavel, 2006). This is because, as the subtitle expounds, of "The Social Structure of Irrelevance." One of the most interesting features of the recent U.S. monuments debate has been how that structure of irrelevance has changed; this is, again in Zerubavel's (2006) terms, because of what he identifies as "the social organization of denial" (p. 5).

Not only is attention socially organized but so too are even basic emotions such empathy. Who do we learn to see as part of our communities, and who do we learn to see as outsiders? Whose views are we taught to take into account, and whose to ignore? Which pasts are we led to celebrate and which to disavow? To be sure, this emphasis on social structure can itself sometimes sound like an excuse. Because we are constrained by circumstances, are we ever fully responsible? But social structure enables as much as it constrains. So just as social pressures can discourage empathy and responsibility, they can also underwrite them. Understanding that we are taught when to look and when to look away, then, is an essential step in underwriting epistemic and commemorative responsibility, and changes in it. To be sure, most of us have failed—continue in an infinity of ways to fail—to meet this responsibility. We cannot take the whole world on our shoulders. But perhaps we can take the monument down the street off of someone else's and cultivate a national memory—more properly national memories—in such a way that unites rather than divides? Understanding that we are perhaps not the source of our own ignorance but still responsible for it may be just a small bit of wisdom from sociology in the current context.

References

Ball, E. (1998). *Slaves in the family*. Farrar, Strauss, & Giroux.
Caplan, L. (2015). The White supremacist lineage of a Yale College. *The Atlantic*. https://www.theatlantic.com/politics/archive/2015/10/the-cause-to-rename-calhoun-college/408682
Coates, T. (2014). The case for reparations. *The Atlantic*. https://www.theatlantic.com/magazine/archive/2014/06/the-case-for-reparations/361631
Cohen, S. (2001). *States of denial: Knowing about atrocities and suffering*. Blackwell.

Erll, A. (2011). Travelling memory. *Parallax, 17*(4), 4–18.
Fine, G. (2001). *Difficult reputations: Collective memory of the evil, inept, and controversial*. University of Chicago Press.
Gordon-Reed, A. (1997). *Thomas Jefferson and Sally Hemings: An American controversy*. University of Virginia Press.
Halbwachs, M. (1992). *On collective memory* (L. Coser, Trans.). University of Chicago Press.
Kern Foxworth, M. (1994). *Aunt Jemima, Uncle Ben, and Rastus: Blacks in advertising, yesterday, today, and tomorrow*. Praeger.
Mosse, G. L. (1991). *Fallen soldiers: Reshaping the memory of the World Wars*. Oxford University Press.
Müller, J. W. (2016). *What is populism?* University of Pennsylvania Press.
Olick, J. K. (2007). *The politics of regret: On collective memory and historical responsibility*. Routledge.
Olick, J. K., & Perrin, A. (2010). Introduction. In J. K. Olick & A. Perrin (Eds.), *Guilt and defense: Theodor W. Adorno on the legacies of national socialism in postwar Germany* (pp. 3–43). Harvard University Press.
Olick, J. K., & Robbins, J. (1998). Social memory studies: From "collective memory" to the historical sociology of mnemonic practices. *Annual Review of Sociology, 24*(1), 105–140.
Renan, E. (1990). What is a nation? In H. K. Bhabha (Ed.), *Nation and narration* (pp. 8–21). Routledge.
Rothberg. M. (2009). *Multidirectional memory: Remembering the Holocaust in the age of decolonization*. Stanford University Press.
Savage, K. (1996). The politics of memory: Black emancipation and the Civil War monument. In J. Gillis (Ed.), *Commemorations: The politics of national identity* (pp. 128–148). Princeton University Press.
Schudson, M. (1989). The past in the present versus the present in the past. *Communication, 11*, 105–113.
Schuman, H., Schwartz, B., & D'Arcy, H. (2005). Elite revisionists and popular beliefs: Christopher Columbus, hero or villain? *Public Opinion Quarterly, 69*(1), 2–29.
Schwartz, B. (2003). *Abraham Lincoln and the forge of national memory*. University of Chicago Press.
Schwartz, B. (2009). *Abraham Lincoln in the post-heroic era: History and memory in late twentieth-century America*. University of Chicago Press.
Simko, C. (2012). Rhetorics of suffering: September 11 commemorations as theodicy. *American Sociological Review, 77*(6), 880–902.
Southern Poverty Law Center. (2019). *Whose heritage: Public symbols of the Confederacy*. https://www.splcenter.org/20190201/whose-heritage-public-symbols-confederacy
Vinitzky-Seroussi, V. (2002). Commemoration a difficult past: Yitzhak Rabin's memorial. *American Sociological Review, 67*(1), 30–51.
Vinitzky-Seroussi, V., & Teeger, C. (2010). Unpacking the unspoken: Silence in collective memory and forgetting. *Social Forces, 88*(3), 1103–1122.
Wagner-Pacific, R., & Schwartz, B. (1991). The Vietnam Veterans Memorial: Commemorating a difficult past. *American Journal of Sociology, 97*(2), 376–420.

Winter, J. (1995). *Sites of memory, sites of mourning: The Great War in European cultural history*. Cambridge University Press.

Young, J. (2002). *At memory's edge: After-images of the Holocaust in contemporary art and architecture*. Yale University Press.

Zerubavel, E. (1996). Social memories: Steps towards a sociology of the past. *Qualitative Sociology, 19*, 283–299.

Zerubavel, E. (2006). *The elephant in the room: Silence and denial in everyday life*. Oxford University Press.

SECTION II
CASE STUDIES OF NATIONAL MEMORY AND POPULISM IN AMERICA

The authors in this section bring several perspectives from the social sciences to the discussion of American national memory. Christina Simko, David Cunningham, and Amy Corning and Howard Schuman pose sociological questions about how views of the past are negotiated and renegotiated, and Jeremy Yamashiro examines some of the psychological dimensions involved. The authors use different conceptual frameworks to study American national remembering, but a point on which they converge is an emphasis on the contestation that goes into creating an account of the past.

In Chapter 5, Simko argues that Donald Trump's "nostalgic temporality," which is steeped in White nationalism and populism, is one of several national narratives contending for predominance in American political discourse. It stands in contrast with the "progressive temporality" of Barack Obama, which acknowledges America's deep flaws but focuses on an unending effort to transcend them in a quest for "a more perfect union." This latter narrative is also characterized by the sort of humility that Strobe Talbott sees as a virtue bequeathed to America by its founders. The third national narrative jockeying for space in this conversation is what Simko calls "traumatic temporality." It recognizes that slavery did not end in 1865 and is consistent with the "politics of regret" (Chapter 4, this volume), making it about as far from Trump's populist vision of the past as one can get.

As an illustration of the traumatic temporality narrative, Simko points to the Equal Justice Initiative's National Memorial for Peace and Justice and companion Legacy Museum in Montgomery, Alabama. In Simko's account, the three narratives she outlines provide competing focal points around which political leaders try to build national discussion. In this capacity, they serve as resources that are part of America's political culture—resources that over time might emerge and re-emerge as part of a national debate that is likely to go on into the future.

In Chapter 6, Cunningham focuses on a concrete case of such mnemonic struggles by outlining an "ecological approach" to study commemorative objects. Instead of looking to a single statue or story as a focus, his "field theory" emphasizes the complex dynamics among objects and stories that can undergo continual change as the field changes. Specifically, he traces how the meaning of the University of Mississippi's Confederate soldier statue has changed over a century as other commemorative objects and texts are placed in its context. In the process, the Lost Cause mythology outlined by Blight (Chapter 3, this volume) has been progressively "loosened within the commemorative landscape" as other objects and narratives are added. Cunningham provides a guide to the nuances of the moves and countermoves in this struggle, including what is *not* said or only vaguely alluded to. His ecological approach adds another item to the analytic toolkit that memory studies can harness to understand how cultural resources in a setting are taken up and used.

In Chapter 7, Corning and Schuman add a different sort of temporal dimension to the analysis of national memory by examining how it changes over decades and across generations. Reporting on years of empirical studies, they document how conflicting images of Christopher Columbus have taken some fascinating twists. The first of these images was of Columbus as the "discoverer" of America, a figure who had emerged as perhaps the leading candidate for America's founding hero. As in the case of the city on a hill narrative (Chapter 2, this volume), Corning and Schuman note that the story of Columbus actually was not always part of American collective memory but, rather, arose in response to political and cultural pressures of a particular era after the American Revolution. It then experienced the vagaries of other pressures, including the need Italian Americans had in the 19th century to shore up the legitimacy of their national belonging.

Corning and Schuman focus primarily on recent struggles and transformations of remembering Columbus. By the 1992 quincentenary of his arrival in the new world, his legacy was being challenged in fundamental ways by new voices that questioned his status as a founding hero. Namely, revisionist historians and Native American activists were condemning Columbus for "bringing slavery, disease, and destruction to America's Indigenous peoples." What happened next provides interesting insight into how top-down efforts to control national memory work. Although official accounts of Columbus changed in the formal instruction in schools, a 1998 survey showed that few people in the general population in the United States had adopted critical views of Columbus. Surveys in 2014 and 2017 indicated a gradual, but possibly accelerating, change in this picture. What Corning and Schuman call the "Simple Traditional" view of Columbus still predominated, but he was no longer taken so uniformly to be the "discoverer" of America.

On the basis of textbook analysis and teacher surveys, Corning and Schuman argue that what students encountered in schools changed considerably in the two decades after their first survey, but something more than mere exposure to new information was at work when it came to the views Americans hold. To be sure, there were signs of change with a decline in "Simple Traditional" assessments of Columbus and an uptick in "Villainous Columbus" views, but these changes varied by generation. Namely, survey results indicate that the younger the respondents, the more likely they were to view Columbus as Villainous. The upshot for Corning and Schuman is that the relationship between textbooks and other cultural images of Columbus, on the one hand, and popular beliefs, on the other hand, may be "longer term and less direct than is often assumed" and may reflect forces such as a critical period in one's life of being exposed to the images that go into national memory. In Corning and Schuman's account, the mechanisms whereby efforts to change views of the past work their way into popular collective memory are complex and only partly understood. The one thing that is clear, however, is that the simple promulgation of new information does not have the direct impact we often seem to assume.

In Chapter 8, Yamashiro introduces ideas from psychological studies that provide further insight into these matters. Using methods from cognitive psychology that tap unconscious processes, he suggests, for example, that Americans may generally be operating with a view of implicit decline in the trajectory of their nation. Societal decline, be it of the West (Spengler, 1922) in general or America in particular, is a long-standing notion in public debate, but Yamashiro examines it as an implicit part of the mentality of the American subjects he studies. In doing so, he introduces the notion of "future thought" that has become part of the study of memory in cognitive psychology and neuroscience in recent years. Instead of limiting themselves to past events, it turns out some of the same psychological and neurological processes involved in remembering are also used to imagine the future. From this perspective, remembering is only part of the story of "mental time travel" that shapes our views, and as Yamashiro notes, this broader view makes it possible to examine ways of thinking that lead to ideas about rising or declining national trajectories. He goes on to note that American views of decline might be organized by a "jeremiad" narrative template around which members of a community organize their views.

Yamashiro also uses tools from cognitive psychology to examine political differences between groups within America. He outlines how differences along a left–right political spectrum appear to be tied to different moral intuitions about what ought to be included in collective remembering. Thus, the divergence between those who privilege social justice and those who privilege "binding values" is reflected in whether events such as slavery, on the one hand, and signing the Declaration of Independence, on the other hand, should be the focus of national remembering. In laying out his line of reasoning, Yamashiro has provided a new set of tools from psychology for understanding some of the intricacies of bottom-up processes that go into shaping national remembering in America.

Reference

Spengler, O. (1922). *The decline of the west*. Alfred A. Knopf.

5

Finding a Way Forward

Memory and the Future in American National Narratives

Christina Simko

"Who controls the past, controls the future," claimed the Party's slogan in George Orwell's *Nineteen Eighty-Four* (1949, p. 33). Scholarship on collective memory clearly shows that the reality is not quite so straightforward. "The past" is rarely a singular construct, but instead a field of struggle in which any group's control is never total.[1] Yet Orwell was quite right that the future is always harnessed to the past. What we are able to imagine is a direct outgrowth of the stories we tell about where we have been.

The tight relationship between memories of the past and visions for the future is exemplified in the four-word slogan that helped propel Donald J. Trump to the U.S. presidency in 2016: "Make America Great Again." These words, which became so ubiquitous that they are often abbreviated "MAGA," are not merely a refrain lifted from the Reagan playbook. They also express and encapsulate a *temporality*: a way of mapping the relationships among past, present, and future (Zerubavel, 2003). Specifically, Trump's nostalgic slogan maps a decline from a glorious past to a present rife with disorder, and it promises that—with the right leadership—the longed-for past can also be restored as the nation's future. "Together, we will lead our party back to the White House, and we will lead our country back to safety, prosperity, and peace," Trump said as he accepted the presidential nomination at the Republican National Convention in 2016. Describing "violence in our streets" and "chaos in our communities," Trump asserted, "Beginning on January 20th, 2017, safety will be restored."[2] At its core, then, Trumpian

---

[1] On fields, see Bourdieu (1984). For an adaptation to memory studies, see Olick (2007).
[2] A full transcription is available at https://www.politico.com/story/2016/07/full-transcript-donald-trump-nomination-acceptance-speech-at-rnc-225974.

nationalism is about memory: seizing upon and fomenting a yearning for a lost past.

As the historian Jill Lepore (2019) notes, academics are not blameless for the resurgence of right-wing nationalism in the United States. Fearing that studying the nation was tantamount to endorsing nationalism, she explains, historians largely abandoned the nation as a unit of analysis beginning in the 1970s. The consequences have been significant. Without public intellectuals who are willing to engage in "the work of providing a legible past and a plausible future" for the American nation, the task falls instead to "charlatans, stooges, and tyrants." In memory studies, as in history, there are significant pressures to set aside the nation as a unit of analysis—to turn our attention instead to "either smaller or bigger things," as Lepore puts it. Studies of the nation may now be dismissed as part of an outdated "second wave" of memory studies that reifies artificially imposed borders and fails to reckon with transcultural flows of ideas (Erll, 2011a). Yet there is perhaps no field better positioned to counteract the work of "charlatans, stooges, and tyrants"—to clarify how storytelling can help bind the republic and shore up democratic norms in the United States—than memory studies. And what is at stake is nothing less than the future, the horizons of possibility that take shape against the backdrop of collective memory.

In this chapter, I juxtapose Trump's nostalgic temporality with two alternatives that hold a prominent place in the contemporary rhetorical and mnemonic landscape. The first is the progressive temporality represented most clearly by Trump's predecessor, Barack Obama, and etched into national memory at the Smithsonian's National Museum of African American History and Culture in Washington, DC. The second is the traumatic temporality evident in the Equal Justice Initiative's (EJI) National Memorial for Peace and Justice and companion Legacy Museum in Montgomery, Alabama, and articulated in public discourse by EJI's founder, Bryan Stevenson. These representations of the American past differ sharply from the sites of memory that Trump embraces, such as the colossal figures of Mount Rushmore that served as the backdrop for the president's Independence Day address in July 2020. But they also differ in significant ways from one another in how they reconstruct the U.S. past and project a path forward.

My primary focus in this chapter is analytical: Most of all, I endeavor to outline and clarify several of the national narratives that are currently contending for predominance in the public sphere—the broad context for the intricate local debates that Cunningham (see Chapter 6, this volume) traces—and in doing so, to underscore the crucial linkage between memory and futurity. Precisely because of this linkage—because struggles over the past are also always contests over the future, debates about who we ought to become—I conclude on a normative note. What is the relationship between the memories at the heart of these three narratives and the "facts," as best as we can establish them? And how do they address the pressing needs of a historical moment in which democracy faces alarming challenges?

"Make America Great Again": Nostalgic Temporality

In his January 2017 inaugural address, Trump began his presidency with a bleak portrait of a once-great society in precipitous decline. His signature promise was to revivify the past in the present: "to *rebuild* our country and *restore* its promise for all of our people" (emphasis added).[3] Reiterating the populist message that defined his campaign, Trump claimed that his inauguration was not merely a transfer of power "from one administration to another, or from one party to another." Instead, "we are transferring power from Washington, DC and giving it back to you, the American People." Trump described a nation beset with social problems:

> Mothers and children trapped in poverty in our inner cities; rusted-out factories scattered like tombstones across the landscape of our nation; an education system, flush with cash, but which leaves our young and beautiful students deprived of knowledge; and the crime and gangs and drugs that have stolen too many lives and robbed our country of so much unrealized potential.

But, he pledged, "This American carnage stops right here and stops right now." Restoring the past—making America great again—would mean reclaiming the nation's "glorious destiny."

The key to achieving this vision would be putting "America First." "We will bring back our jobs. We will bring back our borders. We will bring back our wealth. And we will bring back our dreams," Trump declared. As Trump sought to reinscribe clear national boundaries, who was included in the "we,"

---

[3] The official transcript of Trump's inaugural address is available at https://www.whitehouse.gov/briefings-statements/the-inaugural-address.

the collectivity to whom the jobs, wealth, and dreams for the future rightly belong?

On the surface, Trump oriented his remarks toward "all Americans." He referred explicitly to the nation's racial diversity: "Whether we are Black or Brown or White, we all bleed the same red blood of patriots," he said in the final moments of his inaugural address. Yet such statements have provided only the thinnest rhetorical veil for the White nationalism underlying Trump's ostensibly populist message. In the first year of his presidency, Trump refused to condemn the White supremacists who staged several rallies in Charlottesville, Virginia, protesting the planned removal of an equestrian statue depicting Confederate General Robert E. Lee. On the evening of August 11, 2017, approximately 250 protesters, mostly young White men, staged a torchlit rally, chanting "You will not replace us! Jews will not replace us!" as they marched toward a statue of Thomas Jefferson on the University of Virginia's storied lawn. The next day's "Unite the Right" rally, centered around the Lee statue but spilling out across Charlottesville's downtown, culminated in the death of counterprotester Heather Heyer, who was struck down when a White supremacist plowed into the crowd in a Dodge Challenger. When called upon for comment, Trump remarked that there were "some very fine people on both sides" of the protest.[4]

Even more, Trump underscored the symbolic link between Confederate generals and the founding fathers that the protesters had evoked by gathering around Jefferson's likeness at nightfall and then returning to defend Lee's legacy in broad daylight. Commenting on the events in Charlottesville, Trump predicted a swift slide down a slippery slope, in which the very foundations of the nation—the glorious past he had pledged to restore—would be threatened. "This week, it is Robert E. Lee. . . . I wonder, is it George Washington next? And is it Thomas Jefferson the week after? You know, you have to ask yourself, where does it stop?"[5]

The linkage between one of the Union's creators and the general who led the insurrection that threatened its continuity may seem strange or even incoherent. But there is a clear ideological connection: For all his rhetorical appeals to liberty and equality, Jefferson participated in and perpetuated the institution of slavery that Lee's army mobilized to defend. Moreover, as David Blight (2001) argues, after the Civil War, the reunification of North and

---

[4] Quoted in Gray (2017).
[5] Quoted in Gray (2017).

South into a single nation took shape around a "reconciliationist" narrative that privileged the relationship between northern and southern Whites over full emancipation and citizenship for African Americans. Thus, Confederate soldiers could be honored alongside their erstwhile enemies who fought to preserve the Union.

In fact, the reconciliationist narrative took shape during a several-decade period of postbellum monument-building that served to promote national unity and consensus (Doss, 2010). During this era, the Washington Monument was finally completed, and hundreds of statues depicting Christopher Columbus honored the 400th anniversary of his 1492 voyage. Illustrating the reconciliationist spirit that was afoot, the United Daughters of the Confederacy (UDC) began raising funds for a Confederate memorial in Arlington National Cemetery in 1906. As Erika Doss (2010, p. 22) notes, Black communities were also swept up in this wave of monument-building, erecting statues to heroes such as Crispus Attucks, Frederick Douglass, and Harriet Tubman. Yet truly *national* spaces overwhelmingly remained Whites only. For instance, although the remains of Confederate soldiers were reinterred at Arlington National Cemetery in 1900, and the UDC's memorial was dedicated in 1914, the cemetery remained segregated until 1948. And even though Congress began discussing a monument to honor Black veterans of the Civil War in the 1880s, it would take more than a century to bring it to fruition, with the dedication of the African American Civil War Memorial in Washington, DC, in 1998 (Doss, 2010, p. 23).

The symbolic landscape that took shape in the late 19th and early 20th centuries expressed national pride through monumentality: drawing the gaze upward, both literally and figuratively, toward images of "greatness." Perhaps the ultimate example of postbellum monumentality is Mount Rushmore, a project that commenced in 1927. The original impetus came from South Dakota's state historian, Doane Robinson, as a strategy to attract more tourism. Robinson proposed a monumental carving featuring heroes of the American West, such as Lewis and Clark, Sacagawea, Buffalo Bill Cody, and Oglala Lakota Chiefs Red Cloud and Crazy Horse. Sculptor Gutzon Borglum, a Klansman who had worked on the first iteration of Georgia's Stone Mountain,[6] had other ideas, however. Envisioning Mount Rushmore as a tribute to American expansionism and an embodiment

---

[6] Borglum was fired over financial conflicts with the UDC in 1925, after which his work on a carving of General Robert E. Lee's face was blasted off the mountain.

of Manifest Destiny (Boime, 1991), Borglum's purpose was—in his own words—"to communicate the founding, expansion, preservation, and unification of the United States" through the colossal statues.[7] That the figures literally emerge out of the physical landscape naturalizes westward expansion, the "onetime future of past generations" (Koselleck, 2004, p. 11) that legitimated extraordinary violence and devastation. As Albert Boime (1991) puts it, "Borglum's memorial . . . constituted the crowning touch to western expansion" and "literally etched the magisterial gaze into the conquered landscape" (p. 157).

Today, Mount Rushmore operates under the auspices of the National Park Service (NPS). Since the civil rights movement, the NPS has committed itself to providing "a pluralistic reading of the American experience," which has entailed "a 'toning-down' of the patriotic rhetoric common to [Mount Rushmore's] founders and original promoters" (Glass, 1994, p. 271). Yet Trump's address there in 2020 underscores that the original meanings assigned to national symbols do not simply disappear as ideals and values shift. Rather, as Cunningham (see Chapter 6, this volume) also underscores, memory is cumulative: New interpretations of the past are layered atop the old, remaining available for reuptake in the present (Schwartz, 1991). On July 4, 2020, Trump endeavored to shore up a national narrative rooted in heroic myths of great men—reinforced through monuments whose design inspires awe and reverence, and undergirded by an enduring commitment to the reconciliationist principles that allow Confederate heroes to stand tall alongside the nation's "founding fathers."

With the colossal faces of Mount Rushmore as his backdrop, Trump celebrated the American nation in cartoonish superlatives: It is "the most magnificent country in the history of the world," and "the greatest Americans who have ever lived" are monumentalized on "this magnificent, incredible, majestic mountain."[8] According to Trump, however, this very nation faced an existential threat from outsiders within: "Our nation is witnessing a merciless campaign to wipe out our history, defame our heroes, erase our values, and indoctrinate our children." Specifically, the threat arose out of a "left-wing cultural revolution" whose aim is nothing less than "to overthrow the

---

[7] The National Park Service quotes Borglum on the official website for Mount Rushmore at https://www.nps.gov/moru/learn/historyculture/index.htm.

[8] The official transcript of Trump's address is available at https://www.whitehouse.gov/briefings-statements/remarks-president-trump-south-dakotas-2020-mount-rushmore-fireworks-celebration-keystone-south-dakota.

American Revolution." The critics and iconoclasts seeking to reconstruct the commemorative landscape aimed not to improve the nation but, rather, to undermine it altogether. "Their goal is not a better America, their goal is the end of America."

According to Trump, preserving the nation against such threats demands a revival of monumentality—a vision launched into motion with Trump's July 3, 2020, executive order establishing a National Garden for American Heroes. As the order makes clear, in Trump's America, the past assumes outsize importance. "America owes its present greatness to its past sacrifices," declares the opening line.[9] Again, on the surface, Trump elaborates a multiracial vision, including abolitionists, participants in the Underground Railroad, and civil rights leaders among his list of possible American heroes. Yet his relentless emphasis on past greatness—and his claim at Mount Rushmore that efforts to critically reexamine the past are "a web of lies" in which "all perspective is removed, every virtue is obscured, every motive is twisted . . . and every flaw is magnified"— his fidelity to a White nationalist vision. During his final days in office, Trump's motives—as Talbott (see Chapter 1, this volume) states, "to transmogrify the United States from a representative democracy into a personal dictatorship"— were laid bare in a rally where he incited a violent insurrection at the Capitol, which unfolded while members of Congress were in the midst of certifying his successor's victory.

"A More Perfect Union": Progressive Temporality

For Trump, dissent is a betrayal of the nation's founding principles. For his predecessor, Barack Obama, it is at times the highest form of patriotism.

Just a few weeks after Trump's address at Mount Rushmore, Obama traveled to Ebenezer Baptist Church in Atlanta, Georgia, to eulogize one of his own heroes, Representative John Lewis. Obama, too, grounded his remarks with reference to the founding moment: "This country," he said, "is a constant work in progress. We were born with instructions: to form a more perfect union."[10] In direct contrast to Trump's superlatives, however, Obama

---

[9] The text of Trump's executive order is available at https://trumpwhitehouse.archives.gov/presidential-actions/executive-order-building-rebuilding-monuments-american-heroes/.
[10] A transcript of Obama's eulogy is available at https://www.washingtonpost.com/national/religion/transcript-barack-obamas-address-at-john-lewis-funeral/2020/07/30/41404586-d2ad-11ea-826b-cc394d824e35_story.html.

gestured toward the founders' own humility.[11] "Explicit in those words" of the Constitution's preamble "is the idea that we are imperfect; that what gives each new generation purpose is to take up the unfinished work of the last and carry it further than anyone might have thought possible." Through the Freedom Rides, the March on Washington, the Selma to Montgomery march, and his long career in Congress, Lewis had taken up the mantle and earned a place among the nation's founders. Obama predicted that

> someday, when we do finish that long journey toward freedom; when we do form a more perfect union—whether it's years from now, or decades, or even if it takes another two centuries—John Lewis will be a founding father of that fuller, fairer, better America.[12]

It was precisely this linear progressive temporality, the image of a nation moving steadily forward and upward as each generation undertakes its own efforts to perfect the union, that fueled Obama's improbable ascent to the nation's highest office in 2008. Initially, Obama rose to national prominence with his keynote address at the Democratic National Convention in 2004. At the time, he was a state senator in Illinois, although he would go on to win a seat in the U.S. Senate that November. From there, his rise was meteoric. By March 2008, he was one of just two remaining contenders for the Democratic presidential nomination.

Amidst this tight primary battle against New York Senator (and former First Lady) Hillary Clinton, Obama's campaign faced what appeared to be a mortal threat. ABC News had investigated his pastor, the Rev. Jeremiah Wright of Trinity United Church of Christ in Chicago, and turned up sermons that contradicted Obama's optimistic and patriotic rhetoric. For one, Wright violated one of the most stringent taboos of the 2000s by portraying the United States as complicit in the attacks of September 11, 2001. "We have supported state terrorism against the Palestinians and Black South Africans and now we are indignant because the stuff we have done overseas is now brought right back into our own front yards. America's chickens are coming home to roost." Even more, Wright's commentary forced Obama to address

---

[11] As Spillman (1998) argues, the American founding moment has remained central in national memory partly because of its open-endedness—its ability to be deployed on opposite sides of the same debate.

[12] The quotation is from Obama's eulogy, cited in note 10.

race relations head-on. In one passage that quickly became a sound bite, Wright contended that

> the government gives them [African Americans] the drugs, builds bigger prisons, passes a three-strike law and then wants us to sing "God Bless America." No, no, God damn America, that's in the Bible for killing innocent people. God damn America for treating our citizens as less than human.[13]

Seeking to overcome the damage to his campaign, Obama addressed—and repudiated—Wright's remarks in a speech at Philadelphia's Constitution Center. He began with the words from the preamble that have continued to define Obama's version of the national narrative even into the Trump era: "'We the people, in order to form a more perfect union . . .'—221 years ago, in a hall that still stands across the street, a group of men gathered and, with these simple words, launched America's improbable experiment in democracy," Obama said, "The document they produced was eventually signed but ultimately unfinished."[14]

As both the eulogy and the campaign speech illustrate, for Obama, the Constitution's preamble functions as a kind of secular scripture.[15] According to this view, although its authors were fallible, the text they bequeathed to us contains wisdom for the ages. It falls to each generation to extract—and enact—its true meaning. For instance, Obama argued in Philadelphia that "the answer to the slavery question was already embedded within our Constitution . . . a Constitution that promised its people liberty and justice and a union that could be and should be perfected over time." It was therefore incumbent upon the ensuing generations "to do their part . . . to narrow that gap between the promise of our ideals and the reality of their time." In turn, Obama's eulogy for Lewis in 2020 lionized the lawmaker and activist for his extraordinary role in this ongoing work.

---

[13] See Nasaw (2008) for these and several other excerpts.
[14] A transcript of Obama's speech is available at https://www.npr.org/templates/story/story.php?storyId=88478467.
[15] Philip Gorski (2011) argues that Obama revived and reconstructed the "civil religionist" tradition that Robert Bellah identified in the 1960s and 1970s as the foundation for American collective life. Like Obama, Talbott (see Chapter 1, this volume) underscores the particular significance of the phrase "a more perfect union" among the framers, who projected hopeful futures even while recognizing that perfection would elude mere mortals.

Faith in the wisdom of the secular scriptures underwrites Obama's progressive teleology, his commitment to a narrative that moves optimistically forward. Indeed, more than any other term, the word "forward" captures the essence of Obama's rhetoric. To be sure, his speechmaking acknowledges past violence and atrocity: The Constitution, he said in Philadelphia, "was stained by this nation's original sin of slavery." But Obama directs his gaze and the nation's attention toward the future. In the Philadelphia speech, he explained that his campaign was intended "to continue the long march of those who came before us." He acknowledged and named differences—of race, class, gender, religion, and so forth—but ultimately sought to collapse them in the name of common interests:

> I chose to run for president at this moment in history because I believe deeply that we cannot solve the challenges of our time unless we solve them together, unless we perfect our union by understanding that we may have different stories, but we hold common hopes; that we may not look the same and we may not have come from the same place, but we all want to move in the same direction—toward a better future for our children and our grandchildren.

In the end, the speech worked: rehabilitating Obama's campaign and animating the narrative of hope and change that carried him through the general election and into the White House (see Alexander, 2010). He would continue to emphasize unity—marking the darker elements of the past without dwelling on them; glancing backward fleetingly, then pivoting his gaze steadily ahead—as president. This progressive temporality influenced not only his approach to domestic race relations but also his attitude toward foreign policy. For instance, although he criticized the George W. Bush administration for its so-called "enhanced interrogation techniques" throughout his campaign, when Obama took office, he declined to prosecute the crimes of the past (either literally or rhetorically).

In a certain sense, Obama's outlook embraces and extends a belief in progress that has been integral to the "American experiment" from its beginnings. Yet the substance of the story contains notable differences. Routinely underscoring the place of the civil rights movement in the ongoing quest to perfect the union (see Adams & Vinitzky-Seroussi, 2019), Obama sought to overcome well-documented racial cleavages in American memory. Whereas Black Americans frequently cite the civil rights movement as one of the most pivotal events in modern U.S. history, White Americans seldom share their outlook (Griffin & Hargis, 2008). Obama's "unity" narrative sought to bridge this divide by underscoring the *importance* of the civil rights movement without dwelling on its darker aspects: the violence and humiliation that inspired protesters to action; and the massive White resistance whose legacies endure in residential segregation, the criminal legal system, and the Confederate flags erected over statehouses in places such as Alabama and South Carolina—symbols that continued to fly throughout most of Obama's 8 years in office.

In fact, Obama maintained this progressive narrative even in the face of the White supremacist violence that sparked the ongoing national reckoning with Confederate symbols: the 2015 shooting at Mother Emanuel African Methodist Episcopal Church in Charleston, South Carolina.[16] Charged with eulogizing Reverend Clementa Pinckney, who died along with eight congregants during a Wednesday night Bible study, Obama portrayed the late minister as an embodiment of the nation's steady stride toward a better future:

> Friends of his remarked this week that when Clementa Pinckney entered a room, it was like the future arrived; that even from a young age, folks knew he was special, anointed. He was the progeny of a long line of the faithful, a family of preachers who spread God's word, a family of protesters who sowed change to expand voting rights and desegregate the South. Clem heard their instruction, and he did not forsake their teaching.[17]

In Obama's account, Pinckney is not only integral to the future but also the future made present: "arrived."

Even the shooter became part of Obama's progressive narrative. Although the killer clearly sought "to terrorize and oppress," Obama intoned: "God works in mysterious ways. God has different ideas." For in the end, his act of violence generated a national awakening: "As a nation, out of this terrible tragedy, God has visited grace upon us, for he has allowed us to see where we've been blind." Most of all, the horrific violence in Charleston had

---

[16] In the spirit of the ecological approach that Cunningham develops (see Chapter 6, this volume), it is worth noting that Mother Emanuel is located on Calhoun Street, named for U.S. President John C. Calhoun, whose White supremacist views exerted significant influence on the southern states' decision to secede from the Union.

[17] The official transcript of Obama's remarks is available at https://obamawhitehouse.archives.gov/the-press-office/2015/06/26/remarks-president-eulogy-honorable-reverend-clementa-pinckney.

awakened Americans to the harmful impact of Confederate symbols. "For many, Black and White, that flag was a reminder of systemic oppression and racial subjugation. We see that now." Removing it from places of pride would illustrate the progress the United States has made: "It would be an expression of the amazing changes that have transformed this state and this country for the better, because of the work of so many people of good will, people of all races striving to form a more perfect Union." In the aftermath of the violence at Mother Emanuel—and following an iconic act of civil disobedience, in which activist Bree Newsome removed the Confederate flag that had flown above the capitol in South Carolina since 1961—Republican Governor Nikki Haley oversaw the flag's removal, drawing Obama's praise.

Obama's presidency has come to a close. But a strikingly similar version of the national narrative found a prominent place on the mnemonic landscape in 2016, with the dedication of the National Museum of African American History and Culture. Visitors enter the museum's historical exhibition by elevator, which takes them on a descent from the lobby to the bottom floor. There, the story begins in 15th-century Africa and Europe, tracing how the modern institution of slavery came into being. As the timeline reaches the nation's founding moment, visitors enter a high-ceilinged gallery that both celebrates and complicates the inception of the United States. An exhibit centered around a bronze statue of Thomas Jefferson delves into "the paradox of liberty" in language that plainly evokes Obama's speechmaking:

> The paradox of the American Revolution—the fight for liberty in an era of widespread slavery—is embedded in the foundations of the United States. The tension between slavery and freedom—who belongs and who is excluded—resonates through the nation's history and spurs the American people to wrestle constantly with building "a more perfect Union."

Jefferson is presented as the embodiment of this paradox: Even as he "helped to create a new nation based on individual freedom and self-government," he also "owned 609 slaves." The exhibit notes that Jefferson even enslaved his own children, who "inherited the status of their enslaved mother," Sally Hemings. Behind Jefferson's likeness is a tower of bricks inscribed with the names of many among the 609 people he enslaved.

Jefferson, in short, still holds a place of honor in the national narrative: He is depicted in bronze and credited as the author of the Declaration of Independence, whose words are emblazoned proudly on the museum's wall. But his image is complicated with an explicit account of his hypocrisies. It is also complemented with the stories of Black heroes who are cast in bronze alongside Jefferson. Benjamin Banneker, the exhibit explains, "boldly wrote to Thomas Jefferson" and asked him "to correct his 'narrow prejudices' against Africans." Phyllis Wheatley, "an enslaved girl who had mastered classical English, Latin, and Greek," wrote multilayered poetry and "was held up as a symbol of achievement by international antislavery advocates." Elizabeth Freeman, or "Mum Bett," was mobilized to action after overhearing a conversation about the Massachusetts Constitution: She "seized on its guarantee of liberty" and "helped to end slavery in Massachusetts." Already at the beginning, this exhibit suggests, Black leaders were actively engaged in perfecting the Union, criticizing the contradictions at its core.

In a comprehensive study of Black history museums throughout the United States, Robyn Autry (2017) notes that they overwhelmingly exhibit a progressive narrative structure. Many of the museums deal forthrightly with the horrors of enslavement. But few of them grapple head-on with more recent episodes of racial violence, instead emphasizing stories of triumph over oppression. The National Museum of African American History and Culture is somewhat distinctive in this way. There is, for instance, a clear depiction of the "climate of fear" that prevailed in the segregated South after Reconstruction, and the racially motivated lynchings that were "used . . . to terrorize African Americans" throughout the Jim Crow era. Victims of lynching "were shot, hung, tortured, and burned at the stake," often in front of sizeable crowds—acts of "vengeance" for crimes that were "often unproven or even imaginary." The contradictions at the heart of American political culture are routinely highlighted with exhibit titles such as "Democracy Abroad, Injustice at Home." But the direction of time's arrow nevertheless points unambiguously forward. Progress is even built into the museum's very architecture: After descending via elevator to the bottom floor, visitors gradually ascend as the timeline moves toward the present. When the museum moves into the post-1968 era, panel text explains, "Just as the Civil Rights and Black Power movements pursued goals of justice and equality in the 20th century, Americans must decide how to advance these goals into the 21st century." The story may not be perfectly linear, but ultimately, the question is *how*—not *whether*—progress will continue.

Although presidents and state-funded sites of memory play central roles in narrating the nation, some of the most decisive shifts in national memory have originated with charismatic figures who stand outside official politics.

Perhaps the most influential example is Martin Luther King, Jr., who is now invoked frequently in presidential speechmaking (Adams & Vinitzky-Seroussi, 2019) and whose likeness now holds a place of honor in downtown Washington, DC. Recently, one of the most prominent efforts to intervene in the national narrative has come from Bryan Stevenson, a celebrated civil rights attorney and the founder of the Alabama-based Equal Justice Initiative. EJI began as, and remains, a legal defense organization. Over time, however, its mission has expanded to include memory work that aims to reimagine national narratives in significant ways. EJI's memorial and museum, which opened in 2018, quickly garnered a place in the national spotlight.

Obama's commitment to turning the nation's eyes resolutely forward, to emphasizing progress, is precisely what distinguishes his rhetoric and the National Museum of African American History and Culture from Stevenson and EJI's National Memorial for Peace and Justice and companion Legacy Museum. In repudiating Reverend Wright's words, Obama said that his pastor's "profound mistake" was "that he spoke as if our society was static; as if no progress had been made." Although ultimately hopeful, Stevenson places emphasis on the "static" elements of U.S. history. Progress, Stevenson argues, simply is not possible without gazing steadily backward, taking pause to elucidate how the past continues to cast its long shadow over the present.

"Slavery Did Not End in 1865": Traumatic Temporality

Stevenson's public speechmaking is energetic and even hopeful. But it is also—to borrow one of Stevenson's own favorite terms—sobering. For Stevenson, there is something rotten at the core of the American experiment. He uses different metaphors to home in on that something, likening it to a "disease" that must be treated or "smog" that needs to be cleared.[18] Whatever the metaphor, neither disease nor pollutant can be eradicated by simply continuing to march forward. Instead, the past demands a reckoning.

When the EJI memorial and museum opened in 2018, *The New York Times* observed that the Legacy Museum is quite unlike "conventional" historical museums, "heavy on artifacts and detached commentary." Rather, "it is

---

[18] For the "disease" metaphor, see Stevenson's April 8, 2018, interview with Oprah Winfrey on *60 Minutes* at https://www.youtube.com/watch?v=uHQK1rNd7Qo. For the "smog" metaphor, see Stevenson's April 26, 2018, interview with Jeffrey Brown on *PBS NewsHour* at https://www.youtube.com/watch?v=Z-S3D33_-q8.

perhaps better described as the presentation of an argument" (Robertson, 2018). Indeed, the museum and memorial work in tandem to advance a thesis that Stevenson continually reiterates in public interviews and addresses: namely, that slavery did not end in 1865 but, rather, evolved—first into the terroristic lynchings that sustained White supremacy following the Civil War, then into the degrading system of segregation that marked the Jim Crow era, and finally into today's system of mass incarceration, marred by racial bias.

In short, EJI tells the story of trauma (see also Simko, 2020). At a psychological level, trauma distorts the sufferer's relationship to time. The past intrudes upon the present: Flashbacks, nightmares, and phobias transport the traumatized victim back to the horrors of the past, interrupting the present and interfering with their ability to project new futures (Shay, 1994; Young, 1995). Likewise, EJI tells of a nation that is caught in a cycle of racial violence and oppression. Racial injustice has taken new forms, but—as the protests over the deaths of Ahmaud Arbery, George Floyd, and Breonna Taylor made clear during the spring and summer of 2020—it has never passed away.

As Olick (see Chapter 4, this volume) notes, the United States has long resisted calls to reckon openly with past atrocities. EJI seeks to break through America's silence and denial by confronting the history of Whites' brutality toward African Americans. Even more, EJI argues that this brutality must occupy a central place in national memory. In the Legacy Museum, holograms re-enact the experience of the slave auction block, where family ties were permanently dissevered. Incarcerated people—current and former clients of EJI's defense attorneys—detail the dehumanizing conditions they have faced in the nation's jails and prisons.

The National Memorial for Peace and Justice focuses centrally on recognizing African American victims of lynching. On a hilltop overlooking downtown Montgomery stands a pavilion containing just over 800 Corten steel mini-monuments, each representing a county in which at least one documented lynching occurred. At the entrance to the pavilion, the 6-foot-high monuments are bolted into the ground. Visitors confront them at eye level, where they can read the names of the victims, although many are memorialized as "Unknown." Gradually, however, the monuments begin to lift, eventually rising so far overhead that they evoke the image of hanging bodies. Smaller scale installations situate lynching within the broader context of slavery's horrors and its post-1865 evolution, underscoring EJI's argument that it served to maintain White supremacy even after emancipation. In one sculpture, seven figures bound in shackles represent the agony and brutality of the transatlantic slave trade. As visitors descend from the pavilion, a row of figures with their hands held up in surrender illustrates how the traumatic past continues to reverberate: in incidents of police brutality and in the contemporary system of mass incarceration more generally.

Stevenson and EJI, then, present a very different narrative of 20th-century U.S. history than Obama and the National Museum of African American History and Culture. Direct comparisons illustrate the contrast. When describing the period known as the Great Migration, the African American history museum emphasizes the "pull" factors that drew Black Americans away from the South: "Drawn largely by new jobs in war industries, the first wave of more than 1.5 million people moved during and after World War I, and the second during and after World War II." By contrast, EJI argues that "push" factors predominated: that African Americans who left the South were not merely immigrants in search of better economic opportunities but "refugees and exiles from terror."[19] Likewise, in television interviews, commencement addresses, and meetings with community groups, Stevenson openly criticizes prevailing narratives of the civil rights movement, which he argues have become far too celebratory:

You hear people talking about the civil rights era, and . . . it's starting to sound like a three-day carnival. Rosa Parks didn't give up her seat on day one, and Dr. King led a march on Washington on day two, and on day three, we changed all the laws and racism is over,

he says, with a mixture of moral gravity and humor. "And that's not what happened."[20] Whereas the curators whom Autry (2017) interviewed expressed concern that exhibits on racial violence would undermine the dignity of Black visitors, especially young people, Stevenson argues for unflinchingly confronting even the most difficult histories.

At the same time, EJI emphasizes that America's history of racial violence is not just an African American trauma. It is a *national* burden to bear, akin to what Garagozov (see Chapter 17, this volume) terms the "common

---

[19] The quotation is from EJI's website at https://eji.org/projects/community-remembrance-project.
[20] The quotation is from Stevenson's June 21, 2019, interview with Lester Holt on *NBC Nightly News* at https://www.nbcnews.com/nightly-news/video/lester-holt-in-conversation-with-criminal-justice-reformer-bryan-stevenson-62443077944.

suffering" narrative. To be sure, White and Black Americans bear the scars of the past differently. But even Whites are damaged by their country's history of racial violence. In a *60 Minutes* feature leading up to the memorial's opening, Stevenson argued that the nation's history of lynching has

> done real psychic damage, not just to Black people, but to White people, too. Because you can't bring your child to the public square and have your child watch someone be burned to death, be tortured, to have their fingers cut off, to be castrated, to be taunted, to be menaced, to be hanged like that, and not expect it to have some consequence, some legacy. . . . I don't even think that White people in our country are free. I think we're all burdened by this history of racial inequality.[21]

What the nation requires is *working through* the past, confronting and addressing the traumatic histories that haunt the present and cloud the future.[22] Stevenson often uses the language of "truth and reconciliation" to describe this process. In his view, reconciliation is possible. But racial unity can come about only after a thorough reckoning. Stevenson states, "We want to tell the truth, because we believe in truth and reconciliation, but we know that truth and reconciliation are sequential. We can't get to where we're trying to go if we don't tell the truth first."[23]

In many ways, the future that Stevenson projects—the future for which he expresses genuine hope—is compatible with what Obama imagines. But he has a different roadmap for getting there: one that circles back, retraces U.S. history step by step, and accounts for the past that has bequeathed to us the inequalities and injustices we observe today. Such work is especially difficult in the United States, Stevenson says, because we are "the most punitive society on the planet," as evidenced by the state of the criminal legal system. That is, Americans avoid facing difficult truths because we fear we will be punished. But EJI has other goals in mind. "I'm not interested in talking about America's history because I want to punish America," Stevenson explained in 2018, "I want to liberate America."[24]

---

[21] The quotation is from the Winfrey interview, cited in note 17.
[22] Visions for working through the past have been integral to the literature on trauma since Freud (1950); after World War II, Theodor Adorno (2010) famously considered how a psychoanalytically inspired approach to reckoning with the past could be transferred to the collective level.
[23] The quotation is from the Winfrey interview, cited in note 17.
[24] Quoted in Robertson (2018).

In the buildup to the memorial's opening, he obliquely addressed Trump's MAGA slogan:

> America can be a great nation even though there was slavery, even though there was lynching, even though there was segregation. But if we don't talk about those things we did, we don't acknowledge those things, we're not going to get there.[25]

Greatness is not a past state, but it remains a future prospect.

From Imagination to Reality

Stevenson and his EJI colleagues created the National Memorial for Peace and Justice out of a conviction that narrative matters. After years of working with defendants on Alabama's death row, Stevenson says, "it became clear that race was the big burden." The National Memorial for Peace and Justice and the Legacy Museum are the centerpiece of EJI's effort "to get outside the courts and create a different narrative about race, race consciousness, racial bias, and discrimination in history . . . to create the kind of environment where we could actually win."[26]

Social science confirms Stevenson's instinct that narrative is a constitutive force: in propelling social movements (Polletta, 2006), in shaping electoral politics (Alexander, 2010), in igniting or averting violence (Smith, 2005), and indeed in national memory overall (see Chapter 22, this volume). As we face down the "charlatans, stooges, and tyrants" (Lepore, 2019) who have seized power in the United States and elsewhere—not least by wresting control of national narratives—can memory studies help guide our path? In outlining two of the most powerful and prominent challenges to Trump's nostalgic White nationalism, I also suggest some of the questions we can pose as we adjudicate between them. What national story or stories can provide a constructive path into the future?

First, we should ask whether the stories we tell about the past accurately reflect the nation's history. The relationship between history and memory has long been contested, and I do not want to imply an opposition between them.

---

[25] The quotation is from the Winfrey interview, cited in note 17.
[26] Quoted in Toobin (2016).

Rather, I agree with Erll (2011b) that history is one type of memory. I believe, however, that it is—or ought to be—an epistemically privileged form of memory: As Wertsch (see Chapter 22, this volume) argues, analytic history is an important "antidote or corrective" for national memories that uphold preferred narratives "at the expense of evidence." The Trump administration's reliance on what senior advisor Kellyanne Conway infamously called "alternative facts" testifies to the perils of pure constructivism. History relies on both evidence and argumentation, documentation and interpretation. Although narrative is, by its very nature, reductionistic—never able to capture the past in its full complexity or detail—some narratives fit the evidence better than others.

In particular, if the United States is to endure as a multiracial and multiethnic democracy, it seems especially critical that national narratives account for the legacies of the past in the present. The wealth gap between Black and White Americans and enduring patterns of residential segregation are two well-known legacies. Social scientists have increasingly shown that the lynching violence commemorated at the National Memorial for Peace and Justice has significant legacies in the present as well. Recent scholarship has documented the fear that drove African Americans away from the South during the so-called Great Migration, a period that Karida Brown (2018) aptly relabels the Great Escape (see also Wilkerson, 2012). During the civil rights movement, counties with a history of racially motivated lynching exhibited significantly more Ku Klux Klan activity (Cunningham & Phillips, 2007). Today, states with histories of lynching have more White supremacist hate groups (Durso & Jacobs, 2013) and are more likely to impose the death penalty (D. Jacobs et al., 2005), an institution that is itself bound up with the nation's history of enslavement (Garland, 2010). Empirically speaking, America's past traumas *do* seem to return in every era to haunt the present.

Given the powerful linkage between memories and futures, however, there are other considerations at play. Portraying cycles of violence as inevitable can lead to fatalism (R. Jacobs, 2001), stymying political action. The most motivating narratives sometimes have a looser relationship with the truth than academic history permits: Social change requires that participants be inspired to overcome obstacles, to endure even when the cause may appear hopeless. For instance, the 1960 student sit-ins were thoughtfully coordinated but narrated as spontaneous, providing motivation and compelling more widespread participation (Polletta, 2006). In addition to juxtaposing collective memories with the historical evidence, anyone invested in transformative futures must also ask which storyline is apt to bring about the desired outcome. Here, visions of progress may be crucial, underwriting a conviction that advocacy will be rewarded with change.

By these metrics, both the National Museum of African American History and Culture and EJI, Obama and Stevenson, offer crucial narrative resources for the present. Stevenson and EJI underscore that contra the long-standing American impulse toward progress narratives, the nation remains haunted by its past, by the violence at its very origins. They also provide a site for engaging some of the nation's most painful pasts directly and constructively—a reminder that even if a "more perfect Union" is not our preordained destiny, it can nevertheless become our destination if we are willing to devote ourselves toward that end. Obama and the African American history museum provide an important complement by emphasizing the differences between past and present, the strides taken and the moral and political battles won. Even if the moral arc of the universe does not inevitably bend toward justice, they allow today's would-be politicians and activists to focus on the moments when it has moved in a progressive direction, offering inspiration for generations to come.

References

Adams, T., & Vinitzky-Seroussi, V. (2019). "On cloud nine": Positive memories in American presidential speeches (1945–2017). *Memory Studies*, *12*(1), 11–26.

Adorno, T. W. (2010). The meaning of working through the past. In J. K. Olick & A. J. Perrin (Eds.), *Guilt and defense: On the legacies of national socialism in postwar Germany* (pp. 213–227). Harvard University Press.

Alexander, J. C. (2010). *The performance of politics: Obama's victory and the democratic struggle for power*. Oxford University Press.

Autry, R. (2017). *Desegregating the past: The public life of memory in the United States and South Africa*. Columbia University Press.

Blight, D. W. (2001). *Race and reunion: The Civil War in American memory*. Harvard University Press.

Boime, A. (1991). Patriarchy fixed in stone: Gutzon Borglum's Mount Rushmore. *American Art*, *5*(1–2), 142–167.

Bourdieu, P. (1984). *Distinction: A social critique of the judgment of taste*. Harvard University Press.

Brown, K. L. (2018). *Gone home: Race and roots through Appalachia*. University of North Carolina Press.

Cunningham, D., & Phillips, B. T. (2007). Contexts for mobilization: Spatial settings and Klan presence in North Carolina, 1964–1966. *American Journal of Sociology*, *113*(3), 781–814.

Doss, E. (2010). *Memorial mania: Public feeling in America*. University of Chicago Press.
Durso, R. M., & Jacobs, D. (2013). The determinants of the number of White supremacist groups: A pooled time-series analysis. *Social Problems, 60*(1), 128–144.
Erll, A. (2011a). *Memory in culture*. Palgrave Macmillan.
Erll, A. (2011b). Travelling memory. *Parallax, 17*(4), 4–18.
Freud, S. (1950). Remembering, repeating, and working-through. In J. Strachey (Ed.), *The standard edition of the complete psychological works of Sigmund Freud* (Vol. 12, pp. 145–157). Hogarth.
Garland, D. (2010). *Peculiar institution: America's death penalty in an age of abolition*. Oxford University Press.
Glass, M. (1994). Producing patriotic inspiration at Mount Rushmore. *Journal of the American Academy of Religion, 62*(2), 265–283.
Gorski, P. S. (2011). Barack Obama and civil religion. *Political Power and Social Theory, 22*, 177–211.
Gray, R. (2017, August 15). Trump defends White-nationalist protesters. *The Atlantic*. https://www.theatlantic.com/politics/archive/2017/08/trump-defends-white-nationalist-protesters-some-very-fine-people-on-both-sides/537012
Griffin, L. J., & Hargis, P. G. (2008). Surveying memory: The past in black and white. *The Southern Literary Journal, 40*(2), 42–69.
Jacobs, D., Carmichael, J. T., & Kent, S. L. (2005). Vigilantism, current racial threat, and death sentences. *American Sociological Review, 70*(4), 656–677.
Jacobs, R. (2001). The problem with tragic narratives: Lessons from the Los Angeles uprising. *Qualitative Sociology, 24*(2), 221–243.
Koselleck, R. (2004). *Futures past: On the semantics of historical time*. Columbia University Press.
Lepore, J. (2019, March–April). A new Americanism. *Foreign Affairs*. https://www.foreignaffairs.com/articles/united-states/2019-02-05/new-americanism-nationalism-jill-lepore
Nasaw, D. (2008). Controversial comments made by Rev. Jeremiah Wright. *The Guardian*. https://www.theguardian.com/world/2008/mar/18/barackobama.uselections20083
Olick, J. K. (2007). *The politics of regret: On collective memory and historical responsibility*. Routledge.
Orwell, G. (1949). *Nineteen eighty-four*. Houghton Mifflin Harcourt.
Polletta, F. (2006). *It was like a fever: Storytelling in protest and politics*. University of Chicago Press.
Robertson, C. (2018, April 25). A lynching memorial is opening. The country has never seen anything like it. *The New York Times*. https://www.nytimes.com/2018/04/25/us/lynching-memorial-alabama.html
Schwartz, B. (1991). Social change and collective memory: The democratization of George Washington. *American Sociological Review, 56*(2), 221–236.
Shay, J. (1994). *Achilles in Vietnam: Combat trauma and the undoing of character*. Scribner.
Simko, C. (2020). Marking time in memorials and museums of terror: Temporality and cultural trauma. *Sociological Theory, 38*(1), 55–77.
Smith, P. (2005). *Why war? The cultural logic of Iraq, the Gulf War, and Suez*. University of Chicago Press.
Spillman, L. (1998). When do collective memories last? Founding moments in the United States and Australia. *Social Science History, 22*(4), 445–477.

Toobin, J. (2016, August 15). The legacy of lynching, on death row. *The New Yorker*. https://www.newyorker.com/magazine/2016/08/22/bryan-stevenson-and-the-legacy-of-lynching

Wilkerson, I. (2012). *The warmth of other suns: The epic story of America's great migration*. Random House.

Young, A. (1995). *The harmony of illusions: Inventing post-traumatic stress disorder*. Princeton University Press.

Zerubavel, E. (2003). *Time maps: Collective memory and the social shape of the past*. University of Chicago Press.

6

The Weight of the Past

Ecological Perspectives on a Contested Confederate Monument

David Cunningham

Although we may never be able to affix a definitive end to the contentious tale of the University of Mississippi's (UM) Confederate soldier statue, the beginning of that story can be more precisely located. Its inception dates back not to the statue's initial placement in 1906 but, rather, to the addition of a modest plaque 93 years later and 200 yards away. That plaque, installed in the fall of 1999, accompanied a red maple tree planted in honor of Mae Bertha Carter, whose eight children had courageously desegregated the public schools in Drew, a tiny Delta town located an hour west of the university's campus in Oxford. Seven of the Carter siblings had then gone on to attend and graduate from "Ole Miss," the university's telling nom de plume (Curry, 1996).

Located on the Circle, a teardrop-shaped roadway marking the most visible entrance to campus and ringed by many of the university's most iconic structures, including its main administration building, the plaque's placement was quite central (Rueb, 2019). However, belying—or, more pointedly, due to—Ms. Carter's formidable stature, this tribute has long maintained a low profile. Today, the tree remains dwarfed by the many old-growth hardwoods spread throughout the Circle. The plaque rests flush with the ground, occupying less than 2 square feet.

When I visited the Circle in 2019 with the express purpose of locating and paying homage to the plaque, it took me nearly a half-hour to find it, despite my advance scrutiny of online resources that claimed to triangulate it with nearby buildings. The object itself was largely covered with soil and leaves, and it clearly hadn't been tended to (Figure 6.1). Its text, straightforward and rather severely understated, notes its 1999 placement "In Memoriam" (Ms. Carter had passed earlier that year at the age of 76) and describes its subject simply as the "Mother of Seven Ole Miss Graduates." I learned later that

David Cunningham, *The Weight of the Past* In: *National Memories*. Edited by: Henry L. Roediger and James V. Wertsch, Oxford University Press. © Oxford University Press 2022. DOI: 10.1093/oso/9780197568675.003.0006

Figure 6.1 Mae Bertha Carter memorial plaque at the University of Mississippi

the university administration rejected and struck "freedom fighter" from the original draft version (Susan Glisson & Charles Tucker, personal communication, March 13, 2019). But despite such compromises and the plaque's subsequent public neglect, its placement serves as the defining catalyst of the ensuing two-decade trajectory of struggle over the nearby Confederate soldier's statue—the campus's most prominent, resonant, and charged object.

Looming 30 feet tall over the campus's main entrance, that Confederate monument has long enjoyed pride of place on the Circle. One would need to take great pains to visit the campus without noticing it. Dedicated in 1906, in an era when hundreds of like tributes to the Confederacy were erected in prominent public spaces across the South, the statue itself depicts a soldier, rifle in one hand and the other raised in a salute or show of vigilance— a sentry with the campus at his back. Engravings on the column reinforce the soldier's supposed valor—its front panel offers a dedication "to our Confederate dead, 1861–1865," by the Albert Sidney Johnston Chapter 379 of the United Daughters of the Confederacy, which had commissioned and placed the statue. Elsewhere is a more grandiose tribute: "To the heroes of Lafayette County whose value and devotion made glorious many a battlefield." Emblematic of the White supremacist Lost Cause ideology that motivated the statue's placement, side panels also include quotes from Byron and Simonides, linking the Confederacy to other historical struggles of valiant, principled defenders overwhelmed by more powerful invading forces.

Indeed, as UM historians John Neff, Jared Roll, and Anne Twitty (2016) argue, such Lost Cause ideology served as the statue's raison d'etre, motivating as well as infusing the monument's "purpose, design, placement, and dedication" (p. 1). Twitty recently unearthed the 1906 dedicatory address by then-gubernatorial candidate Charles Scott. Its text valorizes Confederate soldiers not only during the war but also in the Reconstruction period that followed, when those same veterans, Scott asserted, "boldly, aggressively, and intentionally overrode the letter of the law, that they might maintain the spirit of the law and preserve Anglo Saxon civilization." The monument, as Twitty (2020) notes, has always functioned not as a memorial to defeated war dead but, rather, as a tribute to victorious defenders of the values that had motivated Mississippi's secession from the Union.

As such, its mission aligned with that of the overall campus. As the faculty comprising the university's Critical Race Studies Group have observed, the campus environment—which I conceive here as constituting the *ecology* within which any of its constituent objects reside—had long been uniform in its valence, serving as a "bastion to White supremacy" (Combs et al., 2016, p. 341). The campus's overall design reflected and embodied the university's founding mission: to educate the children of the state's White elite, who might otherwise have headed to exclusive schools outside of the South, where they were at risk of exposure to abolitionist ideas challenging those that had long defined southern racial politics.

Iconic spaces throughout the campus resonate with this mission and long have been mobilized to evoke or defend this heritage. In 1962, for instance, the soldier's statue unsurprisingly served as a rallying point for White supremacist forces who sought to prevent the desegregation of the university in the face of James Meredith's admission. The resulting battle led to two deaths and a reported 375 injuries, with the pitched resistance ebbing only after more than 30,000 National Guard troops were deployed to the campus (Eagles, 2009). Prior to the placement of the Carter plaque in 1999, no markers had commemorated the contributions of African Americans to the campus—not the enslaved workers who had constructed many of the campus's most prominent structures, nor the staff that had always sustained the university's operations, nor the Black students and faculty who had helped chart its academic course since 1962. "Such are the ways," observes the poet Natasha Trethewey

(2020), "the monumental landscape . . . has erased the collective history of Mississippi and replaced it with a singular one, meant to glorify whites only."

In interrogating this particular corner of that landscape, I aim to discern how localized processes relate to, and shape, the manner in which national memory relates to lived understandings of material settings. Whereas typical conceptions of national memory emphasize top-down processes by powerful institutions—from elected leaders to the media—I highlight here how national discourse is navigated locally, offering a sort of refractive lens through which to understand one's social and material surroundings. Centering the *trajectory of contestation* over the presence and meaning of a specific object helps illuminate these bottom-up processes through which stakeholders draw on, and refashion, broad memory frames as they orient to the commemorative landscape associated with a particular local institution.

This approach is dually contextual and bounded, in service of aims both specific and general. Offering a close description of the contentious trajectory of a single object on a flagship campus, I highlight the ecological character of the struggle—how meanings imbued in monumental objects, along with the possibilities for reimagining those meanings, are defined relationally, via their orientation to a constellation of like objects in the surrounding landscape. Within a bounded ecological environment, constituent objects exhibit a *valence*, composed of the meanings imbued within its original placement as well as the refashionings of those meanings through subsequent alterations and reinterpretations. Such valences exert cultural pulls over the broader memory and identity that define a place, absorbing competing and otherwise multivalent understandings to convey and communicate an *institutional story*—one that may be oriented nationally but forged within the crucible of a localized community.

Ecological Approaches

At the level of an individual object, valences define and represent the cultural "work" performed by that object. When viewed through a broadened lens, such valences also exert "pulls" on *other* objects, defining the context within which observers view and interpret any particular aspect of the landscape. In this sense, ecological formulations borrow conceptually from field theory, which—when applied to social environments—emphasizes how the actions of specific actors and institutions are conditioned by their self-aware positioning vis-à-vis other actors that occupy the same field (Fligstein & McAdam, 2012). Although material objects may not themselves possess anything analogous to this awareness and ability to adjust their own orientations within their milieus, they do serve as texts on which such meanings can be read by various audiences. These observers, in often multivalent ways, understand an object's presence and significance in interaction with its surroundings, defining the cultural contours of any recognized institution via the constituent elements of the landscape within which the object resides.

Emblematically, institutions such as campuses seek to minimize such multivalent understandings, striving for consistency in this respect—a visual reflection of the core values and guiding mission that defines the institution in toto. Leaders can often go to great lengths to preserve this consistency. When faced with a hard-hitting design for a civil rights monument that would follow the placement of the Carter plaque, for instance, UM Chancellor Robert Khayat (2013) highlighted his "huge problem with the way [the] artwork would alter the campus" given its lack of "compatib[ility] with the university's architecture." "I simply couldn't imagine," Khayat ruminated, "every student, visitor, staff member, or faculty member walking in or out of the Lyceum or library facing the negative, shocking language" (p. 290).

Even with the power to veto the placement of oppositional symbols, maintaining such consistency in practice always is a fraught project. Hazards reside in the social character of public spaces, which ensure that uniformity even in "official memory" is always subject to reconstruction—an act thrown into question by the shifting intentions of those with the authority to place new objects, alter established ones, or advance statements of revised intent to refashion the valence of the milieu or its constituent components (Alderman & Rose-Redwood, 2017; Olick, 2007). Such leadership, of course, is itself subject to renegotiation, shaped by the interplay of multiple, sometimes overtly competing, visions. Furthermore, these guiding viewpoints are also—possibly even predominantly—shaped by the presence of additional audiences to the sites and objects that comprise any institutional space. Through affirmation, critique, or differential attention, those stakeholders activate their own pulls on physical environments, assembling what John Bodnar (1992) refers to as "vernacular memory" that alters the playing field within which those charged with charting institutional mission jockey for position and influence.

Encapsulating the interplay of material objects and social actors, this process of cultural reproduction is subject as well to broader shifts in historical and cultural tides. These exogenous pulls offer a temporal analogue to the spatial ecologies within which memory and meaning are imbued upon objects. Just as proximate and distant sites can, to varying degrees, impose their valence on any given entity, changes in associated meanings over time constitute a gradient that lends dynamism to the spatial ecologies often encapsulated in snapshot understandings of social spaces. An ecological account of the Confederate soldier's statue thus unfolds not only in cross-section as that object's significance is refracted through that of its surrounds but also over time through key inflection points that define phases marked by distinct broader orientations to the object's meanings in the space.

This spatial and temporal ecological character underscores the processual quality of meaning-making (see Chapter 21, this volume) or what Jeffrey Olick (2007) highlights as *"figurations of memory* ... where images, contexts, traditions, and interests come together in fluid, though not necessarily harmonious, ways"* (p. 91). As a fundamentally contextual and relational approach, the perspective developed here offers a general rubric through which meanings and actions around any object are foreclosed or rendered possible. But those contexts cannot accomplish anything in themselves, and the trajectories of commemorative objects are more proximately shaped and ultimately defined by the actors that mobilize around them. The approach here, thus, highlights as well the social infrastructures that enable different constituencies to become active stakeholders within the overall story associated with any object in the landscape. Encompassing the institutions, associations, and social networks associated with the social dimension of a space, social infrastructures define possibilities possessed (or not) by individuals and groups to reaffirm and/or challenge the ecologically construed meanings that permeate the landscape.

The Contentious Trajectory of the Confederate Soldier's Statue at the University of Mississippi

The account here orients to the trajectory of the flashpoint Confederate soldier's statue, emphasizing the shifting valences of its surroundings on the overall campus, the key moments of change within the landscape that serve as inflection points for reinterpreting the significance of any given space, and the social bodies that mobilize around those spaces at any given point. From its placement and dedication in 1906, the Confederate monument served to reflect and bolster the White supremacist valence that permeated the campus. This orientation, as an embodiment of the motivating values characterizing the campus landscape, would not be materially interrupted (despite the pronounced social disruptions that pervaded the campus during the 1960s) until the placement of the Carter plaque more than nine decades later. That act served as an origin point, defining the first of three key phases in the alteration of UM's material landscape. In ways both anticipated and not, the impact of each phase was shaped not only by specific modifications but also by how those discrete additions, refashionings, or removals created more diffuse possibilities for reconceiving the overall campus.

Phase I: Additive Approaches

As the first institutionally sanctioned object on campus that countered the White supremacist renderings that had to that point informed the construction and growth of UM, the Mae Bertha Carter plaque provided a pivotal point of inflection in that trajectory. Prior to 1999, although students and other constituencies had long engaged in what the Critical Race Studies Group terms the "dialectics of protest and reaction" (Combs et al., 2016, p. 342), making claims on university leaders to create a more inclusive campus community, the halting, piecemeal reforms that resulted had not been institutionalized or otherwise challenged the built environment of the university.

The Carter plaque thus constituted a breakthrough. True, the object was small in physical stature. It lacked the "freedom fighter" label or any other overt reference to the struggles through which seven members of the Carter family were able to secure an education from UM. Furthermore, it conceded the "Ole Miss" label, rooted in an antebellum vernacular term for an enslaver's wife, which continues to normalize the campus's prevailing White supremacist foundations even in the face of challenge (Carey, 2016). But such compromises did not eclipse the plaque's significance, transmitted by its presence and recognition of the civil rights struggle and the accomplishments of Black members of the UM community rather than by its particular compositional elements.

This initial shot across the university's White supremacist bow altered the trajectory of the nearby soldier's statue in a number of ways. First, the successful incursion created a sense of efficacy around the possibility of transformation, understood initially by administrative elites as the possibility for *additions* to the campus's landscape in parallel to the existing orthodoxy. This additive logic opened space for progressive constituencies, such as a 1995 Southern Studies class taught by the eminent folklorist William Ferris, to be able to reflect critically on the "symbolism" displayed on campus. As John T. Edge, a student in that class and later the founding director of UM's acclaimed Southern Foodways Alliance, noted, Ferris' course allowed him to consider with his fellow classmates how "inclusive symbols reflect the positive effects of the Civil Rights Movement and the struggle for equal access to education" (as cited in Molpus, 2002, p. 1).

For traditionalist factions within the administration, the addition of such inclusive symbols need not undermine, or even necessarily directly interact with, the campus's primary orientation to Confederate history. Instead, such initiatives could be driven and shaped by an ethic of "parallel chapters" in the university's story. Maintaining this parallelism, of course, required tight management of the civil rights narrative, siloing its presentation to foreclose any direct challenge to Confederate orthodoxy. This effort had shaped the university's management of the Carter plaque, striking phrases such as "freedom fighter" that would place in critical light the many figures commemorated on campus who had labored to deny the freedom of Ms. Carter and Black Mississippians generally.

Such efforts dovetailed with UM Chancellor Khayat's aim to "talk about the promise of [the university's] future without rehashing our widely-known history" (Khayat, 2013, p. 293). This strained partitioning of past and future permeated his more general antipathy toward "race being a part of almost every conversation," requiring what he viewed as an unfortunate continual need to "re-address the same difficult and emotional events of our past" (p. 293). The corresponding additive approach to the campus's commemorative landscape provided, in Khayat's view, a container for recognizing—and wholly enveloping—other sides of the story, which he hoped could serve as a "bookend" on certain events of the past.

This aim motivated and shaped the administration's action around a symbol much more substantial than the Carter plaque: a proposed civil rights monument residing in the heart of the campus. The roots of that proposal extended back to Ferris' 1995 class survey of campus symbols, which, not surprisingly, had found UM's orientation to the civil rights movement "wanting." Determined to change that, students took up the mantle, proposing a new monument and, formalizing their efforts as the Civil Rights Commemoration

Initiative, raising $150,000 to commission an artwork commemorating the struggle for educational equity on the campus and in the state.

Khayat initially praised the initiative, conceding the importance of acknowledging this aspect of the university's history in parallel with an otherwise-unchanged landscape. "Just as the Confederate soldier monument recognizes the role of the university in the Civil War," Khayat asserted in 2001, "this civil rights memorial will recognize the role of the university in that important chapter of the nation's history" ("Civil Rights Campus Memorial," 2001, p. 21). A $75,000 grant received from the state Department of Archives and History earlier that year would, according to Mississippi's largest and most prominent newspaper, the *Jackson Clarion-Ledger* ("Funds Aid Civil Rights Art," 2001), "practically guarantee" that the memorial "would become a reality" (p. 13).

Coinciding with the university's 2002 "Open Doors" commemoration of the 40th anniversary of its desegregation, the Civil Rights Commemoration Initiative's national competition netted 120 submissions. After narrowing the group to 5 finalists, the committee selected Philadelphia-based artist Terry Adkins, whose "outdoor corridor" design depicted four 19-foot gates framing a long pathway intended to represent the arc of key political aims: "freedom" and "justice," "henceforth" and "forevermore." The doors of each also referenced the campus's transformation since Meredith's contested admission; gate doors were etched with the phrases "Teach in fear no more," "Learn in fear no more," and "Unite in fear no more." Such phrasings demonstrated Adkins' emphasis on social change but also on how these issues endure on and beyond the campus. "My idea is basically that the struggle continues," he noted, "The struggle for civil rights isn't over" ("Committee Soon to Pick Model," 2002, p. 16).

Such sentiments challenged Khayat's desired parallelism, which at least implicitly viewed civil rights as a "chapter" with an opening and closing that could coexist with symbols commemorating the university's growth amidst, and due to, earlier "chapters" associated with enslavement and racial segregation. Such concerns were reflected both in the monument's content and in its proposed location, which the Chancellor viewed as "dominating" the space between the Lyceum, where his and other top administrators' offices were located, and the J. D. Williams Library. Responding to the themes emphasized by Adkins, Khayat noted that "'fear' is a negative word. I wanted words like 'courage,' 'opportunity,' 'respect,' 'justice,' those kinds of words. I didn't think 'fear' ought to be on there" (as cited in Jubera, 2005; see also Khayat, 2013, p. 290).

Such concerns were consistent with Khayat's broader orientation, which included admonitions to key staff against invoking the term "racism" to avoid "upsetting" others (Susan Glisson & Charles Tucker, personal communication, March 13, 2019). As a result, university support for the memorial receded over the next 2 years, resulting in construction delays and, ultimately, the abandonment of Adkins' design. The artist viewed the about-face as a "great disservice to the legacy of the civil rights movement and to the University of Mississippi's place within it" (Friedman, 2005). Susan Glisson, the founding director of the university's William Winter Institute for Racial Reconciliation, noted (as cited in Jubera, 2005) that "how decisions are made and whose voices are heard and how race shapes those decisions are at the heart of this story. It's not unique to Mississippi, but because of its history, it resonates here in a way it doesn't in other places."

Khayat's next steps made clear the university's struggle to retain parallelism, minimizing the critical challenge that any civil rights memorial would pose to the ideals suffused within its surroundings. Local sculptor Rod Moorhead and architect James Eley, both White artists with long-standing ties to the university, were hastily enlisted to propose an alternative to Adkins' gates. In contrast to the inclusive, deliberative process undertaken by the Civil Rights Commemoration Initiative, Glisson (as cited in Kanengiser, 2005) described the subsequent design as a "top-down authoritative decision" that failed to "respect . . . the ideas of the civil rights movement."

Moorhead's statue depicted a life-size figure of James Meredith, captured, as memory scholar James E. Young (as cited in Combs et al., 2016, p. 346) noted, "mid-stride" approaching an archway designed by Eley (Figure 6.2). Although reminiscent in form of Adkins' gates, this arch typified Khayat's emphasis on balance. Gone was the word "fear," replaced by four alternatives ringing the monument's capstone: "Opportunity," "Courage," "Perseverance," and "Knowledge." The interior of the archway contained engraved plates with quotes from Khayat, along with Myrlie Evers-Williams, former Mississippi Governor William Winter, and Meredith. The latter was most telling (Figure 6.3). Taken from his 1966 memoir [he was not invited to speak at the ceremony dedicating his statue (see Goudsouzian, 2019)], it notes buoyantly,

> Always, without fail, regardless of the number of times I enter Mississippi, it creates within me feelings that are felt at no other

Figure 6.2 James Meredith statue, part of the University of Mississippi's Civil Rights Memorial

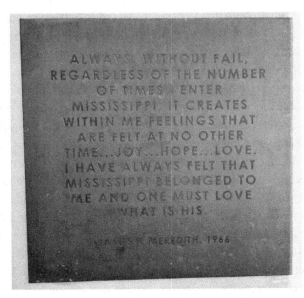

Figure 6.3 Quote by James Meredith, included as one of four plaques within the campus' Civil Rights Memorial

time ... joy ... hope ... love. I have always felt that Mississippi belonged to me and one must love what is his.

The selection had been edited not only for brevity but also to obscure the range of emotion in the original passage. Indeed, between Meredith's reflections on hope and love, he described feelings of "sadness" associated with his sense of Mississippi (Meredith, 1966):

> Sadness because I am immediately aware of the special subhuman role that I must play, because I am a Negro, or die. Sadness because it is the home of the greatest number of Negroes outside Africa, yet my people suffer from want of everything in a rich land of plenty, and, most of all, they must endure the inconvenience of indignity.

If such details sought to reconcile the civil rights memorial with the complex figure it honors [imperfect even in that aim, as Meredith has on multiple occasions called for destroying the object that, in his view, depicted him as a "false idol" and "public relations tool for the powers that be at Ole Miss, frozen in gentle docility" (quoted in Goudsouzian 2019: xxii)], the civil rights memorial intentionally avoids any reckoning with its more prominent Confederate surroundings. Tucked between the Lyceum and library, behind the Circle on which the Confederate soldier's statue continued to grandly overlook the university's main entrance, Meredith's statue orients mainly to the ground it traverses, separated from view of the more heavily trafficked spaces dedicated to the many White supremacist figures who had long occupied a prominent place in the university's broader narrative.

As such, as an untethered addition to the landscape, the presence of the Meredith statue fails to provide a basis for direct critical reflection on the role played by the segregationist and neo-Confederate forces that sought to resist Meredith's admission to the university and, by extension, deny the rightful presence of all Black students, faculty, and staff on campus. Even so, the site's counterhegemonic civil rights focus provided a touchpoint for critique and resistance by those seeking to restore the campus's single-minded White supremacist valence. In early 2014, the Meredith statue was vandalized, with White students shouting racial epithets and placing a noose around the figure's neck. Although the act of racist resistance was decried by the administration as counter to the university's values, the Critical Race Studies Group viewed it as more accurately serving the inverse function: to align the Meredith statue with the "prevailing symbolic environment ... saturated with affectionate references to the Old South" (Combs et al., 2016, p. 339). This alignment interrupted the unstated parallelist separation between Meredith and emblems of enslavement and segregation, highlighting still-salient continuities of support for the values motivating the White students' racist resistance.

Phase II: Contextualization

Even prior to the desecration of the Meredith statue, such juxtapositions within the historical landscape, and the additive mode of engagement that enabled them, had become increasingly untenable. Khayat's successor Dan Jones proclaimed reconciliation as one of his core priorities upon his installment in 2009 (Susan Glisson & Charles Tucker, personal communication, March 13, 2019). By 2012, he had broadened the purview of a standing committee on "Sensitivity and Respect" to take "an earnest and hard look at how to address race and related issues" on campus. Following the noose incident, Jones hosted consultant visits by historians Ed Ayers and Christy Coleman, who had led similar initiatives in Richmond, Virginia, to help "establish a more balanced view of history" on campus.

Charged specifically with a focus "on history, on symbols, and on monuments," Ayers and Coleman highlighted an issue whose considerable stakes Wertsch addresses (see Chapter 22, this volume): the lack of a "coherent narrative" at UM. "The Confederate Memorial and the James Meredith monument," Ayers and Coleman observed, "seem to stand at polar opposites, with vast blank spaces of time and struggle missing." Their core recommendations sought to tackle that issue directly. One in particular—a call to "offer more history, putting the past into context, telling more of the story of Mississippi's struggles with slavery, secession, segregation, and their aftermath"—became a key pillar in Jones' 2014 Action Plan for the university community (University of Mississippi, 2014a).

In some ways, the recommendation did not deviate with the university's additive initiatives under Khayat. Framed around "balancing the way history is represented," one key initiative would involve proposals to add "meaningful new symbols" to the campus landscape. Jones referenced the Meredith statue as one example and welcomed consideration of "further opportunities" in that vein. He also pointedly removed from the table proposals that would subtract from the existing landscape. Lauding Richmond's efforts to balance their city's symbols, Jones noted that those campaigns had productively

Figure 6.4 Confederate soldier's statue at the University of Mississippi

advanced "without attempts to erase history, even some difficult history, and without removing existing statues and building names" (University of Mississippi, 2014a).

But alongside these reinforcements of the parallelisms offered under Khayat, Jones also noted the possibility to "offer context" for existing symbols. Doing so would move beyond the prior additive approach that failed to acknowledge, instruct, or otherwise reckon with the significance of the still-prevailing symbolic valence on the campus. The initial call would be pursued by Jones' successor, Morris Stocks, who occupied the Chancellorship on an interim basis following Jones' exit[1] in 2015 and quickly appointed a four-member committee to pen the text for the marker that would contextualize

---

[1] A year after his shepherding of the Confederate statue issue on campus, Jones' contract was not renewed by Mississippi's Board of Trustees of State Institutions of Higher Learning. Although a number of issues were at play in his dismissal, media stories consistently noted that he had been removed in large part due to rifts that emerged between him and board members based on, as CNN reported, his "measures aimed at dissociating the school from its Confederate history" (McLaughlin & Gallman, 2015).

the Confederate soldier statue (Figure 6.4). One member of that committee, Andy Mullins (personal communication, March 14, 2019), noted that this text, ultimately drafted by retired university historian David Sansing, was discussed and approved "in a hurry." In March 2016, the bronze-and-metal plaque was installed directly in front of the statue (Figure 6.5).

"As Confederate veterans were passing from the scene in increasing numbers, memorial associations built monuments in their memory all across the South," the plaque explained, before noting that the statue had subsequently become "a rallying point" for "a rebellious mob gathered to prevent the admission of" James Meredith in 1962 (University of Mississippi, 2016a). Portraying the monumental site as a "reminder of the University's past and of its current and ongoing commitment to open its hallowed halls to all who seek truth and knowledge and wisdom," the script omitted any overt reference to enslavement, Jim Crow, or the Lost Cause movement that had motivated the United Daughters of the Confederacy's erection of the statue in 1906. As such, the contextualization sought to balance, rather than overcome, the long-standing triumphalist narrative associated with the statue.

Controversy over the text erupted swiftly. Noting the plaque's pronounced silences, the National Association for the Advancement of Colored People (NAACP) called for the university to "wholly distance itself from these symbols of racial terror," and the UM History Department released a

Figure 6.5 Confederate soldier's statue plaque, second version

statement highlighting the text's failure to fulfill the university's original call to tell "more of the story of Mississippi's struggles with slavery, secession, segregation, and their aftermath." The historians, who had been "caught off-guard" by the original plaque's appearance and thereby forced into a "reactive mode" (Anne Twitty, personal communication, March 11, 2019), proposed an alternative that deconstructed "Lost Cause" mythology and characterized the monument as an effort to "recognize the sacrifice of Mississippians who fought to establish the Confederacy as a slaveholding republic" (University of Mississippi, Department of History, 2016). Support for that proposal from a number of prominent historians throughout the country broadened the struggle's locus, along with its corresponding stakes (Mitchell, 2016).

Although initially resistant to changing text that he viewed as both literally and figuratively "set in stone," less than a month after the plaque's unveiling, recently installed Chancellor Jeffrey Vitter capitulated to such concerns, announcing the original committee's desire "to consider further input and reexamine whether the plaque's language should be changed." Seeking to incorporate a broader range of voices in the conversation, Vitter expanded the body charged with drafting any revised text to 14 members and solicited input from the public via an online interface (Andy Mullins, personal communication, March 14, 2019; Sigler, 2016; James Thomas, personal communication, March 14, 2019; University of Mississippi, 2016b).

The committee's process incorporated ideas from members of the history faculty, who also hosted two community forums and crafted a detailed report expanding on the department's original critical appraisal (Neff et al., 2016). Placed in October 2016, the revised plaque retained something of the apologetic tone from the original while incorporating phrases from the historians' proposal, including explicit acknowledgment that Confederate monuments "were often used to promote an ideology known as the 'Lost Cause,' which claimed that the Confederacy had been established to defend states' rights and that slavery was not the principle cause of the Civil War." Such hybridization was particularly evident in the following line: "Although the monument was created to honor the sacrifice of local Confederate soldiers, it must also remind us that the defeat of the Confederacy also meant freedom for millions of people" (Vitter, 2016).

The iterative struggle that resulted from the decision to contextualize the site by modifying but not relocating the Confederate statue highlights the impact of that measure on its surroundings. Initial debate had involved differences in how, precisely, to reposition the object in question: as a site of mourning that now reflected outmoded values, or as a site of oppression testifying—as the historians put it—to the "belief... in white racial supremacy" (University of Mississippi, Department of History, 2016) embodied in the Lost Cause narrative. But, ultimately, both iterations of the plaque had a more general effect: amplifying the statue by calling attention to its enduring significance. By choosing not to alter the object itself or its location on campus, the statue remained a more ambiguous, contested space, its significance open to negotiation. Within the context of the university's parallel efforts to navigate the competing values that define its contemporary identity, retaining the statue's position of prominence, contextualized solely by an accompanying plaque, precluded a definitive statement on the object's commemorative significance. Instead, the statue's orientation to broader university values remained in flux, subject to change (as evinced by the plaque's dual versions) while the object of interest—the statue itself—remained fixed.

Although such an approach thus failed to produce a stable proximate outcome, the university's reckoning with the Confederate statue created a foundation for institutionalizing its approach across the campus's overall commemorative landscape. From the perspective of many on campus, Vitter lacked personal investment in such changes and was "ill-equipped" to build on any momentum around these issues spurred under Jones (Susan Glisson & Charles Tucker, personal communication, March 13, 2019; Anne Twitty, personal communication, March 11, 2019). But even so, a *New York Times* feature on the university's efforts to reconcile its history referred to this developing approach as part of a broader "movement called contextualization," which Vitter (as cited in Saul, 2017) explained was "predicated on the principle that it's better to educate and contextualize rather than remove or move or erase."

To pursue such work, Vitter established the Chancellor's Advisory Committee on History and Context to continue addressing the charge from the 2014 Action Plan to further contextualize its past. In 2017, the committee released its final report, recommending that seven campus sites in total be contextualized. Adhering to the methodology employed with the Confederate statue, five of these sites were recognized with plaques clarifying their association with Confederate figures or slavery. But two other sites were transformed more completely. The Paul B. Johnson Commons added "Sr." to the name, clarifying that the space does not commemorate Paul B. Johnson, Jr., the segregationist politician charged, as lieutenant governor, with opposing Meredith's admission to the university in 1962, but rather his father, who served as the state's governor in the early 1940s. The committee additionally recommended the renaming of Vardaman Hall, which has long honored another former governor, the staunch White supremacist James K. Vardaman. Cognizant of how such a move deviated from the university's established bounded understanding of "contextualization," the committee's report drew on a set of principles for renaming institutionalized at Yale University in 2016. The resulting rationale highlighted how Vardaman's legacy—which includes his active advocacy for lynching as a means to maintain White supremacy—was contested at the time (the report notes that W. E. B. Du Bois pronounced that "Vardaman from Mississippi has gone further than any American living or dead in capitalizing race hatred for political gain") and remained "fundamentally at odds" with the university's mission (University of Mississippi, 2017).

The Vardaman recommendation deviated from the university's top-down emphasis on contextualization over "erasure." Correspondingly, whereas the more contained recommendations around the Commons and the placement of plaques have been completed, Vardaman Hall remains in place, with renovations and details around its ostensible renaming still in limbo 3 years after the release of the key committee report. Committee members also understood that any latitude along those lines would not extend to the more iconic Confederate soldier's statue, noting that signals from the Chancellor were "crystal clear . . . that any recommendation around [moving the Confederate] monument was not going to be seen as in the purview of the charge we were given" (Anne Twitty, personal communication, March 11, 2019; see also Middleton & Ladd, 2020).

But those institutional mandates increasingly conflicted with the intensified attention the plaques brought to the statue and its orientation to the surrounding campus. Research on contextualized commemorative landscapes has demonstrated that modifying objects in place can activate those sites as spaces of contestation, spurring increased attention and a greater likelihood of sustained mobilization around the significance of the object's very presence (Simko et al., 2020). Even if some critiqued UM's initiative as placing markers that are "just there," detached from more comprehensive educational efforts (James Thomas, personal communication, March 14, 2019), the move toward contextualization on the UM campus followed this general pattern, exerting an ecological effect in which the meanings attached to the Confederate monument were further destabilized as the valences of cognate spaces shifted—reflected in, and spurred by, bottom-up initiatives such as walking tours organized by the Mississippi Slavery Research Group (Anne

Twitty, personal communication, March 11, 2019). Those efforts, along with the reworded plaques placed at the statue itself, intensified awareness of the statue's White supremacist foundations and functions and spurred further action around its continued presence on campus.

Phase III: Dismantling (and Reamplification)

If not included within the contextualization committee's purview, broader calls to remove the statue had preceded the placement of plaques, drawing upon bases of support rooted in prior like-minded campaigns. An October 2015 vote by the student senate, known as the Associated Student Body, to remove the state flag, which at the time included the Confederate battle emblem in its upper left corner,[2] from the campus emerged in part as a reaction to the Charleston church shootings earlier that year. The senate proposal was co-authored by the campus chapter of the NAACP, which had been reactivated in part to spur this and related actions (James Thomas, personal communication, March 14, 2019). The NAACP had pursued a series of "escalation tactics" leading up to the ultimately successful senate process, including a letter-drop campaign and a rally at the campus flagpole in the Circle that attracted a small but politically significant counterprotest by Ku Klux Klan members and other organized racists (Berryhill, 2015; James Thomas, personal communication, March 14, 2019).

At the time, campus NAACP activists saw taking down the statue as the next step, and several of those students went on to hold leadership positions in student groups active in campaigns targeting the statue over the following 3 years (James Thomas, personal communication, March 14, 2019). This infrastructure for organizing around these issues at UM had been nurtured over the prior two decades by the supportive presence of the William Winter Institute for Racial Reconciliation. Since its 1999 founding, the Winter Institute had been at the center of groundbreaking anti-racist work throughout the state, including support for community processes seeking justice and restoration around the 1955 Emmett Till murder in the Delta and

---

[2] In June 2020, the state legislature passed a bill to remove and relinquish the state flag that had flown since 1894. This move followed a failed 2001 statewide referendum to replace the flag, and the 2015 campaign that successfully removed it from UM and seven other campuses, in addition to a number of counties and municipalities throughout the state (Pettus, 2017; Rojas, 2020; Victor, 2015).

the 1964 Freedom Summer killings in Neshoba County (MacLean, 2009; Whitlinger, 2020).

The Winter Institute also had built a following among a diverse group of students on campus. Its founding overlapped with the emergence of S.E.E.D., the student group responsible for the placement of the tree and plaque honoring Mae Bertha Carter in 1999. Self-identified "FOTIs," or Friends of the Institute, became more visible on campus over the next decade. By 2005, their influence extended to the Associated Student Body, to the point that members could not advance in that body without engaging with racial issues. Susan Glisson, the Institute's founding director, regularly mentored those students, connecting them to Mississippi civil rights veterans and supporting their efforts to organize a "turn your back on hate" counterprotest when White supremacist Richard Barrett came to the campus in 2004. That mentorship extended to several members of Students Against Social Injustice, which helped spur campus referenda around moving the Confederate statue in 2019 (Susan Glisson & Charles Tucker, personal communication, March 13, 2019).

The outcome of those votes, including a unanimous 47–0 tally in the Associated Student Body, demonstrated that clear support for the removal of the statue existed among faculty, students, and staff. Even so, pragmatists on campus viewed this victory as largely symbolic. Beyond the takedown of the state flag, the administration had never displayed support for "erasing" or otherwise subtracting from the university's material landscape. In addition, any such action was ultimately subject to approval by the state's Institutions of Higher Learning (IHL) board, composed of gubernatorial appointees overseeing all eight of the state's public colleges and universities. As a notoriously conservative body that did not view itself as specifically accountable to its constituents in Oxford, few viewed the IHL board as sympathetic to the removal of Confederate iconography from the campus. Its spokesperson did little to dispel that sense when she painted the referenda results as a "hypothetical" rather than as a mandate for change (Rueb, 2019).

So, the series of approvals during the following year—from Interim Chancellor Larry Sparks, the Mississippi Department of Archives & History, and the IHL board—came as a considerable surprise. In late August 2019, Sparks sent an email to the UM community, noting the next steps he had approved for removing the statue to the Confederate cemetery located on the fringes of campus. Referring to the latter space as a "more suitable location," he tellingly described it as "commensurate with the purpose that is etched on [the monument's] side." That take, of course, elevated heritage defenders' claim that the statue served as a memorial to Confederate veterans killed in the war, extending the university's earlier resistance to critique and its failure to acknowledge the Lost Cause ideology that valorized those veterans' fight to maintain enslavement.

This plan to relocate the monument became the subject of renewed controversy and protest when renderings of the refurbished cemetery location were released to the public in 2020. Although the move would de-center the statue by moving it from the entrance to the Circle to the campus's periphery, the final design also called for a costly refurbishment that would amplify the presence of the largely neglected cemetery. Drawings showed a new brick path with the statue as its showpiece, located in the center of a well-lit rotary marking the cemetery's entrance. The ground under which hundreds of soldiers had been buried (absent records identifying most of their identities or the specific locations at which they had been laid to rest) would now be marked with uniform marble headstones set in neat rows, evoking the iconic layout of Arlington Memorial Cemetery in the nation's capital. The University Police Department would be charged with "continuous monitoring" of the space via security cameras installed throughout. To cover the IHL-approved $1.15 million budget, the university's Development office already had begun soliciting gifts from donors (Board of Trustees of State Institutions for Higher Learning, 2020; Middleton & Ladd, 2020).

A groundswell of criticism from 150 individual faculty and nearly two dozen influential groups on campus charged that the plan would create a "shrine" to the Confederacy (University of Mississippi, Department of History, 2020). Subsequent investigations demonstrated that these grand relocation plans had been longer in the making, dating back to the discreet convening of a Chancellor's Working Group for the Cemetery Headstone Project in 2018. That body included three members of the contextualization Advisory Committee, one of whom—Don Barrett—had been the sole vocal proponent of the cemetery project within the advisory group. A trial lawyer and prominent UM alumnus and donor, Barrett was known for his successful legal actions against big tobacco, along with his unabashed defenses of Confederate values and causes. As founder and president of the Jefferson Davis Foundation, he had long worked to raise funds to support a museum and library on the grounds of Beauvoir, the Confederate president's final homeplace on the Mississippi Gulf Coast (Long, 1963; Middleton & Ladd, 2020).

Barrett's influence on the committee's process grew after his co-chair, UM Civil War historian John Neff, passed away in January 2020. Absent Neff's role as a counterbalance to Barrett, the latter's views on the redeveloped cemetery were fully reflected in the final proposal provided to the IHL board (Middleton & Ladd, 2020). Although the baseline design renderings for the space had been released to the public a year earlier along with Interim Chancellor Sparks' announcement of his support for the statue relocation, three additional pages—showing the lighting plan and full-color mock-ups depicting elaborate landscaping and rows of cemetery headstones—surfaced for the first time in the 156-page proposal approved by the IHL in June 2020 (Board of Trustees of State Institutions for Higher Learning, 2020).

Indeterminants and Conclusions

Amidst mounting controversy and a student and alumni protest march to the cemetery as summer heat and COVID-19 pandemic concerns were rising, as of this writing the university's fundraising campaign around the Confederate cemetery restoration remains in limbo. Even so, preparations to relocate the soldier's statue to the space began in July 2020. Construction fencing inlaid with netting to prevent onlookers from seeing in was placed around the perimeter of the Circle as well as the parcel adjacent to the cemetery (Figure 6.6). On July 14, the monument was removed from the campus's entrance, where it had stood for 114 years (Fowler, 2020; Hitson, 2020).

"By proposing to build a million-dollar shrine to White supremacy in this very spot," student Tyler Yarbrough declared during the protest, "Chancellor [Glenn] Boyce has blatantly disregarded the lives of Black students, Black faculty, Black staff and Black alumni." The larger group of 50 implored Boyce to "abandon the plan," chanting "Relocation, not glorification" (Hitson, 2020). As such calls emphasize, the relocated monument would elevate the visibility and stature of the heretofore-peripheral Confederate cemetery, "glorifying" both that space and the statue itself in the process. In so doing, it also would amplify and validate Confederate iconography throughout the main campus, unreconciled with any ascendant narrative enabled by more recent additions and contextualizations.

These ongoing struggles demonstrate the indeterminacy of the contested commemorative landscape. Although the ultimate significance of the changes described here will surely be conditioned by future iterations of the struggle (Danto, 1985), our emphasis here is on uncovering the

Figure 6.6 Confederate soldier's statue removal, Summer 2020

trajectory that has characterized the dynamism of the campus landscape first set into motion by the addition of the Carter plaque in 1999. The previous discussion emphasized three distinct phases in that trajectory to date, characterized by the parallelism inherent in an additive approach to the commemorative landscape, the amplification of critiques of that landscape that followed from the contextualization phase, and the current push to dismantle symbols of White supremacy on campus. As in earlier periods, the outcome of this current phase will be forged within the nexus of dismantling campaigns and elite efforts to resist or circumvent such changes—as represented by the current plan to recast pressures to remove the Confederate soldier's statue as an opportunity to reamplify both the statue and the Confederate cemetery on campus.

This iterative progression also demonstrates the broader stakes associated with struggles around the commemorative landscape. The significance of any given object within that landscape is shaped by, and bears upon, the valences exerted by other sites within its surrounding environment. Recognizing that ecological character points to the importance of extending outward from a bounded analysis of an object. Avoiding interrogations of such objects disaggregated from the settings within which they are enveloped additionally provides a basis for a bottom-up account of the navigation and contestation of national memory frames associated with the Lost Cause and the racialized nature of the nation's democratic project.

Doing so also raises two types of additional bounding questions in Oxford. The first of those relates to the domains within which struggles over the campus's identity unfold. The campaigns around the values embedded in the material landscape have played out in parallel to concerns around discursive symbols long associated with the university. As the hegemony of the Lost Cause narrative loosened within the commemorative landscape—first through the addition of distinct "chapters" of the university's story that recognize the contributions of Black students, faculty, and staff, and then through efforts to more substantially speak across those parallel narratives within more recent contextualization campaigns—university leaders remained steadfast in resisting discursive changes that would align with the material ones they had been willing to initiate.

Such bifurcations became evident in 2014, around Chancellor Jones' response to Ayers and Coleman's recommendation that the university "consider the implications of calling itself 'Ole Miss' in various contexts," given that label's association with enslavement. Without refuting that genealogical interpretation, the Chancellor defused the resulting outcry by assuring the university community that because

> the vast majority of those associated with our university has a strong affection for "Ole Miss" and do not associate its use with race in any way . . . the affectionate term "Ole Miss" is and will continue to be an important part of our national identity.

As a more delimited measure, he charged the provost and chief communications officer with developing a plan to deploy these labels in ways that exhibit a sensitivity to the contexts within which they are received. In practice, the resulting plan elided concerns about the racial connotations of the term, and instead centered mainly on following "traditional convention that the term 'Ole Miss' is strongly associated with athletics and the broad 'spirit' of the university (e.g. the alma mater), and 'The University of Mississippi' is strongly associated with the academic context" (University of Mississippi, 2014b).

These moves decoupled the university's course of action in the material landscape from the broader discursive realm. Within the latter, the separation of UM's academic mission from the "spirit of Ole Miss" evoked earlier efforts to construct parallel tracks to simultaneously recognize and honor Black members of the community and the systems that had long excluded and oppressed them. That model, characterizing the placement of the Carter plaque and Meredith memorial, was predicated on a lack of monumental cross-talk—reproducing the "blank spaces" noted by Ayers and Coleman in 2014 that prevented a more open reckoning with the university's history and identity. Continuing resistance to changes that recognize the connection between material settings and such long-standing discursive traditions highlight as well the workings of the ecological processes advanced here, demonstrating the continuing durability of cultural conventions that serve also to undergird and define the valences exerted by physical spaces on the campus.

A second bounding question relates to the spatial and institutional borders that mark such struggles. The account here of UM's Confederate monument emphasizes how ecological effects have operated within the bounds of the campus. Clearly, however, local actions and claims have been shaped as well by events and movements developing outside of its borders. At different points, struggles over Confederate memory and monumental iconography on other campuses and in other communities—themselves in turn shaped by the rise of the Black Lives Matter movement and precipitating events such as the shootings in Charleston and, in 2020, the police killing of George Floyd—have created broader resources and opportunities for local mobilization on the UM campus.

In addition to these social and political forces at the national and global levels, contestation at UM has oriented to its more immediate off-campus surrounds. Indeed, the Confederate soldier's statue considered here is not even the only such object in Oxford. The monument's virtual twin stands only a mile down the road, outside the county courthouse in the downtown Oxford Square, a social center for both the city and the campus. The connections between these spaces has long been a salient one—the procession marking the dedication of the campus statue in 1906 began at the Square, and a 2019 action by a coalition of neo-Confederate groups to oppose the campus statue removal campaign traced the same route (Betz, 2019; Neff et al., 2016). Connections between stakeholders mobilizing around the fate of both statues and their dual orientation to a parallel campaign that resulted in the placement of a marker recognizing the 1935 lynching in Oxford of

Elwood Higginbotham (April Grayson, personal communication, March 21, 2019; Gregory, 2018) are surely part of the broader story of UM's trajectory. Indeed, such nested ecologies demonstrate the depth to which the legacies of the Lost Cause—and efforts to dismantle those legacies—reside.

References

Alderman, D., & Rose-Redwood, R. (2017, August 28). Confederate memorials and the unjust geography of memory. *CityLab*.

Berryhill, L. (2015, October 18). NAACP: Remove state flag. *Oxford Eagle* (18 October). Retrieved August 1, 2020, from https://www.oxfordeagle.com/2015/10/18/naacp-remove-state-flag

Betz, K. D. (2019, February 23). "Oxford is more than what these individuals came to represent": Confederate rally met with counter-protests, including by athletes. *Mississippi Today*. Retrieved August 3, 2020, from https://mississippitoday.org/2019/02/23/confederate-rally-i-am-here-to-represent-that-oxford-is-more-than-what-these-individuals

Board of Trustees of State Institutions for Higher Learning. (2020). *Agenda: The University of Mississippi, UM-IHL #207-460 Historic Monument Relocation*. Retrieved July 30, 2020, from https://communications2.wp2.olemiss.edu/wp-content/uploads/sites/295/2020/06/IHL-Monument-Submission.pdf?fbclid=IwAR3N6joE1h3Jqsy5l8Qc7Y74xVkMVhOA8bFqzhpIkSxvynqYOZ9XIlXxcak

Bodnar, J. (1992). *Remaking America: Public memory, commemoration, and patriotism in the twentieth century*. Princeton University Press.

Carey, T. J. (2016). *The design of the southern future: The struggle to build White democracy at the University of Mississippi, 1890–1948*. PhD dissertation, Department of History, University of Mississippi.

Civil rights campus memorial gets grant. (2001, May 26). *Jackson Clarion-Ledger*, p. 21.

Combs, B. H., Dellinger, K., Jackson, J. T., Johnson, K. A., Johnson, W. M., Skipper, J., Sonnett, J., Thomas, J. M., and the Critical Race Studies Group, University of Mississippi. (2016). The symbolic lynching of James Meredith: A visual analysis and collective counter narrative to racial domination. *Sociology of Race and Ethnicity*, 2(3), 338–353.

Committee soon to pick model for UM civil rights monument. (2002, May 7). *Jackson Clarion-Ledger*, p. 16.

Curry, C. (1996). *Silver rights*. Harvest Books.

Danto, A. C. (1985). *Narration and knowledge*. Columbia University Press.

Eagles, C. W. (2009). *The price of defiance: James Meredith and the integration of Ole Miss*. University of North Carolina Press.

Fligstein, N., & McAdam, D. (2012). *A theory of fields*. Oxford University Press.

Fowler, S. (2020, July 14). Confederate statue on Ole Miss campus relocated. *Jackson Clarion-Ledger*. Retrieved July 30, 2020, from https://www.clarionledger.com/story/news/2020/07/14/confederate-monument-ole-miss-statue-being-relocated-cemetery/5433553002

Friedman, U. (2005, December 5). Memorial design nixed, professor slams officials. *The Daily Pennsylvanian*. Retrieved July 31, 2020, from https://www.thedp.com/article/2005/12/memorial_design_nixed_professor_slams_officials

Funds aid civil rights art. (2001, April 9). *Jackson Clarion-Ledger*, p. 13.

Goudsouzian, A. (2019). Introduction to the new edition. In J. Meredith (Ed.), *Three years in Mississippi*. University Press of Mississippi.

Gregory, V. (2018, April 25). A lynching's long shadow. *The New York Times Magazine*.

Hitson, H. (2020, July 1). Protests continue: Students, faculty, and alumni march against relocation plans. *The Daily Mississippian*. Retrieved August 2, 2020, from https://thedmonline.com/protests-continue-students-faculty-and-alumni-march-against-relocation-plans

Jubera, D. (2005, October 26). Outcry engulfs campus memorial. *Atlanta Constitution*, pp. A1, A4.

Kanengiser, A. (2005, October 12). Ole Miss releases new memorial design. *Daily Journal*. Retrieved July 28, 2020, from https://www.djournal.com/news/ole-miss-releases-new-memorial-design/article_aa039dce-73c7-5b62-8533-38a048d4eea9.html

Khayat, R. (2013). *The education of a lifetime*. Nautilus.

Long, M. (1963, November 10). A southern teen-ager speaks his mind. *The New York Times Magazine*, p. SM8.

MacLean, H. N. (2009). *The past is never dead: The trial of James Ford Seale and Mississippi's struggle for redemption*. Basic Civitas Books.

McLaughlin, E. C., & Gallman, S. (2015, March 26). *Donors, alums rebel against decision to ax Ole Miss chancellor*. CNN. Retrieved May 22, 2018, from https://www.cnn.com/2015/03/25/us/university-mississippi-ole-miss-dan-jones-ouster/index.html

Meredith, J. (1966). *Three years in Mississippi*. Indiana University Press.

Meredith, J., with Doyle, W. (2012). *A mission from God: A memoir and challenge for America*. Atria Books.

Middleton, C., & Ladd, D. (2020, July 9). The past isn't dead: UM's winding road to a fight over a statue and a cemetery. *Mississippi Free Press*. Retrieved July 30, 2020, from https://www.mississippifreepress.org/4351/the-past-isnt-dead-ums-winding-road-to-a-fight-over-a-statue-and-a-cemetery.

Mitchell, J. (2016, April 12). Ole Miss history profs say Confederate sign must go. *Jackson Clarion-Ledger*. Retrieved May 21, 2018, from https://www.clarionledger.com/story/news/local/journeytojustice/2016/04/12/ole-miss-history-profs-say-confederate-sign-must-go/82933574

Molpus, N. (2002, Fall). Civil rights memorial design selected. *The Southern Register*, 4.

Mullins, A. (2019). Interview with author. Oxford, MS (14 March).

Neff, J., Roll, J., & Twitty, A. (2016). *A brief historical contextualization of the Confederate monument at the University of Mississippi*. Retrieved May 21, 2018, from https://history.olemiss.edu/wp-content/uploads/sites/6/2017/08/A-Brief-Historical-Contextualization-of-the-Confederate-Monument-at-the-University-of-Mississippi.pdf

Olick, J. K. (2007). *The politics of regret: On collective memory and historical responsibility*. Routledge.

Pettus, E. W. (2017, April 24). Biloxi won't fly state flag. *Jackson Clarion-Ledger*. Retrieved August 2, 2020, from https://www.clarionledger.com/story/news/politics/2017/04/24/biloxi-wont-fly-mississippi-state-flag/100862858

Rojas, R. (2020, June 30). Mississippi governor signs law to remove flag with Confederate emblem. *The New York Times*. https://www.nytimes.com/2020/06/30/us/mississippi-flag.html

Rueb, E. S. (2019, March 8). Ole Miss student and faculty groups vote unanimously to relocate Confederate statue. *The New York Times*. https://www.nytimes.com/2019/03/08/us/ole-miss-confederate-statue.html

Saul, S. (2017, August 9). Ole Miss edges out of its Confederate shadow, gingerly. *The New York Times*. Retrieved May 22, 2018, from https://www.nytimes.com/2017/08/09/us/ole-miss-confederacy.html

Sigler, R. (2016, March 30). Plaque on UM Confederate statue to undergo revision? *Oxford Eagle*. Retrieved May 21, 2018, from https://www.oxfordeagle.com/2016/03/30/plaque-on-um-confederate-statue-to-undergo-revision

Simko, C., Cunningham, D., & Fox, N. (2020). Contesting commemorative landscapes: Confederate monuments and trajectories of change." *Social Problems*, spaa067. https://doi.org/10.1093/socpro/spaa067

Trethewey, N. (2020, July 3). Goodbye to a symbol that told Black Americans to "know your place." *The New York Times*. https://www.nytimes.com/2020/07/03/opinion/confederate-flag-mississippi-trethewey.html

Twitty, A. (2020, June 19). Ole Miss's monument to White supremacy. *The Atlantic*. Retrieved August 2, 2020, from https://www.theatlantic.com/ideas/archive/2020/06/ole-misss-monument-white-supremacy/613255

University of Mississippi. (2014). *Action plan on consultant reports and update on the work of the Sensitivity and Respect Committee*. Retrieved May 21, 2018, from http://chancellor.wp.olemiss.edu/wp-content/uploads/sites/17/2013/08/2014-ActionPlanonConsultantReportsandUpdateontheWorkoftheSensitivityandRespectCommittee.pdf

University of Mississippi. (2016a). *UM begins installing plaque offering context for Confederate statue*. Retrieved June 12, 2017, from https://news.olemiss.edu/um-begins-installing-plaque-offering-context-confederate-statue.

University of Mississippi. (2016b, June 30). *Letter from Chancellor: New plaque language, progress on 2014 action plan*. Retrieved May 21, 2018, from https://hottytoddy.com/2016/06/10/letter-from-chancellor-new-plaque-language-progress-on-2014-action-plan

University of Mississippi. (2017, July 6). Ole Miss will rename Vardaman Hall, contextualize several campus spots tied to Confederate history. *Oxford Eagle*. Retrieved May 21, 2018, from https://www.oxfordeagle.com/2017/07/06/ole-miss-will-rename-vardaman-hall-contextualize-several-campus-spots-tied-to-confederate-history

University of Mississippi, Department of History. (2016). *University of Mississippi History faculty statement about the plaque recently installed in front of the Confederate memorial on campus*. Retrieved June 12, 2017, from https://history.olemiss.edu/wp-content/uploads/sites/6/2016/07/History-Faculty-Statement-about-the-Confederate-Memorial-Plaque_4_2_2016.pdf

University of Mississippi, Department of History. (2020). *The university's Civil War cemetery*. Retrieved August 2, 2020, from https://history.olemiss.edu/the-universitys-civil-war-cemetery

Victor, D. (2015, October 27). University of Mississippi lowers state flag with Confederate symbol. *The New York Times*, p. A16.

Vitter, J. (2016). Letter from Chancellor: New Plaque Language, Progress on 2014 Action Plan. *HoddyToddy.com*. Available at: <https://www.hottytoddy.com/2016/06/10/letter-from-chancellor-new-plaque-language-progress-on-2014-action-plan/> (accessed 30 December 2021).

Whitlinger, C. (2020). *Between remembrance and repair: Commemorating racial violence in Philadelphia, Mississippi*. University of North Carolina Press.

7

From Hero to Villain

Stability and Change in Popular Beliefs About Christopher Columbus

Amy Corning and Howard Schuman

Christopher Columbus made landfall in the western hemisphere on an island in the Bahamas, never reaching the North American continent. Yet beginning with the 300th anniversary of his landing in 1792, Columbus's place in American national memory seemed assured. Commemoration of his first voyage became an urgent matter only after the American Revolution, illustrating the need of new nations to "invent narratives and persuade peoples to interpret their personal experiences within national terms and narratives" (Thelen, 1998, p. 373). As Americans searched for cultural forms and traditions that could signal political unity and a common national identity, Columbus emerged as "America's ultimate founding hero" (Schwartz, 1982, p. 390). Founding moments connect people to origins and offer a "sense of shared experience through time" (Spillman, 1998, p. 446), creating national "felt communities of fate" (Olick, 2007, p. 180). Columbus unified citizens of diverse backgrounds by allowing them to see themselves within America's story and to appreciate the values associated with a unique American identity (Barton, 2001; Koch, 1996; Kubal, 2008), including scientific progress, heroic courage and determination, and individual achievement. Columbus also provided an origin story that accommodated ties to the "civilized" European world (in implicit contrast to Native American "savagery"), yet asserted American distinctiveness (Schlereth, 1992; Schwartz, 1982). Van Engen (see Chapter 2, this volume) traces the tailoring of the story of the Pilgrims (including the erasure of Native Americans as well as other inconvenient elements) to similar purpose.

Since the 19th century, Italian Americans, Catholics, and other communities have sought to use Columbus's image to enhance the legitimacy of their national belonging (Paul, 2014). Those efforts generally did not detract from

Columbus's ability to serve as a unifying symbol because they often focused on individual groups' contributions to America's development (Bodnar, 1992). By the time of the quincentenary in 1992, however, Columbus was no longer an undisputed hero or a consensual symbol. He had been "caught in a riptide of conflicting views of his life and his responsibility for everything" that could be linked to 1492 (Wilford, 1991, p. 247). The quincentenary opened up a discursive space (Wertsch, 2018) that made visible distinct communities of memory and the depth of the commitments underlying the controversy —a divide too wide for most of the planned commemorations to bridge successfully (Summerhill & Williams, 2000).

Yet the debates surrounding the quincentenary appeared to have little impact on the general public's image of Columbus during the 1990s. In a U.S. national sample survey conducted in 1998, few Americans viewed Columbus in the heroic terms common in the 19th century, but 85% of respondents described him in simple and positive terms as the explorer who "discovered America," whereas the descriptions of just 4% reflected revisionist views that alluded to atrocities and enslavement of Native Americans by Columbus and successors or to the devastating impact of diseases the Europeans brought to the continent (Schuman et al., 2005).

This contrast between dramatic change in the meaning of Columbus as a cultural symbol—defined through the efforts of elites and activists and visible in public discourse—and the absence of change in individuals' beliefs is the starting point for our study. Much work has been devoted to understanding both malleability and persistence in cultural forms of memory (e.g., Olick, 2007; Schwartz, 1991; Simko 2015; Spillman, 1997). A largely separate body of work has focused on the factors that influence what individuals believe or recall about the past (e.g., Abel et al., 2019; Corning & Schuman, 2015; Roediger & DeSoto, 2014). Our approach to national memory encompasses both cultural symbols and the beliefs of ordinary people, and it seeks to connect the two. Our concern here is to understand whether and how images of the past conveyed by cultural artifacts, practices, and public discourse are related to individuals' beliefs. Specifically, we consider change in cultural representations of Columbus in order to investigate processes of change in the meaning of Columbus to individuals.

We begin by considering cultural representations of Columbus since the quincentenary to understand what information would have been available to the public during the past several decades, and we review more recent survey data on beliefs of the public. Next, we turn to an examination of trends that may have led to change in textbook treatments of Columbus, and to an analysis of textbooks as a potential source of influence on individuals' beliefs. Finally, we bring together the results of our textbook analysis and our survey findings to draw conclusions about the forces contributing to stability and change in public beliefs about Columbus.

Cultural Representations of Columbus: The Quincentenary and After

The quincentenary served to crystallize revisionist views of Columbus, but the roots of those assessments extended into earlier time periods. The civil rights movement and focus on Black identity and Black Power led other marginalized racial and ethnic groups to assert their rights as well (Skrentny, 2002), and a Red Power movement emerged at the end of the 1960s that mobilized Native American activists (Nagel, 1995). Emphasis on the rights of Native Americans helped raise the profile of research by anthropologists and geographers studying the Americas in the period before contact with Europeans. Their investigation of the scope of population loss to European diseases drew attention to the probable size of the Indigenous population before 1492 (Dobyns, 1966; Mann, 2005, p. 94). The research changed the picture of Columbus's landing from "discovery" of an uninhabited wilderness to an "invasion." As one Native American education specialist commented, "It's perfectly acceptable to move into unoccupied land . . . and land with only a few 'savages' is the next best thing" (Mann, 2005, p. 95).

The implications of these conclusions were further amplified by historian and geographer Alfred Crosby in his 1973 account of diseases and other consequences of European arrival and by geographer William Denevan, among others. Denevan (1992) challenged the "pristine myth" of empty wilderness conjured by 19th-century writers such as Longfellow, Thoreau, and Cooper and artists such as Catlin and Church. Far from leaving little imprint on nature, Native Americans actively influenced their environment through building, burning techniques, and an "apparent mania for earth moving" still visible in the mounds scattered across the continent (Parsons, 1985, as cited in Denevan, 1992, p. 377). The revised understanding of Native American civilizations and the impact of disease undermined earlier assumptions about primitive societies incapable of resisting the Europeans.

Against this new image of North America in 1492, the meaning of Columbus himself also changed, in ways likely to reach the general public. Accessible and unvarnished accounts of the oppression and brutality Columbus and his crew visited upon Native Americans were published during the 1970s and 1980s by Francis Jennings, James Loewen, and Howard Zinn. Loewen's book has sold almost 2 million copies and has recently been re-released (Strauss, 2018), and Zinn's book—"probably the only book by a radical historian that you can buy in an airport"—had sold a million copies by the early 2000s (Green, 2003). By the time of the 1992 quincentenary, commentators observed a "marked change in focus from the benefits of Columbus's discovery to its costs, particularly for the victims of European colonialism" (Axtell, 1992, p. 337).

Representations of Columbus and Native Americans Since the Quincentenary

During the first decades of the 21st century, Columbus's image suffered further. New translations of his own writing and other documents reprised his delusional self-confidence, dishonesty, and cruelty (Kolbert, 2002). Additional work highlighted writing by Bartolomé de las Casas, a contemporary witness who chronicled torture and enslavement of Native Americans (Bergreen, 2011), further confirmed by a newly discovered document (Abend & Pingree, 2006). Bestsellers by Charles C. Mann described Native American life before Columbus's arrival and chronicled the global implications of his landing, as did Jared Diamond's 1998 Pulitzer-prize-winning *Guns, Germs, and Steel*, which had sales in the millions. Research from the first decade of the 21st century further supported the view of a "Native North America that was more dynamic, diverse, populous, and integrated than was previously imagined" (Hämäläinen, 2013, p. 6). Analyses of settler colonialism (Tuck & Yang, 2012; Veracini, 2010) placed European conquest of the Americas in global perspective, and new theory and research have increasingly represented work by Indigenous scholars.

Columbus has also been swept up in misgivings about commemoration of previously venerated historical figures. White supremacist violence in 2015 and 2017 and countless episodes of police brutality resulting in the deaths of African Americans have repeatedly returned public attention to Confederate symbols that glorify a racist past and lend support to racism in the present, and the continued presence of monuments to Columbus and others has been questioned as well (e.g., Neuman, 2017). Statues of Columbus have been defaced periodically (Maslin Nir & Mays, 2017), with activists linking Columbus to "terrorism, murder, genocide, rape, slavery" (Weigel, 2017), and some statues have been pulled down by protestors or removed by local government (Associated Press, 2020; Judkis, 2020).

In popular culture, Columbus's contested reputation figured prominently in a 2002 episode of the television series *The Sopranos*. The term "Columbusing" gained currency in 2014 through a sketch video released by the comedy website CollegeHumor titled "Columbusing: Discovering Things for White people." The video turns "Columbus" into a verb denoting Whites' claims to have "discovered" something long known to other groups, and the wide-ranging examples broadly satirize White cultural appropriation—beginning with Columbus's "discovery." The video was quickly promoted by three online outlets (Harris, 2014; Rose, 2014; Stone, 2014) and NPR's *Code Switch* podcast (Salinas, 2014), and the term or concept has been invoked by *The Washington Post* (Fluker, 2012; Judkis, 2017) and *Education Week* (Mead, 2012). Thus, the absurdity of claiming that Columbus "discovered" America has come to stand in for Whites' brazen entitlement and arrogance toward other racial and ethnic groups more generally.

The holiday calendar has begun to reflect greater recognition of Native Americans. A celebration for Indigenous people was proposed in the 1970s at a United Nations–organized conference, but by the end of the 20th century, only a handful of localities and one state, South Dakota, had replaced Columbus Day with Indigenous People's Day ("Indigenous People's Day," 2020). Those changes accelerated in the 2010s, and as of 2020, at least 14 states and the District of Columbia observed Indigenous Peoples' Day or an alternative (Andrew & Willingham, 2020). (By contrast, Canada, New Zealand, and Australia undertook much earlier efforts to recognize Indigenous history as part of a national story and to acknowledge historical injustices.)

Popular representations of Native Americans have increasingly been recognized as disrespectful and have been criticized for perpetuating stereotypes (Fryberg et al., 2008; Leavitt et al., 2015). Revered children's book author Laura Ingalls Wilder's name was removed from an American Library Association award because her books included stereotyped, derogatory depictions of Native Americans (Voners, 2018). Land O'Lakes announced the removal of the Native American "butter maiden" from its packaging (Hauser, 2020, p. B6). The Washington "Redskins" football team, in response to public, economic, and sponsor pressure, decided to drop the name in 2020 (Kilgore & Allen, 2020). Such moves are consistent with calls from Native American advocates and representatives (e.g., Billings & Black, 2018; Reese, n.d.), as well as recommendations from groups such as the American Psychological Association, which issued a resolution in 2001 calling for immediate retirement of stereotyped images. Although not explicitly connected to Columbus, these actions and related discussions in public, academic, and professional spheres ensure that the history of disrespect and destruction of Native American peoples and cultures remains in view.

Columbus Reappraised

Despite the 1998 survey finding that the quincentenary itself had little effect on public beliefs, it seemed possible that continued debate about representations of Columbus and Native Americans might have affected the public's views. Therefore, we repeated our survey question in two further national sample surveys, in 2014 and again in 2017, nearly 20 years after the original 1998 survey. At each time point, cross-section samples of the adult population were interviewed so that although the respondents are not the same, the samples are comparable, allowing us to evaluate change over time in the population as a whole. In each case, our survey question was included in the monthly Surveys of Consumer Attitudes of the University of Michigan. (Sample sizes were 1,511, 503, and 606 in 1998, 2014, and 2017, respectively.)[1]

In each survey, respondents were asked an identically worded open-ended question: "Suppose a nephew or niece about 14 years old had just heard some mention of Christopher Columbus and asked you to explain what Columbus had done. What would you say in just a few words?" The question was designed to be nonthreatening, and respondents were assured that "there aren't any right or wrong answers to the question—just

---

[1] The surveys were carried out via personal telephone interviews. Our question was included near the end of each survey. The 1998 survey sample was landline only, the 2014 sample included both landline and cell phone numbers, and the 2017 sample was cell phone only. Response rates were 60% for the 1998 survey, 10% in 2014, and 7% in 2017. The latter two response rates are calculated according to the RR2 method described in the American Association for Public Opinion Research's *Standard Definitions* (2016). For information on the 1998 survey and response rate, see Schuman et al. (2005).

Table 7.1 Survey Response Coding Categories and Examples of Coded Content

Category	Description and Examples of Content
Traditional portrayals of Columbus	
Heroic traditional	Mention Columbus's "discovery" of America and include some admirable trait or accomplishment: "He was an explorer, he ventured in places where no one had ever went, and I guess he made it possible for all of us to live here in America."
Simple traditional	Mention Columbus's "discovery" or include detail, but do not explicitly mention admirable qualities: "He was the first European to discover North America."
Portrayals that challenge the traditional view	
Other Europeans	Note that others had reached the Western Hemisphere before Columbus, but do not reflect a revisionist critique: "In 1492, was credited with discovering America, but it was actually the Vikings that did that."
Native Americans already here	Priority of Native Americans, but no explicit criticism of Columbus or his treatment of Indigenous people: "Well, it is told in history books he discovered America, however America was already here occupied by Native Americans. He was an explorer."
Villainous Columbus	Most critical responses; recognize the priority of Native Americans and portray Columbus in ways consistent with the revisionist critique: "He thought he found the West Indies and tortured the Native people on the island."

whatever you would say to a young person to explain what Columbus had done." In both years, we began by reviewing a small sample of responses to ascertain whether or not the original 1998 coding categories still fit the types of responses being given. Having determined that they did, we coded the responses as shown in Table 7.1.[2]

Figure 7.1 compares the percentages of responses coded into the five categories at each of the three time points. The waning of Columbus's status over time is clear, especially in the decrease in Simple Traditional conceptions and the increase in Villainous portrayals. The other types of beliefs we

---

[2] Coding of responses was carried out by two coders working independently. Responses that included both positive and critical elements were coded only into the critical category. In each survey, some respondents gave responses that we considered nonsubstantive ("don't know" or responses that were entirely incorrect or uninterpretable). The percentage of these responses remained constant over time at 13.6% in 1998, 13.5% in 2014, and 13.7% in 2017; they are excluded from the analyses.

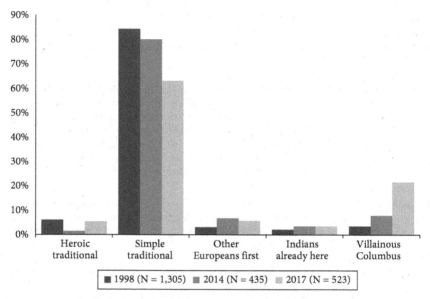

Figure 7.1 Beliefs about Columbus in 1998, 2014, and 2017 surveys.

coded—the more admiring Heroic view of Columbus, as well as emphasis on the earlier arrival of other explorers or on Native Americans already living in the Americas—have changed little, remaining at fairly low levels over time, and we do not consider them further here.

The results shown in Figure 7.1 suggest a gradual but possibly accelerating reappraisal of Columbus by the general public. Although the Simple Traditional view still predominates, Columbus is no longer so uniformly regarded in positive terms as the "discoverer" of America; instead, he is viewed through a more critical lens by a meaningful proportion of the public.

Two Possible Explanations for Change

Our interest lies not only in identifying the existence of change in beliefs but also in understanding why it occurred. We consider two hypotheses about social processes that might account for that change, both of which hinge on the association of Villainous responses to birth cohort.

Increased Public Awareness of Revisionist Representations

Challenges to Columbus's traditional positive status as "the discoverer of America," as well as debates about whether he should be honored, may have become increasingly visible to the general public. Although the 1998 survey revealed little evidence that the 1992 controversies had affected beliefs, continued critical attention to Columbus and protests by Native Americans since the quincentenary—conveyed through news and popular media—might have propelled revisionist representations out of activist and intellectual circles to the wider public. In that case, we would expect exposure to revisionist views to take the form of a period effect, in which all parts of the population who were able to attend to or be influenced by discussions and debates in the media—that is, most adults—would be affected more or less equally. If we plot Villainous Columbus survey responses by birth cohort, a relatively flat curve, with Villainous responses evenly distributed across cohorts, would be consistent with this hypothesis. The height of the curve might rise over time, however, reflecting greater overall endorsement of Columbus's Villainous image.

Education as a Conduit for Critical Representations

The role of education is central to an alternative possibility: that change in public beliefs has occurred primarily because of systematic change in the information about Columbus and Native Americans provided to children and young people through the educational system. Information conveyed through education is designed to be appealing and developmentally appropriate, and it might have a substantial impact on students. Changing educational content "differentiates the knowledge of parent and child" (Ryder, 1965, p. 854), and because early experiences are often formative (Alwin et al., 1991; Krosnick & Alwin, 1989), education is one source of influence that can produce distinctive cohorts. For example, late-20th-century declines in racial prejudice have been partly linked to students' post–World War II exposure to social science curricula in colleges and schools, which presented racial differences as due to environment rather than biology (Quillian, 1996). Cohort differences in the naming of Black historical figures as "famous Americans" have been attributed in part to curricular and textbook changes (Wineburg & Monte-Sano, 2008).

Inspired by the success of demands by Black activists and organizations in the 1960s for "integrated" and positive textbook depictions, other racial and ethnic groups called for similar overhauls (Zimmerman, 2004). Change in textbook treatments of Columbus and Native Americans has been identified for earlier periods and in broad outlines for the 1980s and 1990s (Bello & Shaver, 2011; Fitzgerald, 1979; Schuman et al., 2005), and it seemed worth extending those trends and investigating them in greater detail. This hypothesis centers on the intersection of history and biography (Alwin & McCammon, 2007): Historical change in portrayals of Columbus and Native Americans, communicated through education, intersected with the life course of young people who would have been systematically exposed to those new images as students. According to this hypothesis, Villainous responses should be located mainly among cohorts young enough to have attended school after portrayals of Columbus became more critical.

Relation of Reappraisal to Cohort

Figure 7.2 displays the percentages of Villainous responses given by each birth cohort, plotted separately for each of our three surveys. The curve for all surveys is relatively flat at low levels for birth cohorts on the left of Figure 7.2—cohorts born before about 1970. The youngest respondents in the 1998 survey were born during the 1970s, where a slight upturn of the curve can be detected. Plotted lines for the 2014 and 2017 surveys confirm that upswing and show that it increases further among the even younger respondents present in the later two survey samples.

Exposure through news media and public discourse to revisionist views about Columbus and Native Americans should be approximately the same for all survey respondents, regardless of when they were born. Villainous responses are concentrated among younger cohorts on the right of Figure 7.2, however—a relation that cannot be explained by our first hypothesis. That does not mean that public attention and media coverage have played no role in increasing Villainous responses; in fact, Figure 7.2 shows that the overall height of the line rises at each survey time point, indicating that critical views of Columbus have increased over time among most cohorts.

Turning to our second hypothesis, in all three survey plots, the main upturn begins among cohorts born in the 1970s: In the 1998 and 2017 surveys, the increase begins with the cohort born between 1976 and 1980, whereas in

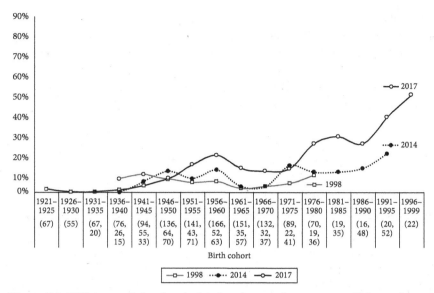

Figure 7.2 Villainous Columbus by birth cohort and survey year. N for each cohort in each survey year shown in parentheses, for each data point plotted (1998, 2014, and 2017).

the 2014 survey it begins with the slightly older cohort, born between 1971 and 1975. In other words, respondents born during the 1970s are the very oldest in our surveys who show possible evidence of systematic change in the image of Columbus conveyed through education. A respondent born in 1975, the midpoint of that decade, would have completed high school in the early 1990s. Thus, if change in education about Columbus and Native Americans can help explain the increase in Villainous responses in Figure 7.2, we would expect that change to have begun during the 1980s or 1990s.

Evaluating Change in Educational Content

We had reason to think that challenges to Columbus's reputation and new portrayals of Native Americans might have been especially pronounced within educational contexts during this time period because of two broader developments: (1) the rise of multiculturalism and (2) changes within the discipline of history that prompted new approaches to historiography and to teaching and learning history. As scholars of color came to greater prominence during and after the civil rights movement, they challenged stereotypes, inaccuracies, and lacunae in scholarship and began to develop a new academic research agenda focused on racial, ethnic, and other groups traditionally excluded from the historical narrative (Novick, 1988; Ramsey & Williams, 2003; Symcox, 2002). Their ideas and research influenced new generations of educators and historians.

Multicultural Education

What began as "multiethnic" education in the 1970s drew attention to the need for teaching, curriculum, and materials that reflected racial and ethnic diversity—in particular, non-European experiences and viewpoints—and gradually expanded into "multicultural education" (Banks, 2009; Sleeter & Grant, 1987). Multicultural approaches gained wider support in response to growing classroom diversity during the 1980s (Sleeter, 1996) and especially the 1990s (Cornbleth, 1995; Ramsey & Williams 2003) when, for the first time, one-third of students attending public elementary or secondary school were members of racial or ethnic minorities (KewalRamani et al., 2007).

By 1990, "multicultural education was being taken seriously" (Sleeter, 2018, p. 7). The National Association for Multicultural Education was established in that year, and the first issue of its journal appeared in 1993. Teacher education programs had begun to advertise faculty positions in multicultural education (Sleeter, 2018). New standards for kindergarten through grade 12 (K–12) social studies teaching, developed in 1994 by the National Council for the Social Studies (NCSS), were designed to help students become "citizens of a culturally diverse, democratic society" (NCSS, 1994, p. vii) and "to construct a pluralist perspective based on diversity" (p. 6).

New Social History

During the same period and in response to some of the same influences, historians rejected a "presidencies and wars" approach, turning their attention instead to the role of larger social forces and of groups previously on the periphery of the historical narrative, especially marginalized racial and ethnic groups, women, and ordinary people (Foner, 1997; Ross, 1998). Professional historians increasingly acknowledged the interpretive and complex nature of history (Appleby et al., 1994; Ross, 1998). History teaching began to emphasize "doing history," even for the youngest students, in order to develop analytical and interpretive skills (Levstik & Barton, 1997).

The controversy over the National History Standards Project (NHSP) illustrates the degree to which these approaches had become accepted among historians and educators. The NHSP was established during the 1990s to develop K–12 history education guidance, and its origins lay in conservative reform efforts to attenuate the influence of multiculturalism in history education. The standards themselves, however, were drafted through a consensus process by participating historians, educators, and members of the public (Nash et al., 1997). Far from promoting the traditional approach sought by the project's political initiators, the history standards conformed to already current academic practice in reflecting a pluralistic orientation and a willingness to challenge traditional narratives, much like the NCSS guidelines. Indeed, NHSP participants believed they had produced "an innocuous document of mainstream history" (Symcox, 2002, p. 163) and were shocked when the standards became a flash point in the culture wars upon their release in 1994. Conservatives denounced the standards for "political correctness" and for inadequately emphasizing a celebratory view of American history and traditional heroes (Cheney, 1994); right-wing critics seized that narrative, and the political firestorm made its way to the U.S. Senate, which condemned the standards. After review by an independent panel, a slightly revised version of the standards was approved, omitting recommended teaching activities but including no major reorientation. Although school districts were reluctant to adopt the standards outright, the controversy served to stimulate interest: 70,000 copies were sold in the first few months and were used by states in developing their own guidelines (Dunn, 2009). By the 2000s, the movement toward cultural pluralism in history was pervasive and influential among academic historians and classroom teachers (Vega, 2006).

Implications for Teaching and Learning About Columbus

The new perspectives prompted greater attention to the culture and history of Native Americans before the arrival of Europeans and to Columbus as the first colonizer. For example, in advance of the quincentenary, the NCSS and the American Historical Association released a joint position statement with recommendations for educators. Among other points, the statement urged teachers to emphasize that "Columbus did not discover a new world and, thus, did not initiate American history" and that the "real America Columbus encountered in 1492 was a different place from the precontact America often portrayed in folklore, textbooks, and the mass media" (NCSS, 1992, p. 147). The statement also encouraged teachers to recognize the "catastrophic mortality rates" suffered by Native Americans as a result of 1492 and to avoid telling "stories of vigorous white actors confronting passive red and black spectators and victims" (p. 148).

The earliest American schoolbooks served to create and disseminate national narratives (see Chapter 2, this volume), and textbooks have done the same in contemporary contexts. VanSledright (2008) writes that "perhaps the single most important repository of the nation-building narrative that provides symbolic shape and substance to [the American] creed is the U.S. history textbook" (p. 113). Change in representations of Columbus and Native Americans, if widely conveyed through textbooks, may have affected the beliefs of young people, helping to account for the relation of Villainous responses to birth cohort identified in our surveys. The timing of likely influence of multicultural education and the turn toward teaching historical thinking in the 1980s and 1990s corresponds well with our results.

Content Analysis of Textbooks

In order to investigate (1) whether we could identify change in educational content on Columbus and early Native American history and (2) whether the timing of any such change matched our survey results, we reviewed a set of 43 American history survey textbooks. The books were written for high school and early college students, and they were published between 1981 and 2016 (just prior to the date of our most recent survey). Textbook use was widespread during the period: Research in 2002 by the U.S. Department of Education showed that 84% of high school students read textbooks at least once a week, and teachers typically followed the textbook narrative (VanSledright, 2008). In a 2014 interview, a sales and marketing coordinator at a major textbook publisher claimed that 70% of college instructors used textbooks (Casper et al., 2014), a figure likely to be even higher at the high school level.

The titles we reviewed were all published by major educational publishing houses and include 6 of the 7 identified by the American Textbook

Council (founded by a conservative commentator; n.d.) as "leading U.S. history textbooks." The total set included 24 different titles; where possible, we included multiple editions so that we could track change within titles over time. (The textbooks analyzed are listed in the Appendix, and quotations in the text are identified by an abbreviated title and date.)

Educators, historians, and other commentators have identified deficiencies in portrayals of Native Americans in teaching and curriculum (Axtell, 1987; Costo & Henry, 1970; Knopp, 1997; Shear et al., 2015; Stanton 2012) as well as inaccuracies and bias in representations of Columbus (Loewen, 1995; Paul, 2014; Phillips & Phillips, 1992). Drawing on their research as well as our own review of a subset of the textbooks, we developed thematic coding categories to capture content that might reflect change. Material relevant to our coding was located in the first chapter or two of each textbook. We also reviewed prefaces, when available, to capture authors' notes about modifications as they introduced new editions. After developing our final codes, the books were coded by two coders working independently.[3]

Our coding categories were of two types, shown in Table 7.2. First, we coded for specific content related to Columbus, his voyages, and his actions, including references to his positive personal qualities, references to his "discovery" of America that did not attempt to qualify the term, references to his search for gold or wealth, and references to his cruelty to or exploitation of Native Americans.[4] We also coded for any acknowledgment in connection with Columbus or Native Americans that the writing of history is an interpretive act or that the story of his landing has traditionally been told from a Eurocentric perspective.

Second, we coded for coverage of Native Americans and their history and culture, as well as the consequences of Columbus's arrival. We coded for references in book prefaces to expanded coverage of early Native American history, for presentation of Native Americans or their cultures as primitive, and for emphasis on the scale of population loss through European disease and depredation. Each of these elements should contribute to students' conclusions about the actions, roles, and significance of Native Americans and European explorers.

Figures 7.3a–d show that four elements of the Columbus narrative have shifted over time, resulting in a less flattering depiction of his voyages and

---

[3] Coding agreement for a 50% subsample was 92%.
[4] The positive Columbus codes were more specific than those used by Schuman et al. (2005), so these results do not align with theirs, although the direction of change is the same.

Table 7.2 Textbook Coding Categories and Examples of Coded Content

Category	Examples of Content
Columbus and his voyages	
Positive personal qualities	"A man of vision, energy, resourcefulness, and courage" (AP, 1983, p. 4) "Columbus was a true leader... respected by his followers" (HUS, 1981, p. 6)
Seeking wealth or gold	"Not averse to acquiring wealth and glory along the way" (LEP, 2002, p. 15)
Cruelty or exploitation of Native Americans	"Columbus was America's first slave trader" (EV, 1990, p. 24) "Columbus, frustrated by his inability to govern the native peoples of Hispaniola, decided to 'subjugate by force of arms.' To terrorize the natives..." (AH2, 2011, p. 7)
Use of term "discover" without qualification	"Word of Columbus's discovery caught Europeans' imaginations" (EV, 1990, p. 23)
Recognize role of interpretation or Eurocentrism	"It is usually said that Europeans discovered America, but it is also true that America discovered Europeans" (MA, 1995, p. 20)
Native Americans before or at the time of Columbus, and consequences of his arrival	
Preface notes expanded coverage of history before Columbus	"An expanded Chapter 1: The First Civilizations of North America surveys the development of cities, agriculture, and civilizations in the pre-Contact Americas, placing greater emphasis on native North American cultures" (NN, 2008, p. xxiv)
Portrayed as primitive, uncivilized	"None of the groups made much progress in developing simple machines or substituting mechanical or even animal power for their own muscle power. They had no wagons or other vehicles with wheels and no horses or oxen to help plow the land" (AH1, 1982, p. 4) "Near-naked natives" (AP, 1991, p. 4)
Emphasis on scale of devastation from disease	"Worst demographic disaster in world history" (APP, 2003, p. 12) "Within thirty years of the first landfall at Guanahaní, not one Taíno survived in the Bahamas.... Overall, historians estimate that the long-term effects of the alien microorganisms could have reduced the precontact American population by as much as 90 percent" (PAN, 2008, p. 24)

activity. Mentions of his bravery and "keen imagination" (EV, 1990, p. 23), etc., are frequent in the earlier books, but positive depictions decline over the decades (Figure 7.3a). References to cruelty or exploitation of Native Americans by Columbus or his crew are rare before the 1990s but become more frequent with each decade (Figure 7.3b). Prior to the 1990s, nearly all

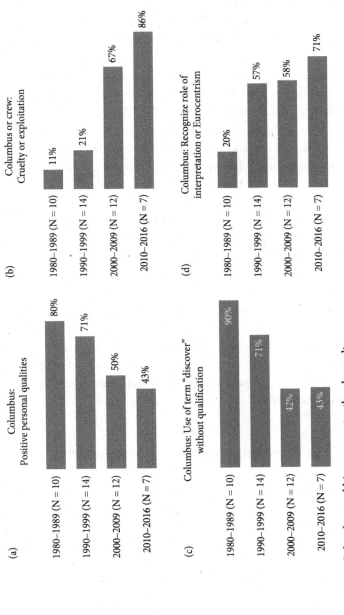

Figure 7.3 Columbus and his voyages: textbook results.

textbooks we reviewed refer to Columbus's having "discovered" America, without any qualification to acknowledge that it was a "discovery" only for Europeans. Over time, the textbook authors begin to distance themselves from the term by enclosing it in quotes or replacing it with the word "encounter" (Figure 7.3c). Finally, from the 1990s on, many of the textbook authors used Columbus and the consequences of his landing for Native Americans to illustrate the situated nature of historical interpretation (Figure 7.3d). We found no consistent change over time for references to Columbus's interest in gold or wealth, so we do not include this content in the figures; the element was evidently part of the narrative during the 1980s and has remained so.

Equally interesting are changes in presentation of Native American history. Prefaces in many editions from the 1990s on included statements noting expanded coverage of early Native American history and cultures; books from the 2010s also mentioned increased coverage, but the percentages were somewhat lower, suggesting that the 1990s and 2000s were a kind of turning point (Figure 7.4a). Native American societies were often depicted as primitive or uncivilized in the earliest books, but those portrayals decreased during the 1990s and later disappeared entirely (Figure 7.4b). Finally, a clear increase in references to the devastating impact of brutality and disease brought by the Europeans occurred in the 1990s (Figure 7.4c). Even with our small number of cases, the trend for seven of our eight content codes is reliable.[5] Only the code for Columbus's interest in wealth showed no association with decade.

Taken together, the data suggest that textbook depictions of both Columbus and Native Americans changed considerably during our time period of interest, especially during the 1990s and 2000s, with most trends continuing into the 2010s.[6]

Connecting the Survey and Textbook Data

We cannot link our survey respondents' beliefs directly to their educational experiences. However, the evidence of major change in textbooks during and after the 1990s corresponds well to the timing of change observed in

---

[5] Using Kendall's tau-c, $p < .05$ for seven of eight cross-tabulations of coded content by decade. [For expanded coverage of early Native American history, which drops off considerably in 2010–2016 once many books had added material (Figure 7.4a), we omit the 2010–2016 decade in testing.]

[6] Increased attention to the early history of Native Americans notwithstanding, curriculum and textbook portrayals of Native Americans or their history continue to be inadequate (e.g., Anderson, 2012; Cummings, 2012; Journell, 2009; Moore & Clark, 2004; Shear et al., 2015).

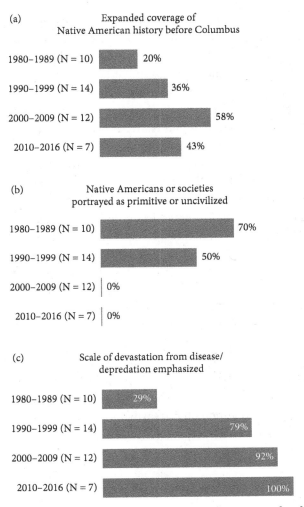

Figure 7.4 Native Americans and Native American history: textbook results.

respondents' beliefs. Cohorts born in the 1970s are the first whose schooling (or any part of it) could have taken place during the 1990s, when revised portrayals of Columbus and Native Americans began to appear in textbooks. As Figure 7.2 shows, respondents born in the 1970s are the oldest to display an increase in beliefs about a Villainous Columbus. Those cohorts would have completed their last years of high school or first years of college during the early 1990s, and they might have been exposed to revisionist views of Columbus and Native Americans at that point. Younger cohorts would have been exposed to those views during more of their educational careers.

The same trends in multiculturalism and new thinking about history and history education that appear connected to change in textbooks have no doubt extended into schools in other ways. The generation of teachers that entered classrooms beginning in the late 1980s and early 1990s would have been trained in multicultural education and new approaches to teaching history. These teachers might have been especially sensitive to deficiencies in history textbook treatments of Columbus and Native Americans, which were discussed in professional publications. Spurred by the quincentenary, articles in a range of practitioner journals recounted the efforts of teachers at all grade levels to challenge their students to think critically about the conventional narrative or made recommendations for doing so (e.g., Bingham, 1991; Brady, 1992; Davis & Hawke, 1992; McGinnis & McGinnis, 1992), and teachers recognized change in their students' awareness (Kubal, 2008). In some cases, teachers reported using the traditional narrative to stimulate students' thinking about what is omitted and from whose perspective the story is told ("contrapuntal pedagogy"; Mason & Ernst-Slavit, 2010). As one teacher described her goals for students related to Columbus, "When you see a story in a book, understand that there are two different stories. American history is largely Eurocentric. Maybe there's another side to this story" (Rosenberg, 1991, p. WC12). At the same time, reports from teacher observation also provide evidence that some teachers continued to present a traditional, Eurocentric narrative (Slekar, 2009; B. Smith, 2000), and VanSledright (2008) observes that teachers willing to encourage students to question official textbook narratives "are remarkable primarily because of their rarity" (p. 119).

The Inertia of Memory

Considering public beliefs about Columbus contributes to our understanding of the inertia (Le Goff, 1985; Olick & Robbins, 1998) of memory in several ways. Stability of public beliefs attunes us to the ways traditional images of Columbus have been buttressed for decades by the annual holiday and associated celebratory events. Other forms of commemoration—works of art and names of schools, cities, and other sites—maintain the visibility of the traditional Columbus. The rhyme still learned by many schoolchildren ("In fourteen hundred and ninety-two, Columbus sailed the ocean blue") brings to mind an image of the explorer on the open sea, and most children's picture books still tell a traditional story (Desai, 2014). Locating Columbus at America's birth confers the benefit of primacy, which influences recall of American presidents and other historical figures (Frisch, 1989; Roediger & DeSoto, 2014). Columbus's connection to European origins is reinforced by conventional historical periodization, which uses his landing to show that "American" history begins in 1492 with European arrival, whereas earlier history is "pre-Columbian" (or "pre-contact")—essentially prehistory (Loewen, 1995; Zerubavel, 1998). Writing unrelated to Columbus employs his name to evoke visionary quests, great deeds, and American origins, in contexts exalted and mundane. A 2005 newspaper article about NASA's future plans quoted an earlier statement by President George H. W. Bush: "Like Columbus ... we dream of distant shores we've not yet seen" (Park, 2005, p. 6). "Turkey is the all-American bird," noted another article, "It was here long before Columbus or the Pilgrims" (Forsyth, 2013). Symbols evoking a national past, like other cultural symbols, are sustained when they serve as the "unspoken backdrop to our thoughts, acts, and messages" (Schudson, 1989, p. 155). Thus, we should not be surprised that 25 years after the quincentenary and despite ongoing critique, beliefs of most of the American public still hew to the traditional image of Columbus "the discoverer." Revisionist ideas have been widely available to ordinary people, but neither the controversies at the time of the quincentenary nor revisionist attention to Columbus in subsequent years have greatly affected the beliefs of older parts of the population. Even among the youngest cohorts, no more than half describe Columbus in Villainous terms.

These forces contribute to persistence of traditional views, but institutional forces promoting critical understanding of Columbus have their own momentum. Change in the information students learned about Columbus and Native Americans occurred in a broader context of new ideas about how to teach history and how to prepare students for life in a pluralist society. Over several decades, those ideas have been institutionalized—however incomplete and controversial the process—through curriculum standards and guidelines, teacher training programs, and textbooks. Education can be a powerful influence on what is remembered: Consistent attention to the Holocaust in Israeli schools has kept that part of the past alive for younger generations (Schuman et al., 2003). If young cohorts' more critical image of Columbus is due to change in the educational content to which they were exposed, institutional forces should extend those beliefs to still younger cohorts as they enter the educational system. The traditional image held by older cohorts is likely to remain stable, but over time, as the older cohorts themselves decrease as a proportion of the population, belief in a traditional Columbus should wane through the process of cohort replacement.

Cultural processes may assist in toppling Columbus from his pedestal. The regularity of the cultural calendar (Schudson, 1989) can become a liability for Columbus, as each Columbus Day brings calls for its replacement with Indigenous People's Day, as well as news reports about states, cities, other localities, and institutions that have already done so. Visual images from attacks on statues of Columbus around the time of the holiday each year show him with bloodied hands, covered in graffiti that ties him to exploitation and enslavement, or lying awkwardly on the ground. Images like these may expedite the transformation of Columbus from founding father to original sinner. Protests and calls for the elimination of Columbus Day reinforce critical views young people may have acquired in school, although they also demonstrate the continuing cultural power of the holiday and statues.

It remains to be determined what meaning Columbus will retain as a symbol of national origins as public beliefs shift in a critical direction. Historical events that evoke shame sometimes figure in national memory (see Chapter 12, this volume). Confronting past atrocities and their ongoing legacies seems crucial to overcoming the burdens they present (see Chapter 5, this volume), but Yamashiro et al. (2019) found that when an American sample was asked to name events representing America's origins, negative events (including slavery and Native American genocide) were infrequently mentioned. It is also possible that Columbus's symbolic relevance to origins will fade, commensurate with increasing recognition of Native Americans' centrality to America's beginnings, subsequent history, and its national imagination. "Americans," an exhibit at the National Museum of the American Indian, employs the ubiquitous presence of Native American imagery in contemporary and historical popular culture to reveal how fundamental Native Americans are to American national identity. "The most American thing ever is in fact American Indians," says Comanche author Paul Chaat Smith (2017), one of the exhibition's curators. In the near term, however, social memberships, including political and religious affiliations, may contribute to fragmentation in how the public understands Columbus's foundational role, with self-identified Republicans less likely than others to associate atrocities with America's beginning, and Catholics especially likely to connect Columbus to origins (Yamashiro et al., 2019). Such patterns may reflect the effects of collaborative remembering processes on remembered content and how memories are structured (see Chapter 20, this volume), different moral bases for collective remembering (see Chapter 8, this volume), as well as motivations for promoting one's own group (see Chapter 11, this volume).

Concluding Reflections on National Memory

"Historians fashion the nation's self-understanding, but they do it without thinking of themselves as agents of the state," write Appleby et al. (1994, p. 155). Change in presentation of Native Americans and Columbus in school was not an "official," coordinated effort imposed from above. The process of change took place over decades, fostered by ideas introduced by new generations of activists, scholars, and teachers. Even initiatives such as the National History Standards Project were broad, consensus-based efforts by a wide range of groups and individuals. Participants resisted overt political control, and the standards that resulted were voluntary (Nash et al., 1997). Moreover, much of what happened in the classroom was up to individual teachers, who confronted on a day-to-day basis the challenge of helping increasingly diverse groups of students connect meaningfully with national history. Students themselves are "active constructors of the meanings of the education they encounter" (Apple, 1992, p. 10). That many disparate educational efforts shared an emphasis on the importance of questioning narratives and recognizing alternative perspectives—both essential tools for managing differences over national memory, as Wertsch (see Chapter 22, this volume), notes—offers grounds for optimism.

Yet other forces work to restrict cultural change. Commentators have raised alarms about revisionism (e.g., Fox-Genovese & Lasch-Quinn, 1999; Schlesinger, 1998). Textbooks are part of "selective tradition" (Williams, 1961), reflecting both publishers' sales imperatives and the dominant American narrative, which lead textbook authors to steer clear of conflict and controversy and maintain an optimistic tone (Foster, 2006). Marginalized racial and ethnic groups receive more coverage than in the past, but as addenda to an overarching narrative of progress (presented largely as the result of individuals' achievements) toward freedom and unity—the American schematic narrative template (Wertsch, 2018) that structures most history education in the United States. The "triumphal national narrative" (VanSledright, 2008, p. 137) is absorbed by younger children (Barton, 2001) and older students alike (Frisch, 1989; VanSledright, 2008; Wertsch & O'Connor, 1994), informing their understanding of the American past and present.

Thus, change in portrayals of Columbus and Native Americans has occurred within the confines of a larger, persistent national narrative.

That collective remembering is a process has been well established by scholars approaching the topic from many disciplinary perspectives (Olick, 2007; Wertsch, 2018; Winter, 2006). Our study affirms the importance of considering that process not only in terms of cultural images of the past but also in terms of images held by individuals. Change in the meaning of national cultural symbols may not influence beliefs of ordinary people in as direct a way as is often assumed; the processes we identify underscore the need to consider alternative, longer term pathways through which cultural representations affect individuals' beliefs about the national past.

Acknowledgments

We are indebted to John Wilkes, Gabriel Reich, Max Broening, Jocelyn Hayes, and Jennifer Tennison for helping locate textbooks and assisting in other ways. The research was supported in part by the National Science Foundation under Grant No. SES-0001844.

Appendix

The following are the textbooks reviewed for this study (preceded by title abbreviation in parentheses, if referred to in text):

America: A narrative history (Brief 3rd ed.). Tindall, G. B., & Shi, D. E. (1993). Norton.
(APP) *America: Past and present* (6th ed.). Divine, R. A., Breen, T. H., Fredrickson, G. M., & Williams, R. H. (2003). Addison-Wesley.
America: Pathways to the present. Cayton, A., Perry, E. I., & Winkler, A. M. (1995). Prentice Hall.
America: The glorious republic (1st ed.). Graff, H. E. (1986). Houghton Mifflin.
America is (4th ed.). Drewry, H. N., & O'Connor, T. H. (1987). Merrill.
(AH1) *American history.* Garraty, J. A. (1982). Harcourt Brace Jovanovich.
American history: A survey (11th ed.). Brinkley, A. (2003). McGraw-Hill.
American history: Connecting with the past (14th, 15th eds.). Brinkley, A. (2012, 2015). McGraw-Hill.
(AP) *The American pageant: A history of the republic* (7th, 8th, 9th, 10th, 11th, 12th, 16th eds.). Kennedy, D. M., Cohen, L., & Bailey, T. A. (1983, 1987, 1991, 1994, 1998, 2002, 2016). Houghton Mifflin.
The American people: A history (1st ed.). Maier, P. (1986). Heath.
The American promise: A history of the United States (3rd, 4th eds.). Roark, J. L., Johnson, M. P., Cohen, P. C., Stage, S., Lawson, A., & Hartmann, S. M. (2005, 2009). Bedford/St. Martin's.

(AH2) *America's history* (7th, 8th eds.). Henretta, J. A., Hinderaker, E., Edwards, R., & Self, R. O. (2011, 2014). Bedford/St. Martin's.

Created equal: A social and political history of the United States. Jones, J., Wood, P. H., Borstelmann, T., May, E. T., & Ruiz, V. L. (2003). Pearson.

(EV) *The enduring vision: A history of the American people* (1st, 2nd, 4th eds.). Boyer, P. S., Clark, C. E., Jr., Kett, J. F., Purvis, T. L., Sitkoff, H., & Woloch, N. (1990, 1993, 2000). Heath.

Give me liberty! An American history (2nd, 3rd eds.). Foner, E. (2008, 2011). Norton.

(HUS) *A history of the United States* (1st, 5th, 6th eds.). Boorstin, D. J., & Kelley, B. M. (1981, 1990, 1996). Prentice Hall.

(LEP) *Liberty, equality, power: A history of the American people* (2nd, 3rd, 5th, 6th eds.). Murrin, J. M., Johnson, P. E., McPherson, J. M., Gerstle, G., Rosenberg, E. S., & Rosenberg, N. L. (1999, 2002, 2008, 2012). Wadsworth Thomson.

Making America: A history of the United States. Berkin, C., Miller, C. L, Cherny, R. W., & Gormly, J. L. (1995). Houghton Mifflin.

(NN) *Nation of nations: A narrative history of the American republic* (2nd, 3rd, 6th eds.). Davidson, J. W., DeLay, B., Heyrman, C. L., Lytle, M. H., & Stoff, M. B. (1994, 1998, 2008). McGraw-Hill.

One flag, one land (1st ed.) Brown, R. C., & Bass, H. J. (1990). Silver, Burdett & Ginn.

(PAN) *A people and a nation: A history of the United States* (8th ed.). Norton, M. B., Sheriff, C., Katzman, D. M., Blight, D. W., Chudacoff, H. P., Logevall, F., & Bailey, B. (2008). Houghton Mifflin.

A proud nation (1st ed.). May, E. R. (1985) .McDougal, Littell & Company.

The United States: A history of the republic (1st ed.). Davidson, J. W., & Lytle, M. H. (1981). Prentice-Hall.

United States history (1st ed.). Reich, J. R., & Biller, E. L. (1988). Holt, Rinehart & Winston.

References

Abel, M., Umanath, S., Fairfield, B., d'Annunzio, G., Takahashi, M., Roediger, H. L., III, & Wertsch, J. V. (2019). Collective memories across 11 nations regarding World War II: Similarities and differences regarding the most important events. *Journal of Applied Research in Memory and Cognition, 8*, 178–188.

Abend, L., & Pingree, G. (2006, October 17). Who really sailed the ocean blue in 1492? Spanish scholars are on a mission to demystify Christopher Columbus's life, long shrouded in a veil of mythic heroism. *Christian Science Monitor*. https://www.csmonitor.com/2006/1017/p05s01-woeu.html

Alwin, D. F., Cohen, R. J., & Newcomb, T. M. (1991). *Political attitudes over the life span: The Bennington women after fifty years*. University of Wisconsin Press.

Alwin, D. F., & McCammon, R. J. (2007). Rethinking generations. *Research in Human Development, 4*(3–4), 219–237.

American Association for Public Opinion Research. (2016). *Standard definitions: Final dispositions of case codes and outcome rates for surveys* (9th ed.). https://www.aapor.org/AAPOR_Main/media/publications/Standard-Definitions20169theditionfinal.pdf

American Psychological Association. (2001). APA resolution recommending the immediate retirement of American Indian mascots, symbols, images, and personalities by schools, colleges, universities, athletic teams, and organizations. Council Policy Manual: Special Populations Policies. https://www.apa.org/about/policy/mascots.pdf

American Textbook Council. (n.d.). *Widely adopted history textbooks*. Retrieved October 20, 2019, from https://www.historytextbooks.net/adopted.htm

Anderson, C. B. (2012). Misplaced multiculturalism: Representations of American Indians in U.S. history academic content standards. *Curriculum Inquiry, 42*(4), 497–509.

Andrew, S., & Willingham, A. J. (2020, October 12). *These states are ditching Columbus Day and celebrating Indigenous Peoples' Day instead*. CNN. https://www.cnn.com/2020/10/12/us/indigenous-peoples-day-2020-states-trnd/index.html

Apple, M. (1992). The text and cultural politics. *Educational Researcher, 21*(7), 4–11.

Appleby, J., Hunt, L., & Jacob, M. (1994). *Telling the truth about history*. Norton.

Associated Press. (2020, July 24). Christopher Columbus statues taken down at two Chicago parks. *The Washington Post*. https://www.washingtonpost.com/national/christopher-columbus-statue-taken-down-at-chicago-park/2020/07/24/a340cf10-cd8c-11ea-99b0-8426e26d203b_story.html

Axtell, J. (1987). Colonial America without the Indians: Counterfactual reflections. *Journal of American History, 73*(4), 981–996.

Axtell, J. (1992). Columbian encounters: Beyond 1992. *William and Mary Quarterly, 49*(2), 335–360.

Banks, J. A. (2009). Multicultural education: Dimensions and paradigms. In J. A. Banks (Ed.), *The Routledge international companion to multicultural education* (pp. 9–32). Taylor & Francis.

Barton, K. C. (2001). A sociocultural perspective on children's understanding of historical change: Comparative findings from Northern Ireland and the United States. *American Educational Research Journal, 38*(4), 881–913.

Bello, M., & Shaver, A. N. (2011). The representation of Christopher Columbus in high school history textbooks. In A. N. Shaver, M. Bello, & E. F. Provenzo (Eds.), *The textbook as discourse: Sociocultural dimensions of American schoolbooks* (pp. 140–161). Taylor & Francis.

Bergreen, L. (2011). *Columbus: The four voyages, 1492–1504*. Penguin.

Billings, A. C., & Black, J. E. (2018). *Mascot nation: The controversy over Native American representations in sports*. University of Illinois Press.

Bingham, M. W. (1991). Teaching the Columbian quincentenary. *OAH Magazine of History, 5*(4), 7–9.

Bodnar, J. (1992). *Remaking America: Public memory, commemoration, and patriotism in the twentieth century*. Princeton University Press.

Brady, P. (1992). Columbus and the quincentennial myths: Another side of the story. *Young Children, 47*(6), 4–14.

Casper, S. E., Dougherty, M., Foner, E., Kinsel, A., Miller, R. M., & Trowbridge, D. J. (2014). Textbooks today and tomorrow: A conversation about history, pedagogy, and economics. *Journal of American History, 100*(5), 1139–1169.

Cheney, L. V. (1994, October 20). The end of history. *The Wall Street Journal*, p. A22.

Cornbleth, C. (1995). Curriculum knowledge: Controlling the "great speckled bird." *Educational Review, 47*(2), 157.

Corning, A., & Schuman, H. (2015). *Generations and collective memory*. University of Chicago Press.

Costo, R., & Henry, J. (1970). *Textbooks and the American Indian*. Indian Historian Press.

Cummings, K. (2012). Invisible Indians: How political systems support the misrepresentation of Indigenous People's history and its effect on Indigenous children. In B. J. Porfilio (Ed.), *The new politics of the textbook: Problematizing the portrayal of marginalized groups in textbooks* (pp. 259–271). Brill.

Davis, J. E., & Hawke, S. D. (1992). Seeds of change: Cutting-edge knowledge and the Columbian quincentenary. *Social Education, 56*(6), 320–322.

Denevan, W. M. (1992). The pristine myth: The landscape of the Americas in 1492. *Annals of the Association of American Geographers, 82*(3), 369–385.

Desai, C. M. (2014). The Columbus myth: Power and ideology in picturebooks about Christopher Columbus. *Children's Literature in Education, 45*(3), 179–196.

Dobyns, H. F. (1966). Estimating aboriginal American population: An appraisal of techniques with a new hemispheric estimate. *Current Anthropology, 7*, 395–416.

Dunn, R. E. (2009). The ugly, the bad, and the good in the National History Standards controversy. *The History Teacher, 42*, 21–24.

Fitzgerald, F. (1979). *America revised: History schoolbooks in the twentieth century*. Little, Brown.

Fluker, C. (2012, October 8). Gentrification in DC: How will we remember those displaced? *The Washington Post*. https://www.washingtonpost.com/blogs/therootdc/post/gentrification-in-dc-how-will-we-remember-those-displaced/2012/10/08/a9eb5ebe-1158-11e2-a16b-2c110031514a_blog.html

Foner, E. (1997). Who is an American? The imagined community in American history. *The Centennial Review, 41*(3), 425–438.

Forsyth, M. (2013, November 27). The turkey's Turkey connection. *The New York Times*. https://www.nytimes.com/2013/11/28/opinion/the-turkeys-turkey-connection.html

Foster, S. J. (2006). Whose history? Portrayal of immigrant groups in U.S. history textbooks, 1800–present. In S. J. Foster & K. A. Crawford (Eds.), *What shall we tell the children? International perspectives on school history textbooks* (pp. 155–178). Information Age.

Fox-Genovese, E., & Lasch-Quinn, E. (1999). *Reconstructing history: The emergence of a new historical society*. Routledge.

Frisch, M. (1989). American history and the structures of collective memory: A modest exercise in empirical iconography. *Journal of American History, 75*(4), 1130–1155.

Fryberg, S., Markus, H. R., Oyserman, D., & Stone, J. (2008). Of warrior chiefs and Indian princesses: The psychological consequences of American Indian mascots. *Basic and Applied Social Psychology, 30*, 208–218.

Green, J. (2003, May 23). Howard Zinn's history. *The Chronicle of Higher Education*. https://www.chronicle.com/article/howard-zinns-history

Hämäläinen, P. (2013). The changing histories of North America before Europeans. *OAH Magazine of History, 27*(4), 5–7.

Harris, A. (2014, June 25). Finally, a perfect term for when White people "discover" things. *Slate*. https://slate.com/culture/2014/06/columbusing-college-humor-video-coins-the-perfect-term-for-when-white-people-discover-old-things-video.html

Hauser, C. (2020, April 17; updated April 20). Land O'Lakes removes Native American woman from its products. *The New York Times*, p. B6. https://www.nytimes.com/2020/04/17/business/land-o-lakes-butter.html

Indigenous People's Day. (2020, July 27). *Wikipedia*. https://en.wikipedia.org/w/index.php?title=Indigenous_Peoples%27_Day&oldid=969869471

Journell, W. (2009). An incomplete history: Representations of American Indians in state social studies standards. *Journal of American Indian Education, 48*(2), 18–32.

Judkis, M. (2017, November 22). "This is not a trend": Native American chefs resist the "Columbusing" of indigenous foods. *The Washington Post.* https://www.washingtonpost.com/lifestyle/food/this-is-not-a-trend-native-american-chefs-resist-the-columbusing-of-indigenous-foods/2017/11/21/a9ca5be6-c8ba-11e7-b0cf-7689a9f2d84e_story.html

Judkis, M. (2020, June 13). Controversial memorials are surprisingly easy to pull down. Fixing the world that built them is harder. *The Washington Post.* https://www.washingtonpost.com/lifestyle/style/controversial-memorials-are-surprising-easy-to-pull-down-fixing-the-world-that-built-them-is-harder/2020/06/13/5c38b7ea-ac2b-11ea-94d2-d7bc43b26bf9_story.html

KewalRamani, A., Gilbertson, L., Fox, M. A., & Provasnik, S. (2007, September). Status and trends in the education of racial and ethnic minorities. National Center for Education Statistics.

Kilgore, A., & Allen, S. (2020, July 13). Washington's name change happened fast, but it was decades in the making. *The Washington Post.* https://www.washingtonpost.com/sports/2020/07/13/washingtons-name-change-happened-fast-it-was-decades-making

Knopp, S. L. (1997). Critical thinking and Columbus: Secondary social studies. *Transformations, 8*(1), 40–65.

Koch, C. M. (1996). Teaching patriotism: Private virtue for the public good in the early republic. In J. Bodnar (Ed.), *Bonds of affection: Americans define their patriotism* (pp. 19–52). Princeton University Press.

Kolbert, E. (2002, October 14 & 21). The lost mariner. *The New Yorker.* https://www.newyorker.com/magazine/2002/10/14/the-lost-mariner

Krosnick, J. A., & Alwin, D. F. (1989). Aging and susceptibility to attitude change. *Journal of Personality and Social Psychology, 57*, 416–425.

Kubal, T. (2008). *Cultural movements and collective memory: Christopher Columbus and the rewriting of the national origin myth.* Palgrave Macmillan.

Leavitt, P. A., Covarrubias, R., Perez, Y. A., & Fryberg, S. A. (2015). "Frozen in time": The impact of Native American media representations on identity and self-understanding. *Journal of Social Issues, 71*(1), 39–53.

Le Goff, J. (1985). Mentalites: A history of ambiguities. In J. Le Goff & P. Nora (Eds.), *Constructing the past: Essays in historical methodology* (pp. 166–180). Cambridge University Press.

Levstik, L. S., & Barton, K. C. (1997). *Doing history: Investigating with children in elementary and middle schools.* Erlbaum.

Loewen, J. W. (1995). *Lies my teacher told me.* The New Press.

Mann, C. C. (2005). *1491: New revelations of the Americas before Columbus.* Knopf.

Maslin Nir, S., & Mays, J. C. (2017, September 12). Christopher Columbus statue in Central Park is vandalized. *The New York Times.* https://www.nytimes.com/2017/09/12/nyregion/christopher-columbus-statue-central-park-vandalized.html?_r=0

Mason, M. R., & Ernst-Slavit, G. (2010, Fall). Representations of Native Americans in elementary school social studies: A critical look at instructional language. *Multicultural Education*, 10–17.

McGinnis, K., & McGinnis, J. (1992). Critical thinking and the quincentenary. *Momentum, 23*(3), 69–70.

Mead, S. (2012, October 8). Nouveau-Columbusing DC schools (Sara Mead's Policy Notebook). *Education Week*. http://blogs.edweek.org/edweek/sarameads_policy_notebook/2012/10/nouveau-columbusing_dc_schools.html

Moore, T. J., & Clark, B. (2004). The impact of "message senders" on what is true: Native Americans in Nebraska history books. *Multicultural Perspectives*, 6(2), 17–23. doi:10.1207/s15327892mcp0602_4

Nagel, J. (1995). American Indian ethnic renewal: Politics and the resurgence of identity. *American Sociological Review*, 60(6), 947–965.

Nash, G. B., Crabtree, C., & Dunn, R. E. (1997). *History on trial: Culture wars and the teaching of the past*. Knopf.

National Council for the Social Studies. (1992). The Columbian quincentenary: An educational opportunity. *The History Teacher*, 25(2), 145–152.

National Council for the Social Studies. (1994). *Curriculum standards for social studies*. https://eric.ed.gov/?id=ED378131

Neuman, W. (2017, September 8). Panel will devise guidelines for addressing monuments deemed offensive. *The New York Times*. https://www.nytimes.com/2017/09/08/nyregion/columbus-statue-de-blasio-monument-commission.html

Novick, P. (1988). *That noble dream: The "objectivity question" and the American historical profession*. Cambridge University Press.

Olick, J. K. (2007). *The politics of regret*. Routledge.

Olick, J. K., & Robbins, J. Social memory studies: From collective memory to the historical sociology of mnemonic practices. *Annual Review of Sociology*, 24, 105–140.

Paul, H. (2014). *The myths that made America: An introduction to American studies*. Transcript Verlag.

Park, R. L. (2005, September 23). The dark side of the moon: NASA's plans. *International Herald Tribune*, p. 6.

Parsons, J. J. (1985). Raised field farmers as pre-Columbian landscape engineers: Looking north from the San Jorge (Colombia). In I. S. Farrington (Ed.), *Prehistoric intensive agriculture in the tropics* (pp. 149–65). International Series 232. British Archaeological Reports.

Phillips, C. R., & Phillips, W. D. (1992). Christopher Columbus in United States historiography: Biography as projection. *The History Teacher*, 25(2), 119–135.

Quillian, L. (1996). Group threat and regional change in attitudes toward African-Americans. *American Journal of Sociology*, 102(3), 816–860.

Ramsey, P. G., & Williams, L. R. (2003). *Multicultural education: A source book*. RoutledgeFalmer.

Reese, D. (n.d.). American Indians in children's literature: About AICL. Retrieved February 8, 2019, from https://americanindiansinchildrensliterature.blogspot.com/p/about.html

Roediger, H. L., III, & DeSoto, K. A. (2014). Forgetting the presidents. *Science*, 346, 1106–1109.

Rose, R. B. (2014, June 25). "Columbusing": A word for when White people claim to discover things. *Jezebel*. https://jezebel.com/columbusing-a-word-for-when-white-people-claim-to-disc-1596239038

Rosenberg, M. (1991, September 29). Schools try a multicultural approach. *The New York Times*, p. WC12.

Ross, D. (1998). The new and newer histories: Social theory and historiography in an American key. In A. Molho & G. S. Wood (Eds.), *Imagined histories: American historians interpret the past* (pp. 85–106). Princeton University Press.

Ryder, N. B. (1965). The cohort as a concept in the study of social change. *American Sociological Review, 30*(6), 843–861.

Salinas, B. (2014). "Columbusing": The art of discovering something that is not new. *CodeSwitch*. https://www.npr.org/sections/codeswitch/2014/07/06/328466757/columbusing-the-art-of-discovering-something-that-is-not-new

Schlereth, T. J. (1992). Columbia, Columbus, and Columbianism. *Journal of American History, 79*(3), 937–968.

Schlesinger, A. M. (1998). *The disuniting of America: Reflections on a multicultural society*. Norton.

Schudson, M. (1989). How culture works: Perspectives from media studies on the efficacy of symbols. *Theory and Society, 18*(2), 153–180.

Schuman, H., Schwartz, B., & D'Arcy, H. (2005). Elite revisionists and popular beliefs: Christopher Columbus, hero or villain? *Public Opinion Quarterly, 69*(1), 2–29.

Schuman, H., Vinitzky-Seroussi, V., & Vinokur, A. (2003). Keeping the past alive: Memories of Israeli Jews at the turn of the millennium. *Sociological Forum, 18*(1), 103–136.

Schwartz, B. (1982). The social context of commemoration: A study in collective memory. *Social Forces, 61*(2), 374–402.

Schwartz, B. (1991). Social change and collective memory: The democratization of George Washington. *American Sociological Review, 56*(2), 221–236.

Shear, S. B., Knowles, R. T., Soden, G. J., & Castro, A. J. (2015). Manifesting destiny: Re/presentations of Indigenous Peoples in K–12 U.S. history standards. *Theory and Research in Social Education, 43*(1), 68–101.

Simko, C. (2015). *The politics of consolation*. Oxford University Press.

Skrentny, J. D. (2002). *The minority rights revolution*. Harvard University Press.

Sleeter, C. E. (1996). *Multicultural education as social activism*. State University of New York Press.

Sleeter, C. E. (2018). Multicultural education past, present, and future: Struggles for dialog and power-sharing. *International Journal of Multicultural Education, 20*(1), 5–21.

Sleeter, C. E., & Grant, C. A. (1987). An analysis of multicultural education in the United States. *Harvard Educational Review, 57*(4), 421–444.

Slekar, T. D. (2009). Democracy denied: Learning to teach history in elementary school. *Teacher Education Quarterly, 36*(1), 95–110.

Smith, B. J. (2000). The K–12 national Seeking Educational Equity and Diversity project: Teaching as a political and relational act. *Women's Studies Quarterly, 28*(3–4), 137–153.

Smith, P. C. (2017, September 20). *The most American thing ever is in fact American Indians*. Talk at the Walker Art Center, Minneapolis, MN. https://walkerart.org/magazine/paul-chaat-smith-jimmie-durham-americans-nmai-smithsonian

Spillman, L. (1997). *Nation and commemoration: Creating national identities in the United States and Australia*. Cambridge University Press.

Spillman, L. (1998). When do collective memories last? Founding moments in the United States and Australia. *Social Science History, 22*(4), 445–477.

Stanton, C. R. (2012). Context and community: Resisting curricular colonization in American history courses. In H. Hickman & B. J. Porfilio (Eds.), *The new politics of the textbook* (pp. 173–194). Sense Publishers.

Stone, A. (2014, June 24). "Columbusing": When White people think they discovered something they didn't. *Huffington Post*. https://www.huffpost.com/entry/columbusing-white-people-collegehumor_n_5526658

Strauss, V. (2018, July 26). It's back in the age of "alternative facts": "Lies My Teacher Told Me: Everything Your American History Textbook Got Wrong." *The Washington Post*. https://www.washingtonpost.com/news/answer-sheet/wp/2018/07/26/its-back-in-the-age-of-alternative-facts-lies-my-teacher-told-me-everything-your-american-history-textbook-got-wrong

Summerhill, S. J., & Williams, J. A. (2000). *Sinking Columbus: Contested history, cultural politics, and mythmaking during the quincentenary*. University Press of Florida.

Symcox, L. (2002). *Whose history? The struggle for national standards in American classrooms*. Teachers College Press.

Thelen, D. (1998). Making history and making the United States. *Journal of American Studies*, *32*(3), 373–397.

Tuck, E., & Yang, K. W. (2012). Decolonization is not a metaphor. *Decolonization*, *1*(1), 1–40.

VanSledright, B. (2008). Narratives of nation-state, historical knowledge, and school history education. *Review of Research in Education*, *32*, 109–146.

Vega, J. E. (2006). Cultural plurality and American identity: A response to Foner's Freedom and Hakim's heroes. *OAH Magazine of History*, *20*(4), 19–22.

Veracini, L. (2010). *Settler colonialism: A theoretical overview*. Palgrave Macmillan.

Voners, M. (2018, June 23). *Children's literature legacy award #alaac18*. Association for Library Service to Children blog. https://www.alsc.ala.org/blog/2018/06/childrens-literature-legacy-award-alaac18

Weigel, B. (2017, August 21). Activist takes sledgehammer to Christopher Columbus monument in northeast Baltimore. *The Baltimore Sun*. https://www.baltimoresun.com/citypaper/bcpnews-activist-takes-sledgehammer-to-christopher-columbus-monument-in-northeast-baltimore-20170821-htmlstory.html

Wertsch, J. V. (2018). National memory and where to find it. In B. Wagoner, (Ed.), *Handbook of culture and memory* (pp. 259–283). Oxford University Press.

Wertsch, J. V., & O'Connor, K. (1994). Multivoicedness in historical representation: American college students accounts of the origins of the United States. *Journal of Narrative and Life History*, *4*(4), 295–309.

Wilford, J. N. (1991). *The mysterious history of Columbus: An exploration of the man, the myth, the legacy*. Vintage Books.

Williams, R. (1961). *The long revolution*. Chatto & Windus.

Wineburg, S., & Monte-Sano, C. (2008). "Famous Americans": The changing pantheon of American heroes. *Journal of American History*, *94*(4), 1186–1202.

Winter, J. (2006). *Remembering war: The Great War between memory and history in the twentieth century*. Yale University Press.

Yamashiro, J. K., Van Engen, A., & Roediger, H. L. (2019, July). American origins: Political and religious divides in U.S. collective memory. *Memory Studies*.

Zerubavel, E. (1998). Language and memory: "Pre-Columbian" America and the social logic of periodization. *Social Research*, *65*(2), 315–330.

Zimmerman, J. (2004). Brown-ing the American textbook: History, psychology, and the origins of modern multiculturalism. *History of Education Quarterly*, *44*(1), 46–69.

8

Psychological Aspects of National Memory

An American Case

Jeremy K. Yamashiro

In this chapter, I review some recent empirical research examining how Americans represent their nation's past in relation to its future and how moral values can impact the form those representations take. Of particular interest is the temporal trajectories implicit in representations of the collective past and collective future, as well as psychological factors influencing which particular events (out of many possible candidates) people nominate for collective remembering. As will be shown, members of different ideological groups converge onto different types of representations, in terms of both content and internal structure. Such processes of convergence are of considerable interest in that shared representations help foster shared group identities and organize collective behavior (Rateau & Moliner, 2012; Roediger & Abel, 2015; Wertsch & Roediger, 2008). On the other hand, controversies over the proper way to represent the nation's past and its future have triggered conflict—at times violent—in a number of countries, including the United States (e.g., Lewis, 2017; Wertsch, 2008); such a psychological approach can also provide insight into these dramatic failures to converge.

Social Representations

In producing their scholarly representations of the past, professional historians must employ rigorous epistemological standards and discipline-specific techniques for finding and interpreting evidence. However, representations of the past may propagate beyond the boundaries of these disciplined professional communities into the larger public, transforming across many reconstructive acts of interpretation and communication (Halbwachs, 1992; Wertsch & Roediger, 2008). Members of a particular community will share many characteristic ways of attending to, organizing, and communicating about particular subjects, and these shared biases will guide convergence onto representations shared by members of a group. That is, because different sectors of the public may vary systematically in the cognitive schemata and social frames they bring to the task of remembering, they may converge onto different representations of the same source material (Moscovici, 1950/2008, 1988). The study of such social representations of history examines how members of particular groups configure historical knowledge and how representations are differentially distributed among members of a population (see Chapter 9, this volume). Importantly, these collective memories fulfill a function beyond simply recounting "the facts" in service of antiquarian interest. They tell the story of how the group came to be in its current state, often taking the form of societal *charters* that teach the normative values on which the society was founded (Hilton & Liu, 2011; Yamashiro et al., 2019).

Collective Temporal Thought

Social representations of history thus concern the collective memories that undergird social, rather than individual, identities (Hirst & Manier, 2008; Wertsch & Roediger, 2008). This approach expands psychology's traditional focus on individual identity, as in research on autobiographical memory's role in self-construction (e.g., Conway & Pleydell-Pearce, 2000), to incorporate memory for the social identity-relevant events in a group's past. Furthermore, in addition to collective memories, social representations of the nation may concern events imagined to occur in the national future, in the form of collective future thought (Szpunar & Szpunar, 2016). I refer to such representations of the collective past and future together under the umbrella term *collective temporal thought* (Yamashiro & Roediger, 2019; for the related but distinct concept of collective mental time travel, see Merck et al., 2016; Michaelian & Sutton, 2017).

Having laid out the general domain of interest—representations of the nation's past and future as they are imagined by members of that nation—I now present some recent empirical work on collective temporal thought. In doing so, I adopt what colleagues and I elsewhere have referred to as a "top-down" approach to the psychology of collective memory (Hirst et al., 2018). In a top-down approach, the researcher selects some collective memory of interest—perhaps flashbulb and event memories for the terrorist attacks of September 11, 2001 (9/11; Hirst et al., 2015), memory for the American presidents (DeSoto & Roediger, 2019), or collective memory for America's origins (Yamashiro et al., 2019)—and describes the psychological characteristics of those mental representations. These characteristics can then provide insights into the sociocognitive mechanisms by which community members converge onto collective memories (Hirst et al., 2018).

Implicit Trajectories of National Decline

Schematic Narrative Templates

Cognitive schemata are dynamic psychological scripts or frameworks of meaning into which newly encountered information can be fit and which structure acts of remembering (Bartlett, 1932). As schemata exert their influence during both perception and recall, representations in memory become progressively more "conventionalized" across multiple acts of recall or communication. Although the schema concept has come to be framed in the language of information processing (e.g., Shank & Abelson, 1977), it is important to remember that Bartlett emphasized both the culture-specific, socially shared nature of schemata and their intimate link with affective attitudes. Schemata allow people to structure information in memory such that it becomes meaningful. Part of what it means to belong to a culture is to structure information similarly to others in that culture, converging on similar ways of meaning-making. Bartlett's sociologist contemporary in France, Maurice Halbwachs (1992), articulated this social aspect of meaning-making even more explicitly. For Halbwachs, *social frames of memory* may refer both to the specific others with whom we regularly remember—who offer a long-term, dependable scaffold to remembering (Sterelny, 2010)—and to the shared ways of meaning-making people acquire during enculturation into a particular social group.

Wertsch's (2002) concept of *national narrative templates* applied the social frames of memory and shared schemata to national memory (see Chapter 22, this volume). National narrative templates are schematic tools for structuring recall of the national past in a way that is shared and culturally meaningful. For instance, four stereotyped episodes compose a ubiquitous Russian national narrative: Russia is peaceful and minding its own business,

Russia is viciously attacked without provocation from the outside, Russia nearly suffers total defeat, but after a long and selfless battle, Russia expels the foreign invaders and rebuilds itself. Russians may recruit this basic schematic plot while recounting a wide range of specific episodes from their nation's past, swapping out the details of the specific invaders—Tatars, Germans, Swedes, French, and Germans again. Importantly, historical representations that do not conform to this schematic structure for meaning-making may appear nonsensical or even immoral to those for whom this national narrative is an important cognitive tool for understanding the past. The recent controversy surrounding the 1619 Project presents an American case in point. The 1619 Project is a series of long-form articles on the legacy of slavery in the United States, published by *The New York Times* in 2019. These articles retell the story of much early American institution building as having been primarily motivated by the defense of slavery, emphasizing the central role the enslavement of Black Americans played in building the nation's foundations. Such a narrative centering brutal exploitation as foundational to America's nationhood is incongruous with the prototypical American narrative, which tends to frame America's history as a continuing struggle to overthrow oppression and progress toward greater freedom. Although some of the controversy surrounding the 1619 Project has concerned quibbles over specific historical details, the primary source of conflict is undoubtedly a clash between the images of the nation presented by the project and America's hegemonic national narrative templates (Serwer, 2019).

The first set of studies I report examined how schematic narrative templates might structure the way Americans represent their nation's past and future. Any attempt to measure the presence of schematic narrative templates faces the problem that a particular act of remembering reveals the template only indirectly; the template exists at a more abstract level than the uttered narrative. One solution to this challenge is to search for systematic biases in the way participants recount their collective memories, drawing from large samples of people hypothesized to share the schematic narrative template. That is, asymmetries and biases in collective temporal thought, particularly regarding cognitive accessibility and affective characteristics, could testify to the underlying presence of schematic narrative templates. If a schematic narrative template is a common cognitive tool that members of a group employ to help structure their collective remembering, then elements important to the template should be relatively more accessible than elements that are less central or which cannot be fit into the narrative.

Cognitive accessibility refers to how easily and fluently some item from memory comes to mind. Such accessibility reliably influences judgment, such as when making estimates of how likely some event is to occur (or has occurred, as the case may be) (e.g., Tversky & Kahneman, 1973). Relatedly, asymmetries in the accessibility of collective memories have been shown to shape judgments about historical influence (see Chapter 11, this volume; Yamashiro & Roediger, 2021). To speak more broadly, some ways of responding to the question, "What are the important events in your nation's history?" will feel obvious, intuitive, and fluent, whereas others will be quite unintuitive and difficult to make sense of, depending on their relation to the national narrative template.

Jeremiad Templates

One schematic template that those who address the American public frequently employ is the jeremiad (Bercovitch, 1978; Murphy, 2008). Jeremiads take their name from the biblical prophet Jeremiah, who addressed the ancient Kingdom of Israel, haranguing the people of the nation for betraying their covenant with God and falling into idolatry and wickedness. This corruption was to be punished by a Babylonian invasion and destruction of the First Temple. American religious and political rhetoric has frequently adopted this biblical metaphor, with the speaker contrasting a morally fallen present to a golden era of righteousness and prosperity in the past. Use of this schematic template appeared in religious and political rhetoric as early as the second generation of Puritan settlers in the Massachusetts Bay Colony and has continued into contemporary discourse concerning events as recent as the 9/11 terrorist attacks, Hurricane Katrina, and President Obama's address to the 2020 Democratic Convention about the increasingly imperiled state of American democracy (Bercovitch, 1978; Blight, 2020; Murphy, 2008). Schematically, four elements comprise a jeremiad's "ritual plotline" (Bercovitch, 1978): (1) a corrupted state of current affairs; (2) images of future disaster resulting from this corruption; (3) the contrast between the fallen present, threatening future, and a golden era in the past, often the era in which the nation's charter was established (Hilton & Liu, 2011); and (4) an exhortation to return to righteousness.

Because of its ubiquity in public discourse addressed to members of the nation, the jeremiad is a schematic template that Americans may be prone to using when they think about the state of their nation, past and future. If jeremiad templates structure Americans' representations of their nation, these representations should demonstrate a trajectory of decline, with foundational events represented positively and present and future events represented relatively negatively. That is, positive events should be more accessible than negative events when people think about their nation's foundation, and negative events should be more accessible when thinking about the nation's future.

Implicit Trajectories of Decline

Yamashiro and Roediger (2019) showed that this indeed was the case. They adapted a retrieval-fluency–based method commonly employed in clinical and autobiographical memory research to detect emotional biases in memory and future thought (MacLeod et al., 1993, 1997; MacLeod & Byrne, 1996). In nonclinical samples, autobiographical memories and personal future thought tend to show positivity biases; that is, people retrieve positive events more fluently than negative events, as measured by the number of events produced during the timed retrieval task. Some clinical samples (e.g., those suffering from depression) show negativity biases in both autobiographical memories and personal future thought. Shrikanth et al. (2018) extended this measure of bias in accessibility to the domain of collective future thought—important events people imagine will occur in their country's future. They demonstrated that both Americans and Canadians show negativity biases in representations of their national futures but not in their personal futures. Subsequent work has indicated that there may be a similar dissociation between personal and collective representations in memory (Shrikanth & Szpunar, 2021).

Yamashiro and Roediger (2019) were interested in the implicit national trajectory that emerged between representations of the national past and collective future—that is, in the change in size or direction of the emotional bias between the two periods. They asked 2,000 American participants to list events in collective memory that were important to America's foundation, as well as events from American history that all Americans ought to remember. Participants rated each event as positive or negative. Participants then engaged in a timed retrieval fluency task in which they were given 1 minute to list all of the events they were either excited about or worried about in their personal future and in their nation's future. For each of the three time frames—national origins, normative collective memory spanning all of American history, and collective future thought—emotional bias was measured as the proportion of events listed that were positive out of all events suggested. Regarding Americans' intertemporal representations of their nation, a clear trajectory of decline emerged, as shown in Figure 8.1.

An unbiased representation of a temporal period would have had a 50/50 split between positive and negative events. In their representations of national origins, participants showed a strong positivity bias, with 68% of events on average being rated as positive by the participant who provided them. This positivity bias reversed when participants imagined important events in their nation's future; here, negative events were more cognitively

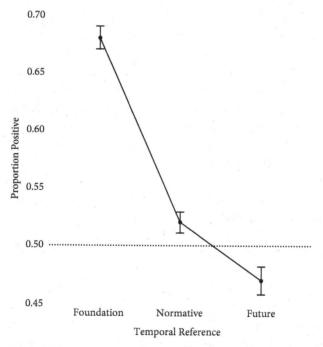

Figure 8.1 Proportion of events rated as positive in representations of America's foundational events (foundation), in the events all Americans should remember (normative), and in imagined events in the national future (future). Means above the dotted line represent positivity biases, and those below it represent negativity biases.
Reproduced from Yamashiro and Roediger (2019).

accessible, and only 47% of the events listed were positive. For the normative collective memories, participants showed a small positivity bias, with 52% of events listed being positive. This last finding suggests that on average, participants believed their fellow Americans ought to remember positive events from their shared history. Regarding the implicit trajectory from national origins into the collective future, judging by the relative cognitive accessibility of positive and negative events, participants showed an implicit trajectory of decline in their representations of the nation, from a strongly positive image of the nation's foundations to an imagined collective future characterized by worrisome events. This is precisely the trajectory that would be expected if a jeremiad narrative of a break with covenant and national decline structured Americans' collective temporal thought (and, to reverse the perspective, the sort of representation of the nation that would make a jeremiad intuitively justified).

Interestingly, this implicit trajectory of decline varied with participants' ideological endorsement of American exceptionalism (see Chapter 2, this volume). The implicit downward trajectory was much steeper in Americans who endorsed American exceptionalism, largely because their representations of national origins were much more positive than those who did not endorse American exceptionalism (Figure 8.2). Somewhat unexpectedly, representations of the national future were comparably negative among both endorsers and non-endorsers of American exceptionalism. Belief in American exceptionalism seemed to correlate with dramatic differences in collective memory but did not seem to exert any influence over imagination for the national future.

Finally, some emerging research suggests that valenced biases in collective temporal thought are sensitive to the specific probe used to elicit events and that different domains of collective temporal thought demonstrate different biases. The positivity biases in collective memory discussed previously, for instance, seem to segregate in specific domains of collective memory, and they certainly do not characterize all domains. The patterning of negativity and positivity biases in different domains of collective temporal thought is suggestive; systematic, parametric work in this area remains to be done. However, we might tentatively suggest that the positivity biases in collective memory reported previously for origin story events and normative collective memories seem to be limited to domains for which there is moralized pressure to maintain positive representations. For example, in contrast to origin stories and normative collective memories, when probed for "important"

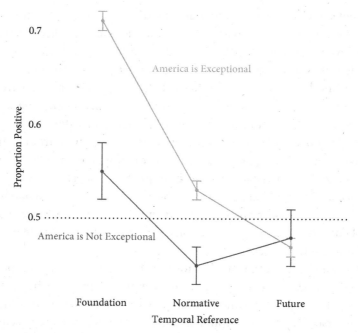

Figure 8.2 Proportion positive for the three temporal domains of reference (foundational events, normative events all Americans should remember, and imagined future events), split by endorsement versus non-endorsement of American exceptionalism. Whereas the negativity bias in collective future thought did not differ, participants who endorsed American exceptionalism showed considerably more strongly positive collective memories, particularly concerning the nation's origins.

or "influential" events in collective memory, people tend to show negativity biases (Liu et al., 2014; Shrikanth & Szpunar, 2021; Topçu & Hirst, 2020). Although negative events may thus predominate in collective memory, they very rarely appear in representations of national origins, and they form a vanishing minority of the events that Americans believe their co-nationals ought to remember (Yamashiro et al., 2019). It bears mentioning, however, that even when a negativity bias appears in collective memory for important events, the implicit trajectory between important events in collective memory and collective future thought remains one of decline, with the negativity bias increasing from collective memory to collective future thoughts. The collective future thought negativity bias, first demonstrated in American and Canadian samples by Shrikanth et al. (2018) and replicated in American

(Yamashiro & Roediger, 2019), British, and French samples (Ionescu et al., 2022), is quite robust, at least across many Western democracies.

Moralized Memory

A developing line of research has begun to probe the moral frames shaping collective memory more directly. Social identities are composed in no small measure of our obligations and commitments (Blustein, 2008), and memory for the events important to these social identities should respond to these values. Values influence which types of events from the national past are considered appropriate to remember, as well as the manner in which they should be remembered. The schematic narrative templates with which people structure their representations of the nation thus go beyond dispassionate plots about history, and indeed often go beyond mere meaning-making; they determine how the national story ought normatively to be told. Burke (1945) referred to this normative element to narratives as their *canonicality*, and White (1981) referred to it as their way of determining the "limits of legitimacy." This normative pressure shaping the way a narrative must be told undoubtedly helps explain why some national narratives can be so remarkably stable across time (Frisch, 1989; Wertsch, 2002). At one extreme, moralized national narratives may in some cases attain the status of "sacred values," which cannot be renegotiated, at least in exchange for material trade-offs (Atran et al., 2007; Ginges & Atran, 2013). Indeed, moralized narratives may undergird "common sense" to such an extent that any attempt at revision would appear to be not just nonsensical but also morally abhorrent.

Moral Intuitions

Whereas classical psychological models of morality focused on the internalization of abstract systems of moral rules (e.g., Kohlberg, 1969), contemporary approaches give much more emphasis to the role played by "fast thinking"—that is, by automatic, emotional, and often unconscious intuitions (Kahneman, 2011). Importantly for our purposes, moral judgments in this fast-thinking mode occur prior to any explicit deliberation, and not as a result of it (Greene & Haidt, 2002; Haidt, 2001). Because of this, their outputs feel intuitive and obvious, and they may guide decision-making without the need for conscious reflection. Critically, however, despite feeling intuitive and obvious, moral intuitions are not necessarily shared universally. For instance, contemporary moral psychology has mapped out systematic divergences in moral priorities across the American liberal–conservative spectrum (Graham et al., 2009). Whereas American liberals tend to strongly moralize issues of fairness and harm, downplaying the importance of authority, loyalty, and purity (sometimes called sanctity), American conservatives moralize issues in all five of these domains roughly equally. Loyalty, authority, and sanctity have been dubbed the *binding values*, in that they serve to moralize attachment to particular groups and traditions. The more universalistic morals of fairness and harm have been referred to as the *individuating values*, serving as they do to protect the rights of individuals to fair treatment and freedom from harm. However, in the context of moral frames shaping memory, I believe it is more appropriate to think of these as social justice values, given that social-identity-relevant memories pertain, by definition, to social groups rather than individuals and that concerns about past harms and injustices extend beyond the treatment of particular individuals.

Moral Frames of Collective Memory

Political divergences in the configuration of moral intuitions correspond with systematic differences in the justifications given when people select events that should be included in a normative national memory. In this study, Americans across the left–right political spectrum listed the top five events they believed all Americans should remember about their nation's past—that is, that should be included in a normative national memory. For each event, they rated a set of possible justifications for remembering the event provided. Participants rated the extent to which binding values motivated their selection (e.g., remembering this event promotes loyalty, it promotes love of country, it promotes respect for legitimate authority, or it promotes respect for tradition) and the extent to which social justice values motivated it (e.g., this event should be remembered because someone was treated unfairly, because someone was denied their rights, because justice demands it, or because someone was harmed).

The different configurations of moral intuitions across the political spectrum first mapped out by Graham et al. (2009) predicted corresponding differences in the moral justifications cited for including particular events in a normative American collective memory. Participants on the political right were more likely to select events because remembering them served to promote the goals of loyalty, respect for legitimate authority, and tradition. For them, national collective remembering should reflect binding values goals. For example, they were more likely to provide events such as the Declaration of Independence, the signing of the Constitution, and the 4th of July, which rated highly on the binding values justifications and relatively low on the social justice values justifications. Participants on the political left, on the other hand, were more likely to suggest that all Americans should remember events in which people had been harmed or injustice had occurred, such as anti-Black atrocities, the civil rights movement, slavery, anti-Native American atrocities, Japanese American internment, and the feminist movement. For these participants, collective remembering should be carried out in the service of social justice so as to mitigate harms and injustices committed in the past. Significantly, these events frequently had very low or negative binding values ratings. Self-identified political moderates seemed to show little systematic preference in the type of moral justifications they employed, although they did show a slight preference for binding values justifications. Americans across the left–right political spectrum thus showed systematically different configurations of moral intuitions, and these intuitions translated into profoundly different ideas about what a normative American collective memory should look like.

Because each event listed had two ratings, one for its mean binding values rating and one for its mean social justice rating, we can graph them in a two-dimensional moral values space. Doing so provides interesting insight into the extent to which moral values act to select for particular representations in specific groups of people. This phase space can be represented by two intersecting axes, one for binding values and one for social justice values, which together map out four quadrants (see Figure 8.3, which graphs only the most frequently mentioned events—bearing in mind that the following analyses included all of the events that participants listed). Each quadrant represents a particular combination of the two classes of moral intuitions. Starting in the upper right quadrant and moving counterclockwise, these are high binding–high social justice, low binding–high social justice, low binding–low social justice, and high binding–low social justice. Participants across the political spectrum were most likely to provide events that fell into the top right quadrant—that is, events scoring highly on both

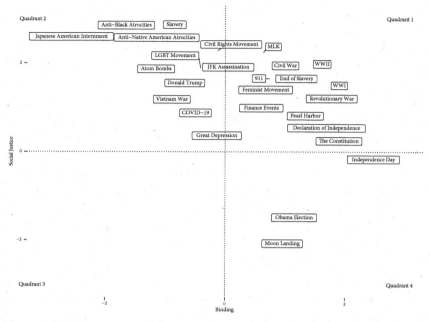

Figure 8.3 Events suggested for a normative American collective memory, graphed by their configuration of binding and social justice values. Along the horizontal axis, memory for events falling further right were more strongly justified by social justice values, whereas those further left were less justified by social justice values. Along the vertical axis, events further up were more strongly justified by binding values reasons, whereas those further down were less justified by binding values reasons.

binding values goals and social justice values goals (the most canonical such event being 9/11, but also including World War II, the end of slavery, and Pearl Harbor). Although both classes of moral intuitions independently motivated collective remembrance, events in which the two classes intersected were overrepresented. In contrast, the bottom left quadrant (low binding—low social justice) was essentially empty. Historical events that were not moralized on either dimension were almost never suggested. The upper left quadrant (low binding—high social justice) was predominantly used by participants on the left, whereas those on the right infrequently suggested events that did not promote binding values goals but did recall instances of historical harm or injustice. Interestingly, those on the left were only very slightly less likely than those on the right to use the mirror-image lower right quadrant (high binding—low social justice). This would seem to suggest that with regard to normative collective memory, binding values goals are somewhat less segregated by political affiliation than are social justice goals.

Conclusion

This chapter surveyed some recent work on psychological approaches to collective memory and collective future thought. This nascent literature suggests that socially shared frameworks of meaning, such as national narrative templates, and other cultural scripts for thinking about the nation's trajectory, such as the jeremiad, can structure collective temporal thought. Events in memory are rendered meaningful via their organization and integration into such symbolic systems. These systems are not for the most part idiosyncratic to individuals (especially concerning such shared objects of thought as the nation) but, rather, are shared by members of a culture. From this perspective, becoming enculturated entails acquiring the habitual tools of thought required for participation in a particular society. Importantly, the psychological impact of such shared schematic structures extends beyond simply providing scripts for telling historical narratives. In addition to their information-structuring function, shared schematic narratives specify which affective attitudes are appropriate to hold in relation to particular junctures in the schema. Schematic representation of the nation's origins, for instance, requires that positive and emulation-worthy events be selected. This positivity bias does not apply to all collective memories—quite the contrary—but it is obligatory for those particular domains of collective memory in which positive representation is moralized. Other aspects of collective memory, it seems, may contain many negative representations, but not this sacralized domain.

The robust positivity bias for representations of national origins poses an important counterpoint to representations of the national future. Far from predicting uniform positivity biases in representations of the nation across temporal domains, strong positivity biases in memory for origins has tended to be associated with negativity biases in collective future thought. This reversal of emotional bias, puzzling on first encounter, makes sense when one considers that public rhetoric frequently contrasts foundational events and the ideals they represent with a present that falls far short of those charter ideals, and further emphasizes looming threats in the collective future. The schema of national decline is itself often employed as a moralized cudgel to goad listeners to return to a state of grace (as defined by the speaker).

Moralizing the schematic templates undergirding collective temporal thought becomes particularly fraught when the values guiding collective remembering diverge between different subgroups. This potential point of conflict was emphasized in the study discussed previously in which moral justifications for collective remembering diverged across the American left–right political spectrum. Recognizing different landscapes of moral intuitions may contribute to our understanding of the current conflicts over public symbols of collective memory, including the removal or destruction of Confederate statues in the United States (and other figures associated with colonial brutalities in other areas of the world), the renaming of schools and military bases, perennial struggles over history textbooks, ethnic studies programs, and many other instances.

The example of the 1619 Project touches directly on this clash of values concerning what remembering the past is *for*. Nikole Hannah-Jones, the 1619 Project's creator, explicitly aimed to reframe America's origin story, placing the injustices and harms inflicted upon Black Americans at the center of America's foundation. Here, the objective is clear: Collective remembering serves the ends of advancing justice in the present by recalling historical injustices and harms. The backlash against the 1619 Project is equally telling. If moral duty requires cultivating respect, loyalty, and love for the nation, remembering events that might complicate these feelings is a violation of the duty underlying collective memory. Under these moral priorities, telling an origin story in which the nation is founded upon brutal exploitation is perceived as profoundly corrosive. Although some of the controversy over the 1619 Project has concerned specific details of the reports, the feelings aroused and rhetorical fireworks surrounding the project suggest that there is more at stake than a disinterested desire to set the historical record straight. As the empirical work cited in this chapter indicates, Americans across the political spectrum experience systematically different intuitions about the moral duties surrounding collective remembering. Whereas those on the left strongly moralize memory for historical injustices and harms, those on the right are more likely to moralize memory that supports respect for legitimate authority and tradition, love of country, and loyalty. The 1619 Project falls right into the moral space where these two poles exert incompatible demands on memory.

It is important to reiterate, however, that although moral intuitions do differ across political affiliations, and some representations such as those presented in the 1619 Project may draw attention to points of incommensurability, in general these differences in values are differences of degree, and not of kind. People across the political spectrum undoubtedly do recognize the full range of moral intuitions, even if they weight them differently. Illustrating this point was the fact that events moralized on both binding value and social justice value dimensions were unquestionably the most frequently selected for collective remembering. That is, the two dimensions are not mutually exclusive, and there is a broad range of collective memories that are endorsed regardless of political orientation. Although obviously not a panacea regarding the points of conflict, recognizing that perceived duties concerning collective remembering can differ in systematic ways may help inform a more sophisticated and nuanced public dialogue as Americans come to terms with their shared past.

In examining systematic biases in representations of the nation, we can detect where these representations converge and begin to describe the social and cognitive factors that make such convergence possible. A program concerning social representations of national memory encourages us to ask precise questions about how factors such as schematic narratives, cognitive accessibility, and moral frames can shape the sorts of representations that are likely to emerge in a particular population of individuals sharing these factors of attraction. It is hoped that such a project can bring insight and understanding into the fraught dialogue over how Americans should represent their nation's past and its future.

References

Atran, S., Axelrod, R., & Davis, R. (2007). Sacred barriers to conflict resolution. *Science, 317*, 1039–1040.

Bartlett, F. C. (1932). *Remembering: A study in experimental and social psychology.* Cambridge University Press.

Bercovitch, S. (1978). *The American jeremiad.* University of Wisconsin Press.

Blight, D. W. (2020, August 21). Barack Obama delivers a jeremiad. *The New York Times.* https://www.nytimes.com/2020/08/21/opinion/obama-convention-2020-speech.html

Blustein, J. (2008). *The moral demands of memory.* Cambridge University Press.

Burke, K. (1945). *A grammar of motives.* Prentice Hall.

Conway, M. A., & Pleydell-Pearce, C. W. (2000). The construction of autobiographical memories in the self-memory system. *Psychological Review, 107*(2), 261–288.

DeSoto, K. A., & Roediger, H. L., III. (2019). Remembering the presidents. *Current Directions in Psychological Science, 28*(2), 138–144.

Frisch, M. (1989). American history and the structures of collective memory: A modest exercise in empirical iconography. *Journal of American History, 75*(4), 1130–1155.

Ginges, J., & Atran, S. (2013). Sacred values and cultural conflict. In M. J. Gelfland, C. Y. Chiu, & Y. Y. Hong (Eds.), *Advances in culture and psychology* (pp. 273–301). Oxford University Press.

Graham, J., Haidt, J., & Nosek, B. A. (2009). Liberals and conservatives rely on different sets of moral foundations. *Journal of Personality and Social Psychology, 96*(5), 1029–1046.

Greene, J., & Haidt, J. (2002). How (and where) does moral judgment work? *Trends in Cognitive Sciences, 6*(12), 517–523.

Haidt, J. (2001). The emotional dog and its rational tail: A social intuitionist approach to moral judgment. *Psychological Review, 108*(4), 814–834.

Halbwachs, M. (1992). *On collective memory* (L. A. Coser, Trans.). University of Chicago Press.

Hilton, D. J., & Liu, J. H. (2011). Culture and intergroup relations: The role of social representations of history. In R. M. Sorrentino & S. Yamaguchi (Eds.), *Handbook of motivation and cognition across cultures* (pp. 343–368). Academic Press.

Hirst, W., & Manier, D. (2008). Towards a psychology of collective memory. *Memory, 16*(3), 183–200.

Hirst, W., Phelps, E., Meksin, R., et al. (2015). A ten-year follow-up of a study of memory for the attack of September 11, 2001: Flashbulb memories and memories for flashbulb events. *Journal of Experimental Psychology: General, 144*(3), 604–623.

Hirst, W., Yamashiro, J., & Coman, A. (2018). Collective memory from a psychological perspective. *Trends in Cognitive Sciences, 22*(5), 438–451.

Ionescu, O., Tavani, J. L., & Collange, J. (2022). Perceived Societal Anomie and the Implicit Trajectory of National Decline: Replicating and extending Yamashiro & Roediger (2019) within a French sample. *Memory Studies,* in press.

Kahneman, D. (2011). *Thinking, fast and slow.* Farrar, Straus, & Giroux.

Kohlberg, L. (1969). Stage and sequence: The cognitive–developmental approach to socialization. In D. A. Goslin (Ed.), *Handbook of socialization theory and research* (pp. 347–480). Rand McNally.

Lewis, N. (2017, August 17). Violence again spurs cities to remove Confederate monuments, but many find hurdles to doing so. *The Washington Post.* https://www.washingtonpost.com/news/the-fix/wp/2017/08/17/violence-again-spurs-cities-to-remove-confederate-monuments-but-many-find-hurdles-to-doing-so

Liu, J. H., Hilton, D., Huang, L. L., et al. (2014). Social representations of events and people in world history across 12 cultures. *Journal of Cross-Cultural Psychology, 36*(2), 1–21.

MacLeod, A. K., & Byrne, A. (1996). Anxiety, depression, and the anticipation of future positive and negative experiences. *Journal of Abnormal Psychology, 105,* 286–289.

MacLeod, A. K., Rose, G. S., & Williams, J. M. G. (1993). Components of hopelessness about the future in parasuicide. *Cognitive Therapy and Research, 17,* 441–455.

MacLeod, A. K., Tata, P., Kentish, J., & Jacobsen, H. (1997). Retrospective and prospective cognitions in anxiety and depression. *Cognition and Emotion, 11,* 467–479.

Merck, C., Topçu, M. N., & Hirst, W. (2016). Collective mental time travel: Creating a shared future through our shared past. *Memory Studies, 9*(3), 284–294.

Michaelian, K., & Sutton, J. (2017). Collective mental time travel: Remembering the past and imagining the future together. *Synthese, 196,* 4933–4960.

Moscovici, S. (1988). Notes towards a description of social representations. *European Journal of Social Psychology, 18,* 211–250.
Moscovici, S. (2008). *Psychoanalysis: Its image and its public.* Polity Press. (Original work published 1950)
Murphy, A. R. (2008). *Prodigal nation: Moral decline and divine punishment from New England to 9/11.* Oxford University Press.
Rateau, P., & Moliner, P. (2012). Social representation theory. In P. A. M. Van Lange, A. W. Kruglanski, & E. T. Higgins (Eds.), *Handbook of theories of social psychology, Volume 2* (pp. 477–494). Sage.
Roediger, H. L., III, & Abel, M. (2015). Collective memory: A new arena of cognitive study. *Trends in Cognitive Science, 19*(7), 359–361.
Serwer, A. (2019, December). The fight over the 1619 Project is not about facts. *The Atlantic.* https://www.theatlantic.com/ideas/archive/2019/12/historians-clash-1619-project/604093
Shank, R. C., & Abelson, R. P. (1977). *Scripts, plans, goals and understanding: An inquiry into human knowledge structures.* Erlbaum.
Shrikanth, S., & Szpunar, K. K. (2021). The good old days and the bad old days: Evidence for a valence-based dissociation between personal and public memory. *Memory, 29*(2), 180–192.
Shrikanth, S., Szpunar, P. M., & Szpunar, K. K. (2018). Staying positive in a dystopian future: A novel dissociation between personal and collective cognition. *Journal of Experimental Psychology: General, 147*(8), 1200–1210.
Sterelny, K. (2010). Minds: Extended or scaffolded? *Phenomenology and the Cognitive Sciences, 9,* 465–481.
Szpunar, P. M., & Szpunar, K. K. (2016). Collective future thought: Concept, function, and implications for collective memory studies. *Memory Studies, 9*(4), 376–389.
Topçu, M., & Hirst, W. (2020). Remembering a nation's past to imagine its future: The role of event specificity, phenomenology, valence, and perceived agency. *Journal of Experimental Psychology: Learning, Memory, and Cognition, 46*(3), 563–579.
Tversky, A., & Kahneman, D. (1973). Availability: A heuristic for judging frequency and probability. *Cognitive Psychology, 5,* 207–232.
Wertsch, J. V. (2002). *Voices of collective remembering.* Cambridge University Press.
Wertsch, J. V. (2008). Collective memory and narrative templates. *Social Research, 75*(1), 133–156.
Wertsch, J. V., & Roediger, H. L., III. (2008). Collective memory: Conceptual foundations and theoretical approaches. *Memory, 16*(3), 318–326.
White, H. (1981). The value of narrativity in the representation of reality. In W. J. T. Mitchell (Ed.), *On narrative* (pp. 5–27). University of Chicago Press.
Yamashiro, J., & Roediger, H. L., III. (2019). How we have fallen: Implicit trajectories in collective temporal thought. *Memory, 27*(8), 1158–1166.
Yamashiro, J., & Roediger, H. L., III. (2021). Biased collective memories and historical overclaiming: An availability heuristic account. *Memory & Cognition, 49*(2), 311–322.
Yamashiro, J., Van Engen, A., & Roediger, H. L., III. (2019, July). American origins: Political and religious divides in U.S. collective memory. *Memory Studies, 15*(1).

SECTION III
COMPARATIVE STUDIES OF NATIONAL MEMORY AND POPULISM FROM AROUND THE WORLD

The chapters in this section use research methods that differ from many of those elsewhere in this volume and reflect the effort to study national memory as an interdisciplinary issue. Instead of historical, ethnographic, or textual analysis, the authors in this section use surveys and questionnaires that yield quantitative data. In contrast to David Cunningham's focused analysis of a monument in Mississippi, for example, these chapters provide a view from 30,000 feet of national memory, and this makes it possible to compare the memory projects of large groups from throughout the world.

The range of methods used in this volume yield different sorts of findings. It can sometimes be tempting for advocates of a particular method to privilege their perspective at the expense of others, but the complexities of national memory call for something broader than any notion that there is a single road to truth. In our view, the goal should be to examine complementary findings generated by different methods to examine insights not available from any method used in isolation. The task is to connect the dots into a more comprehensive picture of national memory.

The studies included in this section go well beyond just documenting differences between various communities' collective memories. Instead, the authors use multiple points of evidence to outline richer pictures of the form such memories take and some of the forces at work that produce them. In Chapter 9, for example, Liu et al. formulate issues in terms of a distinction between "living historical memory" and "historical charters." The former has parallels with the notions of "communicative" memory outlined by Assmann and allow Liu et al. to interpret living historical memories for events such as the terrorist attacks on September 11, 2001 (9/11). Historical charters, in contrast, have to do with the long-term past of a nation and provide a background against which living historical memory gets its meaning and is understood.

Liu et al. have conducted surveys in nearly 40 nations throughout the world to identify various historical charters, which provide a basis for characterizing national communities' general "emotional climate." Among other things, they report the unexpected finding of lower levels of positive emotional climate in wealthier nations such as the United States than in developing countries. This is consistent with the picture Yamashiro (see Chapter 8, this volume) finds of declining historical trajectory in the United States. Taking 9/11 as an example of an event in living historical memory in the United States, Liu et al. suggest why this pattern might exist in noting that the "'War on Terror' used by the Bush administration in justifying two subsequent wars in the Middle East ... served to create an enduring emotional climate of fear and anxiety." In short, the massive data Liu et al. describe from surveys in dozens of countries point to a dynamic interaction between different sorts of remembering that underpin efforts to formulate detailed analyses of memory projects in any particular case.

In Chapter 10, Abel, Umanath, and Barzykowski report on survey research about an event that looms large in the memory of many national communities from around the world: World War II. They report some striking similarities in the responses of more than 1,500 respondents from the 12 nations in which they collected data, raising questions about forces such as the power of Hollywood in shaping national memory worldwide. Their speculation on this point raises issues that beg for further study. Based on their survey questions about the most important events of the war, they also found some points of variation, especially with regard to events that were of particular importance to one's own nation. For example, the Battle of Britain was included by more than half the respondents in the United Kingdom as an important event, but it did not rank high for any of the other 11 groups of respondents.

What is most striking in these data is the extent to which Russia differed from all other national groups in terms of the detail of accurate knowledge about events in World War II and in terms of crucial events that were not listed by any other group as being particularly important. Russia's outsized losses and its massive contribution to the Allied victory over Germany may help make sense of this (see Chapter 11, this volume). But what is more interesting is the extent to which these results reflect deep-seated mental habits that are part of Russia's national memory (see Chapter 22, this volume). These constitute a bottom-up force that is often not fully appreciated by non-Russian observers.

The striking finding that Abel et al. report concerning the difference between Russia and 11 other countries provides an opportunity for collaboration with other researchers and methods. In Chapter 11, Roediger, Putnam, and Yamashiro take up this challenge by introducing another conceptual perspective having to do with collective narcissism and the overclaiming of responsibility. In this case, the focus is on ideas and methods from social psychology about the tendency to overclaim the contribution one makes to group activities. Studies show, for example, that when asked about their contribution to household chores such as taking out the trash, both members of a married couple estimate they did more than 50% of the work. As Roediger et al. note, such tendencies are even more pronounced for larger groups, and indeed they found that people claimed extremely high levels of responsibility for their own national groups. When asked to explicitly take into consideration the contributions of other groups, this narcissistic tendency was reduced somewhat, but not eliminated.

Expanding on this approach in their study of national communities, Roediger et al. found that virtually every group in the 12-nation sample used in Abel et al.'s study had inflated estimates of their contribution to World War II. This finding turns out to be particularly interesting—and loaded—when it comes to how national groups view Russia's contribution to the victory over Germany in World War II. For example, respondents from all 10 countries other than the United States estimated America's contribution to the war effort to be 27%, which exceeded the 20% figure for the Soviet Union when assessed in a similar way—despite the fact that the USSR suffered many times the number of deaths of the United States and inflicted more than 85% of the losses that Germany suffered. In short, the estimates that members of a collective can give of their own group's contribution to historical events seem to reflect much more than objective historical evidence.

By introducing the notion of collective narcissism into the discussion, Roediger et al. raise crucial issues of identity. Umanath and Abel pursue these issues in their discussion of national pride and shame in Chapter 12. They draw from ideas and methods about individual pride and shame found in the research literature in psychology, which provides another illustration of how this discipline can contribute to the study of national memory. For example, they asked American and German undergraduate students to list events in their country's past that they were proud or ashamed of. Perhaps their most surprising finding is that Americans in particular placed greater emphasis on the shameful events from their nation's past than events in which they take pride.

In contrast to standard assumptions that national communities focus on glorious chapters from their past at the expense of shameful episodes, Umanath and Abel paint another picture. Perhaps this is part of the larger issue of viewing America's trajectory as being on a downward path as suggested by Liu et al. in Chapter 9 or by Yamashiro in Chapter 8. Or perhaps it has to do with the fact that the data on which these studies were based were collected in the Donald Trump era of populism, something that appears to be consistent with the assessment of America's national saga outline by Talbott in Chapter 1.

From the perspective of what methods make sense to include in the study of national memory, the use of survey and questionnaire data as reported in the chapters in this section points again to the importance of employing a big tent approach. The data reported unearth several unexpected findings and raise a host of fascinating questions. These are findings that need to be checked and explored further in their own right, but perhaps most important is the implication that scholars using other methods from other disciplines need to join into a larger discussion of how all these pieces fit into a larger puzzle.

9
Social Representations of History, Living Historical Memory, and Historical Charters

Refining Collective Memory Toward a Theory of Political Culture Change

James H. Liu, Sarah Y. Choi, Robert Jiqi Zhang, Roosevelt Vilar, and Moh. Abdul Hakim

Collective memory is an important concept with academic lineage (Olick et al., 2011) in several disciplines. Definitions of this concept can be varied or even vague. Psychology's engagement with this concept has been more recent than that of sociology because the father of this concept was Maurice Halbwachs (1925/1992), a student of Durkheim who refused to acknowledge the validity of individual/biological memory. According to Halbwachs (1925/1992), individual memory is entirely determined by groups in society. Given such a contentious beginning, this concept re-entered the mainstream of psychology much later, through Wertsch's (2002) now classic *Voices of Collective Remembering* and through various authors' work on social representations of history (for reviews, see Hilton & Liu, 2008; Liu & Páez, 2019). A key toward gaining acceptance of the representational view has been the functional value of such an approach in understanding intergroup conflict (Liu & Hilton, 2005).

This chapter attempts to articulate a better understanding of, and terminology for, different aspects of collective memory and show how they are important and useful in different ways. We begin with a distinction made by Assmann (2013) and Assmann and Czaplicka (1995) between communicative and cultural memories. Communicative memories are alive in the hearts, minds, and voices of living people, whereas cultural memories are ritual enactments of history relevant to group identity, mediated institutionally,

James H. Liu, Sarah Y. Choi, Robert Jiqi Zhang, Roosevelt Vilar, and Moh. Abdul Hakim, *Social Representations of History, Living Historical Memory, and Historical Charters* In: *National Memories*. Edited by: Henry L. Roediger and James V. Wertsch, Oxford University Press. © Oxford University Press 2022. DOI: 10.1093/oso/9780197568675.003.0009

through commemorations, statues, religious observances, or even family lineages (e.g., those of royalty). Previous research on social representations of history (SRH) did not distinguish between these two (e.g., see Liu et al., 2009), but we shall endeavor to show why this distinction may be important here. This chapter provides an analysis of different aspects of collective remembering and outlines dynamics between communicative and cultural memories that are theorized to either maintain a country's political culture or lead to collective forgetting and culture change.

Using Assmann's formulation as a starting point, we propose that there are two distinctive aspects of collective remembering crucial to making national political culture: living historical memories and historical charters. One can be thought of as a more peripheral and changing system embedded in communicative memories, and the other is more of an enduring central core of cultural memories (Abric, 1993; Assmann, 2013), but there is also dynamic movement between the two. We interrogate how the terrorist attacks of September 11, 2001 (9/11), reactions to it, and other acts of Islamist terrorism in the Western world have come to dominate the living historical memories of English-speaking countries, producing a climate of fear and anxiety. Together with widespread use of social media, we argue that this has opened the door for populist forms of culture change that depart from America's historical charter, as established by foundational historical events (for the importance of 9/11, see Chapter 8, this volume).

Social Representations of History

More than two decades of research have established solid evidence of typical characteristics of SRH in terms of national histories and world history (for reviews, see Hilton & Liu, 2017; Liu & Páez, 2019). This research typically reports results of surveys from individuals, reported as an aggregate at the country level, often including results of statistical analyses involving comparisons between subgroups (ethnic, linguistic, and regional). Research also often involves comparisons between countries, in keeping with the functional approach to intergroup relations (Liu & Hilton, 2005).

Very briefly, when asked to free recall events and figures important to the history of their nation, collective remembering typically takes a U-shaped curve, where foundational events in the birth of the nation are recalled in conjunction with recent events salient in public affairs. When asked the same questions about world history, free recall takes a J-shaped curve, with strong recency effects, and content is largely focused on politics and war. Free recall of warfare (outside of World War II, which is commonly remembered, and local wars of independence) is less dominant in national histories. But political issues are ever-present.

To make sense of these patterns, Liu and László (2007) argued that social representations of history could be thought of as narratives, where the validity of the narrative hinges on emotional relevance and meaning, communicated via properties as "credibility, authenticity, relevance, and coherence, which in turn are dependent on the proper use of narrative features—time, plot, characters, perspective, narrative intentions, and evaluation" (p. 87). They proposed that ordinary people think of history as a story of the making of an in-group, through processes of politics and war. This might be because, according to historian Charles Tilly (1975), war produced the nation-state and nation-states made war. In addition, in terms of psychology, conflict appears especially narratable because it is central for the plot structure of that most basic of narratives, the folk story (Propp, 1968; see Chapter 22, this volume).

This theorizing involves inferences about deeper patterns of meaning underlying diverse lists of historical events and figures, together with sophisticated analyses of these (Liu & Sibley, 2015). But it may have overestimated the extent to which ordinary people care about, or know about, history. For instance, populist political figures from Donald Trump to Hindu nationalist leaders (Liu & Khan, 2014) have mobilized history to generate support for their political agendas. But empirical research by Taylor et al. (2017) showed little agreement on "when America was great": Less than 40% of their samples nominated consensually important national years for the United States, such as 1776 or 1945. Most people nominated years when they were young themselves. This suggests that Trump's slogan "Make America Great Again" functioned as a symbolic rallying call that evoked feeling more than cognition, and likely did *not* mobilize pre-existing narratives from American history. Similarly, Liu et al. (2014) found that invoking the most important event in New Zealand (and in Taiwan) history did *not* function to mobilize identity and change attitudes in line with the moral implications of foundational historical events.

These and other results led us to question to what extent historical events and figures regularly function as symbolic resources within coherent narratives that ordinary people carry with them in their communities. Historians (Hobsbawm & Ranger, 1983), archaeologists (Kohl & Fawcett, 1995), sociologists (Olick & Robbins, 1998), and education theorists (Carretero et al., 2017) have all argued with theory and evidence that political and administrative elites engage in nation-building through controlling historical representations. There is, however, less evidence on what Kansteiner (2002) describes as the reception side of these attempts to control history. We do not know how individuals receive attempts to construct history as a warrant of legitimacy for the state.

To probe this possible disjuncture, we launched an investigation at the limits of this thesis that history acts as a warrant of legitimacy for the state, by investigating communicative memories across cultures and by clarifying terminology in this area. Communicative memories include childhood autobiographical memories (Wang, 2008), intergenerational family memories (memories in the lives of older members of an intergenerational family, communicated to younger generations; Stone et al., 2014), and lived memories (historical events that have occurred in the person's lifetime; Hirst & Manier, 2002). These are somewhat different phenomena that can be distinguished by level of personal (vs. impersonal) experience. For our purpose, which is to examine the changing character of national political cultures, we focused on aspects of communicative memory that are broadly communicative (encompassing intergenerational experiences and talk) and of societal importance (including impersonal means of communication such as mass media).

Living Historical Memories

According to Liu et al. (2021), living historical memories (LHM) are defined as communicative memories important to society that encompass historical memories unfolding in one's life and in the lifetimes of older persons one knows or has known. LHM are thus conceptualized as being alive in people's hearts and minds, even if they do not reflect firsthand experiences. They are formed by interpersonal and mass communications. But this definition excludes communicative memories that are purely personal, familial, or autobiographical because these are typically not political or implicated in political culture change.

In contrast to top-down social science research suggesting positive links between collective memory and individual-level attitudes of support for the state and groups benefiting from its status quo, psychological research paints a more complicated picture. LHM can give greater opportunity for perceiving inconsistencies in the state's legitimizing ideologies. Kus et al. (2013) showed that in Estonia, LHM facilitated minority ethnic Russians making historical social comparisons (dating back to the Soviet era, when they were the dominant group) that *challenged* the current ideology of the Estonian state. Now dominant ethnic Estonians, and formerly dominant ethnic Russians, enlisted different elements and interpretations of history to bolster their own in-group favoring perceptions of (in)justice and fairness, rather than both endorsing the same view of the past.

LHM can facilitate deeper understanding of social and political arrangements by revealing long-term cause-and-effect relationships that enhance critical reflections on the legitimacy of present-day practices (Watts et al., 2011). Knowledge of history can support critical consciousness, where people achieve greater critical awareness and greater ability to criticize their own country's political and economic system through complex and nuanced knowledge of historical factors that have shaped lives (Freire, 1973; Prilleltensky & Gonick, 1996). For example, greater knowledge of the historical impacts of slavery in the United States or colonization in New Zealand might facilitate more favorable attitudes toward affirmative action for disadvantaged groups (Sibley et al., 2009) through critical consciousness that actions by officials in these countries are not as meritocratic as they would like citizens to believe. This "critical consciousness hypothesis" suggests that LHM could produce *lower* legitimization of political systems and social hierarchies, and lower national identification, rather than the higher levels that the more mainstream "history provides a warrant of legitimacy" hypothesis implies.

An Empirical Study of Counts of Living Historical Memories

To test the previously discussed competing perspectives, Liu et al. (2021) collected data online (stratified for age, sex, and income; $N > 22,000$) from 40 countries throughout the world. The measure of LHM asked participants to free recall "3 historic events that have occurred during the lifetime of people you know (or have known) that have had the *greatest impact on your country*" and rate how positive or negative they considered the events to be. Liu et al. thus obtained measures of the quantity (0–3 free recalls), quality (description of the event), and evaluation (scale of 1–7 from very negative to very positive) of LHM. Only responses coded as historical were included in the analyses reported.

LHM was associated with being older, better educated, more engaged with news media, and lower self-reported socioeconomic status. But these correlations were weak and variable across cultures. Surprisingly, the most consistent correlation of LHM was not with higher education or with paying attention to the news; rather, the number of historical events in living memory a person was able to remember had a negative association ($r = -.20$) with Social Dominance Orientation (SDO), a measure of desire/support for a group-based dominance hierarchy (Pratto et al., 2013). People who had more LHM tended to disagree with items on the SDO scale such as "Superior groups should dominate inferior groups" and to agree with statements such as "Group equality should be our ideal." This relationship was consistent across cultures.

All other correlates of LHM were more variable across cultures. LHM had a significant negative association with system justification ($r = -.128$; Kay & Jost, 2003), meaning that people who could recall more historical memories also tended to disagree with statements such as "Everyone in my country has a fair shot at wealth and happiness." Importantly, the relationship between LHM and system justification was moderated by country-level Human Development Index (HDI; United Nations Development Programme, 2019) so that in more developed countries, LHM had *less* of a negative effect on system justification. HDI is a composite index based on three country-level indicators: life expectancy, education, and per capita income. LHM was thus more closely associated with the *rejection* of system-justifying beliefs in developing countries. Multilevel analyses showed that HDI had a stronger relationship with system justification in countries in which the institutional systems work better (i.e., in high HDI countries; see Vargas-Salfate et al., 2018). This is an outcome in accord with rational thinking because it makes sense for historical memory to be associated with system justification in countries in which the institutions have had more time to develop greater efficiency.

In fact, the correlation of LHM counts with lower levels of ideological support for group dominance and system justification was larger and more consistent across cultures[1] than its association with national identity. Although being able to recall more historical memories was positively associated ($r = .07$) with the statement "I identify with my nationality" in most countries, this relationship was statistically significant in only half of these. In other words, this study suggests that LHM counts are associated with critical consciousness more than with the state's top-down attempts to produce a "suitable history" to bolster its own legitimacy.

In summary, results supported the critical consciousness perspective on two of the three indicators of support for state legitimacy and the status quo. In marked contrast to the expectations of the literature on collective remembering, a measure of LHM counts was associated with a rejection of system justification and the status quo this implies, especially in developing countries. Across cultures, LHM was associated with a rejection of SDO, the idea that some groups are better than others. This form of group-based inequality is often seen in developing countries that are burdened with a colonial legacy. These surprising results, where history as received by individuals is a source of critical consciousness rather than a warrant of legitimacy for the state, are discussed in detail later.

Content Analysis of Living Historical Memories Using Latent Class Analysis

Given the complexity of collective memory, and even smaller facets of collective memory such as LHM, we would be foolish to suggest that the LHM counts reported by Liu et al. (2021) exhaust important aspects of LHM and its relationship to political culture. In fact, one of the first analyses we did was a latent class analysis (LCA) using LHM content from the United States. LCA is intended to capture something like a coherent narrative in the free recall patterns offered by participants. It examines nominations of events [9/11, World War II, the Vietnam War, the assassination of John F. Kennedy (JFK), etc.] and tries to find statistically consistent patterns of which specific items are free recalled together. So it is more concrete than the analyses reported previously, which simply counted how many historical memories of significant events people were able to recall. But because the results were not compelling, they never made it into either of the two

---

[1] Statistically significant in 38 of 40 countries.

Table 9.1 Most Frequently Nominated History Events in Living Historical Memory in the United States[a]

	Event	% of Participants
1	9/11	26.5
2	Trump presidency	12.5
3	Obama presidency	10.0
4	World War II	5.7
5	JFK assassination	5.0
6	Vietnam War	4.5
7	Iraq War	3.4
8	School shootings	3.0

[a] A total of 324 participants nominated at least one historical event.
JFK, John F. Kennedy.

journal articles on our LHM data written since then. Suffice it to say that the overwhelming preponderance of 9/11 in our American sample's LHM precluded clusters of items that appeared to reflect coherent narratives (Table 9.1).

9/11 was by far the most free-recalled event in LHM for Americans, nominated four times more often than World War II. It appeared in three of the four latent classes, which were uncomfortable conglomerates (e.g., 9/11 and the civil rights era) rather than compelling narratives.

Online participants did not appear to be free-recalling historical events according to a meaningful narrative, as hypothesized by Liu and László (2007), or as a schematic narrative template, as theorized by Wertsch (2002; see also Chapter 22, this volume). Rather, for three of the four classes identified by LCA, participants likely free recalled the first thing that came to mind (9/11) and went from there in an idiosyncratic manner. The fourth class, "Three meaningful wars" (anchored by World War II), did not yield useful correlates compared to the three 9/11-dominated latent classes. We also tried LCA on the most commonly free-recalled events in China, with similar results. Neither Americans nor Chinese in these samples automatically appeared to recall historical events according to an obviously meaningful narrative.

Living Historical Memories Evaluation as a Reflection of Emotional Climate in Societies at Different Stages of National Development

Choi et al. (2021) investigated the positivity or negativity of evaluations of the free-recalled events as an aspect of the LHM indicator of the emotional climate of society. *Emotional climate* is defined as the dominant emotions experienced or perceived by members of a society in response to societally shared events (De Rivera, 1992).

LHM is a property of communication, and exposure to communication about collective violence reinforces an emotional climate of fear (De Rivera & Páez, 2007) and threat that motivates prejudice against immigrants (Stephan et al., 2005). In a review of American public opinion, Woods (2011) reported that perceived threat from a terrorist attack had not declined even 6 years after the 9/11 attack (e.g., 50% or more were worried about being personally harmed). This suggests that it is not just the impact of 9/11 but also the actions taken after that traumatic event, such as terrorist attacks in other areas of the Western world and the loud rhetoric of the "War on Terror" used by the Bush administration in justifying two subsequent wars in the Middle East (Powell, 2011), that served to create an enduring emotional climate of fear and anxiety. Because 9/11 has become an enduring refrain in the political communications of the body politic, it has become central in American LHM today.

Not just in the United States but also across other English-speaking countries, and in other Western countries high on HDI, terrorism has become integral to LHM (Choi et al., 2021). As shown in Figure 9.1, there is an almost linear trend of greater negativity among salient events in countries as one moves from left to right; this accords with a shift from mainly developing societies lower on HDI to developed societies higher on HDI (with a few notable exceptions, such as Venezuela, which had been experiencing years of hyperinflation, and Serbia, which was bombed into submission by NATO in the 1990s).

It is not easy to understand why societies such as China, Malaysia, South Africa, India, and Portugal should be more sanguine about their recent (and often troubled) histories than Sweden, the Netherlands, Italy, Greece, and Japan. Category-based coding of the events in LHM offers an explanation.

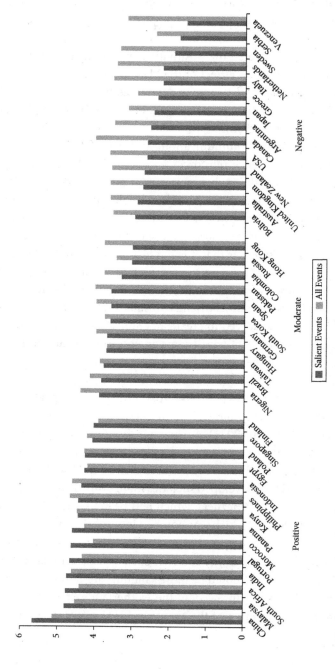

Figure 9.1 Averaged evaluations of salient and combined living historical memory across 39 societies.

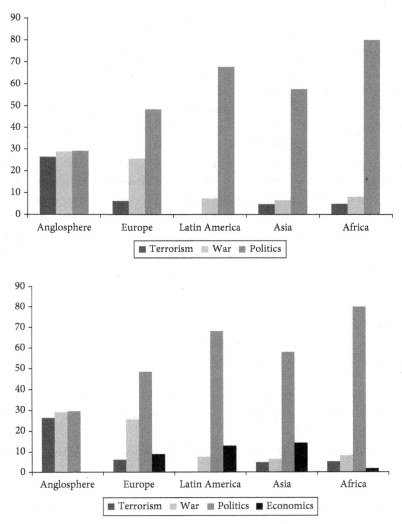

Figure 9.2 Percentages of salient living historical memory categories across regions.

The most positive events in LHM were foundational events in a country's history (a subset of political events in Figure 9.2). Of the 12 societies in which foundational events were named, 10—Morocco (32%), Kenya (27%), South Africa (21%), Singapore (19%), Nigeria (18%), Indonesia (16%), India (16%), Malaysia (13%), China (12%), and Pakistan (9%)—were majority world; Finland (11%) and Poland (6%), from northern and eastern Europe, respectively, were not.

Further category coding revealed that for countries in the Anglosphere (Australia, Canada, New Zealand, the United Kingdom, and the United States), negative evaluations of LHM were largely driven by a high percentage (26%) of free-recalled events related to terrorism (see Figure 9.2). These had an exceptionally low mean evaluation of 1.75, far lower than the average score participants in these societies gave to war (2.63).

In summary, LHM appears to be a dynamic aspect of collective memory that indexes the prevailing emotional climate of a country rather than its enduring values and institutionally embedded historical achievements. The ability of the state to "manufacture consent" in LHM appears to be limited, as correlations suggest it functions more as a symbolic resource for critical consciousness than a warrant of legitimacy for system justification. Critically, nationally foundational events throughout the world were evaluated very positively, endowing developing societies with a positive emotional climate of growth that may energize national identity. Conversely, emotional climate for developed societies, especially in English-speaking societies, was more negative because of the preponderance of the collective remembering of recent negative events (i.e., terrorism).

Historical Charters as the Central Core of Social Representations of History?

Jean Claude Abric's (1993) elaboration of social representations theory may be useful for conceptualizing the relationship between LHM and more enduring aspects of SRH. Abric hypothesized that social representations have a central system (or core) that is stable, coherent, and resistant to change: "Determined by historical, sociological, and ideological conditions . . . marked by the collective memory of the group and the system of norms to which it refers," the central core "constitutes the common collectively shared basis of social representations" (p. 75). For the central core to maintain its stability, it must be surrounded by a peripheral system that acts as "the interface between concrete reality and the central system" (p. 76). Whereas the central system is normative, the peripheral system is functional, being flexible enough to allow for individual differences and sensitive to social context (Wagner et al., 1996). It fulfills the functions of regulating and adapting the central system to meet external constraints, while preserving the stability of the central system.

It is possible to consider LHM as a peripheral system for SRH. Its variability and lack of narrative coherence might then be attributed to individual differences and context-dependent features in individual free recall. But flanked by this periphery, there may still be a common central core that Hilton and Liu (2008) refer to as a *historical charter*: "a widely shared and iconic representation where selective elements of group history, its causes, and consequences have been elaborated into a quasi-legal form that gives moral and sometimes legal implications for group action" (p. 351).

To illustrate this, Hilton and Liu (2008) gave the concrete example of the Treaty of Waitangi in New Zealand. The Treaty, signed by Māori chieftains and the British Crown in 1840, is regarded at the most important event in New Zealand history (Liu et al., 1999). It is considered to be the foundation of the nation's sovereignty (Orange, 2015) and was meant to be a covenant between the British Crown and the Indigenous peoples to form an enduring partnership, as evidenced by the organization of the national museum and by the annual commemoration of the signing of the Treaty. As evidence of the influence of this charter, Māori, who comprise 16% of New Zealand's population, are implicitly (and explicitly) regarded as equally representative of New Zealand as the 70% majority New Zealand Europeans who rule the country today, at least as judged on the Implicit Associations Test by young people (Sibley & Liu, 2007).

However, this covenant was broken in the late 1800s when British colonists waged war to wrestle sovereignty away from Māori. In doing so, they used the language of liberal democracy, claiming to bring enlightened civilization and democracy to Māori, if only they would submit to the British Empire (Liu & Robinson, 2016). Therefore, Sibley et al. (2008) claimed that although the Treaty of Waitangi anchors race talk in New Zealand, how this is translated into concrete policy can be disputed, especially via discourses on equality. For example, Europeans claim that affirmative action to compensate for historical and current injustices against Māori represents unfair and prejudicial treatment (e.g., reverse discrimination) against New Zealand Europeans (Liu & Mills, 2006). Liu (2005) argued that there appear to be two historical charters for New Zealand—one bicultural, representing a partnership between the British and Māori, and the other a liberal democratic charter, celebrating European enlightenment philosophy and British heritage institutions.

Liu and colleagues have never explicitly operationalized either charter (although they have used the Treaty as a stand-in for the bicultural charter in experiments; see Liu et al., 2014). Rather, it is used hermeneutically as an explanatory device. This lack of precision hampers theoretical advance because in the case of the United States, the central question we cannot answer with certainty is whether 9/11 is part of the peripheral system or the central core of American SRH. We shall therefore close this chapter with ideas about the direction of future research needed to advance theory (and practical implications) in this area, through concrete analysis of national memory in a time of populism for the United States.

Dynamics Between Living Historical Memories at the Periphery and Historical Charters as the Central Core of Changing Political Culture

Enough data have been collected to allow interpretive hermeneutics about what an American historical charter might look like. Taylor et al. (2017) provided a snapshot of SRH by asking an MTurk sample of 100 Americans, "Please list the 10 most important events that have occurred at any point in history that, in your opinion, have shaped America's identity" (Table 9.2).

Table 9.2 Most Frequently Reported Nationally Relevant Events of All Time

Rank Order	Event	% of Participants		
		All Subjects	Age ≤ 30 Years	Age > 30 Years
1	American Civil War	69.2	60.6	74.1
2	Attacks on the WTC	69.2	78.8	63.8
3	World War II	52.8	42.4	58.6
4	Declaration of Independence	48.4	39.4	53.5
5	American Revolutionary War	34.1	39.4	31.0
6	JFK assassination	34.1	21.2	41.4
7	Vietnam War	30.8	27.3	32.8
8	World War I	30.8	24.2	34.5
9	Great Depression	29.7	27.3	31.0
10	Women's voting rights	27.5	18.2	32.8

Note: Events are ordered from the most common to the least common based on responses from all subjects. JFK, John F. Kennedy; WTC, World Trade Center.

Adapted from "America was great when nationally relevant events occurred and when Americans were young," by R. J. Taylor, C. G. Burton-Wood, M. Garry, 2017, *Journal of Applied Research in Memory and Cognition*, 6(4), p. 428.

The American Civil War and 9/11 were free recalled most often (69.2%), confirming the centrality of 9/11 not just in LHM but also in SRH. The Declaration of Independence and World War II were the next most frequently nominated events (at near 50%). SRH in America is a story of politics and warfare. Two events signifying civilizational enlightenment (the signing of the Declaration of Independence and women's suffrage) were collectively remembered, together with violence featuring in 7 of the other top 10 events. This is a more bloody history than is reported for some other countries (e.g., Liu et al., 1999, 2002). Although it has elements of a civilizational enlightenment story, land of opportunity is conspicuous in its absence. There is no mention of events related to discovery (e.g., Columbus in 1492, the opening of the Western frontier, or man on the moon). These data suggest, in accord with data on generational differences in the collective memory of Columbus (see Chapter 7, this volume), that the "frontier narrative" of American history is diminishing.

These data, although informative, do not allow us to answer the question, How much of this SRH is influenced by the prevailing emotional climate of negativity in LHM, and how much of this is part of an enduring "schematic narrative template" of aggressive defence of liberty? Yamashiro et al. (2019) painted a different portrait when they asked 2,000 MTurk participants to list five historical events "important to the foundation of America." With this prompt, Americans provided an SRH less oriented toward collective violence and more oriented toward the "land of opportunity" narrative. As shown in Figure 9.3, the Revolutionary War (or War of Independence) was far and away the most important foundational event in American history (free recalled by 62%), but discovery by Columbus was third at 34%, the Pilgrims came in seventh (17%), and westward expansion garnered 5%. An enlightenment narrative representing the civilizing mission of the United States was represented by the Declaration of Independence (No. 2 at 36%), the Boston Tea Party (signifying civil disobedience at 16%), and the Constitution (20%). The Civil War (29%), slavery, and the abolition of slavery were all salient, and the displacement and genocide (10%) against Native Americans warranted two items as well. Hence, equality and diversity narratives were salient as foundational narratives. The shared civilizational heritage with the British Empire (and New Zealand) is evident at No. 5, with British colonization (21%) and taxes (9%). 9/11 comes in at No. 18, with half the nominations as World War II (11%), just above the 5% threshold for inclusion in Figure 9.3. The "city on the hill" narrative celebrated in recent

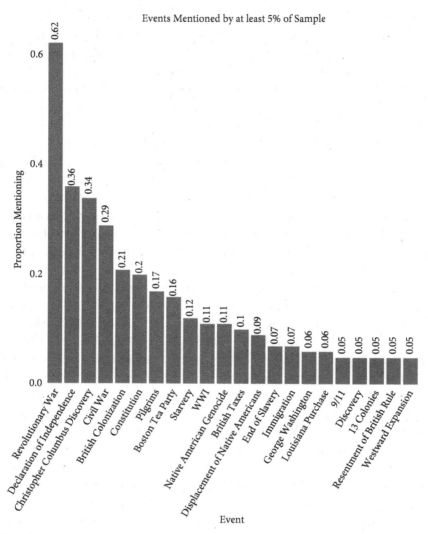

Figure 9.3 Frequency of mention for each of the 22 foundational event categories that were cited by at least 5% of the sample (i.e., 100 people).
Reprinted from "American origins: Political and religious divides in US collective memory," by J. K. Yamashiro, A. Van Engen, & H. L. Roediger III, 2019, *Memory Studies*, p. 9.

years by American presidents (see Chapter 2, this volume) does not appear to be especially salient in the collective memory of ordinary people. Ordinary people might recognize this narrative (and agree with it), but they do not spontaneously recall it.

It is possible to infer a range of narratives from Yamashiro et al.'s (2019) data, but it is not possible to ascertain with any certainty what would be the measurable, central core of an enduring historical charter for the United States. There does appear to be a foundational narrative that is connected to, but distinct from, LHM dominated by 9/11. Some core meanings that might be inferred from commonly free-recalled events include traditional American political values of freedom (i.e., the Revolutionary War and the Declaration of Independence), justice, and equality (i.e., the Civil War, associated with slavery and the end of slavery), together with opportunity (discovery and westward movement) and British heritage (for further exploration of the meaning of these historical events, see Chapter 8, this volume).

Importantly, Yamashiro et al. (2019) note that foundational events were predominantly positive. This accords with Choi et al.'s (2021) previously discussed observations of LHM for developing societies today. The United States is almost 250 years old. It suffered a major terrorist attack on its greatest city in 2001 and has subsequently been engaged in wars abroad that have dragged on for almost two decades, resulting in military victory without strategic success (Afghanistan and Iraq). It makes sense that its emotional climate may tend toward the negative. But this gives rise to the perception of relative decline (Yamashiro & Roediger, 2019), which may in turn explain the appeal of Trump's populist slogan "Make America Great Again." Nostalgia for a golden age in a time of relative decline is a common discourse across cultures (Liu & Khan, 2014). A negative emotional climate for LHM relative to evaluations of the nation's foundational era may be modal; more key is how politicians and other identity entrepreneurs (Reicher & Hopkins, 2001) manage the motivational consequences of this dynamic. Future research into historical charters could follow Abric (1993), who asserts that a representational core is normative: It tells a people what they should do to live up to important traditions, values, and meanings that have served the collective in the past, and it provides useful lessons for the future.

Let us close with a reflection on 9/11. This towering feature of LHM connects to certain aspects of the historical charter of the United States that involve defending freedom from outside threats. This goes back to the Revolutionary War, and it was renewed with a vengeance in World War II. Following victory in World War II, the United States progressively shed peripheral elements of its SRH that limited itself to the Western Hemisphere and added new peripheral, functional representational elements in keeping with its new status as a global superpower. The Korean War followed soon after World War II, and then the disastrous results of the Vietnam War gave pause to further warfare abroad, until the success of the First Gulf War at harnessing mass media to neutralize anti-war protest (Reese & Buckalew, 1995) opened the door for Afghanistan and Iraq. Warfare has become very salient in American LHM, strengthening peripheral elements of its SRH oriented toward the use of military power and extending influence abroad. Seen in this light, the standing of 9/11 is not an isolated event in collective memory but, rather, the manifestation of what might have been a peripheral part of history entering into its representational core. America's historical charter today appears to be "Defender of the Free World," at the cost of being a more humble and caring nation invested in the welfare and equality of its own people. Time will tell if this trend can be reversed.

References

Abric, J. C. (1993). Central system, peripheral system: Their functions and roles in the dynamics of social representations. *Papers on Social Representations, 2*, 75–78.

Assmann, J. (2013). Communicative and cultural memory. In P. S. Varga, K. Katschthaler, D. E. Morse, & M. Takacs (Eds.), *The theoretical foundations of Hungarian 'lieux de mémoire studies (Loci memoriae Hungaricae 1)* (pp. 36–43). Debrecen University Press.

Assmann, J., & Czaplicka, J. (1995). Collective memory and cultural identity. *New German Critique, 65*, 125–133.

Carretero, M., Berger, S., & Grever, M. (Eds.). (2017). *Palgrave handbook of research in historical culture and history education*. Palgrave Macmillan.

Choi, S. Y., Liu, J. H., Mari, S., & Garber, I. (2021, February). Content analysis of living historical memory around the world: Terrorization of the Anglosphere, and national foundations of hope in developing countries. *Memory Studies*.

De Rivera, J. (1992). Emotional climate: Social structure and emotional dynamics. *International Review of Studies on Emotion, 2*, 197–218.

De Rivera, J., & Páez, D. (2007). Emotional climate, human security, and cultures of peace. *Journal of Social Issues, 63*(2), 233–253.

Freire, P. (1973). *Education for critical consciousness*. Seabury.

Halbwachs, M. (1992). *On collective memory* (L. A. Coser, Ed. & Trans.). University of Chicago Press. (Original work published 1925)

Hilton, D. J., & Liu, J. H. (2008). Culture and inter-group relations: The role of social representations of history. In R. Sorrentino & S. Yamaguchi (Eds.), *The handbook of motivation and cognition: The cultural context* (pp. 343–368). Guilford.

Hilton, D. J., & Liu, J. H. (2017). Making history as the narrative of a people: From function to structure and content. *Memory Studies, 10*(3), 297–309.

Hirst, W., & Manier, D. (2002). The diverse forms of collective memory. In G. Echterhoff & M. Saar (Eds.), *Kontexte und Kulturen des Erinnerns: Maurice Halbwachs und das Paradigma des kollektiven Gedächtnisses, Erinnerns* (pp. 37–58). UVK.

Hobsbawm, E., & Ranger, T. (Eds.). (1983). *The invention of tradition*. Cambridge University Press.

Kansteiner, W. (2002). Finding meaning in memory: A methodological critique of collective memory studies. *History and Theory, 41*, 179–197.

Kay, A. C., & Jost, J. T. (2003). Complementary justice: Effects of "poor but happy" and "poor but honest" stereotype exemplars on system justification and implicit activation of the justice motive. *Journal of Personality and Social Psychology, 85*(5), 823.

Kohl, P. L., & Fawcett, C. (Eds.). (1995). *Nationalism, politics and the practice of archaeology*. Cambridge University Press.

Kus, L., Liu, J. H., & Ward, C. (2013). Relative deprivation versus system justification: Polemical social representations and identity positioning in a post-Soviet society. *European Journal of Social Psychology, 43*(5), 423–437.

Liu, J. H., Zeineddine, F. B., Choi, S. Y. F., Zhang, R. J., Vilar, R., & Páez, D. (2021). Living historical memory: Correlations of communicative and cultural memory with national identity, social dominance orientation, and system justification across 40 countries. *Journal of Applied Research in Memory and Cognition, 10*(1), 104–116. https://doi.org/10.1016/j.jarmac.2020.09.007

Liu, J. H., & Hilton, D. (2005). How the past weighs on the present: Social representations of history and their role in identity politics. *British Journal of Social Psychology, 44*, 537–556.

Liu, J. H., & Khan, S. S. (2014). Nation building through historical narratives in pre-independence India: Gandhi, Nehru, Savarkar, and Golwalkar as entrepreneurs of identity. In M. Hanne, W. D. Crano, & J. S. Mio (Eds.), *Warring with Words: Narrative and Metaphor in Domestic and International Politics* (pp. 211–237). New York: Psychology Press.

Liu, J. H., & László, J. (2007). A narrative theory of history and identity: Social identity, social representations, society and the individual. In G. Moloney & I. Walker (Eds.), *Social representations and identity: Content, process and power* (pp. 85–107). Palgrave Macmillan.

Liu, J. H., Lawrence, B., Ward, C., & Abraham, S. (2002). Social representations of history in Malaysia and Singapore: On the relationship between national and ethnic identity. *Asian Journal of Social Psychology, 5*(1), 3–20.

Liu, J. H., & Mills, D. (2006). Modern racism and market fundamentalism: The discourses of plausible deniability and their multiple functions. *Journal of Community and Applied Social Psychology, 16*, 83–99.

Liu, J. H., & Páez, D. (2019). Social representations of history as common ground for processes of intergroup relations and the content of social identities. In D. Matsumoto & H. C. Hwang (Eds.), *The Oxford handbook of culture and psychology* (2nd ed., pp. 586–614). Oxford University Press.

Liu, J. H., Páez, D., Slawuta, P., Cabecinhas, R., Techio, E., Kokdemir, D., Sen, R., Vincze, O., Muluk, H., Wang, F. X., & Zlobina, A. (2009). Representing world history in the 21st century: The impact of 9-11, the Iraq War, and the nation-state on the dynamics of collective remembering. *Journal of Cross-Cultural Psychology, 40*, 667–692.

Liu, J. H., & Robinson, A. R. (2016). One ring to rule them all: Master discourses of enlightenment—and racism—from colonial to contemporary New Zealand. *European Journal of Social Psychology, 42*(2), 137–155. http://dx.doi.org/10.1002/ejsp.2141

Liu, J. H., & Sibley, C. G. (2015). Social representations of history: Theory and applications, methods, measurement and results. In G. Sammut, E. Andreouli, G. Gaskell, & J. Valsiner (Eds.), *The Cambridge handbook of social representations* (pp. 269–279). Cambridge University Press.

Liu, J. H., Sibley, C. G., & Huang, L. L. (2014). History matters: The impact of culture-specific symbols on political attitudes and intergroup relations. *Political Psychology*, 35(1), 57–79.

Liu, J. H., Wilson, M. W., McClure, J., & Higgins, T. R. (1999). Social identity and the perception of history: Cultural representations of Aotearoa/New Zealand. *European Journal of Social Psychology*, 29, 1021–1047.

Olick, J. K., & Robbins, J. (1998). Social memory studies: From "collective memory" to the historical sociology of mnemonic practices. *Annual Review of Sociology*, 24(1), 105–140.

Olick, J. K., Vinitzky-Seroussi, V., & Levy, D. (2011). *The collective memory reader.* Oxford University Press.

Orange, C. (2015). *The Treaty of Waitangi.* Bridget Williams Books.

Powell, K. A. (2011). Framing Islam: An analysis of US media coverage of terrorism since 9/11. *Communication Studies*, 62(1), 90–112.

Pratto, F., Cidam, A., Stewart, A. L., Bou Zeineddine, F., Aranda, M., Aiello, A., ... Eicher, V. (2013). Social dominance in context and in individuals: Contextual moderation of robust effects of social dominance orientation in 15 languages and 20 countries. *Social Psychological and Personality Science*, 4, 587–599.

Prilleltensky, I., & Gonick, L. (1996). Polities change, oppression remains: On the psychology and politics of oppression. *Political Psychology*, 17, 127–148.

Propp, V. (1968). *The morphology of the folktale.* University of Texas Press.

Reese, S. D., & Buckalew, B. (1995). The militarism of local television: The routine framing of the Persian Gulf War. *Critical Studies in Media Communication*, 12(1), 40–59.

Reicher, S., & Hopkins, N. (2001). *Self and nation.* London: Sage.

Sibley, C. S., & Liu, J. H. (2007). New Zealand = bicultural? Implicit and explicit associations between ethnicity and nationhood in the New Zealand context. *European Journal of Social Psychology*, 37(6), 1222–1243.

Sibley, C. S., Liu, J. H., & Khan, S. S. (2009). Who are 'we'? Implicit associations between ethnic and national symbols for Maori and Pakeha in New Zealand. *New Zealand Journal of Psychology*, 38(1), 2–14.

Sibley, C. S., Liu, J. H., Duckitt, J., & Khan, S. S. (2008). Social representations of history and the legitimation of social inequality: The form and function of historical negation. *European Journal of Psychology*, 38, 542–565.

Stephan, W. G., Renfro, C. L., Esses, V. M., Stephan, C. W., & Martin, T. (2005). The effects of feeling threatened on attitudes toward immigrants. *International Journal of Intercultural Relations*, 29, 1–19.

Stone, C. B., van der Haegen, A., Luminet, O., & Hirst, W. (2014). Personally relevant vs. nationally relevant memories: An intergenerational examination of World War II memories across and within Belgian French-speaking families. *Journal of Applied Research in Memory and Cognition*, 3(4), 280–286.

Taylor, R. J., Burton-Wood, C. G., & Garry, M. (2017). America was great when nationally relevant events occurred and when Americans were young. *Journal of Applied Research in Memory and Cognition*, 6(4), 425–433.

Tilly, C. (1975). *The formation of national states in Western Europe.* Princeton University Press.

United Nations Development Programme. (2019). *Human Development Index.* http://hdr.undp.org/sites/default/files/hdr2019.pdf

Vargas-Salfate, S., Paez, D., Liu, J. H., Pratto, F., & Gil de Zúñiga, H. (2018). A comparison of social dominance theory and system justification: The role of social status in 19 nations. *Personality and Social Psychology Bulletin, 44*(7), 1060–1076.

Wagner, W., Valencia, J., & Elejabarrieta, F. (1996). Relevance, discourse and the "hot" stable core social representations—A structural analysis of word associations. *British Journal of Social Psychology, 35*(3), 331–351.

Wang, Q. (2008). On the cultural constitution of collective memory. *Memory, 16*, 305–317.

Watts, R. J., Diemer, M. A., & Voight, A. M. (2011). Critical consciousness: Current status and future directions. New Directions for Child and Adolescent Development, *134*, 43–57.

Wertsch, J. V. (2002). *Voices of collective remembering*. Cambridge University Press.

Woods, J. (2011). The 9/11 effect: Toward a social science of the terrorist threat. *Social Science Journal, 48*(1), 213–233.

Yamashiro, J. K., & Roediger, H. L., III. (2019). How we have fallen: Implicit trajectories in collective temporal thought. *Memory, 27*(8), 1158–1166.

Yamashiro, J. K., Van Engen, A., & Roediger, H. L., III. (2019, July). American origins: Political and religious divides in US collective memory. *Memory Studies*. https://doi.org/10.1177/1750698019856065

10

Decades Later

What World War II Events Are Remembered as the Most Important Ones? Implications of Data Collected in 12 Countries

Magdalena Abel, Sharda Umanath, and Krystian Barzykowski

This chapter is being written in the summer of 2020 and thus almost exactly 75 years after World War II ended in 1945. Even many decades later, the war and its consequences continue to impact our present and linger in people's minds. For instance, when Liu et al. (2005) asked survey participants from 12 different nations to list the most important events of world history, World War II was nominated most frequently in each of the countries. Similar results were also reported by Pennebaker et al. (2006), who asked respondents in 7 countries to nominate the most important events of the past century (World War II placed first) or the past millennium (World War II placed fourth—behind the discovery of the new world, the French Revolution, and the industrial revolution; see also Liu & Hilton, 2005; Liu et al., 2009; Schuman et al., 1998; Scott & Zac, 1993).

Given the huge impact of World War II and its far-reaching, devastating consequences, it is not surprising that it continues to be remembered today. War memorials and monuments in neighborhoods, references in speeches, newspaper articles, and movies, as well as formal education in schools keep the memory of World War II alive. Witnesses who lived through the war are slowly passing away, and indeed, by now many more people have learned and continue to learn about World War II via books, movies, and other types of media (e.g., Kaes, 1990). This change away from the war being remembered as a series of actually lived-through experiences to a more knowledge-based representation has likely changed memories of World War II and is likely to continue changing it. For instance, Zaromb et al. (2014) found that the atomic bombing of Japan by U.S. forces at the end of World War II was

---

Magdalena Abel, Sharda Umanath, and Krystian Barzykowski, *Decades Later* In: *National Memories*. Edited by: Henry L. Roediger and James V. Wertsch, Oxford University Press. © Oxford University Press 2022. DOI: 10.1093/oso/9780197568675.003.0010

viewed as positive by U.S. participants who were alive during World War II but as negative by younger U.S. participants (i.e., college students).

Collective Memory for Past Events and Its Relevance for Events Today

In this chapter, we report and discuss recently collected data on how World War II events are remembered today by people from various countries throughout the world. The project was conducted to gain a better understanding of collective memory for specific events that occurred during World War II. The term *collective memory* refers to memories of past events that are shared by members of larger social groups (Halbwachs, 1925/1992, 1980). An aspect that is stressed by most definitions of collective memory is its contribution to group identity. In contrast to historic accounts of the past, events represented in collective memory do not necessarily have to be factually accurate but can be biased and may thus consist of event interpretations that serve group identity projects (e.g., Hirst & Manier, 2008; Wertsch & Roediger, 2008). Collective memory can be studied from various angles and can refer not only to a shared body of knowledge but also to shared memories that serve to characterize and define a group's "image" and even to a drawn-out process of negotiating and fighting about how the past should be remembered (Dudai, 2002; for reviews, see Hirst et al., 2018; Roediger & Abel, 2015).

Why is it important to examine collective memory for World War II? World War II affected almost all nations throughout the world either directly or indirectly, many of them gravely. The widespread knowledge about the war makes it an ideal case to study in order to examine collective memory for events that have occurred decades earlier. There is, however, another reason that makes it particularly interesting to examine how the war is remembered decades later. As Markovits and Reich (1997) note,

> Collective memory has much more to do with the present than it does with the past. Indeed, one would not be remiss to say that collective memory constitutes the past's instrumentalization for present and contemporary purposes. As such, collective memory is clearly a functionalized phenomenon. It is, in fact, utilitarian for the here and now. Collective memory is the selective use of the past to legitimate present conditions of power. (p. 96)

Consistent with this quote, the repercussions of World War II up to this day continue to determine many political actions throughout the world. For instance, much of Germany's foreign policy was and still is influenced by its legacy as the successor of Nazi Germany (e.g., Markovits & Reich, 1997; Wittlinger & Larose, 2007). In Russia, where World War II is referred to as "the Great Patriotic War," President Putin has been described as using the past, or at least a certain version of it, for national mobilization (Edele, 2017). References to World War II, and the evocation of an underlying schematic narrative template for conflicts more generally, seem to be used to justify and rally support for new military initiatives, such as the Russo-Georgian war in 2008 or the Russo-Ukrainian war that started in 2014 (Siddi, 2017; Wertsch & Karumidze, 2009). Clearly, the way in which past events are remembered today can affect how events unfold in the future, and memory may also be used as a tool of politics (described under the term "politics of history"; Verovšek, 2016). Thus, understanding how the people of various nations remember this global event can inform understanding of how and why nations act the way that they do today.

Some Prior Work on Memory for World War II

World War II and the different ways in which it is remembered have been the subject of extensive research in several academic disciplines, relying on a variety of tools and methodologies. Our goal here is not to review this work in its entirety because that would be a nearly impossible task. Instead, we only aim to review two studies that were conducted rather recently and that directly inspired our own project: Wertsch (2002) and Zaromb et al. (2014). Notably, this prior work was focused on recall of specific World War II events in single mnemonic communities.

Wertsch (2002), for instance, concentrated on Russian memories of World War II and asked 177 Soviet-educated and post-Soviet participants to list the most important events of the war. Being American himself, Wertsch speculated that

> Americans could be expected to respond to a question of major events in World War II by listing items such as Pearl Harbor, D-Day, the Battle of the Bulge, the liberation of the concentration camps by American troops, Guadalcanal, and Hiroshima and Nagasaki. (p. 152)

In contrast to this list of events, the prototypical account of Wertsch's Russian participants included the German invasion of the Soviet Union, the Battle of Moscow, the Battle of Stalingrad, the Battle of Kursk, the Siege of Leningrad, and the Battle of Berlin as the most critical events. Importantly, as work performed more than a decade later demonstrates, Wertsch's (2002) speculations about World War II events that might be important to Americans were quite accurate. Zaromb et al. (2014) asked U.S. citizens to nominate the most important events of World War II. Examining core events that were shared by at least 50% of participants as an expression of collective memory, Zaromb et al. indeed found that the top three events that were nominated most frequently were the attack on Pearl Harbor, D-Day, and the atomic bombings of Hiroshima and Nagasaki. These same events were also nominated consistently across samples of older and younger adults.

Thus, although the United States and Russia fought together on the Allied side during World War II, a comparison of the two studies shows that there does not seem to be a uniform account of the most important events of the war. Indeed, at least for Russian and American participants included in the two studies, there was almost no overlap in which events were remembered as the most important ones. Instead, citizens of the two countries seemed mostly to nominate events that emphasized their own nation's experience of the war as well as the role it played for World War II more generally.

The Current Project

Here, we report on the results of two empirical studies, which applied a very similar method as the prior work by Wertsch (2002) and Zaromb et al. (2014). Participants in both studies completed a larger online survey on World War II. In the first part of this survey, participants were provided with the following instructions and asked to recall the 10 most important events of World War II:

> In the spaces provided below, please list the TEN most important events of World War 2, in your opinion. You may list them as they come to mind, in any order. When listing the event, you do not need to describe the event in detail. Please just provide the name or a short label.

Participants could only proceed to the next part of the survey after listing a minimum of 5 events. Because the task constituted the first part of the survey, the resulting data likely provide a relatively unbiased picture of participants' spontaneous recall of the most important World War II events.

Participants in the study by Abel et al. (2019) were recruited from 11 different countries; participants in the study by Barzykowski et al. (in preparation) were all from Poland. The full surveys were conducted in English, but during event recall, non-native English speakers did not have to produce English event names and could alternatively provide the name they were familiar with in their own language. Other survey parts are described in Chapter 11 in this volume as well as in Roediger et al. (2019).

The questions we aimed to address in this project are the following: Which World War II events are remembered by people of different nationalities? Decades after World War II has ended, is there some agreement—both within and across countries—on which events are seen as the most important ones? Or are nominations of the most important war events mostly characterized by marked differences between countries? Comparing the results reported by Wertsch (2002) and Zaromb et al. (2014), there was indeed prior evidence that even former Allies can remember the war very differently.

The Most Important Events as Remembered by Participants from Eight Former Allied Countries: The Study by Abel et al. (2019)

First, consider events recalled as the most important ones by participants whose countries fought on the victorious Allied side during World War II. We recruited more than 100 participants from each of eight countries, namely from Australia, Canada, China, France, New Zealand, Russia, the United Kingdom, and the United States. The resulting data are complex, but after several rounds of coding, they can be summarized as in Figure 10.1, which shows the top 10 events that were most frequently nominated by participants in each country. Events in the figure are organized from top to bottom, with the most frequently nominated events at the top. The figure is also split into two horizontal parts to visually separate events that were nominated by at least 50% of participants (i.e., core events, shared by the majority of participants within a country; see also Zaromb et al., 2014) from events

China (n = 102)	Canada (n = 121)	USA (n = 135)	Australia (n = 106)	New Zealand (n = 111)	France (n = 106)	UK (n = 116)	Russia (n = 132)
Pearl Harbor (75%)	Pearl Harbor (78%)	Pearl Harbor (91%)	Pearl Harbor (77%)	Pearl Harbor (81%)	D-Day (90%)	D-Day (75%)	Stalingrad (93%)
Atomic Bombs (55%)	D-Day (75%)	D-Day (81%)	Atomic Bombs (67%)	Atomic Bombs (73%)	The Holocaust (72%)	Pearl Harbor (67%)	Battle of Kursk (73%)
D-Day (53%)	The Holocaust (67%)	Atomic Bombs (80%)	The Holocaust (58%)	The Holocaust (61%)	Atomic Bombs (62%)	The Holocaust (59%)	D-Day (66%)
	Atomic Bombs (66%)	The Holocaust (66%)	D-Day (54%)	D-Day 60%	Pearl Harbor (52%)	Battle of Britain (59%)	Leningrad (65%)
			Nazis invade Poland (50%)	Nazis invade Poland (50%)	Appeal of 18 June (50%)	Atomic Bombs (58%)	Battle of Moscow (64%)
						Nazis invade Poland (54%)	Nazis invade USSR (60%)
Nanking (41%)							Battle of Berlin (57%)
Surrender of Japan (38%)	Battle of Britain (42%)	Nazis invade Poland (37%)					
The Holocaust (31%)	Death of Hitler (26%)	Fall of France (26%)	Battle of Britain (31%)	Battle of Britain (48%)	Liberation of France (38%)		
Sino-Japanese War (25%)	Nazis invade Poland(26%)	Nazis invade USSR (24%)	Death of Hitler (26%)	Nazis invade USSR (32%)	Fall of France (29%)	Battle of Dunkirk (45%)	
Stalingrad (24%)	VE Day (25%)	VE Day (22%)	Bombing of Darwin (25%)	Fall of France (23%)	Vichy France (26%)	Stalingrad (32%)	Atomic Bombs (43%)
Marco Polo Bridge (23%)	Stalingrad (21%)	Bombing of London (20%)	Fall of France (24%)	Death of Hitler (22%)	Stalingrad (26%)	VE Day (32%)	Nazis invade Poland (42%)
Nazis invade Poland (22%)	Dieppe Raid (17%)	Battle of Britain (19%)	Singapore's Fall (23%)	Stalingrad (20%)	Vel' d'Hiv Roundup (25%)	USA enters the war (25%)	Pearl Harbor (39%)

Figure 10.1 The top 10 events nominated by participants in each of eight countries formerly on the Allied side of World War II. The top of the figure shows core events that were shared by at least 50% of participants; the bottom shows the rest of the events rounding out the top 10 lists. Countries are presented in ascending order based on the number of core events shared by the majority of participants. In addition, core events were color-coded to facilitate comparisons of event recall across countries.
Adapted from Figures 1 and 2 in Abel et al. (2019).

recalled by fewer participants. In addition, the sequence of countries in the figure is based on the number of core events shared within each group, in ascending order from left to right.

We used different greyscales for events that constituted core events in more than one country to facilitate comparisons across countries. Just from glancing at the color distributions of core events, it becomes evident that there was great overlap across the eight countries and therefore a rather high consensus regarding which events were considered as the most important ones by the majority of participants. D-Day was a core event for all eight countries, whereas Pearl Harbor and the dropping of the atomic bombs on Hiroshima and Nagasaki constituted core events for seven countries (all but Russia). The Holocaust was a core event in six countries (all but Russia and China), and the German invasion of Poland qualified as a core event in three countries (Australia, New Zealand, and the United Kingdom).

Apart from this striking consensus across countries, another issue stands out: Only three countries had unique core events, which were remembered by the majority of participants of these countries but not of any of the other countries. Half of the surveyed French participants listed Charles de Gaulle's radio appeal to French citizens to resist Nazi occupation on June 18, 1940, as one of the most important events of the war. This event is specific to the French experience of the war and was not part of the major collective record in any of the other countries. Indeed, in total, it was only listed by one other participant from the United Kingdom and not by anyone else across the former Allied countries. In contrast, for the UK sample, the Battle of Britain constituted a core event, and although it was not remembered by the majority of participants in any of the other countries, it was part of the top 10 nominated events in four of the other countries (viz., Canada, Australia, New Zealand, and the United States). Perhaps this particular set of countries is not surprising as they all have special relationships with the United Kingdom as its former colonies.

Of all the groups in the study, the Russian respondents nominated by far the highest number of unique core events. Indeed, with seven core events in total, Russian participants showed the highest internal consensus, agreeing the most on which events were the most important ones. The Battle of Stalingrad, the Battle of Kursk, the Siege of Leningrad, the Battle of Moscow, the Nazi invasion of the Soviet Union, and the Battle of Berlin were all unique to the Russian side of the war and not core events for any other Allied country. Russian participants seemed to consider mostly events that occurred on the Eastern Front of the war as important. D-Day made it into the Russian core events as well, but interestingly, many Russian participants referred to D-Day as "the opening of the second front" (a term that was not commonly used by participants in any of the other countries). In short, aside from D-Day, the Russian core events fit perfectly with the events previously reported as critical by Wertsch (2002) more than a decade earlier.

Apparently, for Russian participants, the Eastern Front of the war was not only the first front in battling Nazi Germany's advance but also the most important one. Seemingly, this view was not shared by participants from the other seven former Allied countries included in the survey. The bottom part of Figure 10.1 shows that only two of the core events unique to Russian participants' recall of World War II made it into the top 10 lists of the other countries, namely the Battle of Stalingrad and the German invasion of the

Soviet Union. The contrast in recollected importance for World War II is probably most strikingly illustrated by comparing recall rates for the Battle of Stalingrad across countries. Whereas 93% of Russian participants agreed on Stalingrad being one of the most important events of World War II, the event was only nominated by 20–32% of participants in five of the other seven countries (for the United States and Australia, Stalingrad did not even make it into the top 10 list of events). Of course, in the United States and other countries such as China, Australia, and New Zealand, World War II involved both a European and a Pacific theater. Events listed by Russians ignore the Pacific theater, perhaps because Russians did not participate heavily in that theater until the last few days of the war.

In summary, with the exception of Russia, there was a great deal of overlap across former Allied countries regarding World War II events considered to be most important. In contrast, Russian participants, despite showing the highest internal consensus, almost exclusively nominated events from the Eastern Front of the war, which did not seem to be regarded as so important by participants from the other countries. One reason why participants from other former Allied countries might not have recalled events from the Eastern Front of the war as among the most important ones is that at the time of the events, these countries were not directly involved in them. One country that clearly was directly involved in all events recalled as core events by Russian participants, however, was Nazi Germany. Thus, we turn to the data collected from participants of the three major former Axis countries (Germany, Italy, and Japan) next.

The Most Important Events as Remembered by Participants from Three Former Axis Countries: The Study by Abel et al. (2019)

Participants from Germany, Italy, and Japan were included in the survey, and we again collected data from more than 100 participants in each country. Participants from former Axis countries completed the same event recall task as participants from former Allied countries, and the results are summarized in Figure 10.2.

The color-coding scheme of the core events shared by the majority of participants in a country corresponds to the color coding used in Figure 10.1, and this highlights an interesting finding: Participants from former Axis countries largely agreed on the same most important events as participants

Japan (n = 121)	Italy (n = 146)	Germany (n = 133)
Atomic Bombs 88%	Atomic Bombs 87%	Nazis invade Poland (71%)
Pearl Harbor 74%	D-Day 75%	The Holocaust (68%)
	The Holocaust 68%	D-Day (62%)
	Pearl Harbor 66%	Atomic Bombs (59%)
Potsdam Decl. (36%)		Pearl Harbor (50%)
Battle of Okinawa (34%)		
Air Raid on Tokyo (33%)	Nazis invade Poland (47%)	
The Holocaust (30%)	Allied Invasion of Italy (26%)	Stalingrad (46%)
Battle of Midway (26%)	Italians resist (25%)	VE Day (45%)
Tripartite Pact (26%)	Liberation Day in Italy (23%)	Nazis invade USSR (26%)
Surrender of Japan (24%)	Pact of Steel (22%)	Plots to kill Hitler (26%)
Battle of Iwo Jima (17%)	Stalingrad (21%)	Reichskristallnacht (26%)

Figure 10.2 The top 10 events nominated by participants in each of three countries formerly on the Axis side of World War II. The top of the figure shows core events that were shared by at least 50% of participants; the bottom shows the rest of the events rounding out the top 10 lists.
Adapted from Figures 1 and 2 in Abel et al. (2019).

from former Allied countries. In fact, perhaps surprisingly, these countries did not share any unique core events as part of their recollections of World War II. Pearl Harbor and the atomic bombing of Hiroshima and Nagasaki were core events for all three former Axis countries; D-Day and the Holocaust were also core events for Italy and Germany (but not Japan), and the majority of German participants additionally agreed on the Nazi invasion of Poland as one of the most important events. There were only two core events for Japan, both involving Japan, but with four and five core events that did not all directly involve their own nations, the data from Italy and Germany very much resemble those from the former Allied countries.

As for the majority of Allied countries surveyed in this study, the military actions reflected in the core events of participants from former Axis countries largely followed a Western Allied perspective on the war and, apart from Nazi Germany's invasion of Poland, did not include a single event that happened on the Eastern Front and involved the Soviet Union. This is especially striking to observe in German participants because, as already noted,

Nazi Germany was directly involved in all the events listed as core events by Russian participants. Looking at the remaining events in the top 10 lists of participants from Axis countries, another parallel with Allied countries stands out: Only a few of the unique Russian core events even made it into these lists. For Japan, the top 10 list includes none of these events, and only 21% of Italian participants recalled the Battle of Stalingrad as one of the most important events. The German top 10 list includes two of the unique Russian core events. Remembered by 46% of German participants, the Battle of Stalingrad was close to becoming a core event for Germany. The contrast with Russian participants' recollections of the war, 93% of which considered Stalingrad as one of the most important events, is still puzzling, however.

Overall, participants from former Axis countries largely considered the same events as the most important ones as participants from most former Allied countries. These results are again in stark contrast to the events considered the most important ones by Russian participants, who focused almost exclusively on the Eastern Front of the war. Pondering the data collected in Germany, one could argue that even though Nazi Germany was involved in all the events considered as most important by Russian participants, an important difference is that many of these events were defeats for Nazi Germany. Could this alone explain why the strong focus on events of the Eastern Front of the war by Russian participants was not at least partly echoed by German participants? Barzykowski et al. (in preparation) conducted a follow-up survey to possibly address this question.

The Most Important Events as Remembered by Participants from Poland: The Study by Barzykowski et al. (in Preparation)

Poland's role in World War II is complex. Caught between Nazi Germany and the Soviet Union, the country was invaded by both countries, and its citizens suffered atrocities not only at the hand of the Nazis but also at the hand of the Soviets. Millions of people—many of them Jewish—lost their lives, making Poland the country that lost the highest percentage of its original population in World War II (17.1%; calculations based on Davies, 2007; Darman, 2009).[1]

---

[1] Yet, even this staggering number pales in comparison to the 32.2% of the Jewish population worldwide who were killed in the Holocaust.

During the occupation of Poland, the Polish government operated from exile, first in France and later in Britain. Polish resistance was strong, with Polish soldiers fighting on the Allied side of the war in Europe, Africa, and the Middle East. After the German invasion of the Soviet Union in 1941, the Polish government in exile tried to cooperate with the Soviet Union, hoping that the cooperation would free its country.

These brief reflections on Poland in World War II should make it obvious why Polish recollections of the most important World War II events are particularly interesting to examine. Indeed, after seeing a conference talk regarding the data in Abel et al. (2019), the third author of this chapter approached the first and second authors about this follow-up study, fairly noting that any work on World War II would be incomplete without the perspective of Poland. Due to Poland's geographical location at the Eastern Front of the war, its fate was directly affected by the large battles that were fought there. Thus, Poland was right in the middle of the Eastern Front, which contrasts with several of the other former Allied countries surveyed in Abel et al. (2019). Fighting against Nazi Germany and trying to cooperate with Soviet forces from 1941 onward, Soviet successes on the Eastern Front were not defeats but, rather, victories from a Polish perspective. In addition, for 45 years after World War II, Poland was in the Soviet Union's sphere of influence, and the historic narration, taught mostly in school, has been influenced by the Soviet perspective. Therefore, in subsequent decades, one might expect participants from Poland to show greater overlap with Russian participants regarding World War II events recalled as the most important ones.

We recruited more than 200 participants from Poland (mean age: 27 years) and asked them to complete largely the same survey used in Abel et al. (2019), in English. The first part of the survey again focused on recall of the 10 most important events of World War II. Figure 10.3 shows the top 10 list of events generated by Polish participants. The color coding of events again corresponds to that used in Figures 10.1 and 10.2 and hints at further overlap in recall. Like participants from most other countries, Polish participants most frequently nominated the atomic bombings, Pearl Harbor, and D-Day as the most important events of the war. A fourth core event was unique to the Polish experience of the war and referred to the Warsaw Uprising, in which the Polish resistance tried to liberate Warsaw from Nazi occupation.

Some of the remaining events of the top 10 list referred to events that were nominated as core events by participants from other countries (i.e., the Battle

Figure 10.3 The top 10 events nominated by participants from Poland. The top of the figure shows core events that were shared by at least 50% of participants; the bottom shows the rest of the events rounding out the top 10.
Source: Barzykowski et al. (in preparation).

of Britain, the Holocaust, and the German invasion of Poland), but the bottom three events indeed involved the former Soviet Union. The Soviet invasion of Poland was recalled as one of the most important events by 40% of the Polish participants, whereas the Nazi invasion of the Soviet Union was nominated by 36% and the Battle of Stalingrad by 35%. Broadly speaking, this mirrors the pattern observed for participants from former Allied and Axis countries in Abel et al. (2019): Events on the Eastern Front of the war that were viewed as the most important ones by far by the majority of Russian participants did not have the same importance for the majority of participants from other countries, including Poland. Polish participants tended to agree more on a different set of events, mostly reflecting a Western Allied perspective on the war, and only subsamples of participants within countries listed single events from the Eastern Front of the war as the most important ones. The fact that this same pattern was also observed in the Polish participants' data suggests that events that reflect Soviet contributions to the Nazi defeat may not be as accessible in memory to others, resulting in reduced spontaneous recall of corresponding events decades after the war ended. Apparently, this is the case not only for participants from former Allied countries that were not directly involved in the Eastern Front of the war, or for participants from former Axis countries that were defeated on the Eastern Front, but also for participants from Poland—a country that was geographically located at the former Eastern Front of the war and additionally subject to Soviet influence for decades after the war. The events in the Polish top 10 list that involved the Soviet Union also directly involved Poland, and some of the events may be reflective of the complicated relationship between Poland and the Soviet

Union. The Soviet Union did invade Poland, and Soviet forces also neglected to provide critical support that was expected by Polish resistance fighters (e.g., during the Warsaw Uprising). Thus, although Poland tried to cooperate with the Soviet Union to defeat the Nazis, Soviet atrocities during the war seem to be recollected as part of Poland's collective memory of the war to this day.

Summary of Both Studies

Across the two studies reported here, we surveyed more than 1,500 participants from 12 different countries. When asked to recall the most important events of World War II, these participants generated a total of more than 12,500 events that could be clearly identified, coded, and then analyzed. This revealed a high level of overlap in recalled events across most of the surveyed countries, a conclusion reflected in Table 10.1, which shows the top 10 list of recalled events across all participants from all countries included in Abel et al. (2019) and Barzykowski et al. (in preparation). Roughly two-thirds of participants listed Pearl Harbor and the atomic bombings, making these two events the most frequently nominated events overall. D-Day and the Holocaust were also recalled by more than half of the full surveyed sample, thus constituting core events for the full sample. Stalingrad

Table 10.1 Top 10 Events Nominated Most Frequently by All Participants Included in This Chapter. The greyscales in which some events are shown correspond to those used in Figures 10.1–10.3 and emphasize events shared as core events in more than one country.

Rank	Event Label	% of Participants
1 and 2	Pearl Harbor	66
1 and 2	Atomic bombs	66
3	D-Day	63
4	The Holocaust	53
5	Nazis invade Poland	41
6	Stalingrad	31
7	Battle of Britain	25
8	Nazis invade USSR	25
9	Victory in Europe Day (VE Day)	21
10	Fall of France	18

Adapted from Table 3 in Abel et al. (2019).

was only listed as an important event by approximately one-third of the full sample of participants (including Russian participants) and the Nazi invasion of the Soviet Union by one-fourth—again illustrating that events on the Eastern Front of the war were largely neglected by most non-Russian participants.

The results presented here are surprising in at least two ways. First, the high overlap in which events were considered as the most important ones by participants from various countries was quite unexpected and may indicate that decades after World War II ended, a sort of unspoken agreement transcending at least some countries' borders may have been reached over time (see also Schuman et al., 1998; Scott & Zac, 1993). Rather than an amalgamation of events critical to individual countries, this "agreement" seems to largely comply with a Western Allied perspective on World War II, emphasizing events most consistent with the U.S. involvement in the war. How have participants from so many different countries adopted this version of a shared past? Second, Russian participants deviated in this respect and were the only ones who showed a clear, undeniably Russian view of the past. Given the overall importance of the Eastern Front of the war, one can easily argue that critical events that occurred on the Eastern Front are simply missing from the sets of core events observed in the other surveyed countries. How can national perspectives on the one hand be preserved so strongly over time, but on the other hand not spread and influence others? We discuss these and similar questions in the remainder of the chapter.

How May National Memories Adapt to a Certain Perspective over Time?

There is no single answer to this question, and given that the current project was concerned with cross-national memories of World War II events, it is most likely that several factors contributed to the gradual development of the consensus that we observed across most surveyed countries. In the following, we consider some of them in greater detail, and future work will, we hope, provide empirical answers.

On a micro level, psychological research on small-group interactions has repeatedly shown that collaborative and conversational remembering can increase mnemonic overlap between group members, which may be a starting point for creating shared memories across individuals even in larger social groups (e.g., Congleton & Rajaram, 2014; Rajaram & Maswood, 2017; see also Coman et al., 2016). Chapters 19 and 20 in this volume review this work. Moreover, selectivity during conversational remembering can not only help strengthen certain aspects of the past in memory but also simultaneously induce forgetting of unmentioned details in speakers and listeners (Cuc et al., 2007; see also Abel & Bäuml, 2020; Yamashiro & Hirst, 2020). Although little work has examined similar effects on larger scales, potentially the same mechanisms might also be at work when large audiences are exposed to selective news reports or speeches by politicians who wish to emphasize a specific version of the past (e.g., Stone et al., 2020). In this manner, even larger groups may come to adopt a certain view of the past, increasing overlap not only in what is remembered but also in what is neglected or forgotten.

Nevertheless, the high overlap that was observed across different nations in the current project may also provide support for the view that schematic knowledge structures are involved in collective remembering. Such knowledge structures may be shaped by social interactions and conversational exchanges as well, but arguably, on a macro level, the dominance of Western ideas in education and mass media might hold even greater importance (e.g., Wertsch, 2008). The knowledge we possess affects not only how we recall past events but also how we encode, process, and integrate new events (e.g., Brewer & Nakamura, 1984). Critically, such schemata can exert their influences outside of our conscious awareness. The United States had a direct influence in both Asia and Europe after the war, which may have extended to formal education. Examining textbook coverage of historic events across countries could therefore be promising to study how event recall may be formed by education. In addition, the United States has disseminated its views in further ways. For instance, since the end of the war, American movies, novels, and other media contributions may have made the American view the most easily accessible, despite whatever was learned in formal education, and may thus have continued to influence people throughout the world. If this influence is indeed a decisive factor, then collective memory for international events other than World War II should have been influenced and shaped in similar ways. Future studies could examine this suggestion, potentially also establishing a more direct link between media exposure and collective remembering by additionally examining the output of important media sources across included countries.

Knowledge structures in the form of an underlying schematic narrative template may also help account for the unique pattern observed for Russian participants in the current project (e.g., Wertsch, 2002, 2008). Although Russian participants were not alone in showing a bias toward events involving their own country, they demonstrated a much higher level of internal agreement and cohesion within their group. Their focus on events on the Eastern Front of the war may indeed be justified because Soviet forces carried much of the battle against Nazi Germany from 1941 until June 1944 and contributed critically to the Nazi defeat. Russian participants seem to have been taught and maintain the Russian perspective on the important events of the war, which is reflective of memory of World War II being commemorated, indeed sanctified, in Russia as nowhere else (e.g., Bernstein, 2016; Uldricks, 2009). This commemoration may also be a central contributor to the current Russian identity project, with several instances in which references to World War II have been used to mobilize support for new military actions (e.g., Edele, 2017; Siddi, 2017; Wertsch & Karumidze, 2009).

An aspect that we have largely neglected so far is that memories of World War II may also have been affected and changed due to other historic events that happened since 1945. In light of other global events, the remembrance and interpretation of World War II may have changed. The Cold War holds particular importance here, spanning a long time frame from the end of World War II until the 1990s. During this period, tensions between the United States and the Soviet Union (and their respective allies) reflected a struggle for dominance, both ideologically and geopolitically, in far-flung places throughout the world. Ending with the dissolution of the Soviet Union and countries in Eastern Europe regaining their independence after decades of communist rule, this prolonged period may have been decisive for a polarization of the world and for why a Western Allied, U.S.-centric perspective on world events seems to be dominant now, at least in some of the countries surveyed here.

The considerations so far illustrate that more work is needed to disentangle how and why critical events from world history are remembered the way they are across different countries and across long periods of time. Ideally, such work should be interdisciplinary in order to be able to include and combine different factors by means of different sets of methodological tools. The current project provides support for the view that collective memory can be a shared body of knowledge about the past but can also be related to an identity project that is linked to the "image" of a people as well as a fight about the past and about how it should be remembered (Dudai, 2002; see also Hirst & Manier, 2008; Wertsch & Roediger, 2008). Ultimately, future work may enable us to understand better how people—locally and more globally—come to agree upon a specific version of the past and how even that shared memory can change over time.

Acknowledgments

Krystian Barzykowski was supported by the following grants from the National Science Centre, Poland: grant 2015/19/D/HS6/00641 while working on the data collection and grant 2019/35/B/HS6/00528 while working on the current chapter.

References

Abel, M., & Bäuml, K.-H. T. (2020). Retrieval-induced forgetting in a social context: Do the same mechanisms underlie forgetting in speakers and listeners? *Memory & Cognition, 48*, 1–15.

Abel, M., Umanath, S., Fairfield, B., Takahashi, M., Roediger, H. L., & Wertsch, J. V. (2019). Collective memories across 11 nations for World War II: Similarities and differences regarding the most important events. *Journal of Applied Research in Memory and Cognition, 8*, 178–188.

Barzykowski, K., Umanath, S., Abel, M., Wertsch, J. V., & Roediger, H. L. (in preparation). Collective remembering of World War II in Poland: A complementary Polish-centric perspective.

Bernstein, S. (2016). Remembering war, remaining Soviet: Digital commemoration of World War II in Putin's Russia. *Memory Studies, 9*, 422–436.

Brewer, W. F., & Nakamura, G. V. (1984). The nature and functions of schemas. In R. S. Wyer, Jr., & T. K. Srull (Eds.), *Handbook of social cognition* (Vol. 1, pp. 119–160). Erlbaum.

Coman, A., Momennejad, I., Drach, R. D., & Geana, A. (2016). Mnemonic convergence in social networks: The emergent properties of cognition at a collective level. *Proceedings of the National Academy of Sciences of the USA, 113*, 8171–8176.

Congleton, A. R., & Rajaram, S. (2014). Collaboration changes both the content and the structure of memory: Building the architecture of shared representations. *Journal of Experimental Psychology: General, 143*, 1570–1584.

Cuc, A., Koppel, J., & Hirst, W. (2007). Silence is not golden: A case for socially shared retrieval-induced forgetting. *Psychological Science, 18*, 727–733.

Darman, P. (2009). *World War II: Stats and facts*. Fall River Press.

Davies, N. (2007). *Europe at war 1939–1945: No simple victory*. Penguin.

Dudai, Y. (2002). *Memory from A to Z: Keywords, concepts and beyond*. Oxford University Press.
Edele, M. (2017). Fighting Russia's history wars—Vladimir Putin and the codification of World War II. *History & Memory, 29*, 90–124.
Halbwachs, M. (1980). *The collective memory* (F. J. Didder, Jr., & V. Y. Ditter, Trans.). Harper & Row.
Halbwachs, M. (1992). *On collective memory* (L. A. Coser, Trans.). University of Chicago Press. (Original work published 1925)
Hirst, W., & Manier, D. (2008). Towards a psychology of collective memory. *Memory, 16*, 183–200.
Hirst, W., Yamashiro, J. K., & Coman, A. (2018). Collective memory from a psychological perspective. *Trends in Cognitive Sciences, 22*(5), 438–451.
Kaes, A. (1990). History and film: Public memory in the age of electronic dissemination. *History and Memory, 2*, 111–129.
Liu, J. H., Goldstein-Hawes, R., Hilton, D., Huang, L.-L., Gastardo-Conaco, C., Dresler-Hawke, E., . . . Hidaka, Y. (2005). Social representations of events and people in world history across 12 cultures. *Journal of Cross-Cultural Psychology, 36*(2), 171–191.
Liu, J. H., & Hilton, D. J. (2005). How the past weighs on the present: Social representations of history and their role in identity politics. *British Journal of Social Psychology, 44*, 537–556.
Liu, J. H., Paez, D., Slawuta, P., Cabecinhas, R., Techio, E., Kokdemir, D., Sen, R., Vincze, O., Muluk, H., Wang, F., & Zlobina, A. (2009). Representing world history in the 21st century: The impact of 9/11, the Iraq war, and the nation-state dynamics of collective remembering. *Journal of Cross-Cultural Psychology, 40*, 667–692.
Markovits, A. S., & Reich, S. (1997). The contemporary power of memory: The dilemmas for German foreign policy. *Communication Review, 2*(1), 89–119.
Pennebaker, J. W., Páez, D., & Deschamps, J. C. (2006). The social psychology of history. *Psicología Política, 32*, 15–32.
Rajaram, S., & Maswood, R. (2017). Collaborative memory: A selective review of data and theory. In J. H. Byrne (Ed.), *Learning and memory: A comprehensive reference* (2nd ed., pp. 53–70). Academic Press.
Roediger, H. L., III, & Abel, M. (2015). Collective memory: A new arena for cognitive study. *Trends in Cognitive Sciences, 19*, 359–361.
Roediger, H. L., Abel, M., Umanath, S., Shaffer, R. A., Fairfield, B., Takahashi, M., & Wertsch, J. V. (2019). Competing national memories of World War 2. *Proceedings of the National Academy of Sciences of the USA, 116*, 16678–16686.
Schuman, H., Akiyama, H., & Knäuper, B. (1998). Collective memories of Germans and Japanese about the past half-century. *Memory, 6*, 427–454.
Scott, J., & Zac, L. (1993). Collective memories in Britain and the United States. *Public Opinion Quarterly, 57*, 315–331.
Siddi, M. (2017). The Ukraine crisis and European memory politics of the Second World War. *European Politics and Society, 18*, 465–479.
Stone, C. B., Luminet, O., Jay, A. C., Klein, O., Licata, L., & Hirst, W. (2020, January). Do public speeches induce "collective" forgetting? The Belgian King's 2012 summer speech as a case study. *Memory Studies*.
Uldricks, T. J. (2009). War, politics and memory—Russian historians reevaluate the origins of World War II. *History & Memory, 21*, 60–82.

Verovšek, P. J. (2016). Collective memory, politics, and the influence of the past: The politics of memory as a research paradigm. *Politics, Groups, and Identities, 4*(3), 529–543.

Wertsch, J. V. (2002). *Voices of collective remembering.* Cambridge University Press.

Wertsch, J. V. (2008). The narrative organization of collective memory. *Ethos, 36,* 120–135.

Wertsch, J. V., & Karumidze, Z. (2009). Spinning the past: Russian and Georgian accounts of the war of August 2008. *Memory Studies, 2,* 377–391.

Wertsch, J. V., & Roediger, H. L., III. (2008). Collective memory: Conceptual foundations and theoretical approaches. *Memory, 16,* 318–326.

Wittlinger, R., & Larose, M. (2007). No future for Germany's past? Collective memory and German foreign policy. *German Politics, 16*(4), 481–495.

Yamashiro, J. K., & Hirst, W. (2020). Convergence on collective memories: Central speakers and distributed remembering. *Journal of Experimental Psychology: General, 149,* 461–481.

Zaromb, F., Butler, A. C., Agarwal, P. K., & Roediger, H. L. (2014). Collective memories of three wars in United States history in younger and older adults. *Memory & Cognition, 42,* 383–399. doi:10.3758/s13421-013-0369-7

11

National and State Narcissism as Reflected in Overclaiming of Responsibility

Henry L. Roediger, III, Adam L. Putnam, and Jeremy K. Yamashiro

Individual identity is shaped by the groups to which we belong—our family, our church, the schools we attend, the company for which we work, the sports teams with which we affiliate, and the city and state and country in which we are raised. Because of pervasive group affiliations, individual characteristics—height, weight, gender, personality, and so on—play only a partial role in "individual" identity. We can probably predict much more about a person from the groups to which they belong than from any particular individual characteristic.

Because the groups to which we belong shape our identity, we often feel proud of them. It is as if "I am a member, it must be a good organization." Thus, we show school pride when we are in high school or college; many of us are still loyal to these sports teams as we age, or we become fans of the team in our hometown. In this chapter, we are concerned with allegiances to much larger entities: the country in which people are born and, in the United States, the state in which people are born and raised. We argue that even affiliations to these larger communities play a role in individual identity and, in turn, individuals believe these communities have had greater influence and responsibility than more objective observers might grant them.

We use *imagined community* for nations and states as framed in Benedict Anderson's (1983) work on the creation of national consciousnesses. A nation is, he argued, an idea that must be socially constructed but which, once established, can motivate powerful feelings of allegiance. Any given person is unlikely to encounter even a tiny fraction of the other members of their "nation," but nonetheless they can feel a strong bond with them. We argue that in the United States, many people also feel an allegiance to the state in which they grow up. Like nations, states are social constructions. A person working for a corporation in downtown Atlanta may have little in common with a peanut farmer in Plains or a chicken processor in Gainesville, but nonetheless all three are Georgians. They study Georgia history in school; root for the Braves in baseball; and identify, to a greater or lesser degree, with their state.

Scholars of nationalism, in particular, have written compellingly of the pride that people take in their own nation. In school, students are often taught the uplifting parts of a nation's story, with the more negative parts downplayed. One public display of pride occurs at the opening ceremony at the Olympics every 4 years. When each nation's team marches in, waving their country's flag, spectators can witness the team's great pride in their nation, whether they are from large countries such as Russia or China or from small ones such as Monaco and Estonia. When the American team arrives, chants of "USA! USA!" fill the arena from the U.S.'s numerous fans. The same is true at the state level within the United States. When the University of Mississippi plays the University of Alabama in football, most residents of Mississippi and Alabama take note and root for their state's team.

Such group-centric sentiment is, in a sense, commonplace. Seemingly every group shares a sense of group pride, one that we argue is usually inflated. But is there a way of measuring such egocentrism or, as we have called it in several publications, national and state narcissism? We suggest there is, and we here review applications of the technique in the context of national and U.S. state groups. The technique is one to measure the overclaiming of responsibility, and we describe its origins in the next section.

Overclaiming of Responsibility

Ross and Sicoly (1979) began this line of research by conducting straightforward studies of people in small groups, including married couples. The researchers asked questions of each member separately, such as "How often do you take out the trash?" or "How often do you care for the children?" with a scale of 150 arbitrary units and with "wife" at one end and "husband" at the other end. The totals routinely added to greater than 150 (or more than 100%) when the contributions of the two were summed. As the authors state, "Individuals tend to accept more responsibility for a joint product than other contributors attribute to them" (p. 322).

In another study, Ross and Sicoly (1979) asked members of college basketball teams to name a turning point in their most recent game, with the prediction being that players would ascribe the turning point to their own team.

Sure enough, of the players who answered the question, 80% attributed the turning point to their own team and only 11% to the other team. (The other 9% of the players said both teams.) The authors also asked the players to explain the outcome of the game, whether it was a win or a loss. Only 8% of the players invoked properties of the other team in their answer, whereas 92% credited or blamed the win or loss on their own team's play. Ross and Sicoly's work persuasively showed that people tend to claim more responsibility for themselves (and their group) than is warranted.

The overclaiming effects obtained by Ross and Sicoly (1979) have been obtained by many researchers using other groups and other contexts (e.g., Brawley, 1984; Kruger & Gilovich, 1999; Kruger & Savitsky, 2009). Of particular interest for our purposes, Schroeder et al. (2016) showed that overclaiming of responsibility increased with group size. They demonstrated this partly by reanalyzing an earlier study by Caruso et al. (2006) that examined claims of responsibility in the writing of academic papers with three to six authors; overclaiming increased with the number of authors. In addition, Schroeder et al. (2016) reported experiments showing that the larger the group participating in some task, the greater the overclaiming. However, they showed that overclaiming could be moderated or, in one study, eliminated if people were asked to consider and estimate other group members' contributions before their own.

These studies served as a springboard for our own. How great would overclaiming of responsibility be when people were asked to estimate the contributions of their own country to world history or to fighting in World War II? How great would overclaiming be for citizens assessing their state's contribution to U.S. history? Later in the chapter, we examine possible reasons for overclaiming, and we weigh the evidence for them.

National Narcissism

Nationalism is on the rise throughout the world and has been for some years. In 2020, the United Kingdom, United States, India, Israel, China, Turkey, Russia, and other countries were led by men who tout their country's achievements and do not cooperate well with leaders from other countries. In the United States, Donald Trump proudly announced his "America First" policy, echoing some American leaders of the past who had argued that the focus of the United States should be in taking care of itself and remain isolated from the problems and affairs of other countries. However, even before this recent rise in nationalism, people in the United States had a long history of considering their country exceptional (e.g., Gingrich, 2011), as a beacon of democracy and freedom. Leaders of other nations may scoff at these claims (e.g., Putin, 2013), but American presidents from John Kennedy through Barack Obama have discussed the United States in these terms. Americans often look to "the city on a hill" speech given by John Winthrop in 1630 as the origin of American exceptionalism. Van Engen (2020) provides an interesting history and discussion of the reception of the speech and of the concept of American exceptionalism over time.

The wide acceptance in the United States of American exceptionalism implies that many Americans are egocentric about their country. But are Americans any more egocentric than people from, for example, Russia, China, or India—or, for that matter, Canada or Indonesia? How could we possibly find out? We adapted the methods developed for studying individual-level overclaiming to examine overclaiming on behalf of the groups to which people belong in an attempt to answer this question.

Our first project arose almost by chance. James Liu, a social psychologist in New Zealand, was planning a large cross-national study of how people in 35 countries perceived world history. He asked Jim Wertsch to participate, and Wertsch passed the request along to Henry Roediger, the first author of this chapter. Roediger agreed to help, along with Franklin Zaromb, then a graduate student. We read through Liu's survey and made comments, and Roediger asked if he could add one item near the end of the questionnaire. Liu said yes. The item examined claims of responsibility by citizens of each country for world history. Specifically, the item was "What contribution do you think the country you are living in has made to world history?" The 6,831 college students in the sample provided an estimate on a scale from 0 to 100, where 0% indicated that the country made no contribution to world history and 100% indicated that all contributions came from the country. Students took the survey in their own language. This critical survey question was near the end of the survey, which was good for our purposes. The preceding items asked many questions about events and figures in world history, most of which naturally did not pertain to each student's own country. We thought at the time that our question's placement at the end of the survey might lower estimates of responsibility.

Of course, our question is an odd one because there is no correct or incorrect answer. Psychologists distinguish between objective tests (e.g., the SAT or GRE) that have correct answers and projective tests that have no correct or incorrect answers. The reason for projective tests is to allow the test-taker to project themself into answers on the test. Thus, people from Fiji, in answering how much their country has contributed to world history, tell us nothing objective about world history but, rather, tell us what the people believe about their country and its role in world history. Of course, for most countries, the percentage should be vanishingly small ("world history," after all, covers a huge time span, and most modern countries did not exist for the majority of that time). The United Nations counts 193 countries, with others missing for various reasons (e.g., North Korea and Palestine). Because people in the United States constantly hear about American exceptionalism, we predicted that they would score high on the overclaiming of responsibility for world history relative to people from other countries (despite the fact that written U.S. history is relatively short compared to that of many other countries). We were wrong.

The data from our one-question study were published in Zaromb et al. (2018) and are summarized in Table 11.1, with countries arranged from those claiming the greatest responsibility at the top to those claiming the lowest at the bottom. Recall that students should have estimated a very small percentage, but despite surveying students in only 35 countries, the total amount of responsibility claimed across the surveyed countries was 1,156%! Students from 4 countries claimed more than 50% responsibility: Russians, 60%; British, 55%; Indians, 54%; and Hong Kong Chinese (perhaps identifying as British and/or Chinese for this purpose), 51%. The United States came in 22nd, with a relatively modest (but still ludicrous) 30%, behind Canada (40%), Portugal (38%), and Fiji (36%). We see from the data that students in all countries greatly inflate their country's influence on world affairs relative to any kind of reasonable baseline (although we cannot know what such a baseline is). This outcome occurs despite the fact that we studied college students, whose general knowledge of world history is probably greater than that of the general population, and that the question was placed at the end of a long survey with many events and names from world history. Despite these factors, estimates of one's own country's responsibility for world history were remarkably high. Schroeder et al. (2016) predicted that the larger the group, the greater the overclaiming of responsibility, and their prediction is borne out in the estimates of the claimed influence of countries. Confrontation with the vast community of nations seemed to engender not national humility but, rather, group-centric overclaiming.

Table 11.1 Estimated Contribution of Each Country to World History[a]

Country	n	Estimated Contribution (%)	95% CI
Russia	214	60.8	57.4, 64.2
United Kingdom	92	54.6	49.4, 59.8
India	154	53.9	49.7, 58.1
Hong Kong	140	51.0	46.5, 55.5
Malaysia	198	48.7	44.7, 52.7
Italy	129	44.2	40.0, 48.4
China	185	41.9	38.7, 45.1
Philippines	330	41.2	38.1, 44.3
Brazil	190	40.7	37.2, 44.2
Canada	189	40.2	36.4, 44.0
Indonesia	182	39.4	35.6, 43.2
Portugal	191	37.9	34.7, 41.1
Fiji	159	35.8	30.3, 41.3
Colombia	159	34.4	30.2, 38.6
Spain	209	33.8	30.8, 36.8
Japan	105	33.5	27.1, 39.9
Germany	147	32.7	28.9, 36.5
Mexico	192	32.6	29.2, 36.0
Singapore	218	32.5	28.8, 36.2
Bulgaria	226	29.9	27.1, 32.7
Peru	76	29.7	24.8, 34.6
United States	251	29.6	26.6, 32.6
Pakistan	98	29.1	23.8, 34.4
Tunisia	118	28.5	22.6, 34.4
Australia	167	25.9	22.0, 29.8
Austria	189	23.4	20.2, 26.6
Argentina	328	23.3	21.1, 25.5
Belgium	130	23.0	19.4, 26.6
South Korea	218	22.4	19.5, 25.3
Taiwan	291	21.1	18.2, 24.0
Netherlands	196	20.1	17.7, 22.5
Hungary	181	19.3	16.1, 22.5
New Zealand	137	17.7	13.9, 21.5
Norway	165	12.3	9.6, 15.0
Switzerland	144	11.3	8.7, 13.9

[a]As rated by residents from each country from Zaromb et al. (2018).
CI, confidence interval.

Adapted from "We Made History: Citizens of 35 Countries Overestimate Their Nation's Role in World History," by Zaromb et al., 2018, *Journal of Applied Research in Memory and Cognition*, 7, 521–528, with permission from Elsevier.

In the Zaromb et al. (2018) study, we asked students to focus only on their own country. Prior research has shown that if people are explicitly told to consider the contributions of other entities, they moderate claims of their own contributions (Ross & Sicoly, 1979; Schroeder et al., 2016). We examined whether this idea would extend to collective overclaiming in the next study. Roediger et al. (2019) reported a study examining claims of responsibility of Allied and Axis countries participating in World War II. More than 100 people each from 11 different countries participated by completing a survey devoted to the war; the survey asked general knowledge questions, asked the participants to list the 10 most important events of the war, and also asked (for Allied countries), "In terms of percentage, what do you think was [your country's] contribution to the victory of World War 2? In other words, how responsible was your country for the victory of the war?" This was the question asked of people from Australia, Canada, China, France, New Zealand, Russia, the United Kingdom, and the United States. People from the Axis powers of Italy, Japan, and Germany were asked, "Germany, Italy and Japan fought on the same side for 6 years during World War 2. What percentage of the war effort was provided by [your country]?" In all cases, participants saw a scale from 0 to 100 with a slider below it. They moved the slider to indicate the percentage assigned to their country.

The percentage responsibility results for the eight Allied countries are shown in the leftmost bars in Figure 11.1. Just these eight countries claimed 309% of responsibility for winning the war, for an average of approximately 39% per country. However, there was obviously great disparity among countries. Three countries claimed more than 50% responsibility, topped by Russia (representing the former Soviet Union) at 75%. The United States and the United Kingdom came in at 54% and 51%, respectively. Once again, we see great overclaiming of responsibility, our indicator of national narcissism. And keep in mind that many other countries participated on the Allied side. If we define a participating Allied country as one that had at least 1,000 soldiers killed in the war, then there are 19 other allies that were not included in our study.

Critically, for people of all 11 countries, we asked about the victory in a second way: "In terms of percentage, how much do you think each of the following countries contributed to the Allied victory of World War 2? In other words, how responsible was each country for the Allied victory of World War 2?" with the names of 8 Allied countries (including the subject's own country) listed in alphabetical order and with a ninth listing of "Other countries." The

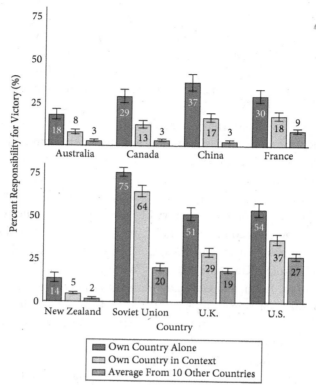

Figure 11.1 Allied contribution to the war effort as estimated by citizens of the Allied countries in the study by Roediger et al. (2019). Perceived percentage contribution to the war effort is depicted for eight former Allied countries. Ratings of each country's contribution to victory were provided by (1) participants concerning their own country's contribution, (2) participants concerning their own country's contribution when asked in the context of seven other Allied contributions, and (3) when participants in 10 other former Allied and Axis countries rated each country's contribution. Error bars represent 95% confidence intervals.

Reprinted from "Competing National Memories of World War II," by Roediger, H. L., et al., 2019, *Proceedings of the National Academic of Sciences of the USA*, 116(34), 16678–16686. Copyright 2018 by the authors. Reprinted with permission.

survey required that the numbers add to 100% before the person could move on to the next question. We asked this question of Axis countries, too, but we asked them about the allies with the same list of countries. As discussed previously, prior work with small groups has shown that when people must assess the contributions of others, they moderate their own estimates of responsibility. As seen in the middle bars in Figure 11.1, we found this same moderation with all 8 Allied countries. On the one hand, people in 4 countries lowered their estimates by half or more—Australia, Canada, China, and New Zealand. On the other hand, people in the United States, United Kingdom, and (to a lesser extent) France moderated their estimates by less than half. Russians, estimating the contribution of the Soviet Union, only decreased from 75% to 64%. Even when seeing the names of the other allies, the total "moderated" percentage responsibility was still 191% —lower than 309% but still displaying robust overclaiming.

The bars on the right in Figure 11.1 display the percentage responsibility given by people from the other 10 countries for any specific country (i.e., the ratings of people from the country itself were excluded). So, for example, people from the other 10 countries judged that Australians were responsible for 3% of the victory. These estimates sum to 96%, which is more reasonable than the other data but doubtless still too high with so many countries omitted. One notable feature of these data is that people from the other 10 countries estimated that the United States contributed more to the effort in World War II (27%) than did the Soviet Union (20%), a statistically significant difference. This finding is doubtless a surprise to people of the former Soviet Union because they fought Germany for several years in Europe before the United States, United Kingdom, and other countries mounted an offensive there. Deaths of military personnel in the war totaled approximately 417,000 for the United States and between 9 and 11 *million* for the Soviet Union.

Why does such great overclaiming occur? We discuss several possible reasons later, after reviewing other results based on U.S. states. The results reviewed here show that in both estimates of contributions to all of world history and of contributions to World War II, people of most countries show a large overclaiming of responsibility effect—one that is so extreme that we refer to it as reflecting national narcissism (for converging evidence, see Abel et al. 2019).

State Narcissism

After seeing the striking collective overclaiming effects in our national narcissism studies, we were curious to determine if such overclaiming also occurred when participants considered a smaller (yet still imagined) community: the home states of U.S. residents. The three authors grew up in different areas of the country, yet we agreed in our predictions as to which states would overclaim the most. We expected that the original 13 colonies would provide high ratings, due to the role that they played in the founding of the country. Furthermore, we also expected that states that currently have a large population and cultural impact (California) or unusual pride about their state (Texas) would also provide high ratings.

As an additional measure, we had the American sample rate not only their home state but also other states. While Virginians might think highly of their state's contributions, it also seems likely that people from Missouri or Idaho (or any other state) would also think Virginians had contributed a lot. Although an overclaiming question is always going to be a projective test to some degree, having nonresident ratings would presumably provide a more balanced assessment of the consensus baseline for a state's contribution to U.S. history. Doing so would allow us to examine how much more people thought of their home state than others did.

To do so, we conducted a pair of large studies, with each sample recruiting approximately 40–68 residents from each of the U.S. states (Churchill et al., 2019; Putnam et al., 2018). After reporting which state they considered their "home state," participants read the critical question, essentially the same question from our national narcissism survey but adapted for the US states:

> You said you grew up in [home state]. In terms of percentage, what do you think was [home state's] contribution to the history of the United States? In other words, how responsible was [home state] for the historical developments in the United States? Keep in mind there are 50 states and that the total contribution for all states has to equal 100%.

Participants then used a slider to make their rating between 0% and 100%. Following the critical question, we also had participants make a similar judgment for 10 other randomly selected states. These out-of-state ratings for each state allowed us to calculate a consensus baseline estimating the contribution attributed to that state by nonresidents, who could have come from any of the other 49 states. Because both of our studies used identical question phrasing, we have combined the data from Churchill et al. (2019) and Putnam et al. (2018); these aggregated data are presented here for the first time in Table 11.2. This combined data set had a total sample size of 5,113 participants, with home state

Table 11.2 Resident Ratings, Out-of-State Ratings, and Narcissistic Indices with Effect Size from Aggregate Data Set Drawn from Putnam et al. (2018) and Churchill et al. (2019)[a]

U.S. State	Resident (n)	Nonresident (n)	Mean Resident Rating (SD)	Mean Nonresident Rating (SD)	Narcissistic Index	Cohen's d
Virginia	117	1,000	41.43 (26.56)	25.62 (23.97)	15.81	0.63
Delaware	87	1,025	31.91 (28.75)	17.27 (19.85)	14.64	0.60
Massachusetts	111	672	38.66 (27.48)	25.08 (23.38)	13.58	0.53
New Jersey	107	978	26.16 (22.72)	13.21 (16.71)	12.95	0.66
Georgia	92	934	27.92 (26.24)	15.28 (18.44)	12.64	0.57
Louisiana	100	969	27.34 (23.82)	16.67 (19.33)	10.67	0.49
South Carolina	103	677	24.94 (23.90)	15.46 (18.12)	9.48	0.45
New Hampshire	99	1,022	24.36 (25.34)	14.98 (19.59)	9.38	0.42
Wyoming	83	964	17.07 (21.28)	8.31 (13.77)	8.76	0.50
Connecticut	110	1,009	25.39 (24.72)	16.67 (19.79)	8.72	0.39
Pennsylvania	112	975	34.11 (26.83)	25.67 (24.99)	8.44	0.33
Rhode Island	90	1,032	20.80 (23.43)	12.51 (17.52)	8.29	0.40
California	158	961	27.49 (22.10)	19.38 (20.16)	8.11	0.38
Kansas	104	925	17.63 (17.79)	9.67 (14.19)	7.96	0.50
Florida	109	1,007	20.61 (21.08)	12.96 (17.37)	7.65	0.40
Missouri	127	989	18.86 (18.45)	11.59 (15.80)	7.27	0.42
North Carolina	105	972	22.74 (23.20)	15.58 (19.13)	7.16	0.34
Hawaii	86	950	17.03 (17.32)	9.88 (16.05)	7.15	0.43
Montana	86	968	15.22 (16.97)	8.46 (13.05)	6.76	0.45

(continued)

U.S. State	Resident (*n*)	Nonresident (*n*)	Mean Resident Rating (SD)	Mean Nonresident Rating (SD)	Narcissistic Index	Cohen's *d*
New York	123	624	31.60 (25.64)	25.01 (22.68)	6.59	0.27
North Dakota	80	995	14.56 (18.46)	8.19 (13.61)	6.37	0.40
Nebraska	97	904	13.00 (16.57)	6.83 (11.62)	6.17	0.44
Tennessee	100	692	18.12 (20.37)	12.08 (15.96)	6.04	0.33
Ohio	113	1,000	18.40 (18.64)	12.45 (17.07)	5.95	0.33
Oklahoma	96	1,018	15.29 (18.65)	9.46 (13.84)	5.83	0.36
Idaho	99	1,012	13.67 (17.31)	7.88 (12.72)	5.79	0.39
Vermont	85	693	17.71 (20.97)	11.95 (16.91)	5.76	0.30
Illinois	117	998	18.23 (18.30)	12.75 (15.85)	5.48	0.32
Oregon	93	1,006	16.21 (17.34)	10.79 (15.03)	5.42	0.33
Alabama	106	962	17.85 (18.88)	12.61 (16.84)	5.24	0.29
South Dakota	94	646	11.88 (14.65)	7.33 (12.59)	4.55	0.33
Nevada	89	1,000	13.85 (16.74)	9.4 (13.98)	4.45	0.29
Maryland	139	1,002	21.97 (20.37)	17.99 (20.63)	3.98	0.19
Michigan	115	960	13.83 (14.12)	9.87 (13.84)	3.96	0.28
Minnesota	104	642	11.63 (13.04)	8.11 (12.70)	3.52	0.27
Indiana	106	990	13.08 (15.05)	9.89 (15.35)	3.19	0.21
Utah	98	964	12.38 (17.92)	9.43 (14.89)	2.95	0.18
New Mexico	95	992	11.55 (14.01)	8.90 (14.31)	2.65	0.19
Kentucky	105	999	15.11 (14.13)	12.60 (17.32)	2.51	0.16
Alaska	77	972	11.14 (12.60)	8.72 (14.37)	2.42	0.18

Arkansas	95	969	12.62 (12.13)	10.21 (14.87)	2.41	0.18
Texas	127	974	21.79 (17.95)	19.53 (20.24)	2.26	0.12
Wisconsin	100	1,021	10.96 (13.54)	9.45 (14.35)	1.51	0.11
Iowa	90	1,001	9.91 (12.57)	9.37 (14.52)	0.54	0.04
Maine	96	980	12.74 (16.44)	12.25 (17.27)	0.49	0.03
Arizona	102	991	9.96 (11.26)	9.48 (14.26)	0.48	0.04
Mississippi	98	984	15.41 (14.56)	15.00 (18.81)	0.41	0.02
West Virginia	93	936	16.62 (18.70)	16.37 (20.64)	0.25	0.01
Colorado	89	1,001	10.88 (11.03)	10.89 (16.19)	-0.01	0.00
Washington	106	987	12.24 (15.54)	14.67 (21.38)	-2.43	-0.13

[a]Mean resident and mean non-resident ratings stand for the proportion of American history attributed to each state by resident raters and out-of-state raters, respectively. States are ranked by Narcissistic Index. Cohen's d represents the effect size for the difference between resident and nonresident ratings for each state.

SD, standard deviation.

ratings drawn from an average of 102 participants from each state [standard deviation (SD) = 15]. The consensus baseline ratings were drawn from an average of 939 participants for each state (SD = 115). The states are ordered in terms of what we call the Narcissistic Index, which is explained later.

The first column in Table 11.2 provides the names of the states; the second column presents the number of participants from each state; and the third column shows the number of out-of-state people who rated that state. The fourth column in the table presents the average resident rating for the 50 states, and the fifth column presents the average rating from nonresidents. A few specific points are worth noting. First, the average resident rating was 19% across all states in column 4. Given that a purely mathematical approach would suggest 2% as a reasonable starting estimate, 19% is remarkably high. Second, there was a wide range of estimates among the resident ratings. The most modest state was Iowa at 10% (still a high number compared to 2%), whereas others were anything but modest: Virginians claimed 41% responsibility for U.S. history, and people from Massachusetts, Pennsylvania, Delaware, and New York all claimed greater than 30%. The variability suggests that people from certain states are more likely to claim responsibility than those from other states. Finally, overclaiming is certainly occurring. Summing the average response from each state yields a staggering total of 945%, replicating a level of overclaiming that the editor of the Putnam et al. (2019) paper referred to as "ludicrous."

By collecting ratings from nonresidents, we were able to obtain an estimate of how much people from outside a state thought that state had contributed. With those ratings, we calculated what we called a Narcissistic Index by subtracting the nonresident ratings from the resident ratings. These data are shown in column 5 of Table 11.2. Cohen's d's represent the effect size for the difference between resident and nonresident ratings for each state. Figure 11.2 presents a heat map of narcissistic indices drawn from the pooled Putnam et al. (2018) and Churchill et al. (2019) data. Across the entire country, Americans showed a mean state Narcissistic Index of 5.80% (95% confidence interval: 4.69, 6.91; Cohen's d = 0.32). However, we again see wide regional variability, with numbers ranging from a low of −2.43% in Washington to 15.81% in Virginia. (We expect many outside-the-state raters may have been thinking of Washington, DC, rather than Washington state, which may account for the one negative rating.) Notice that our predictions seem largely fulfilled: The Narcissistic Index is high for the states of the

NATIONAL AND STATE NARCISSISM 223

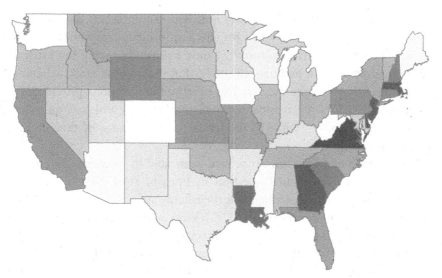

Figure 11.2 Choropleth map of state narcissism from the combined data sets of Putnam et al. (2018) and Churchill et al. (2019), representing data from 5,113 American participants. Darker color represents greater collective overclaiming for the home state, relative to a consensus baseline. White fill represents negligible or no collective narcissism—that is, in lighter states, home state ratings approximately equaled out-of-state ratings.

original 13 colonies and California, but Texas, on the other hand, provided a relatively modest value. Wyoming surprised us by being grouped with the 13 colonies in terms of the Narcissistic Index.

Another question we wondered about was whether we could possibly reduce the large amount of overclaiming. Given the prior work showing that drawing attention to the other members of a group (e.g., Ross & Sicoly, 1979; see also Roediger et al., 2019; Schroeder et al., 2016), we predicted that having people consider the scope and breadth of U.S. history—most of which happened outside of their home state—would lower people's claims of responsibility for their home state. To do so, in Putnam et al. (2018) we had half of our American sample take a quiz about U.S. history before answering the critical question, with the other half taking the quiz after answering the critical question. In the quiz, participants first had to generate a list of the 10 most important events in U.S. history and then answer 15 multiple-choice questions on topics ranging from the Revolutionary War to the Space Race.

To our surprise, taking the history quiz before completing the rating of contribution to state history had no effect on subjects' responses: across all 50 states Americans who took the quiz before answering the critical question provided an estimate of 18.4% for their home state, whereas Americans who took the quiz after answering the questions provided an estimate of 18.2%. Thus, it appeared that simply taking a history quiz was not enough to cause people to moderate their estimates of their home state's contributions.

Other manipulations, however, have been able to moderate claims of responsibility. An additional question in Putnam et al. (2018) required Americans to provide an estimate for their home state, the three states they thought had contributed the most to U.S. history, and a category representing the other 46 states; in this context, home state claims were reduced to an average of 10%. On the other hand, a follow-up study (reported in the supplemental materials of Putnam et al., 2019) showed that removing the reminder from the state narcissism question about the total contribution of all states equaling 100% increased the average estimate to 38% per state, more than doubling what it was originally. This finding suggests that the estimates of state narcissism provided previously are in some ways underestimates. Nonetheless, these findings provide more evidence for collective overclaiming—the idea that people will overclaim responsibility for their group.

Why Do State and National Overclaiming Occur?

When we present these findings, people are not only amazed by the basic phenomenon but also quickly offer hypotheses about *why* such overclaiming occurs. In our experience, most conjectures revolve around people's presumed narcissistic and egocentric tendencies—we value our own group and its contributions far more than the contributions of others. However, any psychological phenomenon with effect sizes as large as those found in our collective overclaiming studies likely arises from multiple mechanisms (Schroeder et al., 2016). In recent work, we have attempted to specify some of the psychological factors underlying collective overclaiming. There are at least two broad classes of psychological mechanism that likely contribute to collective overclaiming: motivational and cognitive factors.

Motivational Factors

One reason collective overclaiming might occur is that it is emotionally satisfying to think of our group as having played an important and influential role in history, and judgments are adjusted to satisfy this motivation (Kruger, 1999; Taylor & Brown, 1988). Of course, people vary in the extent to which they are motivated by in-group affection. In addition, given that most people possess many intersecting social identities, they likely vary in which specific groups they invest with in-group affection. In any case, individuals who are more motivated by a desire to regard their group positively should also overclaim more historical influence for those groups to which they are attached. This mechanism is supported in Ross and Sicoly's (1979) original studies in which, when group members were asked to evaluate their contribution to a negative outcome, overclaiming was reduced.

Group-oriented concern should be particularly influential when it is morally charged—that is, when people moralize loyalty to their group, respect for legitimate authority, and the sanctity of their group. Endorsement of these group-oriented moral values—referred to collectively as the *binding values*—varies across different political and cultural populations (Graham et al., 2009). For the purposes of our discussion on collective overclaiming, endorsement of binding values should create powerful psychological pressure to represent the collective past in a way that is favorable to the in-groups to which loyalty and respect are directed. Indeed, empirical work bears this out. As described previously, Churchill et al. (2019) had participants from each of the 50 U.S. states rate the proportion of U.S. history attributable to their home state and to 10 other states selected at random. They calculated a state narcissism index as in Putnam et al. (2018). Churchill et al. (2019) additionally administered the Moral Foundations Questionnaire (MFQ), which is a set of 36 questions in which people rate the extent to which various moral considerations are important to them. Responses on the MFQ can then be used to calculate the extent to which individuals endorse five "moral foundations" or domains of moralized concern: loyalty, respect for legitimate authority, sanctity/purity, harm/care, and fairness (Graham et al., 2009). Mean scores for the loyalty, authority, and sanctity foundations yield an index of binding values endorsement. Higher endorsement of binding values positively predicted a higher state narcissism index, indicating that people who were more strongly motivated by group-oriented moral values inflated their group's influence over history relative to a consensus baseline.

Binding values could lead to collective overclaiming both because an inflated sense of historical influence is more emotionally satisfying to those endorsing binding values and more indirectly by motivating selective attention when faced with historical information. Such selectivity can result in a bias in availability, discussed in the next section.

Cognitive Mechanisms

Availability

In addition to motivational factors such as moral influences on collective remembering, a number of more strictly cognitive factors probably also contribute to collective overclaiming. Central among these is the *availability heuristic* (Tversky & Kahneman, 1973). The availability heuristic is a cognitive shortcut in which people substitute a difficult question—"What is the probability of an event?"—with an easier one—"How easily do instances of this event come to mind?" In their original studies of overclaiming, Ross and Sicoly (1979) argued that married couples each claimed to have done more housework than their partner not because they thought highly of themselves but, rather, simply because instances of their own contributions came to mind more easily than instances of their partner's contributions. We have tested this mechanism of a bias in judgment driven by asymmetrical availability in a series of recent studies.

Yamashiro and Roediger (2021) examined whether an asymmetry in the cognitive availability of in-group versus out-group historical events predicted the extent of collective overclaiming. Participants from three American states—Virginia, Massachusetts, and California—estimated the proportion of American history attributable to people from their home state, as well as from the other two states. State narcissism indices were calculated as in prior work. Participants additionally engaged in a timed retrieval fluency task, in which they were given 1 minute to list as many important events as they could think of that had occurred in each of the three states. Asymmetrical bias in availability in favor of the home state—what we called the *parochial knowledge bias*—was calculated as the difference in average number of events listed for the home state minus the mean number of events for the other two states. That is, we measured how many events a person could name from their own states minus the average number they could retrieve about other states. Participants who showed a stronger parochial knowledge bias did tend to show more collective overclaiming. The role of an asymmetrical collective memory was further supported by a second study that showed selectively retrieving only events from the two non-home state targets led to a decrease in collective overclaiming. Together, these studies suggested that when people make judgments about historical influence, which is a rather difficult question, they substitute this difficult problem for an easier one, which is how easily important historical events from each group come to mind.

Because these studies used real home states as targets, they could still not rule out the possibility that some of the effect might be attributable to the social–motivational factors discussed previously. In a second project, we attempted to avoid the influence of identification with real social groups and prior knowledge by utilizing artificial states in a fictional country (M. Q. Ross et al., 2020). Participants read about a fictitious country (Olaram) that was composed of a set of territories. They then rated how much they thought a single territory (Adivigan) had contributed to the history of this fictitious country. We found that people still overclaimed responsibility for a target territory, even though it was completely fictional and thus unlikely to trigger any sort of ego-protection mechanisms. Participants provided higher estimates of historical contributions when more detail was provided about the target territory, indicating that having more accessible information about the target territory led to higher estimates.

Support Theory
Availability, then, seems to hold an important place among cognitive mechanisms underpinning collective overclaiming. We have recently begun moving to integrate this mechanism within the broader umbrella of support theory, which is a descriptive model of how people make decisions under uncertainty (Tversky & Koehler, 1994). The central premise of support theory is that rather than evaluating events themselves, people evaluate descriptions of events. For example, when asked to estimate the probability that in the next year either (1) 1,000 people will die in a natural disaster or (2) 1,000 people will die in an earthquake, tornado, or natural disaster, they usually choose the second option, even though it is merely an "unpacked" version of the first option. This *unpacking* makes specific examples seem more vivid and plausible than the vague category label of "natural disaster." Support theory incorporates a number of cognitive biases, including availability (Tversky & Kahneman, 1973), representativeness (judging likelihood based on similarity to a prototypical representation; Kahneman & Tversky, 1972), anchoring and

adjustment (using initial decision points to guide future decision-making; Tversky & Kahneman, 1974), and even focalism (a tendency to pay attention exclusively to the question or hypothesis under examination and to neglect alternatives; Klar, 2002). In the context of overclaiming, support theory predicts that overclaiming occurs because people focus on their own (or their group's) contributions, and they fail to adequately unpack the contributions of the other group members. This theoretical prediction has been supported by work examining overclaiming in small groups (Schroeder et al., 2016) and in collective overclaiming contexts, both with real countries (as described previously; Putnam et al., 2018) and in fictitious countries (M. Q. Ross et al., 2020).

Overestimation of Small Numbers
One final cognitive mechanism that helps explain collective overclaiming numbers is a tendency for people to overestimate small numbers. For example, in the realm of demographics, most Americans tend to estimate that approximately 20% of Americans publicly self-identify as LGBT, but the true percentage is closer to 3% (Gates & Newport, 2012; Newport, 2015). This tendency to overestimate small numbers appears, however, in a number of domains, including estimating perceptions of physical stimuli (Landy et al., 2018). Although it is impossible to know how much any state truly contributed to American history (and, of course, how much a country contributed to world history), we do know that any such number will by necessity be small or even tiny. A mathematically reasonable anchor for U.S. states would be 2% (i.e., 100% of American history divided by 50 states) with adjustment up or down based on what people know about American history, but this obviously is not the tactic most people use. Thus, some of the overclaiming we have shown can be attributed to the overestimation of small numbers.

Extensions and Implications

What are the sources of overclaiming of responsibility? We argue that overclaiming is the result of the collective memories people share as members of a group, which form part of personal identity. These collective memories are shaped by top-down (government-driven) forces, bottom-up (people-driven or grassroots) forces, and the interaction of both. We consider top-down forces first, and we mostly use U.S. history as an example.

Other writers in this book emphasize similar forces at work in other countries. In short, we argue that top-down forces such as governments play a major role in shaping collective memories but that bottom-up forces from the people are at work, too.

Governments in almost all countries mandate the teaching of history, and textbooks often have to be approved either by a government agency or by a group of citizens empowered to select the textbooks. Because such approval is necessary, textbook writers often steer clear of controversial material or material that casts the country in a poor light. In his essay "What Is a Nation?" Ernst Renan (1882/2018) specifically noted that people of a nation tend to forget or minimize the unfortunate aspects of its past. He wrote, "Forgetfulness, and I would even say historical error, are essential in the creation of a nation" (p. 251). Writing about France but with extensions to other countries, he wrote, "Unity is always achieved by brutality: The joining of the north of France with the center was the result of nearly a century of extermination and terror" (p. 251). Renan focused on forgetting because he believed that collective memory of the past represents a great part of what makes a nation. He asked what people of a nation have in common. It is not language, because many languages may be spoken; for example, in Houston, Texas, approximately 140 languages are in use in homes, yet most of the people there are American citizens. Neither race nor national origin makes a nation, because most countries have people who identify with different races and who emigrated from various places (or whose ancestors emigrated). Finally, religion does not qualify, because citizens may be of many faiths. So, what does make a nation? According to Renan, one key element is "the possession in common of a rich legacy of memories" (p. 261); it is collective memories that makes a nation. Renan argues these memories should be positive memories to remember the glories of common efforts in the past.

If a nation revels in its past glories and minimizes its negative actions, its government-sponsored textbooks are likely to be written that way. At least in the United States (but probably in every country), textbooks have traditionally been written as if to follow Renan's ideas. Until very recently, U.S. texts minimized negative elements of U.S. history. Christopher Columbus is glorified for having discovered the West Indies and America, but until recently, little or nothing was written about his horrific treatment of the largely peaceful natives that he met. In general, the genocide of Native Americans through both war and disease is rarely described in texts. Likewise, the horrors of slavery are usually mentioned in textbooks but given short shrift. James Loewen (2007), in his book *Lies My Teacher Told Me*, writes extensively about how generations of popular U.S. history textbooks used in high schools fall short in describing the complex or negative aspects of events. (The subtitle of the text is *Everything Your American History Textbook Got Wrong*.) In addition, *History in the Making* by Kyle Ward (2007) shows how history books have evolved in their portrayal of the same events during the past 200 years, probably due to both top-down and bottom-up influences.

Recently, textbook publishers have become more sophisticated by including special coverage of controversial topics for different states (Goldstein, 2020). The Second Amendment to the U.S. Constitution provides "the right to bear arms." In California's edition of the text, a sidebar appears next to the Second Amendment noting that the U.S. Supreme Court has provided exceptions to the amendment for cases in which guns have been regulated. In Texas's edition of the textbook, the sidebar has been dropped from the text and only blank space appears where the exception statement is noted for California students.

All these examples show how top-down influences change the way history is portrayed, which in turn shape the collective memories that people hold. Of course, sometimes changes are due to new evidence coming to light, such as the DNA evidence showing that Thomas Jefferson was the father of the children of his slave, Sally Hemings (Gordon-Reed, 2008). But other times, textbook writers simply emphasize or omit certain facets of complicated events to seek approval of their book.

The examples just provided illustrate how states and elites can try to control what people in the nation know about history. We turn now to consider the bottom-up influences, the influences from individuals, and we can ask why people in different areas of the same country can believe different representations of history. The senior author of this chapter grew up in the South, in Danville, Virginia. It was (and is) known as the Last Capital of the Confederacy because Jefferson Davis held his last full cabinet meeting there while he and others were fleeing south from Richmond. Roediger also went to two schools named after Robert E. Lee: a middle school and then Washington & Lee University. Growing up in the South in the 1950s and 1960s, one learned the legends about the Lost Cause, the chivalrous southern gentleman, the belief in states' rights, and so on. Some of this information was not learned from formal textbooks but, rather, from the culture in which one existed. Novels, movies, stories, and landmarks helped tell the story of the South, one that others say was an imagined history that bore little resemblance to the truth, to the horrors suffered by Black people in slavery and in the fights for civil rights. The historical record is being corrected in the modern South, although the Lost Cause myth lingers. In short, what one learned growing up in the South in the 1950s and 1960s was not the authorized view of history in the nation but, rather, a regional view of a certain period of history that was inculcated via bottom-up influences from the surrounding society as well as from top-down influences from books approved by the government. The same is doubtless true in certain ways in other areas of the country.

Previously, we suggested that the cognitive processes of individuals can lead to overclaiming of responsibility, implicating bottom-up processes. Our judgments are based on what information is available to us, and this information can arise from either top-down or bottom-up sources; thus, the availability heuristic is an example of a force that represents the interaction of top-down and bottom-up processes. The tendency to focus on one event or aspect of an event (focalizing, in support theory) is another example of a bottom-up process. For example, in our study of perceptions of nations' responsibilities for the victory in World War II, our first framing of the question ("How much did your country contribute to the victory?") led people to focus only on their country and not to think of other nations. However, our second framing, when we asked people to consider their own country in the context of 7 others, with percentages of responsibility to be assigned to all of them (and the category of "other countries"), led to much different results. For example, people in the United Kingdom claimed 51% responsibility in the first framing of the question, but that dropped to 29% in the second framing when they were confronted with deliberately thinking about contributions of other countries. Even the second, more moderate, contribution was higher than the percentage contribution attributed to the United Kingdom by people of 10 other countries (19%). Of course, as we noted, there is no way to say what is the correct percentage for each country, but even with the second framing it is likely that all countries overclaim responsibility; the total percentages of just the 8 countries surveyed still led to 190%. This number highlights another person-driven characteristic that leads to overclaiming—the inability of even well-educated people to reason well with small numbers. In summary, at least some of the streamlining and simplification that we see in the formation of collective memories might be related to basic bottom-up processes.

Is Narcissism the Correct Term?

Throughout this chapter, as well as in our prior work, we have referred to the dramatic overclaiming of responsibility as reflecting national and state narcissism. Some have complained to us that this is adjectival overreach. Psychologists have a long history of creating mischief by applying terms of individual psychology to the social psychology of groups. For example, because the murder of Jews and others in Nazi Germany was not much discussed for 15–20 years after the war by the survivors, one sometimes hears that their memories must have been repressed, thus bringing to bear a term from the Freudian lexicon to memories of victims. However, no one can seriously think that the victims of the concentration camps forgot about their experiences; they simply did not often share their memories. The same was true of the horrors of war of many returning soldiers who refused to talk about their experiences. Using the term "repression" for their reticence to speak about the events is a mistake.

Is referring to dramatic overclaiming as narcissism a similar mistake? After all, we are arguing that cold cognitive mechanisms such as the availability heuristic can account for the effects in individuals. And we are not arguing that the individuals who display national or state narcissism are narcissistic as individuals.

The definition of narcissism usually refers to great selfishness with three primary characteristics: a grandiose sense of self-importance, a sense of entitlement, and exploitation of others. At least at the national level, certainly countries frequently display these characteristics. We have thousands of years of history of one country or empire conquering others and imposing their "superior" system on others; this is true from the Roman empire to the British empire, extending to American "manifest destiny" during the 1800s in conquering the Native Americans who lived in the western United States. At the state level, we can see the excessive state pride that leads to rivalries among states at many levels (not just on the football field, as in an example discussed previously). The U.S. Civil War was based on states with different world views of what was right, even if one side (incredibly, to modern eyes) argued that slavery was a right to their states. Thus, because of the self-adulating, prideful nature of national and state egocentrism, we believe that the term narcissism is useful as a shorthand for the condition.

Conclusion

The self-pride that people have in their groups is an oft-noted phenomenon. One intent of the research we report is to provide a measure of such pride for large groups, which we have called national and state narcissism for the groups we measured. We believe the overclaiming paradigm that was originally developed to measure the contribution of individuals in small groups serves this purpose. The questions we posed to people from different countries and states referred to their belief in their countries' contributions to world history, to the victory (or loss) in World War II, and, for Americans', belief in the influence of their state on the history of the United States. In all cases with these large groups, we showed dramatic overclaiming, which we believe justifies our descriptors of national and state narcissism. We view our use of the overclaiming paradigm as providing a concrete way for quantifying (or operationalizing) how people feel about the role of their state/nation in history, a quality missing in prior research and speculation.

Many factors may account for such overclaiming of responsibility. Support theory, supplemented by other factors, supplies a useful framework. People tend to "focalize" (or focus) on the issue at hand without considering alternatives. When confronted with alternatives that they must unpack, judgments about the focal event being judged become more reasonable. In addition, people use the information they have available to make a judgment. If people in the United Kingdom know a lot about the contribution of the country to World War II but know little about the contribution of the Soviet Union, their judgments will be similarly lopsided. In addition, people seem to have difficulty dealing with small percentages. Even when people in the Putnam et al. (2018) experiment were reminded that there were 50 U.S. states, the percentages assigned to states were almost always much higher than 2%.

Finally, we argued that overclaiming of responsibility, reflecting national narcissism, is a function of both top-down influences, driven by governments and citizen commissions in the writing of textbooks, and bottom-up forces coming from the cognitive processes in individuals and the social milieu in which they exist.

References

Abel, M., Umanath, S., Fairfield, B., Takahashi, M., Roediger, H. L., & Wertsch, J. V. (2019). Collective memories across 11 nations for World War II: Similarities and differences regarding the most important events. *Journal of Applied Research in Memory and Cognition, 8*(2), 178–188. https://doi.org/10.1016/j.jarmac.2019.02.001

Anderson, B. (1983). *Imagined communities: Reflections on the origins and spread of nationalism.* Verso.

Brawley, L. R. (1984). Unintentional egocentric biases in attributions. *Journal of Sport Psychology, 6,* 264–278.

Caruso, E. M., Epley, N., & Bazerman, M. H. (2006). The costs and benefits of undoing egocentric responsibility assessments in groups. *Journal of Personality and Social Psychology, 91*(5), 857–871.

Churchill, L., Yamashiro, J. K., & Roediger, H. L. (2019). Moralized memory: Binding values predict inflated estimates of the group's historical influence. *Memory, 15*(1), 1099–1109.

Gates, G. J., & Newport, F. (2012). *Special report: 3.4% of U.S. adults identify as LGBT.* Gallup. https://news.gallup.com/poll/158066/special-report-adults-identify-lgbt.aspx

Gingrich, N. (2011). *A nation like no other: Why American nationalism matters.* Regnery.

Goldstein, D. (2020, January 12). Two states. Eight textbooks. Two American stories. *The New York Times.* https://www.nytimes.com/interactive/2020/01/12/us/texas-vs-california-history-textbooks.html

Graham, J., Haidt, J., & Nosek, B. A. (2009). Liberals and conservatives rely on different sets of moral foundations. *Journal of Personality and Social Psychology, 96*(5), 1029–1046.

Kahneman, D., & Tversky, A. (1972). Subjective probability: A judgment of representativeness. *Cognitive Psychology, 3*(3), 430–454.

Klar, Y. (2002). Way beyond compare: Nonselective superiority and inferiority biases in judging randomly assigned group members relative to their peers. *Journal of Experimental Social Psychology, 38*(4), 331–351.

Kruger, J. (1999). Lake Wobegon be gone! The "below-average effect" and the egocentric nature of comparative ability judgments. *Journal of Personality and Social Psychology, 77,* 1–12.

Kruger, J., & Gilovich, T. (1999). "Naive cynicism" in everyday theories of responsibility assessment: On biased assumptions of bias. *Journal of Personality and Social Psychology, 76*(5), 743–753.

Kruger, J., & Savitsky, K. (2009). On the genesis of inflated (and deflated) judgments of responsibility. *Organizational Behavior and Human Decision Processes, 108*(1), 143–152.

Landy, D., Guay, B., & Marghetis, T. (2018). Bias and ignorance in demographic perception. *Psychonomic Bulletin & Review, 25*(5), 1606–1618.

Loewen, J. W. (2007). *Lies my teacher told me: Everything your American history textbook got wrong.* Atria Books.

Newport, F. (2015). *Americans greatly overestimate percent gay, lesbian in U.S.* Gallup. https://news.gallup.com/poll/183383/americans-greatly-overestimate-percent-gay-lesbian.aspx

Putin, V. (2013, September 12). A plea for caution from Russia. *The New York Times.* http://www.nytimes.com/2013/09/12/opinion/putin-plea-for-caution-from-russia-on-syria.html?mcubz=2

Putnam, A. L., Ross, M. Q., Soter, L. K., & Roediger, H. L. (2018). Collective narcissism: Americans exaggerate the role of their home state in appraising U.S. history. *Psychological Science, 29*(9), 1414–1422.

Reed-Gordon, A. (2008). *The Hemingses of Monticello: An American family*. Norton.

Renan, E. (2018). What is a nation? (Qu'est-ce Qu'une Nation?, 1882) In M. F. N. Giglioli (Ed.), *What is a nation? And other political writings* (pp. 247–263). Columbia University Press.

Roediger, H. L., Abel, M., Umanath, S., Shaffer, R. A., Fairfield, B., Takahashi, M., & Wertsch, J. V. (2019). Competing national memories of World War II. *Proceedings of the National Academy of Sciences of the USA, 116*(34), 16678–16686.

Ross, M., & Sicoly, F. (1979). Egocentric biases in availability and attribution. *Journal of Personality and Social Psychology, 37*(3), 322–336.

Ross, M. Q., Sterling-Maisel, O. A., Tracy, O., & Putnam, A. L. (2020). Overclaiming responsibility in fictitious countries: Unpacking the role of availability in support theory predictions of overclaiming. *Memory & Cognition, 48*(8), 1346–1358.

Schroeder, J., Caruso, E. M., & Epley, N. (2016). Many hands make overlooked work: Over-claiming of responsibility increases with group size. *Journal of Experimental Psychology: Applied, 22*, 238–246.

Taylor, S. E., & Brown, J. D. (1988). Illusion and well-being: A social psychological perspective on mental health. *Psychological Bulletin, 103*(2), 193–210.

Tversky, A., & Kahneman, D. (1973). Availability: A heuristic for judging frequency and probability. *Cognitive Psychology, 5*(2), 207–232.

Tversky, A., & Kahneman, D. (1974). Judgment under uncertainty: Heuristics and biases. *Science, 185*(4157), 1124–1131.

Tversky, A., & Koehler, D. J. (1994). Support theory: A nonextensional representation of subjective probability. *Psychological Review, 101*, 547–567.

Van Engen, A. (2020). *City on a hill: A history of American exceptionalism*. Yale University Press.

Ward, K. (2007). *History in the making: An absorbing look at how American history has changed in the telling over the last 200 years*. The New Press.

Yamashiro, J. K., & Roediger H. L. (2021). Biased collective memories and historical overclaiming: An availability heuristic account. *Memory & Cognition, 49*, 311–322.

Zaromb, F. M., Liu, J. H., Paez, D., Hanke, K., Putnam, A. L., & Roediger, H. L. (2018). We made history: Citizens of 35 countries overestimate their nation's role in world history. *Journal of Applied Research in Memory and Cognition, 7*(4), 521–528.

12

United States's and Germany's Collective Memories of Pride and Shame for American and German History

Sharda Umanath and Magdalena Abel

Members of a national community can hold a sense of national identity (Schildkraut, 2014; for a theoretical account, see David & Bar-Tal, 2009). For individuals, their autobiographical or self-relevant memories shape their sense of self, their personal identity (Baddeley, 1988). National identities are likely similarly influenced by what a nation of people remembers together about their shared past—collective memories. Although the term *collective memory* has already been defined several times in this book, here we refer to it as a simplified, highly biased, highly emotional shared account of the past that forms and informs the identity of a group (Abel et al., 2018; Halbwachs, 1980; Hirst & Manier, 2008; Wertsch & Roediger, 2008). Our focus is on examining some of the biases and emotionality present in collective memories. The work discussed in this chapter was aimed at determining (1) what residents of two countries believe are the defining highly emotional events in their country's past and (2) the extent to which these events are projected outward to members of other collectives, extending prior work on vicarious memories at the individual level.

National Identity: Collective Memories and a Country's Sense of Self

Social identity theory (Tajfel & Turner, 1986) holds that people typically think positively about the self as well as the groups to which they belong. Extending this theory, some research suggests that national identity may be shaped by an overemphasis on the contribution, importance, and uniqueness of one's

Sharda Umanath and Magdalena Abel, *United States's and Germany's Collective Memories of Pride and Shame for American and German History* In: *National Memories*. Edited by: Henry L. Roediger and James V. Wertsch, Oxford University Press. © Oxford University Press 2022. DOI: 10.1093/oso/9780197568675.003.0012

group (i.e., reflecting an "inflated image" of a group; e.g., Golec de Zavala et al., 2009). Interestingly, recent work in the field of collective memory tells a rather coherent story of not only egocentrism or a focus on the (collective) "self" but also positivity when people remember their shared national past—something Roediger and colleagues have termed "national narcissism." Note that this is somewhat different from Golec de Zavala and colleagues' "collective narcissism," which includes not only in-group favoritism but also the sense that one's group is not sufficiently recognized by others, leading to out-group hate (see Golec de Zavala & Lantos, 2020). The work on national narcissism empirically focuses on the in-group exceptionalism aspect without clear measures or direct discussion of lack of recognition and hostility toward other groups.

First, a series of studies indicates that members of a collective tend to overestimate their group's contribution to larger histories. For example, Americans were asked to estimate their state's contribution to the history of the United States. When the average estimates for residents of each state were totaled together, the sum came to 907% (Putnam et al., 2018). Similarly, when participants from 8 major former Allied countries were asked to estimate their nation's contribution to the victory of World War II, the sum of each country's average percentage contribution totaled 309% (Roediger et al., 2019; see Chapter 11, this volume). And, perhaps most striking, when participants from 35 countries were asked to provide how much of world history could be attributed to their nation, the estimates totaled to 1,156% (Zaromb et al., 2018). For a much more thorough discussion of this research into collectives' exaggerated senses of their contributions, see Chapters 9 and 11 in this volume.

Second, in addition to considering that their own country contributed heavily to more broadly shared historical events, people of a nation tend to judge that the particular events involving their country were of great importance historically. In the study by Abel et al. (2019), and as discussed in Chapter 10 in this volume, participants were asked to generate the most important events of World War II. Despite agreeing on some particularly transformative events (e.g., the attack on Pearl Harbor and the Holocaust), almost every country had at least one idiosyncratic event in their top 10 list of most frequently nominated events. For example, Chinese participants nominated the Nanking Massacre, Australian participants listed the bombing of Darwin, and Japanese participants recalled the Battle of Okinawa. A separate study of Poland shows that in addition to events commonly recalled across many other countries, the Warsaw Uprising and the Soviet invasion of Poland are still being recalled as important events by Polish participants today (see Chapter 10, this volume). These singular events were essentially only highly important to their country alone.

Connecting the collective level to the level of individual memory, a related extension is seen in Taylor et al. (2017). In reference to Donald Trump's 2015 presidential campaign slogan "Make America Great Again," American participants were asked to specify when exactly in its history they thought America was at its greatest. Nationals of different age groups indicated that the country was great particularly during their lifetimes and specifically during their youth (the reminiscence bump period between the ages of 10 and 30 years; see Rubin & Schulkind, 1997), showing a personally egocentric take on their nation's past (for related claims, see Chapter 9, this volume).

Taken together, these lines of work suggest that national identity may be primarily shaped by nationals' pride in their shared past, which in turn shows a skewed tendency to portray one's country in a glorious light.

Pride and Shame for Events in One's Country's Past

In this section, we focus on Americans' and Germans' consideration of their *own* national histories. We were interested in understanding what residents of two countries believe are the defining highly emotional events in their country's past. As discussed previously, if national identity is as egocentric and even narcissistic as some research (see Chapter 11, this volume) suggests, then a country's identity is likely defined by the events of which its people are proud. As a first step in testing this hypothesis, in a first study, we asked 94 American and 106 German undergraduates to try to nominate 10 events, deeds, and acts that made them feel proud to be from their country. (They had to provide a minimum of 5.) As a counterpoint, we also asked participants to generate 10 events that made them ashamed of their nationality. It has been observed that groups emphasize their positive shared past by passively leaving out negative historical acts (e.g., Sahdra & Ross, 2007) or by actively de-emphasizing shameful pasts (e.g., Sibley & Liu, 2012). Here, struggling to think of other, non-prideful national events may be part and parcel of a national narcissistic perspective [see Sahdra & Ross (2007) on "collective forgetting"]. Thus, we predicted that participants from each sample would generate more events of which they were proud than ashamed. For brevity, in the following, we reference the events that participants nominated as evoking pride as "proud events" and those that made them feel ashamed as "ashamed events."

On average, Americans generated significantly more events about their own country than Germans. This pattern emerged regardless of event type (proud or ashamed) when considering their own country's pasts. Surprisingly, Americans nominated significantly more ashamed events than proud ones ($M = 8.66$ versus 8.09). For Germans, there was no difference in the number of proud versus ashamed events they listed ($M = 5.85$ versus 5.90). Note that a higher average number of events signals a higher variety in events that participants provided. That is, more events really indicate more *different* events provided by individuals.

The sheer number of events that participants nominated does not provide information regarding what particular events were most associated with pride (or shame). Thus, we examined the most frequently nominated events to better understand the shared aspect of collective memories around pride and shame for one's nation. The complete lists of the 10 most frequently self-nominated proud and ashamed events for the two countries are provided in Tables 12.1 and 12.2. Consistent with prior work, we had

Table 12.1 United States Top 10 Most Frequently Self-Nominated Events[a]

Proud Event	%	Ashamed Event	%
Abolition of slavery	43.6	Slavery	75.5
World War II	42.6	Treatment of Native Americans	59.6
Barack Obama	40.4	Japanese American internment camps	42.6
Space Race/moon landing	40.4	Vietnam War	40.4
Civil rights movement/Civil Rights Act	39.4	Donald Trump	38.3
Legalization of same-sex marriage	38.3	Atomic bombing of Japan	30.9
Declaration of Independence	36.2	Racial segregation/Jim Crow laws	30.9
Women's suffrage	36.2	Iraq War	25.5
Revolutionary War	32.0	Racism and discrimination	25.5
U.S. Constitution	22.3	Civil War	19.2

[a]Events shown in bold are those that were in the German top 10 most frequently nominated events when taking on the American perspective.

Table 12.2 Germany Top 10 Most Frequently Self-Nominated Events[a]

Proud Event	%	Ashamed Event	%
Fall of Berlin Wall/reunification	77.1	Holocaust	68.9
Admittance/treatment of refugees	57.1	Nazism	57.6
National soccer performance	29.5	World War II	41.5
Democracy	24.8	World War I	35.9
European Union	22.9	Current rise of far right	31.1
German economic miracle	18.1	Adolf Hitler	26.4
Tech, innovation, and important inventions	15.2	Berlin Wall/post-war division of Germany	22.6
Angela Merkel	14.3	Racism and discrimination	17.9
German Constitution	14.3	Admittance/treatment of refugees	16.0
Resistance against Nazis	14.3	German Democratic Republic	15.1

[a]Events shown in bold are those that were in the American top 10 most frequently nominated events when taking on the German perspective.

hypothesized that participants would show a greater consensus regarding proud events than ashamed ones in their own country's past. Such a pattern would reflect greater coherence in the prideful collective memories that are speculated to form the backbone of national identity. Yet, this was not the case. Remarkably, there were no proud events that more than 50% of the American sample listed. We refer to such events nominated by the majority of participants as "core" events because they are likely to be the most reflective of highly *shared* collective memories. Indeed, the only core events that Americans produced were ashamed ones (slavery and the treatment of Native Americans). In contrast, again, German participants were quite balanced with two proud core events (the fall of the Berlin Wall/German reunification and admittance and treatment of refugees) and two ashamed ones (the Holocaust and Nazism).

Thus, participants were able to generate just as many (if not more, in the case of the American sample) ashamed events as proud ones for their own country. In addition, there was just as much (or even more, in the case of the American sample) agreement on what particular events participants felt ashamed of compared to what they felt proud of in their respective country's history. In the context of the evidence discussed previously regarding national narcissism, these findings are quite surprising.

Events Defining National Identity

In a second study, we asked explicitly about national identity and subsequently examined the emotional tone of those key events rather than having participants separately generate proud and ashamed events. From our first study, we had little means for determining whether these proud and ashamed events were those key events that shape people's sense of national identity. For example, perhaps participants were able to generate many ashamed events and even agree on them with others, but in fact, these events were not considered particularly central to their sense of national identity. Indeed, it could be that many more of the events central to one's perception of their country's national identity evoke pride. Thus, following the methodology of previous work by Taylor et al. (2017), we asked participants to nominate events that had in one way or another shaped the national identity of their own country. Specifically, 125 American and 127 German participants were asked to list the 10 most important events from history that, in their opinion, have shaped their country's identity. After generating the list of national identity events, they were then re-presented with each event and asked to categorize how they felt about each: proud, ashamed, both, or neither. Participants subsequently completed this same task for the respective other country, but here we focus on their responses regarding their own national identities.

We first examined the overall proportions of events that participants categorized as proud, ashamed, both, and neither. See Figures 12.1 and 12.2 for the American and German breakdowns, respectively. Overall, Americans categorized the highest percentage of events related to their national identity as proud (37%), followed by neither (25%), ashamed (22%), and both (16%). For Germans, the highest percentage of national identity events were categorized as being neither something participants were proud of nor ashamed of (38%), followed by ashamed (31%), proud (25%), and both (6%). Although for Americans, the greatest percentage of national identity events were categorized as ones that participants were proud of, it is of note that this percentage is rather low; participants labeled just over one-third of these most important events as proud ones. For Germans, only one-fourth of all nominated events were proud ones, and the largest percentage of national identity events did not conjure either pride or shame but was instead neutral with regard to these particular emotional tones. Overall, these data also do not align with what we might expect if national narcissism was defining these national identities.

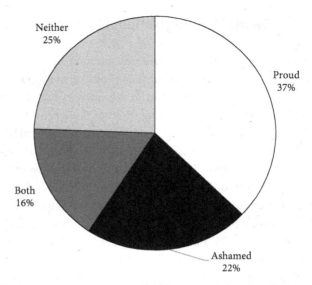

Figure 12.1 American proportions of self-nominated national identity events categorized as proud, ashamed, both, or neither.

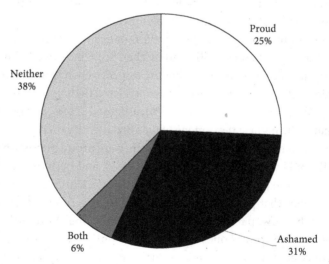

Figure 12.2 German proportions of self-nominated national identity events categorized as proud, ashamed, both, or neither.

UNITED STATES'S AND GERMANY'S COLLECTIVE MEMORIES   243

Table 12.3 United States Top 5 Most Frequently Self-Nominated National Identity Events and Their Emotional Tone Categorization Percentages[a]

Event	Overall	Emotional Tone Categorization (%)			
		Proud	Ashamed	Both	Neither
Civil War	74.4	20.4	22.6	33.3	23.7
World War II	64.8	24.7	28.4	25.9	21.0
September 11, 2001	58.4	8.0	9.6	20.5	61.6
Revolutionary War	57.6	69.4	6.9	4.2	19.4
Declaration of Independence	44.4	74.5	5.5	9.1	10.9

[a]Events shown in bold are those that were in the German top 5 most frequently nominated events when taking on the American perspective.

Another approach to these data is to examine the most frequently nominated events. What are the particular events the samples agreed upon as being the most important for shaping their respective national identities? When asked directly about the events that shape the national identity of the United States, the majority of American participants agreed on four different events. In rank order, these core events were the Civil War; World War II; the terrorist attacks on September 11, 2001; and the American Revolution. Interestingly, the breakdowns of emotional tone categorizations by those who listed these events are quite varied (Table 12.3). The categorizations for the Civil War and World War II were spread across the four options. September 11 was categorized more often than not as neither (61.6%). Indeed, only the American Revolution was categorized as proud by the majority of the sample. Notably, this list of events perfectly replicates the most frequently nominated national identity events observed in Taylor et al. (2017).

For Germany, three core national identity events emerged: the fall of the Berlin Wall/reunification, World War II, and World War I. In contrast to the American variety in emotional tone categorization, there was a clear majority consensus on participants' feelings toward the events (Table 12.4). For the fall of the Berlin Wall/reunification, people were overwhelmingly proud, whereas for World War II and World War I, they were ashamed. For World War I, all remaining participants who did not categorize it as ashamed

Table 12.4 Germany Top 5 Most Frequently Self-Nominated National Identity Events and Their Emotional Tone Categorization Percentages[a]

Event	Overall	Proud	Emotional Tone Categorization (%) Ashamed	Both	Neither
Fall of Berlin Wall/reunification	77.2	73.5	0	6.1	20.4
World War II	68.5	1.1	85.1	0	13.8
World War I	65.4	0	53.0	0	47.0
Berlin Wall	45.7	3.4	32.8	6.9	56.9
Nazism	44.9	0	84.2	1.8	14.0

[a]Events shown in bold are those that were in the American top 10 most frequently nominated events when taking on the German perspective.

labeled it as neutral, invoking neither pride nor shame for their country. The labeling of the emotional tone of these core national identity events begins to provide the outlines of how people feel about their national identities and suggests that they are not solely defined by pride.

Evidence (or Lack Thereof) for "National Narcissism"

The current work suggests that collective memory and national identity may not be shaped by pride alone or even primarily by pride. Despite expectations of American exceptionalism (e.g., Wang et al., 2012), the current U.S. sample nominated more ashamed than proud events and showed greater consensus around what they felt ashamed of, without even one proud event being agreed upon by more than half of the participants. Americans did show egocentrism in that they were able to generate more events when considering their country's past in comparison to the number of events that they were able to list for pride and shame in Germany's past (see the section titled Vicarious Collective Memory). When directly asked about their country's national identity, despite the highest percentage of events being categorized as proud, that percentage was still low—just over one-third of all the events generated. The core national identity events varied greatly in participants' sense of their emotional tone, with just one event being labeled by a majority as something they were proud of. This is consistent with results obtained by

Zaromb et al. (2014), who found that although their samples of older and younger adult Americans included the atomic bombings of Japan as among the most important events of World War II, older adults rated the event as positive, whereas younger adults generally rated it as negative. Although age was not of relevance to the current sample of undergraduate students, these data align with the idea that an event's importance is separable from its perceived emotionality.

Germans also showed little national narcissism. Instead, they repeatedly exhibited a balanced perspective of their past, internally and in considering another country's past. They nominated a similar number of proud and ashamed events for their own country. Their core events were also balanced, with the majority agreeing on two proud and two ashamed events. In explicitly considering their national identities, they did show much more consensus regarding the emotional tones of their core events than did Americans. However, across the three core events, one was primarily considered with pride, whereas the other two were considered primarily with shame—again showing a more balanced sense of identity. They even nominated, on average, a similar number of proud and ashamed events for Americans as they did for themselves, not displaying egocentrism in generating events (see the section titled Vicarious Collective Memory).

Overall, it seems that similar to individual identities, positive, negative, and even neutral memories serve important roles for collective identities, rather than exclusively pride in past actions. How can we reconcile these data with findings that people tend to be nationally narcissistic? One possibility is that the national narcissism seen in the recent literature on collective memory may be a function of *comparison* rather than identity, a phenomenon also observed in individuals. For example, Hopkins and Murdoch (1999) empirically demonstrate the influence of an "other" in individuals' sense of national identity (see also Hopkins et al., 1997). Their British participants' responses about national group stereotypes changed as a function of whether there was a comparison group. That is, one group only considered the national in-group (the British), whereas another was additionally asked to consider an out-group (Americans). The frequency of particular adjectives used to describe the British national in-group changed if the participants had been asked to consider Americans as well (e.g., "reserved" was endorsed more often in the two-group condition than in the one-group condition). Thus, the authors note that national identity is relational and affected by comparison groups.

The questions asked of participants in the current work were unlikely to elicit comparisons to other nations—participants were asked directly only about their own country's internal sense of collective self and separately, later on, asked only about another country's internal sense of collective self. In contrast, when asked about contributions of a collective, participants are inherently asked to consider their collective's contribution as a piece of some larger pie to which others must also have naturally contributed as actors in the events (see Chapter 11, this volume). People know other countries were involved in World War II (Roediger et al., 2019), in American history (Putnam et al., 2018), and, of course, in world history (Zaromb et al., 2018), so asking about one collective's contribution to the whole would immediately evoke a sort of relativism or comparison as participants attempt to answer. In deciding whether one's own collective contributed more or less than others, it is no longer surprising that participants would inflate their own collective's role. These factors likely play much less of a role when no relative comparison is activated and participants are asked only to look inward, as it were. Then, as seen here, a more balanced, or even critical, sense of national identity seems to emerge, shaped by more than just collective memories of pride.

As mentioned previously, exposure to and accessibility of information likely also affect these inflations. Participants very likely know more about their own country, its role, and its important events than about any other country. Similarly, this could be why people from a country generate country-specific events when asked to list important events of a larger global occurrence (i.e., World War II; Abel et al., 2019; see Chapter 10, this volume). Rather than any sense of narcissism per se, the observed egocentrism could simply be a lack of knowledge.

Vicarious Collective Memory: Outsiders' Perspectives on National Identity

Moving beyond a country's own sense of self and the collective memories that shape that national identity, we were curious about the outward projection of the egocentrism of national identity. At least with regard to autobiographical memories, individuals can have vivid vicarious memories of events that happened to other people (Pillemer et al., 2015). Can collective memories be recalled vicariously as well? Little is known about the degree to which important collective memories of another nation are easily accessible or even known to outsiders. Wertsch and Karumidze (2009) note that national narratives can serve as "part of an effort to explain—and often to justify actions to domestic and international audiences" (p. 388). Examining collective memories for World War II, Roediger et al. (2019) showed in the context of an event recognition test that participants across 11 nations had basic knowledge of the events surrounding World War II, including events that did not directly involve their own country. From Abel et al. (2019) and Chapter 10 in this volume, it can also be observed that people of a nation can demonstrate a broader sense of global events involving World War II beyond the exclusive perspective of their own country. Many of the events considered the most important in World War II that were nominated by more than 50% of a sample of each country directly involved other nations and not the nominators' nation. For example, more than 50% of participants from Australia, Canada, China, France, New Zealand, the United Kingdom, Germany, and Italy identified the Japanese attack on Pearl Harbor as well as the American atomic bombings of Japan as among the most important events of World War II, even though those events primarily involved only the United States and Japan. However, in those studies, participants were not asked to consider any particular perspective. Basic awareness that events occurred does not necessitate an understanding of the emotionality of critical events in another nation's past that then influence that country's sense of self. In addition, from a national narcissism stance, one could guess that members of one national community might have a very poor sense of another country's collective memories because of their own self-centered biases. Thus, we hoped to address the potential ability of people to take on the perspective of another country and identify what is important to that collective's shared identity. That is, can nationals of one country capture or characterize the events that are central to another country's identity?

As discussed previously, participants from the United States and Germany in Studies 1 and 2 were asked to generate sets of proud and ashamed events from their own country's past. After doing those two tasks, participants were provided with the following prompt and asked to consider the other country's perspective:

> Please recall up to ten events, deeds, or acts from [the other country's] history to present day that you think might make [nationals from that country] feel [ashamed/proud] to be from [the other country].

The full data are available in Choi et al. (2021). For many reasons, we would expect that participants would generate more events for their own country (discussed previously) than for another country's past. Indeed, Americans did list significantly more events when reflecting on their own country ($M_{ashamed}$ = 8.66, M_{proud} = 8.09) compared to when taking on the German perspective ($M_{ashamed}$ = 5.06, M_{proud} = 5.48). Interestingly, this was not true for Germans; they generated a similar number of events regardless of which country they were considering (self: $M_{ashamed}$ = 5.90, M_{proud} = 5.85; other: $M_{ashamed}$ = 6.39, M_{proud} = 5.62). When examining just those events that participants nominated for the other country, Americans listed more proud events than shameful ones for Germany (seen in the previous means). In contrast, Germans generated more ashamed than proud events for America (also seen in the previous means). In fact, the greatest number of events they generated out of the four tasks was for American shame, just as Americans did for themselves.

We then considered the degree of overlap between the most frequently provided specific events that nationals from a given country nominated for themselves and the ones that those from the other country included. In Study 1, this could be examined through the proud and ashamed events that participants listed. For example, how many of the 10 most agreed upon proud events that Americans considered for themselves did Germans also generate when taking on the American perspective?

Regarding the American past, German participants generated seven of the same most frequently nominated proud events and eight of the same most frequently nominated ashamed events as Americans did for themselves. These overlapping events are bolded in Table 12.1. Specifically, for core events, Germans had no proud core events for Americans, just as Americans did. For the ashamed events, Germans had only one: Donald Trump. Although Donald Trump was in the top 10 most frequently nominated ashamed events for Americans as well, it was not agreed upon by at least 50% of the sample. Similarly, although slavery and the treatment of Native Americans were in the top 10 from the German sample, they were not shared by a majority.

Regarding the German past, American participants generated four of the same most frequently nominated proud events and eight of the same most frequently nominated ashamed events as Germans did for themselves. The events are bolded in Table 12.2. Specifically, for core events, Americans did not reach a majority consensus on any proud events for Germans (whereas

Germans generated two for themselves). The fall of the Berlin Wall/reunification, a core event for Germans, was the most frequently nominated event by Americans. For ashamed events, Americans provided the same two core events for Germany as did German participants (the Holocaust and Nazism), as well as nominating a third core event (World War II, which ranked third in Germany's top 10 list but was not nominated by 50% of German participants).

In our second study, wherein we directly asked participants to consider the events that shaped their nation's identity as well as the events that shaped the other nation's identity, we can also examine the overlap of specific events. For the American national identity, Germans generated three of the same top five most frequently nominated national events as Americans did for themselves (September 11, the Declaration of Independence, and World War II; all bolded in Table 12.3). For core events, the majority of Germans agreed on one of the American self-generated events (September 11) and had a differing one: Barak Obama. For the German national identity, Americans also generated three of the same top five most frequently nominated national events as Germans did for themselves (World War II, World War I, and the fall of the Berlin Wall/reunification, all bolded in Table 12.4), with two of the same core events as well (World War II and World War I). Americans also shared one differing core event: the Holocaust.

Although the overlap between the self and other perspectives was not perfect, these data indicate that participants did have a rather large capacity to take on the perspective of another country's people. This was evident with regard to events that those "others" might be proud and ashamed of as well as with regard to events that were considered important for shaping the other nation's identity. The impressive overlap seen in these data can be interpreted in a variety of ways. One explanation is that citizens may spontaneously consider their own country's history from a more global perspective, nominating events that foreigners would know about, understand, and maybe even agree with. Another explanation is that the overlap reflects the degree to which a country is able to effectively project its identity and culture outward clearly enough so that others can identify them. Apart from politics and formal education, possible avenues for such dissemination could be movies, music, and pop culture more generally. In either case, one collective's understanding of a different collective is affected by knowledge of that other nation's past. Here, we might suspect that participants from these two countries have reasonably high knowledge of the other country. Taken together, these data suggest that perspective taking and something like vicarious memories (Pillemer et al., 2015) are possible at the collective level.

Limitations and Future Directions

The current work was intended (1) to empirically clarify what kinds of memories make up national identities and (2) to examine the extent to which these memories are understood by outsiders. Generally, we found that national identities are shaped by more than pride in a country's past and that members of another nation can have quite a bit of insight into what a country believes are its important historical events. Of course, the limitations of this work and its generalizability must be addressed. Most obviously, the samples of Americans and Germans were not necessarily representative of their respective nations. Both were groups of undergraduate students from particular institutions (the Claremont Colleges in Southern California and the University of Regensburg in the southeast of Germany). Political affiliations and various other characteristics of the participants (e.g., their age and their sense of belongingness in their nation) could have affected the results. Beyond the representativeness of these samples for their respective nations, we must consider the generalizability of samples from just two countries. The United States and Germany are both generally considered Western, educated, industrialized, rich, and democratic (WEIRD; Henrich et al., 2010) countries. They also share many other characteristics, as well as their interactions in their respective national pasts that might have affected the degree of overlap in self versus other perspective-based event nominations. In addition, like all nations, they have singular historical events and unique aspects as well. It is unknown whether similar patterns of data would be found in other nations for both the self and other collective perspectives.

Yet, the fact that people of one nation mostly agreed with how people of a different nation view themselves may suggest that these data are somewhat generalizable in an interesting way. If either sample was so very narrow as to not be at all reflective of their country's perceptions, the other nation should not show any similarity to their thoughts about themselves. Instead, there is a great deal of overlap. And this overlap occurred despite the prompts simply saying "American" or "German" without any other information (e.g., "student" or where within the country the imaginary other person might be from). That is, participants were given a very generic perspective to consider and were not primed to think about any one type of person from the other country in particular. Thus, it would be difficult to claim that students from one country automatically considered the student perspective for the other country or had any specific leaning toward a region or any other more narrowly identifying information.

The current work is an early step toward understanding the interplay of collective memories with national identities from an empirical psychological perspective. Future work is needed to corroborate and extend these findings in more representative samples within the countries examined here and across many other national collectives. There are also numerous avenues going beyond the methodological considerations discussed previously in addressing the limitations of the current studies. For example, participants in our studies did not have an opportunity to share *why* a given event was considered an important part of the nation's past. What characteristics or aspects of particular events made participants consider them as among the top most prideful or shameful events in their own or another country's history? Although in the second study, participants categorized the events as evoking pride, shame, both, or neither, participant-generated explanations would allow for better understanding and contextualization of these national events. When considering the most important events in shaping their or another country's national identity, the same question can be asked: What about those events make them so influential? Not only would answers to these questions elucidate existing national identities but also they would provide insight into the top-down (e.g., state-approved textbooks in history classes and media) versus bottom-up (e.g., family conversations and personal experiences) sources that form and maintain collective memories and, in turn, national identities.

The current findings demonstrate the possibility that subsets of nationals within a country can agree more on what they are ashamed of rather than proud of, whereas there is a great deal of variation regarding what people are proud of. We empirically highlight that the composition of national identity is more complicated than a body of prideful and glorious shared memories. Pride is not everything.

Acknowledgments

The data discussed in this chapter are published in the following peer-reviewed journal article: Choi, S. Y., Abel, M., Siqi-Liu, A., & Umanath,

S. (2021). National identity can be comprised of more than pride: Evidence from collective memories of Americans and Germans. *Journal of Applied Research in Memory and Cognition, 10*(1), 117–130. We thank Henry L. Roediger, III, and James Wertsch for their feedback on the conception of these studies.

References

Abel, M., Umanath, S., Wertsch, J. V., & Roediger, H. L., III. (2018). Collective memory: How groups remember their pasts. In M. L. Meade, C. B. Harris, P. Van Bergen, J. Sutton, & A. J. Barnier (Eds.), *Collaborative remembering: Theories, research, and applications* (pp. 280–296). Oxford University Press.

Baddeley, A. (1988). But what the hell is it for? In M. M. Gruneberg, P. E. Morris, & R. N. Sykes (Eds.), *Practical aspects of memory: Current research and issues: Vol. 1. Memory in everyday life* (pp. 3–18). Wiley.

Choi, S. Y., Abel, M., Siqi-Liu, A., & Umanath, S. (2021). National identity can be comprised of more than pride: Evidence from collective memories of American and Germans. *Journal of Applied Research in Memory and Cognition, 10*, 117–130.

David, O., & Bar-Tal, D. (2009). A sociopsychological conception of collective identity: The case of national identity as an example. *Personality and Social Psychology Review, 13*, 354–379.

Golec de Zavala, A. G., Cichocka, A., Eidelson, R., & Jayawickreme, N. (2009). Collective narcissism and its social consequences. *Journal of Personality and Social Psychology, 97*, 1074.

Golec de Zavala, A., & Lantos, D. (2020). Collective narcissism and its social consequences: The bad and the ugly. *Current Directions in Psychological Science, 29*, 273–278.

Halbwachs, M. (1980). *The collective memory* (F. J. Didder, Jr., & V. Y. Ditter, Trans.). Harper & Row.

Henrich, J., Heine, S. J., & Norenzayan, A. (2010). The WEIRDest people in the world? *Behavioral and Brain Sciences, 33*, 61–83.

Hirst, W., & Manier, D. (2008). Towards a psychology of collective memory. *Memory, 16*, 183–200.

Hopkins, N., & Murdoch, N. (1999). The role of the "other" in national identity: Exploring the context-dependence of the national ingroup stereotype. *Journal of Community & Applied Social Psychology, 9*, 321–338.

Hopkins, N., Regan, M., & Abell, J. (1997). On the context dependence of national stereotypes: Some Scottish data. *British Journal of Social Psychology, 36*, 553–563.

Pillemer, D. B., Steiner, K. L., Kuwabara, K. J., Thomsen, D. K., & Svob, C. (2015). Vicarious memories. *Consciousness and Cognition, 36*, 233–245.

Putnam, A. L., Ross, M. Q., Soter, L. K., & Roediger, H. L., III. (2018). Collective narcissism: Americans exaggerate the role of their home state in appraising US history. *Psychological Science, 29*, 1414–1422.

Roediger, H. L., Abel, M., Umanath, S., Shaffer, R. A., Fairfield, B., Takahashi, M., & Wertsch, J. V. (2019). Competing national memories of World War II. *Proceedings of the National Academy of Sciences of the USA, 116*, 16678–16686.

Rubin, D. C., & Schulkind, M. D. (1997). The distribution of autobiographical memories across the lifespan. *Memory & Cognition, 25*, 859–866.

Sahdra, B., & Ross, M. (2007). Group identification and historical memory. *Personality and Social Psychology Bulletin, 33*, 384–395.

Schildkraut, D. J. (2014). Boundaries of American identity: Evolving understandings of "us." *Annual Review of Political Science, 17*, 441–460.

Sibley, C. G., & Liu, J. H. (2012). Social representations of history and the legitimation of social inequality: The causes and consequences of historical negation 1. *Journal of Applied Social Psychology, 42*, 598–623.

Tajfel, H., & Turner, J. C. (1986). The social identity theory of intergroup behavior. In S. Worchel & W. G. Austin (Eds.), *Psychology of intergroup relations* (pp. 7–24). Nelson-Hall.

Taylor, R. J., Burton-Wood, C. G., & Garry, M. (2017). America was great when nationally relevant events occurred and when Americans were young. *Journal of Applied Research in Memory and Cognition, 6*, 425–433.

Wang, Q., Conway, M. A., Kulkofsky, S., Mueller-Johnson, K., Aydın, Ç., & Williams, H. (2012). The "egocentric" Americans? Long-term memory for public events in five countries. In M.-K. Sun (Ed.), *Trends in cognitive sciences* (pp. 183–190). Nova Science.

Wertsch, J. V., & Karumidze, Z. (2009). Spinning the past: Russian and Georgian accounts of the war of August 2008. *Memory Studies, 2*, 377–391.

Wertsch, J. V., & Roediger, H. L., III. (2008). Collective memory: Conceptual foundations and theoretical approaches. *Memory, 16*, 318–326.

Zaromb, F., Butler, A. C., Agarwal, P. K., & Roediger, H. L. (2014). Collective memories of three wars in United States history in younger and older adults. *Memory & Cognition, 42*, 383–399.

Zaromb, F. M., Liu, J. H., Páez, D., Hanke, K., Putnam, A. L., & Roediger, H. L., III. (2018). We made history: Citizens of 35 countries overestimate their nation's role in world history. *Journal of Applied Research in Memory and Cognition, 7*, 521–528.

SECTION IV

CASE STUDIES OF NATIONAL MEMORY AND POPULISM FROM AROUND THE WORLD

The chapters in this section examine case studies of national memory from around the world. In one way or another, they bring us back to the general claim of this book that we need to go beyond top-down forces to understand national memory. Cultural, psychological, and social factors must be taken into account, often serving as constraints on the efforts of state authorities. This idea takes explicit form in Rauf Garagozov's chapter title, in which he asserts that neither leadership nor political elites may be necessary for collective memory to mobilize a national community.

The authors in this section use a variety of methods to examine the bottom-up forces involved in national memory, and they suggest that these forces can be quite long-lasting and resistant to change. As Yadin Dudai notes in Chapter 13, this can be the case even in the absence of a state territory or sovereignty to encourage memory. For him, this involves a "textual epitome" or "credo" that has provided the foundational core of Jewish collective memory for millennia. This credo has persevered in part because of its ingenious, compact textual organization, but it has also been the object of regular semantic recitation and ritual re-enactment. In ways that echo the ideas of Liu et al. (see Chapter 9, this volume) about historical charters and of Wertsch (see Chapter 22, this volume) about narrative templates, Dudai's account reminds us of the importance of schema-like representation in the textual and cognitive processes involved in national memory.

Dudai takes the interdisciplinary project of studying national memory into new territory by approaching human cultures as "biocultural 'supraorganisms'" and drawing on everything from neurocognitive science to historical studies. He views the powerful yet flexible form of representation involved in the credo as making it possible to maintain a common Jewish identity project across more than 130 generations, while at the same time incorporating new historical episodes such as the Holocaust into the textual life of this community.

Taking up national memory struggles in another region of the world, in Chapter 14 Carol Gluck provides a perspective on how deeply embedded cultural forces can push back against state efforts to provide citizens with a usable past. She examines recent efforts in Japan, China, and South Korea to revise official history in the service of nationalism, but she goes on to argue that "the state alone did not create the patriotic passions." Instead, crucial threads of national memory thrived in "the vernacular terrain" of these societies, often led by dogged efforts of "memory activists." And echoing ideas about the transcultural turn in memory studies, she notes that popular culture and transnational sources also get into the act by contributing to "the unending process of recasting a nation's past."

In Chapter 15, Zhao Ma examines a paradigmatic case of state authorities' efforts to control national memory. In this case, Chinese authorities tried to use popular media to control how the Korean War is remembered. Namely, a state-owned corporation produced *My War*, a 2016 movie about the Korean War, with the intent of replacing a narrative about a socialist and internationalist crusade with one that celebrates Chinese nationalism. In Ma's telling, the goal was to "wash off" the "century of humiliation" narrative that has framed Chinese memory since the mid-19th century and serves as a narrative template (see Chapter 22, this volume) or perhaps what Liu et al. (see Chapter 9, this volume) call a national charter. The outcome, however, was that the Chinese state "failed miserably at the box office, and its nationalist and statist narrative drew heavy criticism on social media." In addition to getting pushback in the marketplace, Ma notes that the film encountered resistance from the cosmopolitan viewers in today's People's Republic of China, providing another illustration of the need to study the transcultural turn in collective memory. The bottom line for Ma is that even a powerful state that can devote massive resources to a popular media project and can control alternatives may find it difficult to be effective in its top-down effort to control national memory.

In Chapter 16, Nutsa Batiashvili examines efforts to shape national memory in the Republic of Georgia, a setting with relatively weak top-down control compared to a country such as China. In this case, the struggle is between groups trying to grab control of a national narrative rather than a top-down effort by established state authorities. Batiashvili formulates this in terms of how radically opposed "counterpublics" struggle to control national memory in the context of the political vacuum following the collapse of the Soviet Union. A far-right organization, Georgia March, has aspired to dominate statist discourse and has sought to impose its views steeped in anti-elitist populist nationalism devoted to issues such as halting the flow of immigrants. Its efforts have been opposed in this context by an ideologically diverse network of liberal youth, the Society for Spreading Freedom, a pro-Western group that has pursued its agenda of having Georgia integrate into the European Union.

At first glance, this might be taken to suggest two distinct national narratives vying for power, but what Batiashvili shows is that the two sides carry on their struggle largely within the confines of a single general narrative about Georgia's Golden Age. Although the opposition between "authentic" and "ordinary people," on the one hand, and "foreigners" and "globalist" forces, on the other hand, might seem straightforward, it plays out within a single semiotic space in Batiashvili's account. This is possible because of the internal heterogeneity, indeed "bivocalism," of the semiotic space, which allows the counterpublics to harness different threads of the same semiotic means to carry out their struggle. An important insight of Batiashvili's is that the competing voices operate in a kind of close proximity; indeed, they are two sides of the same coin and can be found within an individual member of the Georgian national community as well as between groups. This adds an important element to claims about top-down control and bottom-up resistance by encouraging us to recognize that each side of the opposition might have the other embedded in it.

In Chapter 17, Rauf Garagozov takes up a case that involves other countries in Georgia's neighborhood of the South Caucasus, but a case that involves quite different projects in national identity and memory. In the post-Soviet era, Azerbaijan and Armenia have engaged in violent conflict over Nagorno Karabakh, a region that came to be settled by Armenians but was within the border of Azerbaijan. It is a case study of how national memories can contribute to tragic outcomes in the form of military conflict. Between the armed clashes in the 1990s and the wars in 2016 and 2020, tens of thousands of lives have been lost in this case, and this situation has encouraged the view that the enemies are locked in a conflict that shows little sign of getting beyond its frozen condition.

Garagozov begins his chapter by documenting how powerful collective memory can be in organizing populations, even without the leadership of political elites. His vivid description of the explosive mobilization of the Armenian population in 1988 is ominous, and the degree to which Soviet authorities in Moscow misread the power of national identity provides a reminder of how little we may appreciate the forces at work in such cases. But along with the portentous and discouraging picture Garagozov paints, he provides a small note of optimism. Drawing on methods used in cognitive psychology to detect implicit attitudes, he suggests that there may be a crack, however small, in the wall that seems to separate the national communities in this case. Namely, his evidence suggests that the Azerbaijani subjects in his studies simultaneously hold both positive implicit attitudes and strong negative explicit attitudes toward Armenian adversaries. What is particularly striking is that this was the case for Azerbaijani internally displaced people. Garagozov argues that it might be traced to their use of a narrative of common suffering for all people who had experienced internal displacement. Almost in spite of themselves, they seem to retain a way of viewing their situation that provides a means for some connection with their adversaries. Garagozov conducted his studies before the latest round of warfare over Nagorno Karabakh in 2020, so the question remains whether things might change, but his findings on implicit memory provide a ray of hope and beg for more study.

13
Persistence of Collective Memory over 3,000 Years

The Case of Ancient Versus Modern Israel

Yadin Dudai

Memory, the ability to retain and reconstruct information about past experience, is a faculty of many types of information-processing systems. The human brain is such a system. So is a social group. The shared pool of information concerning factual or fictional, recent or remote past experience of the group is commonly referred to as *collective memory*. "Collective memory" is an umbrella term "that has as many interpretations as interpreters" (Wertsch, 2002). Collective memory of the remote, absolute past, which is no longer capable of being personally experienced and recollected by contemporary individuals, is considered the "historical memory" of the group (Halbwachs, 1950). I use the term collective memory to denote historical memory as well. Collective memory can refer to the memory of various types of human groups, including cultures and nations, and as such has an immense potential to mobilize and fuel national movements.

In this chapter, I present preliminary observations and remarks concerning the collective memory of the Jewish culture from a vantage point of the "science of memory" (Roediger et al., 2007). I make the argument that Jewish collective memory should be considered, unless otherwise indicated, as the memory of a culture rather than a nation, and I use the terms collective memory and "cultural memory" interchangeably. However, the re-enactment of remote core elements of Jewish cultural memory has contributed in recent generations to the revitalization of an influential national movement that culminated in the establishment of the modern state of Israel. This has contributed to accelerated evolution of Jewish cultural memory and its differentiation into subnarratives that differ, inter alia, in their national orthodoxy, geographical distribution, religious hue, and populist flavor.

Yadin Dudai, *Persistence of Collective Memory over 3,000 Years* In: *National Memories.* Edited by: Henry L. Roediger and James V. Wertsch, Oxford University Press. © Oxford University Press 2022. DOI: 10.1093/oso/9780197568675.003.0013

The Conceptual Framework

I consider human cultures as biocultural "supraorganisms" (Hölldobler & Wilson, 2009) that store distributed experience-dependent, behaviorally relevant representations over hundreds and thousands of years. Similarly to other memory systems (Dudai, 2002), these supraorganisms encode, consolidate, store, modify, and express memory items in the concerted activity of multiple types and tokens of subcomponents of the system. However, whereas in the individual brain the subcomponents are specialized cells, synapses, and brain circuits that can store information up to the individual's lifetime, in cultures the memory traces are encoded in large distributed assemblies composed of individual brains, intra- and intergenerational interacting brains, and multiple types of artifacts that interact with brains.

My approach is anchored in concepts and findings of neurocognitive science. In the overall approach to the analysis of memory, I follow Marr (1981) in assuming that information processing systems can be heuristically described as operating on three levels, listed here top-down: the *goal* of the system ("the computational theory"), the *algorithms* used to obtain the goal, and *implementation* of the algorithms in hardware. It follows that similar goals and algorithms can be implemented on different types of hardware—for example, in vivo or in silico, or animate and inanimate. Marr's three-level taxonomy is not free of scholarly opposition (Peebles & Cooper, 2015), and among others, interdependence of algorithms and hardware should be taken into consideration. Yet the three-level account is useful in approaching the analytical and experimental dissection of information processing systems, memory systems included. I find it convenient as an additional starting point in the investigation of the mechanisms of collective memory because it promotes exploring the applicability of research on memory in the brain, on which quite a lot is already known, to research on collective memory. Ultimately, the value of such exploration will be gauged only by its ability to yield productive testable explanations and models and not only similes and metaphors. But similarity of phenomena observed in the memory of individuals and of collectives is still a reasonable starting point. Such similarity has been noted: memory phases (Braudel, 1980; Candia et al., 2019), serial position effects (Roediger & DeSoto, 2014), reminiscence bumps (Schuman & Scott, 1989), false recollection (Welzer, 2010), effect of psychological distancing (Zaromb et al., 2018), and induced forgetting (Stone & Hirst, 2014).

The Model System

Scientific practice encourages the selection of model systems for the investigation of research questions. The selection of Jewish cultural memory illustrated in this chapter is not done solely because I am Jewish but also because several attributes render it suitable for the investigation of long-term cultural memory. These include long yet identifiable past, continual to present (more than 130 generations; Liverani, 2014); rich archeological, textual, and historical research; memory traces that for millennia have exceeded the sphere of interest of the specific culture; memory maintained mostly in the absence of the supportive binding of the physical borders of a homeland; importance of memory and re-enactment of the past is inherent in the culture; and geopolitical and cultural developments in recent centuries that promote the potential for observing differentiation of collective memory on the fly.

At this point in the discussion, it is apt to readdress the question of why it is memory of a culture rather than of a nation. Definitions of "nation" vary greatly, from the highly concrete to the theoretical. Two examples cited by Smith (2010) illustrate the spectrum: "A nation," said Joseph Stalin, "is an historically constituted, stable community of people, formed on the basis of a common language, territory, economic life, and psychological make-up manifested in a common culture"; compare this to "the nation: . . . an imagined political community—and imagined as both inherently limited and sovereign" (Anderson, 2006, cited in Smith, 2010, p. 11). Yet the Jews lacked throughout most of their existence both territory and sovereignty. Even today, more than 70 years after the establishment of the state of Israel, approximately half of world Jews live outside it, and most of them consider themselves members of other nations.

The Approach

One straightforward method to take a snapshot of cultural memory is to test its recall or recognition in contemporary individuals. Such tests are commonly considered to tap into semantic memory (Roediger & Crowder, 1976) as opposed to episodic memory, which reflects personal experience. As discussed later, the traditional semantic–episodic dissociation is not always applicable in this context. The "stimulus" that had been the source of the collective memory trace may have a well-documented, verifiable historical source or remain a mystery. Sometimes, archeology, geology, and anthropology manage to dispel the mystery engulfing even prehistoric collective engrams (Matchen et al., 2020; Nunn & Reid, 2016). In other cases, ancient artifacts or texts are identified that reflect events at the time of their composition or recount earlier events or myths and had served as the kernel of the remote memory. This is the case for a critical element of the "core memory" of the Jewish culture.

What is core memory? The concept stems from research on individual human memory (Dudai, 1997). In attempts to estimate the capacity of human episodic memory, one identifies a rather limited reservoir of elemental experiences that keep surfacing in free recall and serve as anchors for the reconstruction of richer recollections. These were dubbed "core personal episodes" (Dudai, 1997). It is of note that core sets of events were also reported in collective memory (Zaromb et al., 2014; see Chapter 10, this volume). I define here the core memory of a culture/nation as the minimal set of cross-generational mnemonic items that are considered by members of that culture/nation to define their collective origin, history, and distinctiveness.

The Saving Story, the Original Core of Jewish Collective Memory

The foundation core of the collective memory of the Jewish people is encapsulated in the terse text of Deuteronomy 26, 5–9. These 63 Hebrew/112 English words are the epitome of Israel's postulated ancient history, termed in Biblical studies the *Credo* (von Rad, 1962, Note 1972), alias *the saving history* or *the confession of the first fruit*. It is composed of five maxims that together comprise the origin myth of the Jewish people (not yet called "Jews" at that time), which is centered around the saving from slavery in Egypt by God, Yahweh (i.e., exodus from Egypt; the reason for the term confession of the first fruit will become apparent soon). The five maxims are the following:

1. A wandering Aramean was my ancestor;
2. He went down into Egypt and lived there as an alien;
3. The Egyptian treated us harshly, we cried to Yahweh, the God of our ancestors;
4. Yahweh brought us out of Egypt with a terrifying display of power, signs and wonders;

5. He brought us and gave us this land, a land flowing with milk and honey.

It is hypothesized by the majority of Biblical scholars that the Credo represents the outcome of amalgamation over more than 30 generations of multiple ancient narratives from multiple regions of the land of the Bible (Finkelstein, 2013; Na'aman, 2014; Noth, 1972; Schmid, 2012). Discussion of these hypotheses far exceeds the scope of this chapter. The same applies to the question of the historical veracity of the events claimed in the Credo (e.g., Cline, 2014; Levy et al., 2015; Liverani, 2014). Suffice it to say that from the point of view of memory research, once the Credo is considered as a memorandum consolidated already over more than 2,300 years, the earlier ontogeny of its narrative(s) and the historical veracity at the time of its composition are inessential for the investigation of its subsequent fate in collective memory.

The Credo was intended from the outset to serve as an item to be remembered by its anonymous author(s)/redactor(s). Several lines of evidence support this assumption. First, this was the only text in the Bible that had to be recited by biblical law at least once annually by every adult (male) member of the community, not only by priests. This had to be done during the first-fruits ceremony, in which farmers traveled in the summer to the temple with offerings of the first products of the soil, acknowledging Yahweh as the source of their land fertility and the true owner of its products as well as the guide of Israel's history (Tigay, 1996). The "saving history" alias "confession of the first fruit" hence came engulfed in a procedural mechanism that promoted its encoding into both personal and collective memory. We return to this mnemonic strategy later. After the destruction of the Second Temple in Jerusalem in the first century AD, an alternative mnemonic procedure was introduced to ensure annual recitation, by integrating the saving story into the earliest Passover Haggadah (second and third century AD; Bokser, 2002). Over time, elements of the saving story were also integrated into prayer cycles.

Second, the text was equipped with mnemonic devices. A salient one already at the beginning of the text is alliteration (in Hebrew, the first three words start each with Aleph and are exceptionally memorable, ארמי אבד אבי, *Arami Oved Avi* = A wandering Aramean was my ancestor). Another mnemonic device throughout the text is poetic parallelism. Third, the short narrative is remarkably full of action and dramatic. Altogether, a text to remember.

What Is Remembered?

Although the Credo is a good starting point for gauging Jewish cultural memory over the ages, and its influence on Jewish self-identity and national aspirations cannot be overestimated, it is clearly not expected to have remained in isolation over thousands of years in the depository of Jewish collective memory. We set out to also identify the spectrum of items that have been accumulated in that memory since the Credo was formulated.

Toward this end, we subjected a total of 679 adults (aged 18–91 years) in two major Jewish communities, Israel and the United States (New York City), to a free recall test. In this low-resolution preliminary analysis, the issue of cultural subgroups was ignored, nevertheless, to reduce excessive variability in exposure to traditional and secular sources of information, ultraorthodox sects were not tested in both locations. The test was as follows: Individuals were requested to participate in what was defined as a simple, short, memory questionnaire with one question only, without being told beforehand what this question was going to be. The test was preceded by a 2-minute oral introduction, in which the notion of collective memory was defined. The printed instructions on the test forms handed to the participants were as follows:

> What in your view are the 10 most important elements of the Collective (Shared) memory of the Jewish People throughout the ages but before the establishment of the state of Israel in 1948. Please provide intuitive, fast answers, 1–2 words each. No need to explain your selection. The order of items in the list is not important.

The instructions were in Hebrew in Israel, in Amharic for Ethiopian Jews in Israel, and in English in the United States. The only personal information requested was age and gender. The task was completed in approximately 10 minutes. A total of 6,384 replies were thus obtained.

Contemporary Israelis came up with 4 items at the top of their list. The Holocaust was listed by 81% of the participants. Fifty-three percent listed at least one event that took place in Palestine during half a century before the establishment of the modern State of Israel in 1948, including pre-independence immigration waves and clashes between Jew and Arabs. Exodus (i.e., the Saving Story) was listed by 50%, and the destruction of the Temple(s) in Jerusalem was listed by 45%. Because each participant was allowed to list up to 10 items, many included more than one event that took place in Palestine in the aforementioned half century before the establishment of the state. Hence, of the total replies, 15% referred to these local recency events, whereas 10% referred to the Holocaust and 7% each to Exodus and the destruction of the Temple(s). The probability of recall of the aforementioned items as well as of the other most frequently recalled items was independent of age, demonstrating collective memory stability over at least three generations.

Recency, Bumps, and Lacunae

Multiple phenomena stand out in a plot of the magnitude of recall versus the factual or fictional time of the recalled event (Figure 13.1). First is a recency effect, in line with a previous report on collective memory (Roediger & Crowder, 1976). Second is multiple reminiscence bumps, a concept borrowed from personal autobiographical memory (Bernsten & Rubin, 2004; see also Schuman & Scott, 1989). The earliest of these refers to the Saving Story (Exodus). Additional ones are traces of traumatic events: destruction of the First Temple

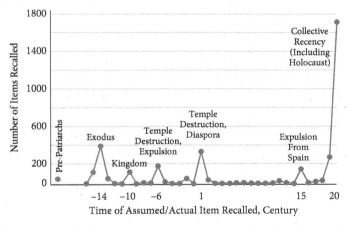

Figure 13.1 Remote and long-term cultural memory. Israeli Jewish adults ($N = 379$; aged 18–91 years; average age, 56 years) were instructed to list in free recall up to 10 memory items that they consider as the most important in Jewish collective memory since ancient times to 1948 (the date of declaration of the state of Israel). The total number of answers was 3,564. The graph depicts the number of items recalled versus the century that these items are traditionally believed or historically known to refer to. Major events are indicated to illustrate the historical narrative of the culture.

in Jerusalem and the Babylonian exile (6th century BC); destruction of the Second Temple and the deportation of the local population by the Romans into the Diaspora (1st century); the expulsion of the large Jewish population from Spain (15th century); and the Holocaust (included in Figure 13.1 under "collective recency").

A "mnemonic lacuna" is detected for events between the 1st and the 15th century. This extended period was not devoid of major historical and cultural events in Jewish life, including the flourishing of Jewish scholarship in Europe, on the one hand (e.g., the golden age of Jewish culture in Spain in the 8th through the 13th century), and terrible pogroms, on the other hand. The former left a rich corpus of religious and secular writings, and the latter were recorded either in real time or soon afterwards (e.g., Bar-Yakov, 12th century/1970; HaCohen, 1575/1992). Relevant information is also included in present-time history books and school curricula, but specific events do not surface intuitively in the recollection of the shared past. This lack of consolidation into collective memory raises the possibility that inhibitory mechanisms were engaged. One possibility that comes to mind, given demographic estimates (DellaPergola & Even, 2001; Jacobs, 1906), is that the low density of contemporary Jewish populations prevented integration into collective memory. The minimal population density and kinetics of information transfer required for effective encoding of an item in collective memory are cardinal questions that interface with multiple research frontiers in collective behavior of populations, social structure network, percolation theory, and epidemiology (Brazowski & Schneidman, 2020; Hagen et al., 2018; Lee et al., 2010; Saberi, 2015; Walters et al., 2018). This question far exceeds the scope of the current discussion.

Another possibility is retroactive interference (Dudai, 2002) by successive trauma, leading to disrupted consolidation, inhibition of expression, or summation of memory of earlier events with that of the most salient one at the end of the series (e.g., the expulsion of the Jews from Spain, which is well remembered). A remarkable example of the concept in Jewish cultural memory is in the Talmud:

> A parable, to what is it like, to a man who was travelling on the road when he encountered a wolf and escaped from it, and he went along relating the affair of the wolf, he then encountered a lion and escaped from it, and went along relating the affair of the lion, he then encountered a snake and escaped from it, whereupon he forgot the two previous incidents and went

along relating the affair of the snake. So with Israel, the later troubles make them forget the earlier ones. (Babylonian Talmud, Berakhot, 13:71)

Retroactive or proactive interference may have also affected the fate of memories of earlier events in Jewish history. One example is Jeconiah's exile. Jeconiah was the king of Judah dethroned by Nebuchdneszzer II, king of Babylon, and taken into captivity in 592 BCE together with thousands of Jerusalem's elites. This was no doubt a highly traumatic event, yet today, scholars excluded, few remember it. Another example is Shesbazzar, the First Prince of Judea who led the return of the Jewish elite to Jerusalem to rebuild the Temple by decree of King Cyrus of Persia in 538 BCE. The first Jewish prince who returned from the banks of the rivers of Babylon surely made a strong impression on contemporary Jews. Yet his memory disappeared from the collective. One can come up with the possibility that Jeconiah and Shesbazzar did not survive in collective memory because of proactive (Shesbazzar) or retroactive (Jeconiah) interference by the destruction of the First Temple (586 BC). The role of retroactive and proactive interference in collective forgetting deserves a full discussion elsewhere.

Split Engrams

The U.S. Jewish cohort came up with 3 items at the top of their list. The Holocaust was listed by 71% of the participants. Fifty-seven percent listed at least 1 item that reflected current Jewish family and community traditions, including holiday meals and dishes that originated or were shaped in eastern European Jewry and imported to the United States in the late 19th and early 20th centuries. Exodus (the Saving Story) was listed by 42%. Because each participant was allowed to list up to 10 items, many included more than 1 item that referred to the aforementioned family traditions and folklore. Hence, of the total replies, 26% referred to these traditions, whereas 9% referred to the Holocaust and 7% Exodus and the Saving Story. The U.S. participants clearly prioritized folklore from the forsaken European diaspora over Zionist history.

The test was also performed on Ethiopian Jews in Israel. They were members of a Jewish community (Beta Israel, "the House of Israel") who lived in Ethiopia in small villages alongside Christian and Muslim communities, and have been isolated from mainstream Jewish communities for more than a millennium. We identified members of the community in Israel who were raised in Ethiopia and immigrated to Israel when they were older than age 25 years. Although a relatively small sample, the data were rather clear. First and second on their list were the elements of the core memory in the Credo: 73% of the participants listed the Exodus (Saving Story) and 37% at least one of the Patriarchs. In terms of percentage of total answers, 24% referred to the Exodus and 12% to the Patriarchs. Only 2% of the answers mentioned the Holocaust.

Persistence and Updates

Taken together, the data indicate three main processes: (1) preservation of an ancient core memory over thousands of years; (2) memories of a few collective traumas have been added to the collective memory in the past > 100 generations (Figure 13.2); and (3) differentiation is taking place in Jewish collective memory, evident in separation of the memory of "collective recency" as a function of geography. Social, ideological, and geographical differentiation, accompanied by splintering of collective memory, occurred in Judaism many times in the past—for example, between Jews in the land of Israel and those in the diaspora already before the 1st century (Barclay, 1996); between Ashkenazi and non-Ashkenazi populations from the Middle Ages onward (Gerber, 1992; Polonsky, 2010); between sweeping religious movements and sects from the 17th and 18th centuries onward (Biale et al., 2018; Scholem, 1973); and between orthodox and progressive movements in the Enlightenment (Feiner, 2002), and subsequently among reform, orthodox, conservative, and nonpracticing Judaism (Plaut, 2015). Some of these multiple dissociations still evolve. However, the unique situation at the present time is the involvement of an independent Jewish state, hence blurring the long-term detachment of culture from nation (e.g., Boyarin, 2015), and the fact that the process can be analyzed in real time. "Nation-locked recency" dominates in the country in which the national narrative fits the original core memory (Israel), and "culture-locked recency" dominates in the community in which new national identity was acquired (the United States). It is of note that in Beta Israel, who were separated from mainstream Jewish communities worldwide for more than 1,000 years, memory of events from ancient Israel remained the main element in their Jewish collective memory (see Figure 13.2).

PERSISTENCE OF COLLECTIVE MEMORY 269

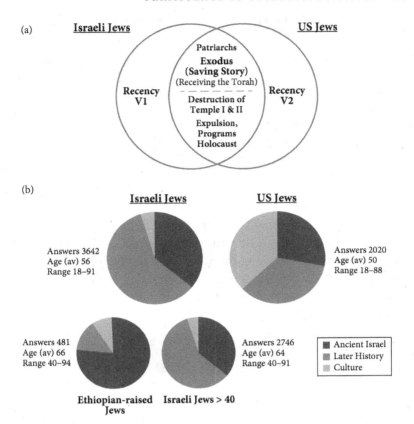

Figure 13.2 (a) Schematic depiction of the major elements of the core collective memory in two major contemporary Jewish populations, in Israel and in the United States, that together comprise close to 90% of world Jewry. The shared core was supplemented in recent generations with different "collective recency": That in the Israeli group refers to pre-1948 historical events leading to the establishment of the state of Israel, whereas the U.S. group refers mainly to family and community traditions and folklore originating in the culture of Jewish immigrants from Europe in the late 19th and early 20th centuries. (b) Type of content of collective memory (ancient Israel, later history, and cultural traditions) in Israeli Jewish participants, U.S. Jewish participants, and Jews in Israel raised in Ethiopia and immigrated to Israel at older than age 25 years. An Israeli population of a similar age group is presented as control.

On Memory Storage

What makes some memories persist, whereas others fade away? Much is already known about what keeps memory going in the brain at multiple levels of neurocognitive organization (Kandel et al., 2015). In collective memory, much has been learned from the vantage point of the social sciences (Olick et al., 2015; Wertsch & Roediger, 2008); new strata of information, particularly about algorithms and mechanisms, are expected to be contributed by application of big data analysis (Candia et al., 2019; Turchin et al., 2018), cognitive sciences (Roediger & Abel, 2015), and the brain sciences (Gagnepain et al., 2020; Zadbood et al., 2017).

Analyses of mechanisms of memory persistence benefit from dissection into time domains. In the brain and cognitive sciences, this refers to short-term, intermediate-term, long-term, and remote memory (Dudai, 2002; Kandel et al., 2014). It is of interest to comment on a few observations concerning short- and long-term time domains in collective memory in general and the context of Jewish cultural memory in particular.

Short-Term Collective Memory

Estimates of the life span of information that enters into collective memory can nowadays be obtained from measuring the decay in the use of cultural products on the Web. The life span of the use of citations, songs, movies, and biographies on the Web was reported to be less than three generations (20–30 years each), even after these cultural products have shifted from the active communication phase (e.g., Hirst & Echerhoff, 2012) into passive accessible stores (Candia et al., 2019). Collective acquired flood aversion in villagers along the Vltava River in the Czech Republic depended on living witnesses and faded away within two generations (Fanta et al., 2019).

The aforementioned findings are in line with a rolling, sliding-window transition of collective information capable of being personally experienced and recollected by contemporary individuals into collective memory that is already "absolute," "dead past," "historical" (Halbwachs, 1950); with "communicative memory" of living experiences transmitted in the framework of individual biographies versus that of the absolute past (Assmann, 2011); and with the concept of the short-term "histoire événementielle" of the French Annales school, which is the domain of the chronicler as opposed to long-term, slower processes that are the domain of the historian (Braudel, 1980).

Long-Term Collective Memory

Having noted that short-term collective memory decays within a few generations, how do some collective memories consolidate into a long-term, persistent phase? "Consolidation" was originally used in the cognitive and brain sciences to denote a process that takes place right after encoding and culminates in a stable long-term engram (Dudai, 2004). However, in recent years it became evident that consolidation of items in memory in the brain may never come to a full closure and that engrams are labile throughout their lifetime (Dudai, 2012; Dudai et al., 2015). It is tempting to assume that collective memories also consolidate and reconsolidate over time to acquire new content and social and emotional valence. For example, the Saving Story is supposed to represent consolidation of multiple stories that took place over many generations (Finkelstein, 2013; Na'aman, 2014; Noth, 1972; Schmid, 2012). In this case, the end product, a text, remained subsequently robust over time, but its construal as reality, myth, or guide for action remained labile.

Major items in Jewish collective memory, some traced back scores of generations ago, are not consolidated even in their content, let alone the manner they are construed in historical, cultural, and, more recently, national context. Their updating and reconsolidation benefit from updated multidisciplinary scientific knowledge. Examples include the relative importance of the kingdom Judea versus the Northern kingdom in the early history of Israel (Finkelstein, 2013), the proportion of the population exiled from Jerusalem after the destruction of the First Temple in the 6th century BC (Lipschits, 2005), and the role of the Diaspora in Jewish life even before the destruction of the Second Temple in Jerusalem in the 1st century (Barclay, 1996). Modifications of this type are detected first in scholarly debates but ultimately affect collective memory in the population at large.

That engrams of remote events are updated over time is a reflection of saliency and viability (Dudai, 2012). This brings back the quest for the mechanisms of transformation of collective engrams into a long-term, viable form. A few observations concerning the long-term Jewish collective memory may contribute to the understanding of attributes and boundary conditions of the process in general.

The Role of Trauma

Major items that entered the repertoire of Jewish collective memory after the Saving Story (itself containing traumatic elements) refer to collective trauma: destructions of the Temple and the resulting mass expulsions, expulsion from Spain, and the Holocaust. This fits with what we know about the effect of trauma on the memory of individuals (LeDoux, 1998); the kinetics of decay portrayed for neutral collective information (Candia et al., 2019) is clearly not valid for traumatic experience. In individuals, severe trauma can lead to memory that lasts a lifetime. Recent data point even to the possibility of biological mechanisms of transgenerational transmission of traumatic experiences (Yehuda & Lehrner, 2018), which may augment transgenerational transmission of the experience by instruments of collective memory. Third-generation Holocaust survivors display increased anxiety (Hoffman & Shrira, 2017), and it is yet unclear how long this *personal* expression of collective memory will persist into subsequent generations.

A bird's-eye view of the repertoire of major elements in Jewish collective memory tends to reinforce the view that, at least until very recently, it is "lachrymose memory" [paraphrasing Baron (1928) on Jewish history]. A glance at the history of nations suggests a decisive role for trauma but also for victories, national landmarks, and cultural achievements (MacGregor, 2016; Nora, 2010). History did not provide the Jewish people with many significant victories, and most of their history deprived them of physical homeland, but it did provide them with outstanding cultural achievements. It is of note that the latter are not too popular in contemporary Jewish collective memory, whereas the memory of trauma reigns.

The Advantage of Planning Ahead

As noted previously, it is evident that the Saving Story was composed at the outset with the intention that it will be remembered until the end of cultural time. This intention was translated into the introduction of mnemonic literary devices in the text, as well as into the formulation of religious and social procedures that will ensure recitation of the text on a regular basis by the entire community.

The Power of Text

Texts propagate cultural memory in many cultures. Epic poems (e.g., the Iliad) were recited and improvised by bards for millennia (Lord, 2000).

In this form of memory transmission, the entire group is exposed to the information, but a professional elite masters and expresses it. The Saving Story may have emerged from such types of orally reliant stories, but it was ultimately crystalized into a terse set of statements that can be easily recited by regular peasants. Furthermore, it can be recited by individuals independent of community and homeland, hence acquiring properties of an antidote to collective amnesia in diaspora. But the text itself was insufficient to achieve the goal; the instrument became effective only by the addition of procedures.

The Power of Routines
Procedures and rituals are likely to augment the persistence of items in collective memory by inducing recurrent retrieval. This should be particularly effective if performance is enforced by religious law or social convention. The latter pencil in the collective calendar cycles of collective "prospective memory." This "memory of things to do" is considered in psychology to apply to short- and medium-term tasks (McDaniel & Einstein, 2007), but the collective supraorganism acts on a much slower timescale.

The postulated enhancing power of repetitions in collective memory brings to mind the observation that active repetition (test) is more effective than passive re-exposure to study material (McDermot et al., 2007). It is tempting to assume that similarly, active re-enactment in the course of a ritual will be more effective than just bringing the memory to mind passively. This re-enactment is what Jewish tradition demands in the act of recollecting the Saving Story. In the Passover Seder, the instruction is to specifically re-enact the memory episodically:

> In every generation a person must regard himself as though he personally had gone out of Egypt, as it is said: "And you shall tell your son in that day, saying: It is because of what Yahweh did for me when I came forth out of Egypt." (Mishnah Pesachim 10:5, and Passover Haggadah)

Furthermore, probably to facilitate this re-enactment in subsequent generations, in the Haggadah, Pharaoh is not mentioned as a specific Pharaoh by name (Ramses II?) but, rather, as a generic term—a villain who fits into a narrative template (see Chapter 22, this volume) with which one could identify any contemporary tyrant responsible for the hardship of the Jewish population.

A Tripartite Algorithm

The procedural cycles "hold–re-enact–hold" and "semantic–episodic–semantic," involved in maintaining the Saving Story over generations, echo a tripartite algorithm of the structure A–B–A (where A and B are states of the system), which operates in long-term memory in the brain. It reflects the fact that in animate systems, engrams are not monotonous fixed records (Dudai, 2012). Two examples illustrate this algorithm. First, in memory consolidation and reconsolidation, representations shift from an active form (in encoding or retrieval, respectively) to an inactive form (storage) and then again to an active form (recurrent retrieval) (Nader, 2003). Second, personal experience is converted over time from an episodic to a semantic form, but in recollection of some events, retrieval re-enacts the memory again into an episodic form that re-engages a richer repertoire of brain circuits before returning into a semantic representation (Furman et al., 2012).

The tripartite type of algorithm can be depicted as a process of compression–decompression–compression, and it may reflect selective pressure favoring minimization of energy spending during prolonged storage (Furman et al., 2012). This argument may apply to collective memory as well.

Damnatio Memoriae

The question regarding what keeps a memory remembered has a complementary question: What keeps a memory forgotten? In testing the collective memory of contemporary Jewish populations, a striking observation was that although Jesus was a Jew, and the rise of Christianity was probably the most influential event in Jewish history in the past two millennia (Mitchell & Young, 2006), almost nobody mentioned Jesus or the birth of Christianity as part of Jewish collective memory (<0.3% of the answers). This clearly is not because of lack of knowledge. Not a perfect damnatio memoriae, but still effective collective denial, which can be traced back already to the early days of the religious conflict (Goldstein, 1950).

A Memory in the Other

Psychology and neuroscience inform us that memory in individuals is markedly affected by the memory of others in the group (Dudai & Edelson, 2016). Similarly, collective memory of a distinct group may also be affected by other groups. In this context, recurrent in discussion of the survival of Judaism is the notion that a significant force in defining and preserving it over the ages was anti-Semitism and Christianity, which considered Jews as The Other (Sartre,

1948; for a recent bold discussion, see Boyarin, 2019). Persistence of memory, collective memory included, is hence not exclusively dependent on endogenous mechanisms. Incidentally, this argument seems to render the aforementioned repression of Jesus' memory an intriguing topic for a psychoanalytic approach to Jewish collective memory. But that's a whole different story.

When Collective Re-Enactment Unsettles Collective Memory

As long as generations adhere to proper sets of rites and procedures, collective memory can persist even in the absence of geographical and sociopolitical communality. But over time, distance, diverging history, and societal and cultural changes can disunite the collective engram. This is why the collective memory of the Jewish people is now in a crisis, again.

First, the rites that kept the memory going for millennia, originally anchored in widespread religious practice, are weakened in parts of the culture by secularization. Second, the State of Israel is a game changer. The Zionist revival was facilitated by unique social, economic, and geopolitical constellation (Bartal, 2005), but it was always motivated and justified by the collective memory, including by the last tenet of the Credo ("He brought us and gave us this land"). The translation of that core memory into reality promotes a split in the collective memory between the sovereign nation and the Diaspora. With ongoing assimilation into the local society, the collective memory of Jewish communities outside Israel, especially in the United States, is expected to further drift away from the Israeli version (Mnookin, 2018; Wertheimer, 2018). Within the scope of this brief commentary on memory, suffice it to say that it is yet unclear how such drift will ultimately affect Jewish collective memory as a whole. Evaluation of deep philosophical and social currents in modern versions of the culture, which are currently viable mostly in the Diaspora, should be definitely dissociated from folkloristic trends; lochs and bagel and gefilte fish are unlikely to serve as the proper replacement for the Credo in keeping Jewish memory going in the long term.

A cultural memory of more than 3,000 years has survived remarkably without a national territory, aided by wisely encapsulating its core in a condensed message and inventing procedures that re-enact that message each generation anew. But when this re-enactment has culminated not only in retrieval of the memory but also in geopolitical realization of the ancient message encoded in it, a dominant element in the collective memory gained a strong, local nationalistic flavor, and the collective memory as a whole started to quiver uncomfortably. Dreams may support memory better when they do not come true.

Acknowledgment

Support of the Braginsky Center for the Interface between Science and the Humanities at the Weizmann Institute of Science is gratefully acknowledged. I thank Abebe Medhaine for assistance in testing the Ethiopian-raised population.

References

Anderson, B. (2006). *Imagined communities*. Verso.
Assmann, J. (2011). *Cultural memory and early civilization: Writing, remembrance, and political imagination*. Cambridge University Press.
Barclay, J. M. G. (1996). *Jews in the Mediterranean diaspora. From Alexander to Trojan (323 BCE–117 CE)*. University of California Press.
Baron, S. W. (1928). Ghetto and emancipation: Shall we revise the traditional view? *Menorah Journal, 14*, 515–526.
Bartal, I. (2005). *The Jews of Eastern Europe, 1772–1881*. University of Pennsylvania Press. [Birth of Jewish Modern Nationalism]
Bar-Yakov of Bonn, E. (1970). *The book of memoirs* [in Hebrew]. Bialik Institute. (Original work published in the 12th century)
Bernsten, D., & Rubin, D. C. (2004). Cultural life scripts structure recall from autobiographical memory. *Memory & Cognition, 32*(3), 427–442.
Biale, D., Assaf, D., Brown, B., Gellman, U., Heilman, S. C., Rosman, M., Sagiv, G., & Wodzinski, M. (2018). *Hasidism. A new history*. Princeton University Press.
Bokser, B. M. (2002). *The origins of the seder: The Passover rite and early Rabbinic Judaism*. JTS.
Boyarin, D. (2015). *A traveling homeland: The Babylonian Talmud as diaspora*. University of Pennsylvania Press.
Boyarin, D. (2019). *Judaism: The genealogy of a modern notion*. Rutgers University Press.
Braudel, F. (1980). *On history*. University of Chicago Press.
Brazowski, B., & Schneidman, E. (2020). Collective learning by ensembles of altruistic diversifying neural networks. *arXiv*:2006.11671 [cs.LG].
Candia, C., Jara-Figueroa, C., Rodriguez-Sickert, C., Barabasi, A.-L., & Hidlago, C. A. (2019). The universal decay of collective memory and attention. *Nature Human Behaviour, 3*, 82–91.
Cline, E. H. (2014). *1177 B.C.: The year civilization collapsed*. Princeton University Press.
DellaPergola, S., & Even, J. (Eds.). (2001). *Papers in Jewish demography 1997*. The Hebrew University.

Dudai, Y. (1997). How big is human memory, or, on being just useful enough. *Learning & Memory, 3*, 341–365.
Dudai, Y. (2002). *Memory from A to Z: Keywords, concepts, and beyond.* Oxford University Press.
Dudai, Y. (2004). The neurobiology of consolidations, or, how stable is the engram. *Annual Review of Psychology, 55*, 51–86.
Dudai, Y. (2012). The endless engram: Consolidations never end. *Annual Review of Neuroscience, 35*, 227–247.
Dudai, Y., & Edelson, M. (2016). Personal memory: Is it personal, is it memory? *Memory Studies, 9*, 275–283.
Dudai, Y., Karni, A., & Born, J. (2015). The consolidation and transformation of memory. *Neuron, 88*, 20–32.
Fanta, V., Šálek, M., & Sklenicka, P. (2019). How long do floods throughout the millennium remain in the collective memory? *Nature Communications, 10*, 1105. https://doi.org/10.1038/s41467-019-09102-3
Feiner, S. (2002). *The Jewish Enlightenment.* University of Pennsylvania Press.
Finkelstein, I. (2013). *The forgotten kingdom: The archeology and history of northern Israel.* Society of Biblical Literature.
Furman, O., Mendlesohn, A., & Dudai, A. (2012). The episodic engram transformed: Time reduces retrieval-related brain activity but correlates it with memory accuracy. *Learning & Memory, 19*, 575–587.
Gagnepain, P., Vallée, T., Heiden, S., Decorde, M., Gauvain, J.-L., Laurent, A., Klein-Peschanski, C., Viader, F., Peschanski, D., & Eustache, F. (2020). Collective memory shapes the organization of individual memories in the medial prefrontal cortex. *Nature Human Behaviour, 4*, 189–200.
Gerber, J. S. (1992). *The Jews of Spain: A history of the Sephardic experience.* Free Press.
Goldstein, M. (1950). *Jesus in the Jewish tradition.* Macmillan.
HaCohen, J. (1992). *Vale of tears* [in Hebrew]. The Sephardic Library. (Original work published 1575)
Hagen, L., Keller, T., Neely, S., DePaula, N., & Robert-Copperman, C. (2018). Crisis communications in the age of social media: A network analysis of Zika-related tweets. *Social Science Computer Review, 36*(5), 523–541.
Halbwachs, M. (1950). *La mémoire collective.* Editions Albin Michel.
Hirst, W., & Echerhoff, G. (2012). Remembering in conversations: The social sharing and reshaping of memories. *Annual Review of Psychology, 63*, 55–79.
Hoffman, Y., & Shrira, A. (2017). Shadows of the past and threats of the future: ISIS anxiety among grandchildren of Holocaust survivors. *Psychiatry Research, 253*, 220–225
Hölldobler, B., & Wilson, E. O. (2009). *The superorganism: The beauty, elegance and strangeness of insect societies.* Norton.
Jacobs, J. (1906). Statistics. *Jewish Encyclopedia.* http://www.jewishencyclopedia.com/articles/13992-statistics
Kandel, E. R., Dudai, Y., & Mayford, M. R. (2014). The molecular and systems biology of memory. *Cell, 157*, 163–186.
Kandel, E. R., Dudai, Y., & Mayford, M. R. (Eds.). (2015). *Learning and memory: A Cold Spring Harbor perspectives in biology collection.* Cold Spring Harbor Press.
LeDoux, J. (1998). *The emotional brain: The mysterious underpinnings of emotional life.* Simon & Schuster.
Lee, S., Ramenzoni, V. C., & Holme, P. (2010). Emergence of collective memories. *PLoS One, 5*(9), e12522. doi:10.1371/journal.pone.0012522

Levy, T. E., Schneider, T., & Propp, W. H. C. (2015). *Israel's exodus in transdisciplinary perspective: Text, archeology, culture, and geoscience.* Springer.
Lipschits, O. (2005). *The fall and rise of Jerusalem.* Eisenbauns.
Liverani, M. (2014). *Israel's history and the history of Israel.* Routledge.
Lord, A. B. (2000). *The singer of tales* (2nd ed.). Harvard University Press.
MacGregor, N. (2016). *Germany: Memories of a nation.* Penguin.
Marr, D. (1981). *Vision.* Freeman.
Matchen, E. L., Phillips, D., Jourdan, F., & Oostingh, K. (2020). Early human occupation of southeastern Australia: New insights from ^{40}Ar/^{39}Ar dating of young volcanoes. *Geology, 48,* 390–394.
McDaniel, M. A., & Einstein, G. O. (2007). *Prospective memory: An overview and synthesis of an emerging field.* Sage.
Mitchell, M. M., & Young, F. M. (Eds.). (2006). *The Cambridge history of Christianity: Origins to Constantine.* Cambridge University Press.
Mnookin, R. H. (2018). *The Jewish American paradox: Embracing choice in a changing world.* PublicAffairs.
Na'aman, N. (2014). The Jacob story and the formation of Biblical Israel. *Tel-Aviv, 41,* 95–125.
Nader, K. (2003). Memory traces unbound. *Trends in Neurosciences, 26,* 65–72
Nora, P. (2010). *Rethinking of France: Kes Lieux de Memoire: Vol. 4. Histories and memories.* University of Chicago Press.
Noth, M. (1972). *A history of Pentateuchal traditions.* Scholars Press.
Nunn, P. D., & Reid, N. J. (2016). Aboriginal memories of inundation of the Australian coast dating from more than 7000 years ago. *Australian Geographer, 47,* 11–47.
Olick, J. K., Vinitsky-Seroussi, V., & Levy, D. (2015). *The collective memory reader.* Oxford University Press.
Peebles, D., & Cooper, R. P. (2015). Thirty years after Marr's *Vision*: Levels of analysis in cognitive science. *Topics in Cognitive Science, 7,* 187–190.
Plaut, W. G. (2015). *The rise of reform Judaism: A sourcebook of its European origins.* JPS.
Polonsky, A. (2010). *The Jews in Poland and Russia: Vol. I.* Littman Library of Jewish Civilization.
Roediger, H. L., III, & Abel, M. (2015). Collective memory: A new arena of cognitive study. *Trends in Cognitive Science, 19,* 359–361.
Roediger, H. L., III, & Crowder, R. G. (1976). A serial position effect in recall of United States presidents. *Bulletin of the Psychonomic Society, 8*(4) 275–278.
Roediger, H. L., III, & DeSoto, K. A. (2014). Forgetting the presidents. *Science, 346,* 1106–1108.
Roediger, R. L., III, Dudai, Y., & Fitzpatrick, S. (Eds.). (2007). *Science of memory: Concepts.* Oxford University Press.
Saberi, A. A. (2015). Recent advances in percolation theory and its applications. *Physics Reports, 578,* 1–32.
Sartre, J. P. (1948). *Anti-Semite and Jew.* Schocken Books.
Schmid, K. (2012). *The Old Testament: A literary history.* Fortress Press.
Scholem, G. (1973). *Sabbatai Sevi: The mystical messiah.* Princeton University Press.
Schuman, H., & Scott, J. (1989). Generations and collective memories. *American Sociological Review, 54,* 359–381.
Smith, A. D. (2010). *Nationalism* (2nd ed.). Polity Press.

Stone, C. B., & Hirst, W. (2014). (Induced) Forgetting to form a collective memory. *Memory Studies, 7*(3), 314–327.
Tigay, J. H. (1996). *The JPS Torah commentary: Deuteronomy.* Jewish Publication Society.
Turchin, P., Currie, T. E., Whitehouse, H., et al. (2018). Quantitative historical analysis uncovers a single dimension of complexity that structures global variation in human social organization. *Proceedings of the National Academy of Sciences of the USA, 115*(2), E144–E151.
von Rad, G. (1962). *Old Testament theology: Vol. I. The theology of Israel's historical traditions.* HarperCollins.
Walters, C. E., Mesle, M. M. I., & Hall, I. M. (2018). Modelling the global spread of diseases: A review of current practice and capability. *Epidemics, 25,* 1–8.
Welzer, H. (2010). Re-narrations: How pasts change in conversational remembering. *Memory Studies, 3*(1), 5–17.
Wertheimer, J. (2018). *The new American Judaism.* Princeton University Press.
Wertsch, J. V. (2002). *Voices of collective remembering.* Cambridge University Press.
Wertsch, J. V., & Roediger, H. L., III. (2008). Collective memory: Conceptual foundations and theoretical approaches. *Memory, 16*(3), 318–326.
Yehuda, R., & Lehrner, A. (2018). Intergenerational transmission of trauma effects: Putative role of epigenetic mechanisms. *World Psychiatry, 17,* 243–257.
Zadbood, A., Chen, J., Leong, Y. C., Norman, K. A., & Hasson, U. (2017). How we transmit memories to other brains: Constructing shared neural representations via communication. *Cerebral Cortex, 27,* 4988–5000.
Zaromb, F., Butler, A. C., Agarwal, P. K., & Roediger, H. L., III. (2014). Collective memories of three wars in United States history in younger and older adults. *Memory & Cognition, 42,* 383–399.
Zaromb, F. M., Liu, J. H., Paez, D., Hanke, K., Putnam, A. L., & Roediger, H. L., III. (2018). We made history: Citizens of 35 countries overestimate their nation's role in world history. *Journal of Applied Research in Memory and Cognition, 7,* 521–528.

14

National Pasts as Political Presents

War Memory in East Asia

Carol Gluck

It is not altogether clear why the wave of nationalism and populism surged in such diverse national contexts at the same contemporary moment in the second decade of the 21st century. What is clear, however, was the nearly universal use of history as an instrument in the nationalist arsenal. Although the weaponization of the past by political regimes appeared in different guises around the world, most of them tended toward revisionism of the right. The overheated memory politics of such revisers-in-chief as Putin in Russia, Orbán in Hungary, Duda in Poland, Modi in India, Xi in China, Erdoğan in Turkey, and Bolsonaro in Brazil was often ascribed to the rise of their illiberal governments. In my view, things were not so simple. The reformulation of national pasts to suit political presents was nothing new. National history in its modern form consists of the stories nations tell themselves and teach their children, partly to create domestic unity and identity and partly to gain international stature as a nation in a world of nations. The past is always in play and always selective, even when it is more or less accurately presented. The question then is how present-day nationalist and populist figures were remaking national memory and to what ends.

No doubt that the memory boom of the past four decades made history a more pressing political imperative than it might otherwise have been. Although the seizure of memory derived from multiple sources, confronting the horrific aspects of World War II played a major role in the expanded public presence of the past in the second half of the 20th century. If, as some say, the events of the French Revolution set the European historical agenda such that the 19th century spent itself catching up with its putative future (Runia, 2014, pp. 6–9), then it is possible that the events of World War II set a memory agenda such that decades later societies were still catching up with their past. The emphasis on trauma and victimhood in collective memory ran parallel with the focus on redress and apology associated with what one scholar called our "Guilted Age" (Rushdy, 2015). And both emphases, which came to encompass broad swaths of national pasts, from slavery and treatment of Indigenous peoples to colonialism and systemic racism, came to the global fore in part through the long and difficult process of remembering World War II.

In the politics of revisionist memory in East Asia, which is my subject, and also in Eastern Europe, the war remained a major force of contention into the third decade of this century. In Japan, as in Hungary, Poland, Russia, China, South Korea, and other places, nationalist–populist revisionism prominently included state manipulation of war narratives by current political leaders. The chronology was comparable in the two regions. In the early 1990s, geopolitical events challenged the dominant Japanese story created immediately after the end of the war. In the fall of 1945, the American-led Occupation oversaw a change in name from the Greater East Asia War, as Japanese knew it, to the Pacific War—from Pearl Harbor to Hiroshima, 1941 to 1945—which was of course the war Japan fought against the United States. This intentionally selective past resulted in the near disappearance of the China War, a total war waged aggressively by Japan for 8 years, beginning in 1937, and a military quagmire that was the reason for the attack on Pearl Harbor in the first place. Having reduced the Asian war to a transpacific conflict, the close U.S.–Japan alliance during the Cold War froze the narrative in place in a manner congenial to many Japanese and Americans alike. That era drew to a close with the so-called rise of Asia in the 1980s, followed by the end of the Cold War after 1989, at which geopolitical point the United States ceased to be the sole power that seemed to matter in Japan's foreign relations. After nearly 50 years, Japanese were called upon to confront their wartime actions in Asia, so long occluded in the well-rehearsed Pacific War story. As China and South Korea challenged Japan to face up to its "history problem" and acknowledge its aggression and atrocities in Asia, the politics of war memory became a flammable national and international issue.

An analogous shift occurred in Eastern Europe after the demise of the Soviet Union in 1991. War stories long frozen in a uniform anti-fascist narrative imposed under the Soviet memory regime erased the range of war experience in countries such as Poland, invaded and brutalized by both Nazi Germany and the Soviet Union; the Baltics, not only occupied but also annexed by the USSR; and East Germany, transformed by postwar fable into an entire population of anti-fascists, leaving the Nazi past behind on the other side of the Berlin Wall. Liberated from the Soviet perspective, Eastern Europeans from the Baltics to the Balkans hailed new nationalist narratives of doubled victimization by Nazis and Soviets during the war and by the Soviet Union through the Cold War decades.

The unfreezing of long-dominant war stories led to increasing memory conflicts—between Japan and China and between Japan and South Korea in East Asia, and between Russia and the Baltics, Poland, and others in Eastern Europe. So it was said that in these two regions, the "postwar" era truly began—or at least began anew—in the 1990s. During that decade, the changes in war memory unfurled under the banner of resurgent nationalism, not populism, which came later to some countries and not at all to others. Chinese President Xi Jinping might be considered a populist of a sort, but not so Japanese Prime Minister Abe Shinzō. Yet both undertook similarly nationalistic revisions of public memory in the 2010s, especially but not only of World War II. Because the distinction matters, I hyphenate nationalism–populism, suggesting that in the realm of national history and public memory, nationalism rather than populism took precedence, not only chronologically but also ideologically. A Populist International might not exist, but nationalism was the international coin of the age, and not for the first time— think of the late 19th century—if with intensified global effect. Nor was national memory ever the monopoly of the state or its controversies confined solely within state borders. Perhaps the greatest change in recent years lay not in the role of national history but, rather, in the heightened popular sensitivity to history as collective memory, the explosion of academic memory studies, and the widespread effort to understand how public memory works in the hope of understanding or affecting it or, as in my case, both.

The Comfort Women and the Politics of Memory in East Asia

The political shifts in the 1990s set the scene for a new and turbulent phase in the politics of war memory in East Asia. Asian governments demanded that Japan face up to its wartime actions in Asia, including the Nanjing Massacre, biological experimentation, chemical warfare, forced labor, colonial brutality in Korea, and the issue that came for a time to swallow the others: the "comfort women," referring to the tens of thousands of women who served in Japanese military brothels across wartime Asia. During three decades of controversy from the early 1990s to the early 2020s, the comfort women issue both revealed and rode the waves of nationalism in the region and also connected with transnational memory norms and practices. As such, it is a useful lens through which to examine the processes of formation and transformation of public memory—its relation to nationalisms (plural), to the state, to civil society, and to the global memoryscape.

The comfort women "came into memory" during the 1990s. They had never been a secret, appearing in public forums as different as the Allied Tokyo War Crimes Tribunal in the 1940s, vernacular novels, plays, newspapers, visual art, scholarship, and even Japan's parliament, which discussed relief for Japanese comfort women in the 1960s. But they had been morally and politically invisible, first because of what I think of as the "familiarity blindness" that accompanied the acceptance of military brothels as normal practice and later because their wartime "shame" and postwar lack of social power made it easy for Japan and their own governments in South Korea and elsewhere not to "see" them as worthy of enshrining in public memory. Although Japanese progressives had opposed the Pacific War story for decades, it was the political pressure *from outside*, first from South Korea and China, which created the context for the Asian comfort women, like other victims of Japanese wartime actions, finally to become visible. Yet the real drivers of memory change came *from below*: from civil society, not the state. In 1991, Kim Hak-sun, a South Korean former comfort woman, told her story in public for the first time and together with two others lodged a class-action lawsuit against the Japanese government, demanding compensation, apology, and other forms of redress. The Japanese prime minister offered a diplomatic apology in 1992, followed by a direct acknowledgment of coercion by the chief cabinet secretary in the Kōno statement of 1993. By this time, feminists, memory activists, progressives, and human rights advocates were taking up the cause of the comfort women, not only in Asia, including Japan, but also at the United Nations, in Asian Canadian and Asian American activist circles, and among international observers as appalled by the past system of Japanese "comfort stations" as they were by the present "rape camps" in Bosnia during the war in the former Yugoslavia.

References to the "Asian comfort women" appeared throughout the juridical and human rights arguments that led to the landmark designation of rape as a crime against humanity in the 1998 Rome Statute establishing the International Criminal Court. Meanwhile, in the public sphere, former comfort women from East and Southeast Asia came forward with their stories, as they and their supporters continued their efforts to be acknowledged and remembered, often with little help or even resistance from their own governments in South Korea, the Philippines, and other places. Through the 1990s, the testimonies of individual comfort women made the voices of the victims audible and, in "the era of the witness," persuasive (Wieviorka, 2006). National and international media magnified their personal pasts as well as the transnational activism on their behalf. An international "people's tribunal" held in Tokyo in 2000, where comfort women from across Asia testified about the brutality of their experience, found the Japanese military, government, and the emperor, too, guilty of crimes against humanity (Kim, 2001). The first comfort woman statue was erected in 2011 in front of the Japanese embassy in Seoul on the occasion of the 1,000th weekly demonstration on behalf of the former comfort women—demonstrations that continue to this day. Similar statues appeared in other places in South Korea, China, the United States, the Philippines, Germany, and elsewhere, spreading the image of injustice far beyond its places of origin. What I call the *vernacular terrain* of public memory—that of civil society, media, and popular culture—had far greater impact on the comfort women's coming into memory than any state, court, or government official (Gluck, 2007).

In 1995, the Japanese government reacted to the pressure from outside, in Asia, and from below, in civil society, by creating the Asian Women's Fund to recognize and compensate the surviving former comfort women. Because the compensation was privately, not state, funded, some comfort women, especially in South Korea, refused the "atonement payments," as they were called in Japanese, and criticized the apology that accompanied them as insufficient (Kumagai, 2014). That same year, the 50th anniversary of the end of the war, Japanese Prime Minister Murayama stated his "profound remorse" and "heartfelt apology" to the peoples of Asia for the suffering caused by Japan's "colonial rule and aggression" (Murayama, 1995). And in 1996, the Ministry of Education approved middle school textbooks that for the first time included mention of the comfort women. In 2005, on the 60th anniversary of the end of the war, the Japanese prime minister repeated the apology made by his predecessor 10 years earlier. Meanwhile, right-wing ideologues and conservative politicians continued to hold unreconstructed views of Japan's "war for self-defense and the liberation of Asia" (Rekishi kentō iinkai, 1995). They denied direct government involvement in the military comfort stations as well as any use of coercion in recruiting young women, and by 2006 they had succeeded in driving the comfort women out of most middle school textbooks (Guex, 2015). Yet Japanese public memory seemed nonetheless to have entered a new, more inclusive phase, in which colonialism and atrocities in Asia were at last becoming part of the war story. Public opinion polls revealed a shift in views of the war toward increasing acknowledgment of aggression, approval of compensation and apology, and concern for the "neighboring countries" in Asia. This shift occurred almost entirely because of the efforts of memory activists whose message was transmitted in the media and popular culture to publics in Japan and elsewhere as well.

The Politics of National Pasts

Yet in 2015, during the commemoration of the 70th anniversary of the end of the war, the comfort women became for the first time the main geopolitical flashpoint between Japan, South Korea, and China, with echoes as far as the United States and Germany. Asian leaders who had not mentioned the comfort women in their commemorative speeches 10 years earlier now made them a center of diplomatic contention. The Japanese government—with the same ruling Liberal Democratic Party in power that had apologized for the comfort women in 1993—dug in and denied any coercion in the recruitment of women and girls on the part of the Japanese military. After nearly 25 years of national, regional, and global exposure to the suffering of the comfort women; after testimonies, field reports, United Nations investigations, and archival research in nine countries; after public opinion polls and streams of films, novels, television, *manga*, and internet sites; after what even Japanese courts—which consistently ruled against the comfort women—admitted as the "irrefutable historical evidence" of their brutal experience; after the comfort women had become registered and lodged in many precincts of public memory—after all that, the Japanese government would have the world believe that the women were either prostitutes or individuals who volunteered to enter sexual service in the imperial Japanese military.

How did this happen? It would be reasonable, and not entirely wrong, to blame the arch-conservative regime of Japanese Prime Minister Abe Shinzō and his like-minded ministers and supporters. Under their aegis, national history once again became nationalistic history, ignoring seemingly established facts in favor of narratives glorified by pride and patriotism. It mattered that this particular prime minister was himself a fervent nationalist, with a record of consistently right-wing views of the war from the time he was first elected to parliament in 1993. He joined the parliamentary Committee for the Examination of History, which denied that the "Greater East Asia War" was a war of aggression and referred to the Nanjing Massacre and the comfort women as fabrications. By 1996, he was a member of the Group of Young Diet Members Concerned with Japan's Future and History Education and increasingly prominent among the growing clamor against what right-wing revisionists condemned as "masochistic history" for its focus on the negative rather than the positive parts of Japan's past (Iwasaki & Richter, 2008). In 2004, Abe stated that "there was no such historical fact as the military comfort women," and during his second campaign for the premiership in 2012, he promised, if elected, to retract his party's 1993 apology (Narusawa, 2013). Once elected, he retracted his pledge of retraction when it became clear that public opinion in Japan and abroad had come too far to swallow such a move. In power from 2012 to 2020, Abe softened his rhetoric only slightly, continuing to the end to deny forcible recruitment of the comfort women, a denial that put him at odds with history as many had by then come to understand it.

The revisionist pattern at work with Abe and his supporters was neither silence nor suppression but, rather, the more common distortion by repeatedly selective use of the facts. It is a fact that a number of the tens of thousands of comfort women were prostitutes or impoverished young women desperate to support their families, although many of the latter were tricked by civilian middleman recruiters to think they were signing up for different work. But the Abe government transmuted this fact into a global argument of "no coercion of anyone," ignoring the evidence that many young girls were indeed forcibly taken and, once in service, were compelled to remain as often cruelly treated sex slaves of the Japanese military. To support its position, the government had to argue that the testimonies of the former comfort women were unreliable, subjective, and manipulated by their supporters—a viewpoint out of line with the prominence accorded voices of victims in the changing transnational landscape of war memory. The prime minister and his supporters also deployed the deflective—and defective—moral argument that other militaries also had military brothels, while Abe continued to repeat his calls for a patriotism worthy of Japan as a "dignified and beautiful country" (Abe, 2006).

Like other nationalist-populist leaders of the time, Abe evoked the national past first and foremost in the service of domestic politics. In electoral terms, this meant appealing to the conservative base of his party as well as to such organizations as the powerful Nippon Kaigi (Japan Conference), the largest right-wing network in Japan today and a staunch supporter of Abe. In policy terms, fanning nationalist sentiments aligned with Abe's campaign to strengthen Japan's military and national security posture in what he called "proactive pacifism" and his opponents in Japan and Asia labeled incipient militarism. These objectives included articulating the doctrine of collective security, which succeeded, and revising the "Peace Constitution," which did not.

Nor was Japan's stature in the world to be sullied by repeated references to the comfort women. The Foreign Ministry mounted a global policy of objecting to every new statue of the comfort women, no matter where it was located, pressuring leaders in Busan, Manila, Taipei, Atlanta, San Francisco, Berlin, and other places to remove the statues, mostly without success. The Japanese government even submitted an amicus brief in an unsuccessful suit filed in 2014 by Japanese Americans against the city of Glendale, California, for the removal of its statue; in 2017, the U.S. Supreme Court refused to hear the case. Such puny diplomatic punches as Osaka's termination of its sister-city relationship with San Francisco in 2018 joined more typical retaliatory moves such as the (short-term) removal of the Japanese ambassador to Seoul and the consul-general in Busan in protest over the statue in that city. In fact, it began to seem as if every time Japan or its envoys protested a statue in one place, a new statue popped up in another. Even as it continued tilting at statues, the government mounted a strenuous campaign to prevent the United Nations Educational, Scientific, and Cultural Organization (UNESCO) from registering the documentary collection of *Voices of the Comfort Women* in the Memory of the World Register. Outraged by the earlier inclusion of documents of the Nanjing Massacre, the Abe government withheld its considerable funding to UNESCO in order to block the nomination of the comfort women submitted by an international alliance of groups from nine countries. Japanese pressure led to a postponement of the nomination and an internal crisis in UNESCO's evaluation process (Suh, 2019, pp. 91–107), but it won no skirmishes in the field of international opinion. In fact, much of Japan's expressed diplomatic "disappointment" over the statues and its self-righteous castigation of China and South Korea for making history an "instrument of politics" (government spokesmen, strangers to irony, all) was directed toward domestic audiences. For whom else is nationalism meant in the first instance but the nation?

When it came to war memory, Japan's nationalism was matched, sometimes bettered, by that of its neighbors, particularly South Korea but also

China and others. For Koreans, the comfort women represented gender discrimination but even more the oppressiveness of 35 years of Japanese colonial rule. In the name of the main Korean organization working on their behalf, the comfort women were referred to as a "volunteer corps," the Japanese colonial euphemism for forced labor (Soh, 2008, pp. 57–58).[1] This language avoided confusion with the "comfort women" in the camptowns around American military bases in postwar South Korea (Moon, 1997), but it also placed the issue squarely in a postcolonial context, where it drew energy from deep-rooted anti-Japanese sentiments that had animated Korean nationalism since Japan annexed the peninsula in 1910. South Korean advocates faced criticism from activists in other countries for placing nationalist above feminist perspectives, for focusing on Korean comfort women to the exclusion of their counterparts across Asia, and for emphasizing colonial grievance over the violation of human rights. In this respect, the discourse on the comfort women in South Korea exhibited the wider phenomenon of "victimhood nationalism" that afflicted so many memory cultures by the turn of the century (Lim, 2010).

Claiming national victimhood meant controlling the narrative, not only in public expression but also in the courts. When a Korean scholar wrote a book that described both forced and (genuinely) voluntary sexual service, including prostitutes, she was sued in 2015 for defaming the honor of the victims and 2 years later found guilty in an appeals court of "distortion of the facts." Whereas Abe and his Japanese supporters viewed all the comfort women as willing sex workers, South Koreans regarded them all as having been dragooned—by the Japanese military, not by Korean middlemen. The comfort women issue in Korea appeared "almost sacred," with any criticism of the victims or the statues as "taboo" (Onchi, 2020). Despite the existence of more reasoned opinion in each country, when it came to political uses of the past, each side selected the facts that suited its national story and stuck to them, no matter what (Pak, 2013). In South Korea, as in Japan, the nationalist appeal of the comfort women issue made it an increasingly useful tool in domestic politics as the topic gained national and international prominence in the 2010s.

In 2011, South Korea's Constitutional Court ruled that the Korean government's failure to gain compensation for the former comfort women

---

[1] The official English name of the organization, founded in 1990, is the Korean Council for the Women Drafted for Military Sexual Slavery by Japan, which makes explicit the meaning of the more general term "volunteer corps" in this context.

violated their constitutional rights, an unusual juridical move that made political demands on the party in power. Responding to this and to public opinion, President Park Geun-hye, in office from 2013 to 2017, at first made the comfort women a sticking point in Korean–Japanese relations, condemning Japan because of its "regressive remarks" and denial of "correct history." Her successor from the liberal opposition party, Moon Jae-in, while rolling back many of Park's policies, found it politically expedient to keep the spotlight on the comfort women, labeling the military brothel system a crime against humanity, much to the displeasure of the Japanese government. And it was no accident that in 2018 the day chosen for a new national day in memory of the comfort women was August 14, which although it was the date the first comfort woman came forward with her story in 1991, also fell on the eve of the far more widely known and emotionally felt commemoration of the liberation of Korea from Japanese colonial rule on August 15, 1945. In short, whether conservative or liberal, whether in the service of national dignity or transnational human rights, the politics of nationalism suffused and determined the South Korean narrative of the comfort women no less than it did its counterpart in Japan.

Needless to say, such uses of the national past in domestic politics had powerful repercussions in the international context. Historical issues—colonialism, comfort women, and forced labor—dogged Korean–Japanese relations for years, reaching a new peak, or nadir, in the 2010s. In the heated diplomatic contention over the disputed islands in the seas between Japan and Korea, the comfort women appeared frequently in anti-Japanese rhetoric. In December 2015, responding to regional concerns and pressure from the United States and others to "put history behind them" (Kerry, 2014), the Korean and Japanese foreign ministers met to resolve the comfort women dispute in a "final and irreversible" agreement. The bilateral agreement established a Reconciliation and Healing Foundation to provide compensation for the surviving comfort women, together with the promise of a letter of remorse in the name of the Japanese Prime Minister. The outcry against the agreement from the Korean public was strong and immediate. Not only had the comfort women themselves not been consulted but Japanese negotiators had also demanded that the Korean government seek to remove the now iconic comfort woman statue from in front of the Japanese embassy in Seoul. It also asked that Koreans cease using the term "sex slaves," which, although it had become common in global discourse on the comfort women, remained a particular thorn in the side of Abe and his conservative supporters. Both these demands were not only diplomatically tone-deaf but also beyond the control, or political will, of the South Korean government. Far from being either final or irreversible, the agreement was criticized by President Moon as emotionally unacceptable to the Korean people; in 2019, he unilaterally dissolved the foundation.

The comfort women issue remained unresolved, even as a Korean court ruled in favor of comfort women in early 2021, basing its judgment on human rights violations and claiming that Japan's usual recourse to the principle of sovereign immunity did not therefore apply. The Japanese government immediately rejected the ruling, which required it to pay compensation to the plaintiffs. Talk of seizing Japanese assets in South Korea re-emerged amid yet another "rift" in bilateral relations (Onchi, 2021). This repeated the pattern of 2018, when Korean courts issued landmark rulings against Japanese corporations for the use of Korean forced labor during the war, bringing this aspect of the "history problem" to join the comfort women at the top of the geopolitical agenda. At that time, the two governments engaged in hostile forms of economic and political retaliation, which were later moderated in policy but with little concomitant cooling in the realm of public opinion. Nationalist sentiments reigned supreme, bringing the regard for one another of these two close Northeast Asian allies to the lowest ebb in a long time. In the affective politics of national history, this was an instance of both countries behaving badly—a nearly global phenomenon in these nationalist–populist times.

Patriotic Passions

Yet in recounting such heated politics of the past, the positions taken by nationalist–populist governments were nowhere near the whole story. It is both more complicated and more disturbing to recognize that it took more than an arch-nationalist prime minister in Japan to urge public memory rightward, and backward. It took more to stir up anti-Japanese feelings among South Koreans than two presidents—one conservative, one liberal—using the comfort women as political capital. It took more to create hostility toward Japan among Chinese youth than President Xi Jinping praising the "great victory of the national spirit with patriotism at its core" in the Chinese People's War of Resistance Against Japanese Aggression or, as he liked to call it in order to celebrate China's global contribution, the World Anti-Fascist War (Xi, 2020).

Except in totalitarian states—and maybe even there—governments seldom control war memory, however much they may try to do so. They do of course influence popular views of the past through national education, rhetoric, ceremony, and memorials, but much of the action and reaction in the changing landscape of public memory takes place in society. This brings us back to the vernacular terrain of memory, where war stories are both produced and consumed, and where memory activists, mass and social media, popular culture, and personal pasts interact with and counteract one another. Populism, after all, makes its appeals to the people, and nationalism depends on identification with the nation. When it comes to revisions of national history, nationalist–populist success in so many different countries at roughly the same time cannot be explained in economic, social, or political terms alone. It is also, and sometimes mostly, a matter of emotion.

In East Asia, as elsewhere, in the years since the end of the Cold War, nationalistic sentiments were roused and patriotic passions ignited in a kind of ricochet that often deflected state messages even as they were being absorbed. The changing attitudes of Asian youth exemplified the sometimes unintended reverberations in the vernacular terrain. In Mao's China, Japan's leaders, not its people, had been blamed for the conflict, while all praise went to the Chinese Communist Party for leading the heroic resistance in a "people's war" against the Japanese (writing the Chinese Nationalists out of the story, for obvious political reasons). Reaching for unity after Mao's death, patriotic education and national commemoration of the war expanded during the 1980s, symbolized by the opening of the Nanjing Massacre Memorial Hall in 1985, with "300000," the totemic number of victims, looming large on its façade. The nationalist fervor of younger Chinese erupted during the 1990s, initially in the context of intensified patriotic education in the wake of the 1989 democracy protests in Tienanmen Square. By the end of the decade, the familiar evil twins of Japanese devils during the war and Western imperialists during the "century of humiliation" had sprung to electronic life on the internet. Riled by frequent mention of Japan's "history problem," which included textbook revisions, politicians visiting Yasukuni, the shrine of Japan's war dead, frequent but unrequited demands for apology, and the high-profile territorial dispute over the islands in the East China Sea, young Chinese cyber-nationalists signed petitions by the millions, fueling passions against "pigJapan." In 2005, tens of thousands of so-called angry youth took to the streets, throwing rocks and eggs at Japanese establishments in riots that even began to worry Party leaders. Fearing the protests might get out of hand and turn in its direction, the Chinese government began to subdue them, as if attempting to put the genie of its anti-Japanese discourse back in the bottle. Not only the internet but popular culture also fanned the flames, especially on television, which had diversified enough to follow government rules and still meet audience demand. In 2012 alone, more than 70 anti-Japanese television series aired on national and regional stations, featuring orgiastic amounts of blood and gore at the hands of Japanese (Xuecun, 2014). Chinese youth in the hundreds of millions played video games, among them government-sponsored "patriotic games" like "Anti-Japan War Online" (2005) and "Shoot the Devils" (2014), in which players shoot Japanese war criminals, but also products of the vast commercial gaming industry, including "The Invisible Guardian" (2019), said to present a more nuanced view of the war against Japan (Davis, 2019).

Much of the seemingly habitual anti-Japanese sentiment in the 2000s was hostility without history, fed by internet memes and violent television dramas and untouched by substantial historical knowledge of the war. And Chinese youth could rant against Japan online while obsessively consuming *anime* and other products of Japanese popular culture, even as the Nanjing Massacre and other atrocities remained central to their image of Japan. Their protests were often driven by Japan's official actions, whether revised history textbooks or politicians' denials of wartime atrocities. The protesters were also electronically connected across national borders, notably to Chinese American memory activists in such organizations as the Global Alliance for Preserving the History of World War II in Asia, headquartered in San Francisco. In this respect, it was "historical issues" as much as history itself that so negatively affected Sino-Japanese relations: In 2015, 70% of the Chinese polled expressed antipathy toward Japan because of its "lack of a proper apology and remorse over the history of invasion of China" (Genron NPO, 2015). This public receptivity to patriotic nationalism was as determining as the history policy of the Chinese Communist Party, which while controlling and censoring, did not alone explain the spread of anti-Japanese zeal. Indeed, Beijing's attitude to such memory activism as the reparations movement on behalf of Chinese comfort women has been characterized as "Don't support, don't discourage" (Hornby, 2015). With this policy, the government could clamp down on demonstrations but do little to contain what I call the "hate nationalism" that roiled numbers of Chinese youth. In China, as in other places throughout the world, patriotic passions seemed to feed a need for national pride and identity, which was manipulated but not entirely manufactured by the state.[2]

South Korean youth developed their own version of hate nationalism during the first two decades of the century. The messages ricocheted at slightly different angles, in that young Koreans were at first closer to Japanese popular culture, notably after the Korean government in 1998 began to lift the bans on Japanese music, manga, television, and film; they also traveled to Japan in greater numbers in the years before the massive influx of young Chinese tourists. But young Koreans—and indeed, young Korean Americans, too—seemed to have inherited colonial resentment against Japan from their parents and grandparents, while Korean schools and museums purveyed an array of anti-Japanese messages relating to the colonial period, wartime atrocities, forced labor, and the comfort women, as well as Korean claims on the islands disputed with Japan. None of these factors was new, but the increasingly high-profile memory politics of the 2010s, both within Korea and across Japanese–Korean relations, brought the comfort women and forced labor into seemingly reflexive patriotic currency. As with Chinese youth, much of the heated language circulated on the internet and in Korean social media, which filled with calls to join the "No Japan" campaign, at one point in 2019 linking the comfort women issue to the boycott of the popular Japanese clothing brand Uniqlo.

And what of Japanese youth? How did the ricochet of nationalist messages travel among younger generations exposed to revisionist history and inflamed memory politics since the mid-1990s? Unlike in China or Korea, where anti-Japanese sentiment often suffused public discourse, the general tenor of opinion was not pointedly hostile to China or South Korea, even as conservative nationalists like Abe whitewashed the history of the war and even as Japanese continued their habitual discrimination against the resident Korean minority in Japan. During the 1990s, public opinion polls showed an increasing acceptance of Japan's responsibility for "aggressive war" and acknowledgment of the comfort women system and the need to compensate its victims. But after the "history problem" came to the geopolitical fore in the late 1990s, Japanese youth were exposed to a stream of provocations, including the patriotic messages of the bestselling revisionist *manga* of Japanese cartoonist Kobayashi Yoshinori, the constant calls from China and

---

[2] For the all-important interaction between top-down and bottom-up representations of the past, see Chapters 8, 11, 17, and 19 in this volume.

Korea for apologies from Japan, and the viperous stew of anti-Japanese sentiment on the internet, to which young Japanese responded with their own version of hate nationalism, which had less to do with the government line and much to do with the "social contagion" of memory linked to an aroused and defensive national pride (see Chapter 20, this volume).

Japanese youth, like their counterparts in China and South Korea, often had little trouble separating their antipathies from their lifestyles. Young Koreans continued to learn Japanese and travel to Japan, young Japanese consumed three "Korean waves" of popular culture, and droves of young Chinese studied in Japan. Moreover, their views ebbed and flowed, responding strongly to the ricochet of memory messages at one point and seeming to forget about them when they again heard the siren calls of Uniqlo, K-pop, or *anime*. Yet, revved up by the nationalist rhetoric of war memory, knowing not very much of war history, these generations of East Asian youth gained a learned antipathy toward one another that, like many attitudes of youth, may well stay with them and influence the regional future far longer than any of the present political regimes and their nationalistic revisers-in-chief.

A similar ricochet of messages among the general public surrounded the politics of apology, which strongly colored the nationalisms of war memory in all three countries. Beginning in the 1990s, Japanese leaders repeatedly issued apologies for wartime actions and atrocities, and just as repeatedly South Koreans and Chinese condemned them as insufficient and insincere. International voices chimed in, including parliamentary resolutions in 2007 in the United States, the European Union, the Netherlands, and other countries demanding that Japan recognize, compensate, and apologize to the former comfort women. In 2014, the U.S. Congress even passed a law calling for the same. Meanwhile, the Japanese government publically paraded its official statements of apology, from 1992 to the present, asserting that in regard to the comfort women, "feelings of remorse and apology articulated by previous Cabinets will be upheld as unshakable" (Ministry of Foreign Affairs, 2018). Although such statements had little lasting impact on the East Asian geopolitics of memory, they did indeed affect opinion within the three societies, where the apology issue succeeded in arousing the patriotic passions that did so much to sour bilateral relations in each case. In Japan, every apology seemed to generate a nationalist denial by a right-wing revisionist or a conservative politician in a pattern one scholar described as "contrition-then-backlash" (Lind, 2008, pp. 93–94). Although such denials had the effect of keeping issues like the comfort women in public view, thus contributing to the growing Japanese recognition of wartime injustice, they also raised the nationalistic temperature, with apologies and denials ricocheting off one another over three decades. To Koreans and Chinese, the denials negated the apologies, so they continued their insistent calls for a genuine expression of remorse. Meanwhile, complaints of "apology fatigue" became more common among Japanese, with a thickening layer of nationalist umbrage threatening to erase some of the earlier gains in public recognition of Japan's wartime responsibility.

Again, this ricochet of memory effects occurred in relation to, but not in control of, official views of the past. In short, historical revisionism at the top succeeds only when it interacts with other factors to arouse patriotic passions which resonate with strains of national identity that are themselves fundamental to the modern nation-state. Whether liberal or conservative, the political uses of history demand this kind of engagement of public memory with national identity, for better and for worse.

Limits to History Remaking

Memory effects do not always ricochet in the same direction; the process of memory-making is not singular; societies are not monolithic; personal pasts remain individual; and even hyper-nationalism has its limits. Despite the turbulence in East Asian war memory over the past three decades, knowledge of and attitudes toward the comfort women in Japan did not revert to the time before the comfort women "came into memory" in the 1990s. Despite Abe and his right-wing supporters, polls continued to show that the public did not abandon its recently shaped views about the wrongfulness of military sex slavery; young people did not need to learn about the comfort women in middle school to know what they thought about a system that recruited and ensnared young Asian girls into brothels. Japanese who responded to a defensive nationalism spurred in part by continual calls for apology did not necessarily accept the government's revisionist history and its denial of the coercion of the comfort women.

Moreover, the comfort women issue no longer rested solely in the hands of Japanese. It had become what I call a "traveling trope," which stood for unacceptable sexual violence against women, not unlike the way the Holocaust came to signify genocide the world over. For there now existed a transnational matrix of memory that interwove with and affected memory politics at home. At the United Nations, the comfort women were cited in connection with the human rights of women, with trafficking, and with calls to recognize the "rights of memory" of victims of past abuses. Like Auschwitz, Hiroshima, Stalingrad, or Nanjing in the collective memory of World War II, the comfort women came to connote more than the historical facts themselves, nor did they belong solely either to the nation that perpetrated or the nations that suffered the injustice. Yet the historical facts remained facts, however much the emotions around them were politicized by all sides. With a different government in place in Japan, these facts might well be faced with a different memory politics that removes the comfort women "issue" from the geopolitical agenda in East Asia, especially if it serves the national and regional interests of the nations involved.

The politics of apology is likely to move in similar directions, not least because it is now part of what I think of as a "global memory culture," which evolved over the decades since 1945, in good part through the processes of remembering World War II. The norms and practices of this global memory culture include apologies, which are expected both from leaders to their own people and from states to other states. That Japan is not exempt from these norms and practices is suggested by the fact that when the Liberal Democratic Party briefly fell from power in 1993 and 2009, the new prime ministers immediately changed tack, whether by eschewing visits to Yasukuni Shrine or making "apology tours" to Asian nations that suffered from Japan's wartime actions. Once another political party—or even a more liberal form of the present party—comes to power, apologies are likely to be offered and, if given in the right spirit and without backlash denials, accepted.

Another, less edifying prospect is also possible, not because of the government and its view of history but because of the receptivity of the Japanese (and Chinese and Korean) people to patriotic passions and the comforts of national self-esteem. If enough has changed in the vernacular terrain that the shifts in Japanese war memory since 1990 are sufficiently undercut and overlaid with a defensive nationalism, then nationalism might win the day and lose the past. For it is changes in the vernacular terrain that explain the support for the nationalist history purveyed by Japan's prime minister (and the presidents of China and South Korea), not the prime minister (and presidents) who explain the popular support for their views. If the memory effect that transposed history to identity were to continue on its current nationalistic course, then the facts might not seem to matter all that much. Jacques Rancière (2014) wrote that "the times of memory-history are not the same as those of truth-history"

(p. 62). It remains possible for "memory-history" to prevail, as in the myth of the Lost Cause in the South's view of the American Civil War or in Russia's coded narratives of repeated victory over an external enemy (see Chapters 3 and 22, this volume). While such memory-history is inscribed in the national identities of China as the central kingdom, Japanese exceptionalism, and Korean postcolonial nationalism, it is also true that views of World War II can change to accommodate, as they have in Western Europe, if not reconciliation then at least overlapping narratives that former enemies can collectively live with in an evolving context of regional and global relations.

Whatever the future of warring national histories in East Asia, the relation between memory-history and truth-history presents a challenge to academic historians like myself. Because in my analysis, the dynamics of public memory unfolds centrally in the vernacular terrain, that must be the site of effective intervention, if one is so minded to intervene, as I am. Indeed, the reason I began to study memory in the first place was to seek an alignment between what I call good memory and good history of World War II in Asia. I understand good memory to encompass efforts to include the unincluded and the victims, whether individual, collective, or national, in the war stories that dominate in each country; by good history, I mean an adherence to the facts of what Rancière called truth-history. Historians who would enter the public fray need to speak the language of memory, which means understanding the politics of historical revisionism pursued by nationalist–populist leaders as well as the patriotic passions that arouse their people. It also means participating in the media and messages of the vernacular terrain rather than trusting that academic history-writing will set the record straight. Yet, because public memory is not a thing but a process, it can and does change, sometimes quite quickly and in surprising ways. The comfort women are a case in point: A group of elderly, often poor and powerless women survivors from nine countries across Asia who did not know one another came into global memory, supported by advocates of different and sometimes conflicting views, and influenced the way the world views and international law judges violations of the human rights of women. Theirs is both a sad and an encouraging tale.

National pasts have been determined by political presents since the advent of the modern nation-state, so the current nationalist-populist revisions of history in so many countries around the world are in one sense timeless and in another acutely representative of the current historical moment. If national discourses sometimes seem besieged by memory and mired in history, it might help to recall the pronouncement of the White Queen in *Through the Looking Glass*: "It's a poor sort of memory that only works backward." While attending to views of the past, we might also turn our eye to the future, which is, after all, the only part of history we can actually affect.

References

Abe, S. (2006). *Utsukushii kuni e* [Toward a beautiful country]. Bungei shunju. Revised in 2013 as *Atarashii kuni e: utsukushii kuni e kanzenban*.
Davis, K. (2019). Chinese video game highlights complex reality of war with Japan. *Sixth Tone*. https://www.sixthtone.com/news/1003680/chinese-video-game-highlights-complex-reality-of-war-with-japan
Foreign Ministry of Japan. (2018). Issues Regarding History: History Issues Q&A. https://www.mofa.go.jp/policy/q_a/faq16.html
Genron NPO. (2015). *11th Japan–China opinion poll analysis report on the comparative data*. https://www.genron-npo.net/en/opinion_polls/archives/5315.html
Gluck, C. (2007). Operations of memory: "Comfort women" and the world. In S. M. Jager & R. Mitter (Eds.), *Ruptured histories: War, memory, and the post-Cold War in Asia* (pp. 47–76). Harvard University Press.
Guex, S. (2015). The history textbook controversy in Japan and South Korea. *Cipango: French Journal of Japanese Studies*, 4. https://journals.openedition.org/cjs/968
Hornby, L. (2015, March 20). China's comfort women. *Financial Times*.
Iwasaki, M., & Richter, S. (2008). The topology of post-1990s historical revisionism. *Positions: East Asia Cultures Critique*, 16(3), 505–537.
Kerry, J. (2014, March 1). *The New York Times*.
Kim, P. (2001). Global civil society remakes history: The Women's International War Crime Tribunal. *Positions: East Asia Cultures Critique*, 9(3), 611–620.
Kumagai, N. (2014). Asia Women's Fund revisited. *Asia-Pacific Review*, 21(2), 117–148.
Lim, J. (2010). Victimhood nationalism in contested memories: National mourning and global accountability. In A. Assmann & S. Konrad (Eds.), *Memory in a global age: Discourses, practices and trajectories* (pp. 138–162). Palgrave Macmillan.
Lind, J. (2008). *Sorry states: Apologies in international politics*. Cornell University Press.
Moon, K. (1997). *Sex among allies: Military prostitution in U.S.–Korea relations*. Columbia University Press.
Murayama, T. (1995, August 15). *Statement by Prime Minister Murayama "On the occasion of the 50th anniversary of the war's end" (August 15 1995)*. Ministry of Foreign Affairs of Japan. https://www.mofa.go.jp/announce/press/pm/murayama/9508.html
Narusawa, M. (2013). Abe Shinzo: Japan's new prime minister a far-right denier of history. *Asia-Pacific Journal: Japan Focus*, 11(2), 3879.
Onchi, Y. (2020, December 29). "Comfort women" settlement fails to settle Japan–South Korea row. *Nikkei Asia*.
Onchi, Y. (2021, January 8). South Korean court orders Japan to pay former "comfort women." *Nikkei Asia*. January 8, 2021.

Pak, Y. (2013). Cheguk ŭi wianbu: singminji chibae wa kiŏk ŭi t'ujaeng [Comfort women of the Empire: Colonial rule and struggles over memory]. *Ch'op'an*. For her views in English, see https://parkyuha.org/archives/4368

Rancière, J. (2014). *Figures of history*. Polity Press.

Rekishi kentō iinkai [Committee for Examination of History]. (1995). *Daitōa sensō no sōkatsu* [Summary of the Greater East Asia War]. Tentensha.

Runia, E. (2014). *Moved by the past: Discontinuity and historical mutation*. Columbia University Press.

Rushdy, A. A. H. (2015). *A guilted age: Apologies for the past*. Temple University Press.

Soh, C. S. (2008). *The comfort women: Sexual violence and postcolonial memory in Korea and Japan*. University of Chicago Press.

Suh, K. (2019). History wars in the memory of the world: The documents of the Nanjing massacre and the "comfort women." In R. Edmondson, L. Jordan, & A. Prodan (Eds.), The UNESCO *Memory* of the World Programme: Key *aspects* and *recent developments* (pp. 91–107). Springer.

Wieviorka, A. (2006). *The era of the witness*. Cornell University Press.

Xuecun, M. (2014, February 9). China's television war on Japan. *The New York Times*.

Xi, J. (2020, September 2). Xi focus: Xi stresses carrying forward great spirit of resisting aggression. *Xinhuanet* [Speech commemorating the 75th anniversary of the end of the war]. http://www.xinhuanet.com/english/2020-09/04/c_139340869.htm

15
How China Remembers the Korean War and the Limit of Statist Nationalism

Zhao Ma

On July 27, 1953, guns fell silent on the Korean peninsula following the signing of the armistice. But the political campaign inside of China continued, not to mobilize the masses to shed blood for their North Korean ally but, rather, to celebrate the living heroes, commemorate dead martyrs, and keep the revolutionary memory alive for generations to come. In 1958, a national memorial was built in Dandong on the China–North Korean border; 2 years later, the Korean War, known in China as the "Resist America and Aid Korea War," became a permanent exhibition at the newly built Military Museum of the Chinese Revolution in Beijing. Throughout the 1950s, eight Chinese national literary journals published more than 2,500 pieces of work that took the Korean War as subject matter (Chang, 2018). Chinese filmmakers participated in the effort of remembering the war by churning out 19 films in nearly half a century after the armistice. Among them, the large majority (14 films) were made in the Maoist era (1950s–1970s), 3 in the immediate aftermath of his death (early 1980s), and 2 in the 1990s. Some films venerated the Chinese soldiers for defeating America, South Korea, and their allies on the front lines; others honored the masses at home for their steadfast support for the war efforts. Several of them became propagandistic and cinematic masterpieces or "red classics."

These cultural projects carried out a propagandistic and didactic mission—to glorify combat, mourn the dead, ennoble the cause, and celebrate national unity and China's relationship with its socialist allies. For those who participated in and even died in the war, their heroic deeds were enshrined in memorials, consecrated in museums, mythicized in the world of words, and celebrated on screen. Their contributions and sacrifices were woven into the glorious history of the Chinese Revolution and the People's

Republic. For the new generation who did not live through the war, the 3 years of bloodbath were entombed in grand architecture and graced by fine words to help them grapple with the enormity of the war and its complex legacies.

In 2016, some six decades after the Korean War ended and nearly 18 years after the last film about the war was made, the state-owned China Film Group Corporation produced a new movie, *My War*. It describes the course of combat of two Chinese Volunteer Army units. One is a "cultural work team" (*wengong tuan*)—a noncombat unit led by Meng Sanxia and composed mostly of female soldiers whose primary task is to boost the morale of other troops. The team experiences the excitement of marching to the battlefield, thrillingly dodging the U.S. air raids and mines laid in ambush, breaking through an encirclement under the veil of night, and finally helping treat the wounded in a brutal battle. The other unit is the "sharp blade vanguard company" (*gangtie xianfenglian*)—an expertly trained force tasked to carry out a series of intensely challenging tasks, including dashing across the Sino-North Korean border under enemy air attack, engaging in close combat with mechanized enemy infantry battalions, cutting off the path of the enemy's retreat, and seizing the enemy's high ground position. Most of the soldiers, including the head of the company, Sun Beichuan, perish over the course of the action, but the company successfully completes the tasks given to it by its commanders.

Upon its release, cultural officials showered praise on the film. "*My War* painstakingly depicts the massive sacrifice of the Chinese Volunteer troops," Zhang Wei, the Executive Vice President of the Chinese Film Critics Association, commented. "It shows the war as a carnage when lives were lost in massive numbers. It is shockingly realistic and a rare rendition of the war [in China]" (Yang, 2016). "Through the art of film," Rao Shuguang, Secretary-General of the state-sponsored Association of Chinese Filmmakers, remarked, "*My War* effectively conveys and expresses the sense of patriotism and heroism in a way that young audiences can 'readily accept' (*leyu jieshou*)" (Yang, 2016).

In sharp contrast to praise lavished by cultural officials, a strong voice of disapproval flooded social media. "I will not watch *My War*," the Hong Kong–based English newspaper *South China Morning Post* stated in 2016, quoting Lin Qi, a history professor at Harbin Normal University, who posted on his Weibo microblog. "As more historical facts are revealed, people are becoming increasingly aware of the cruelty of that war and its hurt to the nations and people involved," Lin emphasized (Zhou, 2016). Another scathing review reads as follows (S. Wang, 2016):

> The war ended some sixty years ago, and since then the international situation has been turned upside down: former enemies [of China] are now friends in close contact; an old ally [with whom China] forged friendship in blood is now a trouble-maker frequently "testing nuclear bombs" on China's doorsteps. Yet, [the film] maintains the outdated political stance and ideological value to make a film for contemporary viewers, which makes [contemporary viewers] feel that [filmmakers] are as if living in their own dream.

There was also a post on social media featuring a picture of one viewer sitting in an empty cinema where the film was shown, followed by a one sentence comment: "Your war, one man's show" (Dingdong, 2016). Amid the polarizing reviews, the film greeted viewers in cinemas nationwide. It grossed a mere 35.92 million yuan at the box office during the first month after it hit theaters, which ranked it at 122nd out of 196 films at the Chinese box office in 2016 (Niaojia, 2020).

So why does a film made to promote "the sense of patriotism and heroism" fail miserably at the box office and draw heavy criticism on social media at a time when Chinese nationalism, as one China observer notes, "operates almost like a state religion under Xi Jinping" (Brown, 2018)? In search of answers, this chapter examines the effort by contemporary Chinese filmmakers and state sponsors to remember the Korean War campaign against the backdrop of China's shifting foreign policy and an emerging cosmopolitan viewership. In the years following the war, there was a consistent effort by the cultural arm of the Chinese Party-state to prescribe and preserve a form of national memory that remembered the Korean War as a sacred mission to defend the Chinese socialist homeland, grow revolutionary heroism, and advance the communist internationalist cause. To be sure, such an ideologically coded and socialist memory came under challenge after China disavowed Maoism in the early 1980s and the Cold War ended in the early 1990s. Neither was it immune from the seismic shift of the bilateral relationship with North Korea, as China refused to endorse North Korea's nuclear program and even participated in a regime of international sanctions to punish its old ally.

From the late 1990s onward, the socialist memory has been gradually replaced by a China-centered, nationalist memory that has introduced a host of changes, such as significantly downplaying the Sino-North Korean alliance (Ma, 2017). The shift from a socialist to a nationalist framework of remembering the Korean War is part of a larger cultural enterprise initiated by the post-socialist Chinese state to remember the broader Chinese Communist Revolution (including the armed struggles before 1949 and high socialism under Mao) on the silver screen. As a result, a series of "main melody" films, which promote socialist values and receive Chinese state financial support, have been produced; they have attempted to obscure the communist objective that initially inspired the revolution and ignore the bitter cost of lives and properties lost in the relentless and ruthless political campaigns, while highlighting another set of much brighter developments attributed to the Communist Party's leadership—regaining independence, building a stronger state apparatus, and industrializing the economy—all of which constitute the core of contemporary Chinese nationalism.

The Korean War in China's national memory has shifted from a socialist crusade to a nationalist mission. Yet, the Chinese state remains at the center in both narratives. It is credited with leading soldiers to fight and defeat enemies, rallying popular support for the war effort, and ultimately accomplishing a nationalist feat that washed off the "century of humiliation," growing people's confidence in being citizens of a "New China." This unchanging and underlining statist narrative functions, to borrow James Wertsch's words, as the "narrative template ... sufficiently entrenched to remain intact even as national memory [undergoes] radical transformations at the surface level of specific narratives" (see Chapter 22, this volume). The statist narrative template seeks to forge a pro-government collective memory that celebrates the Communist Party-state's "great, glorious, and correct" leadership while suppressing memories lingering on the political or moral margins (e.g., wartime experiences of Chinese prisoners of war). In this way, this chapter echoes Rauf Garagozov's findings that "collective memory has the capacity to serve as such a coordinating device for organizing collective actions, mass mobilization, and mass movements" (see Chapter 17, this volume). The officially sanctioned collective memory and its statist framework offer a venue for the Chinese masses to imagine their participation in the larger revolutionary process that the Korean War had attempted to defend and advance, helping the Party-state mold the spiritual world of the Chinese public for generations.

Some scholars have emphasized the effectiveness of the contemporary Chinese state to combine old socialist propaganda institutions and new market tools to impose some unity on and clarity of the memory of the past revolution. The current political leaders have decisively abandoned but not openly repudiated Mao's political radicalism; they have harnessed the reformulated memory of the revolutionary past to build a post-revolutionary future. For example, while studying the patriotic education campaign since the early 1990s, Dong Wang argues that the new school curriculum redefines the meaning of the Communist Revolution, not so much as a working-class revolt against global capitalism but, rather, as a century-long struggle to restore the "wealth and power" of the Chinese nation. "The legitimacy-challenged Chinese Communist Party," Wang stresses, "has used history education as an instrument for the glorification of the party, for the consolidation of national identity, and for the justification of the political system of the CCP's one-party rule in the post-Tiananmen and post-Cold War eras" (Z. Wang, 2012, p. 9). However, this chapter shifts focus to the discord between politics and cultural production, the discrepancy between past history and the present geopolitical situation, and tensions between how the state has attempted to reformulate the memory of the Korean War and how such attempts have been received (or contested and rejected) by the market and many contemporary filmgoers. The discord, discrepancy, and tensions bring to light the unresolved legacies of the Korean War and the unfinished task to remember the Chinese Revolution at the time when statist nationalism is challenged by cosmopolitan viewers.

"Why We Fight:" Remembering the Korean War on the Silver Screen, 1953–1998

The first Chinese feature film that took on the Korean War as the subject matter was *Cutting the Devil's Talons*, produced in 1953 by the state-owned Shanghai Film Studio. The 87-minute film is set in a military industrial complex, located in northeast China, where scientists and engineers are working around the clock to develop a new type of anti-aircraft weapon to be used by Chinese troops on the North Korean battlefields. A Nationalist secret agent sneaks onto the Chinese mainland, makes his way to the northeast, and secures a job in the industrial complex by faking his identity and exploiting the security team's inexperience. The film also depicts a Nationalist agent seeking help from remnants of imperialist forces hidden in a Catholic Church. But before he can steal the weapon design and assassinate the chief engineer, the agent is caught by vigilant factory workers and communist security officers.

As the first Korean War film made in the immediate aftermath of the war, *Cutting the Devil's Talons* played a part in reiterating the Party's wartime propaganda line by defining the war in unequivocal and absolute terms of revolutionary patriotism. The war presented a national emergency. Threats abounded: The U.S.-led United Nations forces were moving across the 38th Parallel toward the Chinese border and the U.S. bombing campaign was targeting Chinese troops and civilians. Washington's hostility and aggression emboldened enemies within China—the Nationalists attempted to make a comeback while imperialist saboteurs were agitated to take actions to undermine revolutionary rule. The sense of China being threatened and attacked by foreign enemies struck a patriotic chord with the Chinese public, who had experienced a painful past of the Chinese nation victimized by foreign invasions. Therefore, as the film depicts, when the communist government decided to enter the war, the Chinese people across class lines answered the call to arms and contributed to the war effort in different ways; scientists and engineers worked tirelessly to develop new weapons while factory workers and security staff diligently guarded industrial secrets. Their support for the war effort became the best expression of patriotism. Yet, the patriotism was ideologically encoded. The "Chinese people" in the film come from particular class groups: workers, intellectuals, and revolutionary cadres and officials. Under communist rule, members of these groups were promised basic political rights, means of livelihood, work opportunities, and respect and trust. As the country's new "masters" (*zhuren*), they were expected to support and defend the revolutionary state and carry the revolution forward. Finally, the film, as a counter-espionage film (*fante pian*)—a burgeoning genre in China's socialist cinema—was clearly inspired by another mass movement, the Suppression of the Counter-revolutionary Campaign, launched in December 1950, merely 2 months after China started combat in Korea. The campaign attempted to seek out and eliminate domestic political enemies. As such, patriotism meant not only fighting enemies abroad but also requiring the "Chinese people" to build a system of "participatory surveillance"—that is, "a mode of surveillance in which the masses act as surveillance agents instead of surveillance subjects in order to safeguard national security" (Lu, 2017).

Three years after *Cutting the Devil's Talons*, the Changchun Film Studio produced a 2-hour war epic, *Battle of Shanggan Ridge*, based on a protracted military engagement in the fall of 1952 during America's Operation

Showdown, also known as the Battle of Triangle Hill. In the film, a Chinese infantry company is ordered to reinforce a hilltop position. Upon arrival, they are pounded relentlessly and repeatedly by enemy assault from both ground and air. After suffering heavy casualties, the company is forced to give up the above-ground fortifications and retreat into tunnels. In the second part of the film, Chinese soldiers fight against the enemy's superior firepower and physical hardships such as hunger and thirst. In the end, resilience and perseverance prevail. Chinese troops not only successfully defend their tunnels but also reclaim the hill. Upon its release in early 1957, *Battle of Shanggan Ridge* exploded in national popularity and instantly became a hugely successful piece of cinematic propaganda.

Among its many achievements, *Battle of Shanggan Ridge* expanded the meaning of revolutionary patriotism. Like its predecessor *Cutting the Devil's Talons*, the film celebrated national unity; it also defined the Chinese mothernation through the lens of class by filling the rank and file of revolutionary heroes with soldiers from worker and peasant backgrounds. Furthermore, *Battle of Shanggan Ridge* sought to strengthen the cultural bonds between Chinese soldiers at the front and civilians at home, evoking a sense of cultural pride, or cultural nationalism, among viewers. For a notable example, the film shows soldiers resting in a dingy and squalid tunnel in the middle of a fierce battle. Then the theme song of the film, "My Homeland," is played, accompanied by images of Chinese iconic landmarks such as the Great Wall and the Yellow and Yangtze Rivers. The way the camera moves from China's majestic mountains and rushing rivers to remarkable agricultural harvests and peaceful scenes inscribes cultural greatness on physical space and material growth. "Potent cultural symbolism is deployed," Paul Pickowicz (2010) argues, "to represent China as a collective cultural and spatial entity to which all citizens are steadfastly loyal" (p. 359, see also Liu 2019, p. 50). The montage of images of the cultural homeland, together with the theme song, enshrined the war mission as a monumental enterprise in which the Party, the army, and ordinary people worked together to restore Chinese pride after suffering at the hands of foreign enemies for more than a century.

Films made in the 1960s and 1970s not only placed Chinese soldiers' sacrifice and achievement in the domestic context of defending socialist China but also placed North Korea, the Sino-North Korean alliance, and communist internationalism front and center in defining and remembering the war mission. Notably, North Korean women feature prominently in several Chinese films, such as *On the 38th Parallel*, *Raid*, *Heroic Sons and*

Daughters, and *Raid on White Tiger Regiment*, to animate the internationalist mission. Women in these films are shown living in a country devastated by war: houses in ruins, families destroyed, and reeling from the death of beloved family members. But they emerge from personal and family tragedies to contribute to the war effort in a variety of ways: rebuilding communities, sheltering Chinese troops, attending to wounded soldiers, and repairing roads and rails damaged by American air attacks. In handling these auxiliary tasks, women and Chinese soldiers forge close bonds, as the former regard the latter as sons, brothers, or fathers. It is through these close physical contacts and intense emotional exchanges that the political mission, namely communist internationalism, was translated into a series of familial responsibilities featuring Chinese soldiers supporting, rescuing, and caring for North Korean women and children. These familial imaginaries in films fed into a massive effort on the part of the Chinese communist state to educate ordinary Chinese in their new role as socialist citizens and leaders of the international communist movement.

The Korean War, as many scholars have persuasively argued, was more than a defensive war to protect China's major industrial base in Manchuria and to safeguard the northeastern border. It also presented the Chinese communist state a great opportunity to mobilize people to support the global campaign against a perceived imperialist invasion and colonial oppression (J. Chen, 1994). Thus, the campaign to embrace an alliance with North Korea cultivated an internationalist consciousness among the Chinese that prepared them to fight to expand the revolution beyond China's national borders. Films continued the internationalist movement from war to peace, helping Chinese people forge cultural and emotional bonds with allies to fight in a common communist internationalist cause against colonial subjugation and imperialist invasion for years to come.

Out of 19 Korean War films made before *My War*, 17 are "war films" (*zhanzhengpian*), covering nearly all branches of service and military specializations. In these films, Chinese soldiers are shown fighting like David against Goliath in a variety of precarious situations—outgunned and outnumbered by opponents and lacking basic food and medical supplies. But they ultimately emerge triumphantly from incredible hardships. Their sacrifices spoke to some essential political qualities, such as revolutionary patriotism, socialist heroism, and anti-Americanism, shared by soldiers and civilians alike, which enabled them to score a victory in North Korea and prepared them to fight and win future wars.

After the August First Film Studio (affiliated with the People's Liberation Army) produced *Shining Star on the Battlefield* in 1983, Chinese filmmakers seemed to lose interest in the Korean War. They instead embarked on a new mission to film China's "reform and openness" (*gaige kaifang*). Although they occasionally revisited the many 20th-century wars that comprise the Communist Party's revolutionary history, they tended to focus on the genres of war against Japanese invasion and the civil war against the Nationalists. Throughout the late 1980s and 1990s, only two films were made featuring the Korean War, and after 1998 the genre fell into oblivion. It was not until 2016 that *My War* was made to bring the past war to life for audiences in the new millennium.

Friend or Foe: Filming China's Relations with the Korean Peninsula

Unlike previous Korean War films that were produced exclusively by mainland Chinese crews, *My War* was directed by Oxide Chun Pang from Hong Kong. Pang had produced a number of successful commercial films, mostly thrillers and crime dramas, before accepting the invitation by China Film Group Corporation to direct *My War*. In an interview with an entertainment reporter, Pang surmised that he was chosen for the job primarily because of his experience of directing *Out of Inferno*, featuring daring Chinese firefighters rescuing desperate civilians who are trapped in a burning skyscraper (Cao, 2016). It was a "main melody" film but also successful at the box office. In other words, the production company expected Pang to make *My War* both politically correct and commercially appealing. But once Pang agreed to shoot the film, he was told that there were strings attached: The two enemies that China fought during the war—the United States and South Korea—were off limits from mentioning in the film, China Film Group Corporation insisted (Cao, 2016). The requirement was not entirely surprising, given the fact that approximately 60 years after the war ended, China had not only normalized relationships with these two former enemies but also become the important trading partner with both of them. It seems that China was ready to let go of the bitter past. But soon afterwards, China Film Group Corporation made a new decision to instruct the production team to include a few scenes of American soldiers and add narration to explain the history of the war. The decision came, as Pang recalled, as Sino-U.S. tensions in the South China Sea had intensified (Cao, 2016). The twisting and turning over whether to show old foes in the film illustrates that the remembrance of the war is deeply involved with contemporary politics and affected by current events. This reinforces the claim that collective memory has much to do with the present, selectively using the past to legitimize contemporary power, something Abel et al. illuminate in Chapter 10 in this volume. It affects not only how we recall past events but also how we deal with new ones.

As previously argued, the Chinese reference to the Korean War as the Resist America and Aid Korea movement crystalized the image of Washington as revolutionary China's archenemy in the official narrative and recent memories of the war. The same narrative and memory also condemned South Korea as a "running dog" (*zougou*), "gang of bandits" (*feibang*), and "puppets" (*kuilei*). In sharp contrast, there was a "special relationship" between China and North Korea (Ma, 2017). Both countries were victims of imperialist invasion in the modern era; the shared victimhood helped transcend racial differences and foster an alliance between two countries, "as close as lips and teeth," to fight for and gain independence through a revolution led by communist parties. Both countries were forced to fight in self-defense against Washington's imperialist ambition and interventionist policies during the Korean War, the argument goes, and in doing so they both contributed to the global communist revolution. However, the revolutionary notion of friend and foe, ally and enemy, has been turned upside down over the course of China's post-Mao reform and by the North Korean leaders' missile program and nuclear ambitions.

After China officially launched economic reforms in 1978, its relationship with North Korea remained stable and cordial throughout the 1980s. Constant and regular state visits reinforced official ties between the two governments and the two ruling political parties. Cultural exchanges also occurred. For example, in 1982, the Chinese state-run Changchun Film Studio imported and dubbed a 20-episode North Korean spy thriller, *Unsung Heroes*. Hundreds of thousands of Chinese watched it on television; many remembered a memorable moment or quote from it, and female viewers wished to own the tight leather coat worn by the lead actress Kim Jung-hwa (Teng, 2014). But beneath the friendly surface, gaps between the two countries' development strategies were widening and tensions mounting. The new generation of Chinese leaders moved to push Chinese domestic and foreign policy out of Mao's revolutionary ethos. Domestically, signature projects of high socialism, such as the People's

Commune, were dismantled. With regard to foreign relations, Deng Xiaoping made remarks in 1984 that "peace and development are the two overriding issues in the world today," which captured his effort to reorient the direction and priority of Chinese foreign policy from continuing the global communist revolution to "[draw] broadly and deeply on the inputs of the advanced capitalist countries: technology, science, managerial skills, machinery and equipment, capital, and export markets" (Garver, 2016, p. 349). North Korea, in comparison, adopted a different path: to double down on central planning and a command economy, to ratchet up hostility with Washington and its allies, and to actively prepare a transition of power from Kim Il-sung to his son Kim Jong-il.

The bilateral relationship worsened significantly in 1992 as a result of China's unilateral decision to normalize diplomatic relations with South Korea (Qian, 2006). From the early 1990s to the turn of the 21st century, China broke international sanctions imposed after the pro-democracy demonstrations of 1989, massively privatized state-owned assets, and finally joined the World Trade Organization in 2001 to integrate its economy with the global supply chain. During the same period, North Korea, under the helm of Kim Jong-il, was plunged into an existential crisis, as its export market disintegrated and financial aid was exhausted after the Soviet Union and the Eastern Bloc collapsed. In the post-Cold War period, Kim Jong-il grew more economically reliant on China. But, despite China's disapproval, he became increasingly aggressive in developing missile technologies and nuclear capability. After Kim Jong-un assumed power in 2011, he accelerated nuclear and missile testing. In 2016, the year when *My War* was released, North Korea conducted two nuclear tests and launched more than 15 missiles. The international community reacted swiftly by imposing sanctions against Pyongyang. China joined the international sanction regime by cutting off Pyongyang's coal exports, thereby choking off one of its few sources of hard currency.

While Beijing's relationship with Pyongyang soured as the nuclear crisis escalated, its relationship with Seoul had been growing exponentially since normalization. The centerpiece of the bilateral cooperation was trade. By one analysis, the two-way merchandise trade between China and South Korea grew from $90 billion in 2004 to $276 billion in 2015, and the trade in services rose from $10.6 billion to $35.8 billion in the same period. By the time the two countries signed the Free Trade Agreement in 2015, China stood as "the biggest trade partner, the largest export market, the biggest source of imports, and the largest overseas investment destination for Korea" (Li et al., 2016). In addition to trade, both Beijing and Seoul supported the denuclearization of the Korean Peninsula, and they supported the use of multilateral diplomacy, primarily through the "six-party talks," rather than military strikes to denuclearize the peninsula. But the lack of progress in diplomatic negotiations and Pyongyang's open defiance against international pressure began to put a strain on Seoul's relations with Beijing. In July 2016, the Park Geun-hye administration agreed to deploy the Washington-backed anti-missile Terminal High Altitude Area Defense system in response to Pyongyang's nuclear and missile tests. China objected to the deployment out of concerns that the system could be used to intercept Chinese missiles and surveil Chinese territory. Beijing voiced its objection and even threatened to impose economic sanctions on South Korean companies doing business in China but to no avail.

Therefore, the nuclear and missile crisis confronted China with a dilemma in its relations with the two Koreas: It opposed Pyongyang's nuclear ambitions but appeared unable to stop its belligerent actions; it shared with Seoul the long-term vision of keeping the peninsula nuclear-free but failed to work out a short-term solution to freeze the North's weapon program. More pressures on Pyongyang strained its relations with its old ally, whereas inaction or ineffective policies only alienated Seoul, its new partner.

Filmmakers of *My War* faced a similar challenge in how to portray North and South Koreans at a time when the historical definition of ally and enemy had been overturned by current events and geopolitics. The solution was to leave out Koreans in this film about the Korean War. In the beginning part of the film, Sun Beichuan is ordered to lead his company to block the retreating American troops. Just after they arrive at the predetermined ambush site, they encounter the vanguard of the armored U.S. troops as the battle is about to start. Just as the Chinese soldiers quickly enter their positions to prepare for battle, the figure of a North Korean guide suddenly appears. This shot takes less than a second, and it is the only appearance of a Korean in the whole film. Not having a main Korean character (hero or villain), the film also makes no reference to historical campaign slogans such as "Resist America and Aid Korea" and "Down with American imperialists." In their place, the film adopts terms such as "save peace" (*zhengjiu heping*) and "extinguish the flames of war" (*pumie zhanhuo*) that appear politically ambiguous and ideologically neutral. Again, an account of the past was shaped by the needs of the present.

It is important to note that references to North Korea mattered significantly in previous films, especially from the Maoist era. Scenes featuring North Korean People's Army officers and soldiers fighting side by side with their Chinese comrades convey a strong sense of communist camaraderie and internationalism. North Korean civilians, especially women, provide cover and care for wounded soldiers, which exemplified the civilian–military unity and the essence of Mao's people's war. However, filmmakers of *My War* erased nearly all traces of North Korea in the new rendition of the war. While removing China's old ally from screen, *My War* also kept fewer scenes for former foes. South Koreans are absent throughout the film; American GIs are shown in the film, but they garner neither a decent number of speaking lines nor close-up shots. When the movie shows a battle scene, the viewers mainly see the enemy's view from behind their leather boots, helmets, and weapons. There are very few scenes of fighting in close quarters between the enemy and Chinese troops.

It seemed that both the production team and China Film Group Corporation had agreed to move forward to leave out both former ally and enemy in remembering the past revolutionary war, as doing so allowed them to insulate the memory of the past from the geopolitics of the present. However, one incident occurred just a week before *My War* was released in theaters that instantly brought back present politics front and center in remembering the past.

A week before *My War* was released in theaters, a 2-minute promo was aired on Chinese TV and internet to generate buzz among potential moviegoers.[1] The promo gives an account of a group of elderly Chinese tourists who have come to Seoul for sightseeing. On the tour bus, a South Korean tour guide, a young and beautiful woman with a radiant smile, greets them for what she thinks is their first trip to the South Korean capital. After her welcome remarks, one tourist interrupts her and proclaims that members of this group had all come here approximately 60 years ago. This remark puzzles the Korean guide because she does not see any travel record on their passports. At this point, other Chinese tourists chime in and reveal that they are Chinese Korean War veterans who "once carried the red flag" and overtook Seoul during the war. The promo ends with these Chinese gray-haired veterans inviting the Korean tour guide and viewers to watch the new movie, *My War*, for a full account of history.

---

[1] See https://www.youtube.com/watch?v=01SPeYukUAE (accessed June 7, 2020).

The short video starred more than a dozen Chinese "red stars" who built their film careers and popularity among movie fans in the era of high socialism, from the 1950s to the 1970s. Many either participated in the war campaign or starred in Chinese Korean War films. One of them, Yu Lan (1921–2020), visited the North Korean war front during the war.[2] Another actor in the promo, Zhang Yongshou (1934–), fought in North Korea as a member of a cultural work unit and after the war portrayed a shrewd and courageous combat hero in a Korean War film masterpiece, *Raid*. In other words, these "red stars'" performances brought revolutionary combat to life for Chinese viewers who were far removed from the battlefield or the revolutionary era. Characters they played and films they made became building blocks of a pedagogical project to script and preserve memories of the revolution. It is also rather clear that producers of the short promo sought to invoke some revolutionary nostalgia and enlist "red stars" for box office success.[3] However, after the promo was broadcast, it backfired almost immediately, igniting a tide of unfavorable reviews and harsh criticisms on Chinese social media. The very incident exposed the government's failed attempt to shape public memory of war, further revealing the deep divide between the bygone notion of revolutionary patriotism and unofficial memory of the war.

Some critics found the promo "absolutely senseless." "Speaking of the 'Steel Knife Company' and 'hold the red flag and take over Seoul' was a naked display of force," one bluntly stated, "lacking in basic sympathy for the war trauma of the people of South Korea. . . . Their homeland was devastated by the war . . . [and they] . . . continued to suffer the painful division of the Korean nation" (S. Wang, 2016). Some bloggers directed their criticism at the war itself. "As more historical facts are revealed," reported the *South China Morning Post*, quoting a Chinese history professor's post on the Weibo microblog, "people are becoming increasingly aware of the cruelty of that war and its hurt to the nations and people involved" (Zhou, 2016). "Today, we can say for sure that, for every party involved in the conflict, the decision to cross the 38th Parallel was either a mistake in itself or a reaction to a mistake," wrote another commentator, "Eventually all mistakes added up together cost

---

[2] Yu's husband, Tian Fang (1911–1974), played the role of a political commissar in the Korean War film *Heroic Sons and Daughters*. His performance successfully portrays the touching image of a calm, amiable senior volunteer political leader and revolutionary father.

[3] The promotional materials claim that the film drew inspirations from a "red classic" novel *Reunion* (*Tuanyuan*) by Ba Jin (1904–2005), who penned the novel in 1961 based on his experience of visiting the battlefield twice during the war and living on the North Korean front for nearly a year (Huang, 2007).

millions of lives and proved that the war was a colossal mistake in world history" (Haojiangke, 2016b). Others called into question the value of the Sino-North Korean alliance, both in the past and at present, "retelling the history under the outdated framework of a political standpoint and value system" (S. Wang, 2016). One critic charged that the people who produced and promoted *My War* "are living in a fantasy created by themselves" (S. Wang, 2016). It is clear that the "red stars" in the promo and their critics used two vastly different sets of criteria to evaluate the political significance and historical meaning of the war. In the eyes of the former, the war was a revolutionary enterprise across national borders, involving tremendous sacrifice but resulting in a heroic victory. For the latter, the war was internecine strife between North and South Korea. It was also a proxy conflict in which smaller nations were turned into pawns to fight on the chessboard of the great powers. Such a view is rooted in a different understanding of China's relations with the two countries on the Korean Peninsula and China's role in the intra-Korean relationship, informed by current geopolitical events as opposed to the revolutionary ambitions of the Maoist era.

From Statist Nationalism to a Cosmopolitan Memory: A Counternarrative?

By the end of *My War*, Sun Beichuan has led his troops to attack the enemy-held 537 Highland. The battle is difficult, and Chinese soldiers suffer heavy casualties. Sun himself is also mortally wounded. In the final moments of his life, he looks forward to the upcoming victory and asks another soldier, "What do you say, will anyone remember what we did today?" His comrade replies in a definitive tone, "People will certainly remember!" The exchange between a dying war hero and his fellow soldier is designed to recognize the Chinese servicemen's sacrifice with the utmost respect. Words they utter could also transform a tragic loss into something of larger and more solemn purpose. But upon closely examining Sun's question, the target of memory, or "what we did today," appears a bit vague. Is he referring to this specific battle on the 537 Highland or the broader war mission? The answer also lacks clarity. Is the soldier referring to their glorious sacrifice in the combat, the future revolutionary movement, or merely the dread of death? To be clear, the words of revolutionary martyrs carry significant and symbolistic meanings in Chinese political culture and socialist cinema. They enshrine the dead and call the living to achieve the noble cause that the dead have died for. However, in *My War* at the moment when clarity is needed, its producers present ambivalence and ambiguity.

Such ambivalence and ambiguity, this chapter argues, are a result of the official narrative in transition, from defining China's war mission in terms of communist internationalism to regarding it as a symbolic achievement of statist nationalism. However, *My War* shows that such a narrative transition is incomplete and even contentious. The new narrative appears vague, probably as the state intended, in order to "absorb various interpretive diversions" such as those discussed by Nutsa Batiashvili in Chapter 16 in this volume. However, there is a "mnemonic standoff" that draws the line between official accounts of history propagated by the political elites and the informal, unsanctioned versions of the past that circulate beyond the state rhetoric (see Chapter 16, this volume). As the statist narrative attempts to shrink and homogenize the disparate memories under one all-encompassing statist framework, criticisms of *My War* present a cosmopolitan outlook and individual differences.

Before *My War*, previous socialist filmmakers and cultural officials attempted to capitalize on the scenes of Chinese soldiers' heroic deaths and their last words to rally viewers' support for revolutionary causes. One notable example is in the Korean War masterpiece, *Heroic Sons and Daughters*. The film opens to a ferocious battle; a young and exuberant soldier, Wang Cheng, and his unit are ordered to defend a position against American assault. Wang sees his comrades fight bravely but fall one after another, and finally he finds himself surrounded by enemies. As enemies close in on him, Wang calls the division headquarters to aim the artillery shelling at him—"fire at me" (*xiangwo kaipao*). In the end, Wang exclaims, "My beloved superior officers, comrades, Commissar Wang: Victory always belongs to us!" before blowing himself up with a Bangalore torpedo amid dozens of frightened American soldiers. The film makes it clear that Wang's words "fire at me" and his action represent a glorious act of self-sacrifice for a splendid victory.

Furthermore, to ensure viewers understand the full meaning of victory for which Wang sacrifices his life, the film shows an oath-taking ceremony scene in which the leader of a platoon named after Wang declares,

> All the soldiers of our Wang Cheng Platoon swear to our people in our homeland, to the brave Korean people, to the head officers, and to the father

of our hero. We will always follow the spirit of Comrade Wang Cheng, carry forward the glory of Comrade Wang Cheng, ardently love our country and the Korean people, fight heroically, work tirelessly, kill the enemy and defeat the American invaders. The flag of our hero always flutters.

To drive home the message of devoting oneself to the cause of the revolution, Commissar Wang Dong encourages the soldiers:

> Comrades, we must uphold the revolutionary spirit of Comrade Wang Cheng, fight side by side with the heroic Korean People's Army, resolutely eliminate American invaders, in return for the loving care that our fellow countrymen and the Korean people have shown for us.

In addition, the film's theme song contains a poem recitation:

> Our Wang Cheng is a soldier of Mao Zedong, an indomitable hero, and a person made of special material. What helped him grow his heroic spirit? It was his infinite love for the Korean people and his teeth-gnashing hatred for the aggressors. There are tens of thousands of soldiers like Wang Cheng in the Chinese People's Volunteer Army. They are the pride and glory of our great homeland.

Remarks made by key characters are deployed at key moments of the film to reinforce the central political message that had framed the official definition and memory of the Korean War—that the war was an ultimate showdown between two opposing blocs as the rising communists were fighting to defeat the demoralized capitalists. That victory did not belong to one person, one army unit, or one country for the time being; rather, it belonged to the entire international socialist camp as an invaluable contribution by the nascent People's Republic of China to the world revolution. That blood shed by Chinese martyrs would launch China onto the world stage to lead the world revolution in the foreseeable future. This way, the war was defined in both internationalist and futurist terms; the internationalist and futurist meanings reiterated throughout the film preclude ideological ambivalence and political ambiguity.

In contrast, the two oath-taking ceremonies featured in *My War* are tight-lipped on the internationalist significance of the war while moving decisively to define it in absolute domestic terms of national salvation and rejuvenation.

The film shows, right before Chinese troops depart to the battlefield, company commander Sun Beichuan vowing on behalf of his soldiers: "Every time we fight, some of our brothers will never come back. They are our role models, glorious role models, motivating us to charge forward. We come for victory, to fight for the motherland." He seems to concentrate on the "motherland" and suggest that the "motherland" is a product of the "victory." But he neither explains what will enable and prepare soldiers to win the victory nor identifies some of the essential political attributes and ideological characteristics of the motherland. Without explaining the linkage between "victory" and "motherland," the film fails to give the war mission and soldiers' sacrifice a larger purpose.

After Sun Beichuan takes the oath, another senior officer steps forward to make a speech to boost soldiers' morale:

> We are a glorious force. Our predecessors came out of the Jinggang Mountains and experienced countless hardships. Their fresh blood was shed on the Xiangjiang River, the Dadu River, the Yellow River, and the Yangtze River; again and again they were victorious. Today we will tread on their bloodstains and advance. New hardships and new victories beckon from ahead. Defeat and retreat do not belong to us.

It is important to note that the remarks invoke several epic events: It was in the Jinggang Mountains that Mao built the communist Red Army and developed the first communist rural base in the late 1920s; at the battle of the Xiangjiang River in 1934, the Red Army fought its way through a series of Nationalist blockades and embarked on the Long March; in 1935, the Red Army crossed the Dadu River to capture a Nationalist stronghold and secure a safe pathway to escape Nationalist encirclement; in 1937, the Red Army crossed the Yellow River to join the Anti-Japanese War; and, finally, in 1949, the communist troops crossed the Yangtze River to overtake the Nationalist capital Nanjing and win the civil war.

By invoking sacred battlefields, the film seeks to find a rightful place for the Korean War in the founding myth of the Communist Party and the Red Army. In this myth, the Red Army grew from bands of partisan fighters struggling to survive in inhospitable terrains and economic backwaters to a modern armed force standing toe to toe with the world's most powerful military. Chinese soldiers' sacrifice and victory turned the Korean War into an apex of the communist revolution and a chapter of glory and greatness.

Through the mouth of the senior officer, the film is also trying to finally clarify the relationship between victory and motherland left unanswered by Sun Beichuan. By placing the army at the center, the film lets the army own the victory as the custodian of the security of the motherland and the well-being of its people. It is not surprising to see that *My War* adopted such strong terms of nationalism under the statist framework to define the meaning of the war and soldiers' sacrifices. Researchers have pointed out that contemporary nationalism is rooted in two overriding concerns—national independence and territorial sovereignty—and the statist framework celebrates the Chinese Communist Party as the ultimate guardian of Chinese national salvation and rejuvenation (Cabestan, 2005; Z. Wang, 2012; Zhu, 2001). Under such state-centered nationalism, the nationalist enterprise becomes synonymous with the success of the Party and its revolutionary mission.

However, the statist nationalism failed to strike a chord with many viewers. One critic commented (Haojiangke, 2016a),

> Military and war films are normally filled with patriotic, nationalist, and heroic sentiments. [These sentiments] provide recurrent themes and almost guarantee box-office success. Nonetheless, today's world calls us to oppose to war, critically rethink [past] wars, stop potential wars in the future, learn lessons from [past] wars, understand the cruelty of war, all of which are far more meaningful than mere acts of glorifying heroes or commemorating victories.

The critic was calling for a more nuanced view of the war, not only celebrating what China gained politically and militarily but also remembering the enormity of loss sustained by all parties involved in the conflict. That neither gains nor losses can be measured solely in grand political terms at the state level. Individuals bore the brunt of killing and devastation of the war; what they had lived through and suffered should not be ignored or sidelined.

If the previously cited critic was calling out what was missing in the statist narrative, other critics went further by directly challenging the existing framework of statist nationalism as they saw it manipulating the memory of the war. Lunanyibing commented: "What *My War* really shows is a type of national ideology, one without reflection on war, without consideration for human nature, without historical clarity, without vigilance for the future" (Henochowicz, 2016). Another critic remarked (Dingdong, 2016),

> [The film] continues to romanticize the war and its participants. It attempts to find a powerful and effective way to declare that China's decision to enter the war was just, to sow divisions among people who share different political beliefs and antagonize countries that have different political systems, to idealize the notion that citizens should make sacrifice for the sake of national interest, to paint a rosy picture of the war, and to let viewers "indulge" in a fantasy [as they watch] a hail of bullets raining down [on screen].

These two remarks contradict nearly every piece of the statist narrative. According to the critics, the war was first and foremost a brutal conflict, a carnage. If the statist narrative seeks to either ignore the life lost or grace the death and destruction with fine words, both critics draw people's attention back to the hellish reality of the war and give voice to the bitter memory of suffering. The sheer horror of the war and the enduring pain are personal as well as universal, transcending racial differences and political antagonism. To be clear, wartime propaganda promoted a shared victimhood between China and North Korea in order to unite two countries to fight for a common communist internationalist purpose. Approximately 60 years later, both critics were proposing a new sense of shared victimhood that encompassed Chinese, South Koreans, and even Americans in an attempt to collectively heal the historical wound and to achieve some degree of political reconciliation in the age of globalization. By rejecting statist nationalism, the critics embraced a more cosmopolitan memory of the Korean War.

Conclusion

After 2 years and 9 months, more than 1.5 million Chinese troops had fought and approximately 180,000 soldiers had made the ultimate sacrifice on the Korean battlefields.[4] During and in the long aftermath of the

---

[4] For decades, the Chinese government regarded the Chinese casualties figure a top military secret and refused to release it to the public for fear of damaging the morale of the army and civilian population. However, the restriction has been lifted in recent years. The *History of the Resist America, Aid Korea War*, compiled by the Chinese Academy of Military Science, estimates that more than 360,000 Chinese soldiers were killed and wounded in the war (Junshi kexueyuan junshi lishi yanjiubu, 2000). Moreover, the Memorial of the War to Resist America and Aid Korea, working in collaboration with the Ministry of Civil Affairs, estimates that China suffered 183,108 combat casualties in the war (H. Chen & Yan, 2010).

war, the communist state crafted a grand statement, or statist framework, to commemorate the death and sacrifice and to call the people to continue the unfinished revolution that these martyrs had nobly advanced. Ultimately, official historians would write the Korean War campaign into the founding myth of the communist nation as one of the "three major movements in the formative years of the nation," along with the Land Reform Movement and the Campaign to Suppress Counter-Revolutionaries. Grand terms such as "heroism," "patriotism," and "internationalism" took over headlines and front pages of official media and took a firm grip on the public memory of the war in the socialist era, from the 1950s to the 1980s.

Sixty years after the outbreak of the war, in 2010 then-Vice President Xi Jinping gave a keynote speech on the anniversary of China's entry into the Korean War:

> The great Korean War demonstrated the new China's national prestige and the military might of the people's army. It showed that a weak army can defeat a strong enemy. Our victory in the Korean War was achieved despite great disparity in strength.... The great Korean War made a great contribution to world peace and to human progress. Our victory in the Korean War protected the Democratic People's Republic of Korea and the infant People's Republic of China. It deeply influenced and changed the political structure of Asia and the world after WWII. This victory was a convincing demonstration that China was a nation with no fear of violence, one that had the determination and strength to maintain world peace. This victory greatly improved our country's status in the world, inspired the oppressed nations to strive for independence and liberation, and advanced world peace and human progress.

Xi's remarks struck patriotic, heroic, and anti-American chords of memory with a friendly audience—gray-haired veterans and their family members—at a carefully staged state ceremony. It is rather clear that 60 years after the war ended, Chinese top leaders continued the effort that attempted to seal the memory of the war in its original statist framework. *My War* is a smaller part of the same commemorative work, but it faces an audience that is more diverse, critical, and cosmopolitan.

Critics of *My War* live in a new geopolitical moment, when China dwells on a new grand strategy, no longer attempting to overthrow the U.S.-led global governance but embracing the international capitalist market. Former enemies have become "strategic partners"; the cooperative relationships between Beijing, Washington, and Seoul power global economic growth and safeguard regional security. In contrast, old ally North Korea has descended into one of the most isolated states, a hermit kingdom. A Chinese president has not set foot on North Korean territory from 2005 to 2019, whereas in 2016 alone, President Hu Jintao met several times in person or over the phone with his American and South Korean counterparts, President Barack Obama and President Park Geun-hye, respectively. As the revolutionary alliance between China and North Korea falls apart, and as the internationalist meaning of the Korean War loses its interpretive vitality, the Chinese government has decided to rewrite history by remembering the war while forgetting its wartime ally. However, critics of *My War* do not shy away from geopolitics; rather, they are keenly aware of China's evolving foreign policy and the shifting alignment of stakeholders in the regional security system. Such a global and multilateral framework enables critics to contemplate the legacies of the Korean War beyond Chinese nationalist and statist terms.

In addition to the new geopolitical moment, critics of *My War* are operating in "a new integrated pan-Asian cultural space" where "Hong Kong gangster films, Japanese anime, Korean television dramas, and Chinese martial arts films freely cross cultural, linguistic, and national boundaries," as Michael Berry (2016, p. 1) notes. This pan-Asian cultural marketplace does not erase the bitter national memory of those bloody conflicts that have torn apart East Asia and ravaged each and every East Asian nation in modern times, nor does it heal all historical wounds for all parties involved in those conflicts. However, the pan-Asian cultural marketplace helps grow some degree of cross-cultural awareness and further undermines the Chinese government's hegemonic grip on the memory of China's Korean War campaign.

Movies Cited

Battle of Shanggan Ridge (*Shangganling*), dir. Lin Shan, Sha Meng, 1956.
Cutting the Devil's Talons (*Zhanduan mozhao*), dir. Shen Fu, 1953.
Heroic Sons and Daughters (*Yingxiong ernu*), dir. Wu Zhaodi, 1964.
My War (*Wo de zhanzheng*), dir. Oxide Pang Chun, 2016.
On the 38th Parallel (*Sanba xianshang*), dir. Shi Wenzhi, 1960.
Out of Inferno (*Taochu shengtian*), dir. Xside Chun Pang, 2013.
Raid (*Qixi*), dir. Xu Youxin, 1962.

Raid on White Tiger Regiment (*Qixi baihutuan*), 1972
Shining Star on the Battlefield (*Zhandi zhixing*), dir. Wei Long, 1983.
Unsung Heroes, dir. Ryu Ho-son and Ko Hak-lim, 1978.

References

Berry, M. (2016). Introduction: Divided lenses. In M. Berry & C. Sawada (Eds.), *Divided lenses: Screen memories of war in East Asia* (pp. 1–18). University of Hawaii Press.

Brown, K. (2018). "Chinese Nationalism: The Dog That Barks in the Night," The Diplomat, November 16. Available at https://thediplomat.com/2018/11/chinese-nationalism-the-dog-that-barks-in-the-night/, accessed on June 1, 2020.

Cabestan, J.-P. (2005). The many facets of Chinese nationalism. *China Perspectives*, 59, 1–21.

Cao, L. (2016). "Zhuanfang Wode zhanzheng daoyan Peng Shun, bei aiguo zhuyi bangjia le?" [Interview with Chun Pang, director of My War and hostage of patriotism?]. Available at https://ent.qq.com/a/20160913/027389.htm, accessed on May 27, 2020.

Chang, B. (2018). *Xiaoyan Zhong de xianhua: Kangmei yuanchao wenxue xushi ji shiliao zhengli* [*Flowers amid gun-smoke*]. Renmin chubanshe.

Chen, H., & Yan, H. (2010, October 26). 183108: Kangmei Yuanchao Jinianguan gongbu zhiyuanjun xisheng renshu [The Resist America and Aid Korea Memorial releases the casualty figures of the Chinese Volunteer Army]. *Xinhua News*. Retrieved April 12, 2017, from http://news.xinhuanet.com/mil/2010-10/26/c_12704264.htm

Chen, J. (1994). *China's road to the Korean War: The making of the Sino-American confrontation*. Columbia University Press.

Dingdong. (2016, September 16). *Wode zhanzheng guangshou feiyi de yinmi yuanyin* [*Why does* My War *stir up a widespread controversy?*]. Retrieved August 27, 2020, from http://dingdong550.blog.sohu.com/322821618.html

Garver, J. (2016). *China's quest: The history of the foreign relations of the People's Republic of China*. Oxford University Press.

Haojiangke. (2016a, September 8). *Jintian zenme jianghao "dangnian juzhe hongqi jin Hancheng" de gushi* [*Carried the red flag to take over Seoul: How do we retell the history*]. Retrieved October 27, 2016, from http://www.ifuun.com/a2016927389882

Haojiangke. (2016b, September 14). *Dangnian juzhe hongqi jin hancheng, shi bukan huishou de canlie* [*Carried the red flag to take over Seoul: The unbearable memory of heartbreaking sacrifice*]. Retrieved August 8, 2020, from https://freewechat.com/a/MzA5MDQwMTgwNA==/2653568599/1

Henochowicz, A. (2016, September 14). Ad for Korean War film offends netizens. *China Digital Times*. Retrieved April 12, 2017, from https://chinadigitaltimes.net/2016/09/ad-korean-war-film-offends-netizens

Huang, Y. (2007). *1951–1953 Zhongguo de wenren yu Zhongguo de junren* [*Chinese writers and Chinese servicemen*]. Lingnan meishu chubanshe.

Junshi kexueyuan junshi lishi yanjiubu. (2000). *Kangmei yuanchao zhanzhengshi* [*History of the Resist America and Aid Korea War*]. Junshi kexue chubanshe.

Li, S., Tu, X., & Liu, B. (2016). Part III: South Korea's economic relations with Northeast Asia—Progress and implications of the China–Korea FTA. *Korea's Economy*, 31. Retrieved August, 11, 2020, from http://keia.org/sites/default/files/publications/koreaseconomy_ch3_progress_implications_of_the_china-korea_fta.pdf

Liu, M. Y. (2019). *Literati lenses: Wenren landscape in Chinese cinema of the Mao era.* University of Hawaii Press.

Lu, X. (2017). The might of the people: Counter-espionage films and participatory surveillance in the early PRC. In K. Fang (Ed.), *Surveillance in Asian cinema: Under Eastern eyes* (pp. 13–32). Routledge

Ma, Z. (2017). War remembered, revolution forgotten: Recasting the Sino-North Korean alliance in China's post-socialist media state. *Cross-Currents: East Asian History and Culture Review, 22,* 54–82.

Niaojia. (2020). *Neidi piaofang niandu zongpaihang: 2016 nian dianying [Box-office rankings, 2016: Domestically produced films)*] (last updated February 12, 2020).

Pickowicz, P. (2010). Revisiting Cold War propaganda: Close readings of Chinese and American film representations of the Korean War. *Journal of American-East Asian Relations, 17*(4), 352–371.

Qian, Q. (2006). *Ten episodes in China's diplomacy.* HarperCollins.

Teng, W. (2014). Cong Wuming yingxiong dao Yingxiong wuming: Zhongguo dalu dui Chaoxian dianzhan dianying de fanyi yu chongxie [Unsung heroes: Translation and rewriting a North Korean sky film in China]. In W. Xiaoming (Ed.), *Dianshiju yu dangdai wenhua [Television drama and contemporary culture]* (pp. 136–140). Sanlian shudian.

Wang, S. (2016). *Buyao yi aiguo de mingyi wu dixian: Ping dianying Wode zhanzheng xuanchuanpian [The shameless demonstration of patriotism: Comments on the promo of* My War]. Retrieved May 27, 2020, from https://cul.qq.com/a/20160911/014245.htm

Wang, Z. (2012). *Never forget national humiliation: Historical memory in Chinese politics and foreign relations.* Columbia University Press.

Xi, J. (2010, October 25). *Xi Jinping's speech at the 60th Anniversary Symposium of the Korean War.* ChinaScope. Retrieved August 20, 2020, from http://chinascope.org/archives/6344

Yang, X. (2016). *Zhuanjia: dianying Wo de zhanzheng zai Zhongguo zhanzhengpian shi shang feichang shaojian [Film experts' opinion:* My War *is a rare war film].* Retrieved December 22, 2020, from https://www.chinaxwcb.com/info/31665

Zhou, L. (2016, September 14). Controversial Chinese teaser for film on Korean War revives debate on China's role in the deadly conflict. *South China Morning Post.*

Zhu, T. (2001). Nationalism and Chinese foreign policy. *China Review, 1*(1), 1–27.

16
Using a Golden Age
National Memory of Georgia's Favorite King

Nutsa Batiashvili

Introduction

What is national memory? The term implies some form of consensus, a representation of a past that is broadly shared throughout a national community. Yet, scholarship on memory politics and collective remembering has demonstrated that nations constantly struggle with conflicting interpretations of past events, and these often underlie culture wars and social dissent. Empirically grounded approaches to understanding the collective memory of a national community stress the importance of narrative tools as the medium of remembering. Widely shared narrative templates (see Chapter 22, this volume) absorb various interpretive diversions and can spread so easily because they can be adopted to fit quite distinct historical circumstances. As such, they are capable of generating various layers of meaning and transmitting them through simple, myth-like codes. Such an approach to forms of remembering assumes that narratives can become embodied. They can function as implicit cognitive habits that underlie not only a society's political reasoning but also the kind of affective engagement with the political that Lauren Berlant (1991) calls "national fantasies."

In my treatment of national memory, I concentrate on the usage of memory symbolism by radically opposed "counterpublics" (Warner, 2002). I approach national memory as an affectively charged symbolic idiom of political expression whereby the same symbols can be used to articulate two very different conceptions of nation and peoplehood. As multivocal structures of meaning, I argue that national memory can anchor both, what Michael Billig (1995) calls "banal nationalism" and a radical, xenophobic ethnonationalist agenda.

In this view, memory can serve both as a unifying and as a splintering agent. Populist nationalists deliver this dual affect through the hyperbolization of memory narratives: The affective impulse behind their line of reasoning creates a sense of commonality because the frames, symbols, and language they use are so intimate, familiar, and easy to process. In Georgia, for instance, they designate Middle Eastern migrants as "genetic enemies" to insinuate upon the collective memory narrative that frames Georgia's past as an unending sequence of invasions, predominantly by Muslim invaders. At the core of this invocation is not a logic that equates a migrant with a medieval Shah but, rather, the affective response that this equation can trigger. The very splintering implication can run counter to the idea of a nation and an understanding of peoplehood upon which both national and democratic sovereignty are founded. It does so first and foremost by positing an opposition between the "elite" and the "people" as a fundamental dividing line that obstructs the notion of horizontal unity upon which the ideas of nationalist and democratic sovereignty are founded.

The "bivocal" narrative of Georgian collective memory that I explore in this chapter provides an example for understanding how this occurs through a process whereby multiple voices (in this case two) are entrenched in a single symbolic form. The notion of bivocality places emphasis on "voicing" as an act of semiosis that engenders varieties of discursive registers. The dialogic interplay between distinct voices that takes place in the discursive standoffs between nationalist populists and their counterpublics can provide insight into the nature of cultural semantics that both unites and divides national publics. In my examination of opposing uses of national memory narratives and symbols, radical nationalists are shown to appeal to a common memory of Georgia's Golden Age. Using narratives for affectively persuasive communication (see Chapter 9, volume), their efforts are geared toward combatting political opponents that paradoxically rely on the exact same memory symbols for their articulation.

My argument has two parts. First, I make a point about the protean nature of memory symbols that makes it possible for the same narratives and historical figures to be harnessed for contradictory national stances. But I argue that there is a limit to how far the meaning of any symbol can be stretched. Second, I outline particular implications that the use of memory in the political domain has for the definitions of "the people" and thus for the enactments of national sovereignty.

In my treatment of national memory as a core cultural mechanism that shapes political discourse, I take my cue from Ernst Cassirer. In *The Myth of the State* (1946), he argued that conceptions of the political order and especially that of a nation-state are founded on the tropes and metaphors that are inherently produced not through discursive or rational reason but, rather, through mythic abstraction. Politics in Cassirer's view is fundamentally a work of symbolic forms, and these in essence are affective, emotion-driven constructions that rely on religious thought rather than on discursive logic.

"National identity," writes Liah Greenfeld (1993), "in its distinctive modern sense ... is an identity which derives from membership in a 'people' " (p. 7). As it underwent multiple transformations in its meaning, *nation* came to mean "*a unique* sovereign people" (Greenfeld, 1993, p. 8). Along with many others, Greenfeld argues that as a superior entity, the nation is perceived as fundamentally homogeneous, where lines dividing various classes, social strata, or subcultural entities are overlooked as superficial. This is an important starting point for her argument because "the location of sovereignty within the people and the recognition of the fundamental equality among its various strata" (p. 10) are not only at the core of the national idea but also the very foundations of democratic order.

Taking Greenfeld's argument further, my point is that both the *uniqueness* of the sovereign people and the boundaries that constitute *the people* or its constitutive other are largely defined through a medium such as national memory. This does not mean that national memory dictates some sort of ethnic particularism or parochialist approach to identity but, rather, that national memory harnesses the symbolic arsenal through which contests over peoplehood, forms of sovereignty, and qualities of uniqueness can take place. Edmund Leach's (1954) point that "myth ... is a language of argument, not a chorus of harmony" (p. 278) is a reminder that national memory involves what Mikhail Bakhtin (1983) would call a heteroglossic vocabulary of terms and grammars, rather than prescribing a univocal model of identity, through which contestation over forms of governance and notions of peoplehood can be conducted within one "mnemonic community" (Zerubavel, 2003).

The case I examine here speaks to this malleable nature of mythical symbols and explores national memory as a cultural repertoire that can be harnessed for contradictory national stances. In her analysis of contradictory evocations of the Medea mythology in post-Soviet Georgian politics, for example, Tamta Khalvashi (2018) makes a point about the potential of mythical symbols to "generate contradictory imaginaries" (p. 6). She envisions mythical symbols as "imaginative horizons" (Crapanzano, 2004) and stresses that these horizons not only function as conceptual schemas for understanding the present but also "contain potential to produce unintended consequences" and "evoke dimensions of experience that lie beyond their immediate meanings" (p. 5).

To be sure, the idea that symbols of the sort envisioned by Cassirer—depending on the context and the intention of their users—have the capacity to continuously generate and mediate new layers of meaning has a long tradition in scholarly literature in disciplines beyond anthropology. Bakhtin's (1983) understanding of the utterance provides perhaps one of the most pronounced and elaborated philosophies of the sign's polysemic potential. The notion of voice that I emphasize suggests that the use of symbols, much like the utterance for Bakhtin, "is an activity that enacts differences in value" (Wertsch, 1991, p. 51) and that meaning is almost always a product of the tension between distinct points of views and disparate intentionalities that are themselves entrenched in symbolic forms.

This does not entail, however, that symbols have a limitless range of signification. They are effective communicative instruments because of their capacity to actualize particular values, to execute a particular logic and enable forms of cultural intersubjectivity that would be impossible without some restraint that the internal grammatical or syntactical structure of symbols implicitly enacts. A similar point has been argued in anthropological literature. Specifically, Arjun Appadurai's (1981) objection to the idea that "charters have no inherent limits, except those of expediency" (p. 201) emerged in response to widespread assumptions about a relativist conception of cultural thought. Appadurai not only suggested that there are culture-specific frameworks and norms that govern "debatability" of symbolic meanings but also questioned whether these norms operate on the basis of universal constraints. The literature on narrative studies will perhaps provide a set of arguments that symbolic forms are partially restrained by their inherent, universally operable logic of functioning. This could to some extent be shaped by the wiring of our neural structures as well as universals of social experience.

Building on these traditions, I offer an understanding of national memory as a reservoir of conceptual tools that have their own semantic affordances. As fundamentally heteroglossic instruments, they can be effectively used to communicate across various publics and produce an illusory consensus upon which the politics of affective persuasion can be constructed. The symbolic forms I envision involve a tension between two tendencies (centripetal and centrifugal) and the two poles of meaning—one pushing it toward a stable core center of meaning and the other pulling it apart in different directions. Meaning is expressed at the level of social practices that enact this tension in politically evocative ways. The scope of heteroglossia and the presence of various voices in any text or symbolic form is itself a product of complex sociohistorical processes, and these act both as enabling and as restraining mechanisms for how symbolic forms function. In the section titled "Apparitions of David," I trace lineages of semiosis that lend various layers of meaning to the national memory of Georgia's Golden Age king.

As an artifact of the historical discourses from different epochs, contemporary evocations of King David (1073–1125) enunciate distinct voices that creatively re-accentuate the core values through his image. Memory symbols afford various agencies, various iterations of possible pasts and possible futures, and various genealogies of affect, and they can support these even when the mythologies produced within and through them are semantically well organized and discursively sealed. David the Builder is a fascinating example in that sense. As a symbolic medium, he is an inalienable possession of every Georgian. There is virtually no argument over the assessment of his character or his politics and a nationwide consensus on the significance of his political, military, and cultural reforms. Most Georgians even agree on the order of the list of his accomplishments and yet along with this centripetal tendency, his figure, his epoch, and his politics serve as the foundation for centrifugal forces in Georgian society. They are a testament to the political stances of starkly opposing publics and virtually irreconcilable versions of peoplehood, citizenship, and statehood.

The Sovereign, the People, and Polarized Nationhood

LIKA: Do you have a favorite Georgian king?

IOSEB: David the Builder.

LIKA: What would you say about David the Builder's politics? Say for instance his tax policy, that he had reduced taxes for migrants, for the settlement of Kipchaks...

IOSEB: Most certainly this was very good, stimulating... motivation. This was the 12th century, do not forget that.

LIKA: In the 12th century we had one of the most progressive kings...

IOSEB: Yes the most liberal thinker. But he was a dictator. Yes David was great, how can I assess him, I don't know.... This was the greatest victory of our history. We haven't had a victory like this. What can I say he was a great man and I love him greatly.

LIKA: In your view, if in those times it was essential for Georgia to have people of different nationalities, say for the sake of the economic development...?

IOSEB: There was the sword then.

LIKA: There was the sword then and now there is trade. Without trade or integration we will not survive, if we Georgians are the only ones remaining [in this country], we will simply not survive.

—Interview by Lika Khazaradze with Ioseb, a Georgian March[1] member, Cafe "Tea House," Tbilisi (November 1, 2018)

With the global surge of nationalist populism, Georgia has experienced dissent among Georgian youth that has strained the country. It is described by some as part of culture wars waged between progressive and regressive visions involving a split between democratic and nationalist, liberal and conservative, of modern and traditional views. In this context, two movements have come to dominate public politics: a predominantly far-right organization Georgian March (*qartuli marshi*) and a much more ideologically diverse network of chiefly liberal youth, the Society for Spreading Freedom (*tavisuflebis gamavrcelebeli sazogadoeba*, mostly referred to as *tavgasebi*, the plural form of the abbreviation). Primarily mobilized as counterprotests to one another, these two networks have voiced concerns over Georgian politics in distinctly nationalist sentiments, but although the symbols they employed had a single source in a common national memory, their rhetoric rested on very different understandings of peoplehood and political order.

The excerpt from a conversation between a liberal-thinking student Lika and Ioseb, a member of the Georgian March, is perhaps one of the more benign instantiations of the competing visions of these groups. The mention of David the Builder comes as no surprise in the conversation. Georgian March is a movement of marching men who carry banners with the king's images through the streets of Tbilisi, whereas for Lika, David IV is an icon of Georgian national memory who signifies a variant of a political order in which ethnic plurality is in no way an impediment to strong statehood. Her

---

[1] Georgian March is a radical nationalist movement described in more detail below.

reference to Kipchaks[2] has to do with one of David IV's prominent reforms aimed at building a regular, professional army by bringing in and settling Turkic nomadic people from the Eurasian steppes (Rayfield, 2012). This is one of the reasons that in contemporary parlance King David is described as a "liberal" king.

Ioseb agrees with this, but for him Georgia of the Middle Ages could be safeguarded by the use of "a sword" to fight intruders or "genetic enemies" as Georgian March leaders refer to migrants from the Middle East. His assertive remark "There was the sword then," cutting Lika's question short, points to a modern geopolitical predicament in which real political process is concealed from the view of the ordinary people. In his view, the enemy and their intentions are always veiled and camouflaged, which is an inherent part of a populist creed that conjures up covert schemes of conspiracy between global(ist) forces and local elites. Ioseb's comment "There was the sword then" insinuates that the medieval world of open wars and conquests was the world of politics in plain sight. The sword was an overt and a fair weapon of warfare, as opposed to camouflaged information tricks that global elites use to brainwash ordinary people.

Much like other populist movements in Europe, Georgian March has a radical nationalist and anti-elitist ideology and is primarily concerned with illegal immigration and protecting the boundaries of the nation as a cultural and ethnographic, rather than a political, entity. Although the appeal of Georgian March is to the idea of popular sovereignty and resembles global trends of populist movements, the rhetorical tactics of its leaders rely on a very specific culturally grounded idiom of political expression. At the heart of their propaganda is language that is marked by constant references to the nation's memory narratives, a language that voices concerns over issues such as "genetic enemies," Georgian family values, "Georgian 'gen-fund" (genetic purity), and Orthodoxy and authentic "Georgianness." It also instills panic based on conspiracy theories about secret alliances of political, media, and corporate elites with global forces. Directed against immigration, drug

---

[2] Kipchaks (also Qipchaqs) Medieval confederation of Turkic nomadic tribes, mostly inhabiting Eurasian Steppes. As part of the King David's attempt to build a regular army, forty thousand Kipchak families were settled in Georgia. In exchange for supplying the King's army with a man and a horse from each family, they were given landholdings and pasture lands. According to historical sources (see Rayfield, 2012), at the time Kipchaks were famous mercenaries serving Hungarian and Egyptian leaders and had established ties with Russians. King David further strengthens his ties with Kipchaks by divorcing his Armenian wife Rusudan and marrying the daughter of the Kipchak chief Gurandukht.

liberalization, unrestricted sale of Georgian land to foreigners (particularly to persons of Arab and Iranian origin), and feminist and anti-homophobic movements, Georgian March perceives a global conspiracy to exterminate the Georgian "genetic fund" (*genop'ondi*), debase Georgian family values, and threaten Georgian land and sovereignty.

Contrary to Georgian March's traditionalist appeal, the Society for Spreading Freedom (SSF) is part of the emerging youth culture that is indissolubly linked to the projects of modernity; to Georgia's European Union–integrating agenda; and to the kind of culture of emancipation that came into being in the first decades of the 21st century through hybrid spaces such as nightclubs, vegan cafes, hubs of liberal intellectualism, and feminist movements. These fields of cultural production exist where Georgian forms of self-expression merge with "European" or "Western" ones. The "Rave Revolution," now a popular coinage, is used to describe some of the manifestations of these semi-politicized movements that at one point used the motto "We dance together, we fight together" in an effort to push back against state intervention in the domain of nightlife. The SSF mobilizes political sentiments primarily around the issue of Russian occupation and repeatedly stresses the threat of territorial conflicts with Russia. Members of SSF criticize the government for the inability to secure state borders, and they constantly raise the problem of occupied territories. Apart from this, SSF members position themselves as a movement for civil rights, gender equality, and religious and cultural pluralism and that represents a variant of Georgian modernity founded on democratic institutions, with European integration being one of its primary goals.

Whereas Georgian March sees a conspiracy between these modernist agendas and global forces to destroy pure Georgian culture and genetic material, SSF members are convinced that *marshelebi* (literally Marchians) are themselves Putin-funded ultra-nationalists executing Putin's full-fledged occupation plan. To an outsider, claims about Georgian nationalists' executing Putin's agenda may seem like an absurdly senseless contradiction. Yet, to Georgians it sounds like a banal possibility because the logic of this allegation is grounded in the same bivocal narrative that envisions the nation's past as a constant oscillation between heroism and treason. Treason is just as much entrenched in the representations of the national narrative as heroism and martyrdom. In common political parlance, "collaborationism" is an often-used term that refers to this historical pattern and an inclination of Georgians to strike deals with outside forces.

Radical nationalists make use of the same narrative logic for their own ends. Much like populist movements elsewhere, Georgian March harnesses the dichotomy of elites versus "the people" and views politics as a spectacle put on for ordinary people that camouflages the hidden agenda of conspiracies of the media, nongovernmental organizations, businessmen, and political parties. The elites represent globalist forces operating against the will of the people and line up with the corporate interests of transnational corporations and foreign states. Thus, Georgian March instrumentalizes national memory and devises a local variant of these oppositions to claim that Georgianness is under threat from outside enemies (Russia, the West, and the "genetic enemies," along with transnational corporations), but the outside forces are aided by internal traitors (e.g., liberals). Their claim that "we are the occupants of our own selves" conveys this logic.

Scholars of nationalism and populism have argued extensively that populist nationalism appeals on the basis of affect rather than rational deliberation or institutional order, and as such exerts pressure on the "liberal settlement" (Mazzarella, 2019, p. 55). It "exempts itself from any form of rational justification, since it primarily aims at mobilizing through emotional appeals focused on a dialectic of hope and fear" (Emden, 2018, p. 16). However, this does not mean that populist nationalism avoids justification of any kind; rather, it relies on reasoning modes that are rooted in culturally shared semantics with a distinct moral and affective logic.

The fact that the same semantic codes and symbolic structures can become vehicles for radically opposed interpretations of sovereignty, citizenship, political order, and peoplehood has to do with a broader problem that underlies the current crisis of "liberal settlement" and concerns the key concepts of democracy: "the people" and "the demos." Symbolic media, particularly national memory and mnemonic symbols, give cultural and moral grounding to the notions of peoplehood. The question of who we are or how we ought to be pertains to someone or something from distant history. Memory provides an instrumental idiom for what Chantal Mouffe (2013) calls "passionate negotiations" on who constitutes "the people."

Definitions of peoplehood, and consequently, forms of popular sovereignty, when placed in the context of the nation, become entangled in particular forms of moral judgments that are in their own turn not absolute, universal, or derived from pure reason. Instead, these moral judgments reflect culturally attuned forms of political imagination. National memory serves in this both as the source of passion and as the very "semiosphere"

(Lotman, 1990) through which "the people" and the constitutive "other" are articulated. This is used by populist nationalists in their appeal to the "authentic" and "ordinary people" and in their claims against "foreigners" and "globalist" forces.

The argument about the malleable nature of memory symbols set out at the beginning of this chapter addresses the power of populist nationalists' logic. In their effort to promote radical nationalist and an anti-Western populist agenda, they have mobilized symbols that have broad legitimacy and are widely shared both as interpretive tools of the political and as identity anchors. Instead of contesting broadly accepted narratives and interpretations of these historic symbols, radical nationalists have tended to accentuate or vocalize one particular aspect from the spectrum of meanings entrenched in the symbolism of national heroes to radicalize the notions of peoplehood.

Hence, populist nationalists tend not to invent new meanings for voicing their own version of mythical icons, but merely harness existing layers of meanings. This is possible because memory symbols are already invested with multiple grids of meaning and provide opportunities for various ways of re-accenting and re-voicing. They come with multiple accents and voices embedded in them in the first place. In the following discussion, I trace the voices and semantic morphology entrenched in the icon of King David IV ("David the Builder") in order to explicate the multivocality of the symbols and to demonstrate how a single icon can mediate starkly contested visions (Turner, 1967).

The Bivocal Narrative

The Golden Age narrative in Georgia has a paradigmatic quality as the single most important source of proud historical reference. This narrative emerged in the 19th century as Georgian intellectuals and founding fathers strove to come up with symbolic forms that would make nationhood conceivable. Their efforts were shaped by the complex reality of a religiously, ethnically, and culturally diverse landscape of the South Caucasus. In this context, the idea of Georgia as a political totality was formulated as a mnemonic abstraction. The elusive image of historical unity concocted by the 19th-century founders was one of persistent struggle for freedom and cultural integrity in the face of multiple invasions over centuries. Further patterned and crystalized by Soviet historiography, the Georgian national narrative, like many others, can be formulated in terms of several mutually interacting *motifs* as envisioned by the Russian Formalist Vladimir Propp (1968). The result is an account of Georgia that takes the following form:

> Aim: Unification of Georgian territories with the 12th-century Golden Age as an exemplary precedent
> Setting: Constant invasions because of Georgia's strategic location
> Action: Struggle for freedom and cultural preservation (language, faith, cultural uniqueness)
> Impediment: Internal weakness—traitors, collaborators, inability to unite
> Outcome: survival, preservation of culture and national integrity

These motifs not only describe the pattern of historical development but also convey the nature of the Georgian national narrative and produce conceptions of the political order. Above all, this representation of the past has the potential to produce particular images of the outside world and to generate countless versions of threats that can come from it.

As a pervasive source of "national fantasies" (Berlant, 1991), this account has the potential to invigorate political sentimentalities. In addition to the radical, xenophobic, or ethnocentric nationalist publics, the narrative also serves as an implicit schema for political reasoning among proponents of liberal democracy and modern civic nationalism. As a model of political conception, it can sustain the kind of fantasy of the future that one Georgian commentator referred to as "the romanticism of breakthrough" (Khvedeliani, 2019), a fantasy that mobilizes specific dreams and hopes in the realm of the political. But more important this narrative is a conceptual basis for conjuring up the sovereign agency on which a viable statehood can be built. It serves not merely as a story that represents happenings in the past but also as a symbolic form that supplies a logic for interpreting, enacting, and engaging with the political in the present.

My proposal that a plotline can yield an extractable logic of this sort in this case is an elaboration of ideas of Propp (1968) and one of the founders of Tartu schools of semiotics, Isaak Revzin (1975). Propp's principal postulate is that folk tales are made up of objectively identifiable constants, which are the "functions" of the dramatic personae. These are the basic components that "serve as stable, constant elements in a tale, independent of how and by whom they are fulfilled" (p. 21). Revzin elaborated on dramatic functions and suggested that two types of predicates (constructs) can be found in folk tales as well as epic texts: ones that express constant and inherent characteristics of actors and ones that reveal action or transformation. These elements explain not "referential semantics" but "inner semantics that serve to form links within the text"; hence, they show the ways in which text is made into a coherent whole (Revzin, 1975, p. 83).

Revzin's (1975) inner semantics is what provides a coherent core and a centripetal force of the symbolic forms, and this restrains what Bakhtin (1983) identified as the centrifugal proclivities of these forms. This is why memory symbols have the capacity to be used and reused in a wide range of contexts but still retain a constant "function" [in Propp's (1968) terms] that shapes the fundamental dialectic of relations between actors and actions.

Central to the logic of the Georgian narrative template is the function of the nature of Georgianness itself. National character is expressed through a dialectic between progressive and regressive forces, heroism and treason, unity and dissent. At any given moment, these tensions serve as a logic for conceiving the agentive capacity of the Georgian people. In particular, the interaction between these forces determines the outcome of any historical challenge, such as defeating a powerful enemy or uniting Georgian territories. I refer to this form of duality in terms of "bivocality" (Batiashvili, 2018), a form of the political discourse that makes possible simultaneous contradictory claims about Georgianness.

The Golden Age narrative provides a script for how impediments to victory can be overcome: a strong king, military force, cultural revival, annihilation of dissent, and extermination of traitors (hence, the agentive capacity). It affords the elements of a self-assured Georgian identity, from heroism to civilizational potential. But in the end, the Golden Age narrative and all the main motifs in the narrative of King David the Builder also enact the idea of Georgian bivocality. The inclination toward dissent and internal frictions in this ideal narrative appear once again as the main impediment to realizing Georgia's civilizational and political aspirations. King David is himself an embodiment of bivocality because he bears the traces of prescriptions for how these weaknesses should be overcome.

Apparitions of David

In various apparitions of King David, from 19th-century feuilletons to 21st-century political contests, we find undeniable indicators of the bivocal nature of the texts (whether written or spoken). *Davit Aghmashenebeli* (literally David the builder[3]) ruled Georgia from 1089 until 1125 and is considered as the principal architect of the Georgian Golden Age. King David reflects the potential to enact distinct conceptions of political order, and depending on the context of his evocation, he epitomizes different virtues of character and of kingship. As a symbol of national memory, the image of this king retains the logic by which relations of power and the potentialities of Georgian identity are expressed.

To use Revzin's (1975) terms, while the "referential semantics" of the king's image fluctuates in the context of various intentionalities, the "inner semantics" of this symbol is invariably present in most of its invocations. By replicating the general grammar of the national narrative, the inner semantics of this mythical configuration develops through the dialectic of Georgia's bivocal tendencies. King David appears in Georgian history not as some sort of Deus ex Machina, not as a contingency that inadvertently transforms the nature of relations, but as a logical and inevitable product of the Georgian essence. As such, he is part of the cosmological order that the national mythologies conjure up. This is why at various points of the political conjuncture he is posited as an example of Georgianness and not as an exception to it.

In his reflections on memory and forgetting in national development, Georgia's 19th-century founding father Ilia Chavchavadze revived or simply reinvented the image of King David in a commemorative text published on January 26, 1888. In this mythical image, Chavchavadze instructs his public on what qualities the secular version of the king's memory (vis-à-vis his religious commemoration as a king saint) should celebrate. As Nikoloz Aleksidze (n.d.) notes in his work on sainthood and body politic,

> Ilia Chavchavadze acted as a locomotive behind every project to reanimate Georgia's medieval history and historical imagery. His project of secularizing religious imagery and thus sacralising the mystical body of the Georgian nation proved to be the most successful nationalist project of the era.

---

[3] In Georgian, the terms *aghmashebeli* (builder) and *aghmshenebloba* (construction) have broader connotation that extend beyond material construction. The prefix *agh* indicates upward movement in *mshenebloba* (construction) and denotes a variety of practices that have to do with bringing strength and prosperity. In contemporary parlance the word *aghmashenebeli* functions as a singular index to the King David IV. There is a recently founded political party "*strategia aghmashebeli*" (strategy the builder) which employs symbolism of David the Builder for the promise of radical reforms aimed at stength and prosperity of the Georgian state.

As Aleksidze (n.d.) writes, "Chavchavadze's aim was to replace the Georgian pantheon and saturate it with exclusively national saints associated with the Georgian body politic and dissociated with the established Russian Imperial discourse" (p. 198). In Chavchavadze's (1888) formulation, David the Builder appears first and foremost as a supreme authority that unites the Georgian political body. "This truly noble man," writes Chavchavadze, "congregated Georgians. Rebuilt the ravaged country, scattered and dispersed the enemy, and today if we are in our home, this is perhaps more of his merit, his work" (p. 1).

In reality, Georgia's culturally composite (multiethnic and multireligious) nature presented a challenge to the nation-making projects of the 19th- and 20th-century intellectual elite. Various attempts to accept and recognize this diversity involved reiterating historical experiences that could serve as a constructive precedent. This is why Chavchavadze (1888) dedicated a good portion of his letter to the "generosity and forbearance" of King David to the people of different religions and ethnicity, further stressing that he had demonstrated these virtues in the times of the "complete supremacy" of his rule. Finally, Chavchavadze's evocation of the king serves his nation-making program by depicting the king's virtues as an example of the national essence:

> The better and the greatest actors of the nation are nothing more than the ones who speak out and realize desires and thirsts of the nation.... They are the living examples of how high a nation can reach under some conditions. (p. 1)

The magnanimity of these actors and their prevalence in history are a testament to the virtues, strength, and potential of the nation. Chavchavadze states,

> If there were noble and prominent men of my blood and flesh yesterday, what is the reason for them not to appear tomorrow ... the nation finds its soul and heart, its trainer, its strength and potential, its icon and example in its heroes. (p. 1)

In contrast to such magnanimity, a Soviet history textbook, sanctioned if not altogether scripted by Joseph Stalin, celebrated the absolutist power established by King David. Georgia's Golden Age narrative was crafted as part of the Soviet epistemological agenda of inventing the notion of the Eastern Renaissance. Written by Georgia's two prominent historians in the 1940s, this history textbook was drafted in full coordination with Stalin and in compliance with his extensive comments. As the transcripts of the meetings that took place in Stalin's Sochi residence demonstrate, David the Builder served as an embodiment of the absolutism that served the Soviet leader's agenda of legitimizing his own regime. The discussion of the king's policies took place in the milieu of the Soviet ruler's famous remark, "Ya za absolutism" ("I am for absolutism"). Consequently, the version included in the history textbooks of the 1940s fully endorsed and crystalized the variant of the narrative suggesting that the territorial or political integrity of Georgia is attainable only under the conditions of strong centralized power (Kartsivadze, 2019).

Also during the Soviet period, Konstantin Gamsakhurdia (1875–1975), a Georgian novelist known for his literary revivals of the Middle Ages, published a novel—a tetralogy on David IV that covered the biography and heroic acts of the king at some length. Gamsakhurdia's image of David the Builder strongly reaffirmed the storyline produced by the Stalin-sponsored history textbook. His son, Zviad Gamsakhurdia, however, who served as the first president of the independent post-Soviet Georgia before he was toppled by the violent coup of 1991–1992, evoked the image of the heroic king with a somewhat different emphasis.

Zviad Gamsakhurdia came into power through the national movements that surged during the late Soviet period and led the Georgian movement as a fervent intellectual whose political capital rested on the sheer charisma of his rhetorical feats. In addition to his political activities, Gamsakhurdia spoke and wrote extensively on Georgia's historic development, ethnogenesis, and its role in the Christian Oecumene, and he founded his political program on essentialist visions of Georgian ethnoreligious unity. His legitimacy was undermined among the opposition and also the international community by the fact that Gamsakhurdia propagated an image of "the ruler" that posited himself not as an administrator, political manager, or a bureaucrat but, rather, as a spiritual guide of the nation that had a civilizational mission.

During his 1990 visit to Gelati Academy, a center of scholarship established by David the Builder, Zviad Gamsakhurdia spoke at length about the missions and virtues of the king, who "combined the struggle with Georgia's foes and the building of the Georgian state with an extensive religious, philosophical, and scholarly activity." For Gamsakhurdia (1990), David the Builder was first and foremost an outstanding and incomparable example

> of a king and a commander-in-chief being such an outstandingly erudite scholar, as well as a poet and creator of spiritual culture. And our ideal today too should be such activity. Our great kings followed this tradition not only when Georgia was felicitous, free and powerful but in the dark periods of her history as well.

At the time of his Gelati lecture, Zviad Gamsakhurdia did not face the challenge of territorial or ethnic dissent, although he might have envisioned one. In contrast, Mikhail Saakashvili, the third president of independent Georgia (2004–2013), was confronted with ethnoterritorial conflicts that had been waged in the early 1990s. Indeed, this was the principal pledge of his presidency and accounts for why the most portentous part of his inaugural ceremony took place at the Gelati monastery. There, he made an oath at the grave of King David IV, pledging that no enemy would see Georgia's evaporation from the world map (Wertsch & Batiashvili, 2012). Eventually, Saakashvili's administration adopted the national flag that is historically linked to Georgia's Golden Age, which among other things reinvigorated historical speculations about King David's participation in the Crusades. Hence, in addition to the Christian symbolism, the modern Georgian flag is associated with the might of King David's unified state and the close ties of his period with the European world.

King David monopolized power through military reform, territorial expansion, expulsion of Turkic tribes, and the markedly fierce response to any attempt at contesting centralized rule. One of the most frequently remembered decisions during his rule is the church reform intended to eliminate all forms of dissent from centralized rule. He is thus venerated as the great king who embodied both secular and religious authority.

In the discourse of contemporary liberals and conservatives, King David's policies are articulated in two very distinct iterations of political order. First, Georgia's contemporary religious leaders and conservative groups highlight the king's saintly image to their advantage. They point to his religious reforms as the "unification of the Georgian Church," with the implication that these reforms laid the grounds for the Orthodox Church to serve as a substitute for the secular state, especially in times of "extreme hardship and fragmentation," when the church provided the "firm foundation of Georgians' spiritual unity" (Gogiashvili, 2008, p. 289). In contrast, for contemporary liberal critics of the Orthodox hegemony in Georgia, King David's reform provides the very basis of legitimacy for attacking and debasing church authority. His reform in their discourse is interpreted as a direct intrusion and a strike against religious authority.

The previously quoted conversation between the Georgian "marcher" and the liberal student about a "favorite king" is an abridged version of the kind of polemic in question. Despite the insurmountable alienation between their political stances, the exchange between Lika and Ioseb takes as a common starting point what King David means as a model of the political order. If for Ioseb, King David's rule illustrates traditionalist values, cultural purity, and ethnoreligious sovereignty, for Lika, David the Builder is above all a testament to Georgia's cultural plurality and is an exemplary model of the radical reformer who assumes power first and foremost by undermining religious hegemony. Lika and Ioseb are able to skip through chains of texts in this culturally intimate exchange because despite their political alienation and diverging interpretive stances to the "favorite king," they are both aware of all possible iterations of this mnemonic symbol. This is why abridged utterances on there being "the sword then" and paradoxical sentences on the "twelfth century *liberal* king" make sense to both of them.

In thinking about the nature and the political function of national memory, the King David example can provide a guiding principle for understanding how distinct counterpublics operate together in a single mnemonic community. Various apparitions and uses of King David in political discourse have served to harness distinct variants of the political order and with that have helped suture multivocal interpretations of "the people," "the demos," and the forms of sovereignty. Diverse registers of King David's symbolism, nevertheless, circulate within the Georgian public sphere in the same way that different speech genres or registers of language are distributed within a single linguistic community. We may speak in only one of them, but in most cases we know how to understand the others. This mutual interpretability, circulation, and reciprocal basis of the memory symbols is perhaps the most solid foundation of the shared national memory.

Conclusion

This chapter makes two arguments about the nature of national memory. Building on a particular example, it shows how national memories are formed and how contextual forces that have to do with power regimes, cultural dynamics, and civilizational alliances shape the process of semiosis around mnemonic symbols. I concentrate on the single most pervasive icon of Georgian national memory, David the Builder, the medieval king who in national memory marks Georgia's Golden Age (hence the moniker Builder). I trace instances in Georgia's modern history in which his evocations are linked to transformations ranging from the Russian imperial period to contemporary populist politics. David the Builder is significant, as most of the dominant cultural symbols are, not as a stand-alone, singular figure that embodies specific memories of the glorious past, but his pervasiveness has to do with the extent to which the memory of him embodies the dominant national narrative. The value of King David as a symbolic form is in his ability to espouse Georgians' sense of superiority and a version of collective identity that drives Georgia's political culture. Uses of the Golden Age memory in Georgian political discourse demonstrate the heteroglossic nature of memory symbols that makes it possible for an icon such as King David to become the media of expression for deeply conflicting stances and ideologies. It also demonstrates that there is a limit to how far the meaning of any symbol can be stretched and that various political evocations of memory symbols always enact this bivocal tension entrenched in them. These evocations enable new layers of meaning to be entrenched in the symbol but at the same time reiterate and reinstate its stable value of signification.

The second argument I make has to do with the idea that national memory is a primary medium through which the notion of "peoplehood" is conceived, and this has direct implications for understanding not only nationalism but also the democratic dilemma. Whereas democratic forms of political order primarily depend on a clear understanding of peoplehood and popular sovereignty, there is in fact no universal logic that can be used to define the boundaries of any "national community." Indeed, this might be one of the most problematic abstractions of political thinking.

References

Aleksidze, N. (n.d.). *Holy bodies and body politic: Sanctity, gender and polity in medieval and modern Caucasia*. Edinburgh University Press.
Appadurai, A. (1981). The past as a scarce resource. *Man, 16*(2), 201. https://doi.org/10.2307/2801395

Bakhtin, M. (1983). *The dialogic imagination: Four essays by M. M. Bakhtin. Contemporary Sociology*, *12*, 311–312. https://doi.org/10.2307/2068977
Batiashvili, N. (2018). *The bivocal nation: Memory and identity on the edge of empire*. Palgrave Macmillan.
Berlant, L. (1991). *The anatomy of national fantasy: Hawthorne, utopia, and everyday life*. University of Chicago Press.
Billig, M. (1995). *Banal nationalism*. Sage.
Cassirer, E. (1946). *The myth of the state*. Yale University Press.
Chavchavadze, I. (1888). Davit Aghmashenebelis mosakhseniebeli dghisatvis [For the commemoration of David the Builder]. *Iveria*.
Crapanzano, V. (2004). *Imaginative horizons: An essay in literary-philosophical anthropology*. University of Chicago Press.
Emden, C. (2018). *Contesting citizenship: Populist nationalism and the paradox of democracy*. Public lecture, Graduate School of Humanities, University of Bern, Switzerland.
Gamsakhurdia, Z. (1990). The spiritual ideals of the Gelati Academy. Lecture delivered at the Lado Meskhishvili Drama Theatre, Kutaisi, Georgia, May 20.
Gogiashvili, O. (2008). *Ilia dghes: Ideologia, politika* [Ilia today: Ideology, politics].
Greenfeld, L. (1993). *Nationalism: Five roads to modernity*. Harvard University Press.
Kartsivadze, M. (2019). Stalin's Cult in Georgian Colours: The Development of the First Official History Textbook of Georgia and the Emergence of Georgian Stalinism (Unpublished MA Dissertation). University College London, London, United Kingdom.
Khalvashi, T. (2018). Horizons of Medea: Economies and cosmologies of dispossession in Georgia. *Journal of Royal Anthropological Institute*, *24*, 804–825.
Khvedeliani, G. (2019). Interview Ghamis Mtavari [Night Mtavari]. https://www.facebook.com/TvMtavari/posts/179769950059790
Leach, E. (1954). *Political systems of highland Burma: A study of Kachin social structure*. Harvard University Press.
Lotman, Y. (1990). *Universe of the mind: A semiotic theory of culture*. Indiana University Press.
Mazzarella, W. (2019). The anthropology of populism: Beyond the liberal settlement. *Annual Review of Anthropology*, *48*(1), 45–60. https://doi.org/10.1146/annurev-Anthro-102218-011412
Mouffe, C. (2013). Politics and passion: The stakes of democracy. In J. Martin (Ed.), *Chantal Mouffe: Hegemony, radical democracy, and the political* (pp. 181–191). Routledge.
Propp, V. (1968). *Morphology of the folktale* (L. Scott, Trans.). University of Texas Press.
Rayfield, D. (2012). *Edge of empires: A history of Georgia*. Reaktion Books.
Revzin, I. (1975). *General semiotic analysis of Propp's Three Postulates: Analysis of the Fairy Tale and the Theory of Textual Cohesion [in Russian]*. In E. M. Melatinski & C. Y. Neklyudov (Eds.), *Typological studies in folklore: Edited volume in memory of V. I. Propp* (pp. 77–92). Наука.
Turner, V. (1967). *The forest of symbols: Aspects of Ndembu ritual*. Cornell University Press.
Warner, M. (2002). Publics and counterpublics. *Public Culture*, *14*(1), 49–90. https://doi.org/10.1215/08992363-14-1-49
Wertsch, J. V. (1991). *Voices of the mind: A sociocultural approach to mediated action*. Harvard University Press.
Wertsch, J. V., & Batiashvili, N. (2012). Mnemonic standoffs in deep memory: Russia and Georgia. In I. Markova & A. Gillespie (Eds.), *Trust and conflict: Representation, culture and dialogue* (pp. 37–48). Routledge.
Zerubavel, E. (2003). *Time maps: Collective memory and the social shape of the past*. University of Chicago Press.

17
Collective Memory and Mass Movements
When Mobilization Requires Neither Leadership nor Political Elites

Rauf Garagozov

On the Saturday afternoon of February 13, 1988, dozens of ethnic Armenians gathered in the central square named for Lenin in Stepanakert [a small town in Azerbaijan, then the capital of Nagorno-Karabakh Autonomos Oblast (NKAO)]. The participants demanded "reunion" (*miatsum*) with the neighboring Armenian Soviet Socialist Republic (SSR). The local police—also ethnic Armenians—circled the crowd but did not intervene, and after shouting slogans for a while, the crowd safely dispersed. Just 1 week later, on Saturday, February 20, 1988, approximately 30,000 people rallied in the central square of Yerevan, the capital of the Armenian SSR, which is several hundred kilometers from Stepanakert, in support of the demands of the Karabakh Armenians. Two days later, on February 22, more than 100,000 Armenians rallied in the same square in Yerevan in support of the same demands. The next day, on February 23, there were 300,000 protesters in Yerevan streets in support of the demands of the Karabakh Armenians. Two days after that, on February 25, approximately 700,000 people (nearly one-fourth of the total population of the Armenian SSR) rallied in Yerevan in support of the demands of the Karabakh Armenians. In less than 2 weeks, a mass mobilization of Armenians reached its crescendo of ethnopolitical protest.

Rallies of such a magnitude appeared to be completely unexpected by the Soviet authorities, and they wrestled with the question: What caused such a large-scale ethnopolitical mobilization of Armenians in such a short time, and not just in Nagorno-Karabakh but also hundreds of kilometers away in Yerevan? It was clearly alarming to Moscow authorities to face disobedience and dissent that were growing by the day in the neighboring Soviet republics of Armenia and Azerbaijan.

Rauf Garagozov, *Collective Memory and Mass Movements* In: *National Memories*. Edited by: Henry L. Roediger and James V. Wertsch, Oxford University Press. © Oxford University Press 2022. DOI: 10.1093/oso/9780197568675.003.0017

To be sure, Moscow authorities realized that they were facing an outbreak of furious nationalism, but because they operated within the conceptual constraints and theoretical dogmas of Marxism, they were unable to develop an effective strategy for dealing with growing national sentiment and inter-ethnic tension. Marxist ideology instructed them to seek a cure for the problem in socioeconomic development, and Moscow allocated 400 million Soviet rubles (approximately $64 million, a huge amount at that time) for the socioeconomic and cultural development of the NKAO, a region with a population of 189,000 people. These measures did not stop the protests, however. Instead, they escalated and turned into a vicious cycle of mutual violence and confrontation and later a full-scale war between Armenia and Azerbaijan.

Moscow's misunderstanding of the driving forces of nationalist mobilization is illustrative, but the ethnopolitical mobilization described previously poses a challenge not only to the proponents of Marxist ideology but also for other dominant theories in political science. The question of what caused such a rapid and large-scale ethnopolitical mobilization of Armenians can hardly be answered from the perspectives of "realism" or "unmet needs." There is no evidence that any severe social, economic, cultural, or even political discrimination against the Armenian minority existed. Indeed, in comparison with other regions of the Soviet Union, they enjoyed a quite high level of economic prosperity and had cultural and political autonomy (Cornell, 1997). It can also be argued that the conflict was not simply caused by some age-old hatred. The Armenians and Azerbaijanis have much in common culturally and got along fairly well and did not fight until the beginning of the 20th century.

The mass mobilization in Armenia in the winter of 1988 also challenges theories of ethnic mobilization focusing on leadership and manipulative elites (Broers, 2019). It is tempting to point to top-down efforts by state authorities or cultural elites to account for outbreaks of the sort that happened in 1988, but in this case the import of bottom-up cultural forces is clear. These seemed to be operating in accordance with what Pierre Bourdieu (1977) called the "conductorless orchestration" (p. 80) that guides many aspects of everyday practice.

How then to explain these developments? I begin with two questions: (1) How can we explain the speed and size of ethnic mobilization of Armenians? and (2) What could be the cause for such mobilization? In order to address these questions, I draw on two perspectives: one that derives from coalitional psychology and a second developed by the narrative approach to conflict and collective memory. The first question can best be explained by using coalitional psychology. Coalitional psychology holds that in the course of evolution, humans have developed cognitive mechanisms that allow them to make or join alliances and are important for survival (Boyer, 2018; see Chapter 18, this volume). Cognitive mechanisms have evolved such that humans are able to compute very quickly and at an unconscious level the possible risks (gains and losses) associated with joining a coalition or making an alliance with other individuals. One form of coalition is ethnic belonging, which requires a cognitive process that interprets incoming information from an ethnic point of view and assesses benefits and costs of joining a group in a way that cannot be predicted from an individual's previous experience (Boyer, 2018). It is argued that coalitions come into competition because they strive to achieve the same goals.

Coalitional psychology is primarily about mobilizing support against other groups, and it suggests that rapid ethnic mobilization reflects the mental mechanisms noted previously that make it possible to make decisions instantaneously and nearly automatically. Discussing the possibility of creating large-scale alliances, Boyer (see Chapter 18, this volume) points to the necessity of "coordination" as an important precondition for the process to be developed. In this regard, he writes,

> In the emergence of social movements, coordination does require such "focal points"—that is, expected choices that all members know that others will expect too. Coordination requires mutual knowledge—that is, a set of representations that (1) most members hold in roughly similar forms and (2) most members expect other members to hold. This can take the form of a common, coherent ideology, made more similar in different minds by repeated instruction and rehearsal. Another coordination tool, particularly important in ethnic coalitions, consists in sharing historical or legendary narratives that provide a rationale for the existence of the group and for its relations to other groups.

I use this observation to argue that collective memory has the capacity to serve as such a coordinating device for organizing collective actions, mass mobilization, and mass movements. Collective memory studies can also provide insight regarding the second question: What triggers or "activates" this cognitive mechanism? What is the reason for mobilization in a particular case? I also contend that achieving sustainable peace and reconciliation between adversaries requires some sort of social engineering with memories of the conflicting parties. In the following sections, I delineate these theses in greater detail.

Collective Memory as a Driving Force for Mass Mobilization

Collective memory in social movement literature is often considered in rather simplistic terms as a process that is shaped by collective actions and collective representations (Eyerman, 2004). I argue that collective memory is not only shaped by social movements but also, in some cases, serves as an independent force powerful enough to drive collective actions and social movements. There is widespread belief among those who study mass movements and ethnic conflicts that collective memory can fan them into something bigger. In many cases, collective memory is not differentiated from notions such as "bad histories" of the groups involved, historical myths, "ancient hatreds," or identified as the aggregate of individual memories. This conceptual vagueness diminishes its utility as an analytical category. As a result, the idea that collective memory may play an important role in mass movements and ethnic conflicts is often reduced to stating that it was merely one factor among others. However, there are ideas and empirical findings that can provide more specific understanding of the function of collective memory in mass movements and conflicts—in particular, the model of collective memory developed by James Wertsch (2002; see Chapter 22, this volume), the narrative approach to conflict (Cobb, 2013), and my own studies (Garagozov, 2019).

Narrative Roots of Collective Memory

Narrative is a complex category, the interpretations of which can vary greatly. Here, we follow the common understanding of it as a story, with an ordered sequence of events that are connected in a meaningful way that offers a certain understanding of the world and human experience for a specific audience (Hinchman & Hinchman, 2001). Pointing to the narrative dimension of social life, scholars have tried to distinguish the main properties and functions of narrative (Bruner, 1991). In this regard, the sociocultural model of collective memory developed by Wertsch (2002) suggests that we consider collective memory as mediated by specific kinds of cultural tools, particularly "textual resources" in the form of narratives.

The focus on the narrative dimension of collective memory opens up new perspectives on understanding how collective memory can function in societies and among generations. In pursuing this idea, Wertsch (2002) proposed making a distinction between "specific narratives" and "schematic narrative templates." According to Wertsch, specific narratives are surface texts that include concrete information about the particular times, places, and actors involved in events from the past. In contrast, schematic narrative templates provide the recurrent constants of a narrative tradition. They do not include any concrete information but are instead cookie-cutter plots that can be used to generate multiple specific narratives.

By way of illustration, (Wertsch, 2002) gives an example of the Russian schematic narrative template, which he calls the Expulsion-of-Alien-Enemies. Based on these theoretical premises, I have explored the Armenian cultural memory by analyzing Armenian historical narratives as a specific type of "mnemonic device" or cultural tools promoting collective remembering (Garagozov, 2015). One of the most important shared narratives that binds the Armenian mnemonic community together concerns Armenians' repeated "sufferings" at the hands of the "infidels": first the Persian fire worshippers, then the Muslim Arabs, followed by the Mongol "pagans," and later the Turks. The Armenian tradition of historical writing has a well-developed schematic narrative template that I term "a faithful people though surrounded and tormented by enemies." This narrative template consists of the following basic components: (1) the initial situation (the "Golden Age") in which the Armenian people are living in a time of valor and fame, which is undermined by hostile intrigues, as a consequence of which (2) hostile forces descend on the Armenians, as a result of which (3) the Armenians experience huge torment and suffering; (4) if they remain steadfast in their faith, they overcome their enemies, but if they depart from the faith, they suffer defeat (Garagozov, 2015).

The Armenian tragedy that took place in Ottoman Turkey in 1915 only strengthened the ethnic overtone of the Armenian schematic narrative template. Since then, this narrative template has taken on the following formula: "The Christian Armenians surrounded and tormented by Muslim Turks." According to it, Turks and, to some extent, Azerbaijanis, whom Armenians also count as Turks, were positioned in Armenian popular memories as their main enemies. Beginning in the 1960s, the Armenian tragedy of 1915 had become increasingly reframed in Armenian communities as the "Armenian genocide" within a narrative that is currently at the core of Armenian memory politics. These memories are preserved via various cultural artifacts (literature and art) and social institutions (i.e., museums, memorials, and exhibitions) and are supported by the "memory politics" pursued in the society. This memory had become what I called *painful* collective memory and a particular type of cultural pattern, by which I mean a group's tenacious and structuralized ideas about its past, the actions and motivations of its heroes, and the deeds of aliens that are abundant in official and unofficial histories.

The pattern may blend with other sides of collective experience and even become explicated in individual and group behavior (Kroeber & Kluckhohn, 1952). This narrative tool kit mediates Armenians' thinking and perceptions of the past, motivations of historical protagonists and their deeds, and in a sense serves as an "instruction for life: what is to be done and not to be done in life" (Brockmeier & Harre, 1997, p. 276). From this point of view, Armenian collective memory can function as a sort of coordination device for collective actions and rapid mass mobilization in situations that are perceived as a threat.

We can now formulate the answer to the question posited previously: What brought tens of thousands of Armenians out into the streets of Stepanakert and Yerevan? It was the Armenian collective memory pattern that "prescribed" and pushed people to go to the rally. As Broers (2019) astutely notes,

> Behind the mass mobilisation that brought Armenians onto the streets in their hundreds of thousands in February 1988 lay the popular memory of genocide at the hands of Turks in the Ottoman Empire in 1915–16. By then genocide had become a pervasive interpretive routine that was no longer meaningfully "hidden," being expressed in forms as diverse as official commemorations conceded by the Soviet state since the 1960s, the art and architecture of the ArmSSR, everyday proverbs warning against naive friendship with Turks, and popular songs celebrating World War I–era fedayi (Armenian guerrillas fighting Ottoman forces). As a narrative of victimisation this routine legitimated violence as resistance. (p. 42)

Although we now have a better idea about the forces at play in mass mobilization in Armenia, the picture would be incomplete without a more careful look at what initiated the Armenians' protests in Stepanakert (NKAO) in Azerbaijan that actually triggered the large-scale process in the Armenian SSR. What gave rise to a small rally of Karabakh Armenians on Lenin Square in Stepanakert on February 13, 1988? It had a prehistory of 2 years when a letter-writing and petition-collection campaign was held among local Armenians. Community members were asked to sign the letters with requests and demands to Moscow authorities to "solve the Nagorno-Karabakh issue" (de Waal, 2003, p. 20).

It is also worth noting that "the Nagorno-Karabakh issue" was raised by Armenian activists whenever the Soviet regime went through periods of relative liberalization (Broers, 2019). Letters and petitions were framed in terms of "victim" narratives of "historical injustices" allegedly committed against the Armenians in 1921, which was when the communist rulers (allegedly Stalin) decided to "take away" Nagorno-Karabakh from Armenia and "transfer" it to Azerbaijan. The victim narrative, even if it was at odds with historical facts (Broers, 2019), effectively reminded the local community about the historical injustice and the pattern of Armenia's painful collective memory noted previously. One can assume that the activation of such types of collective memory may have various consequences, one of which is the generation of strong emotions and affects among its constituency.

Collective Memory and Emotion

The interconnection between collective memory and emotion is increasingly recognized in recent scholarship. However, there are still many issues that remain understudied. For instance, can memory of events that occurred before an individual's own lifetime but to the person's ethnic or national group trigger a strong emotional response and shifts in their attitudes and behavior? Some research (Lambert et al., 2009) and empirical observations provide evidence of such effects. Apparently, people can experience joy and a sense of pride for the achievements of their nation or, conversely, guilt, anger, and sadness for misconduct and crimes committed by compatriots in the past.

In addition, memory of emotions such as humiliation and resentment can cause intense negative feelings in individuals, such as anger or fear. These memory-induced emotions can lead to certain attitudinal shifts in individuals. However, it would be misleading to equate the mechanisms underlying emotional effects induced by individual memory with those in collective memory: Individual memory and collective memory are different in important respects, and collective memory cannot be treated as the sum of individual memories. In the case of individual memory, a neurobiological basis and cognitive mechanisms of the individual determine the interconnection between memory and emotions. In the case of group or collective memory, there is no such single neuro-bio-cognitive "substrate."

How, then, can we explain the empirical fact that certain memories of the group's historical past can evoke strong emotions and feelings in a large number of people who belong to the group? Some studies in collective emotions provide us with insights in this regard. In particular, I refer to Margaret Gilbert's (2014) analysis of collective emotions. She argues that collective emotions are based on what she calls joint commitment, which "instructs the parties to act in a certain way" (p. 25). Employing the concept of social norms, she claims that strong emotions can arise even in the absence of relevant personal emotions due to the social norm adopted in a given society, which requires the formation of certain collective emotions that individuals react to without those being correlated with their own personal emotions. Following this line of reasoning, we may assume that collective memory is much more oriented toward social norms and social representations compared to individual memory. Taking into account the peculiarities of the Armenian collective memory, which is to great extent centered on the narrative of the "Armenian genocide," one can only imagine how easily negative feelings and emotions and consequently negative attitudes toward Azerbaijanis (Turks) are evoked by victim narratives that remind the Armenian community about historical injustice and humiliation.

Although the Karabakh conflict is unique in certain respects, some parts of this conflict have broader currency. It is about the interconnection between collective memory and mass mobilization in a process that can be modeled as follow: The initial stage—what I call the "activation" of collective memory pattern—takes place through the appearance of victim narratives that remind the audience of historical injustice and humiliation and that encourage the audience to interpret certain events of the present in a specific way. It is well known that propaganda is most effective when it corresponds to the attitudes of the audience or when it links a new idea consistent with existing attitudes of the audience (Kinder & Sears, 1985). In this connection, the most powerful narratives in terms of influence are those that follow the schematic templates particular to a given culture because they correspond well with the already existing pattern of collective memory. Due to this correspondence, these narratives have the power to impact the minds and feelings of members of ethnic or national groups in ways that never cease to amaze outside observers. And the specific narratives that reflect these schematic templates and are used in public discourse and mass media can be a harbinger of future conflict.

There can be various reasons and forces involved in the emergence of such narratives and their wide dissemination in public discourse. Without doubt, one such force is the turbulent surge of nationalism, which surfaces in oversimplified historical accounts that often resemble myth. A surge of nationalism is often observed in societies that have just acquired freedom of the press and begin to take a path of democratization (Snyder & Ballentine, 2000). In this connection, the territory of the former Soviet Union or the former Yugoslavia should be mentioned as recent natural laboratories. These suggest that ethnic conflicts were invariably preceded by the appearance and broad circulation in mass media of specific historical narratives. One example is a specific victim narrative that appeared in the press in 1986 and anticipated the future conflict in Yugoslavia: the memorandum of the "genocide of the Serbs" in Kosovo that was signed by many members of the Serbian Academy of Sciences (Gagnon, 2000). The political elites of the former Yugoslavia created, published, and disseminated this memorandum and other kindred narratives (especially popular at that time were narratives about Serbian defeat in battle in Kosovo in 1389), and this reminded their people about past grievances, atrocities, and humiliation and stimulated the process of Serbian ethnopolitical mobilization, eventually resulting in ethnic war.

The Model of Progressive Narrative Transformation

The narrative approach views conflicts as competing stories and conflict resolution as narrative transformation and the creation of a common (shared) narrative (Cobb, 2013). In this regard, two questions are of particular concern: (1) What kinds of narratives are conducive to reconciliation between adversaries? and (2) Which strategies for dealing with narratives found in intergroup conflicts are effective? As a way of addressing these questions, I have developed a theoretical model of narrative intervention called progressive narrative transformation (Garagozov, 2019). The main goal of this method is to find or construct the kinds of narratives that would lessen confrontational attitudes such that they could be more or less easily "bought" by the conflicting parties. For this enterprise, one searches for common points in conflicting groups' versions of either national historical narratives or personal stories that are likely to encourage rapprochement. This idea derives from previous studies on the psychology of reading in which certain iterative elements of prosaic texts, or "rhythmic structures," promote dialogue and better understanding (Garagozov, 1997). After establishing "points for dialogue," another cycle of narrative transformation that makes them slightly closer to each other can be carried out.

Using this model, we developed four types of narrative: "common suffering" (narrative 1), "common cultural traits" (narrative 2), "blaming a third party" (narrative 3), and the "apology" (narrative 4). These narratives are listed in the Appendix.

Throughout a series of experiments, we examined how these narratives influenced the dynamics of intergroup attitudes in the context of the Armenian–Azerbaijani dispute over Nagorno-Karabakh. Because these experiments are described elsewhere (Garagozov, 2019), I provide only a brief overview here. First, however, a few words of introduction about this research may be useful. The research project is titled "The Armenian–Azerbaijani Nagorno-Karabakh Conflict: Internally Displaced Persons (IDPs) and Traumatic Memories," and it deals with the context of the "frozen" conflict over Nagorno-Karabakh. In fact, "frozen" is something of a misnomer because it has involved both frequent skirmishes and occasional larger flare-ups such as the Four-Day War of 2016. Since the outbreak of armed warfare in 1992 between Armenia and Azerbaijan over the 4,400 square kilometers of the territory of Nagorno-Karabakh, Armenian forces have occupied no less than 12,000 square kilometers of territory, comprising not only Nagorno-Karabakh but also seven adjacent territories amounting to approximately 16% of the prewar territory of Azerbaijan. In terms of human cost, this conflict has caused up to 30,000 casualties and more than 1 million IDPs and refugees (Popjanevski, 2017). One of the consequences of the Karabakh conflict is that many IDPs have traumatic memories and a particular type of refugee social identity.[1]

---

[1] A crucial update: While the work on this manuscript was in progress, the conflict over Nagorno-Karabakh was unfrozen again and full-scale fighting ("the second war") between the Azerbaijani army and the Armenian military forces began in the Karabakh on September 27, 2020.

An Experimental Study: The Interplay of Narrative, Collective Memory, Attitudes, and Emotions

Across several studies, we have examined how using the four previously outlined narratives as priming stimuli influences the dynamics of intergroup attitudes and emotions as reflected in direct (explicit) and indirect (implicit) measures. The basic technique is one in which subjects read a narrative and are then assessed for how much it affects their performance on a subsequent measure that assesses attitudinal and emotional responses. In the study, two groups of Azerbaijani respondents—551 IDPs and 445 non-IDPs (a total of 996, including 483 men and 513 women, aged 18–73 years)—read narratives under two different conditions, either in focus groups or in individual interviews.

Explicit attitudes were measured directly by asking social-distance questions regarding an attitude (e.g., "How would you feel about having Armenians as neighbors?"). Implicit attitudes were measured through a "Superlab" computer program allowing for sequential evaluative priming. This part of the study focused on "implicit attitudes," which are not part of conscious reflection and may even contradict explicit attitudes. Numerous studies in the United States, for example, have documented racist tendencies at an implicit level of processing even when people are deeply committed to anti-racist attitudes at the explicit level (McConnell et al., 2008). In the studies reported here, the focus was on how subjects' performance on implicit attitude measures was affected by exposure to the four narratives that served to set the context or "primed" them for seeing the stimuli.

Measures of implicit attitudes typically rely on having subjects respond to stimuli that they see for only a very short time (less than 1 second) and to which they must respond to as quickly as possible. Following in this tradition, a photo of the Armenian president (at the time of study), Serzh Sargsyan, was presented for 500 milliseconds while a positive or a negative word appeared on the participant's screen. The four possibilities for positive words were sympathy, love, friendship, and kindness; the four negative words were corrupt, hostile, terrible, and hate. Participants were instructed to ignore the picture and to indicate the valence of the word by pressing one of two keys on the keyboard, marked "good" or "bad," and to respond as quickly as they could within a response window of half a second. The primary dependent variable we used as a reflection of implicit attitude was error rate. For example, because the image of Sargsyan was expected to generate negative associations for Azerbaijani respondents, low error rates were expected on negative word trials. In contrast, the prime-induced tendency to hit the "bad" key would be expected to lead to higher rates of errors on positive word trials. That is, to the extent that Sargsyan's face elicits more errors on positive than negative words, there is evidence of negative associations with Sargsyan. An index of relative positivity was constructed for each participant by subtracting the error rate on positive word trials from the error rate on negative word trials (for further details, see Garagozov, 2019). Results of explicit and implicit measurement are shown in Figures 17.1 and 17.2.

Emotional experience was assessed through a battery of self-reported items adapted from the Positive and Negative Affect Schedule (Watson & Tellegen, 1985). We formed two general indices of affect (positive vs. negative affect). Across all of the studies, principal component analyses consistently revealed two distinct components corresponding to the dimensions of general negative and general positive moods. For the general negative mood

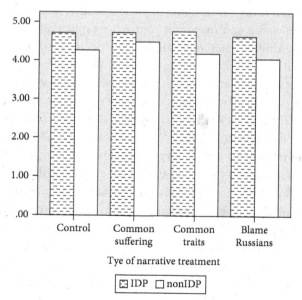

Figure 17.1 Explicit (social distance) attitude, by narrative treatment type and respondent's status. Narrative manipulation did not significantly affect social distance. IDPs were higher than non-IDPs on the social distance measure. Higher numbers indicate higher social distance toward Armenians. IDP, internally displaced persons.

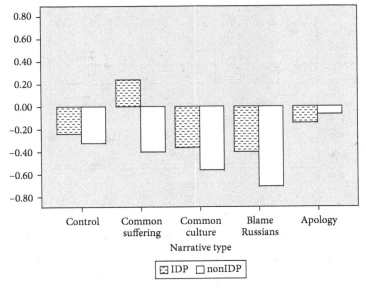

Figure 17.2 Implicit attitude, by narrative treatment and participant's IDP status. IDP participants in the "common suffering" narrative condition had statistically significant positive implicit attitudes toward President Sargsyan in comparison with the control group. Lower numbers indicate more negative attitudes toward Sargsyan. IDP, internally displaced persons.

component, the highest loading items included irate, angry, sad, irritated, nervous, upset, mad, tense, dejected, edgy, and unhappy. For the general positive mood component, the highest loading items included pleased, relaxed, and comfortable. Both indices had adequate internal reliability: Cronbach's alpha for the average of negative items was 0.93; for the average of positive items, alpha was 0.77. For present purposes, however, it was useful to form a general index of negativity affect by subtracting, for each respondent, the positive mood average from the negative mood average. Hence, higher scores on this general index indicate the presence of relatively negative current affect.

An index of empathy was measured in subjects under two experimental conditions (reading a neutral text vs. a common suffering narrative) using an emotional response questionnaire adapted from Batson et al. (1983) and used in the study by Barnett et al. (1985). Empathy was defined as a response to perceiving another person in need that included a set of congruent vicarious emotions which are more other-focused than self-focused, including feelings

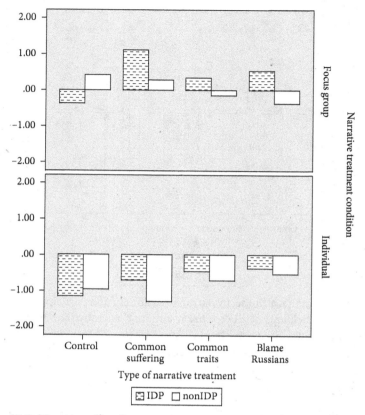

Figure 17.3 Negative affect, by narrative treatment, narrative treatment conditions, and respondent's status. Narrative treatment type combined with status of respondent had an effect on negative affect. All three types of narratives, especially the "common suffering," tended to increase the level of negative affect among IDPs. Higher numbers indicate higher level of negative affect. IDP, internally displaced persons.

of sympathy, compassion, tenderness, and the like. Results of emotions and empathy measurement are shown in Figures 17.3 and 17.4.

One of the most interesting aspects of our findings is that the subjects in our study simultaneously held positive implicit attitudes and negative explicit attitudes about an adversary. Whereas the explicit attitudes manifested by the social distance scale were highly negative under all types of narrative treatment, implicit attitudes toward Armenians were positive for those IDP participants who read the common suffering narrative. This pattern of

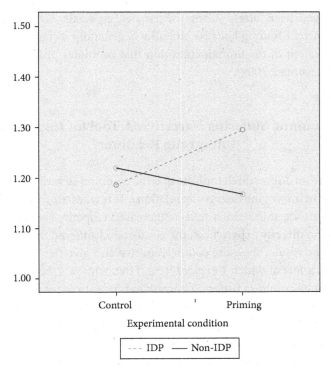

Figure 17.4 Level of empathy, by experimental condition and respondent's IDP status. IDP, internally displaced persons.

attitudes came as a surprise. One might suppose that Azerbaijani IDPs who had suffered the most from Armenians would have greater, rather than less, negative attitudes toward the Armenian president. Another interesting aspect of these results is that the level of negative affect among the participants who recollected and shared their experiences and discussed the narratives in small groups was significantly higher than that among the participants who read the narrative in an individual setting. Most unexpected in this regard was that negative affect was even higher among non-IDPs in focus group narrative treatment than for IDPs, who had experienced more trauma and belonged to a group that had suffered more and experienced many losses, namely of their homes, goods, and, in some cases, family members.

A third interesting finding from our research is that people can simultaneously hold negative affect and empathy about an adversary when primed with the common suffering narrative. The priming effect of the common suffering narrative was particularly strong for females, especially IDP females. This is an important finding because empathy is generally recognized as a central component of the human condition that promotes prosocial behavior (Batson & Ahmad, 2009).

Common Suffering Narrative: A Tool for Improving Intergroup Relations?

Findings from our research indicate that the common suffering narrative can play a role in improving intergroup relations. This takes the form of a positive implicit attitude shift, which reflects increased empathy even among individuals who directly experienced the conflict and suffered the most from it. Some of the results are quite counterintuitive and give rise to a number of questions, a few of which I explore here. First, why was the negative effect of priming by common suffering narratives higher in focus groups than for subjects who read the narratives alone, and why did this difference exist even among non IDPs? This raises the further question of what it is about focus group discussions that has this impact. How is it that the common suffering narrative, which was so strongly rejected by IDPs explicitly and produced strong negative affect, yields a positive implicit attitude shift and empathy toward their adversary in the same people? Let me start with the first question about the amplification of negative affect in focus groups. Departing from Margaret Gilbert's (2014) concept of collective emotions as joint commitment within a group based on social norms, we see the activation of painful collective memories involving "the ongoing talking and thinking about the event by the affected members of society or culture" (Pennebaker, 1992, p. 2). This process serves as a reminder of social norms regarding the Karabakh conflict, which for Azerbaijanis involves collective trauma (Garagozov, 2016). Something about the social processes involved in focus groups seems to enhance negative affect.

Regarding the next questions, two theoretical perspectives provide some insight. One perspective derives from cognitive science and posits that explicit attitudes tend to rely on a higher level of cognitive processing that includes logical, verbal, and symbolic representation as opposed to implicit attitudes, which are more automatic and follow principles of similarity and associations (Fazio & Olson, 2003). In our studies, narratives are used as priming stimuli, and their impact can be understood with the help of studies in the social psychology of intergroup relations. The relevant studies concern the role of social categorization in intergroup relations, an insight that came to form the basis of the common in-group identity model (Gaertner & Dovidio, 2012). In this model, the recategorization of an individual from out-group to in-group identity can lead to attitude shifts and increased empathy. From this principle, it follows that implicit attitudes can be affected by priming manipulations that alter the accessibility of associations toward some object or person and may also change the standards used for category membership or even affect how attitude objects are classified (Gawronski & Bodenhausen, 2006; Mitchell et al., 2003).

Building on these ideas, we used double priming to provide a measure of implicit attitudes. This involved first presenting a common suffering narrative and then the very short exposure of the image of Sargsyan. Because implicit attitudes are conceptualized as multifaceted representations in memory, variations in the stimulus context can affect not only whether a stimulus triggers activation of group-related memory contents but also particular aspects of those contents (Wittenbrink et al., 2001). In this context, the "common victim identity" induced by a common suffering type of narrative evokes not only those aspects of the image of Sargsyan as a bitter enemy but also a particular Armenian who had suffered from the conflict.[2]

There is no reason to expect that IDPs would have positive sentiment toward someone such as President Sargsyan, who was engaged as the commander of militant groups in the Khojaly Massacre, one of the most notorious incidents of bloodshed in the protracted conflict (De Waal, 2003). However, the implicit attitudes of Azerbaijani IDPs toward the Armenian people, recategorized through a common victim identity, appear to have been more positive. The suffering that they have experienced in their life as displaced persons and refugees may make them especially sensitive to suffering, even of an enemy if that adversary is recategorized with a common victim identity. As for the next point concerning empathy, it seems unlikely at first glance that individuals with strong negative affect would experience empathy toward their adversary. However, research findings suggest that some specific emotions might stand out from general negative or positive affect (Schwarz & Clore, 2007). For instance, sympathy can stand out as a single emotion (Kriesberg & Dayton, 2012; Tam et al., 2008), and empathy can exist as a single emotion with strong impact that is experienced by subjects. In this

---

[2] Sargsyan was from Nagorno-Karabakh.

regard, a potential answer can be made again by using the common victim identity categorization model. In turn, the narrative approach developed by Cobb (2013) provides new insights for understanding the effects of the common suffering narrative, especially among IDPs. She describes how the suffering type of narrative shared between Hutu and Tutsi women helped them to come together and organize a small community ("Duhozanye") after the Rwanda genocide. She explained this effect within the narrative framework suggesting that certain transformations of the conflicting narratives can lead to a possible resolution of conflict. Because conflicting narratives are essentially "sealed" narratives that resist any transformation, reducing narrative closure is considered as a way of unsealing such narratives (Cobb, 2013). Cobb argues that reducing the conflicting narratives' closure can be achieved in "liminal space," which is a place where people are made marginal and inferior and are set apart from the existing social structures. Cobb considers narratives of suffering "as a way to create such a liminal space in which identity itself can be unhinged and new ways of speaking and being, through community are created" (p. 107).

Taken from this perspective, the positive implicit attitude shift among IDPs registered in our experiments may be considered as a reflection of a certain identity shift (unhooking) that is elicited by a common suffering type of narrative. The effect of the common suffering narrative is salient for IDPs because they are already close to a liminal space as individuals who have been removed from their accustomed social world with its habitual social relations, social status, hierarchy, social order, and authority.

Conclusion and Implications

Our study shows that some cases of mass mobilization need not involve the heavy hand of state authorities or the political elite, at least to the extent it is often assumed. If such a hand is involved, it takes the form of the "department" of collective memory and collective emotions, and its actions would be triggered by aggravating events and narratives. In this regard, our research identified painful collective memory as a powerful force that both feeds ongoing conflict and feeds off of it. The skillful exploitation of painful collective memory can evoke strong negative emotions even among those who have not personally experienced the traumatic events at issue. Ethnic entrepreneurs, populists and nationalists of different sorts, are able to serve as "memory activists" (see Chapter 14, this volume) who instigate confrontational attitudes and negative emotions toward others.

At the same time, our study suggests that the model of progressive narrative transformation can serve as a method of narrative intervention in seemingly intractable conflicts. Namely, it points to the power of common suffering narratives as a means for shifting toward positive implicit attitudes and increased empathy toward an adversary. This can occur even among individuals who had experienced traumatic events personally and who were exposed to indoctrination via numerous confrontational narratives inculcated through socialization over decades.

This reasoning suggests that the common suffering narrative can create a window of opportunity for individuals to circumvent the death grip that the powerful forces of identity and memory and a "culture of violence" (Bar-Tal, 2013) have on them. It provides a pathway for transcending the limits imposed on their identity, if only for the short term and at the level of implicit attitudes. In this regard, the common suffering narrative and other related and more elaborated narratives, when conveyed through mass media, the educational system, or small-group dialogues and workshops (especially with individuals or groups most affected by the conflict, such as IDPs, refugees, and victims of violence), can serve as a narrative nudge toward peace in a protracted conflict. This can become a point of departure for subsequent positive changes in negatively charged intergroup relations.

Appendix
Four Types of Narratives About Nagorno-Karabakh and Armenian–Azerbaijani Relations

Narrative 1: Common Suffering

The Armenian–Azerbaijani Nagorno-Karabakh conflict created enormous hardships for both peoples. Tens of thousands of people from both sides lost their lives, or were disabled; hundreds of thousands became refugees, displaced persons, or lost all their property. The following photos—of an aged Armenian woman who lost her house and relatives, and a young Azerbaijani woman with a child who lost her relatives, home, and all property—are clear examples of these hardships.

Narrative 2: Common Cultural Traits

In spite of the Armenian–Azerbaijani Nagorno-Karabakh conflict, there are a lot of common things to Armenians and Azerbaijanis, including traditions, cuisine, music, family relations and daily lives. Both peoples have many features in common that distinguish them from other nations. That's why Azerbaijanis and Armenians often intermarried in the period before conflict started.

Narrative 3: Blaming a Third Party

Many people believe that the Armeno–Azerbaijani Nagorno-Karabakh conflict started and is still not resolved because Russia had interests in seeing conflict in the Caucasus.

Narrative 4: Apology

The "apology" narrative was taken from a statement of Armenian human rights activist Giorgi Vanyan (2011):

I feel a sense of shame for suffering caused to tens of thousands of people, to the Karabakh war victims, their relatives and friends, all who have experienced hardships and loss. I feel guilty about not being able to prevent a flare-up of the conflict that brought death and suffering to tens of thousands of civilians in Azerbaijan. I feel guilty about not being able to do anything to prevent this conflict. I must admit that since the inception of the conflict Azerbaijani people have experienced many hardships and injustices. On behalf of my people, I apologize for all these.

References

Barnett, M. A., Thompson, M. A., & Pfeifer, J. R. (1985). Perceived competence to help and the arousal of empathy. *Journal of Social Psychology*, 125, 679–680. http://dx.doi.org/10.1080/00224545.1985.9712044

Bar-Tal, D. (2013). *Intractable conflicts: Socio-psychological foundations and dynamics*. Cambridge University Press. https://doi.org/10.1017/CBO9781139025195

Batson, C. D., & Ahmad, Y. N. (2009). Using empathy to improve intergroup attitudes and relations. *Social Issues and Policy Review, 3*(1), 141–177. https://doi.org/10.1111/j.1751-2409.2009.01013.x

Batson, C. D., O'Quin, K., Fultz, J., Vanderplas, M., & Isen, A. M. (1983). Influence of self-reported distress and empathy on egoistic versus altruistic motivation to help. *Journal of Personality and Social Psychology, 45,* 706–718.

Bourdieu, P. (1977). *Outline of a theory of practice.* Cambridge University Press. https://doi.org/10.1017/CBO9780511812507

Boyer, P. (2018). *Minds make societies: How cognition explains the world humans create.* Yale University Press.

Brockmeier, J., & Harre, R. (1997). Narrative: Problems and promises of an alternative paradigm. *Research on Language and Social Interaction, 30*(4), 263–283. doi:10.1207/s15327973rlsi3004_1

Broers, L. (2019). *Armenia and Azerbaijan: Anatomy of rivalry.* Edinburgh University Press.

Bruner, J. (1991). The narrative construction of reality. *Critical Inquiry, 18*(1), 1–21.

Cobb, S. (2013). *Speaking of violence: The politics and poetics of narrative in conflict resolution.* Oxford University Press. https://doi.org/10.1093/acprof:oso/9780199826209.001.0001

Cornell, S. E. (1997). *Conflict theory and the Nagorno-Karabakh conflict: Guidelines for a political solution?* Triton.

De Waal, T. (2003). *Black garden: Armenia and Azerbaijan through peace and war.* New York University Press.

Eyerman, R. (2004). Cultural trauma: Slavery and the formation of the African American identity. In J. C. Alexander, R. Eyerman, B. Giesen, N. J. Smelser, & P. Sztompka (Eds.), *Cultural trauma and collective identity* (pp. 54–105). University of California Press.

Fazio, H. R., & Olson, A. M. (2003). Implicit measures in social cognition research: Their meaning and use. *Annual Review of Psychology, 54,* 297–327. https://doi.org/10.1146/annurev.psych.54.101601.145225

Gaertner, S. L., & Dovidio, J. F. (2012). Reducing intergroup bias: The common ingroup identity model. In P. A. M. Van Lange, A. W. Kruglanski, & E. T. Higgins (Eds.), *Handbook of theories of social psychology* (Vol. 2, pp. 439–457). Sage.

Gagnon, V. P. (2000). Ethnic nationalism and international conflict. In M. E. Brown, O. R. Cote, S. M. Lynn-Jones, & S. E. Miller (Eds.), *Nationalism and ethnic conflict* (pp. 132–168). MIT Press.

Garagozov (Karakozov), R. (1997). Chronotopical schemes of action as instrumental basis of sense production. In L. Dorfman, P. Martyndale, D. Leontiev, G. Cupchik, V. Petrov, & P. Machotka (Eds.), *Emotions, creativity and art* (Vol. 2, pp. 145–166). Perm State Institute of Culture.

Garagozov, R. (2015). *Collective memory: How collective representations about the past are created, preserved and reproduced.* Nova.

Garagozov, R. (2016). Painful collective memory: Measuring collective memory affect in the Karabakh conflict. *Peace and Conflict, 22*(1), 28–35. https://doi.org/10.1037/pac0000149

Garagozov, R. (2019). Narrative intervention in interethnic conflict. *Political Psychology, 40*(3), 449–465. https://doi.org/10.1111/pops.12531

Gawronski, B., & Bodenhausen, G. V. (2006). Associative and propositional processes in evaluation: An integrative review of implicit and explicit attitude change. *Psychological Bulletin, 132,* 692–731. https://doi.org/10.1037/0033-2909.132.5.692

Gilbert, M. (2014). How do we feel: Understanding everyday collective emotion ascription. In C. Sheve & M. Salmela (Eds.), *Collective emotions: Perspectives from psychology, philosophy, and sociology* (pp. 63–77). Oxford University Press. doi:10.1093/acprof:oso/9780199659180.003.0002

Hinchman, L. P., & Hinchman, S. K. (2001). Introduction. In L. P. Hinchman & S. K. Hinchman (Eds.), *Memory, identity, community: The idea of narrative in the human sciences* (pp. i–xvi). State University of New York Press.

Kinder, D., & Sears, D. (1985). Public opinion and political action. In G. Lindzey & E. Aronson (Eds.), *Handbook of social psychology* (Vol. 3, pp. 659–741). Random House.

Kriesberg, L., & Dayton, W. B. (2012). *Constructive conflicts: From escalation to resolution* (4th ed.). Rowman & Littlefield.

Kroeber, A. L., & Kluckhohn, C. (1952). Culture: A critical review of concepts and definitions. *Papers of the Peabody Museum of American Archaeology & Ethnology, 47*(1), 181–198.

Lambert, A., Scherer, N., Rogers, C., & Jacoby, L. (2009). How does collective memory create a sense of collective? In P. Boyer & J. Wertsch (Eds.), *Memory in mind and culture* (pp. 194–220). Cambridge University Press.

McConnell, A. R., Rydell, R. J., Strain, L. M., & Mackie, D. M. (2008). Forming implicit and explicit attitudes toward individuals: Social group association cues. *Journal of Personality and Social Psychology, 94*(5), 792–807. doi:10.1037/0022-3514.94.5.792

Mitchell, J. P., Nosek, B. A., & Banaji, M. R. (2003). Contextual variations in implicit evaluation. *Journal of Experimental Psychology: General, 132*, 455–469. https://doi.org/10.1037/0096-3445.132.3.455

Pennebaker, J. W. (1992). *On the creation and maintenance of collective memories.* Unpublished manuscript, The University of Texas.

Popjanevski, J. (2017). International law and the Nagorno-Karabakh conflict. In S. E. Cornell (Ed.), *The international politics of the Armenian–Azerbaijani conflict* (pp. 23–48). Johns Hopkins University Press.

Schwarz, N., & Clore, L. G. (2007). Feelings and phenomenal experiences. In A. Kruglanski & E. T. Higgins (Eds.), *Social psychology: Handbook of basic principles* (2nd ed., pp. 385–407). Guilford.

Snyder, J., & Ballentine, K. (2000). Nationalism and the marketplace of ideas. In M. Brown, O. R. Cote, S. M. Lynn-Jones, & S. E. Miller (Eds.), *Nationalism and ethnic conflict* (pp. 61–96). MIT Press.

Tam, T., Hewstone, M., Kenworthy, B. J., Cairns, E., Marinetti, C., Geddes, L., & Parkinson, B. (2008). Postconflict reconciliation: Intergroup forgiveness and implicit biases in Northern Ireland. *Journal of Social Issues, 64*(2), 303–320. https://doi.org/10.1111/j.1540-4560.2008.00563.x

Watson, D., & Tellegen, A. (1985). Toward a consensual structure of mood. *Psychological Bulletin, 98*, 219–235. https://doi.org/10.1037//0033-2909.98.2.219

Wertsch, J. V. (2002). *Voices of collective remembering.* Cambridge University Press. https://doi.org/10.1017/cbo9780511613715

Wittenbrink, B., Judd, C. M., & Park, B. (2001). Spontaneous prejudice in context: Variability in automatically activated attitudes. *Journal of Personality and Social Psychology, 81*, 815–827. https://doi.org/10.1037//0022-3514.81.5.815

SECTION V
CONCEPTUAL FRAMEWORKS FOR THE STUDY OF NATIONAL MEMORY AND POPULISM

In the general introduction to this volume, we stated that our goal was to bring together leading scholars from disciplines in the humanities and social sciences to enhance the study of national memory and populism. The five chapters in this section contribute to this by expanding on the list of conceptual and methodological approaches to be consulted.

In Chapter 18, Pascal Boyer argues that we need to go beyond the usual list of suspects when trying to account for how national communities are mobilized. He specifically questions views that focus on the powers of tribalism or demagogic leaders and argues instead for the need to understand underlying cognitive capacities involved in coalition-building. Drawing on evolutionary psychology, he notes that these capacities are part of standard mental functioning for all humans. In this view, the proclivity for alliance-building grows out of capacities that have emerged over millennia and can make all of us susceptible to mass mobilization efforts.

In building this line of reasoning, Boyer does not rule out the role of symbolic tools such as narratives in organizing large groups, especially ethnic ones. But he views this as a "coordination tool" that facilitates the formation and reproduction of coalitions rather than the lead factor in creating them. For him, narratives provide a rationale for the existence of the group rather than function as some sort of causative force. Boyer's formulation provides a new perspective on why national groups can devolve into unremitting opposition regardless of the particular issue they are debating and be impervious to information based on evidence and rational argument. It also provides new insight into how populist leaders can succeed by taking advantage of cognitive proclivities to view the world in terms of coalitions.

In Chapter 19, Alin Coman adds to our conceptual tool kit in another way by harnessing a distinction between "static" and "dynamic" approaches to the study of collective memory. The former is used, for example, when asking people what they individually recall about events such as the terrorist attacks on September 11, 2001. In contrast, analyses concerned with the dynamical approach examine how memories are shaped through social interaction. Coman goes on to advocate an approach that examines how dynamical processes contribute to emotionally charged memories shared by members of communities, making them distinct from one another. He provides an entire agenda of research projects for how to proceed, starting with analyses of dyadic interaction and moving to larger groups such as nations.

Coman outlines several ways that particular aspects of social life shape memory. For example, he notes that collective remembering is motivated by group membership, sometimes in subtle and surprising ways. Thus, American participants who studied a story about atrocities carried out by European settlers on Native Americans remembered fewer such incidents if the colonizers were described as "early Americans" than if they were called "European settlers." For him, this is part of a larger discussion of how social processes and group membership can induce forgetting as well as remembering. He also addresses the issue of what sorts of narratives make for better "vehicles" for information and how different sorts of narratives may appeal to different national communities. He rounds out his list of tasks to be examined under the heading of dynamical studies of memory with a discussion of "collective future thought" and how it can shape concrete policy decisions, concluding with sobering observations about how accepting accounts of national conflicts based on memories of age-old hatreds led Bill Clinton to forego intervening in the 1994 Rwandan genocide.

In Chapter 20, Suparna Rajaram, Tori Peña, and Garrett D. Greeley bring ideas from other areas of cognitive psychology to bear in their discussion of how collective memories emerge in small group interaction. Their research takes on added significance in an era when the very nature of how groups build collective narratives has undergone significant change with the rise of the internet and social media. Their focus on a person-drive, bottom-up approach to collective memory leads them to pursue the study of individual and small group processes of "collaborative remembering," which in turn provides insight into how memories converge in groups and can distinguish one group from another.

Their discussion challenges the assumption that two heads are better than one when it comes to remembering. Indeed, they review findings about "collaborative inhibition" that show how collaboration in small groups can impair memory, and they go into detail about when and how such inhibition occurs. Findings about "social contagion" are also of great interest and have implications for how false or erroneous information can be incorporated into one's memory—an issue of particular importance at a time of concern with the echo chambers facilitated by social media. Finally, these authors review findings that show how members of groups that collaborate can develop aligned memory structures that affect the processing of incoming experiences and information.

In Chapter 21, Elizabeth J. Marsh, Matthew Stanley, and Morgan K. Taylor bring another set of concepts and methods from cognitive psychology to explore issues of national memory in a time of populism. Namely, they examine some surprising cognitive factors that encourage people to accept incorrect beliefs that can have a tenacious hold over people. Noting that access to knowledge does not necessarily protect one from susceptibility to misinformation, they go on to examine the role of motivational and cognitive factors in memory. Their account of the latter is particularly informative. It starts with the observation that humans routinely use cognitive shortcuts and heuristics to make judgments about truth, which is a pattern that usually yields correct answers in maximally quick and efficient ways, but one that can also cause mistakes.

Building on these ideas, Marsh et al. delve more deeply into a cognitive process that involves how shifting accessibility to knowledge can change the way information is accessed and remembered. For example, asking subjects to reflect on their national identity affected their performance on a seemingly unrelated task of remembering the U.S. states. These are the sorts of studies of what cognitive psychologists call "priming" that could have some unexpected implications for national memory. In the end, Marsh and co-authors suggest that some of the very advantages cognitive systems have evolved to deal with routine tasks of understanding and remembering may have the disadvantage of supporting populist beliefs.

In Chapter 22, James V. Wertsch examines the power of narratives in shaping national memory. Although narrative is far from the only construct required in the study of national memory, it plays a central role in many accounts and can be especially useful as a point of common interest when trying to form interdisciplinary collaboration. Wertsch argues for the need to approach narratives as "cultural tools" that help humans "size up" events, including important events in national memory. In an effort to develop a research agenda for understanding the role of narratives, Wertsch outlines distinctions among "specific narratives," "narrative templates," and "privileged event narratives" and examines how claims of "narrative truth," as opposed to "propositional truth," are related to them.

Wertsch harnesses these ideas in an illustration concerned with the struggle between American and Chinese authorities to control the narrative of the COVID-19 pandemic. Each side relied on its own cultural tools to size up the event, and because narrative templates were involved, the confrontation became increasing vexed and frustrating for everyone. Wertsch notes that this is not an unusual situation in international debates about the past and emphasizes the bottom-up forces that shape national memory in powerful yet little recognized ways. He provides some suggestions on how such mnemonic standoffs might be managed before they spin out of control and lead to even more conflict. These include recognizing the power of narrative forms to shape memory, the need to harness objective historical analysis as a check on memory, practicing cognitive humility when we make assertions about the truth of our accounts of the past, and working with students to develop helpful mental habits with regard to national memory.

18

Mass Movements and Coalitional Psychology

Mobilization Requires Neither Tribalism nor Gullibility

Pascal Boyer

Common views about nationalism and populism are often based on the assumptions that (1) "tribalism" is a strong human urge or instinct that motivates adherence to groups or nations and (2) propaganda from demagogic leaders, by recruiting this tribal urge, can lead large masses of people to adopt irrational (and generally damaging) beliefs. These two themes have remained commonplace in the social sciences from Gustave Le Bon's (1897) description of crowd psychology to 20th-century visions of powerful propaganda (Bernays, 1928/2005).

But both assumptions are misleading. The evidence from anthropology, human evolution, and experimental psychology supports a more complex picture, suggesting that (1) affiliation to groups and communities is not a brutish urge but, rather, the outcome of complex, context-dependent, rational capacities for alliance-building; and (2) people's cognitive systems have robust defenses against persuasion attempts so that political propaganda is in general ineffective, even in the case of nationalism or "populism."

Does this mean that there is no danger in demagoguery and chauvinism? No. In fact, the danger is probably greater than we would usually assume. Because of the group dynamics I describe here, incitement to ethnic hatred, for instance, can have extremely damaging effects without the tribal instincts and popular gullibility we usually imagine. To understand why this is the case requires that we investigate the processes that underpin group formation, beliefs in group identity, and the motivation to demonstrate commitment to a group.

Why Would Anyone Be Committed to Their Group?

Reflections on nationalism or ethnic strife often rely on the assumption that human beings are naturally tribal or "groupish," as psychologists sometimes state—that they "need to belong" (Baumeister & Leary, 1995, p. 497). As Baumeister and Leary note, talking about a tribal urge does not help if we want to know how social groups are formed and how they support collective action.

Unfortunately, psychologists contributed to making the "groupishness" assumption more compelling by describing, for instance, how participants in laboratory experiments seem to bond to their "minimal group" (Tajfel, 1970; Tajfel & Turner, 1986). In these famous studies, an experimenter assigns participants to either one of two groups on the basis of clearly accidental criteria—for example, their preferences for one or another set of abstract paintings. In a subsequent, ostensibly unrelated task, participants are asked to provide judgments about individuals of both groups—for example, in terms of friendliness or attractiveness or intelligence—or to allocate goods (points or money) between all participants. The result, replicated many times, is that people generally favor members of their own "group"— for example, they give them more goods or judge them more attractive or intelligent (Diehl, 1990). The seemingly inescapable conclusion is that humans are so "groupish" that they will favor the members of *any* group to which they belong, however flimsy the grounds on which they "belong."

In fact, the results do not support such a strong conclusion. In these experimental situations, each participant allocates goods (or symbolic accolades) to others, and each of them knows—this is the crucial point— that they will receive similar goods from others. So the results suggest that people expect the "minimal group" to be a minimal circle of exchange, within which there is more reciprocity than with non-group members. Indeed, when experimenters remove this reciprocity—that is, participants distribute those "goods" to others but do not expect others to know where the goods came from, nor do they expect to receive anything—people show no special in-group favoritism (Karp et al., 1993; Kiyonari et al., 2000). So the interpretation based on groupish instincts is not quite correct. People in these studies view the arbitrary category as sufficient grounds to expect some reciprocity—that is a striking result, for sure, but not quite the same as evidence for a spontaneous commitment to whatever group they find themselves in.

This story contains several important lessons for us as we investigate nationalism and ethnic passion. First, it shows that computations guide people's behaviors. What we may see, from the outside, as emotional and inchoate is in fact emotional and computational. Second, these computations may be largely unconscious. People who favor their own "group" in the minimal group studies are generally unaware of the fact. Efficient systems in the mind deliver the appropriate intuitions, that this or that person is attractive or deserving, without making apparent the computations that led to such intuitions. Third, apparent commitment to the group is a matter of individual strategic motivations. Rather than trying to fuse into a collective, people are pursuing specific interests given the available incentives. Fourth, the incentives greatly depend on what an agent expects others to know about the agent's behavior. This implies that signaling, making sure that others know what you did and where you stand, is an important aspect of the interactions that build groups. As discussed in this chapter, all these factors are crucial to understanding mass mobilization and the role of ideology and propaganda in mass movements.

From Alliances to Groups: Human Coalitional Psychology

Social groups are obviously very diverse, from office cliques to bands of marauders, from trade unions to military platoons, and from tribes to entire nations. One should not try to put forward a general theory of groups, a morphology of such vastly disparate collections of agents. Rather, we should focus on the process of formation, the way agents manage to join others agents into alliances, and describe the psychology that supports such behavior.

There are alliances in other animal species, especially among close relatives such as chimpanzees, but those are transient, unstable, and limited in what they achieve and how many individuals they bring together (Harcourt & de Waal, 1992). By contrast, human alliances or coalitions can last for a long time, and they can enlist great numbers of agents in the pursuit of an unlimited variety of goals. This occurs as the outcome of a set of psychological adaptations, inherited dispositions, and capacities that motivate participation in alliances, and it helps individuals extract benefits from such behavior (Kurzban & Neuberg, 2005; Neuberg et al., 2010).

For alliances to emerge, participants must hold specific mental representations. First, they must represent a certain goal, such that it is better obtained through joint effort than individually. Second, each individual must represent that the other members have a roughly similar representation of the goal. Otherwise, members of the alliance would not expect coordinated effort from others. Third, one must discount one's own costs in working for that common effort. Coalitional work, like other forms of collective action, requires behavior that may seem altruistic—that is, conferring a benefit to others at one's own cost. But the cost is offset by expected future gains from the collective venture—whether that expectation is warranted or not. Fourth, one must expect that others, too, will discount their effort. Fifth, one should expect others to have that expectation about oneself. Finally, one should represent all costs (or benefits) by the rival coalitions as benefits (or costs) to oneself so that one is motivated to increase (or decrease) them (Medina, 2007; Pietraszewski, 2013, 2016).

Obviously, no one represents these principles explicitly. They remain tacit assumptions. No one needs to be taught explicitly how to form alliances, how to feel about defectors, or how to reward commitment. These representations and motivations come naturally, from childhood, to normal humans in all human cultures, in remarkably similar ways (Tooby & Cosmides, 2010). Indeed, the principles are so natural that their description in game-theoretic or economic terms, as in the previous paragraph, may seem to consist largely of platitudes—platitudes, that is, for any member of the species that shares this particular cognitive machinery.[1]

Groups and Power: Beyond Folk Sociology

In this evolutionary perspective, groups are the outcome of aggregated and coordinated individual behaviors, motivated by people's appraisal of the advantages of building or joining alliances. This allows the study of groups to avoid those commonsense or folk theories that we routinely use to make sense of the social world around us, and particularly our "folk sociology," a system of assumptions that organize many of our explicit notions about

---

[1] Naturally, to say that these strategic capacities are a result of natural selection does not mean that they are "innate," in most of the vague senses of that term. Humans are not borne with them, no more than they are born with teeth or sexual urges. It does not mean that coalitional motivations occur automatically, regardless of the environments in which organisms operate. On the contrary, the evolutionary picture suggests highly flexible strategic dispositions that compute costs and benefits as they occur in one's environment. Finally, the evolutionary hypothesis clearly does not imply that evolved capacities or motivations are "good" or commendable in any sense.

groups and power and that prove to be generally misleading (Boyer, 2018, pp. 216–237).

One major feature of our folk sociology, found in the most diverse societies, is that we spontaneously construe human groups as agents. For instance, we talk about villages or social classes or nations as entities that want this, fear that, make decisions, fail to perceive what is happening, reward people or take revenge against them, are hostile toward other groups, and so on. Also, we tend to assume that it is possible to describe the behavior of groups in terms of a generic agent. For instance, a debate about wages, about the consequences of having a minimum wage, are conducted in terms of what the "employees" and "employers" will do. In the same way, people will say that "women" want this or "men" do that—again, taking a generic agent as a simplified description of a specific population. This description of groups in terms of generic agents (e.g., "the workers," "Latinos," "farmers," etc.) suggests either that their beliefs and motivations are fairly similar within a group or, more minimally, that an aggregate of most members' beliefs and intentions is a good index of group-level behavior. But, as most social scientists know, emergent phenomena of interaction between individuals result in population-level dynamics that just do not correspond to individual-level facts (Schelling, 1971, 1978).

A second assumption of folk sociology is that power is a kind of substance attached to particular individuals, and its operation is analogous to a physical force. This is manifest in such phrases as "she has power," "she lost power," "his power increased," and so on. This is not just a Western or European way of speaking. Such metaphors are familiar from many tribal societies, chiefdoms, and early states (Boyer, 2018, pp. 218–219). In the conventional metaphors of English, people have power and exercise power. We conceive of someone with power as able to "push" others toward certain behaviors (as a physical force can move objects); we say that people who did not follow the leader were "resisting," that they were not "swayed," they will resent being "pushed around," etc.

These conceptions of social facts and processes are based on loose and misleading conventional metaphors (Lakoff & Johnson, 1980). Obviously, we all know that social groups are not literally agents and that power is not a force, but such metaphors do orient one's thought in particular directions, all the more so if we are not aware of their implications. But the metaphors are very misleading, and that is particularly important when trying to understand a phenomenon such as mass mobilization.

Commitment and Signaling

There are many obstacles on the way to efficient alliances (which explains why they are rare even in social species). Coalitions are a form of collective action, in which each individual invests time, effort, resources, or safety, with the expectation that the combined investment of many others will bring about benefits for all participants—think of a trade union as a simple example. The emergence of such collective action faces the major hurdle of free-riding. If collective action brings benefits, then it brings even greater benefits to those who managed to avoid paying any costs—for example, you did not go on strike but you get the pay hike that was negotiated as a result of the strike. Because all potential participants know this fact, they should all free-ride and collective action would never occur—the game-theoretic conclusion seems unavoidable. But collective action does occur because various tricks make it possible to overcome the ever-present threat of free-riding.

The main defense against free-riding and defection is our capacity and motivation to monitor other people's behavior, as well as the capacity and motivation to share that information with many others. The universal prevalence of gossip is only one among many symptoms of the human urge for acquiring information about others. Most of human evolution occurred in small-scale communities, where one's dealing with others, their cooperative or selfish behaviors, would have been a matter of largely shared information. The effect of such a situation is clear in the fact that reputation effects are so important in guiding people's behavior, in motivating cooperation as well as punishment for free-riders (Krasnow et al., 2016; Sperber & Baumard, 2012).

The logic of collective action implies that commitment should be highly valued. People who are willing to endure hardship in the pursuit of the common goal are highly valued as alliance partners. Conversely, defection and other behaviors that signal a lack of commitment usually trigger strong aversive reactions. People are very keen to monitor commitment and defection because investing resources and effort in a coalition is disastrous if others free-ride on the common achievements or if they defect when it is their turn to invest (e.g., if members of one's platoon run away when the going gets tough). That is why we are often so eager to detect signals of commitment in others, such as public statements that one is a member of the group or actual contributions in time, effort, and resources.

This explains why signaling is a crucial part of our coalition psychology. People need to communicate to others that they are members of the coalition and that they are committed to coalitional solidarity. Wearing ethnically marked clothes or a uniform, cutting one's hair or beard in a particular way, and displaying particular tattoos are all instances of such signals, intended both for outsiders, to signal one's affiliation, and for members of the coalition, to show commitment (Gambetta, 2011).

A common kind of commitment signal consists in "burning bridges"—that is, behaving in a way that would make it impossible to leave the coalition, even if one wanted to do so (Boyer, 2018, p. 50ff). That is the reason why gang members intuitively see the value of gang tattoos, indelible marks of affiliation that exclude a change of heart. Another signal, common in political organizations, consists in displaying one's loyalty to the group by denouncing others inside the organization for their lack of commitment to the cause. For instance, participants in extremist movements, in places as diverse as Nazi Germany and extremist Zionist groups, denounce members of the group who may appear less committed to severing links with rival groups (Finlay, 2007).

Human coalitions are often competitive, pursuing their goals against those of other coalitions. A great part of coalitional psychology consists in mobilizing support against others. Why should that be the case? That is not because human nature is intrinsically antagonistic. More simply, the competitive nature of coalitions lies in the fact that they constitute attempts to recruit social support, and support is what economists call a rival good. The more someone gets, the less is available for others.

Large-Scale Movements and the Problem of Coordination

Redescribing social movements in terms of a coalitional psychology has the advantage of avoiding misleading folk-sociological assumptions—for example, that groups somehow "exist" independently of aggregated individual behaviors or that power is a "force." The coalitional perspective also provides a more precise and psychologically realistic understanding of the dynamics of mass movements.

Social movements are large-scale alliances, which because of their size are faced with issues of coordination. The term "coordination" is best described in game theory, where a typical coordination game is, for instance, the decision to drive on the right or left side of the road. In such situations, the options are equally attractive—there is no intrinsic advantage to either solution—but players only get benefits if they take the same option as others. There are many other varieties of coordination games, and social interaction constantly provides us with situations of complex coordination (Camerer & Knez, 1997).

In the emergence of social movements, coordination does require such focal points—that is, expected choices that all members know others will expect too. Coordination requires mutual knowledge—that is, a set of representations that (1) most members hold in roughly similar forms and (2) most members expect other members to hold. This can take the form of a common, coherent ideology, made more similar in different minds by repeated instruction and rehearsal. Another coordination tool, particularly important in ethnic coalitions, consists in sharing historical or legendary narratives that provide a rationale for the existence of the group and for its relations to other groups (Brubaker et al., 2004; Wertsch, 2002; see Chapter 22, this volume).

Coordination requires that people have a precise enough representation of other people's representations so that these others' behaviors become more predictable. The fact that your neighbor views herself as a Croat, in a situation of heightened ethnic rivalry, makes it slightly easier to predict her reactions to specific events, her attitudes to Serbs and Bosnians, and so forth (Brubaker et al., 2004). Naturally, this does not provide certain knowledge, but it reduces uncertainty—a reduction that is necessary for scaling up cohesive action among a large collection of agents.

Coordination effects are crucial to understanding power dynamics, particularly the extent to which a movement, a dictator, or an entire regime can "gain power" or, on the contrary, remain powerless in the face of oppression. Asymmetries in the level of coordination—for instance, between an oppressive bureaucracy and a liberation movement—explain these power differences and dynamics (Hardin, 1995, p. 28ff). Consider the East European socialist regimes that stayed in place until 1989, although generally despised by the population, as became evident after their sudden downfall. These regimes took great care to boost coordination among the governing class by giving them unified training and a coherent set of ideological principles. At the same time, they were also very careful to dissolve coordination among the populace, mostly by restricting people's ability to communicate by establishing a surveillance system so pervasive that all citizens could legitimately suspect most of their acquaintances to work for the political police (Kuran, 1995).

Oppressive regimes of this kind can subsist without too much outright violence, as long as they can maintain in the populace some measure of pluralistic ignorance. This term denotes a situation in which agents have little, if any, information about other agents' preferences (Bicchieri, 2006, p. 186ff). As many have noted, including some communists, the regime cannot place a party member behind each citizen, and if they did, they would need to monitor the party commissars themselves, and so forth. But what the regime can do is make sure that although everyone guesses that most others hate the regime, no one can be sure about anyone in particular—a situation of very low coordination, in which it is almost impossible to initiate any course of action against the regime. The system was pushed to its extreme with the infamous Stasi of socialist East Germany, with its ubiquitous system of spies and informants (Childs, 1996).

Changes in the balance of coordination can result in sudden power shifts. For instance, the first gradual and then sudden collapse of socialist regimes in Eastern Europe surprised most observers and participants (Ash, 2014). It occurred when the populace managed to become more coordinated—that is, less bound by pluralistic ignorance—at precisely the point when the elites were losing their coordination, mostly because the central authority in Moscow was sending ambiguous or contradictory messages to the bureaucracy. Demonstrations in East Germany, or spontaneous jeers against the dictator Ceausescu in Bucharest, gave each participant direct information about the spread and intensity of opposition to the regime. Also, as the number of participants grew by the day, it became clear to all that the potential cost for participating was low enough to offset the possible cost of repression. Similar dynamics occurred in other countries, notably Hungary and Romania (Kuran, 1995, pp. 261–288).

These processes illustrate a dynamic that is crucial to understanding mass mobilization. Participating in the movement (e.g., demonstrating against a powerful tyrant) comes with expected costs and benefits. The threshold at which people decide to participle varies between individuals. A crucial variable that affects this threshold is each agent's intuition about how many other individuals will participate. Now, each time some individual joins the protest, and is seen doing so, that person increases the perceived number of participants and therefore decreases the perceived cost of participating. This should convince others, whose threshold for participation was just slightly higher, to join too, which in turn lowers the perceived cost and further contributes to increasing the likelihood that yet others will participate. The economist Timur Kuran (1998) described and modeled this dynamic and its dramatic effects in ethnic identification. For example, sudden shifts in the proportion of Muslim men who signal their affiliation with Islamic or secular organizations do not mean that people's attitudes or opinions shift suddenly. Rather, they show that the cost of signaling particular allegiances is affected by cascade dynamics with tipping points (Kuran, 1998).

Epistemic Vigilance: People Are Not Gullible

When we try to understand mass movements and popular enthusiasm for political causes, it is difficult not to assume that the crowds are easily persuaded. History offers many examples of crowds demonstrating fanatical adherence to some leader's discourse—from mass rallies in support of Mussolini or Hitler to the Red Guards storming through China during the Cultural Revolution, endlessly chanting the slogans of Mao Zedong Thought. Obviously, ascribing particular persuasive powers to the "charismatic" leaders explains nothing because the term simply indicates that the leader does have a persuasive influence.

The picture of demagogic leaders exploiting people's tribal urges creates two difficult problems. It implies that there are such tribal urges, which, as discussed previously, is not a plausible description of how movements are formed. In addition, the common picture suggests that the masses are easily persuaded. This is a problem because the alleged gullibility of masses is largely an illusion.

One cherished assumption most people share is that (other) people are gullible. We usually assume that most people acquire their beliefs by just absorbing or accepting what influential others told them, without much critical examination of the statements people endorse. This would explain why (other) people sometimes hold preposterous beliefs that we never would endorse ourselves. Leaving aside the narcissistic aspect of this assumption (see Chapter 11, this volume), how true is it that people are easily persuaded by low-quality information? Until recently, a good part of academic psychology would have endorsed the popular view. It seemed that experimental studies, using many different paradigms, converged on the idea that people were indeed easily persuaded (Gilbert et al., 1990). Among the psychological experiments best known by most non-psychologists are Asch's (1955) "conformity" studies, which seemed to show how people will change their minds to suit the opinions expressed around them. So, it would seem, psychology had clearly demonstrated the power of persuasion in artificial, experimental contexts—suggesting that people would be a fortiori even more malleable in natural situations such as mass rallies.

In a critical re-examination of the original literature, Hugo Mercier (2017) showed that in most cases, the empirical studies either do not show much of a gullibility effect or in fact show precisely the opposite. The famous Asch experiments showed that some subjects followed suggestions and that most did not. With quite a lot of hard work on the part of experimenters and confederates, one can persuade *some* people, some of the time (Mercier, 2017).

In fact, the notion of a mind ready to accept any information others convey should seem, a priori, extremely implausible. Most people know from everyday experience that it is very difficult to convince others of their own beliefs, especially when others have prior knowledge of and opinions about the topics discussed. Far from being open to all manners of new beliefs, minds seem to exert strong resistance to suggestion. This is consistent with the evolutionary assumption that mental systems are functional—that they serve to enhance the fitness of organisms. In that perspective, it would be surprising if our minds were indeed open to suggestion from others. For all aspects of their lives, humans rely on communication and are therefore vulnerable to deception. The risk from harmful communicated information is mitigated by a suite of cognitive mechanisms that evaluate messages—that is, mechanisms of epistemic vigilance (Mercier, 2020; Sperber et al., 2010). These mechanisms weigh messages by scrutinizing their content and their source. People are more likely to accept messages that fit with their prior beliefs or that are supported by arguments they find intuitively compelling (Mercier & Sperber, 2017; Yaniv & Kleinberger, 2000). People are also more likely to accept messages coming from an individual deemed to have their best interests at heart (Bonaccio & Dalal, 2010). Particularly important is the sender's ability to commit to the message: The more the sender can be held responsible if the message turns out to be harmful, the more believable the message (Vullioud et al., 2017). By contrast, when receivers perceive (rightly or not) a conflict of interest between themselves and the sender, they readily discount the message (Sniezek et al., 2004). A wealth of evidence shows that both adults and children exert epistemic vigilance competently (Harris & Koenig, 2006; Mascaro & Morin, 2014).

But What About the Madness of Crowds?

The previous comments on epistemic vigilance seem to fly in the face of familiar facts—that people do endorse strange beliefs, that conspiracy theories abound, and that online websites are filled with "news" that has little contact with actual facts. In short, we tend to think that there are too many examples of human gullibility, showing that people are easily convinced of the most absurd propositions (Mackay, 1841).

This common view is heavily biased toward the irrational and the sensational (Mercier, 2020). Such events occur, but a careful examination of the facts generally suggests a more nuanced account. For instance, many people have heard of the Xhosa prophet Nongqawuse, who during the British conquest of southern Africa allegedly persuaded her fellow Xhosa that the best way to repel the invaders was to burn all the crops and slaughter their cattle, as an ultimate offering to their ancestors. But this oft-cited example of mass delusion becomes less striking if we know more of the details. First, cattle at the time were afflicted with illnesses that made it a viable if unfortunate compromise to kill them before they got sick. Also, many people sacrificed a few of their animals rather than the whole herd. Finally, in many cases, people sacrificed not their own cattle but, rather, the property of distrusted tribal leaders. And when the promised benefits failed to materialize, people stopped paying attention to the prophet (Peires, 1989).

More generally, propaganda may be omnipresent without persuading. A limiting case is Nazi Germany, which would seem the prime exemplar of mobilization through demagoguery. It is true that many Germans were mostly supportive of the National-Socialist anti-Semitic program (Herf, 2006). But even in this case, careful studies show that the effects of rallies and relentless propaganda were very small. That is, people attended to Nazi discourse, joined meetings, and believed Hitler's discourse to the extent that they had prior anti-Semitic beliefs—propaganda itself did not change people's views (Selb & Munzert, 2018).

It certainly is true that cult leaders, for instance, can persuade some people, sometimes, to behave in accordance with extraordinary doctrines, sometimes even leading to collective suicide (Gardner et al., 2008; Guinn, 2017). We may be tempted to view such occurrences as evidence for the overall gullibility and suggestibility of humankind, but they may show the opposite. These exceptional cases demonstrate, if anything, that it takes extraordinary effort to get people to behave in these irrational ways.[2] All this suggests that the ordinary mind in ordinary conditions is not quite as susceptible as we would like to think.

Mass Movements and the Role of Ideological Expression

An evolutionary perspective on coalitions also helps in understanding why people engage in particular kinds of political activity. In many social and political movements, people spend a great deal of time and energy in mostly expressive activities, such as demonstrations, rallies, or, in recent times, internet debates. These expressive activities are puzzling because they do not contribute to realizing the political goals of the movement. Many participants would think that the goal in such activities is to persuade others, to recruit as many supporters as possible for the movement. But research on epistemic vigilance converges with political and historical scholarship in suggesting that political discourse only has a very limited effect (Kalla & Broockman, 2018). These are social phenomena that seem so natural to us that we hardly pause to think about them—but they are natural only because we share the psychology of participants in mass movements.

Does this mean that participation in expressive political activities is simply misguided? Not really, if we take into account the motivations and computations involved in coalitional psychology. Rallies, demonstrations, and the repetition of slogans and propaganda may have specific effects that make them intuitively attractive for members of a coalition, including those discussed next.

Coordination Through Internal Signaling

Large-scale coalitions depend on efficient signaling that increases coordination between members. That is why a great amount of signaling is directed at members themselves. In order to persuade members that continued commitment is a good investment, the leadership has to convey to them that the coalition is numerous, cohesive, and decisive in the pursuit of its goals.

---

[2] Cult leaders, who intuitively know what to do, take great care to recruit vulnerable individuals, isolate them, exhaust them, submit them to schedules of random rewards and capricious favors, and so forth (Dawson, 1998).

That is why many social and political movements favor large-scale meetings, which from the standpoint of mere communication are a waste of time but create powerful signals for all participants. The sheer number of participants in such events conveys a cue of the strength of the coalition. Synchronized chanting and choreography (pushed to an extreme in the Maoist or Nazi cases, but also widespread in many other mass movements) constitute a cue that the coalition is cohesive—that all its members are on the same page, so to speak. Finally, to survive, a coalition needs to demonstrate to its members that everyone is strongly committed, which is why meetings often include passionate speeches and extremist statements of allegiance.

Forced Disclosure

Signaling creates situations in which not sending particular signals is the equivalent of sending a specific one. This is well known in evolutionary biology (Maynard Smith & Harper, 2003), and signaling in social movements may create the same dynamics. The fact that someone is not sending any signals is itself a signal. For instance, Vaclav Havel (1985) famously described how Prague grocers would plant signs with Marxist slogans right in the middle of their vegetables to get the political police to leave them alone. In such a totalitarian regime, anyone who does not signal allegiance to the regime is thereby declaring themself a dissident. More generally, it makes sense for a mass movement to try to exclude silence and indifference. If people have the option of *not* supporting the movement, there is great danger to a coalition's cohesiveness.

This forced disclosure sometimes extends beyond mere adhesion to the regime, and it demands that people adopt a particular slogan or turn of phrase. In this case, even people who express the same ideas as the movement but do not use the approved formulation are viewed as potential defectors. That is, of course, a phenomenon that also occurs in some religious traditions, punishing those who share the beliefs of the movement but fail to state them in the exact terms used in the received creed.

Why Isn't Everyone a "Populist"?

Turning now to a more speculative set of issues, the evidence and models summarized here may help reframe the pressing question, Why are demagogic leaders and "populist" movements successful and seem to be very much on the ascendant throughout the world, from Hungary to the Philippines and Brazil to the United States? In the media as well as intellectual circles, most people who discuss these issues agree that the influence of nationalism and "populism" has increased, is increasing, and should be diminished. And the most common explanations for its success are based on the assumptions discussed here—that people are gullible and that tribalism is an inchoate or primitive motivation. Now that we have (it is hoped) discarded these facile and misleading assumptions, it may seem more pertinent to ask, Why would nationalism and populism *not* be successful? Why isn't everyone a populist nationalist?

A consideration of our evolved psychology may suggest a speculative answer. Most people in most places are familiar with two kinds of social interaction: positive-sum and zero-sum. The former occurs in voluntary exchange, when we trade goods or labor, or in collective action, when we join forces to achieve a common goal. In such contexts, both parties benefit more than they contributed. In contrast, interactions such as warfare, sports competitions, or romantic rivalry are zero-sum: They result in one party losing resources that the other one earns. Different social and historical circumstances provide social environments that vary in the proportion of these two different kinds of social games. People who grow up in stable and safe social environments, with reduced uncertainty about future resources, and in an ethnically homogeneous nation may consider positive-sum games a natural feature of the world and the default assumption when considering interaction between social groups. By contrast, people who are more familiar with social strife, uncertain access to resources, and a more divided polity may come to see zero-sum games as a default setting for group interaction.

There is considerable evidence for this difference and its connection with experienced environments. This is observed, for instance, in measures of generalized social trust—the extent to which people assume that others around them are on the whole cooperative rather than antagonistic (Sønderskov, 2011; Welch et al., 2005). It also appears in people's performance in economic games, where participants have the opportunity to cooperate for everyone's advantage or defect to their own benefit. In these contexts, people from Denmark, for instance, show more cooperative motivation that those from Sicily (Herrmann et al., 2008). This difference does not occur only between nations or cultures. Dan Nettle (2010) showed the same kinds of contrast between different neighborhoods in Newcastle in England. Indeed, if we accept the explanation in terms of early exposure to different social worlds, we would expect such differences to occur as a function of social class and degree of prosperity, much more than ethnicity or culture.[3]

These different attitudes may be relevant to the success or failure of populist movements. Consider, for instance, the issue of mass immigration, which dominates political conflict in many Western countries. People familiar with positive-sum interactions tend to view this new challenge as an opportunity for mutually beneficial interaction. As a result, such people infer that opposition to immigration *must* be rooted in bigotry, xenophobia, etc. By contrast, people more familiar with zero-sum interactions view the arrival of any newcomers in an interaction as a potential threat, as the newcomers have the opportunity to extract benefits without having previously paid their dues.[4] People familiar with zero-sum interactions infer that an immigration supporter *must* be motivated by the desire to harm them and benefit others.

Similarly, a zero-sum orientation makes the contrast highly intuitive, between "elites" and "the people," as two camps with necessarily opposite interests, with the implication that whatever benefits the elites is detrimental to the populace. A zero-sum view also dovetails with a vision of the wealth of nations as a fixed pie, such that the prosperity of some necessarily entails the immiseration of others, a very common view despite the best efforts of economists (Boyer & Petersen, 2018).

So the zero-sum orientation may ground both the populist aspect of modern political movements (an emphasis on downtrodden communities losing out in current economies) and their nationalistic aspect (an emphasis on one's coalition as a closed solidarity circle).

A common view of mass mobilization is that persuasive leaders managed to convince large numbers of people of the truth of their ideology. This suggests that the antidote is to prevent such effects—to counter propaganda before it diffuses through the population. But this may be illusory because the prescription is based on the wrong diagnosis. To put it in the simplest terms, populist nationalism seems to be a response to popular demand, and an evolutionary

---

[3] This adaptability is itself an adaptation—a flexible response to variability in natural and social environments. Life history models (Gluckman et al., 2007) describe the conditions under which, for instance, childhood conditions influence a general attitude toward cooperation, long-term goals, deferred gratification, etc. that appears during child development—that is, it may in fact be an adaptive response to different kinds of environments (Sheskin et al., 2014).

[4] Experimental evidence suggests that newcomers to some alliance are implicitly categorized as potential free-riders, which in turn motivates aggressive motivations against them (Cimino & Delton, 2010).

perspective may explain why the demand increases when people's changed environments activate particular heuristics for representing the social world (Petersen, 2015). Describing the success of populist nationalism in terms of coalitional psychology does not by itself provide much of an antidote, if any is needed. But it may help us understand how social or cultural disruption, growing inequality, and increased uncertainty about economic prospects can make zero-sum ideologies compelling, with the implication that a significant change in these parameters is required for the opposite trend to occur.

Many intellectuals (that may be an occupational disease) tend to think that their own position is the sensible one that a reasonable individual will reach, unless their perception of reality is clouded, their intellectual skills are below par, or their reasoning is swayed aside by powerful passion or the persuasive power of demagogues. This variety of naive realism is probably misguided. We can explain mass participation in social movements, including ethnic chauvinism or xenophobic forms of nationalism, in terms that are less metaphorical, self-serving, and misleading if we take into account the precise combination of evolved motivations and capacities, on the one hand, and highly specific historical conditions, on the other hand, that make them attractive to large numbers of people.

References

Asch, S. E. (1955). Opinions and social pressure. *Scientific American, 193*, 31–35.
Ash, T. G. (2014). *The magic lantern: The revolution of '89 witnessed in Warsaw, Budapest, Berlin and Prague*. Atlantic Books.
Baumeister, R. F., & Leary, M. (1995). The need to belong: Desire for interpersonal attachments as a fundamental human motivation. *Psychological Bulletin, 117*, 497–529.
Bernays, E. L. (2005). *Propaganda*. Ig Publishing. (Original work published 1928)
Bicchieri, C. (2006). *The grammar of society: The nature and dynamics of social norms*. Cambridge University Press.
Bonaccio, S., & Dalal, R. S. (2010). Evaluating advisors: A policy-capturing study under conditions of complete and missing information. *Journal of Behavioral Decision Making, 23*(3), 227–249.
Boyer, P. (2018). *Minds make societies: How cognition explains the world humans create*. Yale University Press.
Boyer, P., & Petersen, M. B. (2018). Folk-economic beliefs: An evolutionary cognitive model. *Behavioral and Brain Sciences, 41*, e158. doi:10.1017/S0140525X17001960
Brubaker, R., Loveman, M., & Stamatov, P. (2004). Ethnicity as cognition. *Theory and Society, 33*, 34.
Camerer, C., & Knez, M. (1997). Coordination in organizations: A game-theoretic perspective. In Z. Shapira (Ed.), *Organizational decision making* (pp. 158–188). Cambridge University Press.

Childs, D. (1996). *The Stasi: The East German intelligence and security service.* New York University Press.

Cimino, A., & Delton, A. W. (2010). On the perception of newcomers: Toward an evolved psychology of intergenerational coalitions. *Human Nature, 21,* 186–202. doi:10.1007/s12110-010-9088-y

Dawson, L. L. (Ed.). (1998). *Cults in context: Readings in the study of new religious movements.* Transaction Publishers.

Diehl, M. (1990). The minimal group paradigm: Theoretical explanations and empirical findings. *European Review of Social Psychology, 1*(1), 263–292.

Finlay, W. M. L. (2007). The propaganda of extreme hostility: Denunciation and the regulation of the group. *British Journal of Social Psychology, 46,* 323–341.

Gambetta, D. (2011). *Codes of the underworld: How criminals communicate*: Princeton University Press.

Gardner, P., Williams, J., & Sadri, M. (2008). Peoples Temple: From social movement to total institution. In D. Dentice & J. L. Williams (Eds.), *Social movements: Contemporary perspectives* (pp. 19–27). *Cambridge*: Cambridge Scholars Publishing.

Gilbert, D. T., Krull, D. S., & Malone, P. S. (1990). Unbelieving the unbelievable: Some problems in the rejection of false information. *Journal of Personality & Social Psychology, 59,* 601–613.

Gluckman, P. D., Hanson, M. A., & Beedle, A. S. (2007). Early life events and their consequences for later disease: A life history and evolutionary perspective. *American Journal of Human Biology, 19*(1), 1–19.

Guinn, J. (2017). *The road to Jonestown: Jim Jones and Peoples Temple*: Simon & Schuster.

Harcourt, A. H., & de Waal, F. B. M. (1992). *Coalitions and alliances in humans and other animals.* Oxford University Press.

Hardin, R. (1995). *One for all: The logic of group conflict.* Princeton University Press.

Harris, P. L., & Koenig, M. A. (2006). Trust in testimony: How children learn about science and religion. *Child Development, 77*(3), 505–524.

Havel, V. (1985). The power of the powerless. In J. Keane (Ed.), *The power of the powerless: Citizens against the state in Central-Eastern Europe* (pp. 27–28). Sharpe.

Herf, J. (2006). *The Jewish enemy: Nazi propaganda during World War II and the Holocaust*: Harvard University Press.

Herrmann, B., Thöni, C., & Gächter, S. (2008). Antisocial punishment across societies. *Science, 319*(5868), 1362–1367.

Kalla, J. L., & Broockman, D. E. (2018). The minimal persuasive effects of campaign contact in general elections: Evidence from 49 field experiments. *American Political Science Review, 112*(1), 148–166.

Karp, D., Jin, N., Yamagishi, T., & Shinotsuka, H. (1993). Raising the minimum in the minimal group paradigm. *Japanese Journal of Experimental Social Psychology, 32,* 231–240.

Kiyonari, T., Tanida, S., & Yamagishi, T. (2000). Social exchange and reciprocity: Confusion or a heuristic? *Evolution and Human Behavior, 21,* 411–427. doi:10.1016/s1090-5138(00)00055-6

Krasnow, M. M., Delton, A. W., Cosmides, L., & Tooby, J. (2016). Looking under the hood of third-party punishment reveals design for personal benefit. *Psychological Science, 27,* 405–418.

Kuran, T. (1995). *Private truths, public lies: The social consequences of preference falsification.* Harvard University Press.

Kuran, T. (1998). Ethnic norms and their transformation through reputational cascades. *Journal of Legal Studies, 27,* 623–659.

Kurzban, R., & Neuberg, S. (2005). Managing ingroup and outgroup relationships. In D. M. Buss (Ed.), *The handbook of evolutionary psychology* (pp. 653–675). Wiley.
Lakoff, G., & Johnson, M. (1980). *Metaphors we live by* (Vol. 111). University of Chicago Press.
Le Bon, G. (1897). *The crowd: A study of the popular mind*. Fisher Unwin.
Mackay, C. (1841). *Memoirs of extraordinary popular delusions and the madness of crowds*. Bentley.
Mascaro, O., & Morin, O. (2014). Gullible's travel: How honest and trustful children become vigilant communicators. In E. J. Robinson, S. Einav, E. J. Robinson, & S. Einav (Eds.), *Trust and skepticism: Children's selective learning from testimony* (pp. 69–82). Psychology Press.
Maynard Smith, J., & Harper, D. (2003). *Animal signals*. Oxford University Press.
Medina, L. F. (2007). *A unified theory of collective action and social change*. University of Michigan Press.
Mercier, H. (2017). How gullible are we? A review of the evidence from psychology and social science. *Review of General Psychology*, *21*, 103.
Mercier, H. (2020). *Not born yesterday: The science of who we trust and what we believe*. Princeton University Press.
Mercier, H., & Sperber, D. (2017). *The enigma of reason*. Harvard University Press.
Nettle, D. (2010). Dying young and living fast: Variation in life history across English neighborhoods. *Behavioral Ecology*, *21*, 387–395.
Neuberg, S. L., Kenrick, D. T., & Schaller, M. (2010). Evolutionary social psychology. In S. T. Fiske, D. T. Gilbert, & G. Lindzey (Eds.), *Handbook of social psychology, Vol. 2* (5th ed., pp. 761–796). Wiley.
Peires, J. B. (1989). *The dead will arise: Nongqawuse and the great Xhosa cattle-killing movement of 1856–7*. Ravan Press.
Petersen, M. B. (2015). Evolutionary political psychology: On the origin and structure of heuristics and biases in politics. *Political Psychology*, *36*, 45–78. doi:10.1111/pops.12237
Pietraszewski, D. (2013). What is group psychology? Adaptations for mapping shared intentional stances. In M. R. Banaji, S. A. Gelman, M. R. Banaji, & S. A. Gelman (Eds.), *Navigating the social world: What infants, children, and other species can teach us* (pp. 253–257). Oxford University Press.
Pietraszewski, D. (2016). How the mind sees coalitional and group conflict: The evolutionary invariances of n-person conflict dynamics. *Evolution and Human Behavior*, *37*, 470–480. doi:10.1016/j.evolhumbehav.2016.04.006
Schelling, T. C. (1971). Dynamic models of segregation. *Journal of Mathematical Sociology*, *1*, 143–186.
Schelling, T. C. (1978). *Micromotives and macrobehavior*. Norton.
Selb, P., & Munzert, S. (2018). Examining a most likely case for strong campaign effects: Hitler's speeches and the rise of the Nazi party, 1927–1933. *American Political Science Review*, *112*(4), 1050–1066.
Sheskin, M., Chevallier, C., Lambert, S., & Baumard, N. (2014). Life-history theory explains childhood moral development. *Trends in Cognitive Sciences*, *18*, 613–615. doi:10.1016/j.tics.2014.08.004
Sniezek, J. A., Schrah, G. E., & Dalal, R. S. (2004). Improving judgement with prepaid expert advice. *Journal of Behavioral Decision Making*, *17*, 173–190. doi:10.1002/bdm.468
Sønderskov, K. M. (2011). Explaining large-N cooperation: Generalized social trust and the social exchange heuristic. *Rationality and Society*, *23*(1), 51–74. doi:10.1177/1043463110396058

Sperber, D., Clement, F., Heintz, C., Mascaro, O., Mercier, H., Origgi, G., & Wilson, D. (2010). Epistemic vigilance. *Mind & Language, 25*(4), 359–393.
Sperber, D., & Baumard, N. (2012). Moral reputation: An evolutionary and cognitive perspective. *Mind & Language, 27*, 495–518. doi:10.1111/mila.12000
Tajfel, H. (1970). Experiments in inter-group discrimination. *Scientific American, 223*, 96–102.
Tajfel, H., & Turner, J. C. (1986). The social identity theory of inter-group behavior. In S. Worchel & W. G. Austin (Eds.), *Psychology of intergroup relations* (pp. 33–47). Nelson-Hall.
Tooby, J., & Cosmides, L. (2010). Groups in mind: The coalitional roots of war and morality. In H. Høgh-Olesen (Ed.), *Human morality and sociality: Evolutionary and comparative perspectives* (pp. 191–234). Palgrave Macmillan.
Vullioud, C., Clément, F., Scott-Phillips, T., & Mercier, H. (2017). Confidence as an expression of commitment: Why misplaced expressions of confidence backfire. *Evolution and Human Behavior, 38*, 9–17. doi:10.1016/j.evolhumbehav.2016.06.002
Welch, M. R., Rivera, R. E. N., Conway, B. P., Yonkoski, J., Lupton, P. M., & Giancola, R. (2005). Determinants and consequences of social trust. *Sociological Inquiry, 75*, 453–473.
Wertsch, J. V. (2002). *Voices of collective remembering.* Cambridge University Press.
Yaniv, I., & Kleinberger, E. (2000). Advice taking in decision making: Egocentric discounting and reputation formation. *Organizational Behavior and Human Decision Processes, 83*, 260–281.

19
Toward a Dynamical—in the Field—Approach to Collective Memory

Alin Coman

On September 30, 2000, video footage showed Muhammad al-Durrah, a 12-year-old Palestinian boy, being fatally shot by Israeli soldiers close to an Israeli military outpost in the Gaza Strip. The footage captured graphic images of Muhammad and his father, Jamal, under fire for an extended period of time, and it culminated in the boy lying motionless in his father's arms. The incident marked the beginning of the Second Intifada—an uprising by the Palestinians against Israeli military occupation, which would lead to more than 4,000 deaths overall. The outrage triggered by this incident among Palestinians was amplified by having an objective video record that gave concreteness to the plight they have endured for many decades (Cook, 2007). Subsequent investigations questioned the objective nature of the recording. The shots, it was argued, could have been fired from a position occupied by Palestinian fighters, whose goal was, supposedly, to inflame the Palestinians and trigger collective violence against the Israelis (Beckerman, 2007).

It is beyond the scope of this chapter to elucidate the truth behind this incident. Importantly for the purposes of this chapter, the way the Israelis and the Palestinians perceived, interpreted, and remembered this incident showcases the fundamental characteristics of collective memories, illustrates its relation to nationalism, and points to research trajectories aimed at understanding the formation of collective memories in real-world contexts.

The study of collective memories—as shared individual memories that bear on people's identities—has experienced a resurgence during the past decade (Hirst et al., 2019; Sutton et al., 2010). This interest has recently proliferated because scholars from diverse disciplines have increasingly recognized that communities base their collective identities and collective actions, to an important extent, on these shared memories (Fivush, & Nelson, 2004; Roediger & Abel, 2015). Given these close connections between memory, identity, and action, one can imagine numerous situations in which one might want to understand why a collective memory takes the form that it does, particularly because it has important consequences. Incidents such as the death of Muhammad al-Durrah, which are frequent throughout the world, motivate a programmatic investigation of how communities come to form memories of the past and how these memories could trigger collective action.

This burgeoning literature has produced significant theoretical and methodological advances in psychology. Two major approaches have developed in contemporary treatments of the formation of collective memories (Hirst et al., 2019). On the one hand, psychologists have studied how people remember highly consequential events by simply asking them to individually recall these events. I call this the static approach to collective memory. With this approach, we have learned how mass media impacts what people remember about the September 11, 2001, terrorists attacks (9/11; Hirst et al., 2009), how remembering U.S. presidents is circumscribed by a well-established recency effect on memory (DeSoto & Roediger, 2019), and how different generations remember different events from the nation's past (Schuman & Scott, 1989; see Chapter 7, this volume). These findings were obtained by studies that asked participants to individually recall or recognize real-world consequential personalities and events.

The complementary approach is one that explores the dynamical nature of collective memories, which primarily investigates how people shape their memories through social interactions (Coman, Brown, et al., 2009; Rajaram & Pereira-Pasarin, 2010; Vlasceanu, Enz, & Coman, 2018). The paradigms used in this approach involve communities of individuals whose memories are assessed both before and after conversational interactions to measure how similar their memories became. Using this approach, it has been found that individual-level cognitive mechanisms (Cuc et al., 2007), the conversational network structure (Coman et al., 2016; Luhmann & Rajaram, 2015), and the timing of conversational interactions (Momennejad et al., 2019) impact how convergent people's memories become following conversations. These two types of approaches have developed independently of one another. They are, however, complementary approaches to collective memory. In this chapter, I argue that the field is ripe for weaving these approaches together for a more adequate understanding of how collective memories of real-world events impact collective behavior.

I advocate for field-oriented studies that could capture the dynamical processes by which emotionally charged memories become shared across individuals who make up distinct communities. To provide theoretical support and methodological scaffolding for this investigation, I first discuss the characteristics of collective memories that make their investigation particularly relevant in the context of nationalism and then identify areas that could benefit from further exploration.

Characteristics of Collective Memories

Existing empirical approaches have thus far neglected to explore the relation between collective memory and nationalism. Several characteristics of collective memories make them of particular interest in this context. First, psychological approaches to collective memories have grounded their investigation in individual-level processes. That is, what allows for collective memories to be formed is how human memory operates at an individual level. Second, collective memories are highly susceptible to social influence, which makes them particularly relevant in contexts in which nationalistic programs are initiated by state and nonstate actors. Relatedly, collective memories are highly dynamic phenomena. That is, they change depending on both top-down (e.g., elites) and bottom-up (e.g., peer-to-peer) influences. Finally, collective memory is, at its core, motivated. In other words, individuals who make up communities have particular motivations that, when activated, bias the remembering processes and, through these processes, affect the underlying collective memory.

Collective Memory Is Grounded in Individual-Level Processes

One question thoroughly investigated in psychological studies of collective memory involves the ways in which it is grounded in individual-level phenomena. The starting point of these investigations is in the malleability of human memory (Loftus, 2005; Schacter, 2001). What allows for the synchronization of memories across communities is the way in which our memories can be shaped after initial encoding, particularly in our social interactions. Given the ubiquity of social remembering—that is, jointly remembering the past along with others—psychologists have become interested in exploring the effects of such interactions on our memories.

As indicated previously, there are numerous instances in which social remembering dramatically alters people's memories. For instance, following exposure to a consequential event (e.g., 9/11), people often encode information about the event. Later, they might be exposed to leaders, pundits, and celebrities recounting this information, as well as discuss it with other individuals. These are all instances of social remembering that impact what people remember subsequently. Extensive work in cognitive psychology has shown that the simple act of retrieving a previously encoded memory strengthens its mnemonic representation. Surprisingly, this selective retrieval results in the forgetting of unmentioned memories related to mentioned memories to a larger extent than of unmentioned, unrelated memories (Anderson et al., 1994). More succinctly, retrieval induces forgetting in related memories. To study this phenomenon rigorously, researchers ask participants to study category–exemplar pairs, such as fruit–apple, fruit–orange, vegetable–broccoli, and vegetable–pea. They then undergo retrieval practice by way of a stem completion task (e.g., fruit-a ___). Practice selectively focuses on some pairs (fruit–apple) but not on other related pairs (fruit–orange) and does not involve whole sets of pairs (e.g., all the vegetable pairs). This design establishes three types of retrieval-practice items: practiced items, unpracticed items related to practiced items, and unpracticed items unrelated to the practiced items (i.e., baseline items). Finally, participants are asked to retrieve the initially presented information in a final recall phase. By analyzing the final recall test, researchers find both a retrieval practice effect (recall proportion of practiced items larger than the recall proportion of baseline items) and a retrieval-induced forgetting effect (recall proportion of items related to those practiced smaller than the recall proportion of baseline items) (Anderson et al., 1994; Karpicke & Roediger, 2007) (Figure 19.1).

Of note, although these initial investigations of retrieval-induced forgetting (RIF) used highly controlled stimulus materials, subsequent investigations have revealed similar findings for real-world events, such as memories of 9/11 (Coman, Manier, et al., 2009). Importantly for the purposes of this chapter, rehearsal and retrieval-induced forgetting effects have been found in settings that involve social remembering, a necessary extension if one wants to investigate communicative effects on memory at a community level. For the most part, in any interaction involving memories, only part of what a speaker is capable of remembering is recollected, producing what the literature refers to as *mnemonic silences* (Stone et al., 2012). This creates a situation in which rehearsal and retrieval-induced forgetting could have an impact on both the speaker and her listeners.

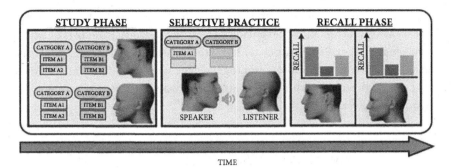

Figure 19.1 Phases of the experimental procedure to study retrieval-induced forgetting. In the dyadic paradigm, pairs of participants study category–exemplar pairs, selectively practice information during conversational remembering, and then individually recall the initially presented information. Practiced information is remembered better than the baseline information, whereas unpracticed information is remembered worse than the baseline level.

The rehearsal effect is observed when a speaker in a conversation repeats something already known to the listener(s). By virtue of the repetition, both the speaker and the listeners have been found to subsequently remember the pre-existing memory better than baseline information (Cuc et al., 2007). At the same time, this research aimed at investigating whether the joint conversational remembering involving speaker–listener dyads triggers similar induced forgetting effects in both interaction partners. In a modified RIF paradigm, pairs of participants studied category–exemplar pairs and then one of the two participants (i.e., the speaker) was asked to selectively practice half of the items from half of the categories, while the other participant (i.e., the listener) simply monitored the speaker's recollection. Finally, the two individuals were asked to individually recall the initially presented information. The results showed that both the speaker and the listener experienced retrieval practice and retrieval-induced forgetting effects following selective practice (but for boundary conditions, see Abel & Roediger, 2018). That is, they both remembered the mentioned information better than baseline information, and they forgot information related to what the speaker mentioned to a larger extent than baseline information. Retrieval induced forgetting for the listener, or socially shared retrieval-induced forgetting (SSRIF), emerges when listeners concurrently, albeit covertly, retrieve along with the speaker. With this concurrent retrieval, the listener retrieves the same material as the speaker and, hence, is more likely to forget items related to what the speaker recalled than unmentioned unrelated items. SSRIF was found for listeners in free-flowing conversations for a wide variety of materials, from lists of words (Barber & Mather, 2012; Cuc et al., 2007) to stories (Coman et al., 2014; Stone et al., 2010) and emotional autobiographical memories (Coman, Manier, et al., 2009). It was also found when attending to audio or video presentations (Coman & Hirst, 2015).

Collective Memory Is Susceptible to Social Influence

As discussed previously, once encoded, a memory remains malleable. It could be updated, restructured, and suppressed upon subsequent recall attempts (Dudai, 2004; Loftus, 2005). One important source of memory change comes from humans' social embeddedness, which involves frequent instances of social influence. These types of influences are of either horizontal or vertical nature.

In horizontal social influence, one's memories are influenced—typically interactively—by one's close social connections, from family members to friends and acquaintances. In a study investigating how people influence each other's memories of 9/11, pairs of New Yorkers jointly remembered their memories of the attacks (Coman, Manier, et al., 2009). It was found that memories that were discussed in the conversation became more accessible, and memories that were related to the discussed ones became less accessible, compared to undiscussed memories and those unrelated to the discussed memories (i.e., baseline). Of note, participants were randomly paired with one another and did not know one another prior to the study. Despite not having a pre-established relationship, they influenced one another's memories of a highly consequential, emotionally charged event. They did not need to have a strong social bond in order to shape one another's memories.

What happens when people who feel connected to one another—such as when they belong to the same community—jointly recall group-relevant memories? Answering this question is of critical importance because collective memory during times of nationalistic fervor is likely to be animated by a community's strongly activated identity. To answer this question, Coman and Hirst (2015) had Princeton students study information about a student-exchange program and listen to either another Princeton student or another Yale student selectively recalling information about the program. In fact, in both cases the selectively recalled information was exactly the same; the only difference was in an introductory statement that gave background information about the speaker. By measuring participants' memories of the initially studied information, it was found that the participants' memories (Princeton students) were shaped to a larger extend by the Princeton speaker than by the Yale speaker, likely because of the shared identity between the speaker and the listener. Horizontal peer-to-peer mnemonic influence has been widely investigated in psychology. There is evidence of this influence between pairs of strangers and intimate couples (Stone et al., 2013), gender-consistent and gender-inconsistent pairs (Barber & Mather, 2012), and attitudinally consistent and inconsistent pairs (Coman & Hirst, 2015). This work has greatly expanded the scope of psychological research to real-world consequential events that are emotionally charged. Despite significant progress, several unanswered research questions on this topic remain: What conditions might lead to maximal mnemonic impact in social exchanges? Is an audio recording of a speaker as impactful as a video of a speaker? Is passive exposure to a speaker as impactful as interactive exchanges between speaker and listener?

Importantly, our memories are shaped not just by contact with individuals who are close in their social circles. In vertical social influence, the impact is unidirectional and takes the form of top-down influence from public sources of information, such as politicians, pundits, and celebrities, to receptive audiences. A burgeoning literature has investigated the nature of this influence on people's beliefs and memories. In a study aimed at causally establishing the impact of newspaper articles on people's conversations, King et al. (2017) convinced 48 small media outlets throughout the United States to publish certain newspaper articles at random intervals over 5 years. The topics addressed in these articles ranged from race to immigration, climate, and food policy, among others. The findings revealed that this intervention increased social media discussions on the particular topic published in the newspaper article by more than 60% relative to a non-intervention baseline. In a more focused investigation of the psychological processes involved in vertical influence, Stone et al. (2020) used a naturalistic event involving a speech by the king of Belgium to assess the impact he had on the audience. In a design that measured people's evaluation of nationally relevant topics both before and after the speech, the results showed that topics mentioned by the king in his speech gained prominence in people's minds, whereas unaddressed topics became less important, in a manner consistent with socially shared retrieval-induced forgetting.

Despite progress in exploring the impact of both horizontal and vertical transmission processes, several areas need further investigation. One of which is the interaction between vertical and horizontal transmission of memories. Elites activate certain memories from the past, which then result in widespread conversation in people's social networks (Katz & Lazarsfeld, 1955). The limited psychological research on this topic has been conducted in fairly controlled laboratory experiments and was devoid of the charged political dimensions that activate memories in the service of collective action (see Coman & Hirst, 2012). This brings to the fore another underinvestigated area in the psychology of collective memory: the activation of memories during periods of conflict and intergroup violence. Slobodan Milošević, the Serbian president during the 1990s, was renowned for using historical events to mobilize identities, a strategy that led to intense periods of violence in the Balkans and resulted in hundreds of thousands of deaths among the warring factions (Holbrooke, 1999) (Figure 19.2). And this is by no means isolated to this particular conflict. It is a frequently employed strategy by authoritarian leaders throughout the world, from Malawi (Posner, 2004) to India (Varshney, 2005) and the United States (Levitsky & Ziblat, 2018). The psychological processes through which memories are used to mobilize identities and action are not properly understood in their real-world context.

Figure 19.2 Slobodan Milošević, the former president of Yugoslavia, speaking at Kosovo Polje in 1989. This event commemorated the Battle of Kosovo that took place in 1389, lost by the Serbs to the Ottoman Empire. The speech increased ethnic tensions between Serbians and Albanians and gave a preview of the civil war that would ensue in the Balkans during the following decade. Milošević, a Serbian, referred to the possibility of "armed battles" in Yugoslavia in the face of pressures from the different regions to become autonomous.

Collective Memories as Dynamic Phenomena

One of the critical characteristics of collective memories is their dynamical nature. Because individual memories are susceptible to social influence, as argued in the previous section, it follows that collective memories are in continuous flux, depending on various factors. These dynamics could be triggered by current public events, commemorations, and public sources of information, such as mass media and social media.

One fruitful area of psychological research that could serve as a springboard for understanding the emergence of collective memory is the burgeoning literature on the effect of communication on memory (Hirst & Echterhoff, 2012). This literature is concerned with the phenomenon that is of interest here—that is, the social transmission of group-relevant memories. Scholars pursuing this line of research often examine instances in which people have discussions with one another about their shared past experiences or mutual knowledge. These interactions can selectively reinforce some and weaken other aspects of the conversational partners' memories. By reshaping the two interactants' memories, these conversations lead to increased similarity between their mnemonic representations. Collective memory thus grows out of a dynamic system that fundamentally depends on communication (Coman, 2015; see also Chapter 20, this volume). Although researchers are beginning to understand the factors moderating communicative influences on memory, critical areas remain underdeveloped (Hirst & Echterhoff, 2012).

First, current investigations are almost exclusively focused on communicative influence on memory at a dyadic level. Existing research examines how communication initiated by one individual can shape the memories of another (Cuc et al., 2007). Research has shown, however, that one cannot explore collective-level phenomena by simply studying isolated dyadic or small group interactions (Epstein, 2007). It is essential to investigate the mechanisms by which the communicative influences at a dyadic level influence the formation of collective memories in larger communities. Recent research provides the theoretical and methodological framework to explore these phenomena in fully mapped social networks (Coman et al., 2016). There is, however, no programmatic investigation that connects micro-level and macro-level processes in a way that could be constructive for understanding nationalism.

It is speculated that the properties governing memory transmission at a local level (i.e., within dyads) bear on the formation of collective memories in larger communities (Roediger & Abel, 2015). Complex interactions and exchanges occurring across a community might mask any effect observed when examining two conversing individuals. Recent research demonstrated that the mnemonic alignment processes triggered during conversations do indeed lead to the emergence of collective memories in small, 10-member, lab-created communities (Coman et al., 2016). Participants first learned category–exemplar pairs about four American Peace Corps volunteers, and they then individually recollected the information in a pre-conversational individual recall. Following this individual recall phase, participants engaged in a series of sequential computer-mediated dyadic interactions as part of 10-member networked communities to jointly remember the initially presented information. In a final post-conversational individual recall phase, participants again individually recalled the initially presented information (Figure 19.3). By computing the pre-conversational and post-conversational

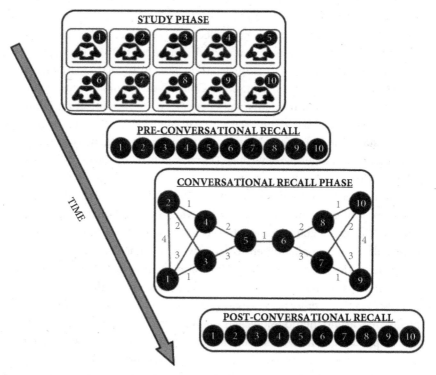

Figure 19.3 The experimental paradigm undertaken to explore the formation of collective memory in social networks. Circles represent participants, and links represent conversations. Red numbers indicate the sequence of conversational interactions.

community-wide mnemonic convergence, it was found that the reinforcement and suppression effects triggered during joint remembering impacted which memories became central to the collective memories of the community and which ones became peripheral. This research constitutes one of the first mechanistic investigations of the emergence of collective memories, providing both the theoretical and the methodological framework for exploring collective memories in more politically charged environments.

Collective Remembering as Motivated Remembering

One important lacuna in the collective memory literature concerns people's motivations during remembering. To understand the formation of collective memories in the real world, one needs to consider how people's motivations affect what they focus on, what they remember, and what they communicate (Higgins & Kruglanski, 2000; Jost et al., 2003; Middleton & Edwards, 1990). Although meaningful progress has been made on this topic (Eitam et al., 2013), there has been no systematic investigation of these processes with regard to the formation of collective memory.

People's motivations have been found to affect what they attend to and what they subsequently remember in an effort to maintain self-continuity (Bluck & Liao, 2013; Sani, 2014). At an individual level, research on mnemonic neglect shows that people tend to selectively forget information that is inconsistent with a positive self-image (Green & Sedikides, 2004; Saunders, 2013). More relevant for our interests in the communication of group-relevant information, individuals' motivations have been found to influence what they decide to communicate and, in turn, how communication affects their memories (Echterhoff et al., 2009). Mirroring these individual-level effects, the intergroup dynamics literature has provided convincing evidence that people tend to focus on (Darley & Gross, 1983; Gaertner & Dovidio, 2005), remember (Fyock & Stangor, 1994), and communicate (Lyons & Kashima, 2003) information that is favorable to one's in-group and unfavorable to out-group members.

Regarding intergroup dynamics, people's motivations drastically affect what they decide to communicate. For instance, a large literature on motivated remembering shows that people do not communicate all they are capable of communicating. Rather, motivated remembering could be seen as an interplay between two complementary strategies: motivated recall and motivated avoidance. On the one hand, individuals tend to remember information that is casting one's group in a positive light and out-groups in a negative light (Fiske, 2003). On the other hand, individuals tend to avoid remembering group-relevant information that is potentially identity threatening, such as past in-group wrongdoings or positive out-group behaviors (Bandura, 1999; Thompson et al., 1997). Rotella and Richeson (2013) have shown, for instance, that American participants who studied a story about the atrocities committed by early colonizers on Native Americans remembered fewer atrocities if the colonizers were labeled as "early Americans" than if they were labeled as "European settlers." This makes it critical, then, for a research program focused on understanding the effect of communication on memory to be concerned not only with what is discussed but also, possibly more important, what is avoided during conversational exchanges. This interplay between motivated recall and avoidance, I argue, meaningfully impacts the formation of collective memories and, thus, needs to be explored more thoroughly.

Motivation—and the communicative context that elicits these motives—may play a key role in modulating SSRIF. Following Echterhoff et al. (2009), Coman and colleagues have shown that relational motives affect the degree to which communication influences memory. As described previously, Princeton students listening to an audio recording of another Princeton student experienced more SSRIF than Princeton students listening to a Yale student. Because the participants were motivated to relate to the Princeton speaker, they were more likely to concurrently retrieve the information with that speaker (for a gender-similarity effect, see Barber & Mather, 2012). To support this conjecture, Coman and Hirst (2015) showed that when participants were primed to think of themselves more generally as students, SSRIF was found regardless of the college affiliation of the speaker.

More relevant for the current chapter, motivated remembering was found to affect the extent to which people forget information following conversational remembering. In other words, when people communicate about the past, they often retrieve information in the service of what they want to accomplish. If they want to defend their group from accusations of violence perpetrated against another group, they will retrieve information about what the other group might have done to deserve the aggression. We reasoned that in situations involving in-group–perpetrated atrocities, in order to morally disengage from one's group responsibility, individuals often emphasize actions that could justify those atrocities. Coman et al. (2014) asked American participants to study stories about four soldiers who were located in Afghanistan. Each soldier's story contained both atrocities committed by the soldier (e.g., water-boarded an Afghani insurgent) and potential justifications for such atrocities (e.g., insurgent withheld information about an upcoming terrorist attack). In a subsequent selective practice phase, participants saw a video of another supposed participant selectively retrieving only the atrocities committed by two of the four soldiers. Finally, all participants were asked to individually remember the initially presented information. Based on previous research on SSRIF, we would expect that participants would forget justifications that were related to the atrocities mentioned in the video (i.e., justifications that were part of the same soldier story as the atrocities). And indeed, we found this pattern when the American participants were told that the soldiers were Afghani. Importantly, when the American participants were told that the soldiers were American, they did not experience forgetting of these justifications. In other words, when the perpetrator was part of the participant's group, the participant was motivated to covertly remember the unmentioned justifications during the listening task, and this motivated retrieval eliminated the typical SSRIF effect.

These findings are highly relevant in the context of nationalism. The implication of this research is that when people remember group-relevant memories, the social and motivation forces around communicating about these memories will accelerate the degree to which the community converges on a similar representation of the past. Often, this representation is sanitized of any wrongdoing and built around a glorious past.

Future Research Trajectories

A number of research trajectories could further our understanding of the impact of collective memories on nationalism. I identify several such trajectories and note that this list is not meant to be exhaustive. Rather, it captures general directions that constitute natural developments for psychological investigations of collective memory.

A Programmatic Study of Narratives

Narratives are vehicles that transmit information. Given their effectiveness in the communicative process, any meaningful investigation of collective memories in the context of nationalism would be well-served by undertaking an empirical exploration of how narratives propagate in social networks and how they motivate people to engage in action (Wertsch, 2008; see Chapter 22, this volume). The story of Mohammed al-Durrah is one that stuck with a population that was oppressed for decades. Given its emotional core, it was amplified during the transmission process, and it motivated people to take action. These processes received little attention in psychological treatments of collective memories, mainly because formalizing an empirical investigation of how narratives impact minds and societies is not a trivial task. Recent attempts in this domain have the potential to answer several critical questions. Are there narrative structures that make for better "vehicles" for information? That is, do they facilitate information propagation through connected communities? Are different cultures differentially sensitive to various narrative structures, depending, for instance, on their schematic narrative templates (see Chapter 22, this volume)? Are Bosnians more likely to encode, remember, and propagate stories of war and conflict compared to Bulgarians?, given the different historical contexts they experienced. Are there generational differences in propagating such stories?

Collective Future Thought

A well-established literature has showed that projecting into the future is dependent on how one remembers the past (Schacter, 2001). For instance, the specificity of how one remembers their past is highly correlated with the specificity one employs to imagine the future. Similarly, the tendency to remember positive autobiographical memories is correlated with how positively one imagines the future (Schacter et al., 2017). In the context of nations, however, there is very little research on how individuals build on the nation's past to imagine its future (but for an example, see Topcu & Hirst, 2020; see also Szpunar & Szpunar, 2016). Both specificity and positivity should impact how one remembers and imagines a nation's past and future. Horizontal transmission of specific and positive collective memories should lead citizens to imagine a specific and positive future, which could play a beneficial role in a national project aimed at building national identity.

Accuracy of Collective Memories

The psychological research on the formation of collective memories has mainly focused on how much people remember from a list of historical events in the static approach (Schuman & Scott, 1989) or how convergent people's memories become after conversations in the dynamical approach (Coman et al., 2016). Little research has explored the accuracy of these collective memories. It is well known that communities often misremember events from the past in self-serving and biased ways (Yamashiro & Roediger, 2021; see Chapter 11, this volume). Consider, for example, the story of Giovanni Palatucci, an Italian police official during World War II, praised as the Italian Schindler. He was credited with saving thousands of Jewish people from extermination and forced migration, culminating in Pope John Paul II's official recognition as a martyr. His life and legacy have been celebrated for decades in Israel, New York, and Italy. In effect, as the examination of more than 700 official documents from the era makes clear, he was a Nazi collaborator and even participated in identifying Jewish people for deportation to extermination camps. It appears that his uncle, a Bishop, petitioned the Italian government to issue a pension to Palatucci's parents following his death and in the process constructed a myth that many Italians were eager to adopt and propagate (Cohen, 2013).

Collective Memory and Action

A neglected area in psychological investigations of collective memories is how they trigger collective action in real-world contexts. I note that this trajectory is difficult to explore empirically, especially if one wants to do field research. The difficulty of conducting these studies should not, however, deter scholars from empirical investigations on this topic. Case studies of these processes reveal the richness of both theoretical and pragmatic insights one could derive (Bar-Tal, 2013). Consider, for instance, the case of Armenia, a nation whose main historical narrative involves the tragic displacement and genocide of its people in the early 20th century by the Ottomans. This plight crystalized in the collective memory of the nation through disputed accounts by the Turkish authorities, yearly commemorations, and political efforts to have the genocide recognized by international actors that energized Armenian diasporas. It solidified the identity of Armenians, and it created a type of national allegiance that, scholars speculate, provided an important advantage for Armenia during the Armenian–Azerbaijan war in the 1990s (Shain & Barth, 2003). In other words, the dispute around the genocide led to more than simply contradictory perspectives on the past; it led to the mobilization of identity and, in turn, to people's willingness to fight for their nation.

Psychological investigations of the processes involved in the mobilization of identities and engagement in collective action are much needed as part of the conversation across the social sciences on this topic.

Conclusion

Psychological investigations of the formation of collective memories have burgeoned during the past decade. Both theoretical and methodological developments have made it easier to ask sophisticated questions about how collective memories form and how they change. Time is ripe for these developments to be calibrated both with other social sciences, which have deep traditions of studying phenomena that are central to collective memory, and with more pragmatic trajectories that include its role in identity mobilization and collective action. Such calibration would likely result in constructive dialogues with political scientists interested in nationalism studies, as well as with practitioners interested in conflict resolution (see Chapter 17, this volume).

An example of an area in which such cross-disciplinary interactions could be constructive is the dispute in nationalism studies involving the origins of ethnic conflict. Approaches that view groups as fixed entities, with a primordial core in ancient history (i.e., primordialist approaches), have a certain representation of current conflict among groups. Ancient hatreds hardened over many generations lie at the core of such conflicts (Bayar, 2009). And so existing conflicts, such as the tremendous ethnic violence that occurred during the Balkan Wars in the early 1990s, have their origin, primordialists claim, centuries earlier with Ottoman conquests of Slavic territories (Kaplan, 1993). An alternative—more credible—perspective (i.e., constructivist approaches) views groups as flexible entities that change over time and whose values, memories, and symbols are continuously in flux. This approach posits that conflicts between groups have their origins in the modern interests of political elites who mobilize people's identities to serve the interests of the elites (Gellner, 1983). Needless to say, endorsing one or the other approach to intergroup conflict results in different prescriptions for solving conflicts: ethnic partition in primordialist approaches or reconciliation attempts and international mediation in constructivist approaches (Sambanis & Schulhofer-Wohl, 2009). As an aside, Bill Clinton's 1993 inauguration speech revealed that he endorsed an ancient hatreds theory of conflict, which, scholars speculate, made his administration hesitant to intervene in Rwanda during the 1994 genocide. Modern psychological research on collective memories has the potential to inform this theoretical dispute in nationalism studies while at the same time offer pragmatic prescriptions to both politicians who aim to minimize the negative effects of conflict and negotiators on the ground.

References

Abel, M., & Roediger, H. L., III. (2018). The testing effect in a social setting: Does retrieval practice benefit a listener? *Journal of Experimental Psychology: Applied, 24*(3), 347–359.

Anderson, M. C., Bjork, R. A., & Bjork, E. L. (1994). Remembering can cause forgetting: Retrieval dynamics in long-term memory. *Journal of Experimental Psychology: Learning, Memory, and Cognition, 20*, 1063–1087.

Barber, S. J., & Mather, M. (2012). Forgetting in context: The effects of age, emotion, and social factors on retrieval-induced forgetting. *Memory & Cognition, 40*(6), 874–888.

Bar-Tal, D. (2013). *Intractable conflicts: Socio-psychological foundations and dynamics.* Cambridge University Press.

Beckerman, G. (2007, October 3). The unpeaceful rest of Mohammed Al-Dura. *Columbia Journalism Review.*

Bandura, A. (1999). Moral disengagement in the perpetration of inhumanities. *Personality and Social Psychology Review, 3*, 193–209.

Bayar, M. (2009). Reconsidering primordialism: An alternative approach to the study of ethnicity. *Ethnic and Racial Studies, 32*(9), 1–20.

Bluck, S., & Liao, H. N. (2013). I was therefore I am: Creating self-continuity through remembering our personal past. *International Journal of Reminiscence and Life Review, 1*(1), 7–12.

Cohen, P. (2013, June 20). Italian praised for saving Jews is now seen as Nazi collaborator. *The New York Times.*

Coman, A. (2015). The psychology of collective memory. In J. D. Wright (Editor-in-Chief), *International encyclopedia of the social & behavioral sciences* (2nd ed., Vol. 4, pp. 188–193). Elsevier.

Coman, A., Brown, A. D., Koppel, J., & Hirst, W. (2009). Collective memory from a psychological perspective. *International Journal of Politics, Culture and Society, 22*(2), 125–141.

Coman, A., & Hirst, W. (2012). Cognition through a social network: The propagation of practice and induced forgetting effects. *Journal of Experimental Psychology: General, 141*(2), 321–336.

Coman, A., & Hirst, W. (2015). Relational motives and socially shared retrieval induced forgetting: The role of social group membership. *Journal of Experimental Psychology: General, 144*, 717–722.

Coman, A., Manier, D., & Hirst, W. (2009). Forgetting the unforgettable through conversation: Socially-shared retrieval-induced forgetting of 9/11 memory. *Psychological Science, 20*, 627–633.

Coman, A., Momennejad, I., Geana, A., & Drach, D. R. (2016). Mnemonic convergence in social networks: The emergent properties of cognition at a collective level. *Proceedings of National Academy of Sciences of the USA, 113*(29), 8171–8176.

Coman, A., Stone, C., Castano, E., & Hirst, W. (2014). Justifying atrocities: The effect of moral-disengagement strategies on socially shared retrieval-induced forgetting. *Psychological Science, 25*, 1281–1285.

Cook, D. (2007). *Martyrdom in Islam*. Cambridge University Press.

Cuc, A., Koppel, J., & Hirst, W. (2007). Silence is not golden: A case for socially shared retrieval-induced forgetting. *Psychological Science, 18*(8), 727–733.

Darley, J. M., & Gross, P. H. (1983). A hypothesis-confirming bias in labeling effects. *Journal of Personality and Social Psychology, 44*, 20–33.

DeSoto, K. A., & Roediger, H. L. (2019). Remembering the presidents. *Current Directions in Psychological Science, 28*(2), 138–144.

Dudai, Y. (2004). The neurobiology of consolidations or how stable is the Engram? *Annual Review of Psychology, 55*, 51–86.

Echterhoff, G., Higgins, E. T., & Levine, J. M. (2009). Shared reality: Experiencing commonality with others' inner states about the world. *Perspectives on Psychological Science, 4*, 496–521.

Eitam, B., Miele, D. B., & Higgins, E. T. (2013). Motivated remembering: Remembering as accessibility and accessibility as motivational relevance. In D. E. Carlston (Ed.), *The Oxford handbook of social cognition* (pp. 463–475). Oxford University Press.

Epstein, J. (2007). *Generative social science: Studies in agent-based computational modeling*. Princeton University Press.

Fiske, S. T. (2003). *Social beings: A core motives approach to social psychology*. Wiley.

Fivush, R., & Nelson, K. (2004). Culture and language in the emergence of autobiographical memory. *Psychological Science, 15*(9), 573–577.

Fyock, J., & Stangor, C. (1994). The role of memory biases in stereotype maintenance. *British Journal of Social. Psychology, 33*(3), 331–343.

Gaertner, S. L., & Dovidio, J. F. (2005). Understanding and addressing contemporary racism: From aversive racism to the common ingroup identity model. *Journal of Social Issues, 61*, 613–639.

Gellner, E. (1983). *Nations and nationalism*. Basil Blackwell.

Green, J. D., & Sedikides, C. (2004). Retrieval selectivity in the processing of self-referent information: Testing the boundaries of self-protection. *Self and Identity, 3*, 69–80.

Higgins, E. T., & Kruglanski, A. W. (2000). *Motivational science: Social and personality perspectives*. Psychology Press.

Hirst, W., & Echterhoff, G. (2012). Remembering in conversations: The social sharing and reshaping of memories. *Annual Review of Psychology, 63*(1), 55–79.

Hirst, W., Phelps, E. A., Buckner, R. L., Budson, A. E., Cuc, A., Gabrieli, J. D., Johnson, M. K., Lyle, K. B., Lustig, C., Mather, M., Meksin, R., Mitchell, K. J., Ochsner, K. N., Schacter, D. L., Simons, J. S., & Vaidya, C. J. (2009). Long-term memory for the terrorist attack of September 11: Flashbulb memories, event memories, and the factors that influence their retention. *Journal of Experimental Psychology: General, 138*, 161–176.

Hirst, W., Yamashiro, J., & Coman, A. (2018). Collective memory from a psychological perspective. *Trends in Cognitive Sciences, 22*(5), 438–451.

Holbrooke, R. (1999). *To end a war*. Knopf.

Jost, J. T., Glaser, J., Kruglanski, A. W., & Sulloway, F. J. (2003). Political conservatism as motivated social cognition. *Psychological Bulletin, 129*, 339–375.

Kaplan, R. (1993). *Balkan ghosts*. Picador Publishing House.
Karpicke, J. D., & Roediger, H. L., III. (2007). Repeated retrieval during learning is the key to long-term retention. *Journal of Memory and Language, 57*(2), 151–162.
King, G., Schneer, B., & White, A. (2017). How the news media activate public expression and influence national agendas. *Science, 358*(6364), 776–780.
Levitsky, D., & Ziblat, S. (2018). *How democracies die*. Crown.
Loftus, E. (2005). Planting misinformation in the human mind: A 30-year investigation of the malleability of memory. *Learning & Memory, 12*, 361–366.
Luhmann, C. C., & Rajaram, S. (2015). Memory transmission in small groups and large networks: An agent-based model. *Psychological Science, 26*(12), 1909–1917.
Lyons, A., & Kashima, Y. (2003). How are stereotypes maintained through communication? The influence of stereotype sharedness. *Journal of Personality and Social Psychology, 85*, 989–1005.
Middleton, D., & Edwards, D. (Eds.). (1990). *Collective remembering*. Sage.
Momennejad, I., Duker, A., & Coman, A. (2019). Bridge ties bind collective memories. *Nature Communications, 10*, 1578–1586.
Posner, D. N. (2004). The political salience of cultural difference: Why Chewas and Tumbukas are allies in Zambia and adversaries in Malawi. *American Political Science Review, 98*(4), 529–545.
Rajaram, S., & Pereira-Pasarin, L. P. (2010). Collaborative memory: Cognitive research and theory. Perspectives in Psychological Science, 5, 649–663.
Roediger, H. L., & Abel, M. (2015). Collective memory: A new arena of cognitive study. *Trends in Cognitive Sciences, 19*(7), 359–361.
Rotella, K. N., & Richeson, J. A. (2013). Body of guilt: Using embodied cognition to mitigate backlash to reminders of personal & ingroup wrongdoing. *Journal of Experimental Social Psychology, 49*(4), 643–650.
Sambanis, N., & Schulhofer-Wohl, J. (2009). What's in a line? Is partition a solution to civil war? *International Security, 34*(2), 82–118.
Sani, F. (Ed.). (2014). *Self-continuity: Individual and collective perspectives*. Psychology Press.
Saunders, J. (2013). Selective memory bias for self-threatening memories in trait anxiety. *Cognition & Emotion, 27*(1), 21–36.
Schacter, D. L. (2001). *The seven sins of memory: How the mind forgets and remembers*. Houghton Mifflin.
Schacter, D. L., Benoit, R. G., & Szpunar, K. K. (2017). Episodic future thinking: Mechanisms and functions. *Current Opinion in Behavioral Sciences, 17*, 41–50.
Schuman, H., & Scott, J. (1989). Generations and collective memories. *American Sociological Review, 54*, 359–381.
Shain, Y., & Barth, A. (2003). Diasporas and international relations theory. *International Organization, 57*, 449–479.
Stone, C. B., Barnier, A. J., Sutton, J., & Hirst, W. (2010). Building consensus about the past: Schema consistency and convergence in socially-shared retrieval-induced forgetting. *Memory, 18*, 170–184.
Stone, C. B., Barnier, A. J., Sutton, J., & Hirst, W. (2013). Forgetting our personal past: Socially shared retrieval-induced forgetting of autobiographical memories. *Journal of Experimental Psychology: General, 142*(4), 1084–1099.
Stone, C. B., Coman, A., Brown, A. D., Koppel, J., & Hirst, W. (2012). Toward a science of silence: The consequences of leaving a memory unsaid. *Perspectives on Psychological Science, 7*(1), 39–53. https://doi.org/10.1177/1745691611427303

Stone, C. B., Luminet, O., Jay, A. C. V., Licata, L., Klein, O., & Hirst, W. (2020, January). Do public speeches induce "collective" forgetting? The Belgian King's 2012 summer speech as a case study. *Memory Studies*. doi:10.1177/1750698019900949

Sutton, J., Harris, C. B., Keil, P. G., & Barnier, A. J. (2010). The psychology of memory, extended cognition, and socially distributed remembering. *Phenomenology and the Cognitive Sciences*, 9(4), 521–560.

Szpunar, P. M., & Szpunar, K. K. (2016). Collective future thought: Concept, function, and implications for collective memory studies. *Memory Studies*, 9(4), 376–389.

Thompson, J., Morton, J., & Fraser, L. (1997). Memories for the Marchioness. *Memory*, 5(5), 615–638.

Topcu, M. N., & Hirst, W. (2020). Remembering a nation's past to imagine its future: The role of event specificity, phenomenology, valence, and perceived agency. *Journal of Experimental Psychology: Learning, Memory, and Cognition*, 46(3), 563–579.

Varshney, A. (2005). An electoral theory of communal riots? *Economic and Political Weekly*, 40(39), 4219–4224.

Vlasceanu, M., Enz, K., & Coman, A. (2018). Cognition in a social context: A social-interactionist approach to emergent phenomena. *Current Directions in Psychological Science*, 27(5), 369–377.

Wertsch, J. V. (2008). The narrative organization of collective memory. *Ethos*, 36(1), 120–135.

Wertsch, J. V., & Roediger, H. L., III. (2008). Collective memory: Conceptual foundations and theoretical approaches. *Memory*, 16(3), 318–326.

Yamashiro, J., & Roediger, H.L., III. (2021). Biased collective memories and historical overclaiming: An availability heuristic account. *Memory & Cognition*, 49(2), 311–322.

20
How Collective Memories Emerge
A Cognitive Psychological Perspective

Suparna Rajaram, Tori Peña, and Garrett D. Greeley

Mary Anne Evans, whom we know as the great 19th-century British novelist George Eliot, asked, "What do we live for, if it is not to make life less difficult to each other?" (Eliot, 1873, p. 253). Indeed, the importance of connectedness and its profound consequences for the well-being of families, communities, as well as nations has occupied many thinkers and writers.

The month of May, which is when the National Memory conference took place in 2019 at Washington University in St. Louis and this chapter began to take shape, is routinely marked by commencement speeches at U.S. colleges and universities. A milestone in the lives of students, commencements mark a celebration of hard-earned credentials and an occasion to build a collective representation of a memorable day with friends and family—an occasion painfully lost along with many others in 2020 to the COVID-19 pandemic. Commencements are also the occasions to collectively reflect on ways in which college graduates may go forth to make our world a better place. In his now famous Kenyon College commencement speech in 2005, the great, late American author David Foster Wallace spoke of the meaning of freedom: "The really important kind of freedom involves attention and awareness and discipline, and being able truly to care about other people and to sacrifice for them over and over in myriad . . . ways every day. . . . That is real freedom." Wallace laid out the blueprint of empathy to forge social interconnectedness, where we use that cognitive ability called imagination to understand what it is like to live in another's shoes and leverage that imagination to be of use to others.

Social connectedness and social connections are thus fundamental ways by which we imagine our world to come together. These shared experiences and stories are, indeed, the memories that glue our social lives. Friends and families and, at much larger scales, societies and nations develop such shared

Suparna Rajaram, Tori Peña, and Garrett D. Greeley, *How Collective Memories Emerge* In: *National Memories.* Edited by: Henry L. Roediger and James V. Wertsch, Oxford University Press. © Oxford University Press 2022.
DOI: 10.1093/oso/9780197568675.003.0020

memory narratives in the service of personal, social, and national goals that bind us together. In our world of growing social connections, both in face-to-face interactions and increasingly on social media platforms, we connect and share information not only with those whom we know but also with strangers. We learn, remember, and share information in these varied contexts, thus constructing our collective narratives both in small groups and in large networks. As the theme of this book asks, how is it then that in this era of globalization we are seeing a rise of populism?

From a memory perspective, we might ask why collective memories emerge in different ways across groups. The concept of collective memory, proposed by sociologist Maurice Halbwachs (1925/1992, 1950/1980), holds an important key to understanding a rise of populism and the formation of national memories. As we note later in this chapter, collective memory has been since conceptualized in many ways across disciplines. In psychology, collective memory usually refers to the overlap in the information that all or most members of a group remember or that all or most members of a group forget. We have adopted this definition to empirically test how cognitive operations shape social transmission of information and emergence of different collective narratives. Our aim in this approach is to understand complex, large-scale group memory phenomena in terms of well-grounded cognitive psychological processes of individual memory.

Collaborative Remembering

How do collective memories emerge? A wide range of perspectives have emerged across disciplines to answer this question. Our approach provides a complementary alternative to the views that collective memories arise in response to top-down processes, often enforced by some authority or by governing or community clusters formed around strong identities. In our work, we ask, what does the individual bring to these situations in terms of their personal past (which is often idiosyncratic), their individual cognitive schemas that develop in response to this personal history, their processing preferences, and the specific learning conditions that bear upon the process of collective memory formation? How does the complex set of cognitive processes that operate within the individual, and across social interactions, interact with the top-down and external informational forces to give rise to similarities in memory representations across a people? Our research explores the roles of the active processing and agency of the individual, their idiosyncratic cognitive histories, and their processing constraints in the context of social transmission of information in which the individual engages. In these ways, our person-driven approach offers a contrasting and complementary alternative to the view that collective memory emerges as a consequence of the top-down forces operating in a situation and proposes a bottom-up processing framework to understand the formation of collective memory.

As cognitive experimental psychologists, we are interested in a key antecedent process, namely collaborative remembering—when a group of people recall the past together—to understand the emergence of collective memory. How does collaborative remembering in groups reshape the memory of each group member and that of the group as a collective?

In psychological research, an interest in the social influences on memory can be traced back to Bartlett's (1932) book on remembering. Bartlett described a series of studies that were usually descriptive in nature and that utilized naturalistic materials. Using this ecological approach, he highlighted the social and reconstructive nature of memory. This approach can be contrasted with more than a century of memory research in cognitive psychology that has been marked by Ebbinghaus's (1885) approach, which advocated strict experimental control. This highly influential approach led to a focus on the study of individual memory ability where great experimental control could be exercised. Our research group has leveraged the theoretical and empirical advances from this extensive body of work to bring together these distinct perspectives and answer questions about the process of memory convergence at a group level. In our research, we examine how the cognitive constituents operating at the individual level give rise to shared memory representations at the collective level (Rajaram, 2011, 2017). We conduct laboratory experiments to understand the process of memory reconstruction in social settings and to specify how the process of collaborative remembering brings about these changes in memory.

We examine the nature of memory typically at two stages, during collaboration and post-collaboration. Testing the nature of memory during collaboration is obviously relevant. However, the second, post-collaborative stage is just as relevant because it reveals the changes that come about in memory because of prior collaboration, even after those social influences are removed. Together, the process of collaborative remembering and its consequences on post-collaborative memory provide a cognitive blueprint for how social influences change individual memories of group members and consequently shape the collective memory of a group.

Are Two Heads Better Than One?

Survey responses have documented a popular and intransigent belief that two heads are better than one when we try to remember the past (Dixon & de Frias, 2007; Dixon et al., 1998; Henkel & Rajaram, 2011). But is this belief true? The answer to this question is far from simple. A complex interplay of cognitive operations come into play when people recall the past together with others. Understanding this interplay can help unlock how the cognitive architecture shapes memory transmission. These answers can, in turn, shed light on how people develop a shared memory representation and why different groups of people can develop different memory representations for the same experience.

In this chapter, we sample from our empirical work to illustrate the cognitive processes that underlie the rise of collective memory. In particular, we focus on the cognitive operations of disruption, forgetting, augmentation, error pruning, and social contagion in social settings to understand how collaborative remembering shapes memory reconstruction. The studies utilize experimental tools that fall under the umbrella of the collaborative memory paradigm. Although our work does not directly interrogate national memories, it identifies the cognitive constituents that give rise to collective memory. Because national memories in many ways reflect collective memory of different groups of people, several elements of our research identify the conditions that can inform how different groups may come to hold different memories of the past.

Testing Collaborative Memory

The prototypical experimental paradigm we have adapted from Weldon and Bellinger (1997) involves three basic steps: (1) an initial study phase in which participants are exposed to information they have to recall later, (2) a delay period that is usually short but can vary in length depending on the goals of the study, and (3) one or more sequential memory tests where participants recall the information they saw before. We have reported an expanded description of these phases in other writings (Rajaram, in press; Rajaram & Pereira-Pasarin, 2010) and provide a brief description here to capture the essential features. In the study phase, participants typically work alone. Researchers have used a variety of study information for participants to view, including word lists, pictures, films, and autobiographical experiences (Basden et al., 2000; Blumen & Rajaram, 2008; Choi et al., 2017; Maswood & Rajaram, 2019; Meudell et al., 1995; Wessel et al., 2015). The delay period usually involves working alone on an unrelated activity such as recalling the names of U.S. presidents, cities, countries, and so on. Finally, the memory tests call for participants to work again alone or work in groups. In our experiments, we have used group sizes similar to those of other psychological experiments reported in the literature, with small groups consisting of two or three but occasionally including larger sizes (e.g., Basden et al., 2000; Choi et al., 2014, 2017; Coman et al., 2016; Geana et al., 2019; Thorley & Dewhurst, 2007; Yamashiro & Hirst, 2014). In our studies, groups usually consist of strangers in order to control for idiosyncratic differences in familiarity among the group members, but researchers can manipulate the nature of the relationship using this paradigm as some have by testing friends, partners, or groups of experts working together (Andersson, 2001; Andersson & Rönnberg, 1995; Johansson et al., 2000, 2005; Meade et al., 2009).

Does Collaboration Improve or Impair Memory?

We mentioned the belief people hold that collaboration benefits memory. Yet, contrary to intuition, individuals contribute fewer memories when working in groups to recall past information than when working alone. The former groups are called collaborative groups, and the recall performance of these groups is usually compared to that of a collection of people known as nominal groups or groups in name only. Nominal groups are composed of an equal number of individuals as the collaborative groups, but instead of working together as members of a collaborative group do, nominal group members work alone to recall the past information. To compute nominal group recall, the redundancies across these individual recall products are removed before pooling the recalls to compute the nominal group product. For example, in the case of triadic (three-person) nominal calculation, if Participant A reported "apple," "orange," and "strawberry," Participant B reported "apple," "orange," and "grape," and Participant C reported "apple" and "pear," the non-redundant pooled recall of the nominal group (by pooling the recall performance of Participants A–C) includes only five items: "apple," "orange," "strawberry," "grape," and "pear." This pooled product serves as the baseline and gives us an indication of the potential for what a collaborative group of equal size could recall. This comparison between the collaborative and nominal groups is more appropriate than comparing a collaborative group to a single individual because the number of group members is equated.

The outcome of interest here is that collaborative groups recall less than the nominal groups, a phenomenon known as *collaborative inhibition* in recall (Basden et al., 1997; Weldon & Bellinger, 1997). Although counterintuitive, collaborative inhibition in group recall has been replicated widely (for a meta-analytic review, see Marion & Thorley, 2016).

Why does collaborative remembering impair memory? It is not because people simply leave the job to others (Latané et al., 1979; Weldon et al., 2000). There are at least two cognitive reasons why people recall less in groups. First, listening to others' recall interferes with the preferred strategies people use for their own recall, and this disruption temporarily lowers recall. If each group member suffers from such retrieval disruption, the group on the whole recalls less (Basden et al., 1997). Second, listening to others not only disrupts an individual's retrieval strategies but also may weaken and inhibit memory representations, thus making these memories difficult to retrieve even when people are no longer in a group (Barber et al., 2015; Cuc et al., 2007; Hirst & Echterhoff, 2012). Recall loss during collaborative remembering can thus have both temporary and far-reaching consequences; people recover some of these memories later, but other memories get inhibited and are forgotten. Thus, memories change through disruption and forgetting.

What then drives the belief that two heads are better than one for memory? Despite the information loss in groups that we just described, this belief may also stem from performance, and the answer to the question lies in the operations of at least three mechanisms that come into play during collaboration. One such mechanism is *re-exposure*, in which listening to other group members recall information provides an opportunity to refresh one's own forgotten memories and increases the likelihood of remembering it later (Blumen & Rajaram, 2008; Rajaram & Pereira-Pasarin, 2007; Weldon & Bellinger, 1997). Interestingly, collaborative recall not only provides an opportunity to an individual to benefit from group members' recall but also provides an opportunity to augment memories through retrieval practice of information that this individual recalls to contribute to the group efforts. In our framework, we refer to this benefit of retrieval practice as *relearning through retrieval*. Thus, memories change through re-exposure and retrieval practice augmentation.

Like the re-exposure process that augments memory, the mechanism of *social contagion* is a similar idea, although it refers to incorporating false or erroneous information into one's own memory that others in the group reported during the collaboration phase (e.g., Maswood & Rajaram, 2018; Meade & Roediger, 2002; Roediger et al., 2001; Thorley & Dewhurst, 2007). Such errors creep into the memory representations of the listeners, who can then spread these errors to others with whom they later interact (e.g., Choi et al., 2017). Thus, memories change through social contagion errors.

Another process that may support intuitive beliefs about the benefits of collaborative remembering is known as *cross-cueing* (Meudell et al., 1992, 1995). Here, the speaker's recall serves as a cue to trigger memories in the listener, who is then able to remember forgotten memories through such cueing. This listener's recall in turn may similarly trigger the recall of forgotten memories in others participating in collaborative recall (Congleton & Rajaram, 2011; Takahashi & Saito, 2004). Thus, memories change through cross-cueing augmentation.

The subjective belief that collaboration helps memory may come from yet another process, one that is rather the opposite of augmentation and cross-cueing. It is the process of *error pruning* during collaborative remembering, where collaborating members correct one another's errors in recall. Such pruning improves memory accuracy for the individual members and for the group as a whole (Rajaram, 2011; Rajaram & Pereira-Pasarin, 2010; Takahashi, 2007; Thorley & Dewhurst, 2009; Weldon & Bellinger, 1997). Thus, memories change through mutual error corrections.

We opened this section with the question, how does remembering in groups reshape each group member's memories? Growing evidence points to the answer that collaborative remembering produces opposing effects on memory. Evidence shows that, on one hand, disruption, forgetting, and social contagion errors hurt memory accuracy, and on the other hand, re-exposure, cross-cueing, and error pruning improve memory accuracy. Memory reconstruction results from such opposing cognitive consequences of collaboration. Figure 20.1 depicts an integrative framework we have developed to map these and additional cognitive processes that come into play when people remember the past together with others.

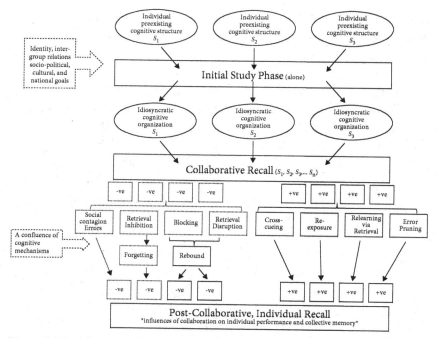

Figure 20.1 A framework to study collaborative memory. Positive and negative notations represent the opposing mechanisms during collaborative remembering. $S_1, S_2, \ldots S_n$ denote participants in experiments. Positive (i.e., +ve) and negative (i.e., −ve) notations represent improvement or impairment in recall. Revised from Rajaram and Pereira-Pasarin (2010) and adapted from Rajaram (in press).

We now turn to the second part of the question we asked at the outset: how do the cognitive mechanisms, activated by collaborative remembering, shape post-collaborative memories? In asking this question, we explore how memories converge across group members and how collective memories emerge as a consequence of collaborative remembering.

Emergence of Collective Memory

Collective memory has been conceptualized in a variety of ways across disciplines. This widespread interest in collective memory has led to a range of definitions that bear similarities and also differences (Hirst & Manier, 2008;

Wertsch, 2008; Wertsch & Roediger, 2008). In social sciences, at the crux of collective memory is the relationship between the collective identity of a group (e.g., nations and villages) and how group members remember their collective past (Olick, 1999; see Chapter 7, this volume).

In psychological research, explorations of collective memory are relatively recent, and here too, a range of approaches are emerging (Roediger & Abel, 2015). For example, some studies have used a survey approach to evaluate the collective memory representations of World War II events across countries (Abel et al., 2019; Putnam et al., 2018; Roediger et al., 2019; Zaromb et al., 2014, 2018; see Chapters 10–12 and 22, this volume). Distinct from this approach, Roediger and DeSoto (2014) developed a memory task in which Americans were asked to recall all the U.S. presidents in their sequential order, to document collective forgetting of historically salient memories. Hirst and colleagues (e.g., Cuc et al., 2007; see Chapter 19, this volume) have used experimental paradigms to show that social sharing of memories can induce forgetting similar details and lead to memory convergence in the information that remains in the memories of conversing partners.

In our approach, we have used the collaborative memory paradigm as an experimental tool to study how individual memories are restructured through collaborative remembering and to uncover how collective memories are formed, shaped, reshaped, and maintained over time. Our goal has been to identify the cognitive building blocks of collective memory, where variables such as identity, goals, intergroup relations, and sociopolitical, cultural, and national goals may interact with the underlying cognitive architecture in collective memory formation (see Figure 20.1).

Measuring Collective Memory

As noted previously, experimental study of collective memory has been less concerned with identity and more with the contents of memory that people share. For the time being, we have taken the same approach in our work, where we measure collective memory as the sum of the information that all former group members remember and the information that all former group members forget. In some cases, collective memory represents the overlaps only in the remembered information or memory overlap across some but not all former group members, depending on the information being recalled and the level of recall it facilitates. Thus, collective memory represents convergence in the remembered and the forgotten information across those who previously collaborated.

Collaborative Remembering and Collective Memory

At the heart of our explorations about collective memory lies the following question: how does group collaboration facilitate the emergence of collective memory? As noted previously, when people remember the past together, they disrupt one another's memories, cause mutual forgetting, and implant their own memory errors in others. These memory deletions and implanted memory errors align memories. Memories also align through the process of augmentation and error correction, when group members re-expose and cross-cue one another to otherwise forgotten memories and correct one another's erroneous recollections. Of key interest here is the cascading effect of these dynamic changes in memory on the post-collaborative memories of those who previously interacted. In other words, through collaborative remembering, people develop a revised version of past events that becomes more aligned than before. Critically, this collective version persists in the individual accounts of the past even after people are no longer in the group setting.

We focus on four attributes of collective memory formation. We begin with a discussion of group configuration or who talks to whom. We then turn to the effects of group knowledge that we call information distribution—that is, who knows what in a group. The flow of information changes depending on who talks to whom, and the content of memory changes depending on who knows what in a group, altering the true and false memories at the collective level. Next, we discuss how repeated joint remembering changes not only the content of memory, or what people remember, but also the structure of memory—that is, how people organize their memories. As we describe later, memory structures represent the architecture of memory at a deeper level and can change group members' propensity for incorporating new memories in the future. Finally, we discuss the effects of joint remembering on modulating the emotional components of post-collaborative memories. We expand on these attributes in the following sections.

Who Talks to Whom and Who Knows What

The concepts of group configuration (i.e., who talks to whom) and information distribution (i.e., who knows what) capture the dynamic nature of real-world social contexts. Mnemonic consequences in these contexts often bring to mind patterns of information transmission in large social networks. However, small groups are particularly useful to consider here because they provide a tractable model to assess face-to-face, real-time information transmission with considerable precision. An example of this idea can be found in Bartlett's (1932) naturalistic study, in which he reported a powerful example of memory transformation when information transmits from one person to the next. In Bartlett's conversational chain, known as serial production, the first individual read a story ("War of the Ghosts"). This person's recall of the story served as learning material for a second individual, and then the second person's recall in turn served as learning material for the third individual, and so on. As versions of the story passed from one person to the next, the details were dropped and distorted and errors were inserted such that the story became increasingly truncated and distorted. In the end, the final version differed greatly from the original story. Roediger and colleagues recently tested this phenomenon with well-controlled study materials and found that not only does serial reproduction from person to person impair memory but also it leads to more forgetting and greater memory distortion compared to repeated reproduction by the same person (Roediger et al., 2014; the Deese–Roediger–McDermott or DRM study lists; Deese, 1959; Roediger & McDermott, 1995).

Who Talks to Whom

Even when all members of a group start out with exposure to the same information, group configuration by itself can exert powerful influences on memory transmission. Everyday variations in group configurations abound, making this a particularly interesting variable. People work with the same team or socialize with the same close others on a regular basis. At other times, people move in and out of social groups or work with different teams. On social media platforms, in some instances people repeatedly interact within the same group, forming echo chambers of ideas, whereas in other instances, people might seek information from a variety of sources (Marsh &

Rajaram, 2019). Empirical illustrations of these scenarios come from studies in which we have compared memory outcomes for individuals who worked in groups or worked individually to recall studied information such as a list of unrelated words, categorically related words, or emotional words across sequential recall attempts. Before we delve into the cascading effects of collaborating in the same versus different groups, it is worth noting that collaborating just once is sufficient to make post-collaborative memories of former group members more redundant compared to those who did not collaborate before (Blumen & Rajaram, 2008). Collaborating twice increases this redundancy, whereby former group members show greater shared memories after two collaborations compared to those who collaborated only once (Congleton & Rajaram, 2014). Furthermore, the size of the collaborative inhibition that occurs during group recall also predicts how likely a group is to develop collective memory; the greater the collaborative inhibition a group exhibits during group recall, the greater its collective memory later, demonstrating a clear relationship between the disruptive aspects of collaborative remembering and the formation of collective memory (Congleton & Rajaram, 2014). We observed a similar relationship in a simulation of 1,000 collaborative groups and 1,000 nominal groups using an agent-based computational model (Luhmann & Rajaram, 2015). Computational agents who "collaboratively recalled" the studied information and exhibited collaborative inhibition also showed far greater post-collaborative similarity compared to pre-collaborative similarity in the output. Nominal groups did not exhibit this pattern.

What happens when repeated collaboration occurs not just with the same group members but with different group members across repeated attempts at recall? We asked this question by comparing individuals who collaborated within the same triad twice, the identical or the insular group condition, and then recalled individually (CCI), or collaborated with different triads of partners each of the two times, the reconfigured or diverse group condition, and then recalled individually (CRI). A third, control condition (III) consisted of an equal number of three recalls where participants worked individually each time and thus provided data for deriving nominal group recall (Figure 20.2). The third and last recall always consisted of individual recall (indicated by the notation "I" in all three conditions) and provided the measure to compare the post-collaborative memory effects of collaborative recall between the CCI and CRI conditions and against the control condition (III). These

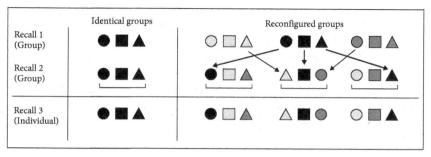

Figure 20.2 An illustration of the group configuration for identical and reconfigured groups. Each shape and each filled color tone represent a different participant within a group.
Adapted from Choi et al. (2014) and taken from Rajaram (in press).

designs are complex but systematic, thereby enabling us to track who recalled what during each of the three recall attempts (Choi et al., 2014, 2017).

As would be expected, groups in both the identical and reconfigured conditions initially exhibited collaborative inhibition in recall, where group recall was lower for both collaborating groups (CCI and CRI) compared to the control, nominal groups (III). Strikingly, this deficit disappeared in the second recall for the reconfigured groups (Figure 20.3, left); when individuals joined forces with new partners, the re-exposure gains from previous recall outpaced the disruption known to occur during group recall and thus eliminated collaborative inhibition.

The interesting question then is the implication of the persisting collaborative inhibition in the identical groups versus its disappearance in the reconfigured groups on the emergence of collective memory. Of interest is also the extent to which exposure to information can vary across these group configurations and consequently influence their collective memory formation. In identical groups, individuals were repeatedly exposed to the memories of the same two partners. By contrast, in reconfigured groups, individuals were exposed to the memories of as many as eight other individuals, either directly or indirectly. Consider, for instance, Participant A, who during the first collaborative recall session heard the recall responses of two partners, B and C, whom we call proximal partners. During the second collaborative recall, Participant A heard the recall responses of two other partners, D and G, who had collaborated in different triads (D with E and F; G with H and I) during the first recall session. As a result, these two partners, D and G, served

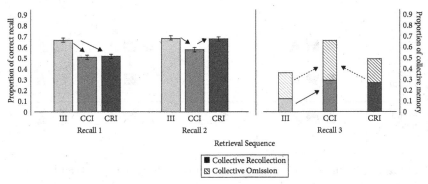

Figure 20.3 Correct recall performance by groups (Recall 1 and Recall 2) and collective memory measures derived from post-collaborative recall (Recall 3) for identical, reconfigured, and nominal (control) groups. (Left) The average proportion of correct recall by nominal groups (III), identical groups (CCI), and reconfigured groups (CRI). (Right) Collective remembering (top stacks) and collective omission (bottom stacks) for the three groups.
Source: Data from Choi et al. (2014).

as proximal partners because they collaborated directly with Participant A. At the same time, D and G also brought with them the influence of their earlier partners with whom they had collaborated during the first recall. These earlier partners, E–H, were thus distal partners to Participant A. As a consequence of these group configurations across the two recall sessions, and the flow of information that resulted from this arrangement, each participant in the CRI (or the Reconfigured) group condition (like Participant A) was exposed to two different pairs of proximal partners in each of two rounds of group recall and an additional four distal partners with whom the second-round proximal partners had earlier collaborated. These configurations are illustrated in Figure 20.3 with shapes and color tones.

The collective memory measure in this design came from the pooled responses of the former collaborators in the third, individual recall. Those who had collaborated earlier showed greater memory overlap than those who never collaborated. Furthermore, those who earlier collaborated in identical groups showed more overlap in the items they later recalled (or failed to recall) than those who earlier collaborated in reconfigured groups (Figure 20.3, right). Therefore, collaborative remembering with the same partners and persistent collaborative inhibition observed for these groups were associated with greater collective memory than for groups in which partners changed across interactions and collaborative inhibition disappeared. Interestingly, this pattern of results was not driven by the identical group members recalling more of the same items; in fact, the reconfigured group members had similar levels of shared recollections. Instead, collective memory for members from identical groups was boosted by more overlapping omissions—that is, more collective forgetting—a pattern that is consistent with the persistent group recall deficit (i.e., collaborative inhibition) observed in this group. Conversely, collaborators from the reconfigured groups, who worked with a broader network of people during group recall, now reported more unique (non-redundant) items and thus less collective forgetting. In essence, identical groups seemed to behave in a manner similar to echo chambers and developed homogenized memories to a greater extent compared to the reconfigured groups.

Who Knows What

In another experimental study that involved an even more complex design, we varied not only who talks to whom but also who knows what (Choi et al., 2017). In any given triad, identical or reconfigured, all group members had previously studied one set of emotional or neutral words and their pictorial depictions (e.g., *hyena, kitten, cow*), two of three members had studied another set of emotional words and their pictorial depictions, and only one member had studied yet another set of emotional words and their pictorial depictions. Thus, for any given group there were some completely shared, some partially shared, and some unshared information to recall later. Among a variety of findings that we observed, of particular interest here are those about false memories (recalling information suggested by another group member but not originally seen by the person being tested). Although diverse groups exhibited greater variety of false memories that arose from the uneven distribution of studied information, insular groups express increased confidence in false memories. In other words, experimental conditions similar to echo chambers appear to increase confidence in false memories. These findings make it clear that insular groups seem to heavily influence the overlap in the content of post-collaborative memories of previous group members. Beyond memory content, what can we say about collaboration's impact on the structure of post-collaborative memories?

Alignment of Memory Structures

The research we have discussed so far shows growing evidence that collaborative remembering plays an important role in changing post-collaborative memories and in producing convergence in what people remember. Here, we consider a deeper facet of memory that goes beyond the contents of memory. A long history of research in cognitive psychology shows that how we organize information has a powerful effect on our ability to later remember information (Congleton & Rajaram; 2012; Mulligan, 2005; Rundus, 1971; Zaromb & Roediger, 2010). Furthermore, the more opportunities we get to study or to recall information, the better we are able to organize information (Tulving, 1962). In other words, the structure of memory exerts a powerful force on what people remember later, and repeated processing of information influences the structure of memory. How might these cognitive principles shape collective memory?

Studies show that when people remember past information together, they begin to organize their memories in similar ways (Blumen & Rajaram, 2008; Choi et al., 2014; Congleton & Rajaram, 2014; Weldon & Bellinger, 1997). In other words, the process of collaboration produces an overlap not only in what people remember later but also in the way they organize this information. As with memory content, the more often people get to collaborate, the more similar their memory structures become. Furthermore, the greater the collaborative inhibition that occurs during group recall, the more similar memory structures become for the group members (Congleton & Rajaram, 2014). Aligned memory structures (schemas) can have far-reaching cognitive consequences by serving as powerful tools for future memory formation. For example, people with similar memory structures are likely to exhibit an affinity to forming and perpetuating similar memories, beliefs, and attitudes, thereby promoting the emergence of a collective narrative (see Chapter 22, this volume). We return to these far-reaching implications of the laboratory findings for collective memory, and by extension for national memories, in the concluding section.

Collaboration Influences Memory for Emotional Information

In addition to the effects of repeated collaboration, group configuration, and information distribution on collective memory formation we have considered so far, the valence of information people remember also matters (Wessel et al., 2015; Yaron-Antar & Nachson, 2006). Interestingly, collaboration brings about different types of changes in post-collective memory for emotional information depending on whether the information is non-personal or autobiographical.

In the study we discussed already in which people recalled previously seen emotional words and pictures (e.g., negative items such as *hyena, wolf*; positive items such as *kitten, puppy*; or neutral items such as *cow, goat*), collaborative remembering enhanced negative memories and led to collective forgetting of positive memories (Choi et al., 2017). These outcomes were particularly pronounced for insular (identical) groups and particularly for information that all group members saw previously. This increase in negative memories after collaboration in identical groups was also evident in later individual recall. In other words, collaboration in identical groups amplified negative memories at both collective and individual levels.

We observed a different pattern when we tested collaborative recall of an autobiographical event that required students to recall a recent exam episode that all of them had individually experienced (Maswood et al., 2019). Collaborative recall led to a reduction in the ratings of negative valence of the exam experience, and it enhanced the positive emotional tone of the narratives that individuals reported afterwards. We examined these emotional changes in the recall of autobiographical information in individual memory rather than for collective memory. Nonetheless, these changes reflect how collaboration produces different influences on memory for non-personal versus autobiographical information.

The differing patterns of post-collaborative memory for non-personal and autobiographical information across these studies are reminiscent of real-life scenarios in which groups often fuel negativity in the discourse on public events (e.g., Rozin & Royzman, 2001), whereas sharing painful memories with others often has therapeutic benefits (e.g., Wessel & Moulds, 2008). The explorations of collaboration on autobiographical memory in our study harken back to the commentaries we noted in the introduction of this chapter about the importance of social connectedness for forging empathy and shared narratives. How will we share and remember the wrenching losses brought about by the COVID-19 pandemic for experiences about graduations, birthdays, hardships, and social isolation, to name just a few of the myriad adversities people throughout the world are facing today? Are personal, autobiographical memories likely to persist or soften and fade over one's lifetime with the passage of time as a healer and with the laws of forgetting operating inexorably (Ebbinghaus, 1885)?

Beyond the memories of the COVID-19 pandemic that may persist or fade in small collective groups such as families and among close others, what about collective memories of the pandemic at large scales over the course of history? Projecting from the surprising lack of public memory for the Spanish flu that struck the world in 1918 and took between 50 million and 100 million lives, Hershberger (2020) recently wrote about the views of leading historians, psychologists, sociologists, anthropologists, and writers on the memory for the COVID-19 pandemic. In this article, Roediger and Wertsch reflected on the ongoing divisive narrative about the pandemic as a barrier to building the type of salience that can promote long-lasting memories. In this context, Wertsch underscores the importance of a central, collective narrative as the key instrument for building and sustaining collective memory. We find resonance with these views in our laboratory findings, obtained with controlled study and test materials, where we found that repeated collaborations in identical groups promote memory convergence, whereas collaborations with changing conversational partners, which brings diversity in the things remembered, reduce memory convergence (Choi et al., 2014, 2017; Congleton & Rajaram, 2014). In Hershberger (2020), Roediger identifies another powerful tool in the iconic images of the pandemic that may serve as anchors to build robust, long-lasting collective memories, in line with the cognitive research on the robustness of memory for pictures (Paivio, 1971) and distinctive information in general.

Conclusion

We close with a brief summary of the key points we made in this chapter and with further reflections on the implications of cognitive experimental research for understanding the emergence of collective and national memories. As one might imagine, remembering with others enhances memory. But critically, it also produces counterintuitive outcomes. People recall less when remembering with others than when remembering alone. Along with such forgetting, people also exhibit memory contagion; they incorporate into their own memories information that others remembered. Such contagion occurs not only for true information but also for false information, underscoring the influence of social connections on our memory. Through the process of collaborative remembering, mechanisms of disruption, forgetting, and social contagion errors reduce the accuracy of what we remember. By contrast, the mechanisms of re-exposure, cross-cueing, and error pruning increase memory accuracy. These seemingly opposing group dynamics align the memories of group members and signal the cognitive markers for how national memories can become homogenized and promote nationalism.

Our findings show that multiple opportunities to collaborate as well as the configuration of the social network are important factors for memory convergence. For example, insular groups promote confidence in false memories, and diverse networks with the influence of many reduce this effect. Group recall also influences memory for emotional information by enhancing negative memories for non-personal information, especially in insular groups, and by reducing the negativity of autobiographical information.

Furthermore, remembering in groups produces overlap not only in what people remember later but also in how they organize this information by bringing closer together the memory structures that group members reorganize through collaboration. Group members who develop aligned memory structures are likely to process new incoming experiences and information in similar ways, thus experiencing persisting effects of collective memory on their future memories, beliefs, and attitudes even after they are no longer in the same group. To understand why these consequences can occur, it is useful to revisit two key cognitive principles discussed previously—disruption and memory organization. Cognitive research on individual memory indicates that the a priori memory structures individuals possess play a crucial role in the ways in which they process new experiences and new information and then recall this information (see Figure 20.1, "Individual pre-existing cognitive structure"). During collaborative remembering, the role of pre-existing cognitive structures becomes evident in that group members disrupt one another's preferred, idiosyncratic ways of organizing recall of their memories, thereby lowering recall. Extrapolating from this evidence, we can infer the role of new, aligned memory structures that people develop after collaborating with one another in shaping future memories. When collaborating members develop new, similar memory structures, they are likely to form and organize memories for new information and experiences in similar ways.

As a result of the cognitive cascade we just described, collective memory for what people remember, and likely even more so the collective memory for how people organize memories, can have a powerful influence on future learning and remembering. Aligned memory structures can guide the development of future narratives for the group members, a process that bridges to the idea of narrative forms that serve as cultural tools for building national narratives that members of a group develop (Wertsch & Roediger, 2008; see Chapter 22, this volume). In this vein, the experimental findings of collective memory structures "indicate that the process of collaboration may instantiate a cognitively based, bottom-up accumulation of shared representations among former collaborators that may act as mini cultural tools they use to access shared representations" (Congleton & Rajaram, 2014, p. 181).

In our experimental studies discussed here, the mini cultural tools of collective memory developed from the operations of group collaboration, group configuration, information distribution, and the emotional nature of information on memory. Talking to others matters, talking to the same versus different people matters, what people know (versus do not know) during the interaction matters, and the valence of information people discuss matters in influencing the formation of collective memory. These mini cultural tools then may serve as laboratory analogs of the foundational idea of national narratives as cultural tools and how nationalism can occur as an emergent property of social networks (see Chapter 22, this volume). In this manner, the influence of many other variables on the emergence of mini cultural tools can be assessed in the laboratory to understand the building blocks of collective memory.

As we highlighted at the beginning, our theoretical framework embodies a person-driven, bottom-up approach to identifying the cognitive mechanisms of learning and memory that shape the formation of collective memory. Our empirical work has been directed toward understanding the manner in which these processes, operating within an individual, influence and converge during social interactions to give rise to collective memory content and structures. These processes are distinct from and complementary to the conceptualization of collective memories as consequences of top-down, government or authority-driven processes. In our view, such complementarity is essential for a comprehensive understanding of the two key components—the person and the context—that are integral to the formation of collective memory.

An important line of questions that follows has to do with translation: how do individuals and groups use collective memory? When do shared representations morph into the scaffolding of nationalistic beliefs or prompt nationalistic actions? How do prior attitudes, echo chambers, and collective forgetting inform new beliefs? Even more broadly, how does collective memory emerge on social media platforms with increasingly large and complex group configurations? These are all questions addressed throughout this volume. The experimental approaches we have discussed in this chapter provide insights into the underlying mechanics of how memories are subject to reconstruction through a social process and can, in turn, inform the emergence of national memories.

Acknowledgments

Preparation of this chapter was supported by National Science Foundation Grant 1456928 to S.R. and National Science Foundation Graduate Research Fellowship 1839287 to T.P.

References

Abel, M., Umanath, S., Fairfield, B., Takahashi, M., Roediger, H. L., III, & Wertsch, J. V. (2019). Collective memories across 11 nations for World War II: Similarities and differences regarding the most important events. *Journal of Applied Research in Memory and Cognition, 8*(2), 178–188. https://doi.org/10.1016/j.jarmac.2019.02.001

Andersson, J. (2001). Net effect of memory collaboration: How is collaboration affected by factors such as friendship, gender and age? *Scandinavian Journal of Psychology, 42*(4), 367–375. https://doi.org/10.1111/1467-9450.00248

Andersson, J., & Rönnberg, J. (1995). Recall suffers from collaboration: Joint recall effects of friendship and task complexity. *Applied Cognitive Psychology, 9*(3), 199–211. https://doi.org/10.1002/acp.2350090303

Barber, S. J., Harris, C. B., & Rajaram, S. (2015). Why two heads apart are better than two heads together: Multiple mechanisms underlie the collaborative inhibition effect in memory. *Journal of Experimental Psychology: Learning, Memory, and Cognition, 41*(2), 559–566. https://doi.org/10.1037/xlm0000037

Bartlett, F. C. (1932). *Remembering: A study in experimental and social psychology.* Cambridge University Press.

Basden, B. H., Basden, D. R., Bryner, S., & Thomas, R. L. (1997). A comparison of group and individual remembering: Does collaboration disrupt retrieval strategies? *Journal of Experimental Psychology: Learning, Memory, and Cognition, 23*(5), 1176–1189. https://doi.org/10.1037/0278-7393.23.5.1176

Basden, B. H., Basden, D. R., & Henry, S. (2000). Costs and benefits of collaborative remembering. *Applied Cognitive Psychology, 14*(6), 497–507. https://doi.org/10.1002/1099-0720(200011/12)14:6<497::AID-ACP665>3.0.CO;2-4

Blumen, H. M., & Rajaram, S. (2008). Influence of re-exposure and retrieval disruption during group collaboration on later individual recall. *Memory, 16*(3), 231–244. https://doi.org/10.1080/09658210701804495

Choi, H. Y., Blumen, H. M., Congleton, A. R., & Rajaram, S. (2014). The role of group configuration in the social transmission of memory: Evidence from identical and reconfigured groups. *Journal of Cognitive Psychology*, *26*(1), 65–80. https://doi.org/10.1080/20445911.2013.862536

Choi, H. Y., Kensinger, E. A., & Rajaram, S. (2017). Mnemonic transmission, social contagion, and emergence of collective memory: Influence of emotional valence, group structure, and information distribution. *Journal of Experimental Psychology: General*, *146*(9), 1247–1265. https://psycnet.apa.org/doi/10.1037/xge0000327

Coman, A., Momennejad, I., Drach, R. D., & Geana, A. (2016). Mnemonic convergence in social networks: The emergent properties of cognition at a collective level. *Proceedings of the National Academy of Sciences of the USA*, *113*(29), 8171–8176. https://doi.org/10.1073/pnas.1525569113

Congleton, A. R., & Rajaram, S. (2011). The influence of learning method on collaboration: Prior repeated retrieval enhances retrieval organization, abolishes collaborative inhibition, and promotes postcollaborative memory. *Journal of Experimental Psychology: General*, *140*, 535–551. https://psycnet.apa.org/doi/10.1037/a0024308

Congleton, A., & Rajaram, S. (2012). The origin of the interaction between learning method and delay in the testing effect: The roles of processing and conceptual retrieval organization. *Memory & Cognition*, *40*(4), 528–539. https://doi.org/10.3758/s13421-011-0168-y

Congleton, A. R., & Rajaram, S. (2014). Collaboration changes both the content and the structure of memory: Building the architecture of shared representations. *Journal of Experimental Psychology: General*, *143*, 1570–1584. https://psycnet.apa.org/doi/10.1037/a0035974

Cuc, A., Koppel, J., & Hirst, W. (2007). Silence is not golden: A case for socially shared retrieval-induced forgetting. *Psychological Science*, *18*(8), 727–733. https://doi.org/10.1111%2Fj.1467-9280.2007.01967.x

Deese, J. (1959). On the prediction of occurrence of particular verbal intrusions in immediate recall. *Journal of Experimental Psychology*, *58*(1), 17. https://psycnet.apa.org/doi/10.1037/h0046671

Dixon, R. A., & de Frias, C. M. (2007). Mild memory deficits differentially affect 6 year changes in compensatory strategy use. *Psychology and Aging*, *22*(3), 632–638. https://psycnet.apa.org/doi/10.1037/0882-7974.22.3.632

Dixon, R. A., Gagnon, L. M., & Crow, C. B. (1998). Collaborative memory accuracy and distortion: Performance and beliefs. In M. J. Intons-Peterson & D. L. Best (Eds.), *Memory distortions and their prevention* (pp. 63–88). Erlbaum.

Ebbinghaus, H. (1885). *Uber das gedachinis*. Dunker & Humblot.

Eliot, G. (1873). *Middlemarch: A study of provincial life: Volume IV, Book VIII: Sunset and sunrise*. Harper & Brothers, New York.

Geana, A., Duker, A., & Coman, A. (2019). An experimental study of the formation of collective memories in social networks. *Journal of Experimental Social Psychology*, *84*, 103813. https://doi.org/10.1016/j.jesp.2019.05.001

Halbwachs, M. (1980). *The collective memory. (La memoire collective)* (F. J. Ditter, Jr., & V. Y. Ditter, Trans.). Harper Row. (Original work published 1950)

Halbwachs, M. (1992). *On collective memory* (L. A. Coser, Ed. & Trans., with an introduction by L. A. Coser). University of Chicago Press. (Original work published 1925)

Henkel, L. A., & Rajaram, S. (2011). Collaborative remembering in older adults: Age invariant outcomes in the context of episodic recall deficits. *Psychology and Aging, 26*(3), 532–545. https://psycnet.apa.org/doi/10.1037/a0023106

Hershberger, S. (2020, August 13). The 1918 flu faded in our collective memory: We might "forget" the coronavirus, too. *Scientific American.* https://www.scientificamerican.com/article/the-1918-flu-faded-in-our-collective-memory-we-might-forget-the-coronavirus-too

Hirst, W., & Echterhoff, G. (2012). Remembering in conversations: The social sharing and reshaping of memories. *Annual Review of Psychology, 63,* 55–79. https://doi.org/10.1146/annurev-psych-120710-100340

Hirst, W., & Manier, D. (2008). Towards a psychology of collective memory. *Memory, 16*(3), 183–200. https://doi.org/10.1080/09658210701811912

Johansson, N. O., Andersson, J., & Rönnberg, J. (2000). Do elderly couples have a better prospective memory than other elderly people when they collaborate? *Applied Cognitive Psychology, 14*(2), 121–133. https://doi.org/10.1002/(SICI)1099-0720(200003/04)14:2%3C121::AID-ACP626%3E3.0.CO;2-A

Johansson, N. O., Andersson, J. A. N., & Rönnberg, J. (2005). Compensating strategies in collaborative remembering in very old couples. *Scandinavian Journal of Psychology, 46*(4), 349–359. https://doi.org/10.1111/j.1467-9450.2005.00465.x

Latané, B., Williams, K., & Harkins, S. (1979). Many hands make light the work: The causes and consequences of social loafing. *Journal of Personality and Social Psychology, 37*(6), 822–832. https://psycnet.apa.org/doi/10.1037/0022-3514.37.6.822

Luhmann, C. C., & Rajaram, S. (2015). Memory transmission in small groups and large networks: An agent-based model. *Psychological Science, 26*(12), 1909–1917. https://doi.org/10.1177%2F0956797615605798

Marion, S. B., & Thorley, C. (2016). A meta-analytic review of collaborative inhibition and postcollaborative memory: Testing the predictions of the retrieval strategy disruption hypothesis. *Psychological Bulletin, 142*(11), 1141–1164. https://psycnet.apa.org/doi/10.1037/bul0000071

Marsh, E. J., & Rajaram, S. (2019). The digital expansion of the mind: Implications of internet usage for memory and cognition. *Journal of Applied Research in Memory and Cognition, 8*(1), 1–14. https://doi.org/10.1016/j.jarmac.2018.11.001

Maswood, R., & Rajaram, S. (2018). Social transmission of false memory in small groups and large networks. *Topics in Cognitive Science, 11*(4), 1–23. https://doi.org/10.1111/tops.12348

Maswood, R., Rasmussen, A. S., & Rajaram, S. (2019). Collaborative remembering of emotional autobiographical memories: Implications for emotion regulation and collective memory. *Journal of Experimental Psychology: General, 148*(1), 65. https://psycnet.apa.org/doi/10.1037/xge0000468

Meade, M. L., Nokes, T. J., & Morrow, D. G. (2009). Expertise promotes facilitation on a collaborative memory task. *Memory, 17*(1), 39–48. https://doi.org/10.1080/09658210802524240

Meade, M. L., & Roediger, H. L., III. (2002). Explorations in the social contagion of memory. *Memory & Cognition, 30*(7), 995–1009. https://doi.org/10.3758/BF03194318

Meudell, P. R., Hitch, G. J., & Boyle, M. M. (1995). Collaboration in recall: Do pairs of people cross-cue each other to produce new memories? *Quarterly Journal of*

Experimental Psychology A: Human Experimental Psychology, 48(1), 141–152. https://doi.org/10.1080/14640749508401381

Meudell, P. R., Hitch, G. J., & Kirby, P. (1992). Are two heads better than one? Experimental investigations of the social facilitation of memory. *Applied Cognitive Psychology, 6*(6), 525–543. https://doi.org/10.1002/acp.2350060606

Mulligan, N. W. (2005). Total retrieval time and hypermnesia: Investigating the benefits of multiple recall tests. *Psychological Research, 69*(4), 272–284. https://doi.org/10.1007/s00426-004-0178-5

Olick, J. K. (1999). Collective memory: The two cultures. *Sociological Theory, 17*(3), 333–348. https://doi.org/10.1111%2F0735-2751.00083

Paivio, A. (1971). *Imagery and verbal processes*. Holt, Rinehart & Winston.

Putnam, A. L., Ross, M. Q., Soter, L. K., & Roediger, H. L., III. (2018). Collective narcissism: Americans exaggerate the role of their home state in appraising US history. *Psychological Science, 29*(9), 1414–1422. https://doi.org/10.1177%2F0956797618772504

Rajaram, S. (2011). Collaboration both hurts and helps memory: A cognitive perspective. *Current Directions in Psychological Science, 20*, 76–81. https://doi.org/10.1177%2F0963721411403251

Rajaram, S. (2017). Collaborative inhibition in group recall: Cognitive principles and implications. In M. Meade, A. Barnier, P. Van Bergen, C. Harris, & J. Sutton (Eds.), *Collaborative remembering: How remembering with others influences memory* (pp. 55–75). Oxford University Press.

Rajaram, S. (in press). *Collaborative remembering and collective memory*. In M. J. Kahana & A. D. Wagner (Eds.), *Oxford handbook of human memory*. Oxford University Press.

Rajaram, S., & Pereira-Pasarin, L. P. (2007). Collaboration can improve individual recognition memory: Evidence from immediate and delayed tests. *Psychonomic Bulletin & Review, 14*(1), 95–100.

Rajaram, S., & Pereira-Pasarin, L. P. (2010). Collaborative memory: Cognitive research and theory. *Perspectives on Psychological Science, 5*(6), 649–663. https://doi.org/10.1177%2F1745691610388763

Roediger, H. L., III, & Abel, M. (2015). Collective memory: A new arena of cognitive study. *Trends in Cognitive Sciences, 19*(7), 359–361. https://doi.org/10.1016/j.tics.2015.04.003

Roediger, H. L., III, Abel, M., Umanath, S., Shaffer, R. A., Fairfield, B., Takahashi, M., & Wertsch, J. V. (2019). Competing national memories of World War II. *Proceedings of the National Academy of Sciences of the USA, 116*(34), 16678–16686. https://doi.org/10.1073/pnas.1907992116

Roediger, H. L., III, & DeSoto, K. A. (2014). Forgetting the presidents. *Science, 346*(6213), 1106–1109. https://doi.org/10.1126/science.1259627

Roediger, H. L., III, & McDermott, K. B. (1995). Creating false memories: Remembering words not presented in lists. *Journal of Experimental Psychology: Learning, Memory, and Cognition, 21*(4), 803. https://doi.org/10.1037/0278-7393.21.4.803

Roediger, H. L., III, Meade, M. L., & Bergman, E. T. (2001). Social contagion of memory. *Psychonomic Bulletin & Review, 8*(2), 365–371. https://doi.org/10.3758/BF03196174

Roediger, H. L., III, Meade, M. L., Gallo, D. A., & Olson, K. R. (2014). Bartlett revisited: Direct comparison of repeated reproduction and serial reproduction techniques. *Journal of Applied Research in Memory and Cognition, 3*(4), 266–271. https://doi.org/10.1016/j.jarmac.2014.05.004

Rozin, P., & Royzman, E. B. (2001). Negativity bias, negativity dominance, and contagion. *Personality and Social Psychology Review, 5*(4), 296–320. https://doi.org/10.1207%2FS15327957PSPR0504_2

Rundus, D. (1971). Analysis of rehearsal processes in free recall. *Journal of Experimental Psychology, 89*(1), 63. https://psycnet.apa.org/doi/10.1037/h0031185

Takahashi, M. (2007). Does collaborative remembering reduce false memories? *British Journal of Psychology, 98*(1), 1–13. https://doi.org/10.1348/000712606X101628

Takahashi, M., & Saito, S. (2004). Does test delay eliminate collaborative inhibition? *Memory, 12*(6), 722–731. https://doi.org/10.1080/09658210344000521

Thorley, C., & Dewhurst, S. A. (2007). Collaborative false recall in the DRM procedure: Effects of group size and group pressure. *European Journal of Cognitive Psychology, 19*(6), 867–881.

Thorley, C., & Dewhurst, S. A. (2009). False and veridical collaborative recognition. *Memory, 17*(1), 17–25. https://doi.org/10.1080/09658210802484817

Tulving, E. (1962). Subjective organization in free recall of "unrelated" words. *Psychological Review, 69*, 344–354.

Weldon, M. S., & Bellinger, K. D. (1997). Collective memory: Collaborative and individual processes in remembering. *Journal of Experimental Psychology: Learning, Memory, and Cognition, 23*(5), 1160–1175. https://psycnet.apa.org/doi/10.1037/0278-7393.23.5.1160

Weldon, M. S., Blair, C., & Huebsch, P. D. (2000). Group remembering: Does social loafing underlie collaborative inhibition? *Journal of Experimental Psychology: Learning, Memory, and Cognition, 26*(6), 1568–1577. https://psycnet.apa.org/doi/10.1037/0278-7393.26.6.1568

Wertsch, J. V. (2008). The narrative organization of collective memory. *Ethos, 36*(1), 120–135. https://doi.org/10.1111/j.1548-1352.2008.00007.x

Wertsch, J. V., & Roediger, H. L., III. (2008). Collective memory: Conceptual foundations and theoretical approaches. *Memory, 16*(3), 318–326. https://doi.org/10.1080/09658210701801434

Wessel, I., & Moulds, M. L. (2008). Collective memory: A perspective from (experimental) clinical psychology. *Memory, 16*(3), 288–304. https://doi.org/10.1080/09658210701811813

Wessel, I., Zandstra, A. R. E., Hengeveld, H. M., & Moulds, M. L. (2015). Collaborative recall of details of an emotional film. *Memory, 23*(3), 437–444. https://doi.org/10.1080/09658211.2014.895384

Yamashiro, J. K., & Hirst, W. (2014). Mnemonic convergence in a social network: Collective memory and extended influence. *Journal of Applied Research in Memory and Cognition, 3*(4), 272–279. https://doi.org/10.1016/j.jarmac.2014.08.001

Yaron-Antar, A., & Nachson, I. (2006). Collaborative remembering of emotional events: The case of Rabin's assassination. *Memory, 14*(1), 46–56. https://doi.org/10.1080/09658210444000502

Zaromb, F. M., Butler, A. C., Agarwal, P. K., & Roediger, H. L., III. (2014). Collective memories of three wars in United States history in younger and older adults. *Memory & Cognition, 42*(3), 383–399. https://doi.org/10.3758/s13421-013-0369-7

Zaromb, F. M., Liu, J. H., Páez, D., Hanke, K., Putnam, A. L., & Roediger, H. L., III. (2018). We made history: Citizens of 35 countries overestimate their nation's role in world history. *Journal of Applied Research in Memory and Cognition, 7*(4), 521–528. https://doi.org/10.1016/j.jarmac.2018.05.006

Zaromb, F. M., & Roediger, H. L., III. (2010). The testing effect in free recall is associated with enhanced organizational processes. *Memory & Cognition, 38*(8), 995–1008. https://doi.org/10.3758/MC.38.8.995

21

Populist Beliefs

Byproducts of an Adaptive System?

Elizabeth J. Marsh, Matthew Stanley, and Morgan K. Taylor

Gun violence is increasing in America. U.S. taxes are the highest in the world. Teenage pregnancy rates are climbing. The solar industry has more jobs than oil. These claims have all been made by politicians (some liberal, others conservative) and are objectively false but believed to be true by many Americans (for additional examples, see Wood & Porter, 2019). We are interested in understanding how people come to believe such claims, with an approach grounded in the basic science of memory. This approach differs from that of social psychologists, political scientists, media scientists, and other researchers who focus on *motivational* factors that underlie belief. That is, much research shows that people are often committed to their beliefs and will reject new information that contradicts their beliefs (e.g., Ecker & Ang, 2019). We build on this important research by highlighting *cognitive* factors that also affect the acceptance and updating of false beliefs. We see the problem filtered through the lens of what we know about the construction, representation, and updating of knowledge more generally. Humans are impressive learners, in part because we rely on shortcuts during learning to increase cognitive efficiency. Such shortcuts evolved because they normally support accurate cognition and correct judgments about truth, but sometimes they lead the learner astray and result in the acceptance of unsupported information, misinformation, and even disinformation. Critically, these shortcuts are fast, and they often take the place of direct retrieval of information—meaning that people may have the knowledge to reject the misinformation and still fall prey to misinformation.

Before reviewing our guiding principles, we provide an example that highlights two important themes: (1) A motivational account is not mutually exclusive with a cognitive account and (2) demonstrated knowledge does not necessarily protect one from susceptibility to misinformation. This example comes from a study about misinformation spread during the Gulf War (Lewandowsky et al., 2005). During the war, as with any fast-changing situation, information was reported, updated, debated, and sometimes retracted. Of interest are specific instances in which the press covered claims that later turned out to be false—for example, about the supposed executions of American prisoners of war by Iraqi forces and the existence of weapons of mass destruction (WMDs). Critical for present purposes is that the experiment focused on claims that were officially retracted by newspapers—meaning that people had a chance to know better. Participants were Americans, Germans, and Australians, who did three tasks. First, they rated their memory for each of a series of events from the war (some true, some false but later retracted, and some fictional ones made up for the experiment). Second, they rated their belief about the veridicality of each claim. Finally, later in the experiment, each individual indicated whether they remembered each claim as retracted by the press. Critically, all three groups of subjects showed similar levels of awareness that the retracted stories were actually retracted—but the Americans reported a higher level of belief in the false retracted claims compared to the Germans and Australians. Motivation likely played a role in updating beliefs; on average, Germans (and to a lesser extent, Australians) did not believe that the war's original purpose was to "destroy WMDs"—meaning that the retractions were a better fit to their justifications for the war than was true of Americans. However, Americans demonstrated as much knowledge about the retractions as did the other participants—an example of how knowing better did not prevent them from holding false beliefs. One key procedural choice in the experiment (which we return to later in this chapter) was to ask about memory for retractions at the *end* of the experiment—meaning that Americans may not have retrieved that information when prompted about their beliefs (previewing one of the principles covered in this chapter: that knowledge can be stored in memory but not retrieved).

In this chapter, we review how cognitive processes can contribute to the acceptance of misinformation. Although our focus is on misinformation, it is important to note that these processes are not rouge ones but, rather, are processes that normally support veridical learning and inferences. Our cognitive system is efficient, relying on heuristics to reduce the processing load. Heuristics are shortcuts that are *normally* correct—for example, a feeling of familiarity upon encountering a company's name might lead you to infer that it is a good company or at least that you have heard of it before, because in the past you have experienced this feeling with companies you know. But the shortcut does not have to be correct; for example, perhaps you just saw an advertisement for the company and that is why the name seems familiar. To the extent that the heuristic is normally correct, it is adaptive, even if it occasionally leads the learner astray. So while the chapter focuses on misinformation, the reader should keep in mind the glass half full version of the chapter: that the cognitive system is designed to promote quick and robust learning.

Here, we focus on the heuristics people use to judge truth (for a review, see Brashier & Marsh, 2020) and how truth judgments are made in the larger context of the noisy and complicated world (for a complementary point, see Chapter 22 in this volume). We highlight how having stored knowledge does not preclude the use of heuristics because it may be stored in memory but inaccessible at a particular point in time. We take a deep dive into this last example, showing how activation of one's national identity can change what comes to mind, even when all participants are similarly knowledgeable.

The Role of Source Information

One frequently used cue to truth is the *source of the information*—not surprisingly, people are more likely to trust and be persuaded by information coming from higher credibility sources than lower credibility ones (e.g., Priester & Petty, 1995; for a review, see Pornpitakpan, 2004). Such behavior is generally rational because higher credibility sources are normally more likely to share correct information. Most interventions for misinformation revolve around the idea that critically evaluating sources is the answer to the problem; for example, the first recommendation in an infographic distributed via the webpage of the International Federation of Library Associations and Institutions (IFLA, 2017) is to "consider the source," followed by "check the author" and to examine supporting sources. Even IFLA's recommendation to ask oneself "Is it a joke?" revolves around source, telling readers "if it is too outlandish, it might be satire. Research the site and the author to be sure." However, people often judge sources heuristically rather than doing research to judge the quality of a source. For example, people are more likely to believe an article with additional citations (Putnam & Phelps, 2017) or trust a native speaker over an accented one (Lev-Ari & Keysar, 2010). And it is not difficult for a malicious actor to pose as a credible source. For example, the website PeaceData.net appeared to be operated by a left-wing U.S. news site but was in fact attributed to Russia (the interested reader will find that the site has been removed, with only warnings by the Federal Bureau of Investigation, Facebook, and *The Washington Post* remaining).

The solution is not as simple as removing the burden of assessing source credibility, although this solution is also a common suggestion. Twitter, for example, uses warning tags to alert users to the possibility of fake news. Facebook has experimented with "disputed by 3rd party fact-checker" tags on posts that algorithms suggest are problematic. One problem is that sources are not mutually exclusive; even if people remember a low-credibility source, they may be unconcerned if they believe the information came from other sources as well (e.g., in our work, people are unbothered when information comes from fictional stories because they believe they encountered it other places as well; E. Marsh et al., 2003). Furthermore, source information is forgotten more quickly than the information itself. This forgetting of source information is actually adaptive given our general goal to have knowledge that can be used flexibly—it is only problematic for the rarer cases when sources are not credible. Social psychologists first documented this "sleeper effect" during World War II (Hovland & Weiss, 1951), and much modern research suggests that misinformation from a lower credibility source is more potent after time has passed (e.g., Underwood & Pezdek, 1998). The problem is that there is another cue to truth that is much less affected by the passage of time: how easily a given statement is processed (*fluency*), which we discuss in the next section.

Fluency as a Cue to Truth

Easy-to-read statements are more likely to be judged as true, as shown in numerous experiments. This interpretation of *processing fluency* is a learned one; based on experience, we have learned that true statements are on average more easily processed than false ones. This correlation occurs because the true statement is on average more likely to be repeated than any one of the infinite possible negations of it (Unkelbach, 2007). Again, it is a heuristic that normally leads us to the correct answer, but the problem is that there are numerous ways to make a false statement fluent.

How does one make a falsehood fluent and easy to read? One way is to simply repeat the statement, a tactic that many used cars salesmen (and politicians) are aware of. For example, consider President Donald Trump's arguments for why a wall is needed on the U.S.–Mexico border. He has repeatedly made claims such as

> In El Paso they have close to 2,000 murders right on the other side of the wall. And they had 23 murders. It's a lot of murders. But it's not close to 2,000 murders right on the other side of the wall in Mexico.

In his 2019 State of the Union Address, he claimed that

> The border city of El Paso, Texas, used to have extremely high rates of violent crime—one of the highest in the country, and considered one of our nation's most dangerous cities. Now, with a powerful barrier in place, El Paso is one of our safest cities.

The truth is much more complicated, but it is clear that El Paso follows national trends of a decrease in violent crime since the mid-1990s, whereas the fence referenced by President Trump was constructed in 2007. However, each time Trump makes a claim about the wall, it becomes more familiar and easier to understand. It does not matter if he uses slightly different language each time (Begg et al., 1985); the claim becomes more *fluent* with repetition.

This effect of repetition on truth is known as the *illusory truth effect*. It has been demonstrated in dozens of studies (see the meta-analysis by Dechêne et al., 2010) and, more important, is not limited to obscure trivia statements. Pennycook and colleagues (2018) used actual headlines in a standard illusory truth experiment, exposing people to one-half of a set of real but fake headlines, such as "Election Night: Hillary Was Drunk, Got Physical With Mook and Podesta" and "Trump on Revamping the Military: We're Bringing Back the Draft." During the exposure phase, all headlines were presented with a photograph to mimic how a news story appears on social media sites such as Facebook. Half the headlines were fake and half were real. Participants then completed a filler task before rating the entire set of headlines for their truth value. As expected, participants rated the fake headlines as truer when the headlines appeared earlier in the exposure phase compared to headlines that only appeared in the test phase.

Recent evidence suggests that repetition can influence truth judgments even in the face of partisan motivations. Murray and colleagues (n.d.) collected more than 100 actual tweets from Donald Trump posted between November 2016 and October 2019. Sample tweets include "Originally, almost all models predicted Dorian would hit Alabama," "California admitted there were a million illegal votes in the 2016 presidential election," and "Chicago is the city with the strongest gun laws in our nation." In an initial phase of the study, participants saw half of the tweets along with the relevant context—namely that they came from Donald Trump. Later, they rated a series of Trump tweets for their truth value (on a scale of 1 to 6); half were old (in that they had been seen earlier in the experiment) and half were new (to the experiment). Old tweets were rated as truer than the new ones—an illusory truth effect—even among Democrats who, as a group, are presumably disposed to disbelieve Trump and even when the tweets were patently false (as determined by Politifact). This study is particularly compelling because it is unlikely participants forgot the source of the statements, given that they were all real tweets from the President of the United States. Furthermore, many of these tweets were likely experienced outside of the experiment—and yet a single additional exposure in the study was enough to boost truth ratings, highlighting the power of the fluency cue.

Repetition is not the only way to make information easier to process. High-contrast font is easier to read than low contrast font and accordingly is rated as truer on average (Reber & Schwarz, 1999). High-quality audios of scientific talks are deemed better quality science than lower quality audios of the same content (Newman & Schwarz, 2018). Similarly, accented speech, for example, is more difficult to process and thus is rated as less true than native speech (Lev-Ari & Keysar, 2010). Simple language (e.g., language that rhymes) leads to higher truth ratings (McGlone & Tofighbakhsh, 2000). And simply adding a photo to a claim increases belief, even if that photo adds no information to support the claim (Newman et al., 2012). Thus, Pennycook et al.'s (2018) study with the actual headlines used two techniques to instill belief—repetition and the presence of a photo—making the claim even easier to process.

Unfortunately, knowing better does not confer immunity against illusory truth. In Pennycook et al.'s (2018) study on fake news, half of the participants had the fake news stories flagged for them during the exposure phase. That is, as has been used by some social media platforms, the fake news headlines were tagged as "disputed by third party checkers" for half of the participants in the study. The illusory truth effect was similar in the two conditions; an explicit warning/negative tag did nothing to help people avoid the fluency cue. Of course, one possibility is that people simply forgot the falsehood tags by the time they did their final set of truth ratings (akin to forgetting a source)—but there are at least two other possibilities. One is a motivational account: Not all people will believe "falsehood" tags provided by "fact checkers" from the mainstream media (which some people assume is biased). For example, many people believe that the 2020 U.S. presidential election was stolen, regardless of the lack of evidence to support such claims (and the almost immediate dismissals of dozens of lawsuits related to this claim). These believers have not forgotten that the media and the courts disputed these claims (effectively labeling them as falsehoods); rather, they simply do not believe that the media and the courts are correct.

A second possibility is cognitive, namely that people know the truth and yet sometimes fail to retrieve it. In our own studies, we have shown that people who demonstrate knowledge of basic facts such as "A kilt is the short pleated skirt worn by Scotsmen" are nevertheless affected by exposure to the false statement "A sari is the short pleated skirt worn by Scotsmen" (Fazio et al., 2015). The illusory truth effect persists regardless of how plausible (or implausible) the repeated statements are (once floor and ceiling effects are taken into account; Fazio et al., 2019). That is, repetition increases belief in statements such as "The United States was founded in 1979" and "The earth is a perfect square"—even though it seems almost 100% certain that people have corrective information stored in memory for these statements. In such cases, people's focus on the false claim (and its fluency) is at the expense of the corrective information coming to mind—an example of Tulving and Pearlstone's (1966) classic distinction between *availability* and *accessibility*. That is, correct information can be stored in memory (available) but not accessible (retrievable), a distinction we return to throughout this chapter.

Tools for Dealing with the Messy World

Consider the challenges facing listeners when parsing President Trump's response to a question about why fewer African Americans than Whites trust the police:

> They have to get better than what they've been doing. I mean obviously that was a terrible thing. And I've spoken about it numerous times in various speeches. And what's interesting is I spoke about it when we launched a very successful rocket—a tremendous program that culminated on that day and obviously it goes on from there.

As another example, here is his reference to the Obama administration's response to the H1N1 pandemic: "And they got very bad marks on the job they did on the swine flu. H1N1, he calls it N1H1. H1N1 got very poor marks from Gallup on the job they did on swine flu." Such statements highlight how spoken language can be a challenge for the listener, given that utterances are often made rapidly, disfluently, and ungrammatically—and sometimes are garbled, muffled, or accented.

Humans have developed multiple strategies for dealing with the complexity of language, two of which we focus on here. First, we simplify the incoming information stream, creating rough representations that only need to be "good enough" for the task at hand—not perfect (Ferreira et al., 2002; Ferreira & Lowder, 2016; Karimi & Ferreira, 2016). Returning to our examples, the reader likely extracted that Trump thinks Obama did a bad job with swine flu—and we doubt the reader remembers that quote verbatim as that level of detail is unnecessary to understand Trump's point. Second, humans are predictors, anticipating what a speaker will say based on constraining factors such as semantic context; correct predictions prime the speaker's upcoming utterance (making it easier to process), and incorrect predictions provide the listener with chances to learn (Bar, 2009). Of course, a rambling speaker may make it almost impossible to make correct predictions about upcoming utterances, putting the listener at a disadvantage. In the case of the second Trump quote in the previous paragraph, the reader may have missed the misinformation in it—namely the reference to Obama polling worse than Trump over the pandemic (Obama's numbers never reached as low as Trump's ratings during the pandemic).

Experimentally, psychologists study this situation with a nonpolitical experimental analog in which participants answer a series of general knowledge questions. Critically, they are explicitly warned that some of the questions will be trick questions that contain errors (and that they should respond "wrong" to those). In some ways, this instruction is akin to the suspicion with which one might receive incoming information from a source one expected to spew misinformation—you know there will be errors and you are trying to catch them while following along. Returning to the experimental analog, of key interest are the responses to general knowledge questions that contain incorrect presuppositions such as "How many animals of each kind did Moses take on the Ark?" Many people fail to notice anything wrong with this question and answer "two," even though later in the study they demonstrate knowledge that the referent should be to Noah, not Moses (the Moses illusion; Erickson & Mattson, 1981). The Moses illusion is robust and persists even when people see sample erroneous questions (Erickson & Mattson, 1981), when the errors are phonologically related to the correct answer (as opposed to semantically related; Shafto & MacKay, 2000), and across younger and older adults (Umanath et al., 2014). The Moses illusion is reduced when a greater proportion of questions contain errors (Bottoms et al., 2010) and when the questions are printed in a more difficult-to-read font (Song & Schwarz, 2008)—both conditions that likely cause vigilance.

The reader may be wondering about the relevance of the Moses illusion to the real world. Two points are important to note. First, failing to notice an error matters because people repeat some subset of the errors at a later time (Bottoms et al., 2010). That is, when people miss contradictions with stored knowledge, they later produce a subset of those contradictions as fact. Second, the effect occurs even if "knowledge" is defined more stringently, by looking at experts' ability to detect contradictions of information in their expert domain. Not only do experts know more than novices (Chi et al., 1988) but also their concepts are more differentiated (Johnson & Mervis, 1997) and organized differently from those of novices (Chi et al., 1981). Experimentally, we defined expertise as being students in a PhD program; although these students may not meet all definitions of expertise, they clearly knew more about their PhD discipline than the control domain. Students were recruited from biology and history departments to answer a series of questions about biology and history, with the explicit warning that they were not to answer any questions with incorrect presuppositions. Embedded in the test were distorted questions from both domains; a history question asked "In what state were the forty-niners searching for oil?" and a biology question asked "Water contains two atoms of helium and how many atoms of oxygen?" (the reader should note that the references should be to *gold* and to *hydrogen*). PhD students were more sensitive in their expert domain, answering fewer trick questions—but they still missed approximately 30% of the errors! A similar pattern occurred when the erroneous presuppositions were bolded and underlined in the questions, meaning that the effect occurred even when the critical terms were "flagged" for readers (Cantor & Marsh, 2017).

Returning to the larger topic of misinformation, the point is that people may be relatively unaware of errors made by politicians or others, so long as the errors are "close enough" to the truth. A listener or reader sometimes fails to notice a mismatch between their simplified representation (e.g., a major figure from the Bible) and what they actually hear or see—but the good news is that they typically do notice blatant errors. That is, a reference to Noah may pass as good enough, but a reference to Nixon would not. Certain linguistic structures provide more camouflage for errors than others; for example, people are less likely to notice an error in the question "How many animals of each kind did Moses take on the ark?" than in the sentence "Moses took two animals of each kind on the ark" (Büttner, 2007). The question presupposes Moses as the sailor on the ark and directs the reader's attention toward retrieving the number "two" from memory. Burying the error later in the question (as opposed to at the beginning) also reduces the chance that people will notice it (Bredart & Modolo, 1988). In other words, it would be easier to slip misinformation by an informed audience if it occurred in complicated speech that camouflaged errors in questions or near the end of a ramble.

Shifting Access to Knowledge

We are all familiar with the dreaded tip-of-the-tongue state, where one knows one knows something but simply cannot retrieve it. During the 2016 U.S. presidential election, this state was nicknamed an Aleppo moment, referring to the time when presidential candidate Gary Johnson asked a newscaster "what's Aleppo?" even though the war-torn Syrian city was prominent in news coverage at the time. Later, he failed to name any world leader when asked during a town hall—eventually referring to a former president of Mexico whose name he could not remember (Vicente Fox). Most people do not think that Johnson did not know any world leaders—rather, for a variety of reasons, he could not at that moment generate the names of leaders he knew about. These incidents are additional examples of Tulving and Pearlstone's (1966) classic distinction between availability and accessibility, discussed previously in this chapter. Information (i.e., the names of world leaders) is stored in memory (available) but not accessible (retrievable). This distinction is particularly well researched in the domain of episodic memory, with an emphasis on understanding the types of retrieval cues that might help people remember events that they are struggling to remember. In contrast, here we focus on shifting accessibility of knowledge.

There are many simple paradigms to study knowledge inaccessibility in the lab; we begin with Brown's (1923) classic demonstration of the phenomena. He asked undergraduates to recall the U.S. states, reasoning that these should be well known to his students. Then, 30 minutes later, he asked them to recall the states again. There was no reason to think that students permanently forgot any states during the 30-minute interval, nor did they have the opportunity to learn any new states—but the two recalls were not identical, highlighting that some knowledge was accessible at one point in time but not the other. Subjects remembered an average of 36 states on the first recall attempt; on average, 2 of these were absent and 5 new states were recalled during the second recall attempt.

What are the cues that drive the fluctuation of access to knowledge? In Brown's (1923) case, he did not provide any specific cues; he simply told students to retrieve the U.S. states. Presumably there was some shift in retrieval cues with time, but because students internally generated their own cues, there is no direct evidence for this explanation. Other studies have directly manipulated properties of retrieval cues to better understand which cues affect the accessibility of knowledge. Well-learned information and information used recently are both (not surprisingly) more likely to be accessible. Multiple cues help (Solso & Biersdorff, 1975). Finally, the target itself can serve as a retrieval cue, albeit an exact one. For instance, when knowledge is marginal (stored but not accessible), individuals are equally likely to regain access to it following exposure (e.g., Berger et al., 1999) or recognizing the target among a list of alternatives (Cantor et al., 2015).

Returning to the problem of misinformation, why should we care if knowledge is temporarily inaccessible? We remind the reader of the example provided at the beginning of the chapter, namely that Americans (when prompted) remembered that claims about WMDs had been retracted—but immediately beforehand indicated that they still believed the claims. To the extent that someone knows something but does not retrieve it, it will not affect belief. In the remainder of this chapter, we take a deep dive into this property to examine how one's national identity can affect what knowledge is accessible at a given time.

An Empirical Example Related to Nationalism

As previously described, not all information stored in memory is always accessible. We sometimes struggle to remember well-known names or the meaning of words we have encountered repeatedly in the past, as well as other types of information. Sometimes, knowledge is not accessible because it has not been used in a long time; other times, something in the environment cues us toward the wrong information or makes it more difficult to access the correct information. In a series of studies recently published in the *Journal of Applied Research in Memory and Cognition*, we investigated whether the activation of one's national identity influences the accessibility of information relevant to that identity (Stanley et al., 2021). Some theorists have argued that our personal identities are complex and multifaceted, composed of many different, contextually activated constructions (H. Marsh & Hattie, 1995; McConnell, 2011). On this view, different identities can be active at different times, and individuals, environments, and institutions all have the power to activate a particular identity across varied contexts. For example, a person's occupational identity as a mechanic might be active at work, but that same person's identity as a father might be active when playing with his children after work. At yet another time, that person's partisan identity might be active when exposed to a political commercial during campaign season, when attending a political rally for a preferred candidate, or when commenting on a political news story on social media. Beyond partisan identities, a person's identity as an American might be active when listening to the Pledge of Allegiance, after exposure to particular symbols (e.g., the American flag or a bald eagle), or when taking a walk through the National Mall in Washington, DC. However, American symbols are not required; one's national identity can also be activated when confronted with an out-group member of another national identity (Wertsch, 2021).

In our studies, we asked whether the activation of one's national identity affects the accessibility of information relevant to that identity. We created a simple laboratory paradigm to examine whether thinking about one's national identity affects the accessibility of knowledge about one's country. Namely, we had participants write about one of two identities (one's national identity, American, or one's self identity), and then we simply asked participants to remember the 50 U.S. states. We followed Brown's (1923) logic that the states are well known to Americans (through school, travel, the media, state-themed postage stamps and quarters, etc.) and are also related to the American identity. No information was taught during the study; it was assumed to exist. At a minimum, there was no reason to believe that knowledge differed as a function of experimental condition, given random assignment to conditions.

Both groups of subjects began by writing about an identity. Subjects in the American identity condition read that

> One of the things we are interested in is the American (United States) identity. Please take some time to think about the way your American identity is important to you. Why and how is your American identity important to you? Please imagine that you are describing to a stranger why and how your American identity is important to you. In 3–7 sentences, please type what you would say to that stranger about the importance of your American identity.

In contrast, participants in the self identity condition were prompted

> One of the things we are interested in is your personal self identity. Please take some time to think about the way your personal self identity is important to you. Why and how is your personal self identity important to you? Please imagine that you are describing to a stranger why and how your personal self identity is important to you. In 3–7 sentences, please type what you would say to that stranger about the importance of your personal self identity.

Subjects had no problems responding to these writing prompts. For example, sample responses in the American identity condition included that

> American identity to me is the ability to walk freely outside without fear of danger. I can go where I please, do what I want to do, and essentially face no restrictions in doing so. Its [sic] a feeling of safety in America knowing that your future is pretty much secured as long as you take care of yourself.

Another subject wrote that

> I am proud to be an American not because I am a nationalist but because I am proud of my countries [sic] history. America has been a beacon of freedom to the world pretty much since it's [sic] inception. It has also been a scientific leader because capitalism allows for very efficient research. America is looked up to by pretty much every country in the world.

Participants in the identity condition wrote responses such as

> My self-identity is important to me because it always keeps me grounded. If I know who I am it saves me from ever acting outside of myself. I think it gives me hope and peace to know who I am, especially in Christ.

Another wrote,

> It's important to me that I have personal integrity. I can't stand liars and value truth. No matter how hard truth may be, it's important to me that it not be obscured. I'm also careful to make sure that, in the pursuit of truth, if I give my word, make a promise, I always keep that promise, stick to my word, no matter how hard it may become. I stand by my friends unconditionally and that's important, too.

After writing about one of their two identities, all participants were asked to recall the 50 U.S. states. To make the task challenging and avoid ceiling effects, they were given only 2 minutes to do so. On average, participants in the American identity condition remembered 22.7 U.S. states, whereas those in the self identity condition remembered 19.9 states. Although the difference between conditions amounted to approximately 3 states, it was still impressive given the overlearned nature of the information. That is, participants had no chance to learn additional states before being asked to recall them, and knowledge of the U.S. states was probably similar between the two groups (given random assignment to conditions).

The reader may be wondering about the claim that the states represent overlearned knowledge, given that people recalled fewer than half of the states. However, it must be noted that the measure here is free recall, not recognition. We predict that if we gave participants a list of states plus foils, they would be at ceiling at identifying the states. Recall is not a perfect measure of what people know, but it is an ideal way of measuring changes in accessibility.

As an aside, we note that preliminary content analyses of recall did not suggest interesting differences in *which* states were recalled or in *when* they were recalled (the order). For example, one might have hypothesized that subjects in the American condition would be more likely to recall the original 13 colonies or other states with particular historical value—but that was not the case. The most recalled states were the most populous ones (California, New York, and Texas). Similarly, recall order did not suggest strategic differences across conditions; it was not, for example, the case that subjects in the American condition were more likely to retrieve the original 13 colonies first. Instead, the state most likely to be recalled first was "Alabama," suggesting that many people used an alphabetical strategy to retrieve the states. Given these results, we did not score the remaining studies for specific state names or recall order.

In a second study, we replicated the effect with two new control conditions. First, we added a no-writing control group, which was not instructed to think of any particular identity (in case the self identity was somehow interfering with recall of the states). Second, a group of participants was asked to write two to five sentences explaining how and why their family identity matters to them. Sample responses from the family identity condition included "My family identity is an important part of who I am. Being married and having children is my life. This creates the person I am. My life revolves around my family" and

> My family is a vital part of who I am. They raised me with the values and morals that have shaped my life and I appreciate the way they approach life. Similarly, my family and I share many important characteristics, so I feel very similar to them. At the same time, my family and I help each other frequently, so this has built very strong reciprocal relationships.

Similar to the first study, participants in the American identity condition recalled approximately three more states than those in the no identity condition and two more states than those in the family identity condition. There was no difference in the number of states recalled between the two control conditions.

Originally, we allowed 2 minutes for recall to make the task challenging; however, later studies showed that the identity priming effect disappeared when people received more time to recall the states. When given 7 minutes or unlimited time to recall states, participants remembered the same number of states regardless of whether they had written about their American or self identities. Our explanation is that activating one's cultural identity primes (speeds retrieval of) related information. The mechanism is essentially what is called "semantic priming" in cognitive psychology, which is demonstrated when, for example, people read or make a word–nonword decision faster after reading a related word. Participants are faster to respond to "doctor" if they have just responded to "nurse" rather than "bread" (Meyer & Schvaneveldt, 1971). Our effects are more about speeded access than, for example, inhibition of some states; thus, with sufficient time, the difference between conditions disappears.

We tested these ideas more directly in a final study using a variation of a cumulative recall paradigm (e.g., Roediger & Thorpe, 1978) to obtain a more fine-grained analysis of recall. After writing about their American or self identities, participants recalled as many states as they could for 1 minute. At the end of each minute, the screen refreshed, the states already recalled were listed, and participants were given an additional minute to recall as many *new* states as they could, taking care to avoid repeating any items. Participants recalled states over six blocks (i.e., 6 minutes total); Figure 21.1 shows the number of additional states recalled each minute. Not surprisingly, participants in both conditions recalled the most states in the first minute and recalled fewer and fewer (new) states as time progressed. Critically, the difference between the two identity conditions was driven by early recall: In the first minute of recall, participants in the American condition recalled more states than did participants in the self condition. Over time, the two conditions recalled similar amounts.

Returning to the issue of nationalism and misinformation, our results highlight how a brief activation of one's American identity changed the accessibility of overlearned information. Our sample was random and not selected for being particularly nationalistic—suggesting that these effects could be much stronger in populations in which the identity was crucial.

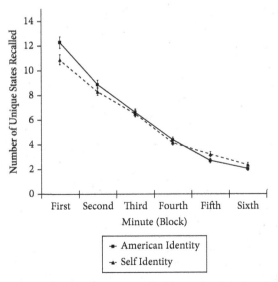

Figure 21.1 Number of unique states recalled in each of six 1-minute blocks, as a function of whether subjects wrote about their American or self identities prior to recalling the states.

Conclusion

Humans take a series of shortcuts when evaluating incoming information: We start biased toward truth (Gilbert, 1991) and use cues such as source and ease of processing as markers for truth. Direct retrieval of knowledge is not a given; it may be inaccessible at a given moment, or our fast but cursory processing of complex information may mean that we do notice discrepancies with what is stored in memory. These shortcuts are adaptive because they promote cognitive efficiency and normally lead people to the correct answers—but they can also lead to misinformation acceptance.

Of course, any one false belief cannot be tied definitively to any one action or mechanism, but we can draw on basic science to identify behaviors or phrasing that likely increase belief in populist ideas. Understanding these properties provides a starting point for solutions; for example, knowing that repetition increases belief highlights why corrections should avoid referring to the targeted myth or error (Lewandowsky et al., 2012). Similarly, interventions aimed at getting people to evaluate sources are unlikely to be successful, unless it means that people avoid a communication altogether (E. Marsh & Yang, 2017). Source information is not always accessed and is quickly forgotten, meaning that interventions focused on source are likely short-term interventions. Finally, we are not optimistic about purely informational campaigns. Aside from people's biases to reject information inconsistent with their beliefs, it is not necessarily protective even for people motivated to reject misinformation.

References

Bar, M. (2009). Predictions: A universal principle in the operation of the human brain. *Philosophical Transactions of the Royal Society: B. Biological Sciences, 364*, 1181–1182.

Begg, I., Armour, V., & Kerr, T. (1985). On believing what we remember. *Canadian Journal of Behavioural Science, 17*(3), 199–214.

Berger, S. A., Hall, L. K., & Bahrick, H. P. (1999). Stabilizing access to marginal and submarginal knowledge. *Journal of Experimental Psychology: Applied, 5*, 438–447.

Bottoms, H. C., Eslick, A. N., & Marsh, E. J. (2010). Memory and the Moses illusion: Failures to detect contradictions with stored knowledge yield negative memorial consequences. *Memory, 18*(6), 670–678.

Brashier, N. M., & Marsh, E. J. (2020). Judging truth. *Annual Review of Psychology, 71*, 499–515.

Bredart, S., & Modolo, K. (1988). Moses strikes again: Focalization effect on a semantic illusion. *Acta Psychologica, 67*(2), 135–144.

Brown, W. (1923). To what extent is memory measured by a single recall trial? *Journal of Experimental Psychology, 6,* 377–382.

Büttner, A. C. (2007). Questions versus statements: Challenging an assumption about semantic illusions. *Quarterly Journal of Experimental Psychology, 60,* 779–789.

Cantor, A. D., Eslick, A. N., Marsh, E. J., Bjork, R. A., & Bjork, E. L. (2015). Multiple-choice tests stabilize access to marginal knowledge. *Memory & Cognition, 43,* 193–205.

Cantor, A. D., & Marsh, E. J. (2017). Expertise effects in the Moses illusion: Detecting contradictions with stored knowledge. *Memory, 25,* 220–230.

Chi, M. T., Feltovich, P. J., & Glaser, R. (1981). Categorization and representation of physics problems by experts and novices. *Cognitive Science, 5,* 121–152.

Chi, M. T., Glaser, R., & Farr, M. J. (Eds.). (1988). *The nature of expertise.* Erlbaum.

Dechêne, A., Stahl, C., Hansen, J., & Wänke, M. (2010). The truth about the truth: A meta-analytic review of the truth effect. *Personality and Social Psychology Review, 14,* 238–257.

Ecker, U. K., & Ang, L. C. (2019). Political attitudes and the processing of misinformation corrections. *Political Psychology, 40*(2), 241–260.

Erickson, T. D., & Mattson, M. E. (1981). From words to meaning: A semantic illusion. *Journal of Verbal Learning & Verbal Behavior, 20,* 540–551.

Fazio, L. K., Brashier, N. M., Payne, B. K., & Marsh, E. J. (2015). Knowledge does not protect against illusory truth. *Journal of Experimental Psychology: General, 144,* 993–1002.

Fazio, L. K., Rand, D. G., & Pennycook, G. (2019). Repetition increases perceived truth equally for plausible and implausible statements. *Psychonomic Bulletin & Review, 26,* 1705–1710.

Ferreira, F., Bailey, K. G., & Ferraro, V. (2002). Good-enough representations in language comprehension. *Current Directions in Psychological Science, 11,* 11–15.

Ferreira, F., & Lowder, M. W. (2016). Prediction, information structure, and good-enough language processing. Psychology of *Learning* and *Motivation, 65,* 217–247.

Gilbert, D. T. (1991). How mental systems believe. *American Psychologist, 46,* 107–119.

Hovland, C. I., & Weiss, W. (1951). The influence of source credibility on communication effectiveness. *Public Opinion Quarterly, 15*(4), 635–650.

International Federation of Library Associations and Institutions. (2017, February 1). *How to spot fake news—IFLA in the post-truth society.* Retrieved January 2021, from https://www.ifla.org/node/11175

Johnson, K. E., & Mervis, C. B. (1997). Effects of varying levels of expertise on the basic level of categorization. *Journal of Experimental Psychology: General, 126,* 248–277.

Karimi, H., & Ferreira, F. (2016). Good-enough linguistic representations and online cognitive equilibrium in language processing. *Quarterly Journal of Experimental Psychology, 69*(5), 1013–1040.

Lev-Ari, S., & Keysar, B. (2010). Why don't we believe non-native speakers? The influence of accent on credibility. *Journal of Experimental Social Psychology, 46*(6), 1093–1096.

Lewandowsky, S., Ecker, U. K., Seifert, C. M., Schwarz, N., & Cook, J. (2012). Misinformation and its correction: Continued influence and successful debiasing. *Psychological Science in the Public Interest, 13*(3), 106–131.

Lewandowsky, S., Stritzke, W. G. K., Oberauer, K., & Morales, M. (2005). Memory for fact, fiction, and misinformation: The Iraq War 2003. *Psychological Science, 16*(3), 190–195.

Marsh, E. J., Meade, M. L., & Roediger, H. L., III. (2003). Learning facts from fiction. *Journal of Memory and Language, 49*(4), 519–536.

Marsh, E. J., & Yang, B. W. (2017). A call to think broadly about information literacy. *Journal of Applied Research in Memory and Cognition, 6*, 401–404.

Marsh, H. W., & Hattie, J. (1995). Theoretical perspectives on the structure of self-concept. In B. A. Bracken (Ed.), *Handbook of self-concept: Developmental, social, and clinical considerations* (pp. 38–90). Wiley.

McConnell, A. R. (2011). The multiple self-aspects framework: Self-concept representation and its implications. *Personality and Social Psychology Review, 15*(1), 3–27.

McGlone, M. S., & Tofighbakhsh, J. (2000). Birds of a feather flock conjointly (?): Rhyme as reason in aphorisms. *Psychological Science, 11*(5), 424–428.

Meyer, D. E., & Schvaneveldt, R. W. (1971). Facilitation in recognizing pairs of words: Evidence of a dependence between retrieval operations. *Journal of Experimental Psychology, 90*, 227–234.

Murray, S., Stanley, M., McPhetres, J., Pennycook, G., & Seli, P. (n.d.). "I've said it before and I will say it again": Repeating statements made by Donald Trump increases perceived truthfulness for individuals across the political spectrum. Unpublished manuscript. https://doi.org/10.31234/osf.io/9evzc

Newman, E. J., Garry, M., Bernstein, D. M., Kantner, J., & Lindsay, D. S. (2012). Nonprobative photographs (or words) inflate truthiness. *Psychonomic Bulletin & Review, 19*, 969–974.

Newman, E. J., & Schwarz, N. (2018). Good sound, good research: How audio quality influences perceptions of the research and researcher. *Science Communication, 40*, 246–257.

Pennycook, G., Cannon, T. D., & Rand, D. G. (2018). Prior exposure increases perceived accuracy of fake news. *Journal of Experimental Psychology: General, 147*(12), 1865–1880.

Pornpitakpan, C. (2004). The persuasiveness of source credibility: A critical review of five decades' evidence. *Journal of Applied Social psychology, 34*(2), 243–281.

Priester, J. R., & Petty, R. E. (1995). Source attributions and persuasion: Perceived honesty as a determinant of message scrutiny. *Personality and Social Psychology Bulletin, 21*(6), 637–654.

Putnam, A. L., & Phelps, R. J. (2017). The citation effect: In-text citations moderately increase belief in trivia claims. *Acta Psychologica, 179*, 114–123.

Reber, R., & Schwarz, N. (1999). Effects of perceptual fluency on judgments of truth. *Consciousness and Cognition, 8*, 338–342.

Roediger, H. L., III., & Thorpe, L. A. (1978). The role of recall time in producing hypermnesia. *Memory & Cognition, 6*(3), 296–305.

Shafto, M., & MacKay, D. G. (2000). The Moses, mega-Moses, and Armstrong illusions: Integrating language comprehension and semantic memory. *Psychological Science, 11*(5), 372–378.

Solso, R. L., & Biersdorff, K. K. (1975). Recall under conditions of cumulative cues. *Journal of General Psychology, 93*, 233–246.

Song, H., & Schwarz, N. (2008). Fluency and the detection of misleading questions: Low processing fluency attenuates the Moses illusion. *Social Cognition, 26*(6), 791–799.

Stanley, M. L., Taylor, M., & Marsh, E. J. (2021). Cultural identity changes the accessibility of knowledge. *Journal of Applied Research in Memory and Cognition, 10*(1), 44–54.

Tulving, E., & Pearlstone, Z. (1966). Availability versus accessibility of information in memory for words. *Journal of Verbal Learning and Verbal Behavior, 5*(4), 381–391.

Umanath, S., Dolan, P. O., & Marsh, E. J. (2014). Aging and the Moses illusion: Older adults fall for Moses but if asked directly, stick with Noah. *Memory, 22*, 481–492.

Underwood, J., & Pezdek, K. (1998). Memory suggestibility as an example of the sleeper effect. *Psychonomic Bulletin & Review, 5*(3), 449–453.

Unkelbach, C. (2007). Reversing the truth effect: Learning the interpretation of processing fluency in judgments of truth. *Journal of Experimental Psychology: Learning, Memory, and Cognition, 33*(1), 219.

Wertsch, J. (2021). *How nations remember: A narrative approach.* Oxford University Press.

Wood, T., & Porter, E. (2019). The elusive backfire effect: Mass attitudes' steadfast factual adherence. *Political Behavior, 41*(1), 135–163.

22
The Narrative Tools of National Memory

James V. Wertsch

We seem to be out of practice when it comes to thinking about nations and nationalism. After spending decades assuming that a globalism would be a permanent fixture of our landscape, an explosion of "new nationalism" (Rose, 2019) has forced us to reassess how we make sense of the world. Developments such as the rise of social media and of China mean that our effort today must be different than it was during the heyday of nation formation in the 19th century, but some themes have remained largely unchanged.

To appreciate the broader historical context, it is useful to start with Ernst Renan's classic lecture "What Is a Nation?" delivered at the Sorbonne in 1882. Renan (1882/1990) began his peroration by listing criteria such as language, religion, and race that are often used in general definitions of a nation. He then outlined why each was inadequate and formulated two abstract forces in their place: a "spiritual principle" and a "rich legacy of memories." The first takes the form of "daily plebiscites" of activities that sustain a nation and can be viewed as a conceptual ancestor of Benedict Anderson's (1991) notion of "imagined communities." In Anderson's telling, these are large-scale collectives bound together not by personal acquaintance but, rather, by acts of shared imagination that rely on public media, maps, and other shared symbolic means. The second, memory, provides the critical foundation on which this spiritual principle operates. Renan was visionary when he wrote that the rich legacy of memory is just as concerned with forgetting and getting history wrong in forming a nation as it is with remembering in the usual sense. He made special note of the practice of omitting or distorting dark and disreputable details in a nation's past. But his discussion remained quite general, leaving us with questions such as the following: How is national memory created and maintained? What sort of mental processes are involved? and How do mnemonic communities maintain beliefs about the past in the face of disconfirming evidence?

In what follows, I address such questions by starting with the notion of *narrative*. This does not mean that all national memory is a matter of narrative. Walter Benjamin (1999), for one, pointed out that images can play a role in this regard, and others rightly focus on other forces. Even in these cases, however, narrative often re-enters the picture as a crucial means of interpretation (Erll, 2011), making it a kind of foundational concept. My focus on narrative also does not entail the idea that stories[1] are some sort of independent agents that carry national memory in their own right. Instead, they serve as "equipment for living" (Burke, 1998) or "cultural tools" (Wertsch, 1998) that shape but do not mechanistically determine patterns of discourse and thought of individuals—a distinction that is important when trying to account for how narratives bind nations together while also leaving room for individual agency and responsibility.

Narrative has long been a topic of general interest in the humanities and social sciences and has been the object of scholarship in its own right (e.g., Scholes & Kellogg, 1966), but my focus is limited to perspectives that are relevant to understanding national memory. For this, a useful starting point is the vision that Alisdair MacIntyre (2015) outlined of moral action, a vision based on the tradition of the first major Western scholar of narrative—Aristotle. For MacIntyre, "man is in his actions and practice, as well as in his fictions, essentially a story-telling animal" (p. 216), and one of the consequences is that "I can only answer the question, 'What am I to do?' if I can answer the prior question 'Of what story or stories do I find myself a part?'" (p. 216).

Narratives as Equipment for Living

MacIntyre (2015) is concerned with the moral world of the individual, but his ideas have implications for national communities as well. Just as we draw on a "stock of stories" (MacIntyre, 2015, p. 216) to know what we are to do in our personal endeavors, we use the narrative resources of a national community when acting as one of its members. Useful insight into how this occurs in everyday life comes from Burke (1998), particularly in his "sociological criticism" concerned with "literature as equipment for living." There, he outlined how narratives are used in everyday settings to size up a situation in effortless

---

[1] I use "narrative" and "story" interchangeably.

ways to make quick decisions about the intentions and actions of ourselves and other humans. In terminology I have used elsewhere (Wertsch, 2021), this amounts to saying that narratives serve as "co-authors" of what we say and think.

The narrative forms used in sizing up situations and actors can be as extended as *War and Peace* or as short and abbreviated as a one-line summary of an event. In her analysis of efforts to rewrite history curricula in post-Soviet Georgia, Nutsa Batiashvili (see Chapter 16, this volume) deals with narrative forms of the first type, but abbreviated narrative forms also play a role in her account, and the latter were the main focus of Burke's (1998) claims about how we size up situations. More generally, his interest was in how the two forms operate in tandem. Consider his comments about Sinclair Lewis's *Babbitt* (1922/1998), a novel about small-town, mercantile New England life in the early 20th century. To call someone a Babbitt is to quickly size him up in a way based on the novel.

But we do not need to reread all 432 pages of the novel on every occasion that we do this; instead, some condensed, schematic form of narrative is assumed. It is a form that is efficient and allows us to make quick, indeed snap, judgments of a situation, often with little more than scant information about the situation. Aristotle touched on this when he suggested a parallel between visual arts and narrative. As summarized by Peter Brooks (1984), the point is that just as in the visual arts a whole must be of a size that can be taken in by the eye, so a plot must be "of a length to be taken in by memory" (p. 11).

Regardless of whether they are extended or are abbreviated and schematic, the central feature of narratives is that they rely on plot to grasp together events that occur in a temporal order into a coherent whole. In this connection, Paul Ricoeur (1991) wrote of how they transform "many incidents *into one* story" through "the operation of emplotment as a synthesis of heterogeneous elements" (p. 21). This is not to say that narrative is the only "cognitive instrument" (Mink, 1978) or form of thinking available to humans. Bruner (1986) contrasted it, for example, to "logico-scientific" thinking. For him, this and story-based reasoning are "two modes of cognitive functioning, two modes of thought, each providing distinctive ways of ordering experience, of constructing reality" (p. 11). The two modes are similar in that they take information and turn it into statements that imply causality, but "the types of causality ... are palpably different" (p. 11). Logico-deductive thinking involves causal forces that operate independently of human intention, whereas narrative thinking is about individuals' intentions and reasons and relies on what Brooks (1984) calls a "strange logic" based on the sense of an ending of a story. The notion of an ending points both to the temporal organization of the events depicted and to their organization through emplotment. These two dimensions of narrative also apply with regard to a story's beginning, something Abram Van Engen examines in Chapter 2 of this volume.

Bruner (1986) suggested that logico-deductive thinking convinces us on the basis of abstract logic, whereas narrative thinking relies on verisimilitude, suggesting different sorts of truth claims—a point that has critical importance for understanding how narratives function in national memory. As members of different national communities, we often can understand and even agree to disagree over values, attitudes, and ideologies, but when it comes to stories about the past, things are different because we assume they can be *true*. This makes differences with others not just a matter of opinion but of truth, which, in turn, can make such differences nearly impossible to negotiate. It might be more appropriate to speak of verisimilitude, as Bruner did, but in fact, we find it difficult not to assume that narrative truth claims take a stronger form, and the result is that we can react to others' accounts of events with surprise and offense, producing outbursts such as "But that's just not true!"

Narrative Truth

Raising the issue of narrative truth does not amount to going down a rabbit hole of relativism, even though it might seem to risk putting us in a position in which truth is taken to be a matter of personal whim or simple power. In my view, this is a risk that can be managed, but more to the point, it is a risk that must be taken to understand the nature of disputes over national memory. Narrative truth is, to be sure, an elusive notion, but it is possible to formulate and apply. As a starting point, I turn to a distinction between it and the more familiar notion of propositional truth. As an example of the latter, consider how we determine the truth of a proposition such as "The Western Allies invaded Normandy on June 6, 1944." We have conventional norms and procedures for arriving at the conclusion that this statement is true and also that a statement such as "The Western Allies invaded Normandy on February 8, 1947" is false. Namely, we use archival documents, eyewitness accounts, and other forms of evidence and judge whether the content of a proposition corresponds with them.

In contrast to this sort of correspondence theory of truth, consider a statement about the overall story of World War II, such as "The turning point in the Allied victory over Germany was the invasion of Normandy on June 6, 1944." This is a statement about narrative truth, and Roediger et al. (see Chapter 11, this volume) note it is something that is widely accepted in the U.S. mnemonic community but rejected in Russia. It is a claim about what the "real" or "right" story of World War II is, and this changes the procedures that apply when trying to assess to its truth. We are no longer in a realm where competing truth claims can be settled solely on the basis of whether a statement corresponds with archival and other forms of evidence. Instead, we start considering issues such as how coherent a story is and whether it attains a sufficient level of verisimilitude to make it acceptable.

This is not to say that the truth of the propositions included in a narrative account is unimportant. It is to say, however, that narrative truth involves something that goes beyond a sum of the propositional truths. Narrative truth involves a judgment about the "emplotment as a synthesis of heterogeneous elements" (Ricoeur, 1991), a judgment that cannot be justified on the basis of the truths of the propositions included in a narrative alone. Mink (1978) made this point in distinguishing scientific theories from narratives, and Cronon (1992) has illustrated it by demonstrating how two historical narratives can include the same information, the same set of propositional truths, yet have quite different storylines.

These points are particularly relevant to national memory because of the way that propositional truth and narrative truth play out against one other. Namely, when encountering a difference over narrative truth, our first inclination is often to turn to propositional truth to resolve it. In the case just noted, for example, someone might attempt to challenge the claim that the real turning point of World War II was D-Day on June 6, 1944, by noting that much larger battles had taken place more than a year earlier on the Eastern Front. Whereas 4,400 Allied troops and 9,000 German troops died on D-Day, more than 1,100,000 Red Army troops and 850,000 Axis troops died in the Battle of Stalingrad. But do such propositional truths settle the question of narrative truth about World War II? Apparently not, at least for the mnemonic communities of the United States and many other nations (see Chapters 10 and 11, this volume). One reason for this is that along with being cognitive instruments, the narrative tools that mediate national memory are part of a collective identity project, and the result is that national communities often resist giving up their accounts of the past, even in the face of evidence that seems to contradict them.

Among other things, this defense of narrative truth is a reflection of "national narcissism" as discussed by Roediger et al. (see Chapter 11, this volume), and it can play out in some surprising ways. Namely, the tensions between propositional and narrative truth take on different forms in the case of one's own national memory and that of others. In the case of others, we often seem to assume that removing the underpinning provided by a single propositional truth in their story will force them to question the truth of an entire narrative, while failing to see the same point in our case.

An illustration of this can be found in Estonians' struggle against Russia over the narrative of the secret protocols of the Molotov–Ribbentrop Pact that led to the forced annexation of their country in 1940. After denying the existence of these protocols for decades, Russian authorities admitted that they existed after all when they were discovered in archives opened after the Soviet Union collapsed—archives that stated exactly what Estonians had claimed. At that point, many Estonians believed that Russians would be forced to acknowledge that the annexation was a crime of aggressive expansionism rather than the result of an invitation by the workers and peasants of Estonia. More generally, they believed that this would lead to an acknowledgment that the entire Soviet period was one of mass criminality and was part of an even longer history of brutal Russian aggression against neighboring nations.

The Estonians were soon disappointed, however, in their hopes that the falsehood of a crucial proposition would undermine the truth of these larger narratives. Instead, the Russian national narrative demonstrated a deep-seated, protean capacity that made it largely impervious to inconvenient facts. To be sure, some of the initial accounts of Russian history that appeared in post-Soviet textbooks acknowledged the illegality, even criminality, of the 1940 annexation, and this led to a "narrative rift" (Wertsch, 2002) in how the story was told. But the damage was soon repaired and the rift overcome. Subsequent accounts interpreted the event as part of Stalin's clever strategy of gaining additional time to prepare for Soviet effort to save the world from fascism. Instead of leading to the collapse of an official account, the Russian response was to sidestep contradictory evidence and retain the larger narrative by taking the real story actually to be about something larger and quite different.

If the truth of a narrative is not determined by the truth of the propositions it includes, what are the forces that shape what the real story is? Unless it is a matter of mere whim or the sheer power of one party over another, it must lie elsewhere. And the most obvious candidate for this force is the deeply held belief systems of members of national communities—belief systems that are typically not consciously articulated and hence are difficult to unearth and address. Once again, this is something that can be examined in terms of narrative, namely by introducing additional distinctions.

Specific Narratives and Narrative Templates

The first distinction I propose in this regard is between "specific narratives," which include concrete information about settings, characters, and events, and "narrative templates," which are more abstract, schematic narrative forms devoid of such information. When we think of national memory, we often think first of specific narratives that include particular events and actors such as those included in history instruction in school. This sort of information is reflected in the data Abel et al. (see Chapter 10, this volume) report about how people in 11 nations remember World War II. The data reveal agreement within national communities and some striking differences between them about concrete events such as Pearl Harbor, the Battle of Stalingrad, D-Day, and so forth, all of which are part of the information included in specific narratives about World War II.

But concrete events and characters are not all that is involved in the rich legacy of memory Renan (1882/1990) saw as underpinning a nation. In addition, other types of narratives in the form of underlying schematic codes distinguish one national mnemonic community from another. And because they operate in unconscious ways and are less accessible to reflection, these can be particularly influential. Schematic forms of representation have been a part of discussions in memory studies since Frederic Bartlett (1932; see also Roediger, 2000) introduced the notion of schema in his psychological research nearly a century ago. And even though the definition of a schema itself remains difficult to define, it is a crucial tool in the study of national memory. Instead of listing the kind of concrete names and dates included in a specific narrative—information that critics often complain clutters up history teaching—schematic narrative templates are general storylines. And they are sufficiently protean that they can accommodate a range of facts, including seemingly contradictory facts, as in the case noted previously about the Russian version of the Molotov–Ribbentrop Pact.

When examining the implications for these claims for the study of national memory, the point is not simply that the narrative tools can be abbreviated and schematic, but that they can be abbreviated and schematic *in different ways in different national communities*. The specific narrative accounts generated by these underlying narrative forms are judged by members of the community to be true, even if that requires "getting history wrong" as Renan (1882/1990) noted. Pointing out errors and lacunae to others, however, often has little impact on their commitment to narrative templates, which are typically the source of history wars, including ones that morph into hot wars such as that between Azerbaijan and Armenia (see Chapter 17, this volume).

To illustrate the notion of a narrative template, consider the Russian "Expulsion-of-Alien-Enemies" schematic storyline that I have described elsewhere (Wertsch, 2021). In contrast to a specific narrative, which can be observed in a surface form, it is a posited hypothetical form, and it can be summarized as follows:

1. An "initial situation" in which Russia is peaceful and not interfering with others.
2. "Trouble," in which a foreign enemy viciously attacks Russia without provocation.
3. Russia comes under existential threat and nearly loses everything as the enemy attempts to destroy it as a civilization.
4. Through heroism and exceptionalism, against all odds, and acting alone, Russia triumphs and succeeds in expelling the foreign enemy.

This narrative template is reflected in multiple specific narratives about particular, concrete events in Russia's past. It provides the habits used in Russia to make sense of everything from the Mongolian invasion of the 13th century to Napoleon's invasion in the 19th century, Hitler's onslaught in the Great Patriotic War, and the invasion of communism and other Western ideas. In all these cases, the plot is about alien enemies who nearly destroy Russian civilization before they are defeated and expelled. The narrative template in this case was sufficiently entrenched to remain intact even as national memory underwent radical transformations at the surface level of specific narratives. Thus, during the Soviet era, questioning the heroic role of the Communist Party in winning the Great Patriotic War was a dangerous practice and could imperil one's career or worse, but soon after the collapse of the USSR, official Russian history textbooks reported that the Party had actually *impeded* the war effort and asserting that the real heroes were the great Russian people.

The radical and disorienting revision of history in this case at first glance seems to suggest that national memory can change suddenly and fundamentally. But at the level of narrative templates, a quite different and much more conservative picture of national memory emerges. The Expulsion-of-Alien-Enemies narrative template suggests a basic pattern that is played out in many different ways, presenting a picture of same story, different characters. Narrative templates provide the underpinning for disputes—sometimes quite heated—over specific narratives and the propositions they contained. In the Russian case, the narrative template at issue has shaped national memory for centuries at an underlying level even as the society underwent multiple massive and violent changes.

This suggests that national memory at this level is largely a matter of mental habits based on schematic narrative templates rather than lists of discrete events. The observation by William James (1890) that habit is "the enormous fly-wheel of society" (p. 121) suggests that the underlying mental habits of a national community can maintain their inertia even as surface behaviors change. James also noted that habit is society's "most precious conservative agent" (p. 121) and plays a role in preserving a social order even in cases in which we see aspects of it that are undesirable and in need of change. From this perspective, it should come as no surprise that it can be so difficult to change habits of emplotting the past.

None of this discussion touches on the issue of whether narrative habits are beneficial or injurious for the national communities involved. For Russia, the Expulsion-of-Alien-Enemies narrative template was clearly beneficial for the all-out mobilization required in the struggle against fascism in World War II. But this same narrative template has had detrimental effects for Russia's neighbors on several occasions as it launched largely unprovoked aggression against them. From their perspective, the Expulsion-of-Alien-Enemies narrative template can make Russia paranoid and dangerous and hence capable of seeing enemies that may not exist. In this regard, it is noteworthy that Russian President Vladimir Putin has sought to justify Russian incursions into Georgia in 2008 and Ukraine in 2014 as preemptive strikes to threats from NATO. This amounts to sizing up the situations as having all the characteristics of Germany before its invasion of 1941 at the beginning of the Great Patriotic War.

Privileged Event Narratives

Narrative templates provide insight into the habits used to size up events, but their abstract, schematic nature leaves something to be desired with regard to understanding the emotional dimensions of national memory. And these emotional dimensions are of particular interest when trying to understand populist movements such as those that Strobe Talbott (see Chapter 1, this volume) outlines. In order to get at this, another conceptual tool is needed, namely "privileged event narratives." This narrative form draws its strength from both a narrative template and a specific narrative. Because it involves an instantiation of a narrative template, it can be depended on to tap into the underlying mental habits of an imagined community with all their unconscious veiled power. But the abstract schematic form of representation this involves makes it less than ideal for eliciting visceral emotion. Narrative templates do not invite us to put ourselves in the shoes of real people who have experienced real feelings of suffering, trauma, and triumph. Privileged event narratives, however, can do this because in addition to reflecting a narrative template, they draw on concrete information included in a specific narrative.

In today's Russian national community, the Great Patriotic War serves as a privileged event narrative. It has been endlessly used by Putin and other Russian authorities in stoking nationalism, and their success in doing so has depended on the emotional appeal of a specific narrative. Namely, it has drawn on the story of suffering and heroism during concrete events such as the Siege of Leningrad and the Battle of Stalingrad. But its appeal also derives from the fact that it fits the more general mold and the habits of the Expulsion-of-Alien-Enemies narrative template. It is this combination that makes it such an effective tool for Russian populism. The result is that the Great Patriotic War has come to occupy such an important place in Russia memory that it sometimes seems to be the *only* event that happened in the 20th century (Gessen, 2017). It should come as no surprise, then, that the most important holiday today in Russia is Victory Day on May 9, which marks the end of the war in Europe in 1945.

A corollary property of privileged event narratives is their preferred status as lenses through which a community views events in the present. It is a favorite part of the rhetorical toolkit of Putin, for example, to bring up the Great Patriotic War, especially the German invasion of 1941, when explaining why Russia has chosen to act as it has in Ukraine during the past decade. These accounts formulate the invasion of the eastern provinces of the country and the annexation of Crimea in terms of the need to resist "fascist" forces that threaten Russians today just as fascist forces did seven decades ago.

This property of being a preferred lens for viewing contemporary events is an aspect of privileged event narratives to be found in any mnemonic community, and we often become aware of how our views differ from those of other communities when we find ourselves wondering why they repeatedly bring up a particular event from the past in ways that seem irrelevant or inappropriate to us. Thus, members of the American national community may know about World War II—even the Russian version of it—but still find it puzzling why Russians want to introduce it into discussions even when it seems unnecessary or irrelevant. In other cases, Americans are even more puzzled when they have little knowledge of an event that serves as a privileged event narrative. This is the case for the "Century of Humiliation" narrative often invoked by Chinese, a case to which I turn in the next section.

Controlling the Narrative

Focusing on the narrative resources used in national memory is more than an academic exercise. It is central to dealing with highly charged efforts to control the narrative of episodes such as the COVID-19 pandemic. This is part of domestic discussions in the United States, but it became particularly heated in nationalist-tinged disputes between the United States and China. In this case, the dispute has been made all the more striking and disheartening because epidemics are often viewed as an ideal place for international collaboration to occur. Such was the case with the international response to SARS, Ebola, and Zika, but discussions of COVID-19 took a decidedly different turn.

U.S. efforts to control the narrative in this case are reflected in remarks by Secretary of State Mike Pompeo and President Donald Trump. They regularly asserted that the first response to the outbreak of the virus in China was slow and involved a cover-up. This line of thought then evolved into a story that included continued refusal by Chinese authorities to share information about what had occurred in Wuhan, the epicenter of the epidemic. This refusal was also depicted as involving mistakes and lies, which led to the spread of the virus throughout the world, making the People's Republic of China responsible for death and economic destruction in the United States and elsewhere. Among the sequelae of this storyline were lawsuits filed by several American political figures against China for the damages it had caused to the United States (Wertsch, 2020).

Not surprisingly, accounts provided by Chinese authorities were quite different. They often acknowledge that authorities were slow to react initially, but after recognizing the dangers of the epidemic, they responded quickly and without further cover-up or withholding of information. These accounts stressed that Chinese medical scientists quickly shared information about the virus with the rest of the world in order to encourage the collaborative effort needed to halt the budding epidemic. The Chinese account also emphasized the quick, aggressive response in locking down Wuhan and other regions, which provided a model of the competence and will required to win the battle over the virus. At a more general level, this was put forth as evidence of the superiority of the Chinese system of public health and governance.

The two sides' accounts of COVID-19 quickly turned into a struggle over narrative control, and this became a story in its own right in media outlets ranging from PBS to Aljazeera and CGTN. Early on, Aljazeera ran an article on "Controlling the Coronavirus Narrative: China's Propaganda Push"[2] that included comments by Steven Tsang, the Director of the SOAS China Institute at the University of London, highlighting the importance that Chinese authorities placed on getting the story correct. He noted that "from the very beginning, controlling the narrative was the single most important mission for the party." This did not mean that party leaders had no concern with public health and the economy, but these were "less important than controlling the narrative. That was the objective."

A few weeks later, PBS NewsHour ran a story on "The U.S.–China Battle to Control the COVID-19 Narrative,"[3] in which U.S. attempts to put forth a countervailing story were discussed. The PBS report included information from multiple perspectives, but much of it was devoted to questioning the triumphal narrative that China was trying to project. The segment started with an account of donations of Chinese aid to Italy, Nigeria, and Venezuela but then shifted to noting that Italy had to pay for the products from China and that Spain and the United Kingdom reported that the personal protective equipment they received was defective. U.S. Secretary of State Mike Pompeo

---

[2] https://www.aljazeera.com/program/the-listening-post/2020/3/14/controlling-the-coronavirus-narrative-chinas-propaganda-push.

[3] https://www.youtube.com/watch?v=tRI1wAdMmRQ.

was then shown complaining that "China didn't share all the information it had. Instead, it covered up how dangerous the disease is." Near the end of this same story, the PBS report included a return volley from Zou Yue, an anchor on the television station China 24, who talked about the failure on the part of the Trump administration and the U.S. government in general. He concluded by observing, "When I saw Governor Cuomo of New York begging the federal government to step in to get ventilators, I thought, 'Wow! What a difference different systems can make.'"

This struggle to control the narrative of COVID-19 played out over subsequent months, and the two sides became increasingly entrenched in their opposing views. In July 2020, for example, the U.S. State Department released a cable from 2018 to support the claim that the virus escaped from a Chinese laboratory near Wuhan due to faulty safety procedures.[4] By that point, the standoff devolved into competing narratives of China and the United States that can be summarized, respectively, as (1) the Chinese government had the will and competence to act aggressively and stop the spread of COVID-19, and it was successful in bringing it to heel; and (2) China failed to act quickly enough to stop the virus from spreading throughout the world and failed to share all the information it had and hence bears responsibility for unleashing the pandemic throughout the world. Both accounts claim to provide the true or real story, which leaves us with the problems outlined previously about how to adjudicate between narrative truths.

As is often the case in such instances, participants in this debate tried to introduce propositional truths in an effort to challenge the narrative truth espoused by the other. In response to the American narrative, Chinese Foreign Ministry spokesperson Zhao Lijian said, "It might be U.S. army representatives who brought the novel coronavirus to Wuhan, Central China's Hubei Province in October 2019."[5] His charge was then refuted by Pompeo, who placed the source of the outbreak in Wuhan and even said there was "'enormous evidence"[6] that the virus came from a Chinese laboratory. In the end, neither side was successful in harnessing facts and propositional truths to undermine the narrative truth of the other. Months after Zhao and Pompeo traded their charges, U.S. leaders continued to insist that COVID-19 should

---

[4] https://www.washingtonpost.com/national-security/state-department-releases-cable-that-launched-claims-that-coronavirus-escaped-from-chinese-lab/2020/07/17/63deae58-c861-11ea-a9d3-74640f25b953_story.html.
[5] https://www.globaltimes.cn/content/1182511.shtml.
[6] https://www.forbes.com/sites/jackbrewster/2020/05/03/pompeo-enormous-evidence-linking-wuhan-lab-to-covid-outbreak/#2f08af871432.

be called the "Chinese virus" because it originated in China,[7] and Chinese authorities continued to insist that there is no definitive proof about the origins of the virus, or even that it could have come from the United States.

Again, this is not to say that propositional truth is unimportant, but it does suggest that it is often impotent when it comes to challenging a group's belief in a narrative truth. And once again, the controversy takes us to the question of what underpins such belief. In this instance, a good candidate for making sense of the Chinese perspective is the Century of Humiliation narrative. This is a privileged event narrative about brutal colonization beginning with the Opium Wars in the mid-19th century and coming to a close with the victory of the Chinese Communist Party in 1949, a victory that allowed the country, as Chairman Mao said, to stand up. This story includes several chapters of humiliation in the form of military defeats and unfair treaties forced on China. In recent years, it is a narrative that is endlessly repeated in schools, commemorative events such as national "Humiliation Day" observed every September 18, and the media, and it has become part of the mental habits of the Chinese mnemonic community. And as such, it has become a favored starting point when making appeals to a form of populist nationalism that emerged after the 1989 Tiananmen Square massacre, when the Chinese Communist Party switched from relying on Marxist to nationalist rhetoric (Wang, 2012).

The Century of Humiliation privileged event narrative shapes views of events in China in ways analogous to how the Great Patriotic War story operates in today's Russia. The narrative tools and mental habits differ in their particulars, but at a general level the upshot is that members of these two national communities have developed mental habits that encourage them to see aggressive intentions where others may not. This surfaced in Chinese reaction to U.S. legal suits that called for compensation for damages against the United States. Observers in the United States differed over the merits of these suits, but they generally understood the logic involved and assumed that Chinese citizens would use the same line of reasoning. But the lawsuits unleashed a nationalist response in China that few Americans were in a position to understand—a response rooted in the Century of Humiliation narrative.

This is reflected in the Chinese term "compensation" ("péi cháng"/赔偿)[8] that was used in the media to report on the suits. It is a term used in one of

---

[7] Trump press interview.
[8] I am indebted to Professor Chen Li of Fudan University for expert advice on this term.

the most infamous chapters of the Century of Humiliation, namely a settlement forced on China after the Boxer Rebellion of 1900. The Boxer Protocol of 1901 employed this term in its "indemnity clause" that forced the Chinese emperor to pay Western powers a large sum as damages for incidents that these powers themselves instigated. This made it very difficult for members of the Chinese mnemonic community to encounter the term péi cháng as part of the lawsuits in 2020 without hearing it resonate with the narrative they routinely use to size up humiliating encounters with Western powers. Regardless of whether the American political figures filing their lawsuits had any inkling of this (they almost certainly did not), it elicited a response that made negotiating differences with China extremely difficult.

Managing National Narratives and Memory

The struggle to control the narrative of the COVID-19 pandemic provides just one illustration of how the underlying schematic codes of memory can constrain nations' views of contemporary events. When combined with the fact that the mental habits associated with narrative templates are conservative and resistant to change, this conservatism lends a sobering note to any plans to negotiate differences between national communities. In fact, however, studies of national memory can provide insight into how such negotiation can be conducted, making them a source of at least tempered optimism.

A good starting point in dealing with this issue is to acknowledge the naiveté of assuming that if people would only listen to one another, they could resolve differences in their national memories. Rather than looking for neat resolution and straightforward agreement over national memory, the more realistic goal may be to *manage* national memory and its worst proclivities. This is a process that will go on for as long as there are discussions about the past, and although it may not be fully satisfying, it is much to be preferred to the alternatives that can produce real conflict such as that described by Rauf Garagozov (see Chapter 17, this volume).

The first dictum for managing national memory, then, is that we need to recognize what we are up against. In particular, we need to recognize the power of underlying codes and habits in co-authoring our thinking and speaking about the past. This includes recognizing how unlikely it is that we will get others to give up a narrative truth by challenging it with propositional truths. Efforts to do so are no more likely to be successful than the Estonians were when they sought to overturn a Russian account of World War II with the appearance of new archival information about the Molotov–Ribbentrop Pact. In such cases, what we are up against is the power of narrative templates and privileged event narratives to shape our accounts of the past, and issues need to be discussed at that level.

A second dictum for managing differences over national memory may at first glance seem to contradict the first. Namely, it is that analytic history should be used as an antidote or corrective to national memory. Elsewhere, I have summarized the difference between national memory and analytic history by saying that the former tends to preserve a narrative at the expense of evidence, whereas the latter tends to preserve evidence at the expense of a narrative (Wertsch & Roediger, 2008). This dictum suggests that using propositional truths to resist narrative truths in national memory is, at best, likely to be an uphill struggle.

Nevertheless, there are benefits to be derived by raising the level of discussion to the sort of rational reflection based on evidence that is the heart of analytic history, at least in its aspirations. With all its weaknesses, this approach sometimes brings to light findings that are difficult to square with deeply held beliefs about the past, and engaging in discussion at this level is one of the best means we have for reining in claims about the past grounded in little more than dogma. Renan (1882/1990) said that every nation gets its history wrong, but this does not mean we should not call out and challenge claims that cannot stand serious scrutiny, and in some cases, the process can produce changes in larger narrative truths.

The third dictum I propose for managing national memory is that national communities need to practice a bit of humility with regard to their beliefs about the past. It is possible that the facts and truths that we take to be obvious may not be so obvious to others. Instead of corresponding to reality, our beliefs may derive from narrative habits that bind us together into a national community. We find it easy to identify flaws in others' accounts of the past, and if we can step back and consider things from a perspective other than what our narrative habits encourage, it is just possible that certainties will be less certain. At the dawn of the nuclear age, Reinhold Niebuhr (1952) made this point by calling on Americans to recognize some of the ironies of their own history and to be more open to considering that their reading of their own and Russian actions was the only one possible.

The final dictum I list for managing national memory goes back to what William James (1890) had to say about habit. He noted that its conservative tendencies can make it a daunting impediment to changing a society's beliefs and actions. But the fact that habit is a product of socialization points to a reason for optimism as well. Namely, by intervening early in the formation of habit, it is possible to change some of the more dire consequences it can have. One of the best practices for developing a broader vision in this regard is to encourage students—indeed, all of us—to make a practice of confronting narratives that differ radically from the familiar ones we have about the past. In its most effective form, this requires trust based on personal acquaintance, reminding us of the need for intercultural and international educational activities, but even when practiced from afar, this can be useful. In short, education—and the earlier, the better—is key to moving beyond fruitless confrontation over the past. And that is part of what motivates the larger conversation in this volume.

References

Anderson, B. (1991). *Imagined communities: Reflections on the origin and spread of nationalism*. Verso.

Bartlett, F. C. (1932). *Remembering: A study in experimental and social psychology*. Cambridge University Press.

Benjamin, W. (1999). *The arcades project* (H. Eiland & K. McLaughlin, Trans.). Harvard University Press.

Brooks, P. (1984). *Reading for the plot: Design and intention in narrative*. Harvard University Press.

Bruner, J. S. (1986). *Actual minds, possible worlds*. Harvard University Press.

Burke, K. (1998). Literature as equipment for living. In D. H. Richter (Ed.), *The critical tradition: Classic texts and contemporary trends* (pp. 593–598). Bedford Books. (Original work published 1938)

Cronon, W. (1992). A place for stories: Nature, history, and narrative. *Journal of American History, 78*(4), 1347–1376.

Erll, A. (2011). *Memory in culture*. Palgrave Macmillan.

Gessen, M. (2017). *The future is history: How totalitarianism reclaimed Russia*. Riverhead Books.

James, W. (1890). *The principles of psychology*. Dover.

Lewis, S. (1998). *Babbitt*. Bantam Dell. (Original work published 1922)

MacIntyre, A. (2015). *After virtue: A study in moral philosophy* (3rd ed.). University of Notre Dame Press.

Mink, L. (1978). Narrative form as cognitive instrument. In R. H. Canary & H. Kozicki (Eds.), *The writing of history: Literary form and historical understanding* (pp. 182–203). University of Wisconsin Press.

Niebuhr, R. (1952). *The irony of American history*. New York: Charles Scribner's Sons.

Renan, E. (1990). What is a nation? In H. K. Bhabha (Ed.), *Nation and narration* (pp. 8–22). Routledge. (Original work published in French in 1882)

Ricoeur, P. (1991). Life in quest of narrative. In D. Wood (Ed.), *On Paul Ricoeur: Narrative and interpretation* (pp. 20–33). Routledge.
Roediger, H. L., III. (2000). Sir Frederic Charles Bartlett: Experimental and applied psychologist. In G. A. Kimble & M. Wertheimer (Eds.), *Portraits of pioneers in psychology* (Vol. 4, pp. 149–161). American Psychological Association.
Rose, G. (Ed.). (2019, March–April). The new nationalism. *Foreign Affairs Magazine*, p. 9.
Scholes, R., & Kellogg, R. (1966). *The nature of narrative*. Oxford University Press.
Wang, Z. (2012). *Never forget national humiliation: History and memory in Chinese politics and foreign relations*. Columbia University Press.
Wertsch, J. V. (1998). *Mind as action*. Oxford University Press.
Wertsch, J. V. (2002). *Voices of collective remembering*. Cambridge University Press.
Wertsch, J. V. (2020). US coronavirus lawsuits pick the scabs of China's 'century of humiliation.' *South China Morning Post*, May 20, 2020. https://www.scmp.com/comment/opinion/article/3085005/us-coronavirus-lawsuits-pick-scabs-chinas-century-humiliation
Wertsch, J. V. (2021). *How nations remember: A narrative approach*. Oxford University Press.
Wertsch, J. V., & Roediger, H. L., III. (2008). Collective memory: Conceptual foundations and theoretical approaches. *Memory*, *16*, 318–326.

Index

Tables and figures are indicated by *t* and *f* following the page number

Abe Shinzō, 282, 285–287, 289, 293, 295
Abric, Jean Claude, 180, 185
academics, and nationalism in
 United States, 66
action. *See* collective action; moral action
Adams, John, 4, 11, 13, 19
 and Jefferson, 12–13
 as realist, 6
 as Revolutionary, 6
 on Webster's Plymouth oration, 22
Adams, John Quincy, 4, 13
Adkins, Terry, 95–96
Adorno, Theodor, 81n22
affect. *See also* emotions
 positive vs. negative, experimental
  measurement of, 354–355, 356*f*, 357–358
African American Civil War Memorial, 69
African Americans. *See also* Black Americans
 and critical view of Columbus, 51
 and Great Migration, 80, 83
 Whites' brutality toward, 79
agents
 generic, 273, 373
 groups as, 373
 of memory, 55
al-Durrah, Muhammad, 389–390, 402
Aleksidze, Nikoloz, 336–337
Aljazeera, on COVID-19 narrative, 465
allegiance, factors affecting, 209
alliances, 371–372
 newcomers to, seen as potential
  free-riders, 384n4
Allied countries
 claimed responsibility for victory in
  WW II, 215–217, 216*f*, 237
 important events of World War II as
  remembered in, 194–197, 195*f*,
  202–204, 203*t*, 237–238

Alt-Right, and Charlottesville debate, 49
alternative facts, 15, 83
America. *See also* United States
 founding moment, deployed on
  opposite sides, 72n11
 history, beginning of, 135
 and United States, differentiation,
  20–21
American exceptionalism, 2, 43–45,
 212–213, 244
 and collective memory, 153, 154*f*
 and future thought, 153, 154*f*
 and implicit trajectory of decline, 153,
  154*f*
American history textbooks
 connection to public opinion (survey)
  data, 132–134
 content analysis of, 128–134, 130*t*, 131*f*
 controversial topics in, 230
 cultural power of, 25n7–n9, 25–26
 influence on individuals' beliefs,
  116–117
 journals reviewing, 25, 25n7
 and nation-building narrative, 128
 as selective tradition, 137
 shortcomings of, 229–230
 titles reviewed, 128–129, 138–139
 treatments of Columbus, 62–63, 116–117,
  124, 128–134, 130*t*, 131*f*, 228
 treatments of Native Americans, 124,
  128–134, 130*t*, 133*f*, 228
 writers of, 25, 25n9
American Indian. *See also* Native
 Americans
 iconography of, 45
Anderson, Benedict, 209, 454
anti-Semitism, and Jewish collective
 memory, 274–275

apology(ies), 281
    to comfort women, 283–286, 294
    demanded from Japan, by other East Asian countries, 291–295
    global memory culture and, 296
apology narrative, 352, 362
Appadurai, Arjun, 327
Appleby, Joyce, 21
Arbery, Ahmaud, 79
Aristotle, 455–456
Arlington National Cemetery
    Confederate soldiers in, 69
    segregation of, 69
Armenian–Azerbaijani relations, 257, 344, 347–348, 352, 352n1, 403, 461
    experimental study (interplay of narrative, collective memory, and emotions), 353–360
    narratives about, types of, 352, 361–362
Armenians
    ethnopolitical mobilizations, 343–344
    historical narratives, as cultural tools, 347–348
    identity mobilization, 258, 403–404
    mass mobilizations, 258, 343–344, 348–349
    narrative toolkits of, 346–349
    schematic narrative template, 347–348
    tragedy of 1915 (genocide), 347–348
    victim narrative, 349–350
Asch, S. E., conformity experiments, 378–379
Asia. *See also* East Asia
    rise of, in 1980s, 281
Asian Women's Fund, 284
Assmann, J., 169–170
atomic bombings (WW II), collective memory of, 247
    and relevance to present, 190–193, 195*f*, 196, 198*f*, 199, 201, 201*f*, 203
atrocity(ies)
    anti-Black, collective memory of, 157, 158*f*
    anti-Native American, collective memory of, 157, 158*f*, 366, 400
    in-group–perpetrated, motivated remembering and forgetting of, 366, 400–401
    in Poland, in WW II, 200, 202

attention, social organization of, 57
attitudes. *See* explicit attitudes; implicit attitudes
Attucks, Crispus, 69
augmentation
    collaborative remembering and, 412, 414–415, 418
    cross-cueing and, 415
Australia
    claimed responsibility for victory in WW II, 215–217, 216*f*
    important events of World War II as remembered in, 194–197, 195*f*, 237
    settler colonialism of, 43
Autry, Robin, 77
availability heuristic, 231
    and overclaiming of responsibility, 226–227
Axis countries
    claimed responsibility for war effort in WW II, 215
    important events of World War II as remembered in, 197–200, 198*f*, 202–204, 203*t*, 237
Ayers, Edward, 48, 99, 110–111

Ba Jin, *Reunion (Tuanyuan)*, 313n3
Bacon, Francis, 7
Bakhtin, Mikhail, 326–327, 335
Balkans, violence in, collective memories and, 396, 404
Baltics, revisionist memory in, 281–282
Baltimore, Maryland, Lee–Jackson monument, removal of, 50
banal nationalism, 324
Banneker, Benjamin, 77
Barrett, Don, 107–108
Barrett, Richard, 106
Bartlett, F. C., 148, 411, 419, 460
Batiashvili, Nutsa, 256–257, 315, 456
Battle of Britain, collective memory of, and relevance to present, 195*f*, 196, 201, 201*f*, 203*t*
Battle of Shanggan Ridge (Chinese film), 305–306, 321
Battle of the Bulge, collective memory of, and relevance to present, 192

INDEX 475

Belgium, king of, speech by, and collective memory/forgetting, 395
beliefs
  cognitive factors and, 434, 441
  false, 434–435, 439–440, 450
  motivational factors and, 434–435, 439–440
Bellah, Robert, 73n15
Bellamy, Wes, 49
belonging, human need for, 370
Benjamin, Walter, 455
Berlant, Lauren, 324
Berlin, Battle of (WW II), collective memory of, and relevance to present, 193, 195f, 196
Berlin Wall, fall of, 36, 39–40
  as German national identity event, emotional tone categorization of, 240t, 241–244, 244t, 249
Berry, Michael, 321
Beta Israel, in Jewish collective memory, 267–268
Biden, Hunter, 16
Biden, Joseph, 16–17, 19
Billig, Michael, 324
binding values, 64, 156–159, 158f
  and overclaiming of responsibility, 225–226
bivocality, 325
  of Georgian collective memory, 257, 324–325, 333–335
Black Americans. *See also* African Americans; 1619 Project
  activism by, 117
  and civil rights movement, 74–75
  Lost Cause and, 38–39
  and monument building, 69
  and psychic damage of racial inequality, 81
  Trump and, 15–16
  and Whites, wealth gap between, 83
Black history museums, 77
Black Lives Matter (BLM) movement, 48, 54, 111
Black Power, 117
Blight, David, 62, 68–69
Bodnar, John, 91
Boime, Albert, 70

Borglum, Gutzon, 69n6, 69–70, 70n7
Bosnia, rape camps in, 283
Boston Tea Party, as foundational in American history, 183, 184f
Bourdieu, Pierre, 344
Boxer Protocol of 1901, 468
Boyce, Glenn, 108
Boyer, Pascal, 365
British colonization, as foundational in American history, 183, 184f
British taxes, as foundational in American history, 183, 184f
Brooks, Peter, 456
Brown, Karida, 83
Brown, Michael, 48
Bruner, J. S., 456–457
Bryant, Zyahna, 49
Burke, K., 455–456
Bush, George H. W., 31, 135
Bush, George W., 74

Calhoun, John C., 47, 75n16
Canada
  claimed responsibility for victory in WW II, 215–217, 216f
  important events of World War II as remembered in, 194–197, 195f, 247
  settler colonialism of, 43
canonicality, of narratives, 155
carrier groups, 55
Carter, Mae Bertha, plaque dedicated to, on Ole Miss (UM) campus, 87–89, 88f, 93–94, 106, 109, 111
Cassirer, Ernst, 327
  The Myth of the State, 326
cell phone camera, 55
Century of Humiliation narrative, 256, 291, 303, 467–468
change, Obama's narrative of, 74
Charleston, South Carolina, Mother Emanuel African Methodist Episcopal Church, shooting at (2015), 47, 49, 75–76, 76n16, 111
Charlottesville, Virginia
  Confederate monuments in, 48, 50, 55, 68
  and end of American exceptionalism, 2
  events in (2019), 47, 55
  Unite the Right rally (2017), 50, 54, 68

chauvinism, 369
Chavchavadze, Ilia, 336–337
China
  anti-Japanese sentiment in, 291–292, 295
  and Century of Humiliation narrative, 256, 291, 303, 467–468
  claimed responsibility for victory in WW II, 215–217, 216f
  and comfort women issue, 282–289, 292
  commemorations of Korean War, 300, 303 (see also Korean War)
  Communist Party leadership in, promotion of, 303
  Communist Revolution in, commemoration of, 300–304
  contemporary nationalism in, 302–303
  and COVID-19 narrative, 368, 464–467
  important events of World War II as remembered in, 194–197, 195f, 237, 247
  Japanese invasion of, 292
  nationalism in, national past and, 256, 291, 296
  patriotic passions in, 292–293
  revisionist memory in, 256, 281
  shift from socialist to nationalist memory framework, 302–303
  statist narrative template in, 303–304, 314–319
  Suppression of the Counter-revolutionary Campaign, 305
  war memory and nationalism in, 288
  youth in, separation of their antipathies and lifestyles, 294
China War, 281
Chinese People's War of Resistance Against Japanese Aggression, 290–291
Christianity, and Jewish history, 274–275
Churchill, Winston, 51
"city on a hill"
  in collective memory of ordinary people, 183–184
  as expression of the church, 28
  as national slogan, 2, 27–31, 45, 212
civil rights movement, 74–75, 80, 83
  University of Mississippi's orientation toward, 94–96

Civil War. See also Lost Cause
  as American national identity event, emotional tone categorization of, 239t, 241–244, 243t
  in American political culture, 182t, 183
  in American political discourse, 45
  Black veterans of, monument to, 69
  commemoration of, 44
  Confederate memory of, 37
  as foundational event in American history, 183, 184f
  and reconciliationist narrative, 69–70
  reunification after, 68–69
Clark, Richard, 49
Clinton, Bill, 31, 366, 404–405
Clinton, Hillary, 72
coalition-building
  cognitive capacities and, 345, 365, 369–371
  as collective action, 372, 374
  competitive nature of, 345, 375
  evolutionary psychology of, 365, 372n1, 372–373, 381, 384–385
  narratives and, 365, 376
coalitional psychology, 371–372, 381, 385
  competition in, 345, 375
  of ethnic mobilization, 344–345
  and mobilizing support, 345, 375
  signaling in, 374–375
Coates, Ta-Nehisi, 47
cognition, shortcuts in, 434
cognitive accessibility, and memory, 149–150
cognitive psychology, 56
  memory research in, 367, 411
cognitive schemata, 148–150
cohesiveness, in coalitions, 382
Cold War, 40, 281–282
  and "city on a hill," 28, 30
  effect on remembrance and interpretation of WW II, 206
Coleman, Christy, 99, 110–111
collaborationism, 331
collaborative groups
  memory transmission in, 420
  recall performance of, 413–414
collaborative inhibition, 367, 414, 420–423, 422f, 424

INDEX 477

collaborative memory, 204
   study of, framework for, 411–413, 416*f*
   testing, 412–413
collaborative remembering, 366, 410–412
   cognitive factors affecting, 427
   and collective memory, 418
   and memory for non-personal vs. autobiographical information, 425–427
   opposing effects on memory, 413–416, 427
   and post-collaborative memory, 411–412, 418
collective action
   coalitional work as, 372, 374
   collective memory and, 345–346, 396, 403–404
collective emotions
   and joint commitment, 350, 358
   social norms and, 350, 358
collective future thought, 366, 402
collective memory, 159, 169, 303. *See also* Georgian collective memory; Jewish collective memory; national memory
   accessibility, asymmetries in, 150
   accuracy of, 402–403
   activation of, 350
   aligned memory structures and, 367, 418, 424, 427–428
   American exception in, 45
   asymmetrical, and collective overclaiming, 226–227
   biases in, 149–155, 159, 236
   bottom-up processes and, 90, 228–231, 368, 391, 411, 428
   changes, over time, 41
   characteristics of, 391–401
   cognitive constituents of, 367, 411–412, 417, 424
   collaborative remembering and, 418
   and collective action, 345–346, 396, 403–404
   communicative influences on, 397–399, 398*f*
   conflicting interpretations in, 324
   consolidation of, 271
   convergence onto, 146–148, 161, 204, 411, 424
   conversational interactions and, 390
   as coordinating device for collective actions, 345
   core events in, 262
   of COVID-19 pandemic, 425–426
   cross-disciplinary approaches to, 404
   definition of, 191, 236, 259, 410, 416–417
   as driving force for mass mobilization, 346
   dynamical nature of, 366, 390–391, 397–399, 403
   emergence of, 266, 397–399, 410, 416–429
   and emotion, 236, 349–351
   and emotional components of post-collaborative memories, 418, 424–426, 428
   and ethnic conflicts, 346
   and future learning and remembering, 427–428
   generational differences in, 183, 238, 390
   group configuration (who talks to whom) and, 418–423, 428
   and group identity, 191
   and identity projects, 205–206, 389–390, 396
   individual-level processes and, 260, 391–394, 393*f*, 410–411
   information distribution (who knows what) and, 418, 423, 428
   long-term, 271–275
   and mass mobilization, 350–351
   measurement, 417–418
   media exposure and, 205
   memory in the Other and, 274–275
   memory structures and, 418, 424, 427–428
   moral frames of, 155–161
   motivation and, 391, 399–401
   narrative and, 346–351
   narrative organization of, 205
   and national identity, 236–238, 250–251
   and national memory, 412
   and nationalism, 389, 391, 401, 428–429
   and nations, 229
   and overclaiming of responsibility, 228–231, 237

collective memory (cont.)
  painful, and conflict, 348–349, 358, 360–361
  for past events, relevance to present, 191–193
  political spectrum and, 156–159
  power of text in, 272–273
  presentist approach to, 51–52
  as process, 138
  psychological approaches to, 147–148, 390–391, 404, 410, 417
  public symbols of, conflicts over, 160 (*see also* Confederate flag(s); Confederate monuments)
  research on, future trajectories for, 401–404
  routines (procedures, rituals) and, 273
  schematic knowledge structures in, 205
  scholarship on, 41
  as shared body of knowledge, 205–206
  short-term, 270–271
  social influence on, 390–391, 394–399, 398*f*
  in social sciences, 404, 417
  as societal charter, 147
  sociological perspective on, 51–55, 410
  static approach to, 366, 390, 402–403
  study of, 389–390
  top-down processes and, 147–148, 228–230, 391, 410–411, 428
  transformation of, 55
  transmission of, 41
  trauma in, 280–281
  tripartite algorithm and, 274
  unsettling of, by collective re-enactment, 275–276
  use of, by individuals and groups, 428–429
  vicarious, 246–250
  victimhood in, 280–281
  for World War II, 190–191
collective temporal thought, 147–148. *See also* future thought; temporality
  asymmetries and biases in, 149–155
colonialism, re-examination of, 45
Columbus, as verb, 119
Columbus, Christopher
  in American national memory, 62, 115, 137–138
  as America's founding hero, 115, 135
  beliefs about, in survey responses, 120–122, 121*t*, 122*f*, 132–134
  collective memory of, generational differences in, 183
  commemoration of, 134–135
  critical versus traditional views of, 46, 51, 116–122, 121*t*, 122*f*, 135, 229
  cultural representations of, quincentenary and after, 116–120
  as "discoverer of America," challenges to, 62–63, 119, 123, 128, 130*t*, 132, 135
  education and views of, 62–63, 123–125
  as foundational in American history, 183, 184*f*
  heroic versus villanous views of, 62–63, 120–125, 121*t*, 122*f*, 125*f*, 132–134
  interest in wealth, 130*t*, 132
  public beliefs about, inertia of memory and, 134–137
  reappraisal, by general public, 62–63, 120–125, 121*t*, 122*f*, 123–125, 125*f*
  revisionist representations of, 123, 135
  statues of, 69, 119, 136
  symbolic relevance to origins, 136
  teaching and learning about, changes in, 62–63, 127–128
  textbook treatments of, 62–63, 116–117, 124, 128–134, 130*t*, 131*f*
  torture and enslavement of Native Americans, 118, 130–132, 130*t*
  as unifying symbol, 115–116
  viewed as villainous, birth cohort and, 123–125, 125*f*, 135–136
Columbus Day, replacement of, with Indigenous People's Day, 119, 136
Coman, Alin, 366
comfort women
  apologies to, 283–286, 294
  compensation for, 284–286, 294
  as issue in politics of memory, 282–295, 297
  issue of, as traveling trope, 295–296
  as "sex slaves," 289
  statues of, 284, 287, 289
  textbooks' treatment of, 284–285
  transnational concern/memory politics and, 295–296

UNESCO and, 287
  as "volunteer corps," 288, 288n1
commitment
  "burning bridges" in, 375
  in groups, 374–375, 382
common suffering narrative, 80–81, 258, 352, 358–361
common victim identity, 359–360
communication
  effect on memory, 397, 400
  motivation and, 399
communicative memory, 165–166, 169–170, 172, 270. *See also* living historical memories
Communism, 36, 40
communist internationalism, in Chinese films, 306–307
community, as founding principle of America, 31
compensation, Chinese term for, 467–468
computations, in people's behavior, 345, 371–372
concentration camp liberation (WW II), collective memory of, and relevance to present, 192
conductorless orchestration, 344
Confederacy. *See also* Lost Cause
  fragmented commemoration of, 54
  in popular culture, 44
Confederate flag(s)
  harmful impact of, 76
  over statehouses, 75–76
Confederate monuments, 35*f*, 36, 38, 88. *See also* University of Mississippi (UM), Confederate soldier statue
  addition of context to, 54
  in Charlottesville, Virginia, 48–50
  conflict about, structure of, 53–54
  defenders of, 53
  removal, 49
  sociological perspectives on, 52–53
  state-sponsored, number of, 44
Confederate soldiers
  in Arlington National Cemetery, 69
  Scott on, 89
conflict
  collective memory and, 346, 396
  narrative approach to, 346, 351–352
  and narratives, 171
  painful collective memory and, 360–361
conflict resolution, 361
  narrative transformation and, 351–352, 360
consistency, in institutional (public) spaces, 91
conspiracy of silence, 57
Constitution, U. S.
  as foundational in American history, 183, 184*f*
  Locke's influence in, 7
  preamble, as secular scripture for Obama, 73, 73n15
  stained by slavery as America's original sin, 74
  Trump's offenses to, 13–14
Constitutional Convention, 10
contextualization, of commemorative landscapes
  contestation activated by, 104
  at University of Mississippi, 99–105
Conway, Kellyanne, 83
Conyers, John, Jr., 47
coordination
  definition of, 375–376
  in game theory, 375–376
  mass movements and, 345, 375–378
  and mutual knowledge, 376
  oppressive regimes and, 377
  and power dynamics, 376
  through internal signaling, 381–382
  and uncertainty reduction, 376
core memory
  of culture/nation, 262
  definition of, 262
counter monument, 44
counterpublics, 257, 324
  in mnemonic community, 340
COVID-19 pandemic
  competing narratives about (China and United States), 368, 464–467
  divisive narrative about, 426
  iconic images of, and collective memory formation, 426
  memories of, factors affecting, 425–426
  Trump's mishandling of, 15

Credo. *See* Saving Story (Credo)
criminal justice system, American, 81
critical consciousness, 173, 175
Crosby, Alfred, 117
cross-cueing, in collaborative recall, 415, 418, 427
crowd psychology, 369
cult leaders, 380–381, 381n2
cultural memory, 169–170, 259. *See also* Jewish cultural memory
 study methods for, 261
culture(s), human
 as biocultural supraorganisms, 255–256, 260
 memory traces in, 260
Cunningham, David, 70, 75n16
Cutting the Devil's Talons (Chinese film), 304–306, 321

D-Day, collective memory of, and relevance to present, 192–203, 195*f*, 198*f*, 201*f*, 203*t*, 460
damnatio memoriae, 274
D'Arcy, Hanna, 46
David the Builder (King of Georgia), 335–336, 336n3
 apparitions of, 335–340
 contemporary evocation of, 328, 339–340
 as icon of national memory, 328–333
 as symbolic, 328, 335–341
Davis, Jefferson, 36, 38–39, 230
 Beauvoir homeplace, commemorative efforts focused on, 107
 "The Rise and Fall of the Confederate Government," 38–39
de Gaulle, Charles, radio appeal of June 18, 1940, collective memory of, and relevance to present, 195*f*, 196
de la Casas, Bartolomé, 118
de Vattel, Emer, *The Laws of Nations*, 11
death penalty, 83
Declaration of Independence
 as American national identity event, emotional tone categorization of, 239*t*, 241–244, 243*t*, 249
 in American political culture, 182*t*, 183
 ideals of, 14
 Jefferson's pride in, 13, 76–77
 Locke's influence in, 7
 and origin of United States, 20
 1776 Project and, 44
defection, from groups, 374–375
demagoguery, 369
 mobilization through, 380
democracy, and dispute/disagreement, 12, 19
democratic order, foundations of, 325–326
Denevan, William, 117
Deng Xiaoping, 310
denial, social organization of, 58
Diamond, Jared, *Guns, Germs, and Steel*, 118
Die Wende, 40
discourse, elite versus popular, 46
disruption (memory), collaborative remembering and, 412, 414, 418, 427
dissent, and patriotism, 71
distancing, psychological, 260. *See also* overclaiming of responsibility
diversity narratives, as foundational, 183
Doss, Erika, 69
Douglass, Frederick, 69
DuBois, W. E. B.
 on "present-past," 36
 on Vardaman, 104
Dudai, Yadin, 255
Dukakis, Michael, use of Winthrop's sermon, 31

E pluribus unum, 14
East Asia
 memory conflicts in, 282
 memory politics in, 282–285
 nationalism-populism in, 282–295
 patriotic passions in, 290–295
 revisionist memory in, 256, 281
East China Sea, disputed islands in, 289, 291
East Germany
 opposition to regime in, 377
 revisionist memory in, 281–282
Eastern Europe
 memory conflicts in, 282
 revisionist memory in, 281–282

Ebbinghaus, H., 411
ecological approaches, 62, 90–92, 411
  and commemorative landscapes, 109–112
  spatial, 91–92
  temporal, 92
ecology
  definition of, 89
  of University of Mississippi campus, 89
Edge, John T., 94
education
  effects on memories, 135
  and event recall, 205
  importance of, 470
  Jefferson on, 8
  meaning of, students as active constructors of, 137
  multicultural, 125–126
  role in changed public beliefs, 123–125
  and "triumphal national narrative," 137–138
Eley, James, 96
Eliot, George, 409
elites
  identity mobilization by, to serve their interests, 404
  and mass mobilization, 344
  and "the people," 325, 330, 332, 384
emotional climate, 166
  in developing versus developed countries, 177–180
  as indexed by living historical memories, 177–180, 178f–179f
  in United States, 185
emotional information, post-collective memory for, 418, 424–427
  non-personal vs. autobiographical, 425–427
emotions. *See also* collective emotions
  collective memory and, 349–351
  individual memory and, 349–350
  and nationalist-populist success, 291
  social organization of, 58
empathy, 359–360
  definition of, 355–356
  experimental measurement of, 355–358, 357f
  and social connections, 409

social organization of, 58
empiricism, founders' belief in, 13
Enlightenment, 19
  European, and founders, 1, 4, 6–9
  Monticello estate as embodiment of, 49
enlightenment narrative, in American social representations of history, 183
Enola Gay, 44
environment
  adaptive response to, 384n3
  experienced, and social trust, 383–384
epidemics, and national collaboration, 464
episodic memory, 261–262, 274
epistemic vigilance, 379
Equal Justice Initiative (EJI), 61, 66, 78–84
equality narratives, as foundational, 183
Erll, Astrid, 83
  on travelling memory, 45n3, 51n5
error pruning, collaborative remembering and, 412, 415, 427
errors
  identification of, 440–443
  linguistic camouflage for, 443
  social contagion and, 415
Estonia
  living historical memories and identity positioning in, 173
  and narrative truth of Molotov-Ribbentrop Pact, 459, 461, 468–469
ethnic conflict, 404
  bottom-up forces and, 344
  collective memory and, 346
  historical narratives and, 351
  top-down forces and, 344
ethnic hatred, incitement to, 369
ethnic identification, cascade dynamics and, 378
ethnic mobilization
  of Armenians, 343–345 (*see also* Armenian–Azerbaijani relations)
  coalitional psychology of, 344–345
  theories of, 344
European Union (EU), and comfort women issue, 294
Evers-Williams, Myrlie, 96
Exodus, in Jewish collective memory, 265, 265f, 267–268

explicit attitudes
  experimental measurement of, 258, 353–354, 354f, 356–357
  social cognition and, 358

fake news, acceptance/processing of, factors affecting, 439–440
false memory(ies), 427
  collaboration and, 423
false recollection, 260
fatalism, 83
Ferris, William, 94
field theory, 62, 90–91
Fine, Gary Alan, 55
first-fruits ceremony, Jewish, 263
firsting process, and national origin myth, 24, 33
Floyd, George, 48, 50, 54–56, 79, 111
fluency
  as cue to truth, 437–440
  processing, interpretation of, 437
folk sociology, 372–373, 375
folk tales, 334–335
forced disclosure, 382
foreign policy
  German, collective memory and, 192
  Obama and, 74
  Trump and, 14–15
forgetting, 454. *See also* retrieval-induced forgetting (RIF)
  collaborative remembering and, 412, 414, 418, 426–427
  collective, 238, 266–267, 274
  induced, 260
  motivated remembering and, 400
  in national memory, 24, 41–42
  Renan on, 229
  retrieval-induced, 204
  selective, 399
  serial reproduction and, 419
  social sharing of memories and, 417
  of source information, 437, 450
former Soviet Union. *See* Russia (USSR, Soviet Union)
foundational events
  in American history, 183–185, 184f
  in living historical memories, in developing versus developed countries, 177–180

founders. *See also* framers
  Confederate "heroes" alongside, 70
  Enlightenment and, 1, 4, 6–9
  principles revered by, 13
Founding Fathers. *See* founders
Fourth of July, celebration of, 20, 20n2
fragmented commemoration, 54
framers. *See also* founders
  concept of "more perfect union," 14, 61, 71–78, 73n15, 84
  as realists, 3
France
  claimed responsibility for victory in WW II, 215–217, 216f
  fall of (WW II), collective memory of, and relevance to present, 195f, 203t
  important events of World War II as remembered in, 194–197, 195f, 247
Franklin, Benjamin, 19
  as Englishman, 6
  personal achievements of, 5, 7
  as philosopher, 5
  as postmaster, 5–6
  and University of Pennsylvania, 5, 5n3
free press
  Franklin's defense of, 5
  Jefferson on, 8
free-riding, 374, 384n4
free speech
  founders' belief in, 13
  Franklin's defense of, 5
free thought, founders' belief in, 13
freedom, defense of, and living historical memories in United States, 185–186
freethinkers, in 18th century, 4
frontier narrative, of American history, 183
future thought, 63
  biases in, 151–155, 159–160
  collective, 147, 159, 366, 402

Gamsakhurdia, Konstantin, 338
Gamsakhurdia, Zviad, 338–339
Garagozov, Rauf, 80–81, 255, 257–258, 303, 468
Garner, Eric, 48
gaslighting, 56
George III (King of England), 1, 10

Georgia. *See also* David the Builder (King of Georgia)
  competing ideologies in, 328–333
  designation of Middle Eastern migrants as "genetic enemies," 325, 330
  Golden Age narrative of, 257, 325, 333–335, 337–338, 341
  national character of, 335
  national narrative of, 333–335
  post-Soviet, history curricula in, 456
  and Russia, 331–332
  Russian invasion (2008), 192
Georgian collective memory, 256–257
  bivocal narrative of, 257, 324–325, 333–335
Georgian March, 257, 329n1, 329–332
German reunification, 40
  as German national identity event, emotional tone categorization of, 240*t*, 241–244, 244*t*, 249
Germany. *See also* East Germany; West Germany
  ashamed events self-nominated in, 238–240, 240*t*, 241–244, 242*f*, 244*t*
  claimed responsibility for war effort in WW II, 215
  and comfort women issue, 284–285
  foreign policy of, collective memory and, 192
  important events of World War II as remembered in, 197–200, 198*f*, 247
  national identity events, emotional tone categorization of, 238–244, 240*t*, 242*f*, 244*t*, 246–251
  proud events self-nominated in, 238–240, 240*t*, 241–244, 242*f*, 244*t*
Gilbert, Margaret, 350, 358
Glendale, California, comfort women statue in, 287
Glisson, Susan, 96, 106
Global Alliance for Preserving the History of World War II in Asia, 292
global memory culture, 296
  and apologies, 296
Gluck, Carol, 256
Golden Age
  in Armenian schematic narrative template, 347
  Georgian, 257, 325, 333–335, 337–338, 341

Goodrich, Charles, 25
Goodrich, Samuel, 25
Gordon, John B., 37
Gordon-Reed, Annette, 50
Gorski, Philip, 73n15
Great Britain, Enlightenment in, 4
Great Escape, 83
Great Migration, 80, 83
Greeley, Garrett D., 366
Greenfeld, Liah, 326
Grotius, Hugo, 11
groupishness, 370
groups. *See also* collaborative groups; nominal groups
  as agents, 373
  carrier, 55
  cohesiveness in, 382
  commitment in, 374–375, 382
  conventional metaphors for, 373
  defection from, 374–375
  and power, 372–373
  social, mnemonic overlap in, 204
Guadalcanal, collective memory of, and relevance to present, 192
Guilted Age, 281
Gulf War, misinformation spread in, 435
gullibility, popular, 369, 378–380

habit(s)
  James on, 462, 469–470
  mental, associated with narrative templates, 468
Halbwachs, Maurice, 52, 56, 148, 169
Hale, Salma, 25
Haley, Nikki, 76
Hamilton, Alexander
  and Jefferson, 12
  warning about despotism, 16–17
Hannah-Jones, Nikole, 160
Havel, Vaclav, 382
Hemings, Sally, Jefferson and, 49–50, 53, 76, 230
Heroic Sons and Daughters (Chinese film), 307, 313n2, 315–316, 321
heuristics, 260, 367, 435–436
  in social representation, 385
  and truth judgments, 436
Heyer, Heather, 68

Higginbotham, Elwood, 111–112
histoire événementielle, 270–271
historical charter(s), 165–166, 170
   American, 182–183, 182*t*, 186
   as central core of social representations of history, 180–182
   as central to changing political culture, 182–186
   definition of, 181
   of United States as "Defender of Free World," 186
historical memory, 259. *See also* living historical memory
history. *See also* living historical memory; social representations of history
   analytic, 83, 469
   as corrective to national memory, 469
   elites' control of, 172
   and memory, relationship between, 82–83
   omissions and distortions in, 454, 461, 469
   politics of, 192
   "pre-Columbian," 135
   teaching of, new approaches in United States, 126–127
   in thinking of American people, 25, 25n7
   as warrant of legitimacy for state, 172–173
history education, cultural pluralism in, 126–127
Holocaust
   as ashamed event, 240*t*, 249
   collective memory of, and relevance to present, 195*f*, 196, 198*f*, 199, 201, 201*f*, 203, 203*t*
   and European collective memory, 43, 43n1, 45, 48
   as German national identity event, emotional tone categorization of, 240*t*
   in Jewish collective memory, 265*f*, 267
   percentage of Jewish population killed in, 200, 200n1
   survivors, and transgenerational transmission of trauma, 272
   teaching about, in Israeli schools, 135

hope
   Obama's narrative of, 74
   Stevenson and, 81
Hopper, Grace, 47
Hu Jintao, 321
Human Development Index (HDI), 174
   nation's position on, and living historical memories, 177, 178*f*
Hungary, 40
   opposition to regime in, 377
   revisionist memory in, 281
Hutcheson, Francis, 7

iconoclasm, 42
   spread of, 50–51
identity(ies). *See also* national identity; individual identity
   activation of, 445
   personal, 236
   social, 155, 236
illusory truth effect, 438–441
imagination, and social connections, 409
imaginative horizons, 327
imagined communities, 209, 261, 454
immigration, 383–384
implicit attitudes
   double priming and, 359
   experimental measurement of, 258, 353–354, 354*f*, 356–357
   identity shift and, 360–361
   priming and, 359
   social cognition and, 358
indifference, social production of, 55–58
Indigenous people. *See also* Native Americans
   in American popular culture, 48
   "pacification" of, 45
Indigenous People's Day, 119, 136
individual identity
   and affiliation to larger communities, 209
   formation of, 209
information. *See also* misinformation
   availability vs. accessibility in memory, 435, 441, 443–444
   exposure to, group configuration and collective memory formation after, 246, 420–423, 421*f*–422*f*

inconsistent with beliefs, people's biases to reject, 450
loss of, in groups, 414
low-quality, persuasiveness of, 378–379
organization, and recall, 424
overlearned, accessibility (recall) of, activation of national identity and, 445–449, 449f
propagation, narratives and, 401–402
retrieval cues for, 444
transmission, in social networks, 419
information processing systems
algorithms, 260
goal of, 260
implementation, 260
three-level taxonomy for, 260
institutional story, 90
instrumentalism, with and about the past, 52
insurrection (January 6, 2021), 71
Trump and, 18
intergroup relations
common suffering narrative and, 80–81, 258, 352, 358–361
priming effect of narratives in, 358–359
social categorization and, 359
intergroup violence
collective memory and, 396
constructivist approaches to, 404
primordialist approaches to, 404
intuitions, moral, 155–161
Israel
commemorative politics in, 54
and Jewish collective memory, 275
and Jewish cultural memory, 259
Israelis, Palestinians' Second Intifada against, 389
Italy
claimed responsibility for war effort in WW II, 215
important events of World War II as remembered in, 197–200, 198f, 247

Jackson, Andrew, 13
Jackson, Thonmas "Stonewall," statue of, in Charlottesville, 50, 55
James, William, 462, 469–470

Japan
apologies demanded from, by other East Asian countries, 291–295
atomic bombing of (see atomic bombings [WW II])
and China, memory conflicts between, 282
claimed responsibility for war effort in WW II, 215
colonialism and atrocities in Asia, 284–285
and comfort women issue, 282–289, 294–295
and global memory culture, 296
and hate nationalism, 294
history of brutality, 43
"history problem" of, 281, 290, 293
important events of World War II as remembered in, 197–200, 198f, 237
Korean forced labor used by, 290, 293
nationalism in, national past and, 256, 286–287, 296
patriotic passions in, 293–294
revisionist memory in, 256, 281, 286
and South Korea, memory conflicts between, 282
wartime actions, as issue in politics of memory, 282–289
youth in, separation of their antipathies and lifestyles, 294
Jeconiah, 267
Jefferson, Thomas, 4, 19, 49
and Adams, 12–13
on education, 8
as Englishman, 8
Enlightenment and, 6–7
on free press, 8
and Hamilton, 12
Monticello estate, 49
paradox of, 76–77
paternity of Hemings's children, 49–50, 53, 76, 230
as Revolutionary, 8
as slaveholder, 49, 53, 68, 76–77
statue of, at University of Virginia, 68
Jefferson Davis Foundation, 107
Jennings, Francis, 118
jeremiad templates, 64, 150–151, 153, 159

Jesus, in Jewish history, 274
Jewish collective memory, 255–256, 259.
    See also Saving Story (Credo)
  Beta Israel in, 267–268
  core of, 262–263, 268, 269f
  culture-locked recency in, 268
  damnatio memoriae in, 274
  differentiation in, 268
  dissociations in, 268
  in Ethiopian Jews in Israel, 267–268, 269f
  events remembered in, experimental test for, 264–265
  Israeli version, 275
  as lachrymose memory, 272
  long-term, 271–275
  memory in the Other and, 274–275
  mnemonic lacuna in, 265f, 266
  nation-locked recency in, 268
  outside Israel, 275
  persistence and updates in, 268, 269f
  planning for, 272
  power of text in, 272–273
  proactive interference and, 267
  recency effect in, 265–267, 265f
  reconsolidation of, 271, 274
  reminiscence bumps in, 265–267
  retroactive interference and, 266–267
  routines (procedures, rituals) and, 273
  secularization and, 275
  split engrams in, 267–268
  traumas added in, 265–266, 268, 272
  unsettling of, by collective re-enactment, 275–276
  updating of, 271
  in U.S. cohort, 267–268, 269f
Jewish cultural memory, 259
  characteristics, 261
  core of, 262
  geopolitical realization of, 275–276
  historical longevity of, 261
  remote and long-term, 265–267, 265f
Jim Crow, 38, 48, 77, 79
Johnson, Gary, 443
Johnson, Paul B., III, 103
Johnson, Paul B., Sr., 103
Jones, Dan, 99–100, 100n1, 103, 110

Kennedy, John F., and Winthrop's "city on a hill," 30, 212
Kessler, Jason, 50
Khalvashi, Tamta, 326
Khayat, Robert, 91, 94–96
Kim Hak-sun, 283
Kim Il-sung, 310
Kim Jong-il, 310
Kim Jong-un, 310
Kim Jung-hwa, 309
King, Martin Luther, Jr., 78
Kipchaks, 328, 330, 330n2
knowledge
  availability vs. accessibility (stored in memory but not retrieved), 435, 441, 443–444
  experts', contradictions with, and truth judgments, 442
  lack of, and national narcissism, 246
  shifting access to (in memory), 367, 443–444
  stored, contradictions with, and truth judgments, 442
Kobayashi Yoshinori, 293
Korean Peninsula
  China's relations with, films about, 308–314
  denuclearization efforts on, 311
Korean War
  in China's national memory, 303, 320
  Chinese casualties in, 319, 319n4
  Chinese commemorations of, 256, 300
  Chinese literary work about, 300
  cosmopolitan memory of, 319
  films about, Chinese, 301, 304–308, 315–319, 321–322
  as Resist America and Aid Korea War (in China), 300, 309
Ku Klux Klan, 83
Kuran, Timur, 378
Kursk, Battle of (WW II), collective memory of, and relevance to present, 193, 195f, 196

land of opportunity narrative, in American political culture, 183
Landrieu, Mitch, 49
language comprehension, 441–442

latent class analysis, of living historical memories, 175–176, 176t
Le Bon, Gustave, 369
Leach, Edmund, 326
leaders
  cult, 380–381, 381n2
  demagogic, 365, 378, 383
Lee, Robert E., 35f, 36, 39
  commemoration of, 230
  statue of, in Charlottesville, 50, 55, 68
  on Stone Mountain Georgia, 69n6
left, use of Winthrop's sermon, 31
left–right spectrum, American, and moral frames of collective memory, 64, 156–161
Legacy Museum (Montgomery, Alabama), 61, 66, 78–79, 82–84
Leningrad, Siege of (WW II), collective memory of, and relevance to present, 193, 195f, 196, 463
Lepore, Jill, 66
Lewis, John, Obama's eulogy for, 71n10, 71–73
Lewis, Meriwether, 49
Lewis, Sinclair, *Babbitt*, 456
liberal–conservative spectrum, American, and moral priorities, 156
Lin Qi, 301–302
Lincoln, Abraham, reputation of, transformation in, 46
literacy, in 18th century, 4
Liu, James, 212
living historical memories, 165–166, 170, 172–173
  across 40 countries, empirical study of, 173–175
  content analysis using latent class analysis, 175–176, 176t
  correlates of, 174
  and critical consciousness, 173, 175
  in developing versus developed countries, 177, 178f
  and Human Development Index, 174
  and national identity, 175
  as peripheral to changing political culture, 182–186
  as reflection of emotional climate, 177–180, 178f–179f

and Social Dominance Orientation, 174–175
and system justification, 174–175
Locke, John, 7
Lodge, Henry Cabot, on Webster's Plymouth oration, 22n5
Loewen, James, 118
Lies My Teacher Told Me, 230
Lost Cause, 36, 62, 230–231
  and Confederate monument at University of Mississippi, 88–89, 101–103, 107, 110
  death of, 39
  defenders of, 53
  iconography of, 44–45
  ideology, emergence of, 37
  as ingrained mythology, 2, 36–37
  language of, 38
  legacies of, 111–112
  mythology of, 44, 297
  as popular movement, 37–38
lynchings, 79
  in American South, 38
  history of, psychic damage caused by, 81
  legacies of, in present, 83
  museum exhibit on, 77
  National Memorial for Peace and Justice exhibit on, 79–80
  in Oxford, Mississippi, marker recognizing, 111–112

Ma, Zhao, 256
MacIntyre, Alisdair, 455
Madison, James, 4, 11, 23, 49
main melody films (China), 303, 308
Manifest Destiny, 70
Mann, Charles C., 118
Mao Zedong/Maoist era, contemporary Chinese attitudes toward, 304, 314, 317
Marr, D., 260
Marsh, Elizabeth J., 367
Martin, Trayvon, 48
Marxist ideology, and misunderstanding of ethnopolitical or nationalist mobilization, 344
mass incarceration, racial bias and, 79–80

488 INDEX

mass media
  and collective memory, 390
  and communicative memories, 172
  and event recall, 205
mass movements, 371, 385
  and coordination, 345, 375–378
  dynamics of, 375–378
  and expressive activities, 381
  as large-scale alliances, 375–378
  origins of, 384–385
  participation in, costs and benefits of, 377–378
  positive-sum orientation and, 383–384
  triggers, 345
  zero-sum orientation and, 383–385
Massachusetts
  and origin story of America, 22, 29
  slavery in, end of, 77
Mayflower Compact, 26
Mayflower story, 22, 29
meaning-making
  process of, 92
  schematic structure for, 148–149
  social aspect of, 148
media, of memory, 55
memorials
  national memory and, 42
  traditional addenda, 44
memory, 259
  autobiographical, 151, 236
  biases in, 149–155
  cognitive accessibility and, 149–150
  consolidation of, 271, 274
  as cumulative, 70
  dissociation between personal and collective representations in, 151
  distortion, serial reproduction and, 419
  figurations of, 92
  and futurity, 67, 83
  history and, relationship between, 82–83
  individual/biological, 169, 260
  inertia of, 134–137
  malleability of, 333, 391
  moralized, 155–160
  organization of, 427
  persistence of, 270
  recurrent retrieval of, 274
  serial reproduction and, 419
  social frames of, 148, 411, 426
  sociological perspective on, 51–55
  sociology of, 56–57
  specific narratives and, 368, 460
  and spiritual principle, 454
  storage of, 270, 274
  structure of, and recall, 424
  tramsmission of, 41
memory activists, 256, 361
  in Japan, 283–285
memory contagion, 426
memory convergence, 403
  in collective memory, 146–148, 161, 204, 366, 411, 424, 426
  community-wide, 398–399
  conversational interactions and, 390
  at group level, 411, 424
  social sharing of memories and, 417, 427
memory-history, versus truth-history, 296–297
memory phases, 260
memory politics
  populism and, 42–43
  regret in, 42–43
memory representations
  different, development of, 412
  shared, development of, 412
memory research, in cognitive psychology, 367, 411
memory studies, 41–42, 66
Mercier, Hugo, 378–379
Meredith, James, 89, 95
  monument, at University of Mississippi, 96–99, 97*f*, 111
Miller, Perry, 28–29
Milošević, Slobodan, 396, 396*f*
minimal group concept, 370–371
minority rights, 46
misinformation
  acceptance of, 367, 435, 450
  in Gulf War, 435
  identification of, 440–443
  susceptibility to, 367, 434–435
misremembering, communities and, 403
Mississippi
  Emmett Till murder in, 105

Freedom Summer (1964) killings in, 106
Institutions of Higher Learning (IHL) board, 106–108
state flag, 105, 105n2
Mississippi State University, and commemorative reconsideration, 50
Mitchell, John, 39
mnemonic communities, 57
mnemonic entrepreneurs, 55
mnemonic silences, 392
mnemonic socialization, 56–57
Molotov–Ribbentrop Pact, 459, 461, 469
Monroe, James, 4, 49
monuments, national memory and, 42
mood, general negative vs. general positive, experimental measurement of, 354–355
Moon Jae-in, 289–290
Moorhead, Rod, 96
moral action, 455
moral foundations, 225
moral intuitions, 155–156
political divergences and, 64, 156–161
moralized memory, 155–161
"more perfect union," framers' concept of, 14, 61, 71–78, 73n15, 84
Morgan, John T., 38
Moscow, Battle of (WW II), collective memory of, and relevance to present, 193, 195f, 196
Moses illusion, 441–442
motivational factors, 367
and beliefs, 434–435, 439–440
and overclaiming of responsibility, 225–226
motivations
coalitional, 371–372, 372n1
and collective memory, 391, 399–401
and communication, 399
and intergroup dynamics, 399–401
and recall vs. avoidance, 399–401
Mouffe, Chantal, 332
Mount Rushmore, 69–70, 70n7
Trump and, 66, 70n8, 70–71
Mullins, Andy, 101
multiculturalism, in education, 125–126
multidirectional memory, 45n3, 51n5

Murayama, Tomiichi, 284
"My Homeland" (Chinese song), 306
My War (Chinese film), 256, 301–321
promo for, 312–314
myth, and contradictory imaginaries, 326–327

Nagorno-Karabakh, 257, 343–344, 349, 352, 352n1
narratives about, types of, 352, 361–362
Nanjing Massacre, 282, 286–287, 291–292
narcissism. *See also* national narcissism; state narcissism
collective, 167, 237
definition of, 232
overclaiming of responsibility as, 232, 237
narrative(s), 455. *See also* common suffering narrative; national narratives
American national, and legacies of past, 83
apology, 352, 362
blaming a third party, 352, 362
canonicality of, 155
as "co-authors," 456
and coalition-building, 365, 376
and collective memory, 346–351
of common cultural traits, 352, 362
contrasted with logico-scientific thinking, 456–457
controlling, victimhood nationalism and, 288
as coordination tool, 365
in creation of national identity, 21n4, 21–23
as cultural tools, 368, 455
and emplotment, 456–458
as equipment for living, 455–457
and fit to evidence, 83
and information propagation, 401–402
moralized, 155–161
and national memory, 325, 455
normative pressures affecting, 155
programmatic study of, 401–402
and scientific theory, differentiation, 458
and social change, 82–84
specific, 347, 368, 460–462
struggles to control, 368, 464–468

narrative(s) (*cont.*)
  of suffering, as liminal space, 360
  as "textual resources," 347
  and truth, 83 (*see also* narrative truth)
  and visual arts, parallel between, 456
narrative templates, 303, 368, 460–462
  and disputes, 462
  mental habits associated with, 468
  national, 148–150, 159
  and national memory, 324, 462
  Russian, 461–462
  schematic, 148–150, 159
  statist, in China, 303–304, 314–319
narrative transformation, and conflict resolution, 351–352
narrative truth, 368, 457–460, 468–469
nation(s), 326
  beginnings of, 20
  definition of, 261, 454
  as unit of analysis, 66
national community(ies), boundaries of, 341
National Council for the Social Studies (NCSS), 126–127
national decline, implicit trajectories of, 63–64, 148–155, 152*f*, 154*f*, 160, 166, 168
national fantasies, 324, 334
National Garden for American Heroes, 71, 71n9
National History Standards Project (NHSP), 127, 137
national identity, 236–238, 326
  activation, and accessibility of relevant information, 445–449, 449*f*
  creation of, 21, 21n3-n4
  events defining, 241–244, 242*f*, 243*t*–244*t*
  influence of "other" in, 245–246
  memory and, 21, 236–238, 250–251
  national pride and, 238, 241
  outsiders' perspectives on, 246–250
National Memorial for Peace and Justice, 61, 66, 78–80, 82–84
national memory, 255–256, 324, 368, 427.
  See also collective memory
  American, remaking by Reagan, 30
  and analytic history, 469
  bottom-up processes in, 90, 228–231, 255, 368, 391, 411, 428
  collective memory and, 412
  conflicting interpretations in, 324
  contemporary values versus older symbols/images and, 52
  contextual forces in, 340–341
  continuous transformations in, 52
  and contradictory national stances, 326
  creation of, 22–23
  as cultural repertoire, 326
  cultural symbols and, 116
  emergence of, 429
  emotional dimensions of, 324, 463–464
  erasure and forgetting in, 24, 41–42, 204
  formation of, 20, 410
  heteroglossia in, 326–328
  individuals' beliefs and, 116
  inertial dynamics of, 52
  instrumentalism with and about the past and, 52
  and lived understandings of material landscape, 90
  management of, 468–470
  memory symbolism and, 324–326
  narrative templates and, 324, 462
  narrative tools mediating, 458–459
  narratives and, 325, 368, 455
  nationalist-populist remaking of, 280
  and peoplehood, 325–326, 341
  and political discourse, 325–326
  propositional versus narrative truth in, 458
  shifts in, charismatic figures and, 77–78
  study methods for, 168
  top-down processes in, 90
  transformations in, 42, 45
  as unifying and splintering agent, 325
  work of, 32
National Museum of African American History and Culture, 66, 76–78, 80, 84
National Museum of the American Indian, "Americans" exhibit, 136
national narcissism, 210–217, 233, 237, 459

and collective forgetting, 238
evidence (or lack of) for, 244–246
as function of comparison, 245–246
and national identity, 241
and overclaiming of responsibility, 217, 237
national narratives, 247
of America, 137–138
as cultural tools, 368, 428
development, 428
national origins, representations of, positivity bias for, 152–155, 159
National Park Service (NPS), 70, 70n7
national sovereignty, 332–333
nationalism, 211–212, 369. *See also* populist nationalism
appeal of, 291
banal, 324
creation of, 21, 21n3
as emergent property of social networks, 428
euphoria of, in America after War of 1812, 21
and historical narratives, 351
influence of, 383
and revisionism, 280
right-wing, in United States, 66
rise of ("new nationalism"), 454
statist, in China, 303–304, 314–319
Trumpian, 65–66
nationalism-populism, in East Asia, 282–295
Native Americans
activism by, 117
in American national memory, 24, 32, 137–138
and critical view of Columbus, 46, 51
displacement, as foundational in American history, 183, 184*f*
genocide of, as foundational in American history, 183, 184*f*
oppression and brutality visted upon, by Europeans, 118, 229
popular representations of, 119–120
population loss to European diseases, 117, 229
pre-Columbian civilizations, 117
stereotyping of, 119–120

symbolic relevance to origins, 136
textbook treatments of, 124, 128–134, 130*t*, 133*f*, 229
treatment of, as ashamed event, 239*t*, 248
Nazism
as ashamed event, 240*t*, 249
as German national identity event, emotional tone categorization of, 240*t*, 241–244, 244*t*
Neff, John, 89, 108
Netherlands, and comfort women issue, 294
Nettle, Dan, 383–384
New England
historians from, 25n9
memory and making of, 2, 26n11
slavery in, national origin myth of America and, 24, 32
Tocqueville on, 27
New Orleans, Louisiana, Robert E. Lee statue, 49
New Zealand
claimed responsibility for victory in WW II, 215–217, 216*f*
historical charters for, 181–182
important events of World War II as remembered in, 194–197, 195*f*, 247
settler colonialism of, 43
Treaty of Waitangi, 181
Newsome, Bree, 76
newspaper articles, effects on conversations, 395
Newton, Isaac, 7
Niebuhr, Reinhold, 469
Nippon Kaigi (Japan Conference), 286–287
nominal groups
memory transmission in, 420
recall performance of, 413–414
Nongqawuse, 380
North America, "pristine myth" about, 117
North Korea
China's relationship with, 302–303, 306–307, 309–312, 321
in Chinese films, 311–312
nuclear capability and missile technologies, 310–311

Obama, Barack, 31, 61, 66, 71–78, 80, 84, 321
  as American national identity event, emotional tone categorization of, 239t, 249
  on Charleston, South Carolina, massacre, 75–76
  and civil religionist tradition, 73, 73n15
  and foreign policy, 74
  presidential campaign, Rev. Wright and, 72–73
  response to H1N1 pandemic, Trump on, 441
  rhetoric of, 74, 78, 212
  "unity" narrative of, 74–75
objective tests, 212–213
Olick, Jeffrey, 92
Olney, Jesse, 25n9
On the 38th Parallel (Chinese film), 306, 321
oppressive regimes, and coordination, 377
origin stories, work of, 32
Orwell, George, *Nineteen Eighty-Four*, 65
Out of Inferno (film), 308, 321
overclaiming of responsibility, 167, 210–211, 233, 237. *See also* national narcissism; state narcissism
  by Americans, 213, 237
  cognitive mechanisms and, 226–228, 231
  collective memory and, 228–231, 237
  increase with group size, 167, 211, 213
  in married couples, 167, 210, 226
  mechanisms accounting for, 224–228, 231
  motivational factors and, 225–226
  as narcissism, 232, 237
  and national narcissism, 217, 237
  for nations in world history, 211, 213, 214t, 237
  overestimation of small numbers and, 228
  in small groups, 210–211
  support theory and, 228
  for World War II, 211, 215, 216f, 237

Pacific War, 281, 283
Paine, Thomas, 5, 19
Palatucci, Giovanni, 403
Palestinians, and Second Intifada, 389
pan-Asian cultural space, 321
Pang, Oxide Chun, 308
Park Geun-hye, 289, 311, 321
parochial knowledge bias, and collective overclaiming, 226–227
Passover rites, 263, 273
past
  "disease" metaphor for, 78, 78n18
  as field of struggle, 65
  instrumentalism with and about, 52
  malleability of, 53
  narratives of, accuracy of, 82–83
  national, in East Asian domestic politics, 285–290
  "smog" metaphor for, 78, 78n18
  top-down and bottom-up representations of, 293n2
  working through, 81, 81n22
Patriarchs, in Jewish collective memory, 268
PBS NewsHour, on COVID-19 narrative, 465–466
PeaceData.net, 436–437
Pearl Harbor, 281
  collective memory of, and relevance to present, 192–203, 195f, 198f, 201f, 203t, 247, 460
Peña, Tori, 366
Pence, Mike, 18
peoplehood, 332–333
  national memory and, 325–326, 341
personal identity, 236
Philippines, and comfort women issue, 284
Pickowicz, Paul, 306
pictures, memory for, 426
Pilgrims
  American cultural and collective memory of, 26n11
  cultural use of, 26, 26n11, 32
  as foundational in American history, 183, 184f
  in national origin myth of America, 21–32, 23n6, 26n11
  as separatists, 29
  spread of story and, 25–27, 32
  story of, content of, 23–24, 32
  Tocqueville on, 27

Pinckney, Clementa, Obama's eulogy for, 75, 75n17
pluralistic ignorance, 377
Plymouth, Massachusetts, in national origin myth, firsting process and, 24
Plymouth Rock, in national origin myth of America, 22n5, 22–23, 23n6, 31
Poland
   important events of World War II as remembered in, 200–202, 201*f*, 237
   memory conflicts with other nations, 282
   Nazi invasion of, collective memory of, and relevance to present, 195*f*, 196, 198*f*, 199, 201, 201*f*, 203*t*
   revisionist memory in, 281–282
   Soviet atrocities of World War II as remembered in, 202
   Soviet invasion of, collective memory of, and relevance to present, 201–202, 201*f*
police brutality, 80, 118
politics. *See also* memory politics
   of affective persuasion, 325, 327
   in American political culture, 182*t*, 183
   of apology, 294, 296
   of history, 192
   memory as tool of, 192
   of regret, 2, 42–43, 61
   and social representations of history, 171
   symbolic forms and, 326
Pollard, Edward A., 38
Pompeo, Mike, 464–467
populism, 369, 383–385
   American, 45
   appeal of, 291
   influence of, 383
   and memory politics, 42–43
   and revisionism, 280
   rise of, in 21st century, 42, 410
   Russian, 463
   Trump's, 61, 67–68, 168
   in United States, 43
populist beliefs, acceptance of, factors affecting, 450
populist nationalism, 257, 329
   emotional appeals of, 291, 332–333
   and historical revision, 297–298
   and hyperbolic memory narratives, 325
   origins of, 384–385
   success of, 384–385
   symbols mobilized by, 332–333
positive-sum games, 383–384
post-collaborative memory(ies)
   collaborative remembering and, 411–412, 418, 424
   emotional components of, 418, 424–426
   group configuration and, 420–423, 421*f*–422*f*
   for non-personal vs. autobiographical information, 425–427
   redundancy of, 420
   structure of, 418, 423–424, 427
power
   conventional metaphors for, 373
   coordination and, 376
   groups and, 372–373
presidents, U.S., memory for, factors affecting, 390
pride, 349
   group, 210
   individual, 167
   national, 167, 210 (*see also* national narcissism)
   in national history, 238–240
   state level, 210 (*see also* state narcissism)
priming, 367, 448
Princeton University, renaming of Wilson school, 50
privileged event narratives, 368, 463–464, 467
   and narrative template, 463
   relevance to contemporary events, 463–464
   and specific narrative, 463
progress, 77–78
   narrative of, 137
   Obama's belief in, 74
progressive narrative transformation, 351–352, 361
projective tests, 213
propaganda
   in Nazi Germany, 380
   persuasiveness of, 380
propositional truth, 368, 457–459, 466–469

Propp, Vladimir, 334–335
psychoanalytic concepts, 56
  of reckoning with past, 81n22
psychology. *See also* coalitional psychology; cognitive psychology
  and collective memory, 169
  crowd, 369
  social, 56
public memory, 291
  formation and transformation of, 283–289
  vernacular terrain of, 256, 284, 291, 296–297
Puritans
  American cultural and collective memory of, 26n11
  and Church of England, 29
  in national origin myth of America, 28–29
  Tocqueville on, 27
Putin, Vladimir
  and Expulsion-of-Alien-Enemies narrative template, 462
  rhetorical toolkit used by, 463
  use of memory politics, 192
  use of privileged event narrative, 463

Rabin, Yitzhak, assassination, commemoration of, 54
racial injustice, 79
racial violence, in America, 80–81. *See also* lynchings
racism
  implicit, 353
  structural, in United States, 39
  Woodrow Wilson and, 50
Raid (Chinese film), 306, 313, 321
Raid on White Tiger Regiment (Chinese film), 307, 322
Rajaram, Suparna, 366
Rancière, Jacques, 296–297
Rao Shuguang, 301
rape, as crime against humanity, 283
Raskin, Jamie, on Trump, 3, 19
Rave Revolution, 331
re-exposure, collaborative recall and, 414–415, 418, 427
Reagan, Ronald, and "city on a hill" expression, 27, 30–31

recency effects, 390
  in Jewish collective memory, 265–267, 265f
reciprocity, in social exchange, 370–372
Reconciliation and Healing Foundation (Korean-Japanese), 289–290
reconciliationist narrative, 69–70
Reconstruction, 48. *See also* Lost Cause
  Scott on, 89
Red Power, 117
red stars (Chinese film stars), 313–314
redress, 281
rehearsal effects, 392–393
relearning through retrieval, 415
reminiscence bumps, 260
  in American history, 238
  in Jewish collective memory, 265–267
Renan, Ernest, 24, 41–42, 460–461, 469
  "What Is a Nation?," 229, 454
repetition
  and collective memory, 273
  and retrieval-induced forgetting, 392–393
  and truth judgments, 439–441, 450
repression, of memory, 232
Republic of Letters, 4
  Jefferson/Adams, 12–13
Republican Party, and Trumpism, 13–14, 16
research methods, 165
resistance, 55
responsibility, social organization of, 58
retrieval-induced forgetting (RIF), 392–393, 393f. *See also* socially shared retrieval-induced forgetting (SSRIF)
revisionism
  in East Asia, 281
  in Eastern Europe, 281–282
  in history education, 137
  limits of, 295–298
  patriotic passions and, in East Asia, 295
  right-wing, 280
Revolution, American
  as American national identity event, emotional tone categorization of, 239t, 241–244, 243t
  as foundational event, 183–185, 184f
  paradox of, in light of slavery, 76
Revolutionary Generation, 4–5, 12

Revzin, Isaak, 334–336
Richmond, Virginia
  commemorative reconsideration in, 50
  Robert E. Lee statue in, 35f, 39
Ricoeur, Paul, 456
Robinson, Doane, 69
Roediger, Henry, 212
Roll, Jared, 89
Romania, opposition to regime in, 377
Rothberg, Michael, on multidirectional memory, 45n3, 51n5
Russia (USSR, Soviet Union), 40
  and Baltics, memory conflicts between, 282
  claimed responsibility for victory in WW II, 215–217, 216f
  contribution to World War II, 167
  and Estonian annexation, 459, 461
  Expulsion-of-Alien-Enemies narrative template, 297, 347, 461–462
  Georgia's relationship with, 331–332
  and Great Patriotic War, 192, 463, 467
  memories of World War II in, 166–167, 192–197, 195f, 203–204
  memory of past, relevance to present, 192, 205–206
  and narrative truth of Molotov-Ribbentrop Pact, 459, 461
  national memory in, factors affecting, 166–167
  national narrative of, resistance to inconvenient facts, 459, 461
  Nazi invasion of, collective memory of, and relevance to present, 193, 195f, 196–197, 198f, 201f, 202–203, 203t
  privileged event narrative in, 463
  revisionist memory in, 281
  and stereotyped narrative episodes, 148–149, 461–462
Rwandan genocide (1994), 366, 404–405
  and conflict resolution, narratives in, 360

Saakashvili, Mikhail, 339
Salovey, Peter, 47
Sansing, David, 101
Sargsyan, Serzh, image of, priming effect, 353–354, 359
Saving Story (Credo), 275

in Jewish collective memory, 255–256, 262–265, 267–268, 271–274
schema, 424, 460
schematic forms of representation, 460
schematic narrative templates, 148–150, 159, 347, 460–461
  and collective memory, 205
  cultural sensitivity to, 402
  and social representations of history, 183
schoolbooks. See textbooks
Schudson, Michael, 53
Schuman, Howard, 46
Schwartz, Barry, 46, 55
Scott, Charles, 89
Seelye, John, 26n11
segregation, 79, 83. See also Lost Cause
semantic memory, 261–262, 274
semantic priming, 448
September 11, 2001 (9/11) terrorist attacks
  as American national identity event, emotional tone categorization of, 239t, 241–244, 243t, 249
  in American political culture, 182t, 183
  collective memory of, 366, 390, 392, 394
  effect on emotional climate, 177
  as foundational event in American history, 183–186, 184f
  and living historical memories, 170, 175–177, 176t
  mass media and, 390
  social influence on, 394
Serbs, ethnopolitical mobilization of, 351
serial position effect, 260
settler colonialism, 43, 118
1776 Project, 44
shame, 349
  individual, 167
  in national history, 167, 238–240
Shesbazzar, 267
Shining Star on the Battlefield (Chinese film), 308, 322
signaling
  in coalition psychology, 374–375
  and forced disclosure, 382
  in groups, 371
  internal, coordination through, 381–382

Simko, Christina, 55
1619 Project, 44, 149, 160–161
slavery. *See also* Lost Cause; 1619 Project; temporality, traumatic
   abolition of, as foundational in American history, 183, 184*f*
   in American political discourse, 45
   and America's foundations, 149
   as America's original sin, 74
   as ashamed event, 239*t*, 248
   defenders of, 53
   evolution into contemporary forms of racial bias, 79–82
   as foundational in American history, 183, 184*f*
   Jefferson and, 49, 53, 68, 76–77
   Jefferson Davis on, 39
   in Massachusetts, end of, 77
   in National Museum of African American History and Culture, 76
   in New England, national origin myth of America and, 24, 32
   public historical consciousness of, 48
   reparations for, 47
   textbook treatments of, 229–230
   in U.S. political culture, 44
Small, William, 6–7
smallpox, inoculation against, 5, 7
Smith, Anthony D., 23
Smith, Paul Chaat, 136
social connectedness/connections, 409–410
social contagion, 294, 367
   collaborative remembering and, 412, 415, 427
Social Dominance Orientation (SDO), 174–175
social groups, mnemonic overlap in, 204
social identity, 236
   values and, 155
social influence
   on collective memory, 390–391, 394–396
   horizontal, 394–396
   vertical, 395–396
social infrastructures, 92
social interaction
   positive-sum, 383–384
   zero-sum, 383–385
social justice values, 64, 156–159, 158*f*
social media
   and collective memory, 429
   echo chambers in, 367, 419
social movement, collective memory and, 346
social psychology, 56
social remembering, effects on memory, 391–392
social representations
   central core of, 180
   convergence onto, 146–148, 161
   of history, 146–147
   peripheral system and, 180
   theory of, 180
social representations of history, 169–172
   historical charters as central core of, 180–182
   as narratives, 171
   research on, 170
social studies, multiculturalism and, 126
social trust
   experienced environment and, 383–384
   generalized, 383–384
socially shared retrieval-induced forgetting (SSRIF), 393–395, 400–401
   motivated retrieval and, 401
Society for Spreading Freedom, 257, 329, 331
sociology, and collective memory, 169
Sons of Liberty, 7
source information
   credibility of, 437
   forgetting of, 437, 450
   and truth judgments, 436–437, 450
South Korea
   anti-Japanese sentiments in, 293, 295
   China's relationship with, 310–313
   and comfort women issue, 282–290, 293
   as enemy of China in Korean War, 308–309
   and forced labor issue, 290, 293
   hate nationalism in, 293
   nationalism in, national past and, 256, 296
   revisionist memory in, 256, 281
   war memory and nationalism in, 287–288

youth in, separation of their antipathies and lifestyles, 294
Soviet Union. *See* Russia (USSR, Soviet Union)
Sparks, Larry, 106–108
Spencer, Richard, 50
spiritual principle, 454
Stalin, Joseph, 337–338
  on nation, 261
Stalingrad, Battle of (WW II), collective memory of, and relevance to present, 193, 195*f*, 196–197, 198*f*, 199, 201*f*, 202–203, 203*t*, 460, 463
Stanley, Matthew, 367
Stasi, 377
state narcissism, 210, 217–224, 219*t*–221*t*, 223*f*, 226, 233
Stevenson, Bryan, 66, 78–82
Stockholm Declaration (2000), 43, 43n1
Stocks, Morris, 100
Stone Mountain Georgia, 69, 69n6
support theory, 227–228, 231, 233
Suppression of the Counter-revolutionary Campaign (China), 305
symbols
  political evocation of, 341
  uses of, in national stances, 325–328
sympathy, 359–360
Szakos, Kristin, 48

Talbott, Strobe, 61, 73n15, 168, 463
Taylor, Breonna, 79
Taylor, Morgan K., 367
temporal depth, 21
temporality, 65. *See also* collective temporal thought
  nostalgic, Trump's, 61, 65–71
  progressive, 61, 66, 71–78
  traumatic, 61, 66, 78–82
terrorism, in living historical memory, in developing versus developed countries, 177–180, 178*f*–179*f*
terrorist attacks. *See also* September 11, 2001 (9/11) terrorist attacks
  effect on emotional climate, 177
  and living historical memories, 170
text(s), in cultural memory propagation, 272–273

textbooks. *See also* American history textbooks
  government-sponsored, 229–230
  Japanese, treatment of comfort women, 284–285
  Soviet, Georgian narrative in, 337–338
Till, Emmett, 105
Tilly, Charles, 171
Tocqueville, Alexis de, *Democracy in America*, 27–28
trajectory of contestation, 90
tranquility (civil peace), Trump's offense against, 14
transitional justice, 43
trauma, 79
  in collective memory, 272, 280–281
  in individual memory, 272
  transgenerational transmission of, 272
travelling memory, 45n3, 51n5
Trethewey, Natasha, 89–90
tribalism, 365, 369, 378
tripartite algorithm, in memory, 274
Trump, Donald J.
  "America First" rhetoric, 31–32, 67, 211–212
  arguments for U.S.–Mexico wall, 437–438
  as ashamed event, 239*t*, 248
  baseless claim of election fraud, 17–18
  betrayal of oath, 13–14
  bigotry of, 15–17
  comments on Charlottesville events, 68
  and Covid pandemic, 15, 464–465
  demagoguery of, 2
  as despotic, 3–4
  disfluent/garbled speech, 440–441
  as disruptive force, 1, 3
  executive order on National Garden for American Heroes, 71, 71n9
  failures as president, 14–15
  falsehoods/lies of, 13, 15, 17–18
  and foreign policy, 14–15
  impeachments of, 16
  inaugural address (2017), 67, 67n3
  and January 6 insurrection, 18
  and justice, 14
  on left-wing cultural revolution, 70–71
  "Make America Great Again" (MAGA) slogan, 65, 82, 171, 185, 238

498   INDEX

Trump, Donald J. (*cont.*)
   as malignant narcissist, 13
   Mount Rushmore address, 66, 70n8, 70–71
   on "*my* people," 14
   nomination acceptance speech (2016), 65n2, 65–66
   nostalgic temporality, 61, 65–71
   Raskin on, 3, 19
   self-serving by, 14
   and tranquility, 14
   tweets, truth judgments about, repetition and, 439–440
   and Ukraine, 16
   and Unite the Right rally, 50, 68
   as White supremacist, 54
truth. *See also* narrative truth; propositional truth
   acceptance/processing of, factors affecting, 439–440
   correspondence theory of, 457–458
   fluency as cue to, 437–440
   judgments about, 367, 439–441, 450
   markers for, processing of, 450
   repetition and, 439–441, 450
   shortcuts supporting, 434, 436
   source of information and, 436–437, 450
truth and reconciliation, 81
truth-history, versus memory-history, 296–297
Tsang, Steven, on COVID-19 narrative, 465
Tubman, Harriet, 69
Tulsa Massacre (1921), reparations for, 47
Twitty, Anne, 89

Ukraine
   Russian actions in, narrative template for, 463–464
   Russian invasion (2014), 192
   Trump and, 16
United Confederate Veterans (U.C.V.), 37–38
United Daughters of the Confederacy (U.D.C.), 37–38, 69n6
   and monument building, 69, 88
United Kingdom
   claimed responsibility for victory in WW II, 215–217, 216*f*
   important events of World War II as remembered in, 194–197, 195*f*, 247
United States. *See also* America
   and allegiance to state, 209
   and America, differentiation of, 20–21
   ashamed events self-nominated in, 238–240, 239*t*, 241–244, 242*f*, 243*t*
   beginning of, 20–21, 33
   citizens' overclaiming of responsibility, 213, 237
   as "city on a hill," 2, 27–31, 45, 212
   claimed responsibility for victory in WW II, 215–217, 216*f*
   collective memory of World War II in, 193
   and comfort women issue, 284–285, 294
   as enemy of China in Korean War, 308–309
   history, regional view of, 230–231
   important events of World War II as remembered in, 194–197, 195*f*, 203–204
   national identity events, emotional tone categorization of, 238–244, 239*t*, 242*f*, 243*t*, 246–251
   proud events self-nominated in, 238–240, 239*t*, 241–244, 242*f*, 243*t*
   western expansion of, 69–70
University of Mississippi (UM)
   academic mission, separation from "Ole Miss" spirit, 110–111
   Action Plan (2014), 99, 103
   African Americans' contributions to, 89
   as bastion of White supremacy, 89
   campus environment, 89
   Carter plaque, 87–89, 88*f*, 93–94, 106, 109
   Chancellor's Advisory Committee on History and Context, 103–104
   Civil Rights Commemoration Initiative, 94–96
   commemorative landscape of, 93–112
   Confederate cemetery redevelopment effort, 106–108
   Confederate soldier statue, 62, 87–88, 92–108, 100*f*–101*f*, 109*f*, 111
   connection with off-campus surrounds and Confederate iconography, 111–112

desegregation of, 89, 95
founding mission of, 89
historical orientation of, Khayat's "parallel chapters" in, 94–96, 110
lack of "coherent narrative," 99
local mobilization on campus of, 111
"Ole Miss" label, 87, 93, 110
"Open Doors" commemoration, 95
physical spaces of, cultural conventions and, 111
S.E.E.D., 106
Sensitivity and Respect committee, 99
and state flag, 105, 105n2
Students Against Social Injustice, 106
White students' racist resistance at, 98–99
William Winter Institute for Racial Reconciliation, 96, 105–106
University of Pennsylvania, Franklin and, 5, 5n3
University of Virginia
Jefferson statue, 68
Jefferson's pride in, 13
and neo-Nazi leaders, 50
unpacking, 227–228
Unsung Heroes (Chinese film), 309, 322

valence(s), of objects, 90–91
values
binding, 64, 156–159, 158*f*, 225–226
individuating, 156–159
and social identity, 155
social justice, 64, 156–159, 158*f*
Vanyan, Giorgi, 362
Vardaman, James K., 103
VE Day, collective memory of, and relevance to present, 195*f*, 198*f*, 203*t*
vernacular memory, 91
vernacular terrain, of public memory, 256, 284, 291, 296–297
victim narrative, Armenian, 349–350
victimhood, in collective memory, 280–281
victimhood nationalism, 288
Vietnam Veterans Memorial, politics of, 43–44, 54
violence. *See also* intergroup violence
in American political culture, 182*t*, 183
in Balkans, collective memories and, 396, 404
collective, communication about, and emotional climate, 177
racial, in America, 80–81 (*see also* lynchings)
Virginia
origin story of America and, 2, 22, 32
statute for religious freedom, Jefferson's pride in, 13
Tocqueville on, 27
Vitter, Jeffrey, 102–103

Wagner-Pacifici, Robin, 55
Wallace, David Foster, 409
Wang, Dong, 304
war memory
East Asian, and revisionism, 295–298
governments and, 291
politics of, 281
state manipulation of, 281
War on Terror, effect on emotional climate, 166, 177
Ward, Kyle, *History in the Making*, 230
warfare
in American political culture, 182*t*, 183
salience in American living historical memories, 185–186
and social representations of history, 171
Warren, Elizabeth, 31
Warsaw Uprising, collective memory of, and relevance to present, 201, 201*f*
Washington, George, 1–2, 4
on character, 11–12
as citizen-soldier, 9, 9n10
at Constitutional Convention, 10
desire for pastoral life, 9–10
Enlightenment ideals and, 8–9
farewell address by, 11–12
first inaugural address, 10
leadership qualities of, 9–11
as president, 10–11
on Revolutionary cause, 9
and statesmanship, 11–12
Washington Monument, 69
wealth gap, between Black and White Americans, 83

Webster, Daniel
  Plymouth oration, 22n5, 22–23
  speeches by, and national origin myth of America, 23n6, 23–24
Wertsch, James V., 83, 99, 137, 148, 212, 303, 346–347, 367–368
  study of Russian memories of WW II, 192–193
  Voices of Collective Remembering, 169
West Germany, collective memory in, Holocaust and, 43, 45, 48
westward expansion, as foundational in American history, 183, 184*f*
Wheatley, Phyllis, 77
White Americans, and psychic damage of racial inequality, 81
White nationalism, Trump and, 68
White supremacism, 52, 83. *See also* University of Mississippi (UM), Confederate soldier statue
  Calhoun and, 75n16
  Lost Cause and, 38
  and South Carolina massacre (2015), 47, 49, 75–76, 76n16
  Trump and, 15, 68
  and violence, 118
  Woodrow Wilson and, 50
White supremacy, 52, 79
  Ole Miss and, 89
Wilder, Laura Ingalls, 119
Willard, Emma, 25–26, 29
  A History of the United States, or Republic of America, 26, 26n10
Wilson, Marcius, 25n9
Wilson, Woodrow, 50
Winter, William, 96
Winthrop, John
  "city on a hill" sermon, 2, 27–32, 28n12, 212
  A Model of Christian Charity, 28, 31
women. *See also* comfort women
  North Korean, in Chinese films, 306–307
women's suffrage, in American political culture, 182*t*, 183
World Anti-Fascist War, 290–291
World War I, as German national identity event, emotional tone categorization of, 240*t*, 241–244, 244*t*, 249

World War II. *See also* World War II, important events of
  as American national identity event, emotional tone categorization of, 239*t*, 241–244, 243*t*, 249
  in American political culture, 182*t*, 183
  collective memory of, 190–191, 247, 296, 417, 463
  commemoration of, 190–191
  Eastern Front, collective memory of, and relevance to present, 197, 199–203, 205
  as foundational event in American history, 183, 184*f*, 185–186
  as German national identity event, emotional tone categorization of, 240*t*, 241–244, 244*t*, 249
  good history of, in Asia, 297
  good memory of, in Asia, 297
  importance in world history, cross-national survey results, 190
  in living historical memory in United States, 176, 176*t*
  memory agenda set by, 280–281
  memory for, prior work on, 192–193
  narrative truth about, 458
  national memories of, adaptation to perspectives over time, 204–206
  as privileged event narrative, 463–464
  relevance to present, 192
  remembrance and interpretation of, other global events affecting, 206
  specific narratives about, 460
World War II, important events of
  American view of, 193
  empirical studies of, 166, 193–194
  as remembered in eight former Allied countries, 194–197, 195*f*, 202–204, 203*t*, 237–238, 247
  as remembered in Poland, 200–202, 201*f*, 237
  as remembered in three former Axis countries, 197–200, 198*f*, 202–204, 203*t*, 237, 247
  Russian view of, 166–167, 192–193
world wars, commemorations of, 42
Wright, Jeremiah, 72–73, 78

Xi Jinping, 282, 290, 302, 320

INDEX   501

Yale University, renaming practices used at, 47, 104
Yarbrough, Taylor, 108
Young, James, 44, 96
Yu Lan, 313, 313n2
Yugoslavia, ethnic conflict in, 351

Zaromb, Franklin, 212
Zelensky, Volodymyr, 16

zero-sum games, 383–385
Zerubavel, Eviatar, 56–57
  Hidden in Plain Sight, 58
Zhang Wei, 301
Zhang Yongshou, 313
Zhao Lijian, 466
Zimmerman, George, 48
Zinn, Howard, 118
Zou Hue, 466